Turkey

a travel survival kit

Tom Brosnahan

Turkey – a travel survival kit
2nd Edition

Published by
Lonely Planet Publications
Head Office: PO Box 88, South Yarra, Victoria 3141, Australia
Branch Office: PO Box 2001A, Berkeley, CA 94702, USA

Printed by
Colorcraft, Hong Kong

Photographs by
Tom Brosnahan

First published
July 1985

This edition
January 1988

National Library of Australia Cataloguing in Publication Data

Brosnahan, Tom.
    Turkey, a travel survival kit.

    2nd ed.
    Includes index.
    ISBN 0 86442 018 8

    1. Turkey – Description and travel – 1960 –.-
    Guide-books. I. Title.

915.61'0438

Tom Brosnahan was born and raised in Pennsylvania, went to college in Boston, then set out on the road. His first two years in Turkey, during which he learned to speak fluent Turkish, were spent as a US Peace Corps Volunteer. He studied Middle Eastern history and the Ottoman Turkish language for eight years, but abandoned the writing of his Ph.D. dissertation in favour of travelling and writing guidebooks. So far his twenty books for various publishers have sold over two million copies in twelve languages. *Turkey – a travel survival kit* is the result of seven years' experience and travel in the country.

Dedication
For my Mother and Father, this one too.

Lonely Planet Credits

Editor	Elizabeth Kim
Maps & Cover Design	Fiona Boyes
Design & Illustrations	Valerie Tellini
Additional Illustrations	Graham Imeson
Typesetter	Ann Jeffree

Thanks to Jim Hart for his hours spent getting our typesetting machine to set the accents properly, and to Hugh Finlay for final proofing and indexing.

Acknowledgements
Several people and organizations have provided very useful assistance in the tremendous task of revising the tens of thousands of facts in this guide, and expanding it for its second edition. Warm thanks are due to Yelman Emcan, General Director of the Promotion and Marketing Directorate of the Ministry of Culture and Tourism in Ankara, and to C. Kâmil Müren, Culture and Information Attache in New York; also to J F Kreindler, Vice President, Corporate Communications, Pan American World Airways, and Merle Richman, Director of Pan Am's Public Relations Department. They helped out without attempting to exert any editorial

influence whatsoever; the opinions expressed in this guide are my own.

Tom Brosnahan.

A note about this guide
This, the 2nd edition of *Turkey – a travel survival kit*, has been brought fully up to date and greatly expanded. In particular, there is much more information on inexpensive hotels, on transportation, and on the eastern and south-eastern regions of the country. Many new maps have been added. Exact prices are quoted in both Turkish Liras (TL) and US dollars. Though Turkey's 30% annual inflation rate will quickly render the lira prices obsolete (perhaps even while this book is being printed), the dollar prices will remain fairly accurate. You will soon become accustomed to doing a quick mental calculation on the lira prices, to bring them up to date. Conversions in this book were done at a rate of US$1 = 714TL, the exchange rate in force as the revision work was being done. At the same rate, A$1 = 460TL; NZ$1 = 365TL; £1 = 1011TL.

This is the only book on Turkey you can buy which acts as a foreign-language phrasebook as well as a guide. Important and useful Turkish words and phrases are translated and followed by a pronunciation key so that you can immediately put them to good use. This saves you buying, carrying and fumbling with two books, and provides the phrases you need precisely when and where you need them. Many people have mentioned that the unfamiliar Turkish language can be the biggest stumbling-block to full enjoyment of a journey through Turkey.

From the publisher

Thanks must also go to all the travellers who used the first edition of this book and wrote to us with information, comments and suggestions: Graeme Archer (A), M J Armitage (UK), Helen Borsky & Dan Thomson (UK), Nicolas Brault (F), Craig Breskin (UK), Jan & Geoff Brown (A), Robyn Chaplin (A), S J Cheetham (UK), Margie Christopherson, Kiran Curtis (UK), Sven Dano (Dk), K L Dickhaut (C), Ingiliz Enstitusu (Tur), Kate Jones-Gillespie (A), Alan Ginsberg (US), Hugh Goddard (UK), Andrew Green (A), Phil Greenwood (UK), Chris Gregg, Sven Hansen (Dk), Soren Hansen (Dk), Andy Hazel & Lucy Casson, Rick Heeks (UK), Mark Henderson (NZ), George Henke (D), Henrietta Hope & Victoria Camero (UK), M J Horner (UK), Barbara Inan (UK), Kryss Kats (UK), Joseph Lemak (US), M Bavatie & S Wheeler (UK), George Main (UK), Chris McGarvey (UK), M & C McGrath (A), Frank Mercer, Claudia Mills & Tom Schroeder (US), F Whitehall & S Davies (US), W Orennan (C), Bram Posthumus (NL), Stephanie Raby, L Ravestein (NL), Choni Rimat (Isr), Rupert Robin (UK), Anya Schiffrin (UK), I W Searle (UK), Deborah Shadovitz (A), Sare Sikstrom (C), Helen Singer (UK), Karl Smith (UK), Celal Taskiran (Tur), Ewan & Fiona Thomson, Peter Thorne (UK), Simon Wallis (UK), Mrs D E Walter (US), Rifat Yildez (Tur).

A - Australia, C - Canada, D - West Germany, Dk - Denmark, F - France, Isr - Israel, NL - Netherlands, NZ - New Zealand, Tur - Turkey, UK - UK, US - USA.

A Request

All travel guides rely on new information to stay up to date and one of the best sources of this information is travellers on the road. At Lonely Planet we get about 100 letters and postcards a week that help us keep in contact with the latest travel developments. So, if you find that things have changed, write to us and let us know. Corrections, suggestions, improvements and additions are greatly appreciated and the best letters will get a free copy of the next edition or another Lonely Planet guide of your choice.

Contents

Introduction

In the minds of most western visitors, the mention of Turkey conjures up vague visions of oriental splendour and decadence, mystery and intrigue. Once in the country, this romantic but shallow stereotype is quickly dumped in favour of a look at the real thing. For 60 years the Turkish Republic has been working to put its imperial past behind it (while preserving the best parts for posterity), and has done remarkably well. Turkey today is a modern, secular and western-oriented country with a vigorous economy. Its people are disarmingly friendly to foreign visitors, the cuisine is outstanding, the cities like vast outdoor museums, the countryside often like a national park.

The visions of oriental splendour originated at least partly from reality. In the last years of the Ottoman Empire, the entire Middle East ruled by the Turkish sultan was up for grabs, and the western powers did whatever they could to gain advantage. This included putting pressure on the sultan by portraying him in the western press as little better than a monster. This negative image built easily on the notion of the 'terrible Turk' left from the days, in the 1600s, when Ottoman armies threatened the gates of Vienna, and thus all of central Europe.

By contrast with this European stereotype, Muslim tourists coming to Turkey today from the Arab countries formerly subject to the sultanate have a view of İstanbul as the glittering imperial capital, fount of culture and seat of the last Caliph of Islam. İstanbul is to an easterner what Rome is to a westerner.

Turks themselves are proud of their imperial past. Not the last centuries, but the times of Mehmet the Conqueror and Süleyman the Magnificent, when the Turkish Empire was the richest, most powerful, most civilized state in the world. And they are fascinated by the depth of history in their homeland, the progression of kingdoms and empires which fostered a dozen great cultures: Hittite, Hellenic, Hellenistic, Roman, Christian, Byzantine, Seljuk, Ottoman and more. But Turks harbour no romantic visions of reclaiming past glories or territories. Kemal Atatürk, founder of the modern republic, set forth the plan in no uncertain terms: preserve the high culture of the past, but get on with the work of the future.

Turkey's past is simply incredible. In fact, the world's oldest 'city' was discovered here, at Çatal Höyük (7500 BC). The Hittite Empire, little known in the west, rivalled that of ancient Egypt, and left behind breathtaking works of art. The heartland of ancient Greek culture is actually in Turkey, including cities such as Troy, Pergamum, Ephesus, Miletus and Halicarnassus. Most Turkish cities have a Roman past, and all have a Byzantine one. The Seljuk Turkish Empire could boast of men like Omar Khayyam and Celaleddin Rumi ('Mevlana', the poet, mystic and founder of the order of Whirling Dervishes).

When you've had your day's dose of history and culture, you can head out to the beach. At Side, on the Mediterranean coast, the Roman ruins are right *on* the beach. Or have dinner at a small fish restaurant on the shores of the Bosphorus. Or sit in a shady tea garden for a little *keyf*. Order a tiny, tulip-shaped glass of hearty Turkish tea (for about US$0.05), enjoy the pleasant surroundings, think over the day's good times, and let it all come together: that's *keyf*. There's no adequate translation; pleasure, contentment, positive outlook, relaxation? It's all part of a normal day in Turkey.

PLANNING WHERE TO GO

Any itinerary is an expression of interest, energy, time and money. Here are some suggestions to help you plan your travels in Turkey. These are *minimal* times, moving fast.

Less Than a Week (3-5 days) İstanbul, with an overnight trip to İznik and Bursa, or Troy and the Dardanelles.

Basic One-Week (7-9 day) Itinerary İstanbul (two nights), Bursa (one), Dardanelles and Troy (one), Bergama, İzmir and Kuşadası (two) with excursions to Ephesus, Priene, Miletus, Didyma; return to İstanbul (one). Spend any extra time in İstanbul.

Two Weeks Add an excursion from Kuşadası via Aphrodisias to Pamukkale/Hierapolis (one to two nights); also take a loop excursion to Ankara, Konya and Cappadocia. Visit the Hittite cities. If you have time left over, spend a day or two on the Turquoise Coast (Antalya, Side, Alanya).

Three Weeks Add a yacht cruise or coastal highway excursion from Kuşadası south to Bodrum, Marmaris, Fethiye, Kaş, Finike, Kemer and Antalya; or second-best, an excursion along the Black Sea coast. Another option is a tour to the south-east, Şanlıurfa, Mardin and Diyarbakır, best done outside of the blazing-hot months of July and August.

Eastern Tour A 10 to 14-day tour for mid-May to mid-October only: a circuit beginning in Ankara or Cappadocia going to Adıyaman (Nemrut Dağı), Diyarbakır, Bingöl, Van, Doğubeyazıt (Mt Ararat), Erzurum, Kars, Artvin, Hopa, Rize, Trabzon, Samsun, Amasya, and returning to Ankara via Boğazkale/Hattuşaş.

Everything You can see an awful lot of the country if you spend six weeks.

Facts about the Country

HISTORY

Turkey's history is astoundingly long – almost 10,000 years. Before giving a summary, here is a table so you can keep the various periods in the right places:

Historical Table

7500 BC: Earliest known inhabitants; earliest human community at Çatal Höyük.

5000 BC: Stone-and-Copper Age; settlement at Hacılar.

2600 to 1900 BC: Old Bronze Age; Proto-Hittite Empire in central and south-eastern Anatolia.

1900 to 1300 BC: Hittite Empire, wars with Egypt; the Patriarch Abraham departs Harran, near Şanlıurfa, for Canaan.

1250 BC: Trojan War.

1200 to 600 BC: Phrygian and Mysian invasions, followed by the great period of Hellenic civilization; Yassı Höyük settlement flourishes; King Midas and King Croesus reign; coinage is invented; kingdoms of Ionia, Lycia, Lydia, Caria, Pamphylia; Empire of Urartu.

550 BC: Cyrus of Persia invades Anatolia.

334 BC: Conquest of simply everything and everybody by Alexander the Great from Macedon.

279 BC: Celts, or Gauls, invade and set up Galatia near Ankara.

250 BC: Rise of the Kingdom of Pergamum (Bergama).

129 BC: Rome establishes the Province of Asia, with its capital at Ephesus (near İzmir).

47 to 57 AD: St Paul's trips in Anatolia.

330 AD: Constantine dedicates the 'New Rome' of Constantinople, and the centre of the Roman Empire moves from Rome to the Bosphorus.

527 to 565: Reign of Justinian, greatest Byzantine emperor; construction of Sancta Sophia, greatest church in the world.

570 to 622: Muhammad's birth; revelation of the Koran; flight ('Hijra') to Medina.

1037 to 1109: Empire of the Great Seljuk Turks, based in Iran.

1071 to 1243: Seljuk Sultanate of Rum, based in Konya; life and work of Celaleddin Rumi ('Mevlana'), founder of the Whirling Dervishes.

1000s to 1200s: Age of the Crusades.

1288: Birth of the Ottoman Empire, near Bursa.

1453: Conquest of Constantinople by Mehmet II.

1520 to 1566: Reign of Sultan Süleyman the Magnificent, the great age of the Ottoman Empire; most of North Africa, most of Eastern Europe and all of the Middle East controlled from İstanbul; Ottoman navies patrol the Mediterranean and Red seas and the Indian Ocean.

1876 to 1909: Reign of Sultan Abdul Hamid, last of the powerful sultans; the 'Eastern Question' arises: which European nations will be able to grab Ottoman territory when the empire topples?

1923: Proclamation of the Turkish Republic.

1938: Death of Atatürk.

Earliest Times

The Mediterranean region was inhabited as early as 7500 BC, during Paleolithic, or Old Stone Age, times. By 7000 BC a Neolithic (New Stone Age) city had grown up at what's now called Çatal Höyük, 60 km south-east of Konya. These early Anatolians developed fine wall paintings, statuettes, domestic architecture and pottery. Artefacts from the site, including the wall paintings, are in Ankara's Museum of Anatolian Civilizations.

The Chalcolithic (Stone-and-Copper Age) period saw the building of a city at Hacılar (HA-juh-LAHR), near Burdur, in about 5000 BC. The pottery here was of finer quality, and copper implements rather than stone or clay were used.

Hittites: The Bronze Age

The Old Bronze Age (2600-1900 BC) was the time when Anatolian man first developed cities of substantial size. An indigenous people now named the Proto-Hittites, or Hatti, built cities at Nesa, or Kanesh (today's Kültepe), and Alaca Höyük. The first known ruler of Kanesh was King Zipani (circa 2300 BC), according to Akkadian texts. You can visit the archaeological site near Kültepe, 21 km north-east of Kayseri. As for Alaca Höyük, 36 km from Boğazkale (see below), it was perhaps the most important pre-Hittite city and may have been the first Hittite capital.

The Hittites, a people of Indo-European language, overran this area and established themselves as a ruling class over the local people during the Middle Bronze Age (1900-1600 BC). They took over existing cities and built a magnificent capital at Hattuşaş (Boğazkale), 212 km east of Ankara near Sungurlu. The early Hittite Kingdom (1600-1500 BC) was replaced by the greater Hittite Empire (1450-1200 BC). They captured Syria from the Egyptians (1380-1316), clashed with the great Ramesis II (1298), and meanwhile developed a wonderful culture. Their graceful pottery, ironwork ornaments and implements, gold jewellery and figurines now fill a large section of the Museum of Anatolian Civilizations in Ankara. The striking site of Boğazkale (bo-AHZ-kahl-eh), set in dramatic countryside, is worth a visit, as is the religious centre of Yazılıkaya nearby. The Hittite religion was based upon worship of a Sun Goddess and a Storm God.

The Hittite Empire was weakened in its final period by the cities of Assuwa ('Asia'), subject principalities along the Aegean coast, which included the city of Troy. The Trojans were attacked by Achaean Greeks in 1250 – the Trojan War – which gave the Hittites a break. But the *coup-de-grace* came with a massive invasion of 'Sea Peoples' from various Greek islands and city-states. Driven from their homelands by the invading Dorians, the Sea Peoples flocked into Anatolia by way of the Aegean coast. The Hittite state survived for a few centuries longer in the south-eastern Taurus mountains, but the great empire was dead.

Phrygians, Urartians, Lydians & Others

With the Hittite decline, smaller states filled the power vacuum. About 1200 BC the Phrygians and Mysians, of Indo-European stock, invaded Anatolia from Thrace and settled at Gordium (Yassı Höyük), 106 km south-west of Ankara. This Hittite city became the Phrygian capital (circa 800 BC). A huge Hittite cemetery and a royal Phrygian tomb still exist at the site. King Midas (circa 715 BC), he of the golden touch, is Phrygia's most famous son.

At the same time (after 1200 BC), the Aegean coast was populated with a mixture of native peoples and Greek invaders. The region around İzmir became Ionia, with numerous cities. To the south was Caria, between modern Milas and Fethiye, a mountainous region whose people were great traders. The Carians sided with the Trojans during the Trojan War. When the Dorians arrived they brought some Greek culture to Caria, which the great Carian king, Mausolus, developed even further. His tomb, the Mausoleum, was among the Seven Wonders of the Ancient World. Of his capital city, Halicarnassus (modern Bodrum), little remains.

Further east from Caria was Lycia, a kingdom stretching from Fethiye to Antalya; and Pamphylia, the land east of Antalya.

As the centuries passed, a great city grew up at Sardis, 60 km east of İzmir. Called Lydia, it dominated most of Ionia and clashed with Phrygia. Lydia is famous not only for Sardis, but for a great invention: coinage. It's also famous for King Croesus, the world's first great coin collector. Lydia's primacy lasted only from 680 to 547 BC, at which date Persian invaders overran everybody.

Meanwhile, out east on the shores of salty Lake Van, yet another kingdom and culture arose. Not much is known about the Urartians who founded the Kingdom of Van (860-612 BC), except that they left interesting ruins and vast, bewildering cuneiform inscriptions in the massive Rock of Van just outside the modern town.

The Cimmerians invaded Anatolia from the west, conquered Phrygia and challenged Lydia, then settled down to take their place as yet one more ingredient in the great mulligan stew of Anatolian people. The stew was simmering nicely, but in 547 BC the Persians brought it to a boil. Though the Ionian cities survived the invasion and lived on under Persian rule, the great period of Hellenic culture was winding down. Ionia, with its important cities of Phocaea (Foça, FO-chah, north of İzmir), Teos, Ephesus, Priene and Miletus, and Aeolia centred on Smyrna (İzmir), had contributed a great deal to ancient culture, from the graceful scrolled capitals of Ionic columns to Thales of Miletus, the first recorded philosopher in the west. While the great city of Athens was relatively unimportant, the Ionian cities were laying the foundations of Hellenic civilization. It is ironic that the same Persian invasion which curtailed Ionia's culture was what caused that of

Alexander the Great

Athens to flourish. On reaching Athens, the Persians were overextended. By meeting the Persian challenge, Athens grew powerful and influential, taking the lead in the further progress of Hellenic culture.

Cyrus & Alexander

Cyrus, emperor of Persia (550-530 BC), swept into Anatolia from the east, conquering everybody and everything. Though he subjected the cities of the Aegean coast to his rule, this was not easy. The independent-minded citizens gave him and his successors trouble for the next two centuries.

The Persian conquerors were conquered by Alexander the Great, who stormed out of Macedon, crossed the Hellespont (Dardanelles) in 334 BC, and within a few years had conquered the entire Middle East from Greece to India. Alexander, so it is said, was frustrated in untying the Gordian knot at Gordium (Yassı Höyük), so he cut it with his sword. It seems he did the right thing, as the domination of Asia – which he was supposed to gain by untying the knot – came to be his in record time. His sword-blow proved that he was an impetuous young man. But then, if you're going to conquer the known world in time to die at the age of 33, you've got to make a few short cuts.

Alexander's effects on Anatolia were profound. He was the first of many rulers who would attempt to meld western and eastern cultures (the Byzantines and the Ottomans followed suit). Upon his death in 323 BC, in Babylon, his empire was divided up among his generals in a flurry of civil wars. Lysimachus claimed western and central Anatolia after winning the battle of Ipsus (301 BC), and he set his mark on the Ionian cities. Many Hellenistic buildings went up on his orders. Ancient Smyrna was abandoned and a brand-new city was built several km away, where the modern city stands. But the civil wars continued, and Lysimachus was slain by Seleucus (King of Seleucid lands, 305-280 BC), another of Alexander's generals, at the Battle of Corupedium (281 BC). Though Seleucus was in turn slain by Ptolemy Ceraunus, the kingdom of the Seleucids was to rule a great part of the Middle East for the next century, based in Antioch (Antakya).

Meanwhile, the next crowd of invaders, Celts or Gauls this time, was storming through Macedonia on its way to Anatolia (279 BC) to establish the Kingdom of Galatia. The Galatians made Ancyra (Ankara) their capital, and subjected the Aegean cities to their rule. The foundations of parts of the citadel in Ankara date from Galatian times.

While the Galatians ruled western Anatolia, Mithridates I had become king of Pontus, a state based on Trebizond (Trabzon) on the eastern Black Sea coast. At its height, the Pontic kingdom extended all the way to Cappadocia in central Anatolia.

Still other small kingdoms flourished at this time, between 300 and 200 BC. A leader named Prusias founded the Kingdom of Bithynia, and gave his name to the chief city: Prusa (Bursa). Nicaea (İznik) was also of great importance. And in south-eastern Anatolia an Armenian kingdom grew up, centred on the town of Van. The Armenians, a Phrygian tribe, settled around Lake Van after the decline of Urartian power. A fellow named Ardvates (ruled 317-284 BC), a Persian satrap (vice-regent) under the Seleucids, broke away from the Seleucid kingdom to found the short-lived Kingdom of Armenia. The Seleucids later regained control, but lost it again as Armenia was split into two kingdoms, Greater and Lesser Armenia. Reunited in 94 BC under Tigranes I, the Kingdom of Armenia became very powerful for a short period (83-69 BC). Armenia finally fell to the Roman legions not long afterwards.

But the most impressive and powerful of Anatolia's many kingdoms at this time was Pergamum. Gaining tremendous power around 250 BC, the Pergamene king picked the right side to be on, siding with Rome early in the game. With Roman help, Pergamum threw off Seleucid rule and went on to challenge both King Prusias of Bithynia (186 BC) and King Pharnaces I of Pontus (183 BC). The kings of Pergamum were great warriors, governors and also mad patrons of the arts, assembling an enormous library which rivalled that of Alexandria. The Asclepium, or medical centre, at Pergamum was flourishing at this time, and continued to flourish for centuries under Rome. Greatest of Pergamene kings was Eumenes II (197-159 BC), who ruled an enormous empire stretching from the Dardanelles to the Taurus mountains near Syria. He was responsible for building much of what's left on Pergamum's acropolis, including the grand library.

Roman Times

The Romans took Anatolia almost by default. The various Anatolian kings couldn't refrain from picking away at Roman holdings and causing other sorts of irritation, so finally the legions marched in and took over. Defeating Antiochus III, king of Seleucia, at Magnesia (Manisa, near İzmir) in 190 BC, the Romans were content for the time being to leave 'Asia' (Anatolia) in the hands of the kings of Pergamum. But the last king, dying without an heir, bequeathed his kingdom to Rome (133 BC). In 129 BC, the Romans established the Province of Asia, with its capital at Ephesus.

An interesting postscript to this period is the story of Commagene. This small and rather unimportant little kingdom in central Anatolia, near Adıyaman, left few marks on history. But the one notable reminder of Commagene is very notable indeed: atop Nemrut Dağı (NEHM-root dah-uh, Mt Nimrod), Antiochus I (62-32 BC) built an astounding memorial. His mammoth cone-shaped funerary mound is framed by twin temples filled with huge

stone statues portraying himself and the gods and goddesses who were his 'peers'. A visit to Nemrut Dağı, from the nearby town of Kâhta, is one of the high points of a visit to Turkey.

Roman rule brought relative peace and prosperity to Anatolia for almost three centuries, and provided the perfect conditions for the spread of a brand-new, world-class religion.

Early Christianity

Christianity began in Roman Palestine (Judea), but its foremost proponent, St Paul, came from Tarsus in Cilicia, in what is now southern Turkey. Paul took advantage of the excellent Roman road system to spread Jesus's teachings. When the Romans drove the Jews out of Judea in 70 AD, Christian members of this Diaspora may have made their way to the numerous small Christian congregations in the Roman province of Asia (Anatolia).

On his first journey in about 47-49 AD, Paul went to Antioch (Antakya), Seleucia (Silifke), and along the southern coast through Pamphylia (Side, Antalya) and up into the mountains. First stop was Antioch-in-Pisidia, today called Yalvaç, near Akşehir. Next he went to Iconium (Konya), the chief city in Galatia; Paul wrote an important 'Letter to the Galatians' which is now the ninth book of the New Testament.

From Iconium, Paul tramped to Lystra, 40 km south, and to Derbe nearby. Then it was back to Attaleia (Antalya) to catch a boat for Antioch. His second journey took him to some of these same cities, and later north-west to the district of Mysia where Troy (Truva) is located; then into Macedonia.

Paul's third trip (53-57) took in many of these same places, including Ancyra (Ankara), Smyrna (İzmir) and Adramyttium (Edremit). On the way back he stopped in Ephesus, capital of Roman Asia and one of the greatest cities of the time. Here he ran into trouble because his teachings were ruining the market for silver effigies of the local favourite goddess, Cybele/Diana. The silversmiths led a riot, and Paul's companions were hustled into the great theatre for a sort of kangaroo court. Luckily, the authorities kept order: there was free speech in Ephesus; Paul and his companions had broken no laws; they were permitted to go freely. Later on in this third journey Paul stopped in Miletus.

Paul got his last glimpses of Anatolia as he was being taken to Rome as a prisoner, for trial on charges of inciting a riot in Jerusalem (59-60). He changed ships at Myra (Demre); further west, he was supposed to land at Cnidos, at the tip of the peninsula west of Marmaris, but stormy seas prevented this.

Other saints played a role in the life of Roman Asia as well. Tradition has it that St John retired to Ephesus to write the fourth gospel near the end of his life, and that he brought Jesus's mother with him. John was buried atop a hill in what is now the town of Selçuk, near Ephesus. The great, now ruined basilica of St John marks the site. As for Mary, she is said to have retired to a mountaintop cottage near Ephesus. The small chapel at Meryemana ('Mother Mary') is the site of a mass to celebrate her assumption into heaven on 15 August.

The Seven Churches of the Revelation were the Seven Churches of Asia: Ephesus (Efes), Smyrna (İzmir), Pergamum (Bergama), Sardis (Sart, east of İzmir), Philadelphia (Alaşehir), Laodicea (Goncalı, between Denizli and Pamukkale) and Thyatira (Akşehir). 'Church' of course meant 'congregation', so don't go to these sites looking for the ruins of seven buildings.

The New Rome

Christianity was a struggling faith during the centuries of Roman rule. By 250 AD, the faith had grown strong enough and Roman rule so unsteady that the Roman emperor Decius decreed a general persecution of Christians. Not only this, but the empire was falling to pieces. Goths attacked the Aegean cities with fleets, and later invaded Anatolia. The Persian Empire again threatened from the east. Diocletian (284-305) restored the empire somewhat, but continued the persecutions.

When Diocletian abdicated, Constantine battled for succession, which he won in 324. He united the empire, declared equal rights for all religions, and called the first Ecumenical Council to meet at Nicaea (İznik, near Bursa) in 325.

Meanwhile, Constantine was building a great city on the site of Hellenic Byzantium. In 330 he dedicated it as New Rome, his capital city; it came to be called Constantinople. The emperor died seven years later in Nicomedia (İzmit), east of his capital. On his deathbed he adopted Christianity.

Justinian

While the barbarians of Europe were sweeping down on weakened Rome, the eastern capital grew in wealth and strength. Emperor Justinian (527-565) brought the Eastern Roman, or Byzantine, empire to its greatest strength. He reconquered Italy, the Balkans, Anatolia, Egypt and North Africa, and further embellished Constantinople with great buildings. His personal triumph was the Church of the Holy Wisdom, or Sancta Sophia, which remained the most splendid church in Christendom for almost 1000 years, at which time it became the most splendid mosque.

Justinian's successors were generally good, but not good enough, and the empire's conquests couldn't be maintained. Besides, something quite momentous was happening in Arabia.

Birth of Islam

Five years after the death of Justinian, Muhammad was born in Mecca. In 612 or so, while meditating, he heard the voice of God command him to 'recite'. Muhammad was to become the Messenger of God, communicating His holy word to men. The written record of these recitations, collected after Muhammad's death into a book by his family and followers, is the Koran.

The people of Mecca didn't take to Muhammad's preaching all at once. In fact, they forced him to leave Mecca, which he did, according to tradition, in the year 622. This 'flight' (*hijra* or hegira) is the starting-point for the Muslim lunar calendar.

Setting up housekeeping in Medina, Muhammad organized a religious commonwealth which over 10 years became so powerful that it could challenge and conquer Mecca (624-630). Before Muhammad died two years later, the Muslims (adherents of Islam, 'submission to God's will') had begun the conquest of other Arab tribes.

The story of militant Islam is one of history's most astounding tales. Fifty years after the Prophet's ignominious flight from Mecca, the armies of Islam were threatening the walls of Constantinople (669-678), having conquered everything and everybody from there to Mecca, plus Persia and Egypt. The Arabic Muslim empires that followed these conquests were among the world's greatest political, social and cultural achievements.

Muhammad was succeeded by 'caliphs' or deputies, whose job was to oversee the welfare of the Muslim commonwealth. His close companions got the job first, then his son-in-law Ali. After that, two great dynasties emerged. The Umayyads (661-750) based their empire in Damascus, the Abbasids (750-1100) in Baghdad. Both continually challenged the power and status of Byzantium.

Coming of the Turks

The history of the Turks as excellent soldiers goes back at least to the reign of the Abbasid Caliph Al-Mutasim (833-842). This ruler formed an army of Turkish captives and mercenaries that became the empire's strength, and also its undoing. Later caliphs found that their protectors had become their masters, and the Turkish 'praetorian guard' raised or toppled caliphs as it chose.

The Seljuk Empire

The first great Turkish state to rule Anatolia was the Great Seljuk Turkish Empire (1037-1109), based in Persia (Iran). Coming from Central Asia, the Turks captured Baghdad (1055). In 1071 Seljuk armies decisively defeated the Byzantines at Manzikert (Malazgırt), taking the Byzantine emperor as a prisoner. The Seljuks then took over most of Anatolia, and established a provincial capital at Nicaea/İznik. Their domains now included today's Turkey, Iran and Iraq. Their empire developed a distinctive culture, with especially beautiful architecture and design; the Great Seljuks also produced Omar Khayyam (died 1123). Politically, however, the Great Seljuk empire declined quickly, in the style of Alexander the Great's empire, with various pieces being taken by generals.

A remnant of the Seljuk empire lived on in Anatolia, based in Iconium (Konya). Called the Seljuk Sultanate of Rum ('Rome', meaning Roman Asia), it continued to flourish, producing great art and great thinkers until overrun by the Mongol hordes in 1243. Celaleddin Rumi, or 'Mevlana', founder of the Mevlevi (Whirling) Dervish order, is perhaps the Sultanate of Rum's outstanding thinker.

The Crusades

These 'Holy Wars', created to provide work for the lesser nobles and riff-raff of Europe, proved disastrous for the Byzantine emperors. Although a combined Byzantine and Crusader army captured

Nicaea (İznik) from the Seljuks in 1097, the Crusaders were mostly an unhelpful, unruly bunch. The Fourth Crusade (1202-1204) saw European ragtag armies invade and plunder Christian Constantinople. This was the first and most horrible defeat for the great city, and it was carried out by 'friendly' armies.

Having barely recovered from the ravages of the Crusades, the Byzantines were greeted with a new and greater threat: the Ottomans.

Birth of the Ottoman Empire

Byzantine weakness left a power vacuum which was filled by bands of Turks fleeing from the Mongols. Guerilla units, each led by a warlord, took over parts of the Aegean and Marmara coasts. The Turks who moved into Bithynia, around Bursa, were followers of a man named Ertuğrul. His son, Osman, founded (in about 1288) a principality which was to grow into the Osmanlı (Ottoman) empire.

Süleyman the Magnificent

The Ottomans took Bursa in 1326. It served them well as their first capital city. But they were vigorous and ambitious, and by 1402 they moved the capital to Adrianople (Edirne) because it was easier to rule their Balkan conquests from there. Constantinople was still in Byzantine hands.

The Turkish advance spread rapidly to both east and west, despite some setbacks. By 1452, under Mehmet the Conqueror, they were strong enough to think of taking Constantinople, capital of eastern Christendom, which they did in 1453. Mehmet's reign (1451-1481) began the great era of Ottoman power.

Süleyman the Magnificent

The height of Ottoman glory was under Sultan Süleyman the Magnificent (1520-1566). Called 'The Lawgiver' by the Turks, he beautified İstanbul, rebuilt Jerusalem and expanded Ottoman power to the gates of Vienna (1529). The Ottoman fleet under Barbaros Hayrettin Paşa seemed invincible. But by 1585 the empire had begun its long and celebrated decline. Most of the sultans after Süleyman were incapable of great rule. Luckily for the empire, there were very competent and talented men to serve as Grand Vezirs, ruling the empire in the sultans' stead.

The Later Empire

By 1699, Europeans no longer feared an invasion by the 'terrible Turk'. The empire was still vast and powerful, but it had lost its momentum, and was rapidly dropping behind the west in terms of social, military, scientific and material progress. In the 19th century, several sultans undertook important reforms. Selim III, for instance, revised taxation, commerce and the military. But the Janissaries and other conservative elements resisted the new measures strongly, and sometimes violently. It was tough to teach an old culture new tricks.

Affected by the new currents of ethnic nationalism, the subject peoples of the empire revolted. They had lived side-by-side with Turks for centuries, ruled over by their heads of communities (Chief Rabbi, Patriarch, etc) who were responsible to the sultan. But decline and misrule made nationalism very appealing. The Greeks gained independence in 1830; the Serbs, Bulgarians, Rumanians, Albanians and Arabs would all seek their independence soon after.

As the empire broke up, the European powers (England, France, Italy, Germany, Russia) hovered in readiness to colonize or annex the pieces. They used religion as a reason for pressure or control, saying that it was their duty to protect the Catholic, Protestant or Orthodox subjects from misrule and anarchy. The Holy Places in Palestine were a favourite target, and each power tried to obtain a foothold here for colonization later.

The Russian emperors put pressure on the Turks to grant them powers over all Ottoman Orthodox subjects, whom the Russian emperor would thus 'protect'. The result of this pressure was the Crimean War (1853-56), with Britain and France fighting on the side of the Ottomans against the Russians.

More reforms were proposed and carried out in the Ottoman Empire in an attempt to 'catch up' several centuries in a few years. The last powerful ruler, Abdul Hamid II (1876-1909), was put on the throne by Mithat Paşa, who also proclaimed a constitution in 1876. But the new sultan did away with Mithat Paşa and the constitution both, and established his own absolute rule.

Despite Abdul Hamid's harsh methods, the empire continued to disintegrate, with nationalist insurrections in Crete, Armenia, Bulgaria, Macedonia and other parts of the empire. The situation only got worse. The Young Turk movement for western-style reforms gained enough power by 1908 to force the restoration of the constitution. In 1909, the Young Turk-led Ottoman Parliament deposed Abdul Hamid and put his weak brother on the throne.

In its last years, though a sultan still sat on the throne, the Ottoman Empire was ruled by three members of the Young Turks' Committee of Union & Progress named Talat, Enver and Jemal. Their rule was vigorous, but harsh and misguided, and only worsened an already hopeless situation. When WW I broke out, they sided with Germany and the Central Powers. The Central Powers were defeated, the Ottoman Empire along with them.

The victorious Allies had been planning, since the beginning of the war, how they would carve up the Ottoman Empire. They even promised certain lands to several different peoples or factions in order to get their support for the war effort. With the end of the war, the promises came due. Having promised more than they could pay, the Allies decided on the dismemberment of Anatolia itself in order to get more land with which to pay 'claims'. The Turks were about to be wiped off the map. As for the last sultans, they were under the control of the Allies in İstanbul and thought only of their own welfare.

The Turkish Republic

The situation looked very bleak for the Turks as their armies were being disbanded and their country taken under the control of the Allies. But a catastrophe turned things around.

Ever since independence in 1831, the Greeks had entertained the *Megali Idea* ('Great Plan') of a new Greek empire encompassing all the lands which had once had Greek influence – the refounding of the Byzantine Empire. During WW I, the Allies had offered Greece the Ottoman city of Smyrna. King Constantine declined for various reasons, even though his prime minister, Eleutherios Venizelos, wanted to accept. After the war, however, Alexander became king, Venizelos became prime minister again, and Britain encouraged the Greeks to go ahead and take Smyrna. On 15 May 1919, they did.

The Turks, depressed and hopeless over the occupation of their country and the powerlessness of the sultan, couldn't take this: a former subject people capturing an Ottoman city, and pushing inland with great speed and ferocity. Even before the Greek invasion, an Ottoman general named Mustafa Kemal had decided that a new government must take over the destiny of the Turks from the powerless sultan. He had begun organizing resistance on 19 May 1919. The Greek invasion was just the shock needed to galvanize the people and lead them to his way of thinking.

The Turkish War of Independence lasted from 1920 to 1922. In September 1921 the Greeks very nearly reached Ankara, the nationalist headquarters, but in desperate fighting the Turks held them off. A year later, the Turks began their counter-offensive and drove the Greek armies back to İzmir by 9 September 1922.

Victory in the bitterly fought war made Mustafa Kemal even more a national hero. He was now fully in command of the fate of the Turks. The sultanate was abolished and after it, the Ottoman Empire. A Turkish republic was born, based in Anatolia and eastern Thrace. The treaties of WW I, which had left the Turks with almost no country, were renegotiated. Venizelos even came to terms with Kemal, signing a treaty in 1930.

Atatürk's Reforms
Mustafa Kemal undertook the job of completely remaking a society. After the republic was declared in 1923, a constitution was adopted (1924); polygamy was abolished and the fez, mark of Ottoman backwardness, was prohibited (1925); new, western-style law codes were instituted, and civil (not religious) marriage was required (1926); Islam was removed as the state religion, and the Arabic alphabet was replaced by a modified Latin one (1928). In 1930,

Constantinople officially became İstanbul, and other city names were officially Turkified (Angora to Ankara, Smyrna to İzmir, Adrianople to Edirne, etc). Women obtained the right to vote and serve in parliament in 1934.

In 1935, Mustafa Kemal sponsored one of the most curious laws of modern times. Up to this time, Muslims had only one, given name. Family names were purely optional. So he decided that all Turks should choose a family name, and they did. He himself was proclaimed Atatürk, or 'Father Turk', by the Turkish parliament, and officially became Kemal Atatürk.

Atatürk lived and directed the country's destiny until 10 November 1938. He saw WW II coming, and was anxious that Turkey stay out of it. His friend and successor as president of the republic, İsmet İnönü, succeeded in preserving a precarious neutrality. Ankara became a hotbed of Allied-Axis spying, but the Turks stayed out of the conflict.

Recent Years
In the beginning years, Atatürk's Republican Peoples' Party was the only political party allowed. But between 1946 and 1950 true democracy was instituted, and the opposition Democratic Party won the election in 1950.

By 1960 the Democratic Party had acquired so much power that the democratic system was threatened. The army, charged by Atatürk to protect democracy and the constitution, stepped in and brought various Democratic Party leaders to trial on charges of violating the constitution. The popular Peron-like party leader, Adnan Menderes, was executed, though all other death sentences were commuted. Elections were held in 1961.

In 1970 there was a gentlemanly *coup d'état* again because the successor to the Democratic Party had overreached its bounds. High-ranking military officers entered the national broadcasting headquarters and read a short message, and the government fell.

Under the careful watch of those same officers, democracy returned and things went well for years, until political infighting and civil unrest brought the country to a virtual halt in 1980. On the left side of the political spectrum, foreign communist elements pumped in arms and money for destabilization and, it is claimed, supported Armenian terrorist elements who murdered Turkish diplomats and their families abroad. On the right side of the spectrum, fanatic Muslim religious elements and a neo-Nazi party caused havoc. In the centre, the two major political parties were deadlocked so badly in parliament that for months they couldn't even elect a parliamentary president. The economy was in bad shape, inflation was 130% per year, the lawmakers were not making laws, crime in the streets by the fringe elements of left and right was epidemic. The military stepped in again on 12 September 1980, much to the relief of the man in the street, and restored civil, fiscal and legal order.

The constitution was rewritten so as to avoid parliamentary impasses. In a plebiscite, it was approved overwhelmingly by the people. The head of the military government, General Kenan Evren, resigned his military commission (as Atatürk had done) and was elected to be the country's new president. Under the interim Consultative Assembly and National Security Council, laws stalemated for years were passed. The old political leaders, seen by the new government to have been responsible for the breakdown of society, were tried (if they had committed crimes) or excluded from political life. The indictment against the head of the now-outlawed neo-Nazi party ran to nearly 1000 pages; he was subsequently convicted.

In 1983, elections under the new constitution were held, and the party less favoured by the military caretakers won. The new prime minister was Turgut Özal, a former World Bank economist. Under the new government, Turkey continues on the course it has pursued since Atatürk: a persistent drive towards an industrialized western economy. How successful this will be is, as with many small countries who pursue such a course, more in the hands of world banks and world markets than in the efforts of the countries themselves.

ATATÜRK

It won't take you long to discover the national hero, Kemal Atatürk. Though he died on 10 November 1938, his picture is everywhere, a bust or statue (preferably equestrian) is in every park, quotations from his speeches and writings are on every public building. He is almost synonymous with the Turkish Republic.

The best popular account of his life and times is Lord Kinross's *Atatürk: The Rebirth of a Nation* (Weidenfeld &

Kemal Atatürk

Nicolson, London, 1964). As portrayed by Kinross, Atatürk is a man of great intelligence and even greater energy and daring, possessed by the idea of giving his people a new lease on life. Like all too few leaders, he had the capability of realizing his obsession almost single-handed. His achievement in turning a backward empire into a forward-looking nation-state was taken as a model by Nasser, the shahs of Iran and other Islamic leaders. None had the same degree of success, however.

Early Years

In 1881, a boy named Mustafa was born into the family of a minor Turkish bureaucrat living in Salonika, now the Greek city of Thessaloniki, but at that time a city in Ottoman Macedonia. Mustafa was smart, and a hard worker in school. His mathematics teacher was so impressed that he gave him the nickname Kemal (excellence). The name Mustafa Kemal stuck with him as he went through a military academy and the War College, and even as he pursued his duties as an officer.

Military Career

He served with distinction, and acquired a reputation as something of a hothead, perhaps because his commanders were not as bold as he was. By the time of the Gallipoli battle in WW I, he was a promising lieutenant colonel of infantry.

The defence of Gallipoli, which saved the capital from British conquest (until the end of the war, at least), was a personal triumph for Mustafa Kemal. His strategic and tactical genius came into full play; his commanders had little to do but approve his suggestions; he led with utter disregard for his own safety. A vastly superior British force (mostly Anzacs) was driven away, and Mustafa Kemal became an Ottoman folk hero.

Though he was promoted to the rank of *paşa* ('pasha', general), the powers-that-be wanted to keep him under control.

They saw him as a 'dangerous element', and they were right. When the war was lost and the empire was on the verge of being disarmed and dismembered, Mustafa Kemal Pasha began his revolution.

The Revolution

He held meetings and congresses to rally the people, began to establish democratic institutions, and held off several invading armies, all at the same time and with severely limited resources. Several times the whole effort almost collapsed, and many of his friends and advisors were ready to ride out of Ankara for their lives. But Kemal never flinched, and was always ready to dare the worst. He was skilful – and fortunate – enough to carry through.

Many great revolutionary leaders falter or fade when the revolution is won. Atatürk was fortunate enough to live 15 years into the republican era, and he had no doubts as to what the new country's course should be. He introduced reforms and directed the country's progress with surprising foresight.

Most importantly, he gave Turks a new, positive image of themselves with which to replace the negative western image of the Ottoman Turk as decadent, sombre, ignorant and incompetent. This western image, which replaced that of the 'Terrible Turk' once there was no longer a threat that Turkey would conquer Europe, was based on a little truth and a lot of politics, but also on religious grounds: Turks were not Christian, and therefore unworthy. Atatürk replaced the Ottoman Turk with a new person who was European and modern in outlook.

Atatürk was the right man at the right time, and Turks believe that without this particular man there is no way Turkey could be what it is today. Rather, it might have ceased to exist; at the least, it would be like one of its Islamic neighbours, with less material and social progress, and no real grounding in democratic traditions.

The Turks look around them at their Islamic neighbours and thank their lucky stars they had a leader of such ability and foresight.

What This Means to You

This all means something to the visitor. There is a law against defaming the national hero, who is still held in the highest regard by the Turks. You won't see cartoons or caricatures of him, and no one mentions him in jest. The battle for nationhood was just too close to ever be anything but a serious matter. A slight directed toward Atatürk is virtually the same as insulting the Turks and their country.

POPULATION

Turkey has a population estimated at 54 million in 1987. Though the great majority of its people are Turks, ethnically and linguistically, there is a significant Kurdish population in the south-eastern region. The Kurds, though Muslims, have their own language and close tribal and family affiliations. Turkey also has small groups of Greeks, Armenians, Laz (a Black Sea people), Assyrians and Jews. The Turkish Jewish community is the remnant of a great influx which took place in the 1500s when the Jews of Spain were forced by the Inquisition to flee their homes. They were welcomed into the Ottoman Empire, and brought with them knowledge of many recent European scientific and economic discoveries and advancements.

GEOGRAPHY & CLIMATE

Most first-time visitors come to Turkey expecting to find deserts, palm trees, camel caravans, etc. In fact, the country is geographically diverse, with snow-capped mountains, rolling steppe, broad rivers, verdant coasts and rich agricultural valleys.

Distances

Turkey is big: the distance by road from Edirne on the Bulgarian border to Kars on the Russian one is over 1700 km. From the Black Sea shore to the Mediterranean is almost 1000 km. Now, 1000 km on flat ground might take only one very long day to drive, but Turkey has many mountain ranges which can lengthen travel times considerably.

Turkey is located between 35° and 42° north latitude, and 25° and 44° east longitude. It has borders with Bulgaria, Greece, Iran, Iraq, Syria and the Soviet Union. Coastline totals almost 8400 km; the Aegean coastline alone is 2800 km long. As for mountains, the highest is Ağrı Dağı (Mt Ararat) at 5165 metres (17,275 feet). Uludağ (Mt Olympus) near Bursa is 2543 metres (8343 feet). Under the empire, snow and ice could be taken from Uludağ, sailed across the Sea of Marmara, and presented to the sultan in İstanbul to cool his drinks.

Climatic Regions

Going from west to east, here's the lay of the land.

Marmara This region includes eastern Thrace from Edirne to İstanbul, rolling steppeland and low hills good for grazing, some farming and industry. The peninsula of Gelibolu (Gallipoli) forms the north shore of the Çanakkale Boğazı (Dardanelles, Hellespont). On the southern shore of the Sea of Marmara are low hills and higher mountains (including Uludağ). The land is very rich, excellent for raising fruits such as grapes, peaches and apricots. Average rainfall is about 670 mm; this is Turkey's second most humid region, with an annual average of 73% humidity.

Aegean This is a region of fertile plains and river valleys, low hills and not-so-low mountains. The ancient river Meander, now called the Menderes, is a good example of the Aegean's rivers. When you see it from the heights of ruined Priene, you'll know where the word 'meander'

comes from. For travelling, the Aegean region presents changing views of olive, fig and fruit orchards on hillsides; broad tobacco and sunflower fields.

Mediterranean The Mediterranean coast is mountainous without much beach between Fethiye and Antalya, but then opens up into a fertile plain between Antalya and Alanya before going to mountains again. All along the south coast, mountains loom to the north. The great Taurus (Toros) range stretches all the way from Alanya east to Adana. Temperatures at Antalya are a few degrees warmer than at İzmir.

Central Anatolia The Turkish heartland is a vast high plateau broken by mountain ranges, some with snow-capped peaks. The land is mostly rolling steppe good for growing wheat and grazing sheep. Ankara is 900 metres above sea level. In summer, it is hot and dry; in winter, chilly and often damp. Late spring and early autumn are perfect.

Black Sea The coast, 1700 km long, has a climate you might not expect in this part of the world. Rainfall is two to three times the national average, and temperatures are moderate. You will see hazelnut groves (on which the economy depends

heavily), cherry orchards and tobacco fields. The root word of 'cherry' is the Turkish *kiraz*, and this is where they came from. The cattle on the outskirts of every town provide milk, cream and butter famous throughout Turkey. At the eastern end of the Black Sea coast, the mountains come right down to the sea, and the slopes are covered with tea plantations. Rainfall and humidity are high. The Black Sea coast is like central Europe, but pleasantly warmer.

South-East Anatolia This region is dry (382 mm rainfall per year) and very hot in summer, as hot as 47°C (117°F). The land

is rolling steppe with rock outcrops. The major rivers are the Tigris (Dicle) and the Euphrates (Fırat).

Eastern Anatolia A mountainous and somewhat forbidding zone, this is wildly beautiful like no other region in Turkey. The average temperature is a cool 9°C (48°F), but varies between a hot 38°C (100°F) and a daunting –43°C (–45°F). Rainfall is average for Turkey, about 560 mm. It's chilly out here except from June through September. The people are not as rich as in other regions, but they do well enough grazing sheep, raising wheat and producing a few other crops.

When to Visit

Spring and autumn are best, roughly from April through June and September through November. The climate is perfect on the Aegean and Mediterranean coasts then, and in İstanbul. It's cooler in Central Anatolia, but not unpleasantly. There is very little rain between May and October.

The best months for water sports are, of course, the warmest: July and August. But the water is just right in May, June, September and October too.

In the hottest months on the coasts you may have to take a siesta during the heat of the day between noon and 3 pm. Get up early in the morning, clamber around the local ruins, then after lunch and a siesta come out again for *piyasa vakti*, 'promenade time', when everyone strolls by the sea, sits in a café, and watches the sunset.

If you plan a trip to eastern Turkey, do it in July and August. Don't venture into the east before May or after September, as there will still be lots of snow around, perhaps even closing roads and mountain passes. Unfortunately, the trip to eastern Turkey in high summer usually includes a pass through the south-east, which is beastly hot at that time.

Temperature Chart

The following chart shows the average daily minimum and maximum temperatures (in C°) for the main centres in Turkey.

RELIGION

The Turkish population is 99% Muslim. A small community of Sephardic Jews, descendants of those who were driven out of Spain by the Inquisition and welcomed into the Ottoman Empire, exists in İstanbul. There are groups of Greek Orthodox, Armenian Orthodox, Byzantine Catholic, Armenian Roman Catholic, Armenian Protestant and a few even smaller sects. But all of these non-Muslim groups make up less than 1% of the population, so to talk about Turkish religion is to talk about Islam.

The story of Islam's founding is covered in the History section.

Principles of Islam

The basic beliefs of Islam are these: God (Allah) created the world and everything in it pretty much according to the Biblical account. In fact, the Bible is a sacred book to Muslims. Adam, Noah, Abraham, Moses and Jesus were prophets. Their teachings and revelations are accepted by Muslims, except for Jesus's divinity and his status as saviour. Jews and Christians are called 'People of the Book', meaning those with a revealed religion that preceded Islam. The Koran prohibits enslavement of any People of the Book. Jewish prophets and wise men, Christian saints and martyrs, are all accepted as holy men in Islam.

But Islam is the 'perfection' of this earlier tradition. Though Moses and Jesus were great prophets, Muhammad was the greatest and last, *the* Prophet. To

city	Jan	March	May	July	Sept	Nov
Ankara	-4 – 4	0 – 11	9 – 22	15 – 30	11 – 26	2 – 13
Antalya	6 – 15	8 – 18	15 – 25	23 – 34	19 – 31	11 – 21
Bursa	2 – 9	4 – 13	11 – 23	17 – 31	14 – 27	7 – 16
Edirne	-1 – 6	2 – 12	12 – 24	17 – 31	13 – 27	5 – 13
İstanbul	3 – 8	3 – 10	12 – 21	18 – 29	16 – 25	9 – 15
İzmir	5 – 12	6 – 16	14 – 26	21 – 33	17 – 29	10 – 19
Silifke	7 – 14	9 – 18	15 – 26	22 – 32	20 – 31	12 – 22
Trabzon	5 – 11	5 – 11	13 – 17	20 – 26	18 – 23	10 – 16

him, God communicated his final revelation, and entrusted him to communicate it to the world. Muhammad is not a saviour, nor is he divine. He is God's messenger, deliverer of the final, definitive message.

Muslims do not worship Muhammad, only God. In fact, *muslim* in Arabic means, 'One who has submitted (to God's will)'; *islam* is 'submission (to God's will)'. It's all summed up in the *ezan*, the phrase called out from the minaret five times a day, and said at the beginning of Muslim prayers: 'God is great! There is no god but God, and Muhammad is his Prophet.'

The Koran

God's revelations to Muhammad are contained in the *Koran-i Kerim*, the Holy Koran. Muhammad, who couldn't read or write, recited the *suras* (verses or chapters) of the Koran in an inspired state. They were written down by followers, and are still regarded as the most beautiful, melodic and poetic work in Arabic literature, sacred or profane. The Koran, being sacred, cannot be translated. It exists truly only in Arabic.

The Islamic Commonwealth

Ideally, Islam is a commonwealth, a theocracy, in which the religious law of the Koran is the only law – there is no secular law. Courts are religious courts. In Turkey and several other Muslim countries, this belief has been replaced by secular law codes. In Iran, the Ayatollah Khomeini has attempted to do away with secular law and return to the exclusive use of Islamic law.

Religious Duties & Practices

To be a Muslim, one need only submit in one's heart to God's will, and perform a few basic and simple religious duties:

– One must say, understand and believe, 'There is no god but God, and Muhammad is His Prophet'.

– One must pray five times a day: at dawn, at noon, at mid-afternoon, at dusk and after dark.

– One must give alms to the poor.

– One must keep the fast of Ramazan, if capable of doing so.

– One must make a pilgrimage to Mecca once during one's life, if possible.

Muslim prayers are set rituals. Before praying, a Muslim must wash hands and arms, feet and ankles, head and neck in running water; if no water is available, in clean sand; if there's no sand, the motions will suffice. Then he must cover his head, face Mecca and perform a precise series of gestures and genuflexions. If he deviates from the pattern, he must begin again.

In daily life, a Muslim must not touch or eat pork, or drink wine (interpreted as any alcoholic beverage), and must refrain from fraud, usury, slander and gambling. No sort of image can be revered or worshipped in any way.

Islam has been split into many factions and sects since the time of Muhammad. Islamic theology has become very elaborate and complex. These tenets, however, are still the basic ones shared by all Muslims.

CUSTOMS

Under the Ottoman Empire (1300s to 1923), Turkish etiquette was highly organized and very formal. Every encounter among people turned into a mini-ceremony full of the flowery 'romance of the East'. Though the Turks have adapted to the informality of 20th-century life, you'll still notice vestiges of this courtly state of mind. Were you to learn Turkish, you'd find dozens of polite phrases – actually rigid formulas – to be repeated on cue in many daily situations. Some are listed in the language section at the back of this book. Pull out one of these at the proper moment, and the Turks will love it.

Turks are very understanding of foreigners' different customs, but if you

A verse of the Koran

want to behave in accordance with local feelings, use all the polite words you can muster, at all times. This can get laborious, and even Turks complain about how one can't even get out the door without five minutes of politenesses. But even the complainers still say them.

Also note these things: don't point your finger directly towards any person. Don't show the sole of your foot or shoe towards anyone (ie, so they can see it). Don't blow your nose openly in public, especially in a restaurant; instead, turn or leave the room and blow quietly. Don't pick your teeth openly, but cover your mouth with your hand. Don't do a lot of kissing or hugging with a person of the opposite sex in public. All of these actions are considered rude and offensive.

Mosque Etiquette

Always remove your shoes before stepping on a mosque's carpets, or on the clean area just in front of the mosque door. This is not a religious law, just a practical one. Worshippers kneel and touch their foreheads to the carpets, and they like to keep them clean. If there are no carpets, as in a saint's tomb, you can walk right in with your shoes on.

Wear modest clothes when visiting mosques, as you would when visiting a church. No tatty blue jeans, no shorts on men or women, no weird gear. Women should have head, arms and shoulders covered, and modest dresses or skirts, preferably to the knees. At some of the most-visited mosques, attendants will lend you long robes if your clothing doesn't meet a minimum standard. The loan of the robe is free, though the attendant will probably indicate where you can give a donation to the mosque. If you donate, chances are that the money actually will go to the mosque.

Visiting Turkish mosques is generally very easy, though there are no hard and fast rules. Most times no one will give you any trouble, but now and then there may be a stickler for propriety guarding the door, and he will keep you out if your dress or demeanour is not acceptable.

Avoid entering mosques at prayer time, (ie, at the call to prayer – dawn, noon, mid-afternoon, dusk and evening, or 20 minutes thereafter). Avoid visiting mosques at all on Fridays, especially morning and noon. Friday is the Muslim holy day.

When you're inside a mosque, even if it is not prayer time, there will usually be several people praying. Don't disturb them in any way; don't take flash photos; don't walk directly in front of them.

Everybody will love you if you drop some money into the donations box.

Body Language

Turks say 'yes' (*evet*, eh-VEHT) by nodding the head forward and down.

To say 'no' (*hayır*, HAH-yuhr), nod your head up and back, raising your eyebrows at the same time. Or just raise your eyebrows: that's 'no'.

Another way of saying 'no' is *yok* (YOHK), literally 'It doesn't exist (here)', or 'We don't have any (of it)'. Same head upward, raised eyebrows.

Remember, when a Turk seems to be giving you an arch look, he's only saying 'no'. He may also make the sound 'tsk', which also means 'no'. There are lots of ways to say 'no' in Turkish.

By contrast, wagging your head from side to side doesn't mean 'no' in Turkish; it means 'I don't understand'. So if a Turk asks you, 'Are you looking for the bus to Ankara?' and you shake your head, he'll assume you don't understand English, and will probably ask you the same question again, this time in German.

There are other signs that can cause confusion, especially when you're out shopping. For instance, if you want to indicate length ('I want a fish this big'), don't hold your hands apart at the desired length, but hold out your arm and place a flat hand on it, measuring from your

fingertips to the hand. Thus, if you want a pretty big fish, you must 'chop' your arm with your other hand at about the elbow.

Height is indicated by holding a flat hand the desired distance above the floor or some other flat surface such as a counter or table top.

If someone – a shopkeeper or restaurant waiter, for instance – wants to show you the stockroom or the kitchen, he'll signal 'Come on, follow me' by waving his hand downward and toward himself in a scooping motion. Waggling an upright finger would never occur to him, except perhaps as a vaguely obscene gesture.

FESTIVALS & HOLIDAYS

The official Turkish calendar is the western, Gregorian one as in Europe. But religious festivals, some of which are public holidays, are celebrated according to the Hicri (HIJ-ree), the Muslim lunar calendar. As the lunar calendar is about 11 days shorter than the Gregorian, the Muslim festivals arrive that many days earlier each year.

Actual dates for Muslim religious festivals are not completely systematic. Rather, they are proclaimed by Muslim authorities after the appropriate astronomical observations and calculations have been made, and then the civil authorities decide how many days should be civil holidays. But to help you know what's going on, the approximate dates of all major festivals for the near future are listed at the end of this section. No matter what month or year you visit Turkey, you can see at once when a lunar-calendar festival will be held.

Muslim days, like Jewish ones, begin at sundown. Thus a Friday holiday will begin Thursday at sunset and last until Friday sunset. For major religious holidays there is also a half-day vacation for 'preparation', called *arife* (ah-ree-FEH), preceding the start of a festival; shops and offices close about noon, and the festival begins at sunset.

Friday is the Muslim Sabbath, but it is not a holiday. Mosques and baths will be crowded, especially Friday morning. The day of rest, a secular one, is Sunday.

Only two religious holidays are public holidays: Şeker Bayramı and Kurban Bayramı.

Festivals

Regaip Kandili According to the lunar calendar, Regaip Kandili is the first Friday in the month of Recep, the traditional date for the conception of the Prophet Muhammad. Mosques are illuminated and special foods prepared. You'll see packets of small, sweetish *simit* bread rings, wrapped in coloured paper, for sale on the streets.

Miraç Kandili The 26th of the month of Recep, Miraç Kandili celebrates Muhammad's miraculous nocturnal journey from Mecca to Jerusalem and to heaven astride a winged horse named Burak. Mosques are illuminated and special foods eaten.

Berat Kandili The 'sacred night' between the 14th and 15th of the month of Şaban, this has various meanings in different Islamic countries, like Hallowe'en (All Saints, Day of the Dead). Mosque illuminations, special foods.

Ramazan The Holy Month, called Ramadan in other Muslim countries, is similar in some ways to Lent. For the 30 days of Ramazan, a good Muslim lets *nothing* pass the lips during daylight hours: no eating, drinking, smoking, or even licking a postage stamp. A cannon shot, and these days a radio announcer, signal the end of the fast at sunset. The fast is broken traditionally with flat *pide* bread if possible. Lavish dinners are given and may last far into the night. Before dawn, drummers circulate through town to awaken the faithful so they can eat before sunrise.

Ramazan can be an ordeal when it falls during the long, hot days of summer; *Ramazan kafası* ('Ramazan head', meaning irritability) can cause arguments to break out. Restaurants may be closed till nightfall, and in conservative towns it's bad form for anyone – non-Muslims included – to smoke, munch snacks or sip drinks in plain view. Business hours may change, and be shorter. As non-Muslims, it's understood that you get to eat and drink when you like, and in the big cities you'll find lots of non-fasting Muslims right beside you, but it's best to be discreet and to maintain a polite low visibility.

The fasting of Ramazan is a worthy, sacred act and a blessing to Muslims. Pregnant or nursing women, the infirm and aged, and travellers are excused, according to the Koran, if they feel they cannot keep the fast.

Kadir Gecesi The 27th day of the Holy Month of Ramazan is the 'Night of Power', when the Koran was revealed and Muhammad was appointed to be the Messenger of God. His duty was to communicate the Word of God to the world. Mosque illuminations, special prayers and foods celebrate the day.

Şeker Bayramı Also called Ramazan Bayramı, İd es-Seğir or İd el-Adha, this is a three-day festival at the end of Ramazan. Şeker (shek-EHR) is sugar or candy; during this festival children traditionally go door-to-door asking for sweet treats. Muslims exchange greeting cards and pay social calls. Everybody enjoys drinking lots of tea in broad daylight, after fasting for Ramazan. The festival is a three-day national holiday when banks and offices are closed. Hotels, buses, trains and airplanes are heavily booked.

Kurban Bayramı The most important religious and secular holiday of the year, Kurban Bayramı (koor-BAHN, sacrifice) is equivalent in importance to Christmas in Christian countries. Traditional date for its beginning is the 10th day of the month of Zilhicce.

The festival commemorates Abraham's near-sacrifice of Isaac on Mt Moriah (Genesis 22; Koran, Sura 37). In the story, God orders Abraham to take Isaac, the son of his old age, up to Mt Moriah and sacrifice him. Abraham takes Isaac up the mountain and lays him on the altar, but at the last moment God stops Abraham, congratulates him on his faithfulness, and orders him to sacrifice instead a ram caught in a nearby bush. Abraham does so.

Following the tradition today, 2½ million rams get theirs on Kurban Bayramı in Turkey each year. For days beforehand you'll see herds of sheep parading through streets or gathered in markets. Every head of household who can afford a sheep buys one and takes it home. Right after the early morning prayers on the actual day of Bayram, the head of the household slits the sheep's throat. It's then flayed and butchered, and family and friends immediately cook up a feast. A sizeable portion of the meat is distributed to the needy, and the skin is often donated to a charity; the charity sells it to a leather products company. Lots of people take to the road, going home to parents or friends. Everybody exchanges greeting cards. At some point you'll probably be invited to share in the festivities.

Kurban Bayramı is a four-day national holiday which you must plan for. Banks may be closed for a full week, though one or two branches will stay open in the big cities to serve foreigners. Transportation will be packed, and hotel rooms, particularly in resort areas, will be scarce and expensive.

Mevlid-i Nebi The 12th of Rebi ul-evvel is the anniversary of the Prophet's birth (in 570 AD). Special prayers and foods, mosque illuminations.

THE CALENDAR

January
All Month Camel wrestling at various locations in the province of Aydın, south of İzmir.

1 January New Year's Day is a public holiday. Decorations in shops, exchanges of gifts and greeting cards, make it a kind of surrogate Christmas, good for business.

15-16 January Camel-wrestling Festival in the village of Selçuk, next to Ephesus, south of İzmir.

February
In February it rains almost everywhere and is chilly and cheerless. The only fun to be had is indoors or at the ski slopes on Uludağ near Bursa. Another ski resort is in the Beydağları mountains near Antalya. Regaip Kandili (see above) falls on 18-19 February 1988 and on 9-10 February 1989.

March
Religious Holidays The movement of the lunar calendar makes March a time of *kandil* festivals (see above). Miraç Kandili is on 14-15 March 1988 and 3-4 March 1989. Berat Kandili occurs on 22-23 March 1989.

April
Religious Holidays The important holy month of Ramazan begins on 18 April 1988 and 7 April 1989, and lasts for 30 days. Berat Kandili is on 2-3 April 1988.
20-30 April Manisa Powergum Festival, when a traditional remedy called *Mesir macunu* or *Kuvvet macunu* ('powergum'), said to restore health, youth and potency, is concocted and distributed in Manisa, near İzmir.
23 April The big national holiday is National Sovereignty Day, when the first Grand National Assembly, or republican parliament, met in Ankara in 1920; it's also Children's Day.
Late April to early May Tulip Festival in Emirgân, a suburb of İstanbul.

May

May begins the tourist season in earnest, and also includes important civil and religious holidays. Sound and light shows begin at the Blue Mosque in İstanbul and last until October.

In Konya, the javelin-throwing game of *cirit* (jirid), played on horseback, takes place every Saturday and Sunday until October.

Religious Holidays The Holy Month of Ramazan is 18 April to 17 May 1988 and 7 April to 6 May 1989. Three days before the end of the Holy Month is Kadir Gecesi. Also, the important festival of Şeker Bayramı falls on the three days immediately following the end of the Holy Month, namely 18-20 May 1988 and 7-9 May 1989.

First Week Selçuk Ephesus Festival of Culture & Art at Selçuk, south of İzmir; folk dances, concerts, exhibits, some in the Great Theatre at Ephesus.

19 May Youth & Sports Day, held to commemorate Atatürk's birthday (1881)

29 May In İstanbul, celebrations remember the conquest of the city from the Byzantines in 1453.

Last Week Festival of Pergamum at Bergama, north of İzmir – drama in the ancient theater, folk dancing and handicrafts exhibits.

June

Sound and light shows take place at the Blue Mosque in İstanbul all month.

First Week The International Mediterranean Festival takes place in İzmir usually at this time.

4-5 June Traditional Rosegrowing Competition at Konya, when roses grown in the region are judged.

7-13 June Music & Art Festival at Marmaris – musical performances, folk dances, exhibitions.

Second Week Traditional Kırkpınar Oiled Wrestling Competition at Edirne; Festival of Troy at Çanakkale, on the Dardanelles near Troy.

Late June to Mid-July The world-class İstanbul International Festival, with top performers in the arts and special exhibitions.

July

In İstanbul, sound and light at the Blue Mosque continues, as does the İstanbul Festival. These are the two highlights of the month, but watch out for Kurban Bayramı.

Religious Holidays Kurban Bayramı, the single most important religious holiday of the Muslim year (equivalent in social disruption to Christmas in Christian countries), begins on 25 July 1988 and 14 July 1989, and may close everything tight for four days to a full week.

1 July The first day of the month is Denizcilik Günü (Navy Day), when seamen, ships and various maritime pursuits are celebrated. It commemorates the day when Turkey regained the right to operate its own ships along its own shores. (Under the empire, this right of *cabotage* had been granted under the Capitulations exclusively to foreign shipping companies.) You'll see decorations, hear speeches, and share in a moment of silence (except for ships' sirens and car horns) at 10 am. No public holiday, though.

5-10 July Nasreddin Hoca Celebrations, in honour of the semi-legendary humorous master of Turkish folklore legends and tales; held in Akşehir, his traditional birthplace.

7-12 July At Bursa, the Folklore & Music Festival is one of Turkey's best folk-dancing events of the year; the Bursa Fair (trade and tourism) starts about the same time.

29-31 July Music, Folklore & Water Sports Festival in Foça, north of İzmir.

August

In İstanbul, sound and light continue at the Blue Mosque. Similar shows begin at the Anıtkabir, Atatürk's Mausoleum, in Ankara.

Religious Holidays Kurban Bayramı, the

most important holiday of the year, begins on 6 August 1987. Remember, this is a four-day holiday.

15 August A special Mass celebrates the Assumption of the Virgin Mary, at the House of the Virgin Mary (Meryemana) near Ephesus. The Catholic Archbishop of İzmir says Mass.

15-18 August Çanakkale Troy Festival at Çanakkale, near Troy – folk dances, music, tours of Mt Ida and Troy.

20 August to 9 September The biggest festival is the İzmir International Fair; for a month the city's hotels are packed and transportation is crowded. The fair has amusements, cultural and commercial-industrial displays.

26 August Armed Forces Day with speeches and parades.

30 August Zafer Bayramı (zah-FEHR, Victory), commemorating the decisive victory at Dumlupınar of the republican armies over the invading Greek army during Turkey's War of Independence in 1922. Several foreign countries, including Greece, invaded Anatolia after WW I. Towns and cities celebrate their own Kurtuluş Günü (koor-too-LOOSH gew-new, Day of Liberation) on the appropriate date when Atatürk's armies drove out the foreign troops during July and August 1922.

September
Sound and light shows continue at the Blue Mosque in İstanbul and at the Anıtkabir in Ankara. The İzmir Fair goes on until 9 September.

1-9 September Bodrum Culture & Art Week, Turkish classical music concerts in Bodrum Castle, art exhibits and water sports shows.

2-4 September Kırşehir Ahi Evran Crafts & Folklore Festival at Kırşehir, when Turkish handicrafts are displayed and modelled in shows.

9 September In İzmir it's Kurtuluş Günü, or Liberation Day. In 1922, Atatürk's armies pushed the Greek invaders into the sea. Lots of parades and speeches.

11-12 September Çorum Hittite Festival, crafts shows, musical performances, tours of Hittite archaeological sites at Çorum near Ankara.

15-18 September Cappadocia Tourism Festival, a grape harvest and folklore festival highlighting the 'fairy chimneys' and underground cities of Cappadocia.

15 September to 5 October Textile & Fashion Fair at Mersin with fashion shows, handicrafts exhibitions, musical and folk-dancing performances.

22-30 September Konya hosts performances by the Whirling Dervish order, based here. On the 24th there's a culinary contest.

26-29 September At Diyarbakır, the Watermelon Festival. One year when I attended, everybody was disappointed because the prize-winning watermelon weighed in at a mere 32 kg. Bad year, they said. No rain.

October
Sound and light shows are supposed to continue in İstanbul at the Blue Mosque, but check in advance.

Religious holidays The Prophet Muhammad's birthday, Mevlid-i Nebi, falls on 22-23 October 1988 and 13-14 October 1989; *kandil*-like celebrations and illuminations.

1-9 October Film & Art Festival in Antalya, with a competition for best Turkish film of the year; other exhibits.

21-29 October Turkish Troubadors' Week at Konya – bards who continue the poetic forms hold contests in repartee, free-form composition and riddles.

29 October Cumhuriyet Bayramı (joom-hoor-ee-YEHT, Republic Day), commemorating the proclamation of the republic by Atatürk in 1923; biggest civil holiday, lots of parades and speeches.

November
Religious Holidays The Prophet Muhammad's birthday, Mevlid-i Nebi, falls on 3-4 November 1987; *kandil*-like celebrations and illuminations.

10 November is the most important day of the month, the day Atatürk died in 1938. At precisely 9.05 am, the moment of his death, the entire country comes to a screeching halt for a moment of silence. Literally everything stops in its tracks (you should too), just for a moment. Car horns and sirens blare. In schools, in the newspapers (the names of which are normally printed in red, but are all in black on this day), on radio and television, the national hero's life and accomplishments are reviewed.

December

All Month Camel wrestling at various locations in the province of Aydın, south of İzmir.

6-8 December St Nicholas Festival, when commemorative ceremonies are held in the 4th-century church of St Nicholas, the original Santa Claus, in Demre near Antalya.

14-17 December (approx) The Mevlana Festival, honouring Celaleddin Rumi, the great poet and mystic who founded the Mevlevi order of Whirling Dervishes, is held in Konya. Hotel space is tight, so try to pin down a room in advance, or be prepared to take a room below your normal standard.

LANGUAGE

Turkish is the dominant language in the Turkic language group which also includes such less-than-famous tongues as Kirghiz, Kazakh and Azerbaijani. Once thought to be related to Finnish and Hungarian, the Turkic languages are now seen as comprising their own unique language group. You can find people who speak Turkish, in one form or another, from Belgrade, Yugoslavia all the way to Sinkiang, China.

In 1928, Atatürk did away with the Arabic alphabet and adopted a Latin-based alphabet much better suited to easy learning and correct pronunciation. He also instituted a language reform to purge Turkish of abstruse Arabic and Persian borrowings, in order to rationalize and simplify it. The result is a logical, systematic and expressive language which has only one irregular noun (*su*, water), one irregular verb (*etmek*, to be) and no genders.

Word order and verb formation are very different from those belonging to the Indo-European languages, which makes Turkish somewhat difficult to learn at first despite its elegant simplicity. Verbs, for example, consist of a root plus any number of modifying suffixes. Verbs can be so complex that they constitute whole sentences in themselves, though this is rare. The standard blow-your-mind example is, *Afyonkarahisarlılaştır-amadıklarımızdanmıymışınız?* 'Weren't you one of those people whom we tried – unsuccessfully – to make to resemble the citizens of Afyonkarahisar?' It's not the sort of word you see every day.

Turks don't expect any foreigner to know Turkish, but if you can manage a few words you'll delight them. For their part, they'll try whatever foreign words they know, usually English or German, but some French, Dutch or Swedish. In this guide I've written the necessary Turkish words into the text wherever possible, so that you won't be at a loss for words. For a full collection of words, see the Turkish Language Guide section at the back of this book.

You may be approached by university students or school children wanting to practise their English. The approach is usually what it's purported to be, although if you're a good-looking young woman and he's a good-looking young Turkish man, he'll figure (naturally), why stop at English? Though foreign men are rarely approached by good-looking Turkish women for English practice or anything else, it does happen. Keep in mind that Turkish men (husbands, fathers, brothers) are very, very sensitive about the honour of their womenfolk.

Facts for the Visitor

VISAS & IMMIGRATION

If you have a valid passport, chances are good that you can enter Turkey and stay for three months, no questions asked. Citizens of Australia, Canada, Eire, Japan, New Zealand, the United Kingdom, the United States, and virtually all the countries of western and central Europe have that privilege. Citizens of some other places – Hong Kong, Jamaica, etc – have it as well.

Because of the Armenian terrorist campaign against Turks and things Turkish, persons with Armenian surnames are sometimes denied entry to Turkey regardless of the passport they carry. Even if you look nothing like a terrorist, the Turks will say they are taking no chances, and will put you back on the plane or across the border. Check with a Turkish consulate in your home country so as not to be inconvenienced.

Don't overstay your visit. If you're going to stay a year, you might want to apply for a residence permit (*İkamet Tezkeresi*), in which case you will have to show means of support. This means savings, a steady income from outside the country, or legal work within the country. The last is very difficult to find. Most people staying for a shorter period, or working without a valid permit (say, as private tutors of English), cross the border into Greece for a day or two every three months rather than bother with the residence permit.

Customs

Upon entering the country, customs inspection is often very cursory for foreign tourists. They may spot-check, but you probably won't even have to open your bags.

Arrival A verbal declaration is usually all you need. You can bring in up to one kg of coffee, five litres of liquor and two cartons (400) of cigarettes. Things of exceptional value (jewellery, unusually expensive electronic or photographic gear, etc) are supposed to be declared, and may be entered in your passport, which guarantees that the goods will be taken out of the country when you leave.

Departure *It is illegal to buy, sell, possess or export antiquities!* Read on.

You may export valuables (except antiquities) that have been registered in your passport on entry, or that have been purchased with legally converted money. For souvenirs, the maximum export limit is US$1000 of all items combined; if two or more similar items are exported, a licence may be required. Also, you may be required to show proof of exchange transactions for at least these amounts. Save your currency exchange slips, and have them ready for the customs officer in the departure area. He may ask you to turn over to him enough currency exchange slips to cover the amount of the purchases.

Your bags may well be checked when you leave the country (both for customs and security reasons), and searching questions will be asked about whether or not you are taking any antiquities with you. Only true antiquities are off-limits (not the many artful fakes). If you buy a real Roman coin from a shepherd boy at an archaeological site, can you take it home with you? Legally not. What happens if you get caught trying to smuggle out a significant piece of ancient statuary? Big trouble.

Only in the matter of carpets is there a difficult 'twilight zone', because particularly old and valuable carpets fall under the heading of 'antiquities'. To export such an item, you're supposed to have a statement from the shopkeeper, the local museum, or some other authority stating that the carpet is not an 'antiquity'. It's a bad situation, because your flight is about to leave, the customs officer says you ought to go back into the city and get a statement (which may take days). Bribery is not the way out. What to do? Have some sort of a statement to appease the officer, or do a lot of agreeable sweet-talking. Also, be ready to go back into the city and get the statement, as a last resort. If your carpet is less than a century old, you should have no problems whatsoever.

To avoid any chance of such unpleasantness, get your rug dealer to write something and sign it if the carpet's really old. This should do: *Bu halı/kilim antika değildir, ihraç edilebilirdir*, 'This carpet/kilim is not an antiquity, it may be exported'. Such a statement may not fill the bill legally, but it's some ammunition just in case the customs officer questions your purchase. And it beats the hassle of looking up some museum director and letting him gobble your time. Most likely, you'll have no problem, and the language barrier will work to your benefit. Unless, of course, you really *do* have a rug of museum quality.

Vehicles Automobiles, minibuses, trailers, towed seacraft, motorcycles and bicycles can be brought in for up to three months without a *carnet de passage* or *triptique*. Drivers must have a valid driving licence; an International Driving License is useful, but not normally required. Your own national driver's licence should pass all right. Third-party insurance such as a 'green card' valid for the entire country (not just for Thrace or European Turkey) or a Turkish policy purchased at the border is obligatory.

MONEY

The unit of currency is the Turkish *lira*, or TL, which was called the Turkish pound (LT) in the Ottoman Empire. The lira is supposedly divided into 100 *kuruş* (koo-

ROOSH), but inflation has rendered the kuruş obsolete. There's talk of a 100-to-one currency switch, which would bring the kuruş back to life. So far it's only talk.

Coins are rare, but you may come across coins of 1, 2½, 5, 10, 20, and 50 liras, and perhaps even higher denominations as time goes by. Notes (bills) come as 10, 20, 50, 100, 500, 1000, 5000 and 10,000 liras.

The exchange rates are:

US$1	=	714TL
£1	=	1011TL
A$1	=	460TL
NZ$1	=	365TL
C$1	=	511TL
DM1	=	355TL

Inflation is about 30% per annum. The exchange rate for hard currency reflects a slow 'creeping' devaluation which offsets this inflation and keeps the actual cost for a foreign tourist gratifyingly low. An adventurous traveller can live on as little as 3500TL (US$4.90) a day, easily on 7000TL (US$9.80) a day. For 15,000TL to 20,000TL (US$21 to US$28) a day, you can live in comfort and even style, so long as you don't stay at a Hilton or Sheraton.

Note All costs in this book are given in US dollars and in Turkish liras converted at a rate of 714TL = US$1.

Changing Money

Always have your passport with you when you change money.

Many tourist shops, travel agencies, expensive restaurants and some hotels have licences to accept foreign currency. The rate may not be quite as good as you get at the bank, though all rates will be pretty close. Most PTT (post office) branches will give you liras for foreign cash, but not for travellers' cheques.

Banks Banks are open from 8.30 am till

noon, and 1.30 to 5 pm, Monday through Friday. Outside those times it's difficult to change money. Plan ahead. There are currency exchange desks at the major entry points to Turkey by road, air and sea. The rate at the entry-point will be pretty close to the one downtown, so it's a good idea to change some money right as you enter – US$25 or US$50 at least.

Almost any bank will change money for you. Look for a sign on or near the front door reading 'Kambiyo - Exchange - Change - Wechsel', which says it all. In the large cities big banks have branches everywhere, even within 100 metres of one another, and exchange facilities may be limited to the more convenient branches. If a bank tells you it can't change your money, don't worry. You won't have to walk very far to reach the next one.

Many banks will post the daily exchange rates for all the major European currencies, plus the Japanese yen and the US dollar. You'll have no trouble exchanging US dollars, pounds sterling,

marks, francs, guilders, kroner, etc. Dollars, marks and sterling seem to go fastest. Eurocheques are readily accepted.

Procedures Changing money, either notes or travellers' cheques, can take anywhere from five to 25 minutes. It depends upon the bank and how cumbersome its procedures are. Usually a clerk must type up a form with your name and passport number, you must sign it once or twice, it must be countersigned by one or two bank officers, and then a cashier in a glass booth *(vezne)* will give you your money. Always take your passport when changing money, and be prepared to wait a while. Be patient. The bank people will often be especially kind to you (particularly in small towns). If the man with the tea tray is circulating, you may be invited to have some tea or coffee (on the bank). Even if the tea-man is not around, your preference may be asked and something ordered specially for you. When Turkish banks become as efficient as the Swiss, there won't be any smiles and free tea, which is a pity.

Commissions Some banks charge a fee for changing travellers' cheques (though not for changing cash notes). The Türkiye İş Bankası, for instance, charges up to 3%, plus the cost of official stamps. Most other banks charge nothing and have the same rate of exchange, so try elsewhere. To find out before you begin, ask *Komisyon alınır mı?* (koh-meess-YOHN ah-luh-NUHR-muh, 'Is a commission taken?')

Exchange Receipts Save your currency exchange receipts *(bordro)*. You will need them to change back Turkish liras at the end of your stay. Turkish liras are worth a lot less outside the country, so you won't want to take them with you. Also, the customs men at the frontier may ask you to show currency exchange receipts if you've bought a lot of valuable souvenirs

such as carpets. They want to make sure you changed money legally to buy them.

The Black Market Turkey's black market is not very vigorous, and it is chancy. Currency exchange violations are serious matters. Don't get caught at it. The black market, small though it is, exists because foreign currency is scarce, not because it's undervalued. Thus, if a Turk is going to Europe or America, he is allowed to purchase US$1000 in hard currency to cover expenses while abroad. To get a few more dollars, some people are willing to pay a bit more than the going rate.

In a shop you may get a better deal if you offer to pay in hard currency, but don't depend on it. The official line will be, 'I have a licence to change money. I'll just take it to the bank. There's no difference in price'. What the shopkeeper actually intends to do with the money is another matter, of course. It doesn't hurt to offer. If he grants a reduction, he can always say, 'OK, just because I'm fond of Australians/Americans/English/etc'.

Travellers' Cheques No problem in exchanging these for Turkish liras in a bank, as long as you have your passport with you. The more expensive hotels, restaurants and shops will accept the cheques, as will car rental agencies and travel agencies. Generally, though, it's better to change cheques for Turkish liras in a bank. But see 'Commissions', above.

Though a wide range of cheques is accepted, the more familiar your cheques are, the better. American Express, Thomas Cook, Eurocheques and the like go quickly. I once changed some Swiss Bankers' Travellers' Cheques with little trouble; the clerk just had to look up the example in her book and compare them.

Credit Cards
Turks are beginning to learn about living

on plastic. The big hotels and expensive shops may accept your credit card. Car rental agencies certainly will. Make sure in advance because not all establishments accept all cards. If you have American Express, Visa, Diners Club and Mastercard/Access/Eurocard, you're probably equipped for any establishment that takes cards. If you only have one or two, ask. Turkish Airlines, for instance, may accept only Mastercard/Access/ Eurocard. The State Railways doesn't accept credit cards. A souvenir shop may accept all four.

A shopkeeper may require you to pay the credit card fee of 5% to 7%, or charges (up to 2200TL, US$3.08) for making credit card arrangements (*provizyon*, pro-veez-YOHN) with a bank. He may not see it as a normal cost of business. Any price, whether marked or haggled for, is assumed to be for cash. As he must pay the credit card company a percentage, and the bank a fee, he may reason that the charge should be passed on to you.

Transferring Money

The speed with which you need to transfer money determines the cost of the transfer. If you have months, send a letter home, ask them to send a cheque, deposit the cheque in a Turkish bank for clearance, and then wait. Of course, banks can telex or wire money in a matter of a day or two (usually), but this may cost as much as US$30 per transfer. Sometimes the transfer fee is a percentage of the amount transferred. Still, if you're in a hurry, you may have to do it.

Though the PTT in Turkey handles postal money orders, I would not recommend this route for anything more than token amounts. The PTT is often difficult to deal with. You'll do better with a bank.

Before transferring money, consider these alternatives: some shopkeepers and other businesses will accept a personal cheque in exchange for a purchase. If you have a Turkish friend to countersign a cheque, you may well be able to get cash from a bank. With some credit cards you may be able to get a cash advance on the card from a bank, or use the card as security to cash a cheque at the card's company office. Even if the amount is limited (US$100 to US$150 per day), it doesn't take many days to build up a substantial sum. A bank may require you to pay a telex charge for a credit card cash advance, but it will not be more than a few dollars.

If it comes to transferring money by bank wire, walk into a large bank, preferably in a large town, find someone who speaks English, and explain the problem. The bank may be able to telex your bank and request the funds, or you may have to call your bank (or a friend) and do it yourself. When the funds arrive at the Turkish bank, take your passport and pick up your money.

Should you want foreign currency, you may find that the bank goes through a maddening, fee-producing exercise: your incoming funds will be converted into Turkish liras, then reconverted to your home currency. The bank pockets the 'spread' between buying and selling currency rates, plus two exchange fees. There may also be a fee for the special service.

Student Discounts

Holders of the International Student Identity Card (ISIC) are officially permitted to enter archaeological sites and museums under the control of the Ministry of Culture & Tourism and the Ministry of Education for free. For students with Turkish student cards, there is usually a special student admission price of 50TL (US$0.07), compared to normal admission prices of 200TL to 500TL or more (US$0.28 to US$0.70). Though the ISIC is your free pass everywhere, there may be some gatekeepers who don't know the official rules, and you may have to ask them to consult the regulations or call a superior. You may run into one or two sites which are not under the control of these ministries, however, and may have to pay the admission fee. The former sultans' palaces, for instance, are under the control of the Grand National Assembly (Turkish parliament), and not the aforementioned ministries.

Students get discounts of 10% on the Turkish State Railways and on Turkish Maritime Lines ships. Turkish Airlines, which used to give very nice student discounts, does not do so anymore. However, the airline does have the offer of a 10% 'family discount' to any husband-and-wife couple, with or without children.

Turkey is part of the WASTEELS and Inter-Rail discount schemes for rail.

EMBASSIES & CONSULATES

İstanbul has many palatial consulates left from the days of Ottoman glory, when foreign powers built splendid embassy compounds to impress the sultan. The embassies are all now in Ankara, the modern capital. But there are helpful consulates or consular agents in İstanbul, İzmir, Adana and a few other port cities.

If you plan to travel from Turkey to Europe by way of Bulgaria, you'll save time and money by picking up a Bulgarian transit visa in İstanbul or Ankara. In fact, they may not be issuing them at the border. See the Getting There chapter for details.

Here is a list of diplomatic missions. To find one, use these phrases:

(Name of country) Büyükelçiliği nerede? (. . . . bew-YEHK-ehl-chee-lee neh-reh-DEH),
'Where is the . . . . embassy?'
(Name of country) Konsolosluğu nerede? (KOHN-sohl-lohs-loo-oo).
'Where is the . . . . consulate?'

Australia (Avustralya)
Embassy: Nene Hatun Caddesi 83, Gazi Osman Paşa, Ankara (tel 127 53 18)
Austria (Avusturya)
Embassy: Atatürk Bulvarı 189, Kavaklıdere, Ankara (tel 125 47 61)
Consulate: Silâhhane Caddesi 59/4, Teşvikiye, Şişli, İstanbul (tel 146-3769)
Bulgaria (Bulgarya)
Embassy: Atatürk Bulvarı 129, Kavaklıdere, Ankara (tel 126 74 55)
Consulate: Yıldız Posta Sokak 15, Gayrettepe, İstanbul (tel 166-2605). In many cases, the Turkish travel agency which sells you the bus or train ticket through Bulgaria will also be able to get a Bulgarian transit visa for you at a cost of about 3500TL (US$4.90).
Canada (Kanada)
Embassy: Nene Hatun Caddesi 75, Gazi Osman Paşa, Ankara (tel 127 58 03)
Denmark (Danimarka)
Embassy: Kırlangıç Sokak 42, Gazi Osman Paşa, Ankara (tel 127 52 58)
Consulate: Silâhhane Caddesi, İzmir Palas Ap 31/1, Teşvikiye, Şişli, İstanbul (tel 140-4217)
France (Fransa)
Embassy: Paris Caddesi 70, Kavaklıdere, Ankara (tel 126 14 80)
Consulate: İstiklal Caddesi 8, Taksim, İstanbul (tel 143-4387)
Germany (Federal) (Federal Almanya)
Embassy: Atatürk Bulvarı 114, Kavaklıdere, Ankara (tel 126 54 65)
Consulate: İnönü (Gümüşsuyu) Caddesi, Ayazpaşa, Taksim, İstanbul (tel 145-0705)
Greece (Yunanistan)
Embassy: Şölen Sokak 8, Çankaya, Ankara (tel 139 04 10)
Consulate: Ağahamam Sokak, Kuloğlu, Beyoğlu, İstanbul (tel 145-0596). If your passport bears any evidence (ie, stamps) that you have been in the Turkish Republic of Northern Cyprus, you will be denied entry to Greece. Have the official stamp a piece of paper instead.
India (Hindistan)
Embassy: Kırlangıç Sokak 42, Ankara (tel 127 52 58 or 127 53 68). Apparently Indian visas are quite easy to get in Ankara, the process taking only about five hours.
Iran (İran)
Embassy: Tahran Caddesi 10, Kavaklıdere, Ankara (tel 127 43 20)

Consulate: Ankara Caddesi, Cağaloğlu, İstanbul (tel 528-5053). Iranian transit visas are, in principle, available to citizens of many countries (excluding the USA), but in practice may be impossible to obtain. If you want to try, get a letter of introduction from your embassy and have it when you apply. Be prepared to wait for months – literally – according to recent reports from readers of this book. Visas, usually seven-day transit visas, are good for only one week from the date of issue. Though US dollars circulate freely in Iran, you will not be able to cash US dollar travellers' cheques.

Israel *(İsrail)*
    Embassy: Farabi Sokak 43, Çankaya, Ankara (tel 126 39 04)
    Consulate: Büyük Çiftlik Sokak, Arif Aras Ap, Teşvikiye, Şişli, İstanbul (tel 146-4125)

Netherlands *(Holanda)*
    Embassy: Şehit Ersan Caddesi 4, Çankaya, Ankara (tel 27 43 26)
    Consulate: İstiklal Caddesi 393, Galatasaray, İstanbul (tel 149-5310)

Pakistan *(Pakistan)*
    Embassy: İran Caddesi 1 (tel 127 23 26)

Sweden *(İsveç)*
    Embassy: Kâtip Çelebi Sokak 7, Kavaklıdere, Ankara (tel 127 35 44)
    Consulate: İstiklal Caddesi 497, Tünel, Beyoğlu, İstanbul (tel 143-5770)

Switzerland *(İsviçre)*
    Embassy: Atatürk Bulvarı 247, Çankaya, Ankara (tel 127 43 16)
    Consulate: Hüsrev Gerede Caddesi 75/3, Teşvikiye, Şişli, İstanbul (tel 148-5070)

Syria *(Suriye)*
    Consulate: Şehit Cemal Sokak 3, Nişantaş İstanbul (tel 148-2735)

UK *(İngiltere, Birleşik Krallığı)*
    Embassy: Şehit Ersan Caddesi 46/A, Çankaya, Ankara (tel 127 43 10)
    Consulate: Meşrutiyet Caddesi 26, Galatasaray, İstanbul (tel 149-8874)

USA *(Amerikan Birleşik Devletleri, Amerika)*
    Embassy: Atatürk Bulvarı 110, Kavaklıdere, Ankara (tel 126 54 70)
    Consulate: Meşrutiyet Caddesi 106, Tepebaşı, Beyoğlu, İstanbul (tel 143-6200)

USSR *(Sovyetler Birliği, Rusya)*
    Embassy: Karyağdi Sokak 5, Çankaya, Ankara (tel 139 21 22, 3)

Consulate: İstiklal Caddesi 443, Tünel, İstanbul (tel 144-3587)

Call before you visit any of these embassies or consulates. Diplomats keep very odd business hours sometimes, and they close up on both Turkish and their own national holidays.

ADDRESSES

Turkish postal addresses are usually written with the name of the main street first, then the minor street and then the number of the building. For example:

Bay Mustafa Adıyok
Geçilmez Sokak, Bulunmaz Cıkmazı
Luks Apartımanı No 23/14
Tophane
İSTANBUL

In this example, *Bay* means 'Mr' (for 'Mrs' or 'Miss', it's *Bayan*, pronounced like the English phrase 'buy an . . .'). The next line has the name of a largish street, 'Geçilmez Sokak', followed by the name of a smaller street, alley, mews or dead end, 'Bulunmaz Cıkmazı', which runs off it. The third line has the name of an apartment building, 'Luks Apartımanı'. As for the numbers, the first one, '23', is the street number of the building; the second, '14', is the apartment or office number within the building. The district, 'Tophane', comes next, then the city.

The address can be written more simply when the desired building is on a large, well-known street. For example:

Bay Mustafa Adıyok
Büyük Cad No 44/10
Taksim
İSTANBUL

In some cases the district of the city is put at the beginning of the second line, as 'Taksim, Büyük Caddesi No 44/10'. In any case, you've got to be familiar with the district names to find a certain address.

Turkey is instituting a system of five-digit postal codes, but they have yet to come into general use. Use the postal code if you have it.

INFORMATION

Every Turkish town of any size has a Tourism Information Office run by the Ministry of Culture & Tourism. The ministry's symbol is the fan-like Hittite sun figure, which you will get used to seeing.

A town may also have a municipal or provincial tourism office. If you need help and you can't find an office, ask for the Belediye Sarayı (behl-eh-DEE-yeh sah-rah-yuh, Town Hall). They'll rummage around for someone who speaks some English, and will do their best to solve your problem.

In İstanbul, there are Tourism Information Offices at Atatürk Airport in the International Arrivals area (tel 573-7399, 573-4136); in Sultanahmet Square at the northern end of the Hippodrome (tel 522-4903); two long blocks from Taksim Square in the Hilton Hotel arcade (tel 140-6300, 140-6864); and on Meşrutiyet Caddesi near Galatasaray Square and the British Consulate, in the İstanbul Bölge Müdürlüğü building.

In İzmir, the Information Office (tel 14-2147) is on Gazi Osman Paşa Bulvarı at Cumhuriyet Meydanı, right next to the Turkish Airlines office in the shops built beneath the Büyük Efes Oteli. Cumhuriyet Meydanı is the square with the equestrian statue of Atatürk.

In Ankara you can go to the ministry itself. It's on Gazi Mustafa Kemal

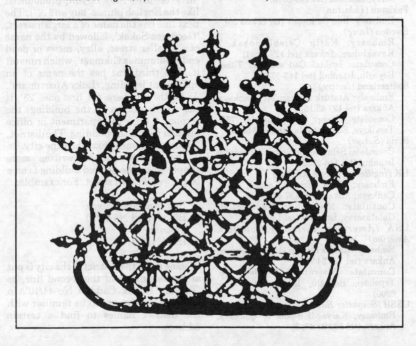

Hittite Sun Figure, symbol of the Turkish Ministry of Culture & Tourism

Bulvarı several blocks west of Kızılay, on the south (left) side of the street. Ask for the Kültür ve Turizm Bakanlığı. The telephone number is 229 09 65.

Here are the addresses of Turkish Culture & Tourism Offices abroad:

Austria
Turkishe Botschaft Informationsabteilung, Mahlerstrasse 3, 1010 Wien; tel 43 (0222) 512-2128, 9; telex 111281 TUINF A

Belgium
Conseiller Culturel et de l'Information, Ambassade de Turquie, Rue Montoyer, 4-1040 Bruxelles; tel 32 (2) 513-8230, 9; telex 25973 TURKTA B

Denmark
Turkish Embassy Information Counsellor Bureau, Vesterbrogade 11A, 1620 Kobenhavn V; tel 45 (1) 223-100, 228-374; telex 22340

France
Turquie, Service d'Information, Champs-Elysees 102, 75008 Paris; tel 33 4562-7868, 4562-7984, 4562-2610; telex 290639

Germany, Federal Republic
Informationsabteilung des Türkischen Generalkonsulats, Baselerstrasse 37, 6 Frankfurt M1; tel 49 (0611) 233-081, 82; telex 4170-081
Informationsabteilung des Türkischen Generalkonsulats, Karlsplatz 3/1, 8000 München 2; tel 49 (089) 594-902, 594-317; telex 528190 INTU D

Italy
Ambasciata di Turchia, Ufficio Cultura e Informazione, Piazza della Repubblica 56, 00185 Roma; tel 39 (6) 462-957, 474-1697; telex 612131 TURTANIT

Japan
Turkish Tourism & Information Office, 33-6, 2-Chome Jingumae, Shibuya-Ku, Tokyo; tel 81 (3) 470-6380, 470-5131; telex J-22856 EMBTURK

Kuwait
Turkish Embassy, Office of the Information Counsellor, PO Box 15518, Deaya, Kuwait, 35456; tel 65 242-4248, 242-4298; telex 46228 TURKISM, KT

Netherlands
Turkish Embassy, Information Counsellor's Office, Herengracht 451, 1017 BS Amsterdam; tel 31 (20) 266-810, 244-006; telex 15521

Saudi Arabia
Turkish Embassy, Information Office, Medina Rd, Km 6, Al-Musaidiya St, PO Box 6966, Jeddah; tel 66 54578; telex 402631 CIBMEM-SJ

Spain
Oficina de Información y Turismo de Turquia, Plaza de España, Torre de Madrid, Piso 13, Off 3, 28008 Madrid; tel 34 (1) 248-7014, 248-7114; telex 44345 TUEL

Sweden
Turkiska Statens Informationsbyra, Kungsgatan 3, 11143 Stockholm; tel 46 (8) 218-620, 218-630; telex 11033 A TELEKC S

Switzerland
Türkisches Generalkonsulat, Talstrasse 74, 8001 Zurich; tel 41 (1) 221-0810; 12; telex 045-813752

United Kingdom
Turkish Tourism & Information, 170-173 Piccadilly, 1st floor, London W1V 9DD; tel 44 (1) 734-8681, 2, 491-0773; telex 895-4905 TTIOF G

United States
Office of the Culture & Information Attaché, Turkish Consulate-General, 821 United Nations Plaza, New York, New York 10017; tel 1 (212) 687-2194; telex 426428
Culture & Tourism Office, Turkish Embassy, 2010 Massachusetts Avenue NW, Washington, DC 20036; tel 1 (202) 429-9844, 833-8411; telex 248366 TURP UR

GENERAL INFORMATION

Time

Turkish time is Eastern European Time, two hours ahead of Greenwich Mean Time except in the warm months (April through September), when clocks are turned ahead one hour. At noon in Istanbul, Ankara or Erzurum, the time elsewhere is:

Paris, Rome	11 am
London	10 am
New York	5 am
Los Angeles	2 am
Perth, Hong Kong	7 pm
Sydney	9 pm
Auckland	11 pm

Weights & Measures

Turkey uses the metric system. For those used to the Anglo-American systems of measurement conversion information can be found at the back of this book.

Electricity

It is 220 volts, 50 cycles as in Europe, though sometimes it's not up to full voltage ('brown-out'). Parts of Beyoğlu in İstanbul, wired by the French over a century ago, used to be on 110 volts, but now everything's 220 volts.

Plugs are of the European variety with two round prongs, but there are two sizes in use. Most common is the small-diameter prong, so if you have these you're in fine shape. The large-diameter, grounded plug as used in Germany and Austria is also in use, and you'll find some outlets (points) of this type. Plugs for these won't fit the small-diameter outlets.

Adapters are not easily available. You've got to rig something up yourself unless you've brought an adapter from Europe and it happens to be the right one. (Adapters for the flat-prong North American-type plugs are sold in many electrical shops. If you have these plugs, and 220-volt appliances, you're unusual and in luck.)

For those who have the good sense to plan ahead, here are the Vital Statistics of the Turkish Plug: prongs 4 mm in diameter, 1.9 cm long; distance from the centre of one prong to the centre of the other 1.9 cm; distance between the prongs 1.5 cm. The European grounded plug, by contrast, has prongs 4.5 mm in diameter, 1.9 cm apart from centre to centre, but only 1.4 cm long.

HEALTH

You need no special inoculations before entering Turkey, unless you're coming from an endemic or epidemic area. If you want to get preventive shots (tetanus, typhoid, etc) get cholera too. The chances are small that you'll run into cholera, but it may come in handy when crossing borders. Health officers far removed from the scene may not keep track of which countries have it.

Medical services are well developed in Turkey. Some doctors speak English, French or German, and have studied in Europe or America. Your consulate can recommend a good doctor or dentist.

For minor problems, it's customary to ask at a pharmacy/chemist's (eczane, edj-zahn-NEH) for advice. Sign language usually suffices to communicate symptoms, and the pharmacist will prescribe on the spot. Even 'prescription' drugs are sometimes sold without a prescription.

Though Turkey manufactures most modern prescription medicines, it's not good to risk running out. If you take a drug regularly, bring a supply. If your medicine is available in Turkey, it will probably be far less expensive here than at home. It may be good to buy a quantity to take home with you. The drug's name may not be exactly the same, though the substance may be.

Food & Water

Turkey is generally a safe country as far as food and water are concerned, but you should take precautions for several reasons.

The first is obvious: sanitary practices are not universally observed, no matter where you are in the world.

The second reason has to do not with the cleanliness of the food but with its familiarity. Most people suffer some consequences from drastic change of diet and water, for each area and each cuisine has its own 'normal' bacteria and its own composition. Some people find it difficult to digest olive oil, or even to stomach pure water that has a high limestone content. Any experienced traveller knows that getting sick from food is mostly by chance, but there are still a few things you can do to improve your chances.

Dining Precautions Take the normal travel precautions. Choose dishes that look freshly prepared and sufficiently hot. You can go into almost any Turkish kitchen (except in the very posh places) for a look at what's cooking. In fact, in most places that's what the staff will suggest, the language barrier being what it is. Except for grilled meats, Turkish dishes tend to be cooked slowly for a long time, just the thing to kill any errant bacteria. If they don't sell on the day they're cooked, they might be saved, and the oil may congeal and become harder to digest. Most of the time meals are reasonably fresh.

As for grilled meats, these may be offered to you medium rare. They'll probably be all right, but if they really look pink, send them back for more cooking (no problem in this). The words you'll need are *biraz daha pişmiş* (beer-ahz da-HAH peesh-meesh, 'cooked a bit more') or *iyi pişmiş* (ee-EE peesh-meesh, 'well done').

Beware of milk products and dishes containing milk that have not been properly refrigerated. Electricity is expensive in Turkey, and many places will scrimp on refrigeration temperature. If you want a rice pudding *(sütlaç)* or some such dish with milk in it, choose a shop that has lots of them in the window, meaning that a batch has been made recently, guaranteeing freshness. In general, choose things from bins, trays, cases, pots, etc that are fairly full rather than almost empty.

Drinking Precautions As for water, you'll find it preferable to stick to bottled spring water as much as possible. It's sold everywhere in clear plastic 1½-litre bottles and is delicious. The tap water is not particularly poisonous (as in some countries), but neither does it taste good. At a roadside *çeşme* (CHESH-meh, fountain or spring), look out for the word *içilmez* (eech-eel-MEHZ, 'not to be drunk') near the water. If what you see is *içilir* (eech-eel-LEER, 'drinkable'), or *içme suyu* (EECH-meh soo-yoo, 'drinking water'), or *içilebilir* (EECH-eel-eh-bee-LEER, 'can be drunk') then everything's all right. Even if the water is pure, its high limestone content may give some people loose bowels at first. This is nothing serious.

Alternatives to spring water include *maden suyu*, naturally fizzy mineral water, and *maden sodası* (or just *soda*), artificially carbonated mineral water. The latter just has bigger bubbles, and more of them, than the former. Both come from mineral springs, and both are truly full of minerals. The taste is not neutral. Some people like it, some don't. It's supposed to be good for you, clean out your kidneys, etc.

Soft drinks, beer and wine are reliably pure, except in rare cases. As for wines, you'll have no trouble with the big names: Doluca, Kavaklıdere, Tekel, Efes Güneşi.

Food Poisoning Even though few people get sick from the food, there are cases of salmonella (food poisoning) and hepatitis. The way to combat them is to remain generally strong, well rested and well fed, and to avoid eating in places which seem to ignore basic rules of sanitation.

The symptoms of food poisoning are headache, nausea and/or stomach ache, diarrhea, fever and chills. If you get it, go to bed, put as many covers on as possible (stay warm no matter what). Drink lots of fluids, preferably hot tea without sugar or milk. Camomile tea, *papatya çay*, is a specific against queasy stomach. Some tea houses serve it, herbal markets sell the dried camomile, and in many parts of Turkey you can even pick the fragrant little daisy-like camomile flowers along the roadside and make the tea yourself.

Until the bout of food poisoning has run its course (24 to 30 hours), drink nothing but plain tea (no milk or sugar), and eat nothing but dry toast or rusks and maybe a little yogurt. The day after, you'll feel weak, but the symptoms will have passed except perhaps for the diarrhea. If you take it easy and eat only bland, easily-digested foods for a few days, you'll be fine.

In almost every case, the few people who get food poisoning while abroad compound the problem by ignoring it, or by continuing to travel or see the sights, or by eating whatever is easiest. Medicines, available with or without a prescription from any *eczane*, can help a serious bout of the illness. But nothing can rebuild your intestinal flora, necessary to good digestion, except time and tender loving care. Most medicines for food poisoning are strong antibiotics. They kill the poisonous bacteria (which your body will kill on its own, in time), but they also kill all the normal, healthful digestive bacteria. Thus antibiotics can actually *prolong* the diarrhea by making it difficult for your digestive system to do its work.

As for hepatitis (*sarılık*, sahr-uh-LUHK), this is a serious viral infection which must be treated carefully. The chief symptoms are fatigue, loss of energy, a yellow cast to the eyes and skin, and odd-coloured brownish urine. If you rest when your body tells you to, you will have no trouble curing yourself. If you push on, the disease can cause serious liver damage or even be fatal. Being a virus, there is no known drug to combat it. Antibiotics can actually make it worse, even fatal, as they put great stress on the liver (which must detoxify them), which is already overburdened.

If you think you have hepatitis, go to a doctor and get an examination and a blood test. If the diagnosis is positive, go to bed and stay there. Eat only easily digestible non-fatty foods such as toast, yogurt, cooked fruits and vegetables. Don't drink any alcohol for six months after diagnosis. You will have to figure on at least a week or two of bed rest, then an easy life for several months. The doctor may prescribe vitamins, especially B-complex. If he prescribes any other medicine, go to another doctor. This is no joke.

Doctors, Dentists & Hospitals

You can find excellent doctors and dentists in the big cities. Ankara has a first-rate medical centre called Hacettepe (hah-JEHT-tehp-peh) plus other hospitals (*hastane*, hahs-tahn-NEH) and clinics (*klinik*, klee-NEEK). Government-supported hospitals are called Devlet Hastanesi (dehv-LEHT hass-tah-neh-see), and you can find them by following the standard European road sign with a large 'H' on it. Clinics run by the Red Crescent (Kızılay, the Turkish equivalent of the Red Cross) are marked by a red crescent. Both provide low-cost health care.

In every city and town of any size you will see signs marking the medical offices (surgeries) of doctors and giving their specialties. *Operatör* means surgeon. *Göz hastalıkları* means the *tıbbî doktör* (medical doctor) treats eye diseases. *Dahili* is internal medicine. *Kadın hastalıkları* are gynecological ailments. A doctor who treats *çocuk hastalıkları* is a pediatrician.

Istanbul has several foreign-run hospitals:

American
   Amiral Bristol Amerikan Hastanesi, Güzelbahçe Sokak, Nişantaş, İstanbul (tel 148-6030)
French
   Pasteur Fransız Hastanesi, Divan Hotel Arkası (behind the Divan Hotel), Taksim, İstanbul (tel 148-4756)
   La Paix Hastanesi, Büyükdere Caddesi, Şişli, İstanbul (tel 148-1832)
German
   Alman Hastanesi, Sıraselviler Caddesi, Taksim (tel 143-5500)

Charges at the foreign hospitals will be higher than at the government-supported Turkish hospitals or Red Crescent clinics. All charges will be much less than you're used to at home, unless your country has a public health plan (such as National Health in Britain).

Care in Turkish hospitals is sometimes not of the highest standards in terms of comfort or convenience. But medical care, as always, depends upon the particular staff members (doctors and nurses) involved. These can be quite good or not so good. The lower staff echelons may be low paid and trained on the job. Supplies are not used in great quantities, so you may not find such things as disposable syringes. As a foreigner, you will probably be given the best possible treatment and the greatest consideration.

Toilets

Virtually every hotel above the lowest class, most apartments, many restaurants, train stations and airports have the familiar raised-bowl commode toilet. You may also meet with the flat 'elephant's feet' variety, a porcelain or concrete rectangle with two oblong foot-places and a sunken hole. This may be daunting at first, but it is actually the best kind of toilet from a physical standpoint. It is also sanitary, in that only your shod feet contact the vessel – you squat, you don't sit on anything. Using it is not as difficult as you may think. Just make sure all the stuff doesn't fall out of your pockets when you squat. Also, bring your own toilet paper. In the government-rated hotels there will be paper. In public conveniences, if there's no attendant, there will be no paper; there will be a spigot and a can for washing (with the left hand). It's a good idea to carry enough paper or tissues with you at all times.

Sometimes the plumbing is not built to take wads of paper, and the management will place a wastepaper basket or can next to the toilet for used paper. Signs in Turkish will plead with you not to throw the paper down the toilet. What you do depends upon your feelings on the matter.

Clean public toilets can be found near the very big tourist attractions such as Topkapı Palace and the Grand Bazaar. In other places, it depends. Look first. Every mosque has a toilet, often very basic, but maybe better than nothing.

DANGERS & ANNOYANCES

Turkey is a safe country, relative to most of the world. Crime is not a big problem. You may feel safer here than you do at home.

Police

One of the reasons Turkey is so safe is martial law. Since the terrible times of the late 1970s, when political extremism made it perilous even to walk along the street, martial law has been in force from time to time in various parts of the country. Though it has now been lifted in most areas, it is still in force in parts of the east and south-east, where there is always some smuggling and Kurdish separatist activity.

Even under the return to democracy and civil rule, Turks are wary of the fringe elements. They remember all too well how difficult life was while chaos reigned.

You'll see a lot of soldiers in Turkey. This is partly because soldiers make up the *jandarma* (gendarmerie) force, and partly because Turkey has universal male military service – every man serves, even if he is partly disabled. With all these men in arms, jobs have got to be found for them. Other reasons are: NATO commitments, a border with the Soviet Union (which has tried several times to take land in eastern Turkey), and a long, proud military tradition which began when Turks formed the elite units under the later Arab caliphs in the 10th and 11th centuries.

Here's the rundown on the police forces:

Polis The green-clad officers with white caps, both men and women, are part of a national force (Polis, poh-LEES) which controls traffic, patrols highways and attends to other police duties in cities and towns.

Belediye Zabıtası The blue-clad officers are called Belediye Zabıtası (municipal inspector), or market police. These men are the modern expression of an age-old Islamic custom of special commercial police who make sure a loaf of bread weighs what it should, that 24-carat gold is indeed 24 carats, that scales and balances don't cheat the customer. You'll see them patrolling the markets and bazaars, and if you have a commercial problem they'll be glad to help. They may not speak much of a foreign language, though.

Jandarma Soldiers in the standard Turkish army uniforms may be of three types. Without special insignia, they're regular army. With a red armband bearing the word 'Jandarma', they're gendarmes, whose job is to keep the peace, catch criminals on the run, stop smuggling, etc. If the soldiers have white helmets emblazoned with the letters 'As. İz.', plus pistols in white holsters connected to lanyards around their necks, they're Askeri İnzibat, or military police who keep off-duty soldiers in line.

Most of these soldiers are draftees inducted into the enormous Turkish army, put through basic training, and sent out to 'guard', jobs that are usually pretty unexciting. They look ferocious – life in the Turkish army is no joke – but basically they are hometown boys waiting to get out. Every single one of them can tell you the precise number of days he has left to serve. Any request from a foreign tourist for help or directions is received as though it were a marvellous privilege.

Theft

In general there is not much problem with theft if you take the normal precautions. These include keeping track of your wallet or other valuables on crowded buses and trains and in markets; not leaving valuables in your hotel room, or at least not in view; and not walking into unknown parts of town when nobody else is around.

Actually, the biggest danger of theft is probably in dorm rooms and other open accommodation where other foreigners can see what sort of camera you have (and can guess its value pretty accurately), or where you stash your money.

Women Alone

Women must be more careful, as in any Mediterranean country. Turkish social customs dictate that a young woman (say, a high school student) not go to a major shopping street without friends or mother; college-aged women usually stroll with friends; women in their prime look purposeful, ignore catcalls, and don't walk on lonely streets after dark. If you're approached by an eastern Romeo, ignore, ignore, ignore. It's best not to say or do anything.

The key is respectability: if you look and act respectable according to Turkish standards, you'll be able to fend off advances easily. A wedding ring helps. It says, 'I've got an Other Half who doesn't like people to fool with me'. If you must say something, say *Ayıp!* (ah-YUHP), which means 'shameful'. Use it all you want to on young kids. But men may take exception if you call them shameful when they're certain that you'll find their masculine charms irresistible.

When searching for a hotel, look for one catering to families *(aile)*. When you go out, look for the section of the tea garden or restaurant reserved for families or women alone. The magic word for a respectable spot is always *aile*, as in *aile salonu* (family dining room) or *aile çay bahçesi* (family tea garden).

Disputes

In general, Turks view foreigners as cultured, educated and wealthy – even if many foreign visitors don't deserve such a view. This means that you will sometimes be given special consideration, jumped to the heads of queues, given the best seat on the bus, etc. In a dispute, if you keep your cool and act dignified, you will generally be given the benefit of the doubt. If it is thought you have powerful friends, you will definitely be given that benefit.

It's difficult to imagine a dispute involving a foreigner coming to the point of blows, as Turks are slow to anger. Don't let it happen. A Turk rarely finds it necessary to fight, but if he does, he wants to win, *whatever* the cost. Knowing that horrible things could happen, bystanders will pull two quarrelling men apart, even if they've never seen them before.

In the case of women travellers in disputes with Turks, you should know that Turkish men feel acutely any insults to their manhood, and will retaliate. Insults to them can include being shouted at or browbeaten by a woman who is not (in their eyes) unquestionably of a higher social status. In general, keep it all formal.

Lèse Majesté

The battle to form the Turkish Republic out of the ruins of the Ottoman Empire was a very tough one, and every Turk has great respect for the accomplishments of Atatürk and the republic. There are laws against insulting, defaming or making light of Atatürk, the Turkish flag, the Turkish people, the Turkish republic, etc. These are normal for many European countries. Any difficulty will probably arise from misunderstanding. At the first sign that you've inadvertently been guilty of *lèse-majesté*, make your apologies. It may seem a trivial thing to you, but if it's important to someone else, you should apologize. An apology will be readily accepted.

Natural Hazards

Earthquakes Turkey sometimes has very bad ones. The big quakes only seem to hit

every eight or 10 years, though, and the same thing happens in many parts of the world, so it's up to Allah.

Undertow & Rip-tide At some of the swimming areas, particularly in the Black Sea near Istanbul, this is a real danger. Undertow can kill you by powerfully pulling you beneath the surface, and a rip-tide does the same by sweeping you out to sea so that you exhaust yourself trying to regain the shore. There may be no signs warning of the danger. Lifeguards may not be present, or may be untrained or unequipped (no boat). Don't trust to luck. You can't necessarily see these hazards or predict where they will be. In either situation, remain calm, as panic can be fatal. Don't exhaust yourself by trying to swim straight back to the beach from a rip-tide, because you'll never make it. Rather, swim to the left or right to escape the rip-tide area, and make for land in that direction. These dangers are usually a problem only on long stretches of open sea beach with surf. In coves and bays, where waves are broken or diverted by headlands, you probably won't be in danger.

Wildlife Turkey has mosquitoes, scorpions and snakes. You will not see many of them, but be aware, as you tramp around the ruins of Ephesus or Priene, that such beasts do live here and may be nearby, at least in summer. There are also wild boar and wolves around, though you won't encounter these unless you hike deep into the bush.

Man-Made Annoyances
Knuckle-Smashers When you close a door, watch out that your knuckles don't bash into the jamb. This happens frequently.

Plumbing Problems The first time you flush a toilet, pull the cord *very gently*. If nothing happens, pull harder. Some of the flushers are made of iron and take a good heavy tug; most of the new ones are made of plastic. If you pull on a plastic one the way you do on an iron one, you'll pull the cord right off the toilet.

If you encounter a flat, 'elephant's feet' toilet, stand back when you flush it. If it flushes well, it may get all over your feet.

The Imperial Auto Give way to cars and trucks in all situations, even if you have to jump out of the way. The sovereignty of the pedestrian is unrecognised in Turkey. If a car hits you, the driver (if not the courts) will blame you for not getting out of the way. This does not apply in a recognised crosswalk controlled by a traffic officer or a traffic signal. If you've got a 'Walk' light, you've got the right of way. Watch out, all the same. The insistence of every Turkish driver that you, as a pedestrian, are merely an annoyance composed of so much protoplasm, will get to you after awhile. Grit your teeth and bear it, murmuring 'When in Rome', etc. A dispute with a driver will get you nowhere.

The Pungent Weed If you're allergic to cigarette smoke, you may have a hard time in Turkey. Though the local cancer prevention society fields a brave effort to stop smoking, this is the land of aromatic Turkish tobacco. Smoking is the national passion. No-smoking areas are virtually unheard of, and would not really be observed if they were, even on planes and trains. OK, some people don't smoke next to the fuel pumps in filling stations. But in general, position yourself near a fresh-air source if possible.

Noise Noise is a source of annoyance in cities. As in many Third World countries, the noise level in Turkey is often high. Choose hotel rooms with noise in mind. Also, Turks are addicted to nightlife and think nothing of staying up until 1 or 2 am in the middle of the week, so watch out for highly amplified bands

and singers. Nightclub noise is particularly insulting when you have spent good money to upgrade your accommodation only to find that the better the hotel, the louder its nightclub.

Air Pollution In winter, air pollution is a problem in the big cities. In Ankara it is a very serious problem, rivalling that of Tokyo and Mexico City. The major heating fuel is lignite (soft brown coal), which produces enormous clouds of heavy, choking particles. In summer there is some pollution from autos, but it's not bad. In winter, especially in Ankara, the air is very bad. If you find your nose running, your eyes watering and itching, and your head aching, that's the pollution. The heating season lasts from 15 October to 1 April.

POST & TELECOMMUNICATIONS

Postal and telecommunication service in Turkey are handled by the PTT (peh-teh-TEH), which stands for *posta, telefon, telgraf*. Look for the yellow signs with black 'PTT' letters.

Mailboxes (letterboxes) and postal vehicles are yellow as well. Every town has a PTT, usually close to the main square. Go here to buy stamps and telephone tokens, to send letters and telegrams, or to make telephone calls (if no other phone is available).

İstanbul's Merkez Postahane (Mehr-KEHZ POHS-tah-neh, central post office) is in the section called Eminönü, several blocks west of Sirkeci Railway Station. Go here for *poste restante* mail. If you are having mail sent, have it addressed this way:

Name
Poste Restante
Merkez Postahane
Eminönü
İstanbul
TURKEY

Turkish Daily News

Turkey's First And Only English Daily

Convenient PTT branches are located in Taksim, Galatasaray, Aksaray and the Grand Bazaar.

Many railway stations and bus stations in Turkey have their own branch PTTs.

Turkish postal and telephone personnel have a reputation for surliness, bad temper and incompetence which is, in many cases, richly deserved.

Postal Rates As of this writing, postal rates are as follows:

destination	letter	postcard
Turkey	20TL	20TL
Europe, UK	100TL	70TL
USA, Canada	150TL	120TL
Australia, NZ	170TL	140TL

These rates will certainly have changed by the time you arrive. Check current rates so that your mail is not delayed.

Express Mail The PTT now operates an express mail, courier-type service called *acele posta servisi* (AH-jeh-leh POHSS-tah sehr-vee-see). If you must have something reach its destination in the fastest possible manner, ask for this.

Mailing Parcels
To mail packages out of the country from

İstanbul, or to receive dutiable merchandise, you must go to the special Paket Postahane (parcel post office) near Karaköy. You must have your package open for customs inspection, and fight a mountain of the world's most frustrating red tape. You'd be far better off mailing your package from another town or city, even if you have to go out of your way to do so. As there is only one post office in a small town, it also serves as the customs office, and small-town clerks are nicer to deal with. Postal clerks in Turkey are as a rule cold and curt, often rude, and sometimes even nasty, though foreigners get better treatment than Turks do. You can't be rude back because there's a law (as in Europe) against 'insulting a public official'.

Telephones
You will find the telephone useful in Turkey. The PTT operates two different telephone systems, the traditional operator type and an automatic ('direct-dial') type. You will find yourself using the automatic system more, as it is faster, cheaper and easier. Automatic phones are yellow and have push-buttons rather than dials.

Tokens For most calls you'll need a *jeton*

(zheh-TOHN, token), or perhaps several. They come in three sizes. The small ones (*küçük jeton*, kew-CHEWK zheh-tohn, 40TL, US$0.06) are for local calls. The middle-sized ones (*normal jeton*, nohr-MAHL, 200TL, US$0.28) are useful mostly for trunk (long-distance) calls within Turkey. The large ones (*büyük jeton*, bew-YEWK, 400TL, US$0.56) are necessary for international calls. Buy your jetons at the post office, from a disabled person outside or near a rank of public telephones. Most PTTs have a sign saying *Satılmış jeton geri alınmaz*, which means 'Jetons, once sold, cannot be returned'.

Types Once you have your jetons, find a phone. The yellow automatic push-button phones are replacing the older sorts, but you may still come upon one of the older ones. You will find one of four types of phones.

The yellow phones have pictographs on them demonstrating their use, and sometimes also instructions in English. These phones are described in more detail below under 'Trunk Calls'.

The desk phones with a small box attached take normal jetons for local calls. These are the ones you find in grocery shops and offices. They are more expensive because they take normal rather than small jetons. Trunk calls can be made only through the slower, more expensive operator system, and usually must be collect (reverse-charge) calls.

For the old black wall telephones, don't put the jeton in the slot on top until your party answers. These phones, also, are useful mostly for local and collect calls.

For the red or gun-metal grey phones, put the jeton in before you dial; if you don't get through, it will be returned to you. These, too, are good mostly for local or collect (reverse-charge) calls.

Trunk Calls For long-distance/trunk calls, use a yellow automatic phone. It may have a sign above it saying 'Şehirlerarası'

which means 'Inter-city'; or 'Uluslararası' or 'Milletlerarası' which mean 'International'. You'll need to know the city and country codes for the place you're calling. These are on display in most PTTs and in some phone boxes (booths).

Look for the little square red light below the push-buttons. Is it lit? It is? Tough luck – the phone is broken. Let's assume the phone works instead. Lift the receiver and deposit a jeton. The yellow phones have slots for all three sizes of jetons. Sometimes the jeton may fall straight through and out the return hole, so re-insert it very gently and let it fall as slowly as possible. If all else fails, try another phone or another size of jeton. The fault is with the phone, not with the jeton.

For a local call, punch the buttons for the local number, and you're on your way.

For a trunk call, look for the little round light in the last box, to the right, of the pictorial instructions above the push-buttons. When this light goes out, push '9'. Then, when you hear the inter-city long-distance tone, push the buttons for the city code, and the local number. For international calls, push '9' twice, then the country code, followed by the city code and local number. For instance, for London, after pushing '9' twice, push '44', then the area code ('1'), then the number. For Melbourne, dial thus: 9-9-61-3 + local number. For the USA and Canada, dial 9-9-1 + area code + local number.

As you talk, watch that little round red light up top, and listen for chimes on the line. Both are indications that it's time to deposit another jeton.

With an operator phone (that is, any phone except the yellow push-button models), place the call with the operator, then wait for the operator to ring you back. The call will go through according to the speed which you designate: *normal* (nohr-MAHL) means 'slowest' in this instance; *acele* (ah-jeh-LEH) means twice as fast; *yıldırım* (yuhl-duhr-RUHM) means 'lightning', five times as fast as *normal*. Five times as fast costs five times as much. After you place the call, you wait a minute or two, or an hour or two – the operator can tell you how long.

Telegraph

You can send a telegram (*telgraf*, tehl-GHRAHF) from any post office in Turkey. Ask for a *telgraf kâğıdı* (tehl-GHRAHF kyah-uh-duh, telegram form), fill it out, and hand it over. For most foreign countries, there is only one rate of service: fast and expensive. A simple telegram to North America may cost US$15, for instance.

If you're sending your wire within Turkey, the clerk will ask you at what speed you want it sent. As with the phone service, *normal* is quite slow; *acele* is fast, and twice as expensive; and *yıldırım* (lightning) costs five times as much as *normal*. Remember that the address is included in the word count.

Telex

The larger cities have some post offices with telex (*teleks*, TEHL-eks) machines and electronic mail capabilities. If your recipient has a telex machine and number, this can be cheaper than sending a telegram. Write out your message, including the telex number if you have it, find a post office with a machine, and the attendant will send the message and give you a receipt and confirmation copy. There are telex machines in İstanbul's major PTTs and in the branch post office in Ankara's Kizilay Square.

The price for a telex, as for a telephone call, depends upon the actual time spent using the line. The PTT telex operator may make mistakes and have to retype the entire message, and you will have to pay for his incompetence and all of this time on the line. An alternative to telex is facsimile transmission, also available in the larger PTTs.

MEDIA
Newspapers & Magazines

The Turks are great readers of newspapers. The local dailies are produced by up-to-date computerized methods, in full colour. Only a decade ago, İstanbul could boast more than a dozen Turkish-language dailies, two in Greek, one in Armenian, one in French and two in Ladino Spanish (spoken by Jews who came from Spain to the Ottoman Empire in the Middle Ages). As everywhere, the number of dailies is dwindling as the more successful papers grow. Several of the Turkish-language dailies now have editions printed in Germany for Turkish workers there, as well as numerous local editions.

Of prime interest to visitors is the *Turkish Daily News*, an English-language daily published in Ankara and sold for 150TL (US$0.21) in most Turkish cities where tourists go. It is the cheapest source of English-language news in print. The big international papers such as the *International Herald-Tribune, Le Monde, Corriere della Sera, Die Welt*, etc are on sale in tourist spots as well, but are much more expensive (900TL, US$1.26 for the *Herald-Tribune*). They may be a day or two late.

Large-circulation magazines including *Newsweek, Time, Der Spiegel* and the like are also sold in tourist spots.

If you can't find the foreign publication you want, go to a big hotel's newsstand or check at a foreign-language bookstore (see Bookshops below for addresses).

Radio & TV

TRT, for Türkiye Radyo ve Televizyon, controls all broadcasting. It's a quasi-independent establishment modelled on the BBC. Western classical and popular music, along with Turkish classic, folk, religious and pop music, are played regularly on both AM (medium-wave) and FM channels. Short news broadcasts in English, French and German are given each morning and evening.

Television is two colour channels, Turkish only, evenings only. The familiar Los Angeles-made series and many of the films are dubbed in Turkish. Occasionally you'll catch a film in the original language.

BBC World Service is often receivable on medium-wave (AM) as well as on short-wave. The Voice of America broadcasts in English on middle-wave, relayed from Rhodes, each morning. The rest of the middle wave band is a wonderful babel of Bulgarian, Romanian, Greek, Hebrew, Arabic, Russian, Persian, Italian and Albanian.

READING

Everyone from St Paul to Mark Twain and Agatha Christie has written about Turkey. It's one of those Middle Eastern countries with an incredibly deep history and culture. You will get far more out of your visit if you read up on the history, the culture and the people before you go.

In a few cases, you might want to carry a specialized guide or history with you on your visit. A list of prominent foreign-language bookstores in Turkey follows this section.

Almanacs

The *Turkish Daily News* (Ankara) publishes the *Turkey Almanac* annually, in English. Its 400-plus large-format pages are packed with statistics and details on the government, the military, the press, trade, agriculture, population, culture, religion and sports – it even includes the musical score of the National Anthem. The price is about US$9.

Anthropology

For a good overview of life during the great days of the empire, look for Raphaela Lewis's *Everyday Life in Ottoman Turkey* (B T Batsford, London; G P Putnam's Sons, New York, 1971; 207 pages, many photographs). It is not easily found in bookshops these days; go to a library.

Archaeology

Ancient Civilizations & Ruins of Turkey (Haşet Kitabevi, İstanbul, 1973 and later editions; 390 pages of text plus 112 pages of photographs; about US$8) by Ekrem Akurgal is a very detailed and fairly scholarly guide to most of Turkey's ruins 'from Prehistoric Times until the End of the Roman Empire'. Good, readable English translation. This is the best handbook for those with a deep interest in detailed classical archaeology.

George Bean (1903-1977) was the dean of western travel writers on Turkish antiquities. His four books cover the country's greatest wealth of Greek and Roman sites in depth, but in a very readable style. These four works were written as guidebooks to the ruins. They contain plenty of detail, but not so much that the fascination of exploring an ancient city or temple is taken away.

If you'd like to go deeply into a few sites, but not make the investments of time, energy and money necessary to cover the entire coast from Pergamum to Silifke, just buy Bean's *Aegean Turkey* (Ernest Benn, London; W W Norton, New York, 1979; 250 pages, diagrams, photos; about US$16). Covers İzmir and vicinity, Pergamum, Aeolis, sites west of İzmir to Sardis, Ephesus, Priene, Miletus, Didyma, Magnesia on the Meander, and Heracleia.

Also by George Bean (and from the same publishers):

Lycian Turkey (1978; 197 pages, diagrams, maps and photos; about US$16). Covers the Turkish coast roughly from Fethiye to Antalya, and its hinterland.

Turkey Beyond the Meander (1980; 236 pages, maps, diagrams, photographs; about US$22). Covers the region south of the Meander (Menderes) River, excluding Miletus, Didyma and Heracleia (which are covered in *Aegean Turkey*) but including sites near Bodrum, Pamukkale, Aphrodisias and Marmaris, and to the western outskirts of Fethiye.

Turkey's Southern Shore (1979; 154 pages, maps, photographs, diagrams; about US$20). Overlaps with *Lycian Turkey* a bit; covers eastern Lycia, Pisidia and Pamphylia, which is roughly the coast from Finike east to Silifke.

Besides these archaeological guides, you'll find shorter, locally produced guides on sale at each site. Most of these include colour photographs (of varying quality). The text, however, is often badly translated, or else doesn't go into much depth. Look closely at one before you buy.

Biography

Atatürk, The Rebirth of a Nation (Weidenfeld & Nicolson, London, 1964 and later; 542 pages, photos) by Lord Kinross is essential reading for anyone who wants to understand the formation of the Turkish Republic and the reverence in which modern Turks hold the father of modern Turkey. It's well written and far more exciting than most novels.

For a fascinating look into the last years of the Ottoman Empire and the early years of the Turkish Republic, read İrfan Orga's *Portrait of a Turkish Family*.

Dictionaries & Phrasebooks

Several companies publish Turkish-English pocket dictionaries, including Langenscheidt/McGraw-Hill. The most useful thing to have is not a dictionary, but a good phrasebook such as *Turkish for Travellers* by Berlitz Publications. Besides lots of phrases and glossaries, this one includes cultural details and information, menu readers, etc.

For a more detailed dictionary, look to *The Concise Oxford Turkish Dictionary*. Similar in scope and easier to find in Turkey is the *Portable Redhouse/Redhouse Elsözlüğü*; this 500-page work on thin paper was actually intended for Turkish students learning English, but it does the job well when you graduate from the pocket dictionary.

For grammars, there's *Teach Yourself*

Turkish in the popular English series. Longer, more expensive, and far more interesting is Geoffrey L Lewis's *Turkish Grammar* (Oxford University Press, London, 1967). You've got to be pretty interested in Turkish (and in grammar) to get this far into it. But if a grammar can be said to read like a novel, this one does.

Fiction

Everybody knows about Agatha Christie's *Murder on the Orient Express*, and so they should. It has some scenes in Turkey itself, though most of the train's journey was through Europe and the Balkans. In any case, it helps to make vivid the 19th-century importance of the Turkish Empire.

Among Turkish authors, the one with the world-class reputation is Yaşar Kemal, whom some compare to Kazantzakis. Kemal's novels often take Turkish farming or working-class life as their subject matter, and are full of colourful characters and drama. There are translations in English of *Memed, My Hawk, The Wind from the Plains* and several others, done by Kemal's wife.

You might also want to look at *An Anthology of Modern Turkish Short Stories*, edited by Fahir İz (Bibliotheca Islamica, Minneapolis & Chicago, 1978).

Guidebooks

This book was written to tell you just about everything you'd need to know on a first or even subsequent trip to Turkey. Other excellent guides exist, however, each with its own special interest.

The excellent French series of Blue Guides published by Hachette has a commendable volume on Turkey, but the latest edition (1978) is in French only. An earlier English translation (1960, 1970) is useful for some detailed archaeological information and out-of-the-way spots, but the writing now seems stilted, the printing crude, and the practical information far out of date. If you see it in a used bookshop, cheap, you might want to pick it up. A new translation of the 1978 French edition is reportedly in the works, but the practical information in that, too, is already far out of date.

Otherwise, the most interesting guides on Turkey are those published by the Redhouse Press of İstanbul. Founded under the Ottoman Empire as part of an American missionary effort, the Redhouse Press now does an admirable job of publishing dictionaries, guidebooks and general works designed to bridge the gap between the Turkish and English-speaking realms. Some of the Redhouse guides have been translated into German, French and Italian. Though only a few Redhouse books turn up in bookshops outside of Turkey, you'll find them readily within the country itself, in decent editions at moderate prices. A good example of a Redhouse work is *Biblical Sites in Turkey* by Everett C Blake and Anna G Edmonds (1982; 200 pages, colour photos, maps; about US\$4). Other guides cover Istanbul and day trips from it.

History
The Ottoman Centuries by Lord Kinross covers the greatness of the empire without weighing too heavily on your consciousness.

The Emergence of Modern Turkey by Bernard Lewis (Oxford University Press, London, 1965 and later; 511 pages, maps) is a scholarly work covering Turkey's history roughly from 1850 to 1950, with a few chapters on the earlier history of the Turks. It tells you nearly everything you want to know about modern Turkey's origins.

Turkey (London, 1955 and later) by Geoffrey L Lewis is a good general introduction to the country, the people and the culture through their history.

Gallipoli by Alan Moorhead is the fascinating story of the battles for the Dardanelles, which figured so significantly

in the careers of Atatürk and Winston Churchill.

The Harvest of Hellenism by F E Peters details Turkey's Hellenic heritage. *Byzantine Civilisation* by Sir Steven Runciman is the standard work on the Later Roman Empire.

Travellers' Accounts
The published diaries and accounts of travellers in Turkey provide fascinating glimpses of Ottoman life. One of the more familiar of these is Mark Twain's *Innocents Abroad*. Twain accompanied a group of wealthy tourists on a chartered boat which sailed the eastern Mediterranean and Black Seas over a century ago. Many of the things he saw in İstanbul haven't changed much.

BOOKSHOPS
As far as Turks are concerned, their country is part of Europe. Western culture is their culture, and if they learn a foreign language it will be English, French or German. Thus it is easy to find bookshops *(kitabevi)* selling works in these languages. The major cities, and most of the resort towns, have bookshops which sell some foreign-language books, newspapers and magazines.

İstanbul
In general, the place to find foreign-language books is in and around Tünel Meydanı, at the southern end of İstiklal Caddesi, and from there northward to Galatasaray.

Sander Kitabevi has a small branch a few doors north-east of the PTT in Galatasaray, on the same side of İstiklal Caddesi. The main store is at Halâskârgazi Caddesi 275-277, Osmanbey, north of Taksim Square. Books are in English, French and German.

Alman Kitabevi ('German Bookstore'), İstiklal Caddesi 481, Tünel, Beyoğlu, has mostly German books, but some in English.

Haşet Kitabevi (Hachette), İstiklal

Caddesi 469, Tünel, Beyoğlu, has perhaps the best selection of French and English books and periodicals.

Redhouse Kitabevi, Rıza Paşa Yokuşu, Uzun Çarşı, in the Old City down the hill from the Grand Bazaar, publishes books in English and Turkish, including excellent guides and dictionaries. It has an English-language bookstore as well.

Sahaflar Çarşısı, the used-book bazaar, is great fun for browsing. It's just west of the Grand Bazaar across Çadırcılar Caddesi, sandwiched between that street and the Beyazit Mosque. One shop here specializes in used foreign-language paperbacks; much of the stock is worthless, however.

The big hotels – Hilton, Sheraton, Etap, Divan – all have little bookshops or newsstands. The one in the Hilton arcade is quite good.

Ankara

Tarhan Kitabevi, Sakarya Caddesi at Atatürk Bulvarı, a few steps north (down the hill) out of Kızılay, is perhaps Turkey's best foreign-language bookstore, with a predominance of books in English but some in French and German as well.

To find the shop, walk out of Kızılay towards Ulus and the old part of Ankara along Atatürk Bulvarı, and take the first turn to the right (a pedestrian street).

İzmir

There are several foreign-language bookstores on Cumhuriyet Caddesi, or İkinci Kordon, the second street in from the waterfront. Look near the NATO headquarters. The Büyük Efes (Grand Ephesus) hotel also has a small shop.

Other Towns

If tourists go there in any numbers, you'll find a newsstand selling international papers and at least some paperback novels, perhaps second-hand.

ACCOMMODATION

Hostels

With hotels and pensions so cheap, few people stay at hostels. When they exist, hostels tend to be extremely basic, intended for low-budget Turkish students from the provinces who are attending university classes.

The Ministry of Youth Affairs & Sports operates a number of hostels and camps in İstanbul, Ankara, İzmir, Bolu, Çanakkale and Bursa. Hostel arrangements change from season to season and year to year. Ask at a Tourism Information Office, or at Gençtur Tourism & Travel Agency Ltd (tel 528 0734), Yerebatan Caddesi 15/3, Sultanahmet, İstanbul. Gençtur works closely with the Ministry of Youth Affairs & Sports.

Hotels

In this guide hotels are listed according to price, except in places with only a few hotels which must be used by all visitors regardless of their price preference.

Bottom End Lodgings in this group are priced from 750TL (US$1.05) per bed up to 7000TL (US$9.80) for a double room. For Turks, these are the rooms used by farmers in town for the market, lorry-drivers resting up, or working-class families on holiday at the seaside.

Rooms priced below about 3000TL (US$4.20) do not usually have private shower or toilet in the room, but may have a *lavabo* (washbasin). Above 3500TL (US$4.90), in small towns you may get private plumbing. Cold-water showers are usually free, as they should be. Hot-water showers may cost 500TL (US$0.70) or so in lodgings where a fire must be built in the hot-water heater. If there is solar water-heating, hot showers are often free (but perhaps not all that hot!)

At the lowest prices, the rooms will be quite bare and spartan, but functional. If you find used sheets on the bed, request clean ones; the owner has got to change them sometime, and it may as well be for you. Say *Temiz çarşaf lâzım* (teh-MEEZ chahr-SHAHF lyaa-zuhm, 'Clean sheets are necessary'). Bedbugs are not unheard of; let me know of any banquets you host so I can warn other readers.

It is sometimes possible to sleep on the roof of a pension or hotel, or camp in the garden, for a minimal fee of 750TL to 1000TL (US$1.05 to US$1.40). Another way to save lodging money is to take night buses on long hauls.

Mid-Range Turkey has lots of hotels which are modern and comfortable but not overly fancy. Facilities in this price range include lifts, some multilingual staff, rooms with private shower or bath and toilet, balconies to enjoy the view, and guarded car parks. Fairly prosperous Turks look upon a hotel room costing about 12,000TL (US$16.80) double as the luxury standard.

In every city and town you'll visit, including many cities in eastern Turkey, you will be able to find a clean, fairly modern room with double or twin beds and private bath or shower for 7000TL to 21,000TL (US$9.80 to US$29.40). There are seaside hotels and motels right on the beach which charge these prices in high season. In most cities, the higher price in this range will apply to the very best hotel in town, which may have a swimming pool, discotheque, bar, television lounge, obsequious staff, etc.

Top End İstanbul has a Hilton, a Sheraton and two Etap hotels. Ankara has the Büyük Ankara Oteli (Grand Ankara Hotel), and will soon have a Hilton and a Sheraton. These few top-class luxury places charge 'international' prices of, say, US$115 to US$150 for a double room. Somehow they get away with it, and always seem to be busy. Group rates and rates on package deals are down in the US$75 to US$80 range for the same room, however. Hotels in this classification are priced at 21,000TL (US$29.40) and up.

Choosing a Hotel
Here are some points to watch.

Inspect the Rooms Don't judge a hotel by its façade. Look at the rooms. I've never had a desk clerk refuse to show me a room. Among the middle range of Turkish hotels there is a tendency to put money into the lobby rather than into the rooms, and so looking at the lobby does not give you an accurate idea of the quality of the guest quarters.

Know the Price Next, prices should be posted prominently at the reception desk. Usually there is very little fiddling around in this regard.

Beware of Noise Turkish cities and towns are noisy places, and you will soon learn to choose a hotel and a room with quiet in mind. In this guide I have done some of the work for you by recommending mostly the quieter places, but you will have to be aware when you select your room. The front rooms in a hotel, those facing the busy street, are usually looked upon as the most desirable by the hotel management, and priced higher than rooms at the rear. Take advantage of this. Ask for *sakin bir oda* (sah-KEEN beer oh-dah, 'a quiet room') and pay less.

Water Pressure In some cities, and particularly in summer, there may be temporary water problems. Water may be cut off for several hours at a time, though many hotels have roof tanks which do away with this problem.

Hot Water As for hot water, it's often difficult to find in summer in the cheaper hotels, unless they have solar water-heaters. Many small hotels have only a single furnace for both hot water and central heating, and they really don't want to run that furnace in summer. Since the summers are warm, even hot, this doesn't present much of a problem. Early spring and late fall are another matter, though. Every desk clerk will say, 'Yes, we have hot water', but when you try to take a shower the new fact will be, 'Ah, the furnace just this minute broke down!'

Believe it or not, the most dependable hot water is in the cheapest pensions, because in these places the *patron* builds a little fire in the bottom of the hot-water tank 30 minutes before your shower appointment, and you bathe in as much steaming water as you want. The extra charge for this luxury is about 300TL to 500TL (US$0.42 to US$0.70). An alternative, fairly dependable hot-water method is the *şofben* (SHOHF-behn), or flash heater. This type runs on gas, and flashes into action as soon as you turn on the hot-water tap. It's activated by water flow through the hot-water pipe. Obviously this sort of heater is not dependent on a central furnace, but it does have other problems. Gas pressure must be sufficient to heat the water, which it sometimes is not; and the flow of water must be strong enough to activate the şofben, which it sometimes is not. Often it's a balancing act, keeping the flow of water fast enough to activate the heater, yet slow enough to make sure the water is hot.

Electricity Electricity may go off for short periods in some locations. This is not much of a problem, however.

Hotel Restaurants These, in general, do not offer good value in Turkey. You may want to have breakfast here for convenience (or because breakfast has been included in the room price), but most other meals should be taken in independent, local places. There are exceptions, of course, as in those remote towns where the one nice hotel in town also has the one nice restaurant.

Unmarried Couples Unmarried couples sharing rooms usually run into no problems, even though the desk clerk sees the obvious when he takes down the

pertinent information from your passports onto the registration form. The cheaper the hotel, the more traditional and conservative its management tends to be. Very simple hotels which are clean and 'proper' want to maintain their reputations. If you look clean and proper there should be no trouble. Lots of allowances are made for odd foreign ways.

Single Women Single women travelling alone or in pairs should look for *aile* (ah-yee-LEH) hotels – places where families stay. Men travel much more than do women in Turkey, and many hotels, from moderate to rock-bottom, cater mostly to men on business. No sharp dividing line, no key word in the hotel's name lets you know that one hotel is good and another not-so-good. In principle, every hotel accepts all potential guests. In practice, you may feel uncomfortable in a place which customarily is filled with men; and they may wonder why you're staying there when there are better *aile* hotels nearby. To locate a suitable hotel, look to see if there are matronly types waiting in the lobby, or just ask, *Bu otel aile için mi?* (BOO oh-tehl ah-yee-LEH ee-cheen mee, 'Is this hotel for families/ladies?') If it's not, the clerk will direct you to a more suitable place nearby.

FOOD & DRINK
It is worth travelling to Turkey just to eat. Turkish cuisine is thought by many to rank with French and Chinese as one of the world's great basic cuisines. If French cuisine is based on ingenuity and originality, and Chinese on quick cooking and interchangeability of ingredients, Turkish cuisine's special genius is excellent, fresh ingredients and careful, even laborious preparation. The ingredients are often very simple, but are harmonized with such care and finesse that the result is incredibly edible. With simple ingredients it's difficult to cover up bad cooking, so bad cooks don't last long.

Restaurants

Restaurants (restoran, lokanta) are everywhere, open early in the morning until late at night. Most are very inexpensive, and although price is always some determinant of quality, often the difference between a 2000TL (US$2.80) meal and a 8000TL (US$11.20) meal is not that great, at least as far as flavour is concerned. Service and ambience are fancier at the higher price.

Full Service First there is the familiar place with white tablecloths and waiter service. It may be open for three meals a day, and will probably be among the more expensive dining places. Most full-service restaurants have some 'ready food' (see below), and prepare grilled meats, particularly in the evening. They also usually serve liquor, wine and beer.

Hazır Yemek Next there is the hazır yemek (hah-ZUHR yeh-mehk, 'ready food') restaurant. Although all restaurants offer some 'ready food' dishes prepared in advance, these places specialize in an assortment of dishes, prepared in advance of mealtime and served on demand. They are basically working-class cafeterias, but with waiter service. You pass by a steam table, which is often in the front window of the restaurant to entice passers-by, you make your choices, and a waiter brings them to you.

There will always be soup (çorba, CHOR-bah), often mercimek çorbası (mehr-jee-MEHK, lentil). Ezo gelin çorbası (EH-zoh GEH-leen) is a variation of lentil soup, with rice and lemon juice. Domates çorbası (doh-MAH-tess) is creamy tomato soup. Şehriye (SHEH-ree-yeh) is vermicelli soup, made with a chicken stock.

Pilav (pee-LAHV) of some sort will always be available. Plain pilav is rice cooked in stock. There may also (or instead) be bulgur pilav, cracked bulghur wheat cooked in a tomato stock.

Many of the dishes will be vegetables-and-meat. Most popular are salçalı köfte (sahl-chah-LUH kurf-teh), meatballs of lamb stewed in a sauce with vegetables; patlıcan kebap (paht-luh-JAHN keh-bahp), eggplant and chunks of lamb; or orman kebap (ohr-MAHN keh-bahp), lamb chunks, vegetables and potatoes in broth. Kuzu haşlama (koo-ZOO hahsh-lah-mah) is lamb hocks in a stew.

Sometimes grilled meats are available in hazır yemek restaurants. Döner kebap (durn-NEHR keh-bahp), lamb roasted on a vertical spit and sliced off in thin strips as it cooks, is the closest thing you'll find to a national dish. Şiş kebap (SHEESH keh-bahp) is meat only, small pieces of lamb grilled on real charcoal.

Sometimes beer is served in these restaurants; more often, it's not. Decor may be non-existent and the letters on the front window may only say 'Lokanta' (restaurant), but the welcome will be warm, the food delicious and very cheap.

With your meal you will receive as much fresh bread as you can eat, for a nominal charge. It's easy to 'overeat with your eyes' in these places, especially when the bread is so good. Soup, pilav, a main course and bread make for a big meal.

Hazır yemek restaurants prepare most of their daily dishes for the noon meal and then just keep them heated (one hopes) until suppertime. The best reason to eat a big meal at noon is that the food is freshest and best then. If you want grilled fish or meat, have it in the evening.

Kebapçı, Köfteci Another sort of restaurant is the kebapçı (keh-BAHP-chuh) or köfteci (KURF-teh-jee). A kebapçı is a man who cooks kebap (roast meat). A köfteci roasts köfte, which are rissoles or meatballs of ground lamb made with savory spices. Though they may have one or two ready-food dishes, kebapçıs and köftecis specialize in grilled meat, plus soups, salad, yogurt and perhaps dessert. Döner kebap and şiş kebap (see above) are the two most common kinds of *kebap*. *Kuşbaşı* (KOOSH-bah-shuh, 'bird's head') is a smaller and finer lamb *şiş kebap*. *Çöp kebap* (CHURP keh-bahp) is tiny morsels of lamb on split bamboo skewers.

If you want any sort of *kebap* or *köfte* well-done, ask for it *iyi pişmiş* (ee-YEE peesh-meesh) or *pişkin* (peesh-KEEN).

*Kebapçı*s can be great fun, especially the ones that are *ocakbaşı* (oh-JAHK bah-shuh), or 'fireside'. Patrons sit around the sides of a long rectangular firepit. The *kebapçı* sits enthroned in the middle, grilling hundreds of small skewers of *şiş kebap* and *şiş köfte* (sheesh KURF-teh), which is *köfte* wrapped around a flat skewer; *Adana köfte* (ah-DAHN-nah) is the same thing, but spicy-hot. The chef hands them to you as they're done, and you eat them with flat bread, a salad, and perhaps *ayran* (ah-yee-RAHN), a drink of yogurt mixed with spring water.

Pideci For those on an adventurer's budget, the Turkish *pideci* is a godsend. At a *pideci*, the dough for flat bread is patted out and shaped something like a boat, then topped with butter and other toppings, immediately baked in a wood-fired oven, and served at once. It's fresh, delicious, inexpensive, sanitary and nutritious. As toppings, if you want cheese say *peynirli* (pehy-neer-LEE); if you want eggs, say *yumurtalı* (yoo-moor-tah-LUH); *kıymalı* or *etli* means with ground lamb. In some parts of Turkey a *pide* with meat is called *etli ekmek*, but it's still the same freshly baked flat bread.

I've recommended numerous *pideci*s in the various places covered by this book. To find your own, ask *Buralarda bir pideci var mı?* ('Is there a *pideci* around here?')

Büfe & Kuru Yemiş Besides restaurants, Turkey has millions of little snack stands and quick-lunch places known as *büfe*

(bew-FEH, buffet). These serve sandwiches, often grilled; puddings; portions of *börek* (bur-REHK, flaky pastry); and perhaps *lahmacun* (LAHH-mah-joon), an Arabic soft pizza made with chopped onion, lamb and tomato sauce. In the bigger büfes in İstanbul, you may have to pay the cashier in advance and get a receipt (*fiş*, FEESH), hand it to the cook, and order your snack. Just tell the cashier *İki lahmacun*, pay, give the *fiş* to the cook, and repeat the order. You'll end up with two of the soft pizzas.

A *kuru yemiş* (koo-ROO yeh-MEESH) place serves dried fruits and nuts. These places are wonderful! Along İstiklal Caddesi in İstanbul you'll find little *kuru yemiş* shops selling pistachios (shelled or unshelled), walnuts, hazelnuts, peanuts (salted or unsalted), dried figs and apricots, chocolate, sunflower seeds and a dozen other good things. Prices are displayed, usually by the kilogram. Order 100 grams (*yüz gram*, YEWZ grahm), which is a good portion, and pay exactly one-tenth of the kilogram price displayed.

Another good place for *kuru yemiş* is the Mısır Çarşısı, the Egyptian or Spice Bazaar in İstanbul's Eminönü section. *Kuru yemiş* shops here will also have *pestil* (pehs-TEEL), fruit which has been dried and pressed into flat sheets. Odd at first, but delicious, it's quite cheap and comes from apricots (*kayısı*), mulberries (*dut*) and other fruits.

Saving Money Several tips can save you lots of money on food. First, order as you eat. Turks order appetizers, eat them, then decide what to have next, and order it. There is no need to order your entire meal at the beginning, except perhaps in the 'international' hotels. Second, don't overeat with your eyes. Often you will be brought to a steam table or cookstove to select your meal, and there's a tendency to order too many courses. Order them one at a time, and remember that it takes 20 minutes for food to 'make you feel full' after you've eaten it.

Third, eat bread. Turkish bread is delicious, fresh, plentiful and cheap. Many Turkish dishes come in savoury sauces; dip and sop your bread and enjoy. For instance, a meal of *kuru fasulye* (beans in a rich tomato sauce with meat stock) with bread and water is delicious, nutritious and ridiculously cheap at about 300TL or 400TL (US$0.42 or US$0.56).

Fourth, don't accept any plate of food which you have not specifically ordered. For example, in İstanbul's Çiçek Pasajı, itinerant vendors may put a dish of fresh almonds on your table. They're not a gift. They'll show up on your bill at a premium rate. The same goes for unwanted appetizers, butter, cheese, etc. If you haven't ordered it, ask *Hediye mi?* (heh-dee-YEH mee, 'Is it a gift?') or *Bedava mı?* (beh-dah-VAH muh, 'Is it free?'). If the answer is no, say *İstemiyorum* (eess-TEH-mee-oh-room, 'I don't want it').

Finally, always check your restaurant bill for errors. As tourism comes to Turkey, so do the common sins of ripping off the tourist. The more touristy a place is, the more carefully you must check your bill.

Meals

Breakfast (Kahvaltı) In a hotel or pastry shop, breakfast (*komple kahvaltı*, kohm-PLEH kah-vahl-TUH) consists of fresh, delicious Turkish bread (*ekmek*, ek-MEHK) with jam or honey, butter, black olives, white sheep's milk cheese and tea (*çay*, CHAH-yee). Sometimes a wedge of processed cheese, like the French 'La Vache Qui Rit', is added or substituted for the sheep's milk cheese.

You can always order an egg (*yumurta*, yoo-moor-TAH), soft-boiled (*üç dakikalık*, EWCH dahk-kah-luhk) or hard-boiled (*sert*, SEHRT). Fried eggs are *sahanda yumurta* (sah-hahn-DAH yoo-moor-tah). Sometimes your bread will come *kızartmış* (kuh-zahrt-MUSH, grilled, toasted). This is the standard breakfast for tourists. If you order an egg or another

glass of tea, you may be charged a bit extra.

Breakfast is not normally included in the hotel room rate, though some hotels do include it. When breakfast is included, the desk clerk will mention it as he quotes the price of the room. *Kahvaltı dahil* (kah-vahl-TUH dah-HEEL) means 'Breakfast is included'.

Turkish bread and tea are usually fresh and good, but because any breakfast can get dull after awhile there are alternatives. Turks may have a bowl of hot chicken soup (*tavuk çorbası*, tah-VOOK chor-bah-suh). If that's not for you, find a place serving *su böreği* (SOO bur-reh-yee), a many-layered noodle-like pastry with white cheese and parsley among the layers, served warm.

Hot, sweetened milk (*sıcak süt*, suh-JAHK sewt) is also a traditional breakfast drink, replaced in winter by *sahlep* (sah-LEHP), which is hot, sweetened milk with tasty tapioca-root powder added and cinnamon sprinkled on top.

Bacon is difficult to find as any pork product is forbidden to Muslims. You may find it in the big hotels in the biggest cities.

Turkish coffee (*kahve*, kahh-VEH) is better as an after-dinner drink than a breakfast drink. You may find some places willing to serve you *Amerikan kahvesi* (ah-mehr-ee-KAHN kahh-veh-see), a less concentrated brew than Turkish coffee. *Fransız kahvesi* (frahn-SUHZ kahh-veh-see, 'French coffee') can be either strong *Amerikan kahvesi* (served black) or it can be coffee-with-milk, which may also be called *sütlü kahve* (sewt-LEW kahh-veh).

Instant coffee, called *neskafe* (NEHS-kah-feh) or *hazır kahve* (hah-ZUHR kahh-veh), is also served most everywhere now.

Lunch (Öğle yemeği) The noon meal can be big or small. In summer, many Turks prefer to eat a big meal at noon and a light supper in the evening. You might want to do this, too.

Dinner The evening meal can be a repeat of lunch, a light supper, or a sumptuous repast. In good weather the setting might be outdoors.

Turkish Specialties

Meze A big meal starts with *meze* (MEH-zeh), all sorts of appetizers and hors d'oeuvres. You'll find *börek* (bur-REHK), pastry rolls or cylinders or 'pillows' filled with white cheese and parsley, then deep-fried. There will be olives *(zeytin)*, white cheese, *turşu* (toor-SHOO, pickled vegetables), *patates kızartma* (pah-TAH-tess kuh-ZART-mah, fried potatoes) or light potato fritters called *patates köfte*. The famous stuffed vine leaves *(dolma)* come either hot or cold. The hot ones *(etli*, eht-LEE, 'with meat') have ground lamb in them. The cold ones are made without meat, but 'with olive oil' *(zeytinyağlı)*.

Salads The real stars of the *meze* tray, however, are the salads and purees. These are mystifying at first because they all look about the same: some goo on a plate decorated with bits of carrot, peas, parsley, olives or lemon slices. Here's where you'll need words to understand:

Amerikan salatası A Russian salad with mayonnaise, peas, carrots, etc.
Beyin salatası Sheep's brain salad, usually the whole brain served on lettuce. Food for thought.
Cacık That's 'jah-JUHK', yogurt thinned with grated cucumber, then beaten and flavoured with a little garlic and a dash of olive oil.
Çoban salatası A 'shepherd's salad', this is a mixed, chopped salad of tomatoes, cucumbers, parsley, olives and peppers (sometimes fiery). If you don't want the peppers, order the salad *bibersiz* (bee-behr-SEEZ). But as the salad was probably chopped up all together at once,

this order means some kitchen lackey will attempt to pick out the peppers. He may miss some. Be on guard.
Karışık salata Same as a *çoban salatası*.
Patlıcan salatası This is pureed eggplant (aubergine), perhaps mixed with yogurt. The best of it has a faintly smoky, almost burnt flavour from the charcoal grilling of the eggplant.
Pilâki Broad white beans and sliced onions in a light vinegar pickle, served cold.
Rus salatası Russian salad. See *Amerikan salatası*.
Söğüş Pronounced 'sew-EWSH', this indicates raw salad vegetables such as tomatoes or cucumbers peeled and sliced, but without any sauce or dressing.
Taramasalata Red caviar, yogurt, garlic and olive oil mixed into a smooth paste, salty and delicious.
Yeşil salata Green salad of lettuce, oil and lemon juice or vinegar.

Main Courses After the *meze* comes the main course. The fish is marvellous all along the coast, especially in the Aegean. Ankara has some excellent fresh fish restaurants, too.

Most popular fish are *palamut* (tunny or bonito), a darkish, full-flavoured baby tuna. *Lüfer* (bluefish), *levrek* (sea bass), *kalkan* (turbot), *pisi* (megrim or brill) and *sardalya* (fresh sardines) are other familiar fish.

Many fish will be grilled *(ızgara)* or fried *(tava)*, especially turbot and tunny. Lüfer and levrek are particularly good poached with vegetables *(buğlama)*. Fresh sardines are best if deep-fried in a light batter.

If you prefer meat, you can order a *karışık ızgara* (kahr-uh-SHUK uhz-gahr-ah), mixed grill of lamb. For beef, order *bonfile* (bohn-fee-LEH), a small filet steak with a pat of butter on top. *Kuzu pirzolası* (koo-ZOO peer-zohl-ah-suh) is tiny lamb chops, charcoal grilled.

Besides grilled meats there are

numerous fancy *kebaps*, often named for the places where they originated. Best of the *kebaps* is *Bursa kebap* (BOOR-sah), also called *İskender kebap*, since it was invented in the city of Bursa by a chef named İskender (Turkish for Alexander). The *kebap* is standard *döner* spread on a bed of fresh, chopped, flat *pide* bread, with a side order of yogurt. After the plate has been brought to your table, a man comes with savoury tomato sauce and pours a good helping on top. Then another man comes with browned butter, which goes on top of the sauce. This stuff is addictive.

Of the other fancy kebaps, *Urfa kebap* comes with lots of onions and black pepper; *Adana kebap* is spicy hot, with red pepper the way the Arabs like it (Adana is down near the Syrian border).

Vegetarian Food Vegetarianism is not prevalent in Turkey. If you merely want to minimize consumption of meat, you will have no problem, as Turkish cuisine has many, many dishes in which meat is used merely as a flavouring rather than as a principal element. However, if you wish to avoid meat utterly, you will have to choose carefully. A good dish to try is *menemen* (MEH-neh-MEHN), tomatoes topped with eggs and baked; it is fairly spicy-hot. Salads, cheeses, *pilavs* and yogurt can fill out the menu. Note that many of the bean dishes such as *nohut* (chick-peas, garbanzos) and *kuru fasulye* (broad beans) are prepared with lamb as a flavouring.

Here are some phrases so that you can explain to the waiter or the chef what you want: *Hiç et yiyemem* (HEECH eht yee-YEH-mehm, 'I can't eat any meat'); *Etin suyu bile yiyemem* (EH-teen soo-YOO bee-leh yee-YEH-mehm, 'I can't even eat meat juices'); *Etsiz yemek var mı?* (eht-seez yeh-mehk VAHR muh, 'Do you have any dishes without meat?'). Chicken is an ingredient in two dessert puddings, and you wouldn't know it from looking at

them or even eating them: *tavuk göğsü* and *kazandibi*. *Yiyemem* means 'I can't eat'. Depending upon your requirements, use it with *et* (meat), *tavuk* or *piliç* (chicken), *yumurta* (egg) or *balık* (fish) to make yourself understood.

Cheese Cheeses are not a strong point in the Turkish kitchen. Though there are some interesting peasant cheeses such as *tulum peynir*, a salty, dry, crumbly goat's milk cheese cured in a goatskin bag, or another dried cheese which looks just like twine, these interesting cheeses rarely make it to the cities, and almost never to restaurant tables. What you'll find is the ubiquitous *beyaz peynir* (bey-AHZ pey-neer), white sheep's milk cheese. To be good, this must be full-fat *(tam yağlı)*, not dry and not too salty. You may also find *kaşar peynir* (kah-SHAHR pey-neer), a firm, mild yellow cheese which comes from *taze* (tah-ZEH, fresh) or *eski* (ess-KEE, aged). The *eski* is a bit sharper, but not very sharp for all that.

Desserts Turkish desserts tend to be very sweet, soaked in sugar syrup. Many are baked, such as crumpets, cookies (biscuits) or shredded wheat, all in syrup.

Baklava comes in several varieties: *cevizli* is with chopped walnut stuffing; *fıstıklı* is with pistachio nuts; *kaymaklı* is with clotted cream. Sometimes you can order *kuru baklava*, 'dry' *baklava*, which has less syrup. True *baklava* is made with honey, not syrup, and though the home-made stuff may contain honey the store-bought stuff rarely does.

As an alternative to sweet desserts, Turkish fruits can't be beat, especially in mid-summer when the melon season starts, and early in winter when the first citrus crop comes in. *Kavun* is a deliciously sweet, fruity melon. *Karpuz* is watermelon.

The standard unsweet dessert, available in most restaurants, is *krem karamel* (creme caramel or flan).

Drinks

Tea & Coffee The national drink is not really Turkish coffee as you might expect, but *çay* (CHAH-yee) – tea. The Turks drank a lot of coffee as long as they owned Arabia, because the world's first (and best) coffee is said to have come from Yemen. With the collapse of the Ottoman Empire coffee became an imported commodity. You can get Turkish coffee anywhere in Turkey, but you'll find yourself drinking a lot more *çay*.

The tea plantations are along the eastern Black Sea coast, centred on the town of Rize. Turkish tea is hearty and full-flavoured, served in little tulip-shaped glasses which you hold by the rim to avoid burning your fingers. Sugar is added, but never milk. If you want your tea weaker, ask for it *acık* (ah-CHUK, clear); for stronger, darker tea, order *koyu* (koh-YOO, dark). You can get it easily either way because Turkish tea is made by pouring some very strong tea into a glass, then cutting it with water to the desired strength.

The tiny glasses may seem impractical at first, but in fact they assure you of drinking only fresh, hot tea. Few Turks sit down and drink only one glass. For a real tea-drinking and talking session, they'll go to an outdoor tea garden and order a *semaver* (samovar) of tea so they can refill the glasses themselves, without having to call the *çaycı* (CHAH-yee-juh, tea-man).

As for Turkish coffee (*Türk kahvesi*, TEWRK kah-veh-see), it is always brewed up individually, the sugar being added during the brewing. You order it one of four ways:

sade (sah-DEH) – plain, without sugar
az (AHZ) – with a little sugar
orta (ohr-TAH) – with moderate sugar
çok şekerli (CHOHK sheh-kehr-LEE) – with lots of sugar

Order *bir kahve, orta* (BEER kah-VEH, ohr-TAH) for the first time, and adjust

from there. The pulverized coffee grounds lurk at the bottom of the cup – stop drinking before you get to them.

Water Turks are connoisseurs of good water, and stories circulate of old men able to tell which spring it came from just by tasting it. *Menba suyu*, spring water, is served everywhere, even on intercity buses.

Water from various springs is sold in 250-ml and 1½-litre clear plastic bottles filled in modern factories. The standard price for a 1½-litre bottle of any brand, sold in a grocery, probably chilled, is 250TL (US$0.35). If you order it in a restaurant there will be a mark-up of 100% to 300%.

Tap water is supposedly safe to drink because it is treated. But it's not as tasty nor as trustworthy as spring water.

Soft Drinks Soft drinks include the usual range of Coca-Cola, Pepsi, Yedigün ('Seven Days', a clear lemon-flavoured soft drink like Seven-Up), Fruko (an orange soda) and others. Most Turks make little distinction between Coke and Pepsi, and if you ask for one will serve you the other without thinking. Few places carry both brands, so you might as well just ask for *kola*, which will yield whatever the shop or restaurant carries.

If you want unflavoured fizzy water, ask for *soda*. Fizzy mineral water is *maden sodası*.

Fruit juices are a favourite refresher, and can be excellent. These used to be only thick juices full of pulp and flavour, but with the advent of modern marketing you will also find watery, sugared drinks of almost no food value. These are usually the ones in the paper containers. The good fruit juices tend to come in glass bottles.

Traditional drinks include *ayran* (ah-yee-RAHN), yogurt mixed with spring water and shaken; it's tart, refreshing and healthful. *Şıra* (shur-RAH), unfermented white grape juice, is delicious but is served in only a few places, and only during the summer. *Boza* is a thick, slightly tangy, very mild-flavoured drink made from fermented millet (like bird seed), served only in winter.

Wine & Beer Strictly observant Muslims don't touch alcoholic beverages at all, but Turkey is a modern country in which the strictures of religion are moderated by the 20th-century lifestyle. *Bira* (BEE-rah, beer) is served almost everywhere. Tuborg makes light *(beyaz)* and dark *(siyah)* beer in Turkey under licence. A local company with a European brew-master is Efes Pilsen, which also makes light and dark. The light is a good, slightly bitter pilsener. Tekel, the Turkish State Monopolies company, makes Tekel Birası (teh-KEHL bee-rah-suh), a small-bubbled (sort of flat), mildly flavoured brew that may be an acquired taste. As of this writing, beer is available in disposable cans, at a premium price. You'll save money, get better flavour, and not contribute to the litter problem if you buy bottled beer.

Turkish wines are surprisingly good and delightfully cheap. Tekel makes all kinds in all price ranges. Güzel Marmara is the cheap white table wine. Buzbağ (BOOZ-baah) is a hearty Burgundy-type wine with lots of tannin. Restaurants seem to carry mostly the wines of the two big private firms, Doluca (DOHL-oo-jah) and Kavaklıdere (kah-vakh-LUH-deh-reh). You'll find the premium Villa Doluca wines, white *(beyaz)* and red *(kırmızı,* KUHR-muh-ZUH) in most places. Kavaklıdere wines include the premium white named Çankaya and the medium-range wines named Kavak (white), Dikmen (red) and Lâl (rose).

Among the more popular regional table wines are those under the Doruk and Dimitrakopulo labels.

Strong Liquor Hard liquor is a government monopoly in Turkey, and what's not made by Tekel is imported by them.

Duties on imported spirits used to be very high but have now dropped significantly, so that your favourite brand will probably cost about the same in Turkey as it does at home. Even so, the locally made drinks will be much cheaper than the imported brands.

The favourite ardent spirit in Turkey is *rakı* (rah-KUH), an anise-flavoured grape brandy similar to the Greek *ouzo*, French *pastis* and Arab *arrak*. *Rakı* comes under several labels, all made by Tekel, the standard one being Yeni Rakı. It's customary (but not essential) to mix *rakı* with cool water, half-and-half and perhaps some ice, and to drink it with a meal.

Tekel also makes decent *cin* (JEEN, gin), *votka* and *kanyak* (kahn-YAHK, brandy). When ordering *kanyak*, always specify the *beş yıldız* or *kaliteli* ('five-star' or 'quality') stuff. The regular *kanyak* is thick and heavy, the five-star much lighter.

There is a Tekel *viski* (VEES-kee, whisky) named Ankara. You might try it once.

For after-dinner drinks, better restaurants will stock the local sweet fruit brandies, which are OK but nothing special.

TIPPING

Restaurants Most of the tipping you'll do will be in restaurants. Some places will automatically add a service charge *(servis ücreti)* of 10% or 15% to your bill, but this does not absolve you from the tip, oddly enough. The service charge goes either into the pocket of the *patron* (owner), or to the maitre d'. Leave 5% on the table for the waiter, or hand it directly to him.

If service is included, the bill may say *servis dahil* ('service included'). Still, a small tip is expected. In any situation, 5% to 10% is fine. Only in the fancy foreign-operated hotels will waiters expect those enormous 15% to 20% American-style tips. In the very plain, basic restaurants you needn't tip at all, though the price of a soft drink or a cup of coffee is always appreciated.

Hotels In hotels, tip the bellboy who shows you to your room and carries your bags. He'll expect about 4% or 5% of the room price. So if your room costs 10,000TL (US$14), give about 450TL (US$0.63). If a bellboy does any other chores, a slightly smaller tip is in order.

Taxis Don't tip taxi drivers unless they've done some special service. Turks don't tip taxi drivers, though they often round off the metered fare. Thus, if the meter reads 489TL, it's common to give the driver 500TL. Taxi drivers may look for a tip from you, but that's only because you're a foreigner and foreigners tip taxi drivers. Dolmuş drivers never expect tips or rounded fares.

Hairdressers In barbershops and hairdressers, pay the fee for the services rendered (which goes to the shop), then about 15% to the person who cut your hair, and smaller tips to the others who provided service, down to the one who brushes stray locks from your clothing as you prepare to leave (5% for that).

Turkish Baths In Turkish baths there will be fees for the several services, but everyone will expect and await tips. You needn't go overboard in this. Share out about 30% or 35% at most to the assembled staff (and they will indeed be assembled for tips as you depart). In a few of the more heavily touristed baths in İstanbul the attendants are insistent. Don't let them browbeat you. Look firm and say, *Yeter!* (yeh-TEHR, 'It's sufficient').

Sleeping Cars If you take a sleeping compartment on a train, the porter will come around near the end of the trip, request an official 10% service charge, give you a receipt for it, and expect a few more percent for himself. If you give him 5% extra, he'll be pleased.

Other Situations There are other situations in which a tip is indicated, but that must be handled delicately. For instance, at a remote archaeological site, a local person may unlock the gate and show you around the ruins. He will probably have official admission tickets, which he must sell you. If that's all he does, that's all you pay. But if he goes out of his way to help you, he deserves a tip. He may be reluctant to accept it, and may refuse once or even twice. Try at least three times. He may well need the money, but the rules of politeness require several refusals. If he refuses three times, though, you can assume that he truly wants to help you only for friendship's sake. Don't press further, for this will insult his good intentions.

In many of these situations, a token gift will be just as happily received as a cash tip. If you have some small item, particularly something distinctive from your home country such as a ball-point pen, you can offer it in lieu of money.

WHAT TO WEAR

For high summer, that is mid-June through mid-September, you'll need light cotton summer clothes, and a light sweater or jacket for the evenings or to wear up on the Central Anatolian plateau. You won't need rain gear at all, except perhaps on the Black Sea coast.

In spring and autumn, summer clothing will still be right but the evenings will be cooler. If you plan to travel extensively in Central Anatolia (Ankara, Konya, Cappadocia, Nemrut Dağı), pack a heavier sweater and perhaps a light raincoat.

Winter wear – December through March – is woollens and rain gear. Though it doesn't get really cold along the Mediterranean, it does get damp, rainy and chilly in most of the country. İstanbul and İzmir get dustings of snow; Ankara gets more. Nemrut Dağı and the eastern region are covered in snow.

Formal or Informal?

How does one dress in a Muslim country? In this one, you dress pretty much as you would for Europe. In high summer, no one will really expect men to have a coat and tie, even when visiting a government official. For the rest of the year, Turks tend to dress formally in formal situations such as at the office or in a good restaurant or nightclub, but informally at other times. Neat and tidy dress is still admired here. Tatty or careless clothes, a sign of nonchalance or independence in other societies, are looked upon as tatty or careless in Turkey.

Anyone can visit a Turkish mosque so long as you look presentable. Your clothes must be neat. No shorts or sleeveless shirts on either men or women; women require skirts of a modest length (knees) and a headscarf. Before you enter a working mosque, that is, one with carpets on its floor, remove your shoes to protect the carpets from soil. Muslims pray on the carpets, so they must be kept clean.

LAUNDRY

There are no coin-operated automatic laundries in Turkey yet, but laundry (çamaşır, chahm-mah-SUHR) is a simple matter. At any hotel or pension, ask at the reception desk, or just short-circuit it and ask a staff member (chambermaid). They'll quickly find someone to do laundry. Agree on a price in advance. The classier the hotel, the more exorbitant their laundry rates. Even so, the rates are no higher than at home.

Figure at least a day to get laundry done. It may be washed in a machine or by hand, but it will be dried on a line, not in a drying machine. In summer, drying takes no time at all. If you wash out a T-shirt at 10.30 am in İzmir and hang it in the sun, it'll be dry by 11 am.

By the way, the word çamaşır (laundry) also means 'underwear' in

Turkish. This can be confusing at times.

Dry-cleaning shops (kuru temizleme, koo-ROO tehm-eez-lem-MEH) are found here and there in the big cities, usually in the better residential sections or near the luxury hotels. Service is similar to that in Europe and America: fast service takes an hour or two if you're willing to pay 50% more; otherwise, overnight or two-day service is normal. Prices are very reasonable, and you'll save money by taking the garments yourself rather than having the hotel staff do it.

SHOPPING

Most shops and shopping areas close on Sunday. This includes the Grand Bazaar and the Spice (Egyptian) Market in İstanbul, and the bazaars in other cities and towns. Grocers' shops may be open on Sunday, though, and there will always be one chemist (pharmacy) in town open.

Haggling

For the best buy in terms of price and quality, know the market. Spend some time shopping for similar items in various shops, asking prices. Shopkeepers will give you pointers on what makes a good kilim, carpet, meerschaum pipe or alabaster carving. In effect, you're getting a free course in product lore. This is not at all unpleasant, as you will often be invited to have coffee, tea or a soft drink as you talk over the goods and prices.

You can, and should, ask prices if they're not marked, but you should not make a counter-offer unless you are seriously interested in buying. No matter how often the shopkeeper asks you, 'OK, how much will you pay for it?' No matter how many glasses of tea you've drunk at his expense, don't make a counter-offer unless you're seriously interested in buying. If the shopkeeper meets your price, you should buy. It's considered very bad form to haggle over a price, agree, and then not buy.

Facts for the Visitor 67

Some shopkeepers, even in the Haggle Capital of the World (İstanbul's Grand Bazaar), will offer a decent price and say, 'That's my best offer'. Many times they mean it, and they're trying to do you a favour by saving time. How will you know when they are, and when it's just another haggling technique? Only by knowing the market, by having shopped around. Remember, even if he says, 'This is my best offer', you are under no obligation to buy unless you have made a counter-offer, or have said, 'I'll buy it'. It's perfectly acceptable to say a pleasant good-bye and walk out of the shop, even after all that free tea, if you cannot agree on a price. In fact, walking out is one of the best ways to test the authenticity of the shopkeeper's price. If he knows you can surely find the item somewhere else for less, he'll stop you and say, 'OK, you win, it's yours for what you offered'. And if he doesn't stop you, there's nothing to prevent you from returning in a half-hour and buying the item for what he quoted.

If any shopkeeper puts extraordinary pressure on you to buy, even though you can't agree on price, walk out of the shop, and consider reporting him to the Belediye Zabıtası (Market Police, see above). It is very un-Turkish and impolite for a shopkeeper to browbeat you. Anyone who does so is not playing by the normal rules of the game.

Value Added Tax

Turkey has a Value Added Tax, called Katma Değer Vergisi, added to and hidden in the price of most items and services, from souvenirs through hotel rooms to restaurant meals. Most establishments display a sign saying *Fiatlarımızda KDV Dahildir*, 'VAT is included in our prices'. Thus, it is rare that the VAT is added to your bill separately, and you should be suspicious if it is.

There is a scheme whereby tourists can reclaim the amount paid in VAT on larger

purchases such as leather garments, carpets, etc. Not all shops participate in the scheme, so you must ask if it is possible to get a KDV İade Özel Fatura (keh-deh-VEH ee-ah-DEH err-ZEHL fah-too-rah, Special VAT Refund Receipt). Ask for this during the haggling rather than after you've bought. The receipt can be converted to cash at a bank in the international departures lounge at the airport, or at your point of exit from Turkey; or the shop will (one hopes) mail a refund cheque to your home after the government has completed its procedures (don't hold your breath).

Things to Buy

Alabaster A translucent, fine-grained variety of either gypsum or calcite, alabaster is pretty because of its grain and colour, and because light passes through it. You'll see ashtrays, vases, chess sets, bowls, egg cups, even the eggs themselves carved from the stone. Cappadocia is a major producing and carving area, and towns like Ürgüp and Avanos specialize in it. But in fact you will find it wherever good souvenirs are sold.

Antiques Turkey harbours a lot of fascinating stuff left over from the empire: vigorous peasant jewellery, waterpipe mouthpieces carved from amber, old Korans and illuminated manuscripts, Greek and Roman figurines and coins, tacky furniture in the Ottoman Baroque style. However, *it is illegal to buy, sell, possess or export any antiquity*, and you can go to prison for breaking the law. All antiquities must be turned over to a museum immediately upon discovery. You may be offered Greek and Roman coins and figurines for sale. Refuse at once. Items only a century or two old are not usually classed as antiquities, though, and only true antiquities are off-limits, not the many artful fakes.

Turkey is one of those countries with treasure troves of antiquities, some of which are smuggled out of the country and fed into the international contraband art market. It's a dirty business. Keep away from it.

Carpets & Kilims Turkey has marvellous carpets and *kilims* (flat-woven mats) at good prices only half or two-thirds what you'd pay at home. Unless you're willing to research patterns, dyes, knots-per-square-cm and so forth, you'll buy what you like for a price that fits your budget.

The very basic examination of a carpet, so that you can look like you know what you're doing, involves the following procedures. Turn a corner over and look at the closeness of the weave. Ask, 'How many knots per square cm?' The tighter the weave, the smaller the knots, the higher the quality and durability. Compare the colours on the back with the colours on the front. Spread the nap with your fingers and look to the *bottom* of the carpet's pile. Are the colours more vivid there than on the surface? If so, the surface has faded in the sun considerably. Take a white handkerchief, wet it a bit, and rub it on the top surface of the carpet. Is there colour on the handkerchief? There shouldn't be; if there is, the carpet's dyes are runny. Look at the carpet from one end, then from the other; the colours will be different because the pile always leans one way or the other. Take the carpet out into the sunlight and look at it there.

That's about all you can do without becoming a rug expert. If you don't trust the dealer's sworn oath that the rug is all wool, all silk, or whatever, ask him to clip a bit of the tassle and burn if for you – if you can recognize the smell of burning silk, wool or nylon.

Carpet prices are determined by demand, age quality, condition, enthusiasm of the buyer and debt load of the seller. New carpets can be skillfully 'antiquated'; damaged or worn carpets can be rewoven (good work, but expensive), patched or even painted. Worn carpets look fairly good until the magic paint washes out. Give the carpet a good going-over, decide if you think it's a good price, and go from there.

Method of payment can be a bargaining point, or a point of contention. Some dealers will take personal cheques, but all prefer cash or travellers' cheques. If you pay with a credit card (and not all shops will have facilities for this), the dealer may require you to pay the fee which the credit card company will charge him, and even the cost of the phone call or telex to check on your credit. If he doesn't require you to pay these charges, it means that you've paid a hefty enough price so that another 6% to 8% doesn't bother him.

If all this seems too much trouble, be advised: it isn't. A good Turkish carpet will easily outlast the human body of its owner, and become an heirloom.

Ceramics The best Turkish ceramics were made in İznik (Nicaea) in the 17th and 18th centuries. İznik tiles from the great days are now museum-pieces, found in museums throughout the world.

Today most of the tile-making is done in Kütahya, a pleasant town with few other redeeming qualities for the tourist. For the very best ceramics, you must go there. Souvenir shops will also have attractive, hand-made tiles, plates, cups and bowls. They're not really high-fired so they're vulnerable to breaks and cracks, but they are still attractive.

The real, old İznik tiles qualify as antiquities. If you go to İznik, you will find a reviving tile industry on a small scale. Some of the items are quite pretty and reasonably priced.

Copper Gleaming copper vessels will greet you in every souvenir shop you peep into. Many are old, sometimes several centuries. Most are handsome, and some are still eminently useful. The new copperware tends to be of lighter gauge;

that's one of the ways you tell new from old. But even the new stuff will have been made by hand.

'See that old copper waterpipe over there?' my friend Alaettin asked me once. We were sitting in his impossibly cluttered, closet-sized shop on İstanbul's Çadırcılar Caddesi, just outside the Grand Bazaar. 'It dates from the time of Sultan Ahmet III (1703-1730), and was used by the *Padişah* (sultan) himself. I just finished making it yesterday.'

Alaettin was a master coppersmith, and his pieces might well have graced the sultan's private apartments – except that the sultanate was abolished in 1922. He charged a hefty price for his fine workmanship but not for the story, which was the gift-wrapping, so to speak.

Copper vessels should not be used for cooking or eating unless they are tinned inside; that is, washed with molten tin which covers the toxic copper. If you intend to use a copper vessel, make sure the interior layer of tin is intact, or negotiate to have it tinned *(kalaylamak)*. If there is a *kalaycı* shop nearby, ask about the price of the tinning in advance.

Inlaid Wood Cigarette boxes, chess and *tavla* (backgammon) boards and other items will be inlaid with different coloured woods, silver or mother-of-pearl. It's not the finest work, but it's pretty good. Make sure there is indeed inlay. These days, alarmingly accurate decals/transfers exist. Also, check the silver: is it silver, or aluminum or pewter? Is the mother-of-pearl actually daughter-of-polystyrene?

Jewellery Turkey is a wonderful place to buy jewellery, especially the antique stuff. None of the items sold here may meet your definition of 'chic', but window-shopping is great fun. Jewellers' Row in any market is a dazzling strip of glittering shop windows filled with gold. Light bulbs, artfully rigged, show it off. In the Grand Bazaar, a blackboard sign hung above Kuyumcular Caddesi ('Street of the Jewellers') bears the daily price for unworked gold of so-many karats. Serious gold-buyers should check out this price, watch carefully as the jeweller weighs the piece in question, and then calculate what part of the price is for gold and what part for workmanship.

Silver is another matter. There is sterling silver jewellery (look for the hallmark), but nickel silver and pewter-like alloys are much more common. Serious dealers don't try to pass off alloy as silver.

Leather & Suede On any given Kurban Bayramı (Sacrifice Holiday), over 2,500,000 sheep get the axe in Turkey. Add to that the normal day-to-day needs of a cuisine based on mutton and lamb and you have a huge amount of raw material to be made into leather items. Shoes, bags, cushions, jackets, skirts, vests, hat, gloves and trousers are all made from soft leather. This is a big industry in Turkey, particularly in and around the Grand Bazaar. So much leather clothing is turned out that a good deal of it will be badly cut or carelessly made. But there are lots of fine pieces as well.

The only way to assure yourself of a good piece is to examine it carefully, taking time. Try it on just as carefully; see if the sleeves are full enough, if the buttonholes are positioned well, if the collar rubs. If something is wrong, keep trying others until you find what you want. Made-to-order garments can be excellent or disappointing, as the same tailor who made the ready-made stuff will make the ordered stuff; and he will be making it fast because the shopkeeper has already impressed you with his 'No problem. I can have it for you tomorrow'. It's better to find something off the rack that fits than to order it, unless you can order without putting down a deposit or committing yourself to buy.

Leather items and clothing are standard tourist stuff, found in all major tourist destinations.

Meerschaum If you smoke a pipe, you know about meerschaum. For those who don't, meerschaum ('seafoam' in German; *Lületaşı*, LEW-leh-tahsh-uh in Turkish) is a hydrous magnesium silicate, a soft, white, clay-like material which is very porous but heat-resistant. When carved into a pipe, it smokes cool and sweet. Over time, it absorbs residues from the tobacco and turns a nut-brown colour. Devoted meerschaum pipe smokers even have special gloves with which to hold the pipe as they smoke, so that oil from their fingers won't sully the fine, even patina of the pipe.

The world's largest and finest beds of meerschaum are found in Turkey, near the city of Eskişehir. Artful carving of the soft stone has always been done, and blocks of meerschaum were exported to be carved abroad as well. These days, however, the export of block meerschaum is prohibited because the government realized that exporting uncarved blocks was the same as exporting the jobs to carve them. So any carved pipe will have been carved in Turkey.

Carving is of a very high quality, and you'll marvel at the artistry of the Eskişehir craftspeople. Pipes portraying turbaned pashas, wizened old men, fair maidens and mythological beasts, as well as many pipes in geometrical designs, will be on view in any souvenir shop. Pipes are not the only things carved from meerschaum these days. Bracelets, necklaces, pendants, earrings and cigarette holders all appear in souvenir shops.

When buying, look for purity and uniformity in the stone. Carving is often used to cover up flaws in a piece of meerschaum; do look over it carefully. For pipes, check that the bowl walls are uniform in thickness all around, and that the hole at the bottom of the bowl is centered. Purists buy uncarved, just plain pipe-shaped meerschaums that are simply but perfectly made.

Prices for pipes vary, but should be fairly low. Abroad, meerschaum is an expensive commodity, and pipes are luxury items. Here in Turkey meerschaum is cheap, the services of the carver are low-priced, and nobody smokes pipes. If you can't get the pipe you want for 5000TL to 10,000TL (US$7 to US$14), or at least only half of what you'd pay at home, then you're not working at it hard enough.

SPORTS

Turks are sports enthusiasts. Football (soccer), basketball and wrestling are the favoured sports. Every city of any size has a large football stadium which fills up on match days.

The famous oiled wrestling matches, where brawny strong-men in leather breeches rub themselves down with olive oil and grapple with equally slippery opponents, take place each spring in Edirne. Another purely Turkish sight is the camel-wrestling matches held in the province of Aydın, south of İzmir, in the winter months. Konya is the setting for *cirit* (jirid), the javelin-throwing game played on horseback. See the Festivals & Holidays section for full details.

Water sports are big in Turkey because of the beautiful coasts and beaches. Yachting, rowing, water-skiing, snorkelling, diving (with or without scuba gear) and swimming are well represented.

Mountain-climbing (*dağcılık*, DAAH-juh-LUHK) is practised by a small but enthusiastic number of Turks, and Turkey has plenty of good, high mountains for it.

Turkey is a good country for hunting animals, from small game to wild boar (there's a boar-hunting festival at Ephesus each spring). However, the Turks are touchy about people bringing guns into the country. Check with a Turkish consulate about regulations and permits for importing a sporting gun.

Skiing is decent on Uludağ, near Bursa, and at a few resorts in the Beydağları mountain range near Antalya. Equipment can be rented at the slopes.

Bicycling has not caught on in Turkey as much as in Europe. Many of the highways have fairly rough surfaces which are not bad for cars and trucks, but a bit bumpy for a bike. The sport may catch on though. Turkey's scenery certainly lends itself to bike touring.

Pages from an 18th-century Turkish prayer book

The Prophet's Rose Tree. The stamen is identified with God; the petals with the Prophet; the leaves with the Caliphs.

The Tree of Bliss. Planted by the Prophet in Paradise, it grows from the heavens towards earth.

Getting There

You can get to Turkey by air, rail, road or sea. Note that if you travel by land you will have to deal with the problem of visas for transit of East European countries. See the section on this topic at the end of this chapter, and also the section on Embassies & Consulates.

AIR

Most international flights arrive at İstanbul's Atatürk Airport, the country's busiest, with a big new terminal; other international airports are at Ankara, İzmir, Adana (down near the Syrian border), and Antalya and Dalaman (on the southern coast). Most foreign visitors arrive in İstanbul because it has the most flights and is also the first place tourists want to see. Antalya and Dalaman receive mostly charter flights filled with vacationers headed for the south coast.

Turkish Airlines (Türk Hava Yolları or THY, symbol TK) has flights to most major cities in Europe, the Middle East and North Africa. The airlines of these destination countries also fly into and out of Turkey.

Transport to and from the airport is covered within the section on each city.

All of the fares mentioned below are subject to change, but they will give you an idea of what to expect.

From Athens, Greece

Olympic Airlines and Turkish Airlines share the route, offering at least four flights per day in summer. Fares for the 70-minute flight are 14,920 Drachmae (US$111) one way, 22,170 Drachmae (US$165) for an excursion (round trip/return ticket).

From Europe

Most of the European national airlines have flights to Turkey, often connecting with flights from North America. The normal one-way/single fare from London to İstanbul is £303 (US$445), but there are excursions as low as £244 to £414 (US$360 to US$610) off-season. High-season (summer) excursion fares are £322 to £497 (US$474 to US$730). Among the scheduled carriers, JAT, the Yugoslavian airline, seems to have the lowest fares via Belgrade to İstanbul, even lower than those quoted above. Lots of people know this, however, and the flights are often full. Reserve your seat well in advance for this one. Also, look at the schedules and fares of other East European airlines such as Tarom of Rumania.

British Airways and Turkish Airlines fly from London to İstanbul, and Turkish Airlines seem to have many discount fares from the British capital. Pan American World Airways, Air France and Turkish Airlines fly from Paris.

From the Middle East

Here is the data on fares to İstanbul from various Middle East cities:

Amman Turkish Airlines and Royal Jordanian share the traffic with about two flights per day. The non-stop, 2½-hour flight costs JD84 (US$245) one way, JD96 to JD114 (US$280 to US$333) for the round-trip excursion ticket.

Cairo Sabena, Egyptair and Turkish Airlines have flights about four days per week, charging E£337 one way (US$250), E£388 to E£455 (US$287 to US$337) for a round-trip excursion ticket on the non-stop, two-hour flight.

Damascus Syrian Arab Airlines, Turkish Airlines and Pakistan International Airlines make the 2½-hour flight four days per week and charge S£2050 (US$168) one way, S£2360 to S£2768 (US$194 to US$227) round-trip excursion.

Tel Aviv El Al has flights three times weekly, charging US$267 one way,

US$338 to US$347 for round-trip excursions.

From India

Aeroflot, the Soviet airline, reportedly has a one-way fare of US$450 from India to İstanbul via Moscow.

From North America

Scheduled Flights Pan American World Airways has been flying the New York-İstanbul route for over 50 years, and still provides efficient and convenient daily service via Paris and Geneva. Regular cabin-class fare is US$1355 one way; excursion fares range from US$889 to US$1725 depending upon season, stopovers, etc.

As of this writing Turkish Airlines does not fly from North America to Turkey, but there is talk of opening up such a route.

Most of the European national airlines fly from New York to their home countries, then on to İstanbul, at fares similar to the Pan Am ones mentioned above. KLM's connections are particularly good, with a layover in Amsterdam of little more than one hour. Pakistan International Airlines (PIA) has a one-stop service from New York to İstanbul, with an even lower excursion fare, but some passengers find the service less than luxurious.

From New York and Chicago, particularly during the summer months, group fares to İstanbul are sold by various tour operators. You do not have to be part of a group, nor do you have to take a tour or buy nights in a hotel. You pay only for the flight (which is on a regular, scheduled airline, not a charter), but you get your ticket at a special low group rate. There may be some restrictions, perhaps that you have to stay more than seven nights and less than 180 nights. From New York, fares are US$290 to US$409 one way, US$549 to US$969 round trip; from Chicago they are US$385 one way, US$639 round trip. For more information

contact a travel agent or get a copy of *JAXFAX Travel Marketing Magazine* (tel (203) 655-8746). Or contact one of these tour operators:

Am-Jet/Amtravel, 501 Fifth Avenue, Suite 2008, New York, New York 10017 (tel (212) 697-5332, 818-0125)

Globe Travel Specialists, 507 Fifth Avenue, New York, New York 10017 (tel (212) 682-8687)

Hürtürk Travel & Tours, 18 West 56th St, Suite 501, New York, New York 10019 (tel (212) 586-2901)

Sunbeam Travel, 274 Madison Avenue, Suite 904, New York, New York 10016 (tel (212) 725-8835, outside New York (800) 247-6659)

Theresa's World Travel, 61-06 Myrtle Avenue, Glendale, New York 11385 (tel (718) 381-1666)

Travel Magic, 555 Fifth Avenue, New York, New York 10017 (tel (212) 972-3036, outside New York (800) 543-0003)

Union Tours, 3175 North Lincoln Avenue, Chicago, Illinois 60657 (tel (312) 472-4620, (800) 331-6221)

VIP Tourism Pirinçcioğlu, 20 East 49th Street, New York, New York 10017 (tel (212) 421-5400).

It is also worth investigating the East European airlines, as well as alternative fares such as the 'open-jaw' ones that let you fly to one city (eg Vienna) and return from another (eg İstanbul). You have to make separate arrangements for transport between the two cities, but the overall savings can be considerable. For example, Tarom, the Rumanian national carrier, always advertises a stand-by fare of US$205 from New York to Vienna, non-stop. JAT, the Yugoslavian airline, often has the lowest direct fare from New York to İstanbul, though you may have to stay overnight in Belgrade.

From Australia

There is no direct route by air from Australia to İstanbul, though there are connecting flights via Athens, Bahrain, Belgrade, Dubai, Frankfurt or London/Heathrow, and Turkish Airlines has a weekly flight to and from Singapore. The return fare to Athens, the closest and most convenient connection to Istanbul, range from A$1569 in the off season, to A$1757 in the shoulder season and A$1851 in the peak season. From Athens you can then continue to İstanbul by land or air.

The cheapest way to get to Turkey from Australia is to fly to Athens and take a boat to one of the islands and then a ferry to the Turkish mainland. This route proves the dictum that the smaller the price the greater the inconvenience.

Charter Flights
You cannot take a charter flight to Greece and then go to Turkey without paying a huge penalty! Several countries (such as Greece) which benefit greatly from charter-flight traffic have enacted a regulation which prohibits charter passengers from leaving the charter destination country for the duration of their stay. Thus, if you fly to Athens on a charter and then legally enter Turkey (ie, have your passport stamped), the officials at the airport in Athens will not allow you to board your return charter flight. You will have to pay for another whole ticket to get home. (If you just take a day-excursion to Turkey, and the Turkish immigration officials do not stamp your passport, you will have no problem boarding your return charter flight.) The regulation is enforced so that the charter destination country reaps all of the benefits of the low charter fare. This regulation does not apply to regular or excursion-fare flights, only to charters.

Thus, if you want to go by charter flight, you must go directly to Turkey. By the way, I have had no news that the Turkish officials enforce the charter regulation, which means that if you take a charter to Turkey, you *can* visit Greece, return to Turkey, and have no trouble boarding your return charter flight.

RAIL
The Orient Express lives on in special

excursion trains, but the fares for these deluxe tours are between US$2500 and US$5500 one way for packages which include transportation from European points to İstanbul aboard restored railway coaches, with lectures and optional side-trips.

Otherwise, there is daily train service from Europe. In 2nd class it is fairly cheap, which is why the cars are usually packed with Turkish 'guest workers' and their families. They want to stash away as much as possible from a stint of hard factory work in Europe, so they don't mind discomfort.

You'll find a lot of cigarette smoking in every car.

There is no romance left on this famed Orient Express route. In 2nd class you're much more likely to meet with delay, discomfort, unpleasantness or worse. You may be able to resurrect a bit of romance if you travel 1st class, preferably in a sleeping car as far as Belgrade, then in a couchette to İstanbul. Another tip is to get off the train in Edirne, the first stop in Turkey. It's an interesting city, well worth a stop. From Edirne to İstanbul the train takes at least six hours, but the bus takes less than four.

From Greece
I'm not sure why they still run the train between Athens and İstanbul. Neither country cares much about it. The schedule says that the 1400-km journey takes a day and a half, departing Athens or İstanbul in the evening, arriving mid-morning about 35 hours later. This schedule (if indeed the train is on time) is about an hour faster than the schedule run in 1908 under the Ottoman Empire. My guess is that the Ottoman train ran on time much more frequently than today's does, which hauls 2nd-class coaches only.

Don't think you'll cut this excruciating time much by going from Thessaloniki to İstanbul. That trip is still about 25 hours – if it's on time. You'd be well advised to take a bus (see below).

From Venice, Italy

You can take a late afternoon train from Venice which reaches Belgrade the next morning; but then you must wait until mid-afternoon to catch an onward train to İstanbul. From Belgrade to İstanbul alone is 26 hours, and thus the entire Venice-İstanbul trip takes a full two days.

From Munich, Germany

The İstanbul Express from Munich is a bit better, taking 39 hours from Munich to İstanbul, 30 hours from Vienna to İstanbul; it hauls couchette cars and, between Munich and Belgrade, sleeping cars. All these travel times apply only if the trains are on time, which they rarely are.

From Paris, France

There is a daily train which takes 57 hours to reach İstanbul.

Fares

Fares are competitive with the bus (see below). If you're young, you can take advantage of the Wasteels BIGE Youth Train, with special low fares. In İstanbul, buy your tickets at window *(Gişe)* No 5 in Sirkeci station. Also, there are special low fares for people under 26 years of age using the Inter-Rail pass.

BUS

The construction of good highways between Europe and Turkey has opened the Middle East to all sorts of vehicles. Turkish bus companies operate frequent passenger services.

From Europe

The past decade has seen the rise of frequent, fairly comfortable and moderately priced bus travel along this route. Several Turkish companies operate big Mercedes buses which are at least as comfortable as the now-neglected trains (usually more so), comparable in price, often faster and perhaps safer. The major

discomfort on the trip may be cigarette smoke.

Bosfor Turizm operates from Paris and Lyon (US$80), Geneva, Milan and Venice (US$63), departing from Paris on this route Monday evening and arriving in İstanbul around noon on Thursday. From Munich they have an express service which departs each Friday and Sunday at noon and arrives in İstanbul about 48 hours later. Cost is US$80, plus US$25 to US$30 for a hotel the second night. From Vienna, an express service departs Tuesday and Friday evenings, arriving in İstanbul Thursday and Sunday evenings (US$63). Bosfor Turizm has sales desks or representatives in the international bus terminals of several European cities; or you can contact them at these addresses:

İstanbul
    Mete Caddesi, Taksim (tel 90 (11) 143-2525, telex 24324 IBOS TR)
Munich
    Seidlstrasse 2, 8 München 2 (tel 49 (89) 59 40 02 or 59 24 96, telex 529388 MBOS)
Paris
    Gare Routière Internationale, 8 place de Stalingrad, 75019 Paris (tel 33 (1) 201-7080 or 205-1210, telex 210192)
Vienna
    Argentinierstrasse 67, Südbahnhof, 1040 Wien (tel 43 (222) 65 06 44, telex 136878 WBOS)

Other Turkish companies ply similar routes. For instance, Varan run buses to İstanbul and Ankara from Metz, Nancy, Strasbourg, Colmar and Mulhouse, departing on Saturday; from Zurich (Saturday morning); from Bregenz, Dornbirn and Innsbruck (Saturday); and from Salzburg and Vienna (Monday and Friday). Here are some addresses:

İstanbul
    İnönü (Gümüşsuyu) Caddesi 17, Taksim (tel 90 (11) 143-2187 or 144-8457)
Innsbruck
    Salurnerstrasse 15 (Tourist Center) (tel 43 (6222) 32 58 44)

Salzburg
    Bahnhof Vorplatz Kaiserschutzenstrasse
    12 (tel 43 (6222) 75 068)
Strasbourg
    18 Boulevard President Wilson (tel 33 (88)
    22 03 87)
Vienna
    Südbahnhof Südtirolerplatz 7 (tel 43 (222)
    65 65 93)
Zurich
    Klingenstrasse 9, Zürich 5 (tel 41 (1) 44 04
    77)

Olympic Bus, Russell Square in London, will sell you a ticket to İstanbul via Thessaloniki for £60 single (£120 return). You arrive in Thessaloniki at 4 am to change buses; the onward bus may be full, which means you may have to wait 24 hours or more for a seat on a later bus. The entire journey from London to İstanbul takes three or four days.

In Holland, Sümag Busreisen (tel (070) 890201), Hoefkade 399, 2526 BW Den Haag runs buses each Saturday (meet at noon for 3 pm departure) from The Hague to İstanbul for Fl 250; the trip takes a minimum of 45 or 46 hours. There is a return bus each Wednesday from İstanbul costing Fl 225. The Sümag agent in İstanbul is Özsel Koll Şti (tel 526-2637), İncili Çavuş Sokak 37/1, Sultan-ahmet, behind the Pudding Shop.

From Athens, Greece

The trip from Athens to İstanbul, which operates at least twice a week, takes 22 to 24 hours, part of that time spent sleeping in a hotel in Thessaloniki. Total cost is about US$40. Here are the agencies:

Athens
    Rika Tours, Marni 44, Platia Vathis (tel 30
    (1) 523-2458, 3686 or 5905, telex 21-9473)
İstanbul
    Ast Turizm, Beşir Fuat Caddesi 8,
    Tepebaşı (tel 90 (11) 144-2006)
Thessaloniki
    Simeonidis Tours, 26th October St No 14
    (tel 30 (31) 54 09 71 or 52 14 45)

There may be other companies running this route as well. If you find a good one, write me so that I can tell other readers.

From Northern Greece

You don't need an international bus to get to Turkey. You can take a Greek bus to the frontier, walk across the border, and catch something to Edirne. From Edirne, there are fast, frequent, comfortable and inexpensive bus services directly to İstanbul.

CAR

Car ferries (see below) from Italy, Cyprus and Syria can shorten driving time considerably. No special car documents are required for visits of up to three months. The car will be entered in the driver's passport as imported goods, and must be driven out of the country by the same visitor within the time period allowed. *Do not drive someone else's car into Turkey.* Normally, you cannot rent a car in Europe and include Turkey (or many other East European countries) in your driving plans. If you want to leave your car in Turkey and return for it later, the car must be put under customs seal.

For stays longer than three months, contact the Turkish Touring & Auto-mobile Club or Türk Turing ve Otomobil Kulübü (tel 90 (11) 140-7127), Halâskârgazi Caddesi 364, Şişli, İstanbul.

The E5 highway makes its way through the Balkans to Edirne and İstanbul, then onward to Ankara, Adana and the Syrian frontier. Though the road is good in most of the countries it passes through, you will encounter heavy traffic and lots of heavy vehicles along the route, as this is a very important freight route between Europe and the Middle East.

Insurance

Your Green Card must be endorsed for *all* of Turkey, both European and Asiatic, not just the European portion (Thrace). If it is not, you will have to buy a Turkish insurance policy at the border.

SEA

Without question, the most romantic way to arrive in İstanbul is by sea. The panorama of the Old City's skyline, with rows of minarets and bulbous mosque domes rising above the surrounding houses, is an incomparable sight. If you can't arrive by sea, don't despair. A trip on a Bosphorus ferryboat will reveal a similar panorama.

Though steamers still ply the Mediterranean from port to port, eventually turning up at İzmir or İstanbul, schedules are erratic. Sometimes fares are not particularly low, as passenger accommodation tends to be deluxe. The Black Sea Steamship Company, a Soviet outfit, runs very comfortable, modern cruise ships during the summer months. You can sometimes book a place on one, and prices will be moderate, but everything will be in Russian, including the chit-chat of your fellow passengers. The occasional Turkish Maritime Lines freighter may take passengers at low fares, but this is not dependable either. Going to Turkey by sea, then, you have three choices.

From Venice, Italy

Turkish Maritime Lines Turkish Maritime Lines (T C Denizyolları, or TML) operates modern, comfortable car-and-passenger ferries from Venice (Italy) to İzmir, departing Venice every Saturday evening from June through September, arriving in İzmir on Tuesday morning. The return trip from İzmir departs Wednesday afternoon, arriving in Venice Saturday morning. One-way fares per passenger in cabins range from US$220 to US$415, breakfast and port taxes included. There is a 'Pullman' class where you get a reclining seat for US$185, breakfast and port tax included. Students get a 10% reduction on fare only (not meals). If you want lunch and dinner, add US$30. Fare for a car, port tax included, is about US$170; for a motor-cycle about US$87.

British Ferries Sealink British Ferries (PO Box 29, London SW1V 1JX, tel (01) 834-8122; or Sealink Travel Centre, Liverpool St Station, London EC2M 7PY) operate the *m/v Orient Express* on the route Venice, Piraeus, İstanbul, Kuşadası, Patmos, Katakolon, Venice, departing Venice every Saturday evening from May through October, arriving Piraeus Monday morning, İstanbul Tuesday morning, Kuşadası Wednesday morning, Patmos Wednesday evening, Katakolon (Olympia) Thursday noon, and Venice Saturday morning. There is time to leave the vessel and explore the port and nearby areas on each day. All meals and port taxes are included in the per-person fares which, between Venice and İstanbul or Kuşadası, are £175 to £425 (US$260 to US$627) single, £315 to £765 (US$465 to US$1129) return. The top fares are for two persons sharing a stateroom; most of the fares are for cabins in which two, three or four persons share. Charge for a car is £130 to £145 (US$192 to US$214) single, £234 to £261 (US$345 to US$385) return.

From Brindisi, Italy

A Greek company called Libra Maritime runs boats and buses connecting Brindisi-Patras-Piraeus-İzmir in 40 hours. The Piraeus-İzmir ferryboat carries cars and passengers, and runs three days per week in the summertime, departing Piraeus on Monday, Wednesday and Friday at 8 pm, and departing İzmir on Tuesday and Thursday at 9 pm, Sunday at 2 pm. The ships are the *Atlas III* and *Atlas IV*. Contact Libra in Piraeus at Plateia Loudovicou 4 (tel (1) 411-7864); in Brindisi at 54 Corso Garibaldi (tel 21 935, 28 004). In İzmir Libra's agent is International Tourism Service (Enternasyonal Turizm Servis, Seyahat ve Gemicilik A Ş).

From the Greek Islands

In the past, Greeks have at times been unwilling to provide information on transport to Turkey, but recent reports are better and it is now fairly easy to find and to buy tickets on the ferries from the Greek islands to Turkey.

The procedure is this: once you've found the ticket office, buy your ticket a day in advance. You may be asked to turn in your passport the night before the trip. The next day, before you board the boat, you'll get it back. There is no problem in this.

In high summer boats run daily from Rhodes to Marmaris, a delightful little resort town on the Turkish Mediterranean, at a cost of 2000 Drachmae (US$15) one way. There is also daily service from Samos to Kuşadası (US$25 one way, US$30 same day round trip, US$45 round trip), from Lesvos (Mytileni) to Ayvalık (US$15 one way, US$25 round trip), from Chios to Çeşme (US$18 one way, US$20 same-day round trip, US$30 round trip) and from Kos to Bodrum. In spring and autumn service is less frequent, perhaps three or four days a week or, at the very beginning and end of the season, only once a week. In winter it is mostly suspended, though a few boats may still run from Rhodes to Marmaris and from Samos to Kuşadası, depending upon demand and weather conditions.

From Famagusta, Cyprus

Turkish Maritime Lines ferries run between Famagusta (Magosa, Cyprus) and Mersin (Turkey), a 10-hour trip operating all year. From October to April, departures are Tuesday and Friday evenings from Mersin, arriving in Famagusta the next morning. In summer (late April through September), departures from Mersin are on Monday, Wednesday and Friday evenings. Return trips from Cyprus, then, depart Tuesday, Thursday and Sunday mornings. The Friday departures from Mersin stop at Famagusta on Saturday, then go on to Lattakia (Lâzkiye), Syria. The TML agent in Syria is the Lattakia Shipping Agencies Company, Port Said St, PO Box 28, Lattakia (tel 33 163, 34 263 or 34 213).

Private companies operate boats and

hydrofoils between Taşucu (Silifke), Turkey and Turkish Cyprus. See the section on Silifke for details.

You should be aware that relations between the Greek Cypriot-administered Republic of Cyprus and the Turkish Republic of Northern Cyprus are not good, and that the border between the two regions may be closed. Also, if you enter the TRNC and have your passport stamped you will later be denied entry to Greece. The Greeks will reject only a stamp from the Turkish Republic of Northern Cyprus, *not* a stamp from Turkey proper.

EAST EUROPEAN VISAS

If you go by rail or road (bus, car, motorcycle, bicycle), you will have to deal with the problem of visas for transit of East European countries.

Yugoslavia Holders of UK, Irish and most European passports need no visa; those from the US, Canada, Australia and New Zealand need a transit visa, good for seven days, obtainable at the border at no cost. Israeli passport holders may run into problems, and may not be granted a visa. South African, Taiwanese and South Korean passport holders will not be granted visas.

Bulgaria You will need a transit visa (good for 48 hours), both on the trip from Europe to Turkey and on the trip back, because the train and the highway pass through Bulgaria. It is about US$8 one way, US$15 round trip for the privilege of passing through. Late reports have it that you cannot get a visa at the border if you are travelling by rail; you *might* be able to get one if you're travelling by bus, but it will involve a great deal of hassle and will cost twice as much. Get some up-to-date information, or better still, get your visa in advance so as to avoid hassle, delay and possible refusal. Visas can be obtained from your nearest friendly Bulgarian diplomatic representative.

In Australia contact the Bulgarian Consulate-General (tel 02 3277581), 4 Karlotta Rd, Double Bay, NSW 2028. In the UK, it's the Bulgarian Legation, 24 Queen's Gate Gardens, London SW7. In the USA, contact the Consular Section, Bulgarian Embassy, 1621 22nd St NW, Washington, DC 20008.

Passport holders from Scandinavian and East European countries do not need visas for Bulgaria. If you carry a South African passport you can't get a visa; you must go around Bulgaria, through Greece.

Getting Around

Turkey has an elaborate public transport system, as private cars are still quite expensive and Turks love to travel all the time. Even the sleepiest village seems to have minibuses darting in and out through the day, and buses running between İstanbul and Ankara depart every few minutes.

AIR

Turkish Airlines (THY) operate flights throughout the country. Most routes begin and end in İstanbul, travelling via Ankara. Thus there are 10 or more flights per day between these two cities, and continuing flights to many other points. Fares (US dollars) and frequencies from İstanbul are:

city	flights/week	fare
Adana	14	40,000TL ($56)
Ankara	80	30,000TL ($42)
Antalya	16	32,000TL ($44.80)
Diyarbakır	7	30,000TL ($42)
Erzurum	8	30,000TL ($42)

Other flights are: Dalaman (one or two daily), Elazığ (four weekly), İzmir (five to seven daily from İstanbul, one or two daily from Ankara), Kayseri (two weekly), Malatya (five weekly), Merzifon (three weekly), Samsun (three weekly), Sivas (twice weekly), Trabzon (daily) and Van (four flights weekly). There are also non-stop flights once a week, on Sundays, between İzmir and Antalya, and twice weekly between Sivas and Malatya.

İstanbul Airlines operates between its namesake city and Adana, Antalya, Diyarbakır, İzmir, Trabzon and Northern Cyprus.

Sönmez Holding Airlines or Sönmez Holding Hava Yolları (tel (241) 45 460), PO Box 189, Bursa is a small airline set up by a large holding company for the convenience of its employees and visitors, but they are perfectly happy to fly you between Bursa and İstanbul. The airline has one small C-212 aircraft which wings from Bursa to İstanbul and back each morning, and again each evening; there's an extra flight on Saturday, but no flights at all on Sunday. Buy tickets at the airport or contact Ottomantur (tel (241) 10 099 or 22 097), Kızılay Pasajı, Çakırhamam, Bursa; Moris Seyahat Agentalığı (tel (1) 149-8510 or 149-8511), Tünel Pasajı 11, Beyoğlu, İstanbul. A bus departs the Ottomantur office in Bursa 45 minutes prior to flight time. To get to İstanbul's Atatürk Airport, take the airport bus from the THY terminal in Şişhane.

Check-in Procedures

It's a good idea to get to the airport at least 45 minutes before flight time. Signs and announcements are not always provided, or understandable, so keep asking to make sure you end up at the proper destination. As of this writing, there is open seating on all domestic flights; you are not assigned a specific seat number, but may sit wherever you choose.

Security

As you approach the airport perimeter, your bus or taxi will be stopped and spot-checked by police looking for terrorists. On a bus, your passport and ticket will be inspected.

As you enter the terminal you will have to put your luggage through an x-ray machine. Before you leave the terminal you will be frisked for weapons, and your hand baggage will be searched. Don't try to carry even a pocket-knife aboard, as they will probably find it, and they certainly won't allow you to carry it aboard. Rather, pack it in your checked luggage.

As you approach the aircraft, all passengers' luggage will be lined up, and you will be asked to point out your bag. It will then be put on board. This is to prevent someone from checking a bag with a bomb in it, then not boarding the plane. So if you forget to point out your bag to the baggage handler, it may not be loaded on board and may be regarded with loathing and distrust.

Turkish Airlines has an enviable record of terror-free flights, for obvious reasons.

RAIL

The Turkish State Railways (T C Devlet Demiryolları, or TCDD) run to many parts of the country, on lines laid out by German companies which were supposedly paid by the km. But some new, more direct lines have been laid during the republican era, shortening travel times for the best express trains.

It's not a good idea to plan a train trip all the way across Turkey in one stretch. Turkey is a big country, and the cross-country trains are a lot slower than the bus. The Vangölü Ekspresi from İstanbul (Haydarpaşa) to Lake Van (Tatvan), a 1900-km trip, takes almost two full days, for example - and that's an express! Train travel among Ankara, İzmir and İstanbul is another matter, however. The top trains on these lines are a pleasure to ride, whether by night or day.

Whenever you take an inter-city train in Turkey, you'd do well to take only *mavi tren, ekspres* or *mototren* trains. These are fairly fast, comfortable, and cheaper than the bus. The *yolcu* trains are much slower and the *posta* trains move at the speed of cold treacle; neither is very comfortable.

Fares

In general, train fares are cheaper than bus fares for the same journey, even if the train is an *ekspres*. The exceptions are the fast *mavi tren* and the couchette and sleeping-berth trains when you avail yourself of those facilities.

Here is a sampling of fares (US dollars) for seats on express trains from İstanbul's Haydarpaşa station to:

city	full fare	student fare	return fare
Adana	3500TL ($4.90)	3200TL ($4.48)	5600TL ($ 7.84)
Ankara	2100TL ($2.94)	1900TL ($2.66)	3400TL ($ 4.76)
Denizli	2200TL ($3.08)	2000TL ($2.80)	3600TL ($ 5.04)
Diyarbakır	4500TL ($6.30)	4100TL ($5.74)	7200TL ($10.08)
Edirne	1000TL ($1.40)	900TL ($1.26)	1600TL ($ 2.24)
Erzurum	4700TL ($6.58)	4300TL ($6.02)	7600TL ($10.64)

Tickets for a trip on one of the many *mavi tren* super-expresses cost about 50% more than for the same trip on a normal express train.

You must also pay considerably more for a berth in a sleeping car, but the price compares well to that for a night in a moderately good hotel. The prices below are given *per person* in US dollars for sleeping compartments with one, two, three or four berths, from İstanbul (Haydarpaşa) to:

city	single	double	triple
Ankara	16,100TL ($22.54)	12,100TL ($16.94)	9,100TL ($12.74)
Diyarbakır	19,500TL ($27.30)	15,500TL ($21.70)	12,500TL ($17.50)
Erzurum	19,700TL ($27.58)	15,700TL ($21.98)	12,700TL ($17.78)
Kayseri	12,200TL ($17.08)	9,700TL ($13.58)	7,700TL ($10.78)
Tatvan	20,000TL ($28.00)	16,000TL ($22.40)	13,000TL ($18.20)

A very comfortable private 1st-class sleeping compartment on the nightly all-sleeper Ankara Ekspresi between Ankara and İstanbul (Haydarpaşa) thus costs about 25,000TL (US$35) for two people, total, for the 12-hour trip. When you realize that this includes both the night's lodging and the night's travel, the price seems very reasonable. If there's a dining car, table d'hote meals are surprisingly good and not overly expensive. Breakfast in the dining car is about 1000TL (US$1.40).

Top Trains

Mavi Tren (Blue Train) Daily 1st-class express between Ankara and İstanbul, about 7½ hours; a bit faster than the bus, more expensive, more comfortable. There are now *mavi trens* on a few other routes as well.

Boğaziçi Ekspresi Daily all-Pullman 1st-class express between Ankara and İstanbul, about 9½ hours; a bit slower than the bus, but cheaper and more comfortable.

Ege Ekspresi Daily 1st-class express between Ankara and İzmir, about 9½ hours, about the same time as the bus, but cheaper and more comfortable.

Ankara Ekspresi Nightly Ankara-İstanbul 1st-class all-sleeping-car train, about 12 hours.

Anadolu Ekspresi Nightly Ankara-Istanbul sleeping-car, couchette and coach train, about 12 hours.

İzmir Ekspresi Nightly Ankara-İzmir coach and sleeping-car train, about 12½ hours.

Buying Tickets

Most seats on the best trains, and all sleeping compartments, must be reserved. This is done when you buy your ticket. Turkish State Railways have installed a computerized reservations system for use in selling tickets for reserved seats, sleeping berths and couchettes on the top trains. Look for the *bilgisayar gişeleri* (computer ticket windows).

Turkish words useful in the railway station are given in the Turkish Language Guide at the back of this book.

As the best trains are very popular, particularly the sleeping-car trains, and as rail travel is generally cheaper than bus

travel, you should make your reservation and buy your ticket as far in advance as possible. A few days usually suffice. If you can't do this, check at the station anyway. There may be cancellations, even at the last minute. I once boarded a night train expecting to sleep in a seat, but I mentioned to the sleeping-car conductors that I preferred a bed. They came and found me after the train departed, and sold me a vacant compartment left by a no-show.

Weekend trains, from Friday evening through Monday morning, seem to be busiest.

Youth & Student Discounts Student discounts of 10% are available on most trains, most routes. In listings of fares, look for the *öğrenci* or *talebe* (student) fare.

If you are under 26 years of age you can buy an Inter-Rail card which allows you unlimited 2nd-class rail travel in Turkey and 19 other European countries plus Morocco, and also a 50% reduction on private trains. Ask at Sirkeci station in İstanbul, or at the station in Ankara.

Cancellation Penalties If you decide not to travel and you seek a refund for your rail ticket up to 24 hours before train departure, you must pay a cancellation fee of 10% of the ticket price. Within 24 hours of departure the fee rises to 25%. After the train has departed the fee is 50%.

BUS

Bus and minibus (dolmuş, see below) are the most widespread and popular means of transport in Turkey. Buses go literally everywhere, all the time, and at low cost. Highways are good and usually uncrowded. Bus service runs the gamut from plain and very inexpensive to very comfortable and moderately priced. It is so cheap and convenient that many erstwhile hitch-hikers opt for the bus. The eight-hour trip between İstanbul and Ankara, for example, costs only 2000TL to 3000TL (US$2.80 to US$4.20), depending on the bus company. Though bus fares are open to competition among companies, and even to haggling for a reduction, the cost of bus travel in Turkey works out to around 350TL (US$0.49) per 100 km – a surprising bargain.

About Bus Travel

A bus trip in Turkey is usually a fairly pleasant experience if it's not too long. Most buses are the Mercedes 0302, big and fairly comfortable. The seat cushions are surprisingly firm though, too firm for comfort on a very long ride. As Turks are great cigarette smokers, you may encounter a significant amount of smoke on the trip. Passengers in the seats near you will offer you cigarettes as an ice-breaker, hoping to strike up a conversation. There's no stigma in refusing. Say *Hayır, teşekkür ederim, içmem* ('No, thank you, I don't smoke') or, if this is a mouthful, just *İçmem* (eech-MEHM) with a smile. Turks, like most people, think it laudable that someone doesn't smoke (or has given up smoking). Besides, the offer was intended as a politeness, a welcome and a conversation opener. It serves this purpose whether you smoke or not.

Though your fellow passengers will be careful not to abuse your privacy, they'll also be curious about where you come from, what language you speak, and how you're enjoying the country. You can talk as much or as little as you like, though it's polite to exchange at least a few sentences.

Shortly after you head out, the *yardımcı* ('assistant') will come through the bus with a bottle of lemon cologne with which to refresh his *sayın yolcular* ('honoured passengers'). He'll dribble some into your cupped hands, which you then rub together, and on your face, and on your hair, ending with a sniff to clear your nasal passages. You may not be used to the custom, but if you ride buses in Turkey much you will get used to it quickly, and probably love it.

If you want a bottle of cool spring water at any time during the trip, just signal to the *yardımcı* and ask *Su, lütfen* ('Water, please'). There's no charge.

Stops will be made every 1½ hours or so for the toilet, snacks or meals and the inevitable *çay* (tea). At some stops boys rush onto the bus selling sweets, nuts, sandwiches and the like, or a waiter from the tea-house (buses always stop at a tea-house) may come through to take orders. But most people welcome the chance to stretch their legs.

Keep your bus ticket until you reach your absolutely final destination. In some cases, companies have *servis arabası* minibuses that will shuttle you from the bus station into the city at no extra charge – if you can show a ticket on the company's line.

You can save money by taking night buses on long hauls (eight or 10 hours or more). Cigarette smoke will be less, the bus will be cooler, and you will save money on a hotel room. You miss the scenery, though.

In eastern Turkey, readers have commented that the Sev-Tur company packs its buses too full, ignoring the law that there be no standees.

The Otogar

Most Turkish cities and towns have a central bus terminal called variously Otogar, Otobüs Terminalı, Santraj Garaj or Şehir Garajı ('City Garage'). In this book I'll stick to Otogar. Besides intercity buses, the Otogar often handles minibuses to outlying districts or villages. Otogars are often equipped with their own PTT branches, telephones with international service, restaurants, snack stands, pastry shops, tourism information booths and left-luggage booths (checkrooms) called *emanet* (eh-mah-NEHT).

İstanbul has several mammoth garages; Ankara and İzmir have one mammoth apiece. Bus companies aiming at the high-class trade may have their own small, private terminals in other parts of town, to save their privileged patrons the hassle of dealing with large crowds at the main terminal. These are mentioned in the text where necessary.

A few small towns have only a collection of bus line offices rather than a proper garage.

Buying Tickets

Though you can often just walk into an Otogar and buy a ticket for the next bus out, it's wise to plan ahead. At the least, locate the companies and note the times for your destination a day in advance. Buses on some routes may fill up, so buying tickets a day in advance is good if you can do it. This is especially important along the south coast, where long-distance bus traffic is less frequent than in the rest of the country.

The word for 'tomorrow', very handy to know when buying bus tickets a day in advance, is *yarın* (YAHR-uhn). Bus departure times will be given in the 24-hour clock, eg 18.30 instead of 6.30 pm.

When you enter an Otogar you'll see lots of people and baggage, buses and minibuses, plus rows of little ticket offices. Competition on some routes is stiff. In most cases, more than one company will run to your desired destination; the cities and towns served by the company will be written prominently at the company's ticket office. It's a good idea to check several ticket offices, asking when the company's next bus leaves. Hawkers near the entrance to the Otogar will approach you as soon as you enter, asking your destination. Tell them, and they'll lead you to a particular company's ticket office. This is fine, except that this company may or may not have the next departure. A few times I have been sold a ticket for the company's next bus (in two hours) when another company had a bus departing – with seats available – in 40 minutes. Let the hawkers lead you, but then ask around at other companies before you buy.

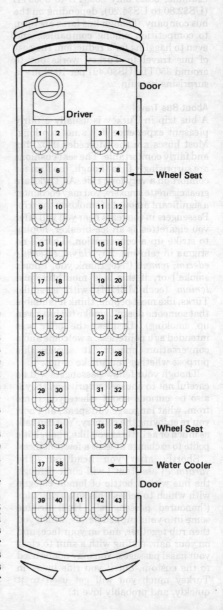

Door

Driver

Wheel Seat

Wheel Seat

Water Cooler

Door

All seats are reserved, and your ticket will bear specific seat numbers. It's very important that you plan your seat strategy rather than leave it up to the ticket seller. He'll have a chart of the seats in front of him. The ones already taken will be indicated. He should (and usually will) offer the chart to you so you can pick your seats, and may indicate the ones he recommends.

The preferable seats, according to Turkish custom, are in the middle of the bus (that is, not right over the wheels, which can be bumpy), and also on the side which will not get the full sun. On the Mercedes 0302 bus, avoid if possible the front two rows (seats 1-8) and the last three rows (33-43); seats 9-28 are the best, but on the shady side.

Though some buses are now air-conditioned, most are not, and in the newer models ventilation is actually worse than in the older ones, so what side you are on can be important. On a four-hour summer afternoon trip from Ankara to Konya, for instance, you'll be too warm if you're on the right-hand (western) side of the bus, while the seats on the left side will remain comfortable.

Once you've bought a ticket, getting a refund can be very difficult, though it's possible. Exchanges for other tickets within the same company are easier.

Minibus & Dolmuş

Turkish jitney cabs and some minibuses (*minibüs* or *münübüs*), are called *dolmuş* (DOHL-moosh, 'filled'). The name comes from the fact that a dolmuş departs as soon as every seat (or nearly every seat) is taken. You can catch a dolmuş from point to point in a city (see below), or from village to village, and in some cases from town to town. Though some minibus routes operate like buses by selling tickets in advance (perhaps even for reserved seats), the true dolmuş does not. Rather, it is parked at the point of departure (a town square, city Otogar or beach) and waits for the seats to fill up.

The dolmuş route may be painted on the side of the minibus, or on a sign posted next to the dolmuş, or in its window; or a hawker may call out the destination.

When the driver is satisfied with the load, he heads off. Fares are collected en route or at the final stop. Often the fare is posted. If it's not, watch what other passengers to your destination are paying and do the same. Though passengers to intermediate stops sometimes pay a partial fare, on other routes the driver (or the law) may require that you pay the full fare. In either case, prices are low, though slightly more than a bus on the same route.

TAXI

Inter-city taxis are expensive, but if you must catch a plane, train or bus in town and you're in a village, you may have to use one. Since 1980, municipalities have set inter-city (and for that matter, intra-city) taxi rates. Before you engage a taxi, if it does not have a meter ask to see the official rate card or *tarife* (tah-ree-FEH). If your destination is not on the *tarife*, you've got to strike a bargain. You needn't tip unless the driver has provided some extra service for you.

CAR

Driving a car to Turkey is a fine idea, though you can get around perfectly well without one. Turkish highways tend to be good and not madly crowded except for the major commerce routes (E5, E24), though city streets are just the opposite. Parking is a real problem in the large cities. Turkish drivers are not particularly discourteous out on the highway, though they tend to drive at high speed, and some are inexperienced. In the cities, discourtesy and madness are universal.

International Driving Permit

You don't really need an International Driving Permit while you drive in Turkey, despite what some travel books say. Your home driving licence, unless it's something weird (say, from Burkina Faso), will be accepted by traffic police officers and by car rental firms. If you'd feel more secure against bureaucratic hassle by carrying an IDP, you can get one through your automobile club at home.

Spares

Spare parts for most cars may be available, if not readily so, outside the big cities. European models, especially Renaults, Fiats and Mercedes, are preferred, though ingenious Turkish mechanics contrive to keep all manner of huge American models – some half a century old – in daily service.

Traffic Police

Police in black-and-white cars (usually Renaults) and green uniforms with white peaked caps set up check-points on major highways in order to make sure that your car documents are in order and that all of the safety features of your vehicle are in working condition. If you are stopped, the officer will ask for your auto registration, insurance certificate and driving license, but when he realizes that you are a foreigner he may just wave you on without a look at your papers. However, he may ask you to turn on your headlamps (high and low beam), hoot your horn, switch on your turning signals and windscreen wipers, etc, to see that all are working properly.

Rental Cars

Cars may be rented in İstanbul, Ankara, İzmir and Kuşadası, Antalya, Alanya and Adana from the larger international rental firms (Hertz, Avis, National/ Europcar, Budget and Dollar/interRent) or from smaller local ones. In İstanbul, Ankara and İzmir/Kuşadası, payment by major credit card is easily available. In other areas ask about payment when you reserve. The company most prominent is Avis. Most popular rental cars are the Fiat ('Murat') 124 and 131, and the Renault 12.

Costs Total costs for a week with unlimited km, including full insurance and tax, might be 157,000TL to 215,000TL (US$220 to US$301) plus the cost of fuel. When you look at a rental company's current price list, keep in mind that the daily or weekly rental charge is only a small portion of what you will actually end up paying, unless it includes unlimited km. The charge for km normally ends up being higher, per day, than the daily rental charge. Fuel, as of this writing, costs about 300TL (US$0.44) per litre. By the way, VAT (KDV) should be included in the rental, insurance and km prices quoted to you. It should not be added to the bottom of your bill.

You should not be afraid to try (with caution) one of the small local agencies, which offer much lower prices than the big firms. I've had good experience with Seytur Ltd (tel (711) 44157 or 44216), Ziyapaşa Bulvarı, Libya Dostluk Derneği Yanı, 290 Sokak 40, Adana. Though there is little fluency in English and no far-flung network for repairs, they are friendly, helpful and surprisingly cheaper than the large firms. Instead of US$270 for a week's rental of a Renault 12 with unlimited km and collision damage insurance, I paid US$177. Other small agencies, in more convenient cities, may do as well.

MOTORCYCLE

Motorcycles and mopeds are becoming more popular in Turkey because they are cheaper than cars to buy and to run. These days, Austrian and German mopeds are the popular items. Motor-cycles tend to be large old Czechoslovak Jawa models that make a distinctive hollow putt-putt.

You can bring your motorcycle to Turkey and have a fine time seeing the country. Spare parts will probably be hard to come by, so bring what you may need, or rely on the boundless ingenuity of Turkish mechanics to find, adapt or make you a part. Or else be prepared to

You'll get the hang of the dolmuş way of life after only a few days in Turkey, and will find it very useful.

Taxi

Most taxis in most cities have digital meters, and they use them. If yours doesn't, mention it right away by saying, *Saatiniz* (saa-AHT-EE-NEEZ, 'Your meter'). The starting rate is 250TL (US$0.35), 260TL in Ankara, more at night. The average taxi ride is 400TL to 700TL (US$0.56 to US$1) in the daytime, slightly more at night.

Ferryboat

In İstanbul and İzmir, public transport is delightfully augmented by ferryboats. White with orange trim (the Turkish Maritime Lines' colours), these sturdy craft steam up, down and across the Bosphorus and the Bay of İzmir, providing city dwellers with cheap, convenient transport, views of open water and (in summer) fresh cool breezes. They are not nostalgic transport toys but a real, even vital, part of each city's transport system. You should take the ferry in each city at least once, enjoying the cityscapes that are revealed from the decks, sipping a glass of fresh tea or a soft drink. The ferries can be crowded during rush hour but there's still lots of air and scenery; and while buses sit trapped in traffic the ferries glide through the water effortlessly, at speed.

In İstanbul, special ferry sailings on a touristic route are operated daily. There's no better way to see the Bosphorus, and the price for a 2½-hour cruise all the way from İstanbul to the Black Sea is only about 750TL (US$1.05).

Logo of the TCDD – the Turkish State Railways

İstanbul

For many centuries this city was the capital of the civilized world. Even though Ankara became the capital of the newly proclaimed Turkish republic in 1922, İstanbul continues to be the Turkish metropolis. It is the largest city (about six million people), the business and cultural centre, the largest port and the first destination for tourists, Turkish or foreign.

In recent years İstanbul has yielded some of its pre-eminence to up-and-coming towns such as Ankara, İzmir and Adana. But it is still, without doubt, the heartbeat of the Turkish spirit. For Ankara, the up-tempo, modern capital city, Turks feel pride; but it is İstanbul, the well-worn but still glorious metropolis, which they love. Its place in the country's history, folklore, commerce and culture is unchallenged.

The First Glimpse

No matter how you arrive, you'll be impressed. The train skirts the southern coast of the Thracian peninsula, following the city walls until it comes around Seraglio Point and terminates right below Topkapı Palace. The bus comes in along an expressway built on the path of the Roman road, and stops next to the Topkapı (Cannon Gate, not to be confused with the palace of the same name) in the ancient city walls. Flying in on a clear day may reveal the great mosques and palaces, the wide Bosphorus (Boğaziçi) and the narrower Golden Horn (Haliç), in a wonderful panorama. But nothing beats 'sailing to Byzantium' – gliding across the Sea of Marmara, watching the slender minarets and bulbous mosque domes rise on the horizon. Even Mark Twain, who certainly had control of his emotions, waxed rhapsodic in his *Innocents Abroad* on the beauties of arriving by sea. Today, though

a cloud of fumes from fossil fuels may obscure the view a bit, it's still impressive.

İstanbul has grown ferociously in the past decade, and now sprawls westward to the airport, 23 km from the centre, northward halfway to the Black Sea, and eastward deep into Anatolia. It is crowded. The Bosphorus, the strait which connects the Black Sea and the Sea of Marmara, is more than 1½ km wide, and the narrower Golden Horn, a freshwater estuary, also helps to preserve a sense of openness and space. More than that, the Bosphorus provides an uncrowded maritime highway for transport to various sections of the city. For several thousand years before the construction of the Bosphorus Bridge (1973), the only way to go between the European and Asian parts of the city was by boat. A second Bosphorus Bridge, north of the first one, is under construction.

As an introduction to Turkey and the Turks, İstanbul is something of a rich diet – too rich for some people. You might enjoy the city more if you come here after having first seen some smaller, more comprehensible and easily manageable Turkish town.

History

İstanbul today is interesting as the Turkish metropolis, but nobody visits just for that reason when the city is 3000 years old. The greatest part of the city's fascination comes from its place in history and from the buildings that remain from ancient times. Without knowing something of its history, a tour of İstanbul's ancient monuments will leave you impressed but bewildered.

Summary Here's a quick summary of its past, so that you'll be able to distinguish a hippodrome from a harem.

1000 to 657 BC Ancient fishing villages on this site.

657 BC to 330 AD Byzantium, a Greek city-state, later subject to Rome.

330 to 1453 AD Constantinople, the 'New Rome', capital of the Later Roman ('Byzantine') Empire. Reached its height in the 1100s.

1453 to 1922 İstanbul, capital of the Ottoman Turkish Empire, which reached the height of its glory in the 1500s.

1922 to present Ankara becomes the capital of the Turkish Republic. İstanbul continues to be the country's largest city and port, and its commercial and cultural centre.

Early Times The earliest settlement, Semistra, was probably around 1000 BC, in the same period kings David and Solomon ruled in Jerusalem and a few hundred years after the Trojan War.

This was followed by a fishing village named Lygos, which occupied Seraglio Point where Topkapı Palace stands today. Later, about 700 BC, colonists from Megara (near Corinth) in Greece settled at what is now Kadıköy, on the Asian shore of the Bosphorus.

Byzantium The first settlement to have historic significance was founded by another Megarian colonist, a fellow named Byzas. Before leaving Greece, he asked the oracle at Delphi where he should establish his new colony. The enigmatic answer was 'Opposite the Blind'. When Byzas and his fellow colonists sailed up the Bosphorus, they noticed the colony on the Asian shore at Chalcedon (Kadıköy). Looking to their left, they saw the superb natural harbour of the Golden Horn, on the European shore. Thinking, as legend has it, 'Those people in Chalcedon must be blind', they settled on the opposite shore, on the site of Lygos, and named their new city Byzantium. This was in 657 BC.

The legend might as well be true. İstanbul's location on the waterway linking the Marmara and Black Seas and on the 'land bridge' linking Europe and Asia is still of tremendous importance today, 2600 years after the oracle spoke. The Megarian colonists at Kadıköy must certainly have been blind to have missed such a site.

Byzantium submitted willingly to Rome and fought Rome's battles for centuries, but finally got caught supporting the wrong side in a civil war. The winner, Septimius Severus, razed the city walls and took away its privileges (196 AD). When he relented and rebuilt the city, he named it Augusta Antonina.

Constantinople Another struggle for control of the Roman Empire determined the city's fate for the next 1000 years. Constantine pursued his rival Licinius to Augusta Antonina, then across the Bosphorus to Chrysopolis (Üsküdar). Defeating his rival (324 AD), Constantine solidified his control and declared this city to be 'New Rome'. He laid out a vast new city to serve as capital of his empire, and inaugurated it with much pomp in 330 AD. The place which had been first settled as a fishing village over 1000 years earlier was now the capital of the world, and would remain so for almost another 1000 years.

The Later Roman, or Byzantine, Empire lasted from the re-founding of the city in 330 AD to the Ottoman Turkish conquest in 1453, an impressive 1123 years. A lot remains of ancient Constantinople, and you'll be able to visit churches, palaces, cisterns and the Hippodrome during your stay. In fact, there's more of Constantinople left than anyone knows about. Any sort of excavation reveals streets, mosaics, tunnels, water and sewer systems, houses and public buildings. Construction of a modern building may be held up for months while archaeologists investigate. Rediscovering Byzantium, to a modern real-estate developer, is an unmitigated disaster.

Several years ago the telephone company discovered an unknown Byzantine cistern while laying underground telephone lines. As no one came forward with the considerable funds needed to explore and document the site, it was resealed and the telephone lines rerouted.

The Conquest Westerners usually refer to 'The Fall of Constantinople', whereas to Muslims it was 'The Conquest of İstanbul'. Though the Byzantine Empire had been moribund for several centuries, the Ottomans were quite content to accept tribute from the weak Byzantine emperor as they progressively captured all the lands which surrounded his well-fortified city. By the time of the conquest, the emperor had control over little more than the city itself and a few territories in Greece.

When Mehmet II, 'the Conqueror' (Fatih), came to power in 1451 as a young man, he needed an impressive military victory to solidify his dominance of the powerful noble class. As the Ottomans controlled all of Anatolia and most of the Balkans by this time, it was obvious that the great city should be theirs. Mehmet decided it should be sooner rather than later.

The story of the conquest is thrilling, full of bold strokes and daring exploits, heroism, treachery and intrigue. Mehmet started by readying the two great fortresses on the Bosphorus. Rumeli Hisar, the larger one, on the European side, was built in an incredibly short three months. Anadolu Hisar, the smaller one on the Asian side, had been built a half-century earlier by Yıldırım Beyazıt, so Mehmet had it repaired and brought to readiness. Together they controlled the strait's narrowest point.

The Byzantines had closed the mouth of the Golden Horn with a heavy chain to prevent Ottoman boats from sailing in and attacking the city walls on the north side. In another bold stroke, Mehmet marshalled his boats at a cove (now covered by Dolmabahçe Palace) and had them transported overland on rollers and slides, by night, up the valley (where the Hilton now stands) and down the other side into the Golden Horn at Kasımpaşa. He caught the Byzantine defenders completely by surprise and soon had the Golden Horn under control.

The last great obstacle was the mighty bastion of the land walls on the western side. No matter how Mehmet's cannons battered them by day, the Byzantines would rebuild them by night, and the impetuous young sultan would find himself back where he started come daybreak. Then he got an offer. A Hungarian cannon-founder named Urban had come to offer his services to the Byzantine emperor, for the defense of Christendom, to repel the Infidel. But finding that the emperor had no money, he went to Mehmet and offered to make the most enormous cannon ever. Mehmet, who had lots of money, accepted the offer, and the cannon was cast and tested in

Sultan Mehmet II

Edirne. The first shot, which terrified hundreds of peasants, sent a huge ball 1½ km, where it buried itself two metres in the ground. The jubilant sultan had his new toy transported to the front lines and set to firing. A special crew worked hours to ready it for each shot, for every firing wrecked the mount, and the gun had to be cooled with buckets of water as well.

Despite the inevitability of the conquest, the emperor refused surrender terms offered by Mehmet on 23 May 1453, preferring to wait in hope that Christendom would come and save him. On 28 May the final attack began, and by the evening of the 29th Mehmet's troops were in control of every quarter. The emperor, Constantine XI Dragases, died in battle fighting on the walls.

Mehmet's triumphant entry into 'the world's greatest city' on the evening of 29 May is commemorated every year in İstanbul. Those parts of the city which did not resist his troops were spared, and their churches guaranteed to them. Those that resisted were sacked for the customary three days, and the churches turned into mosques. As for Sancta Sophia, the greatest church in Christendom (St Peter's in Rome was not begun until 1506), it was converted immediately into a mosque. Mehmet rode into it astride his horse to declare the change.

The Ottoman Centuries Mehmet the Conqueror began at once to rebuild and repopulate the city. He saw himself as the successor to the glories and powers of Constantine, Justinian and the other great emperors who had reigned here. He built a mosque (Fatih Camii) on one of the city's seven hills, repaired the walls and made İstanbul the administrative, commercial and cultural centre of his growing empire.

Süleyman the Magnificent (1520-1566) was perhaps İstanbul's greatest builder. His mosque, the Süleymaniye (1550), is Turkey's largest. Other sultans added more grand mosques, and in the 19th

century numerous palaces were built along the Bosphorus: Çırağan, Dolmabahçe, Yıldız, Beylerbeyi, Küçük Su.

As the Ottoman Empire grew to include all of the Middle East and North Africa as well as half of eastern Europe, İstanbul became a fabulous melting-pot. On its streets and in its bazaars, people spoke Turkish, Greek, Armenian, Ladino, Russian, Arabic, Bulgarian, Rumanian, Albanian, Italian, French, German, English and Maltese. The parade of national costumes was no less varied. But from being the most civilized city on earth in the time of Süleyman, the city and the empire declined. By the 19th century it had lost some of its former glory, though it was still the 'Paris of the East'. Its importance was reaffirmed by the first great inter-nation luxury express train ever run, which connected İstanbul with Paris – the famous Orient Express.

Republican İstanbul Atatürk's campaign for national salvation and independence was directed from Ankara. The founder of the Turkish Republic decided to get away from the imperial memories of İstanbul, and also to set up the new government in a city which could not easily be threatened by gunboats. Robbed of its importance as capital of a vast empire, İstanbul lost a lot of its wealth and glitter. From being the East's most cosmopolitan place, it relaxed into a new role as an important national, more than international, city. But these days it seems to be returning to its former role. More livable than Cairo or Beirut, more attractive than Tel Aviv, more in touch with the Islamic world than Athens, it may just become a 'world capital' again.

Orientation
It's a daunting prospect to arrive in a strange city of six million people whose language is a complete mystery to you. In general, Turks are friendly and helpful, even amidst the frustrations of a

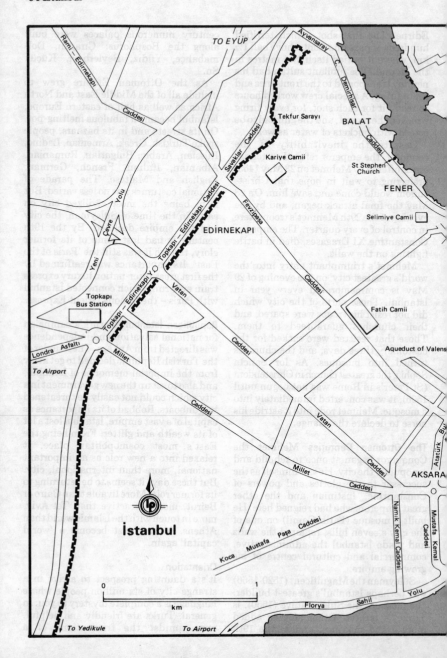

TO EYÜP

Ayvansaray C.

Demirhisar C.

BALAT

Tekfur Sarayı

Savaklar Caddesi

Kariye Camii

St Stephen
Church

FENER

Fevzipaşa Caddesi

Selimiye Camii

EDİRNEKAPI

Topkapı – Edirnekapı Caddesi

Çevre Yolu

Rami – Edirnekapı Caddesi

Yeni Yolu

Topkapı – Edirnekapı Caddesi

Vatan

Topkapı
Bus Station

Fatih Camii

Aqueduct of Valens

Londra Asfaltı

Millet Caddesi

To Airport

Caddesi

Vatan Caddesi

Millet Caddesi

AKSARA

Atatürk Bul

Namık Kemal Caddesi

Mustafa Kemal Caddesi

Mustafa Paşa Caddesi

Koca Mustafa Paşa Caddesi

İstanbul

0 _____ 1

km

To Yedikule

To Airport

Florya Sahil Yolu

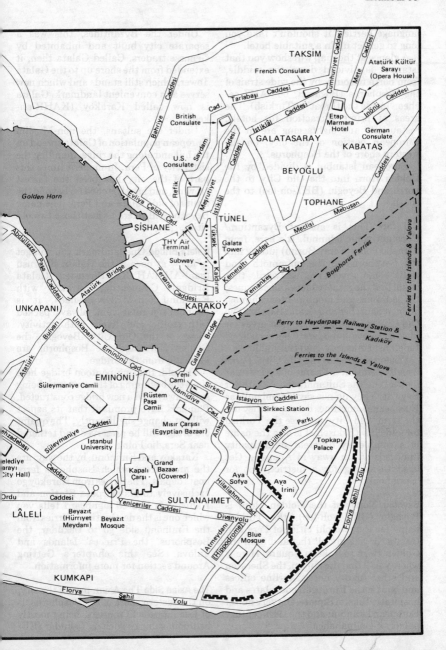

language barrier. It shouldn't take you long to get set up in a suitable hotel.

A glance at the map will show you that İstanbul is divided down the middle, from north to south, by the wide strait of the Bosphorus (Boğaziçi, boh-AHZ-ee-chee, 'Inside the throat' in Turkish). The areas of prime attraction for hotels, restaurants and sightseeing are in the European portion of the city, on the western shore of the Bosphorus.

European İstanbul is divided by the Golden Horn into the Old City to the north and Beyoğlu (BEY-oh-loo) to the south.

Old City This is ancient Byzantium/Constantinople/İstanbul. It's here, from Seraglio Point (Saray Burnu) jutting into the Bosphorus to the mammoth land walls some seven km eastward, that you'll find the great palaces and mosques, hippodromes and monumental columns, ancient churches and Grand Bazaar. The Old City also harbours the best areas for inexpensive and moderate hotel choices: Laleli near Aksaray, and Sultanahmet.

When referring to the Old City, Turks usually mention the name of a particular district such as Sultanahmet, Aksaray or Beyazıt. They do not say 'Stamboul', as Europeans sometimes do; nor do they use the term 'Old City' because the Turkish for 'old city' (Eskişehir) is also the name of a completely different municipality hundreds of km away in Anatolia. Get used to asking for a district, not for 'Stamboul'.

Beyoğlu North of the Golden Horn is Beyoğlu (BEHY-oh-loo), the Turkish name for the two old cities of Pera and Galata, or roughly all the land from the Golden Horn to Taksim Square. Here is where you'll find the Hilton, the Sheraton and other luxury hotels; airline offices and banks; the European consulates and hospitals; Taksim Square, the very hub of European İstanbul; and the 19th-century palace of Dolmabahçe.

Under the Byzantines, this was a separate city built and inhabited by Genoese traders. Called Galata then, it extended from the shore up to the Galata Tower, which still stands and which now serves as a convenient landmark. Galata is now called Karaköy (KAHR-ah-keuy).

Under the sultans, the non-Muslim European population of Galata spread up the hill and along the ridge, founding the sister city of Pera. In modern times this part of the city has been the fastest growing, and has stretched far beyond the limits of old Galata and Pera. The name Beyoğlu still refers to just those two old cities.

Galata Bridge One landmark you will get to know at once is the Galata Köprüsü (gahl-AH-TAH KEUP-reu-seu, Galata Bridge). Connecting Karaköy with Eminönü (eh-MEEN-eu-neu), it is İstanbul's jugular vein, always packed with traffic and lively with activity. Views of the Old City, Beyoğlu, the Golden Horn and the Bosphorus are fantastic from the bridge.

The old, floating pontoon bridge here since the beginning of the century is being swept away, and a new bridge constructed. Planners have promised that its aspect will not change significantly. The quaint old bridge will be preserved and tethered near Seraglio Point.

Karaköy and Eminönü, by the way, are the areas from which Bosphorus ferry boats depart. The ferries from Karaköy go exclusively to Haydarpaşa Station and Kadıköy (a lighted signboard tells you which one is the destination); ferries from the Eminönü side go to Üsküdar, the Bosphorus, the Princes' Islands and Yalova. See this chapter's Getting Around section for more information.

The Asian Side The Asian part of the city, on the eastern shore of the Bosphorus, is of less interest to tourists, being mostly bedroom suburbs such as Üsküdar (EUskeu-dahr, Scutari) and Kadıköy (KAH-duh-keuy). One landmark you'll want to know about is Haydarpaşa İstasyonu (HIGH-dahr-pah-shah ee-stahs-yohn-oo), right between Üsküdar and Kadıköy. This is the terminus for Anatolian trains, which means any Turkish train except the one from Europe via Edirne. If you're headed for Ankara, Cappodocia or any point east of İstanbul, you'll board at Haydarpaşa.

Information
The Ministry of Culture & Tourism maintains several Tourism Information Offices in the city. Besides the ones at Atatürk Airport (tel 573-7399 or 573-4136) and the Yolcu Salonu (International Maritime Passenger Terminal, tel 149-5776), there's one at the western end of the Hippodrome in Sultanahmet Square (tel 522-4903), near the Blue Mosque, Sancta Sophia and Topkapı Palace. In Beyoğlu, the office is in the Hilton Hotel arcade (tel 133-0592), just off Cumhuriyet Caddesi. Get to Taksim Square, ask for 'joom-hoor-ee-YEHT jad-dess-see' or simply 'HEEL-tohn oh-tehl-ee', walk two rather long blocks in the direction indicated, and you'll see the Hilton arcade, with the hotel behind it, on the right-hand side of the street.

The first thing you'll see in İstanbul will be the impressive skyline of the old city. It will take you at least three days to get around and see the major sights. You can easily spend a week at it, for İstanbul offers an awful lot to see.

The sightseeing plan below is organized to show you the most important and accessible sights first, so you can see as much as possible in even a short time. If you have a week, you should be able to see just about everything described here.

Museums are closed on Monday except for Topkapı Palace, which is closed on Tuesday instead, and Dolmabahçe Palace, which is closed on both Monday and Thursday. Also, holders of International Student Identity Cards are admitted free to all sites controlled by the Ministry of Culture & Tourism. You needn't even pay the 'student' entry fee, which is for students with other forms of identification.

OLD İSTANBUL
In the Old City, Topkapı Palace is right next to Sancta Sophia, which is right next to the Blue Mosque, which is right on the Hippodrome, which is right next to the Cistern Basilica, which is only a few steps from the museum complex, which is right next to Topkapı Palace. You can spend at least two days just completing this loop. Start with the palace, which is among the world's greatest museums.

You can get there from Aksaray and Laleli by dolmuş by bus or on foot along Ordu Caddesi, which turns into Yeniçeriler Caddesi, and finally Divan Yolu. Ask the driver if he's going to Sultanahmet. From Taksim it's a bit more difficult. Get a dolmuş to Sirkeci and walk up the hill for 10 minutes (take a short-cut to the palace through Gülhane Park); or take a T1 or T4 circle route bus, which stops right in Sultanahmet. The dolmuş is faster.

Topkapı Palace
It will take you the better part of a day to explore Topkapı Palace. Though it's tempting to nip into Sancta Sophia for a look as you go by on your way to Topkapı, I strongly recommend that you resist the urge. Sancta Sophia has been there for 1500 years, and it will be there when you come out of Topkapı. Start on the palace early in the day, before the bus tours get there. If you don't, you'll end up missing something important (like the Harem or the Treasury), or coming back another day.

Topkapı Palace is open from 9.30 am to 7 pm during July and August, till 5 pm the rest of the year; closed Tuesday. Admission to the palace costs 1000TL (US$1.40), half-price on weekends and holidays; you will buy a ticket for the Harem tour (500TL, US$0.70) at the

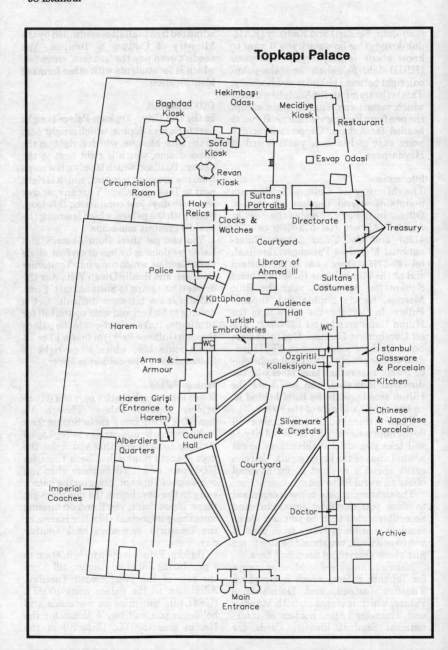

Topkapı Palace

Baghdad Kiosk

Hekimbaşı Odası

Mecidiye Kiosk

Restaurant

Sofa Kiosk

Esvap Odasi

Revan Kiosk

Circumcision Room

Holy Relics

Clocks & Watches

Sultans' Portraits

Directorate

Treasury

Courtyard

Library of Ahmed III

Police

Kütüphane

Sultans' Costumes

Audience Hall

Harem

Turkish Embroideries

WC

WC

İstanbul Glassware & Porcelain

Özgiritli Kolleksiyonu

Arms & Armour

Kitchen

Harem Girişi (Entrance to Harem)

Council Hall

Silverware & Crystals

Chinese & Japanese Porcelain

Alberdiers Quarters

Courtyard

Imperial Coaches

Doctor

Archive

Main Entrance

Harem entrance as you begin the tour.

The palace is called the Seraglio by foreigners (including Mozart, in his 'Abduction from the Seraglio'), an Italian word for the Turkish *saray* (palace).

Topkapı Sarayı (TOHP-kahp-uh sah-rah-yuh) was the residence of the sultans for almost three centuries. Mehmet the Conqueror built the first palace shortly after the Conquest in 1453, and lived here until his death in 1481. Sultan after sultan played out the drama of the Ottoman sovereign here until the 19th century. Mahmut II (1808-1839) was the last emperor to occupy the palace. After him, the sultans preferred to live in new European-style palaces – Dolmabahçe, Çırağan, Yıldız – which they built up the Bosphorus. Under the republic, the Saray became Turkey's finest museum. Mozart's famous opera is performed in the Seraglio every year during the İstanbul International Festival.

Court of the Janissaries Topkapı grew and changed with the centuries, but its basic four-courtyard plan remained the same. As you pass through the great gate behind Sancta Sophia, you enter the first court, the Court of the Janissaries. On your left is the former **Aya İrini Kilisesi or Church of Divine Peace**, now a concert hall where recitals are given during the İstanbul International Festival. There was a Christian church here from earliest times, and before that a pagan temple. The early church was replaced by the present one during the reign of the Byzantine emperor Justinian in the 540s, so the church you see is as old as Sancta Sophia. When Mehmet the Conqueror began building his palace, the church was within the grounds and thus couldn't be used for worship. Ironically, it was used as an arsenal for centuries, then as an Artillery Museum. In the 1970s restoration work began, and it was first used as a concert and exhibit hall soon afterward.

The large Court of the Janissaries, stretching from the church to the Middle Gate, is now a shady park and tour bus parking area, but in the old days this was where the sultan's elite corps of guards gathered to eat the hearty *pilav* provided by him. When they were dissatisfied with the sultan's rule (which meant his treatment of them), they would overturn the great cauldrons of *pilav* as a symbol of revolt. After that the sultan usually didn't last too long. Food was the most important symbol – so important, in fact, that the Janissary corps was organized on commissary lines. Some of the officers had kitchen titles, and the corps was called the *ocak*, 'hearth' or 'cookfire'.

'Janissary' comes from *yeni çeri* (YEHN-ee chehr-ee), 'new levies'. These soldiers were personal servants of the sultan, 'owned' by him, paid regularly and fed by him, and subject to his will. They were full-time soldiers in an age when most soldiers were farmers in spring and fall, homebodies in winter, and warriors only in summer. The Janissaries were mostly recruited as boys of 10 years old from Christian families in the Balkans. Though Islam forbids the enslavement or forcible conversion of Christians and Jews, the Balkans were looked upon as an exception. Saints Cyril and Methodius, 'Apostles to the Slavs', converted the pagan Slavic peoples to Christianity in the 800s, after the revelation of the Koran to Muhammad. So it was very convenient for the Ottoman religious authorities to rule that Slavic Christians 'had made the wrong choice' in converting to Christianity. Since they had been pagans when the Koran was revealed, they could be enslaved now.

The boys were taught Turkish and were instructed in Islam. The brightest went into the palace service, and many eventually rose to the highest offices, including Grand Vezir. This ensured that the top government posts were always held by 'slaves' of the sultan. Those not quite so bright made up the Janissary corps. More than once, in the later years of the empire, they proved that the sultan was their 'slave', and not the other way around.

The reforming sultan, Mahmut II, decided to do away with this dangerous and corrupted palace guard in 1826. Risking his throne, his life and his dynasty, he readied a new, loyal European-style army, then provoked a revolt of the Janissaries and wiped them out, ending their 3½ centuries in this courtyard headquarters.

Janissaries, merchants and tradespeople could circulate as they wished in the Court of the Janissaries, but the second court was different. The same is in a way true today, because you must buy your tickets before entering the second court. The ticket booths are on your right as you approach the entrance. Just past them is a little fountain where the Imperial Executioner used to wash the tools of his trade after decapitating a noble or rebel who had displeased the sultan. The head of the unfortunate was put on a pike and exhibited above the gate you're about to enter.

Ortakapı & Second Court The 'Middle Gate' (Ortakapı, also called the Gate of Greeting) led to the palace's second court, used for the business of running the empire. Only the sultan was allowed through the Ortakapı on horseback. Everyone else, including the Grand Vezir, had to dismount. The gate you see was constructed by Süleyman the Magnificent in 1524, utilizing architects and workers he had brought back from his conquest of Hungary. That's why it looks more European than oriental.

Within the second court is a beautiful, park-like setting. You'll see at once that Topkapı is not a palace on the European plan, one large building with outlying gardens. Rather, it is a series of pavilions, kitchens, barracks, audience chambers, kiosks and sleeping quarters built around a central enclosure, much like a fortified camp. It is a delightful castle and palace all in one.

As you walk into the second court, the great **palace kitchens** will be on your right. They now contain a small portion of Topkapı's incredibly large and varied collection of Chinese celadon porcelain. The greater part of the collection, which is quite vast, is in storage. Another room holds a fine collection of European and especially interesting Ottoman porcelain and glassware. The last of the kitchens, the Helvahane in which all the palace sweets were made, is now set up as a kitchen, and you can easily imagine what went on in these rooms as the staff prepared food for the 5000 inhabitants of the palace.

On the left side of the second court is the ornate **Kubbealtı or Imperial Council Chamber** where the Grand Vezir met with the Imperial Divan (council) on matters of state. The sultan did not participate in these discussions, but kept track sometimes by sitting behind a screen and listening. *Kubbealtı* means 'beneath the cupola'. The squarish tower which is one of Topkapı's most noticeable features is just above the Council Chamber.

Harem The entrance to the Harem is just behind the Kubbealtı. You will have to buy a ticket and take a guided tour; they leave periodically. It's a good idea to see the Harem as soon as possible, because it is open only from 10 am to 4 pm. Line up for the Harem tour before you go to the other parts of the palace. Make sure the guide will be speaking a language that you understand.

Fraught with legend and wild romance, the Harem is everything that you've imagined, even though most of the legends and stories are actually not quite true.

The usual stereotype has an army of gorgeous women petting and caressing, amusing and entertaining, and doing their best to exhaust, a very pampered man. Well, there's no denying that the sultan had it good. But every detail of Harem life was governed by tradition, obligation and ceremony. The sultan could not, unfortunately, just leap into a roomful of beauties and go to it. Every traditional Muslim household had two distinct parts: the *selamlık* or 'Greeting Room' where the master greeted friends, business associates and tradespeople; and the *harem* ('private apartments'), reserved for himself and his family. The harem, then, was something akin to the private apartments in Buckingham Palace or the White House. The *selamlık* was what outsiders saw when they visited.

The women of the Harem had to be foreigners, as Islam forbade enslaving Muslims, Christians or Jews (Christians and Jews could be enslaved if taken as war prisoners, or if bought as slaves in a legitimate slave market). Besides war prisoners, girls were bought as slaves (often sold by their parents at a good price), or received as gifts from nobles and potentates. A favourite source of girls for the Harem was Circassia, north of the Caucasus Mountains in Russia, as Circassian women were noted for their beauty, and parents were often glad to sell their 10-year-old girls.

Upon entering the Harem, the girls would be schooled in Islam and Turkish culture and language, plus such arts as make-up and dress, music, reading and writing, embroidery and dancing. They then entered a meritocracy, first as ladies-in-waiting to the sultan's concubines and children, then to the sultan's mother, and finally, if they were good enough, to the sultan himself.

Ruler of the Harem was the Valide Sultan, or Queen Mother, the mother of the reigning sultan. She often owned large landed estates in her own name and controlled them through black eunuch servants. She was allowed to give orders directly to the Grand Vezir. Her influence on the sultan, on the selection of his wives and concubines, and on matters of state, was very great.

The sultan was allowed by Islamic law to have four legitimate wives, who received the title of *kadın* (wife). If one bore him a child, she was called Haseki Sultan if it was a son, Haseki Kadın if it was a daughter. Each lady of the Harem would do almost anything to get her son proclaimed heir to the throne, thus assuring her own role as the new Valide Sultan. (The Ottoman dynasty did not observe primogeniture, or succession by the first-born son. The throne was basically up for grabs to any imperial son.)

As for concubines, Islam permits as many as a man can support in proper style. The Ottoman sultan could support a lot. Some of the early sultans had as many as 300 concubines, though not all in the Harem at the same time. The domestic thrills of the sultans were usually less spectacular. Mehmet the Conqueror, builder of Topkapı, was the

last sultan to have the four official wives. After him, sultans did not officially marry, but instead kept four chosen concubines without the legal encumbrances.

The Harem was much like a small village with all the necessary services. About 400 or 500 people lived in this distinct section of the palace at any one time. Not many of the ladies stayed in the Harem forever; sometimes the sultan granted them their freedom, and they were snapped up as wives by powerful men who wanted these supremely graceful and intelligent women, and also their connections with the palace.

The Kızlarağası (kuhz-LAHR-ah-ah-suh), or Chief Black Eunuch, was the sultan's personal representative in the running of the Harem and other important affairs of state. In fact, he was the third most powerful official in the empire, after the Grand Vezir and the Supreme Islamic Judge.

The imperial princes were brought up in the Harem, taught and cared for by the women. The tradition of the *kafes* (kah-FESS) or 'cage' was one of many things which led to the decline of the great empire. In the early centuries imperial princes were schooled in combat and statecraft by direct experience: they practised soldiering, fought in battles and were given provinces to administer. In the later centuries they spent their lives more or less imprisoned in the Harem, where the sultan could keep an eye on them and prevent any move to dethrone him. This meant that the princes were prey to the intrigues of the women and eunuchs; and when one of them did succeed to the throne he was corrupted by the pleasures of the Harem, and completely ignorant of war and statecraft. Luckily for the empire in this latter period, there were very able generals *(pashas)* and Grand Vezirs to carry on.

When you walk into the Harem, think of it as the family quarters; as a place of

art, culture and refinement; and as a political entity subject to intense manoeuvring and intrigue. Much of it was constructed during the reign of Süleyman the Magnificent (1520-1566), but a lot was added over the years. The door through which you enter was for tradespeople, who brought their wares here to the black eunuch guards. The tilework in the second room is some of Turkey's finest; the green and yellow colours are unusual in İznik faience. A corridor leads past the rooms of the black eunuchs who guarded the sultan's ladies. In the early days white eunuchs were used, but black eunuchs sent as presents by the Ottoman governor of Egypt later took control. As many as 200 lived in the Harem, guarding its doors and waiting on its women.

The sultan, when he walked these corridors, wore slippers with silver soles. They were noisy, and that was the point: no woman in the Harem was allowed to show herself to the Imperial Regard without specific orders. When they heard the clatter of silver on stone, they all ran to hide. This rule no doubt solidified the Valide Sultan's control: *she* would choose the girls to be presented to the sultan. There was to be no flirting in the hallways.

You enter a small courtyard, around which were the private apartments of the four *kadıns*, or wives. A larger courtyard beyond was the domain of the Valide Sultan, or Queen Mother. Besides being the centre of power in the Harem, this was where each new sultan came after accession to the throne, to receive the allegiance and congratulations of the people of the Harem.

The sultan's private Turkish bath is next. His mother and his four wives each had their own private bath. Other private baths went to the lady responsible for discipline in the Harem and to her assistant, the treasurer. After that, all the women shared a common bath.

Next you enter a few of the sultan's private chambers. There is a 17th-century room with a beautifully decorated fireplace, and a reception room with a fountain. Here the sultan received the ladies of the Harem, or his married female relatives - sisters, cousins and aunts. The fountain obscured the sounds of their conversation so that no one - in this hotbed of intrigue - could eavesdrop.

The sultan's private chamber was first built by Sinan, Süleyman the Magnificent's great architect, but the present decor dates from the 18th century.

Sultan Ahmet I (1603-1617), builder of the Blue Mosque, added a nice little library. In 1705 his successor Ahmet III added the pretty dining room with all the appetizing bowls of fruit painted on the walls.

The Veliaht Dairesi is the apartment of the Crown Prince, where in later centuries he was kept secluded from the world. Note the ingenious little fountains in the windows and the leather-covered domed ceiling. Next to the Crown Prince's suite are the sumptuous rooms of his mother, the Haseki Sultan.

These are the last rooms you see on the tour. You exit into the third, innermost courtyard.

Third Court If you enter the Third Court through the Harem, and thus by the back door, you should head for the main gate into the court. Get the full effect of entering this Holy of Holies by going out through the gate, and back in again.

This gate, the **Bab-i Saadet or Gate of Felicity**, was the entrance into the sultan's private domain. A new sultan, after girding on the sword which symbolized imperial power, would sit enthroned before this gate and receive the congratulations and allegiance of the empire's high and mighty. Before the annual military campaigns in summertime, the sultan would appear before this gate bearing the standard of the Prophet Muhammad to inspire his *pashas* (generals) to go out and win for Islam. Today the Bab-i Saadet is the backdrop

for the annual performance of Mozart's 'Abduction from the Seraglio' during the İstanbul International Festival in late June and early July.

The Third Court was staffed and guarded by white eunuchs, who allowed only very few, very important people to enter. Just inside the Bab-i Saadet is the **Arz Odası or Audience Chamber**. The sultan preserved the imperial mosque by appearing in public very seldom. To conduct official business, important officials and foreign ambassadors came to this little room. An ambassador, frisked for weapons and held on each arm by a white eunuch, would approach the sultan. At the proper moment, he knelt and kowtowed; if he didn't, the white eunuchs would urge him ever so strongly to do so. After that, he could speak to the sultan through an interpreter.

The sultan, seated on the divans whose cushions are embroidered with over 15,000 seed pearls, inspected the ambassador's gifts and offerings as they were passed by the small doorway on the left. Even if the sultan and the ambassador could converse in the same language (sultans in the later years knew French, and ambassadors often learned Turkish), all conversation went through an interpreter. One couldn't have just anybody putting words into the Imperial Ear.

During the great days of the empire, foreign ambassadors were received on days when the Janissaries were to get their pay. Huge sacks of silver coins were brought to the Kubbealtı (Council Chamber). High court officers would dispense them to long lines of the tough, impeccably costumed and faultlessly disciplined troops as the ambassadors looked on in admiration. It all worked for a while.

As you stroll into the Third Court, imagine it alive with the movements of imperial pages and white eunuchs scurrying here and there in their palace costumes. Every now and then the chief white eunuch or the chief black eunuch would appear, and all would deferentially bow. If the sultan walked across the courtyard, all activity stopped until the event was over.

Right behind the Arz Odası is the pretty little **Library of Ahmet III** (1718). Walk to the right as you leave the Arz Odası, and enter the rooms which were once the **Turkish baths** of the Third Court staff. They now contain a fascinating collection of imperial robes, caftans and uniforms worked in thread of silver and gold. You'll be surprised at the oriental, almost Chinese design of these garments. The Turks came originally from the borders of China, and their cultural history was tied closely with that of the Persian Empire and Central Asia. In fact, tribes in China's westernmost province of Sinkiang still speak a dialect of Turkish.

Next to the baths are the chambers of the **Imperial Treasury**. This you won't believe. After a while the display cases filled with rubies, emeralds, jade, pearls and more diamonds than you ever imagined will cause you to think, 'These are not all real, they must be plastic'. They're real.

One of my favourite items in the Treasury is the solid gold throne of Shah Ismail, encrusted with tens of thousands of precious stones. It was captured by Sultan Selim I (1512-1520) in a war with the Persians. Other thrones are almost as breathtaking. Look also for the tiny figurine of a sultan sitting under a baldachin (canopy). His body is one enormous pearl. The Kaşıkçının Elması or Spoonmaker's Diamond is an 86-carat mammoth surrounded by several dozen smaller stones. But the prize for biggest precious stone goes to the uncut emerald which weighs 3.26 kg, or almost seven pounds.

In the midst of all this heavy-duty show of wealth, don't lose sight of the fact that the workmanship, design and artistry exhibited in many of these items is extraordinary in itself.

Next door to the Treasury is the **Hayat**

Balkonu or Balcony of Life. Here the breeze is cool, and it offers a marvellous view of the Bosphorus and the Sea of Marmara.

Fourth Court To reach the palace **restaurant and café**, walk along the rear side of the Third Court and look for the narrow alley which goes north between the buildings. Down the slope and on the right is the **Mecidiye Köşkü or Kiosk of Sultan Abdülmecit**. Admire the view, enter the kiosk and go down the stairs to reach the restaurant. Tour groups fill it up around lunchtime, so plan your visit after noon, or at least a half-hour before.

Four imperial pleasure domes occupy the north-easternmost part of the palace, sometimes called the gardens, or Fourth Court. The Mecidiye built by Abdülmecit (1839-1861), you've already seen as entrance to the restaurant. In the other direction (north-east) is the **Mustafa Paşa Köşkü or Kiosk of Mustafa Pasha**, also called the Sofaköskü.

The gardens around it were once filled with tulips. In fact, the reign of Sultan Ahmet III (1703-1730) is named the Tulip Period because of the rage which spread through the upper classes. Gardens such as this held hundreds of varieties of tulips. Little lamps would be set out among the flowers at night. A new variety of the flower earned its creator fame, entree, and a good deal of money. Tulips had been grown in Turkey from very early times, having come originally from Persia. Some bulbs made their way to Holland in Renaissance times. The Dutch, fascinated by the possibilities in the flower, developed and created many varieties, some of which made their way back to Turkey and began the tulip craze here.

Up the stairs at the end of the tulip garden are two of the most enchanting kiosks. Sultan Murat IV (1623-1640) built the **Revan Köşkü or Erivan Kiosk** in 1635 after reclaiming the city of Erivan (now in the Soviet Union) from Persia. He also constructed the **Bağdat Köşkü or**

Baghdad Kiosk in 1638 to commemorate his victory over that city. Notice the İznik tiles, the inlay and woodwork, and the views from all around.

Just off the open terrace with the wishing well is the **Sünnet Odası or Circumsision Room**, used for the ritual which admits Muslim boys to manhood. Circumcision is usually performed at the age of nine or 10. Be sure to admire the beautiful tile panels.

Back in the Third Court Re-enter the Third Court for a look at yet another set of wonders, the **Holy Relics**. On the north-west side of the Third Court are more exhibition rooms. You can sometimes see the Imperial Baldachin, a tent-like shelter of incredibly heavy embroidered cloth. It was the sultan's audience chamber when on military campaign.

The most impressive exhibits are in the **Hırka-i Saadet suite of the Felicitous Cloak**. These rooms, sumptuously decorated with İznik faience, constituted a Holy of Holy of Holies, in a way. Only the chosen could enter the Third Court, but entry into the Hırka-i Saadet rooms was for the chosen of the chosen on special ceremonial occasions. For in these rooms reside the cloak of the Prophet Muhammad himself, his battle standard, two of his swords, a hair from his beard, a tooth, his footprint and a letter in his own handwriting.

The Felicitous Cloak itself resides in a golden casket in a special alcove along with the battle standard. This suite of rooms was opened only once a year so that the imperial family could pay homage to the memory of the Prophet on the 15th day of the holy month of Ramazan. Even though anyone, prince or commoner, faithful or infidel, can enter the rooms now, you're supposed to acknowledge the sacred atmosphere by reverent behavior.

Other exhibits in the Third Court include another little **library (Kütüphane)**, **Mosque of the Eunuchs (Ağalar Camii)**, miniature paintings, imperial seals and arms. These exhibits are sometimes moved around or closed to make room for special exhibits. In the room with the seals, notice the graceful, elaborate *tuğra* (TOO-rah) or monogram of the sultans. The *tuğra* was at the top of any imperial proclamation. It actually contains elaborate calligraphic rendering of the names of the sultan and his father. The formula is like this: 'Abdül Hamid Khan, son of Abdül Mecid Khan, Ever Victorious'.

Imperial Stables Enter the Imperial Stables (Has Ahırları) from the Second Court, just to the north-east of the main entrance (Ortakapı). Go down the cobbled slope.

The stables are now a museum for the carriages, saddles and other horse-related gear used by the sultans. The usual collection of gold-encrusted coaches, diamond-studded bridles, etc fill the rooms. One gets the impression that the Imperial lifestyle was at least soft, even though it had its complications.

Onward As you leave the palace proper through the Ortakapı, you can walk to your right and down the slope to the museums (see below), or straight to Sancta Sophia. I'll assume, for the moment, that you're heading to Sancta Sophia.

Just after you leave the tall gate of the Court of the Janissaries, take a look at the ornate little structure on your left. It's the **Fountain of Ahmet III**, the one who liked tulips so much. Built in 1728, it replaced a Byzantine one at the same spring. No water these days, though.

The ornate gate across the road from the fountain was where the Sultan entered Sancta Sophia for his prayers. It led to a special elevated Imperial Pavilion inside, which you will see.

Down the narrow street along the palace walls are old İstanbul houses which have been rebuilt under the auspices of the Turkish Touring & Automobile Club, and now serve as a posh hotel.

Sancta Sophia

The Church of the Holy Wisdom (Hagia Sofia in Greek, Ayasofya in Turkish) was not named for a saint; *sofia* means wisdom. Emperor Justinian (527-565) had it built as yet another effort to restore the greatness of the Roman Empire. It was completed in 548 and reigned as the greatest church in Christendom until the conquest of Constantinople in 1453. St Peter's in Rome is larger than Sancta Sophia but it was built more than 1000 years later.

A lot can happen to a building in 1400 years, especially in an earthquake zone, and a lot has certainly happened to Sancta Sophia. But it is still a wonder and a joy to behold. Ignore the clutter of buttresses and supports, kiosks and tombs and outbuildings which hug its massive walls. Try to see the church as it was meant to be seen by its creators.

You can no longer approach the church exactly as a Byzantine would have, walking along a street which led up a hill and straight to the great main door, but you can come close. Enter on the side by Sultanahmet, through what was the Forum of Augustus.

Sancta Sophia is open daily except Mondays, 9.30 am to 4.30 pm and to 7 pm in July and August; the galleries are open from 9.30 to 11.30 am and from 1 to 4 pm; there's a multi-vision show at 3 pm daily except Saturday. Entrance costs 1000TL (US$1.40); half-price on Sunday and holidays.

Now, to recapture the feeling that Justinian had when he first entered his great creation, walk down to the main entrance and stop. Here are the sunken ruins of a Theodosian church (404-415), and the low original steps.

If you enter the church slowly, one step at a time, you will at first see only darkness broken by the brilliant colours of stained-glass windows. As your eyes adjust to the dark, two more massive doorways appear, and far beyond them in the dim light, a semi-dome, blazing with gold mosaics portraying the Madonna and Child, she as Queen of Heaven. Just inside the threshold of the first door the mosaic is clear and beautiful, and the apse beneath it makes a harmonious whole. From where you are standing now, the mosaic of Christ as Pantocrator (Ruler of the World) above the third and largest door is visible except for the august expression on the face.

As you approach, the face of the Pantocrator becomes visible, and in the distance you can also see the apse and lofty semi-dome above it which, big as they are, are dwarfed by a gigantic dome above them. At the same time you are facing the Pantocrator in all his majesty.

When you walk through the second door and toward the immense Imperial Door, the 'gigantic dome' turns out to be only another semi-dome. Halfway to the Imperial Door, a row of windows peeks out above the larger semi-dome and betrays the secret. As you approach the Imperial Threshold the magnificent dome soars above you like the vault of heaven itself, and seems to be held up by nothing. Justinian, when he entered his great creation for the first time, came this far and exclaimed, 'Glory to God that I have been judged worthy of such a work. Oh Solomon! I have outdone you!'

During its years as a church (almost 1000), only imperial processions were permitted to enter through the central, Imperial Door. You can still notice the depressions in the stone by each door just inside the threshold where imperial guards stood. It was through the Imperial Door that Mehmet the Conqueror rode his horse in 1453 to take possession for Islam of the greatest religious edifice in the world. It remained a mosque for almost 500 years. In 1935 Atatürk proclaimed it a museum; the wisdom in this decision is apparent when you consider that both devout Muslims and Christians would like to have it as a place of worship for their religion.

Sancta Sophia

There are bigger buildings, and also bigger domes, but not without modern construction materials such as reinforced concrete and steel girders. The achievement of the architects, Anthemius of Tralles and Isidorus of Miletus, is unequalled. The dome, constructed of special hollow bricks made in Rhodes of a unique light, porous clay, was a daring attempt at the impossible. Indeed, it almost was impossible, because the dome lasted only 11 years before an earthquake brought it down in 559. Over the centuries it was necessary for succeeding Byzantine emperors and Ottoman sultans to rebuild the dome several times, to add buttresses and other supports, and to steady the foundations. The dome is supported by massive pillars incorporated into the walls. In order to appreciate how this works, compare it with the Blue Mosque. And for an acoustic thrill, stand right beneath the centre of the dome and clap your hands.

The Ottoman chandeliers, hanging low above the floor, combined their light with the rows and rows of little oil lamps which lined the balustrades of the gallery and even the walkway at the base of the dome.

Justinian ordered the most precious materials for his church. Note the matched marble panels in the walls, and the breccia columns. The Byzantine emperor was crowned while seated in a throne placed within the square of inlaid marble in the main floor. The nearby choir gallery is an Ottoman addition, as is the *mihrab*, or prayer niche, which shows the faithful the direction in which Mecca lies. The large alabaster urns were added at a later date by Sultan Murat III (1574-1595) as a place where worshippers could perform their ritual ablutions before praying.

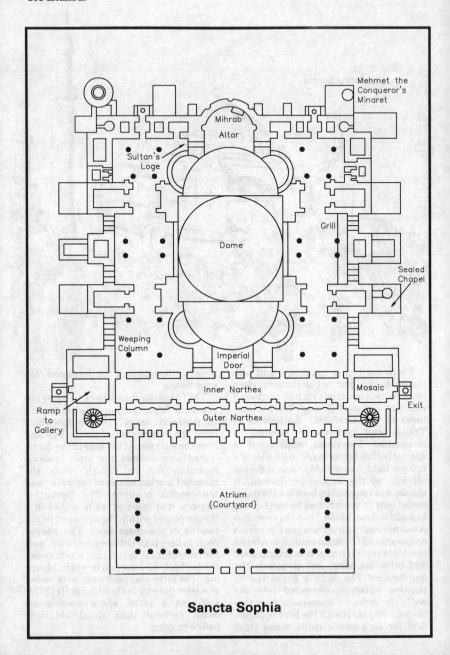

Mehmet the Conqueror's Minaret

Mihrab

Altar

Sultan's Loge

Grill

Dome

Sealed Chapel

Weeping Column

Imperial Door

Inner Narthex

Mosaic

Exit

Ramp to Gallery

Outer Narthex

Atrium (Courtyard)

Sancta Sophia

The large medallions inscribed with gilt Arabic letters were added in the 1600s. Calligraphy is a highly prized art in Islam, and these were done by one of the greatest calligraphers of the 1600s. You'll see these words over and over in Turkish mosques. They are the names of God (Allah), Muhammad and the early caliphs Ali and Abu Bakr.

The curious elevated kiosk, screened from public view, is the Hünkâr Mahfili or Sultan's Loge. Ahmet III (1703-1730) had it built so he could come, pray and go unseen, preserving the imperial mystique.

If you wander around enough you'll come to the 'weeping column'. A copper facing with a hole in it has been put on a column (to the left after you enter through the Imperial Door). Stick your finger in the hole and make a wish. Legend has it that if the tip of your finger emerges damp, you're supposed to get your wish. Wet or dry, you'll feel slightly silly, but none the worse for that.

Mosaics Justinian filled his church with gorgeous mosaics. The Byzantine church and state later went through a fierce civil war (726-787) over the question of whether images were to be allowed or not. (The debated Biblical passage was Exodus 20:4, 'Thou shalt not make unto thee any graven image, or any likeness of anything that is in heaven above, or that is in the earth beneath, or that is in the water under the earth: Thou shalt not bow down thyself to them, nor serve them . . . .') Though the Bible seems clear, the people liked images a lot, and the iconoclasts ('image-breakers') were defeated.

When the Turks took Constantinople there was no controversy. The Koran repeatedly rails against idolatry, as in Sura 16: 'We sent a Messenger into every nation saying, Serve God and give up idols'. Consequently Islamic art is supposed to have no saints' portraits, no pictures of animals, fish or fowl, nor anything else with an immortal soul, and

the mosaics had to go. Luckily they were covered with plaster rather than destroyed. In the 1950s, the American Association for the Preservation of Byzantine Monuments lent the money and expertise to begin restoration of the mosaics. The work is still going on.

From the floor of Sancta Sophia you can see several saints' portraits high up in the semi-circles of the side walls. The best are in the galleries, reached by a switchback ramp which starts at the northern end of the narthex.

Some of the work, though partially lost, is superb. Be sure to go all the way to the far ends of the galleries. At the apse end of the south (right-hand) gallery are portraits of emperors, with a difference. The Empress Zoe (1028-1050), for instance, had three husbands. When her portrait was put here in mosaic her husband was Romanus III Argyrus, but he died in 1034. So when she married Michael IV in that year, she had Romanus's portrait taken out and Michael's put in. But Michael didn't last that long either, and in 1042 his portrait was removed to make way for that of Constantine IX Monomachus. Constantine outlived Zoe, so it is his portrait that you see today. The inscription reads, 'Constantine, by the Divine Christ, Faithful King of the Romans'.

As you leave Sancta Sophia, pass all the way through the corridor-like narthex and through the door at the end of it. Then turn and look up. Above the door is one of the church's finest mosaics, a Madonna and Child; on the left, Constantine the Great offers her the city of Constantinople; on the right, Justinian offers Sancta Sophia.

A few more steps and you're out of the museum. The fountain to the right was for Muslim ablutions. Immediately to your left is the church's baptistry, converted after the Conquest to a tomb for sultans Mustafa and İbrahim. Other tombs are clustered behind it: those of Murat III, Selim II, Mehmet III and various princes. By the way, the minarets were added by Mehmet the Conqueror (1451-1481), Beyazit II (1481-1512) and Selim II (1566-1574).

Hamam Across the road to the left (east) of the park with the fountain is a *hamam* or Turkish bath, now fixed up and in use. Good Muslims perform ritual ablutions before saying the five daily prayers, which makes cleanliness a tenet of the religion. On Friday, the holy day, it's looked upon as especially good to take a steam bath. Every mosque has a steam bath nearby; this was Sancta Sophia's.

Set into Sancta Sophia's enclosing fence, directly across the road from the Turkish bath, is a *sebil*. You'll recognize it as a little café, with an ornate kiosk, sidewalk tables and chairs. A *sebil* was a place where sweet spring water and other refreshing drinks were sold; this one has just been adapted for modern ways. You'll see many others scattered throughout the Old City, mostly closed up, though.

The Blue Mosque

There used to be palaces where the Blue Mosque now stands. The Byzantine emperors built several of them, stretching from near Sancta Sophia all the way to the site of the mosque. You can see a mosaic from one of these palaces, still in place (described in more detail later in this section).

Sultan Ahmet I (1603-1617) set out to build a mosque that would rival and even surpass the achievement of Justinian. He succeeded, but only in part. The Sultan Ahmet Camii or Mosque of Sultan Ahmet, the Blue Mosque, is a triumph of harmony, proportion and elegance, but it comes nowhere near the technical achievements of Sancta Sophia.

The mosque is best appreciated if entered, as at Sancta Sophia, by the main gate, slowly. In this case you can do it right; don't just walk across the park between the two structures, and in the side door. Rather, go out to the At Meydanı, the Hippodrome, and approach the mosque from the front.

The Blue Mosque is the only one in Turkey with six minarets. When it was built, the sacred mosque of the Kaaba in Mecca had six, and another had to be added so that it would not be outdone. Walk toward the mosque, through the outer gate (the hanging chains prevented men from riding in on horseback). As you walk up the steps to the courtyard door, you will see the domes of the Blue Mosque rise heavenward, one after the other. The effect is marvellous.

The layout of the Blue Mosque is the standard Ottoman design as it evolved over the centuries. The forecourt contains an ablutions fountain in its centre. The portico around three sides could be used for prayer, meditation or study during good weather.

The Blue Mosque is such a popular tourist sight that worshippers were in danger of being lost in the tourist crowds. So you'll be asked to enter from a side door, not through the main door. Turn left, walk through the side gate, then turn right. At the side door an attendant will take your shoes; if your clothing is unpresentable, he'll lend you a robe to wear while you see the mosque. There's no charge for this but you may be asked for a donation to the mosque, to which the money will actually go.

Though the stained glass windows are replacements, they still create the marvellous coloured effects of the originals. The semi-domes and the dome are painted in graceful arabesques. The 'blue' of the mosque's name comes from the İznik tiles which line the walls, particularly in the gallery (which is not open to the public). You'll be able to get up close to equally beautiful tiles in the Rüstem Paşa Camii described below.

You can see immediately why the Blue Mosque, constructed in 1609-1616, over 1000 years after Sancta Sophia, is not as great an architectural triumph as Sancta

Sophia. Although the four massive pillars which hold up the dome don't detract from the mosque's breathtaking beauty, they show what an impressive achievement Sancta Sophia is, by showing what's usually needed to hold up a massive dome.

Other things to notice: the imperial loge, covered with marble latticework, to the left; the piece of the sacred Black Stone from the Kaaba in Mecca, embedded in the *mihrab*; the grandfather clock, to be sure the faithful know the exact times of the five-times-daily prayers; the high, elaborate chair *(mahfil)* from which the *imam* or teacher gives the sermon on Friday; and the *mimber*, or pulpit. The *mimber* is the structure with a curtained doorway at floor level, a flight of steps and a small kiosk topped by a spire. This one is particularly notable because of its fine carving (it's all marble), and because it was from here that the destruction of the Janissary corps was proclaimed in 1826 (see under 'Topkapı Palace').

Mosques built by the great and powerful usually included numerous public-service institutions. Clustered around the Sultan Ahmet Camii were a *medrese* or theological school; an *imaret* or soup kitchen serving the poor; a *hamam* or Turkish bath so that the faithful could wash on Friday, the holy day; and shops, the rent from which supported the upkeep of the mosque. The tomb of the mosque's great patron, Sultan Ahmet I, is here as well. Buried with Ahmet are his brothers, Sultan Osman II and Sultan Murat IV.

Textile Museum Parts of the Blue Mosque have been turned into a textile museum officially called the Museum of Kilims & Flat-Woven Rugs (Kilim ve Düz Dokuma Yaygılar Müzesi). The cellars, entered from the north side (toward Sancta Sophia), are where you buy your ticket (9 am to 5 pm, closed Monday; about US$0.15).

On the way into the cellars, you may see a woven nomad's tent, pitched and ready. This was the setting in which many of the *kilims* were made and used.

Inside the building are impressive stone-vaulted chambers. Huge *kilims* are stretched on boards, with descriptive tags written in Turkish and English.

Other exhibits are housed upstairs in the Carpet Museum or Halı Müzesi, at the end of the stone ramp which you can see from the side door where you entered the mosque. The ramp was so that the sultans could ride their nobly caparisoned steeds right up into the shelter of the mosque, dismount, and walk to their loge in safety and imperial privacy.

Turkish oriental carpets are among the finest works of art. The collection here provides a look at some of the best examples.

Mosaics Before the Blue Mosque was built, its site was occupied by the palaces of the Byzantine emperors. The Roman art of mosaic moved, with most other Roman traditions, to Byzantium, and so the palace floors were covered in this beautiful artwork. Though the palaces have long since disappeared, you can sometimes see the mosaics in place at the back, at 22 Torun Sokak.

When archaeologists from the University of Ankara and the University of St Andrew's (in Scotland) dug here in the mid-1950s, they uncovered a mosaic pavement dating from early Byzantine times, about 500 AD. The pavement, filled with wonderful hunting and mythology scenes and emperors' portraits, was a triumphal way which led from the palace down to the harbour of Boucoleon. Fifteen hundred years' worth of dust and rubble have sunk the pavement considerably below ground level.

Other mosaics were saved, providentially, when Sultan Ahmet had shops built on top of them. The shops, originally intended to provide rent revenues for the upkeep of the mosque, have been restored, and they still serve to protect these 5th-century mosaics.

The Hippodrome

This was the centre of Byzantium's life for 1000 years and of Ottoman life for another 400. The Hippodrome (At Meydanı, 'Horse Grounds' in Turkish) was the scene of countless political and military dramas during the long life of this city.

History In Byzantine times, the rival chariot teams of 'Greens' and 'Blues' were politically connected. Support for a team was the same as membership in a political party, and a team victory had important effects on policy. A Byzantine emperor might lose his throne as the result of a post-match riot.

Ottoman sultans kept an eye on activities in the Hippodrome. If things were going badly in the empire, a surly crowd gathering here could signal the start of a disturbance, then a riot, then a revolution. In 1826, the slaughter of the debased and unruly Janissary corps was carried out by the reformer-sultan Mahmut II. Almost a century later, in 1909, there were riots here which caused the downfall of Abdülhamid II and the re-promulgation of the Ottoman constitution.

Though the Hippodrome might be the scene of their downfall, Byzantine emperors and Ottoman sultans outdid one another in beautifying it. Many of the priceless statues carved by ancient masters have disappeared. The soldiers of the Fourth Crusade sacked Constantinople (a Christian ally city!) in 1204, tearing all the bronze plates from the magnificent stone obelisk at the Hippodrome's southern end, in the mistaken belief that they were gold. The crusaders also stole the famous 'quadriga', or team of four horses cast in bronze, which now sits atop the main door to Saint Mark's Church in Venice.

Monuments Near the northern end, the little gazebo done in beautiful stonework is actually a **fountain** (no longer working). Kaiser Wilhelm II of Germany paid a state visit to Abdülhamid II in 1901, and presented this fountain to the sultan and his people as a little token of friendship. According to the Ottoman inscription, the fountain was built in the Hijri (Muslim) year of 1316 (1898/1899 to us). The monograms in the stonework are those of the Ottoman sultan and the German emperor.

The impressive granite obelisk with hieroglyphs is called the **Obelisk of Theodosius**, carved in Egypt around 1500 BC. According to the hieroglyphs, it was erected in Heliopolis (now a suburb of Cairo) to commemorate the victories of Thutmose III (1504-1450 BC). The Byzantine emperor Theodosius had it brought from Egypt to Constantinople in 390 AD. He then had it erected on a marble pedestal engraved with scenes of himself in the midst of various imperial pastimes. Theodosius's marble billboards have weathered badly over the centuries. The magnificent obelisk, spaced above the pedestal by four bronze blocks, is as crisply cut and as shiny bright as when it was carved from the living rock in Upper Egypt.

Many obelisks were transported over the centuries to Paris (Place de la Concorde), London (Cleopatra's Needle), New York, Rome and Florence. A few still remain in Egypt as well.

South of the obelisk is a strange **spiral column** coming up out of a hole in the ground. It was once much taller and was topped by three serpents' heads. Originally cast to commemorate a victory of the Hellenic confederation over the Persians, it stood in front of the temple of Apollo at Delphi from 478 BC, until Constantine the Great had it brought to his new capital city about 330 AD. Though badly bashed up in the Byzantine struggle over the place of images in the church (Iconoclastic Controversy), the serpents' heads survived until the early 1700s. Now all that remains of them is one upper jaw in the Archaeological Museum.

The level of the Hippodrome rose over the centuries, as civilisation piled up its dust and refuse here. The obelisk and serpentine column were cleaned out and tidied up by the English troops who occupied the city after the Ottoman defeat in WW I.

No one is quite sure who built the large **rough-stone obelisk** at the southern end of the Hippodrome. All we know is that it was repaired by Constantine VII Porphyrogenetus (913-959), and that the bronze plates were ripped off by the Fourth Crusaders.

Turkish & Islamic Arts Museum

The Palace of İbrahim Paşa (1524) is on the western side of the Hippodrome. Now housing the Türk ve İslam Eserleri Müzesi, or Turkish & Islamic Arts Museum, it gives you a glimpse into the opulent life of the Ottoman upper class in the time of Süleyman the Magnificent. İbrahim Paşa was Süleyman's close friend, son-in-law and Grand Vezir. He was enormously wealthy and so powerful that the sultan finally had him murdered. Roxelana, Süleyman's wife, had convinced the sultan that İbrahim was a rival and a threat.

The museum is open from 10 am to 5 pm daily; closed Monday. Admission costs 300TL (US$0.42). Labels are in Turkish and English. There is a coffee shop in the museum for refreshments.

Highlights among the exhibits, which date from the 700s and 800s AD up to the last century, are the decorated wooden Koran cases from the high Ottoman period; the calligraphy exhibits, including *fermans* with *tuğras* (imperial monograms); Turkish miniatures and illuminated manuscripts. You'll also want to have a look at the *rahles* or Koran stands, and the many carpets from all periods.

The lower floor of the museum houses ethnographic exhibits. At the entry is a black tent *(karaçadır)* like those used by nomads in eastern Turkey. Inside the tent is an explanation of nomadic customs, in English. Inside the building are village looms on which carpets and *kilims* are woven, and an exhibit of the plants and materials used to make natural textile dyes for the carpets. Perhaps most fascinating are the domestic interiors, including a *yurt* or Central Asian felt hut, a village house from Yuntdağ, and a late-19th-century house from Bursa. One display shows women shopping for cloth, and another a scene of daily life in an İstanbul home of the early 20th century.

The buildings behind and beside İbrahim Paşa's palace are İstanbul's law courts and legal administration buildings.

'Little' Sancta Sophia

The southern end of the Hippodrome is artificially supported by a system of brick arches called the **Sphendoneh**. Take a detour into İstanbul's lively little back streets for a look at this Byzantine feat of engineering. While you're down there, you can visit the small, old Byzantine Church of Saints Sergius and Bacchus (now called the Little Sancta Sophia Mosque or Küçük Aya Sofya Camii), and also the Sokollu Mehmet Paşa Camii (mosque).

Facing south, with the Blue Mosque on your left, go to the end of the Hippodrome and turn left, then right, onto Aksakal Sokak. Soon you'll be able to recognize the filled-in arches of the Byzantine Sphendoneh on your right. Follow the curve around to the right and onto Kaleci Sokak. The next intersecting street is Mehmet Paşa Sokak; turn left and the Küçük Aya Sofya Camii is right there. If the mosque is not open, just hang around or signal to a boy on the street, and someone will come with the key.

Justinian and Theodora built this little church sometime between 527 and 536. Inside, the layout and decor are typical of an early Byzantine church, though the building was repaired and expanded several times during its life as a mosque, after the conquest of Constantinople in 1453. Repairs and enlargements to convert the church to a mosque were added by the Chief White Eunuch Hüseyin Ağa around 1500. His tomb is to the left as you enter.

Go north on Mehmet Paşa Sokak, back up the hill to the neighbouring Mosque of Sokollu Mehmet Paşa. This one was built during the height of Ottoman architectural development (1571) by the empire's greatest architect, Mimar Sinan. Though named for the Grand Vezir of the time, it was really sponsored by his wife Esmahan, daughter of Sultan Selim II. Besides its architectural harmony, typical of Sinan's great works, the mosque is unique because the *medrese* or religious school is actually part of the mosque structure, built around the forecourt.

Walk back up the hill on Suterazisi Sokak to return to the Hippodrome.

Yerebatan Saray

Cross the main road, Divan Yolu, from the Hippodrome. On the north side of the street is a little park with a curious stone tower rising from it. The tower is part of an ancient aqueduct, a segment of this timeless city's elaborate water system. Beneath the park, entered by a little doorway on its north side (on Hilaliahmer Caddesi) is the Cistern Basilica.

This 'Sunken Palace' (its Turkish name) is actually a grand Byzantine cistern, 70 metres wide and 140 metres long. The roof is held up by 336 columns. It was built by Justinian the Great (527-565), who was incapable of thinking in small terms.

The city is positively mined with similar cisterns. Many have been discovered, some still hide in the basements of modern construction, still others remain to be discovered.

Gülhane Park & Sublime Porte

Walk down the hill from Yerebatan Saray, along the main street called Alemdar Caddesi. Sancta Sophia will be on your right. Just past a big tree in the middle of the road, the street turns left, but right before you is the arched gateway to Gülhane Park.

Before entering the park peer through the tangle of buses and crowds, looking to your left. That bulbous little kiosk built into the park walls at the next street corner is the **Alay Köşkü or Parade Kiosk**, from whence the sultan would watch the periodic parades of troops and tradespeople's guilds which commemorated great holidays and military victories.

Across the street from the Alay Köşkü (not quite visible right from the Gülhane gate) is a gate to the Sublime Porte. The gate leads into the precincts of what was once the Grand Vezirate, or Prime Ministry, of the Ottoman Empire. Westerners called the Ottoman prime ministry the 'Sublime Porte' because of a phrase in Ottoman official documents: 'The Ambassador of (wherever) having come to my Sublime Porte . . . .'

In Islamic societies, and in other societies with strong clan roots, it was customary for the chief or ruler to adjudicate disputes and grant favours. To petition the leader, you went to his tent, or house, or palace, stood at the door (hence 'porte'), and waited for a chance to lay it on him. When a western ambassador arrived at the sultan's 'sublime porte', he was looked on as just another petitioner asking favours. In later centuries, ambassadors reported not to the palace but to the Grand Vezirate, which was thus thought to be the Sublime Porte. Today the buildings beyond the gate house the Ottoman archives and various offices of the İstanbul provincial government.

Back up the street and inside the gates of Gülhane Parkı, you'll find a shady refuge (once part of the Topkapı Palace grounds) and a small zoo. Admission to the park is free.

Museums

İstanbul's major collection of 'serious' museums is right between Gülhane and Topkapı. As you pass beneath the arched gateway from Alemdar Caddesi, bear right and walk up the slope along a cobbled road, which then turns to the right. After the turn you'll see a gate on the left. Within the gate are the İstanbul Arkeoloji Müzeleri or **Archaeological Museum, Tiled Kiosk** and **Museum of the Ancient Orient**.

You can also reach the museum complex from Topkapı. As you come out the Ortakapı from the palace, walk into the Court of the Janissaries, then turn right and walk down the hill before you get to the Church of Divine Peace.

The museum complex is open from 9.30 am to 5 pm every day in summer, closed Mondays off-season. Admission to the complex (that is, to all of the museums, on one ticket) costs 500TL (US$0.70); half-price on Saturday, Sunday and holidays. As of this writing the Tiled Kiosk is open only on Tuesday, and the

Museum of the Ancient Orient closes for lunch from noon to 1 pm.

These were the palace collections, formed during the 19th century and added to greatly during the republic. While not immediately as dazzling as Topkapı, they contain an incredible wealth of artefacts from the 50 centuries of Anatolia's history.

The Archaeological Museum houses a vast collection of statues and sarcophagi. One of the most beautiful sarcophagi was once thought to be that of Alexander the Great; today that theory is not held by all. Signs in the museum are in Turkish and French. The upper floor is presently closed. The Ottoman inscription over the door of this imposing structure reads 'Eser-i Atika Müzesi', or Museum of Ancient Works.

Across the court from the Archaeological Museum is the Çinili Köşkü or Tiled Kiosk of Sultan Mehmet the Conqueror. Though once completely covered in fine tilework, you'll see tiles only on the facade these days. Mehmet II

Relief of Alexander (Sarcophagus, Archaeological Museum)

had this built not long after the conquest (1472), which makes it the oldest surviving non-religious Turkish building in İstanbul. It now houses an excellent collection of Turkish faience, appropriately enough. You'll see many good examples of fine İznik (Nicaea) tiles from the period in the 1600s and 1700s when that city produced the finest coloured tiles in the world.

Last of the museums in the complex is the Eski Şark Eserler Müzesi or Museum of the Ancient Orient. Go here for a glimpse at the gates of ancient Babylon in the time of Nebuchadnezzar II (604-562 BC), for clay tablets bearing Hammurabi's famous law code (in cuneiform, of course), ancient Egyptian scarabs, and artefacts from the Assyrian and Hittite empires.

Divan Yolu

The main thoroughfare of the Old City stretches between the gate named Topkapı and the palace named Topkapı. Starting from the Hippodrome and Yerebatan Saray, it heads due west, up one of İstanbul's seven hills, past the Grand Bazaar, through Beyazıt Square and the university to Aksaray Square. Turning north a bit, it continues to the Topkapı (Cannon Gate) in the ancient city walls. In its progress through the city, its name changes from Divan Yolu to Yeniçeriler Caddesi, Ordu Caddesi, Millet Caddesi. At the eastern end, near the Hippodrome, it's Divan Yolu, the Road to the Imperial Council.

The street dates from the early times of Constantinople. Roman engineers laid it out to connect with the great Roman roads heading west. The great milestone from which all distances were measured was near the tall shaft of stones which rises above Yerebatan Saray. The street held its importance in Ottoman times, as Mehmet the Conqueror's first palace was in Beyazıt Square, and his new one, Topkapı, was under construction.

If you start from Sancta Sophia and the

Hippodrome and walk up the slope on Divan Yolu, you will see the little **Mosque of Firuz Ağa**, chief treasurer to Beyazıt II (1481-1512), on the left. It was built in 1491, in the simple style of the early Ottomans: a dome on a square base, with a simple porch out front. The Ottomans brought this style with them from the East or borrowed it from the Seljuk Turks. It changed greatly after they conquered İstanbul, inspected Sancta Sophia and put the great architect Mimar Sinan to work.

Just behind the little mosque of Firuz Ağa are the ruins of the **Palace of Antiochus** (400s), not much to look at these days.

The first major intersection on the right is with Babiali Caddesi. Turn right here and after walking a block you'll be in **Cağaloğlu Square**, once the centre of İstanbul's newspaper publishing. Most of the publishers have moved to large, modern buildings outside the walls. The **Cağaloğlu Hamamı**, a Turkish bath, is just off the square, on the right (see 'Entertainment' for details on taking a Turkish bath).

If instead you turn left (south) from Divan Yolu, you'll be on Klodfarer Caddesi (not a German word, but the name of the Turcophile French novelist, Claude Farrère). It leads to a large open area beneath which lies the Byzantine cistern now called **Binbirdirek**, 'A Thousand-and-One Columns'. You'll see the little doorway to the stairs. If the door is locked, call to a child, who will find the guard. Not as large as Yerebatan Saray, Binbirdirek is still very impressive, if a bit neglected these days.

Back on Divan Yolu, the impressive enclosure right at the corner of Babiali Caddesi is filled with **tombs** of the Ottoman high and mighty. First to be built here was the *türbe* or mausoleum of Sultan Mahmut II (1808-1839), the reforming emperor who got rid of the Janissaries and revamped the Ottoman army. After Mahmut, other notables chose to be buried here, including sultans Abdülaziz (1861-1876) and Abdül Hamid II (1876-1909).

Right across Divan Yolu from the tombs is a small stone **library** built by the Köprülü family in 1659. The Köprülüs rose to prominence in the mid-1600s and furnished the empire with an outstanding succession of Grand Vezirs, generals and Grand Admirals for centuries. They basically ran the empire during a time when the scions of the Ottoman dynasty did not live up to the standards of Mehmet the Conqueror and Süleyman the Magnificent.

Stroll a bit further along Divan Yolu. On the left, the curious *türbe* with wrought-iron grillework on top is that of Köprülü Mehmet Paşa (1575-1661). Across the street, that strange building with a row of streetfront shops is actually an ancient Turkish bath, the **Çemberlitaş Hamamı** (1580).

The derelict, time-worn column rising from a little plaza is one of İstanbul's most ancient and revered monuments. Called **Çemberlitaş** ('The Banded Stone'), or the Burnt Column, it was erected by Constantine the Great (324-337) to celebrate the dedication of Constantinople as capital of the Roman Empire in 330. This area was the grand Forum of Constantine, and the column was topped by a statue of the great emperor himself. In an earthquake zone erecting columns can be a risky business. This one has survived, though it needed iron bands for support within a century after it was built. The statue crashed to the ground almost 1000 years ago.

The little **mosque** nearby is that of Atik Ali Paşa, a eunuch and Grand Vezir of Beyazıt II.

The Grand Bazaar

İstanbul's Kapalı Çarşı ('Covered Market'), the Grand Bazaar, is 4000 shops and several km of streets, mosques, banks, police stations, restaurants and workshops.

Starting from a small *bedesten* or warehouse built in the time of Mehmet the Conqueror, the bazaar grew to cover a vast area as neighbouring shopkeepers decided to put up roofs and porches so that commerce could be conducted comfortably in all weather. Great men built *hans*, or caravanserais, at the edges of the bazaar so that caravans could bring wealth from all parts of the empire, unload and trade right in the bazaar's precincts. Finally, a system of locked gates and doors was provided so that the entire mini-city could be closed up tight at the end of the business day.

Though tourist shops are multiplying in the bazaar, it is still a place where an *İstanbullu* (citizen of İstanbul) will come to buy a few metres of printed cloth, a gold bangle for a daughter's birthday gift, an antique carpet or a fluffy sheepskin. Whether you want to buy or not, you should see the bazaar (remember that it's closed on Sunday). Turn right off Divan Yolu at the Çemberlitaş and walk down Vezir Hanı Caddesi. The big mosque before you is the **Nuruosmaniye** ('Light of Osman'), built between 1748 and 1755 by Mahmut I and his successor Osman III, in the style known as Ottoman Baroque. It's one of the earliest examples of the style.

Turn left through the mosque gate. The courtyard of the mosque is peaceful and green, but with a constant flow of pedestrian traffic heading through it, to and from the bazaar.

Out the other side of the courtyard, you're standing in Çarşıkapı Sokak, Bazaar Gate St, and before you is one of several doorways into the bazaar. The glorious gold emblem above the doorway is the Ottoman armorial emblem with the sultan's *tuğra* (monogram). While you're here, you might want to see an interesting little street behind the Nuruosmaniye Mosque. If you turn right after leaving the mosque courtyard, then right again, you'll be on **Kılıççılar Sokak**, Swordmakers' St. The dingy workshops on both sides of the street have fiery forges in the

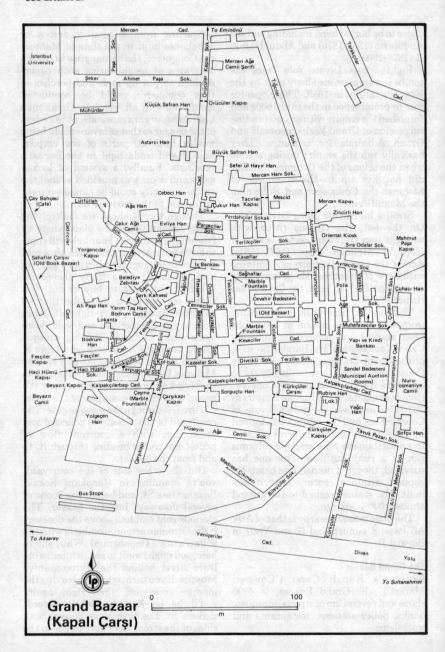

Grand Bazaar (Kapalı Çarşı)

İstanbul University

Mercan Cad. To Eminönü

Tarakçılar

Mercan Ağa Camii Şerifi

Tığcılar Sok.

Örücüler Kapısı

Örücüler Kapısı

Şeker Ahmet Paşa Sok.

Emin Paşa Sok.

Mühürdar

Küçük Safran Han

Cad.

Astarcı Han

Büyük Safran Han

Sefer ül Hayır Han

Mercan Hanı Sok.

Çav Bahçesi (Cafe)

Lütfüllah

Cebeci Han

Tacirler Kapısı

Mescid

Mercan Kapısı

Zincirli Han

Mahmut Paşa Kapısı

Çukur Han Lok.

Perdahçılar Sokak

Oriental Kiosk

Sıra Odalar Sok.

Ağa Han

Cakır Ağa Camii

Evliya Han

Parçacılar Sok.

Aycesme Sok.

Kuyumcular

Sahaflar Çarşısı (Old Book Bazaar)

Yorgancılar Kapısı

Terlikçiler Sok.

Kavaflar Sok.

Aynacılar Sok.

Varakçı

Polis

Çuhacı Han Sok.

Çuhacı Han

Belediye Zabıtası

Sağhaflar Cad.

Marble Fountain

Cevahir Bedesteni

Ağa Sok.

Çuhacı

Ali Paşa Han

Şark Kahvesi

Yarım Taş Han Bodrum Camii

Evliya Han

Resam

Orta

Takkeciler

(Old Bazaar)

Muhafazacılar Sok.

Yapı ve Kredi Bankası

Nuruosmaniye Cad.

Nuruosmaniye Camii

Lokanta

Bodrum Han

Zenneciler Sok.

Basmacılar

Kazaslar

Marble Fountain

Keseciler

Kolancılar

Cad.

Sandal Bedesteni

Sandal Bedesteni (Municipal Auction Rooms)

Fesçiler Kapısı

Fesçiler

Hacı Hüsnü Sok.

Bod. Kum Han Sok.

Kavukçular Sok.

Kol-tuk

Sipahi

Kazaslar Sok.

Divrikli Sok.

Terziler Sok.

Kalpakçılarbaşı Cad.

Beyazıt Kapısı

Kalpakçılarbaşı Sok.

Çeşme (Marble Fountain)

Çarşıkapı Kapısı

Sorguçlu Han

Kürkçüler Çarşısı

Rubiye Han (Lok.)

Yağcı Han

Beyazıt Camii

Yolgeçen Han

Çarşıkapı

Hüseyin Ağa Camii Sok.

Kürkçüler Kapısı

Tavuk Pazarı Sok.

Sofçu Han

Medrese Çıkmazı

Bileyiciler Sok.

Atik Ali Paşa Medrese Sok.

Bus Stops

Kürkçüler Pazarı Sok.

Yeniçeriler Cad.

To Aksaray

To Sultanahmet

Divan Yolu

0   100
m

rear. They no longer make swords here, except the miniature ones to be used as letter-openers. Most of the metalwork is brass souvenirs. Once you've taken a look, head back to the doorway with the Ottoman arms above it.

Inside the bazaar, the street you're on is called **Kalpakçılarbaşı Caddesi**. It's the closest thing the bazaar has to a main street. Most of the bazaar is down to your right in the maze of tiny streets and alleys, though you will want to take a left turn up the steps and into into the **Kürkçüler Çarşısı**, Bazaar of the Furriers.

Street names refer to trades and crafts: Jewellers' St, Pearl-Merchants' St, Fez-Makers' St. Though many trades have died out, moved on or been replaced, there are several areas you should see. The **Sandal Bedesteni** is the municipal auction hall and pawn shop – take a stroll through. **Kuyumcular Sokak**, the second street on the right as you walk along Kalpakçılarbaşı Caddesi, is Jewellers' St, aglitter with tons of gold and gems. The Furriers' Bazaar, mentioned above, now houses shops selling leather clothing and other goods, but it's still an interesting corner of the bazaar.

You should of course have a look in the **Old Bedesten** at the centre of the bazaar, dating from the 1400s. This is sometimes called the Cevahir Bedesteni (Jewellery Warehouse), or Old Bazaar. I'd also recommend explorations into one or more of the *hans* which adjoin the bazaar. A particularly pretty one is the **Zincirli Han**; it's at the far (north) end of Jewellers' St, on the right. By the way, no one will mind if you wander into any of these *hans* for a look around. In fact, you may well be invited to rest your feet, have a glass of tea and exchange a few words.

Don't let the touts get to you. They'll approach you on the main streets and in the tourist-shop areas, but in the bazaar's *hans* and interesting little back streets you won't meet with a single one.

The bazaar has numerous inexpensive little restaurants and cookshops (marked

'lokanta' or 'lok' on the map). If you need a full restaurant there's the Havuzlu Lokantası, but the little places also have very tasty food at rock-bottom prices. See 'Places to Eat' for details on the bazaar's restaurants.

Uzunçarşı Caddesi There is another very interesting route you can follow by starting from within the bazaar. Near the western end of Kalpakçılarbaşı Caddesi, Sipahi Sokak heads north, changes names to become Feraceciler Sokak (Cloakmakers' St), then becomes Yağcılar Caddesi (Oil Merchants' St). You'll see the Şark Kahvesi on your left, then some steps up to a *mescit* (small mosque). Continue straight on, past shops and *han* entrances to Örücüler Kapısı, Gate of the Darners. Cross a main street named Mercan Caddesi (to the left) and Çakmakçılar Yokuşu (to the right), and continue on Uzunçarşı Caddesi.

This, 'Longmarket St', is just what its name says: one long market of wood-turners' shops, clog-makers' cubbyholes, bakeries for *simit* (toasted circular rolls coated with sesame seeds), second-hand clothing merchants and the like. Follow it all the way down the hill and you will end up in the market district in Eminönü, near the **Mısır Çarşısı** (Egyptian Spice Bazaar) and Galata Bridge, and right at the small, exquisite **Rüstem Paşa Camii or Mosque of Rüstem Paşa**. See the section on Eminönü for more information.

Çadırcılar Caddesi The Kapalı Çarşı is surrounded by dozens of little streets also filled with stores and workshops. For your actual purchases, you might do well to escape the bazaar and look for shops with lower rents and thus lower prices. Chief among these, and fascinating in its own right, is Çadırcılar Caddesi, Tentmakers' St. Exit from the bazaar by walking to the west end of Kalpakçılarbaşı Caddesi. Once outside, turn right and you'll be on Çadırcılar.

Old Book Bazaar Just after leaving the bazaar, if you turn right onto Çadırcılar, then left through a doorway, you'll enter the Sahaflar Çarşısı or Old Book Bazaar. Go up the steps and along to the shady little courtyard. Actually, the wares in the shops are both new and old. Of the new, most are in Turkish. Of the old, many are in other languages. It's unlikely that you'll uncover any treasures here, but you can certainly find a curiosity or two.

The book bazaar dates from the Byzantine Empire. Many of the book-sellers are members of a dervish order called the Halveti after its founder, Hazreti Mehmed Nureddin-i Cerrahi-i Halveti. Their *sema* or religious ceremony includes chanting from the Koran, praying, and rhythmic dancing and breathing to the accompaniment of classical Turkish liturgical music. As with all dervish orders, the *sema* is an attempt at close knowledge of and communion with God. The Mevlevi dervishes attempt it by their whirling dance, the Halveti through their circular dance and hyperventilation. But don't expect to wander into a den of mystics. What you'll see are normal Turkish booksellers who just happen to be members of this dervish order.

Out the north gate of the Sahaflar Çarşısı is a pretty tea-garden filled with café tables under colourful umbrellas; university students studying, talking or flirting; and waiters in traditional costume scurrying around carrying trays packed with tiny glasses of fresh tea. It's a good place for a rest. If you want tea, just signal the waiter when you see him with a full tray. For a soft drink, order anytime.

Beyazıt & İstanbul University
The aforementioned tea-garden is right next to the **Beyazıt Camii**, or Mosque of Sultan Beyazıt II (1481-1512). Beyazıt used an exceptional amount of fine stone in his mosque, which he built in 1501-1506

on a plan similar to that for Sancta Sophia, but smaller. It's well worth a look.

The main street here, which started out as Divan Yolu, is now called Yeniçeriler Caddesi. It runs past Beyazıt Square, officially called Hürriyet Meydanı (Freedom Square), though everyone knows it simply as Beyazıt. The plaza is backed by the impressive portal of İstanbul University.

Under the Byzantines, this was the largest of the city's many forums, the **Forum of Theodosius**, built by that emperor in 393. Mehmet the Conqueror built his first palace here, a wooden structure which burnt down centuries ago. After Mehmet built Topkapı he used his wooden palace as a home for aging harem women.

The grand gates, main building and tall tower of the university were originally built as the Ottoman War Ministry, which explains why they are so grandiose and somewhat martial. You used to be allowed up into the tower, which is no doubt still used as a fire lookout post.

The small building at the west side of the square is now a **Calligraphy Museum** (Beyazıt Hat Sanatları Müzesi), open from 9.30 am to 4 pm every day, for 50TL (US$0.07) admission.

Laleli & Aksaray
As you continue west along the main street, now named Ordu Caddesi (Army or 'Horde' Avenue), notice the huge broken marble columns decorated with peacock-tail designs on the left-hand side of the roadway. These were part of the decoration in the Forum of Theodosius. There was a monumental arch here-abouts.

A bit further along, on the right, are more university buildings, and beyond them the hotel district of Laleli. Stay on Ordu Caddesi and you'll soon come to the **Laleli Camii**, an Ottoman baroque mosque built (1759-1763) by Sultan Mustafa III. The ornate baroque architecture houses a sumptuous interior. Underneath it are shops and a plaza with fountain. These were partly to produce rent for the upkeep of the mosque, partly to show off the architect's skill and cunning.

Continue down the hill on Ordu Caddesi and you will enter the confused clamour of Aksaray Square, where there's nothing particularly interesting to see or do. The **Valide Camii** on the square's north-west side is, well, very highly ornamented to say the least. It does not date from any great period of Ottoman architecture, having been built in 1871 by the Valide Sultan Pertevniyal, mother of Sultan Abdülaziz. It used to be attractive, in a way, because it looked like a white wedding cake among the dull, normal structures of Aksaray, but now – with all the exhaust fumes – it's not even white anymore, and traffic flyovers block a good, full view.

Şehzadebaşı & Süleymaniye

The Süleymaniye Camii or Mosque of Sultan Süleyman the Magnificent is İstanbul's largest. A few blocks south-west of it, on the other side of the 4th-century Aqueduct of Valens, is the pretty Şehzade Camii. To the west is the quaint old Municipal Museum. To get to the Süleymaniye from Beyazıt Square, walk around the university. The mosque is directly north of (behind) the university enclosure. Facing the university portal in Beyazıt, go to the left along Takvimhane Caddesi.

The Süleymaniye crowns one of İstanbul's hills, dominating the Golden Horn and providing a magnificent landmark for all of the city. This, the grandest of all Turkish mosques, had to be built between 1550 and 1557 by the greatest, richest, and most powerful of Ottoman sultans, Süleyman I (1520-1566), 'The Magnificent'. The Turks call this sultan Kanuni, 'The Lawgiver', and remember him more for his codification of the empire's laws than for his magnificent style.

Süleyman was a great builder who restored the mighty walls of Jerusalem (an Ottoman city since 1516) and built countless other monuments throughout his empire. He was the patron of Mimar Sinan, Turkey's greatest architect. Though the smaller Selimiye Camii in Edirne is generally counted as Sinan's masterpiece, the Süleymaniye is without doubt his grandest work.

Ottoman imperial mosques were instrumental in repopulating the capital after its conquest. In 1453, much of the city had been abandoned, the Byzantine population had shrunk, and huge areas were vacant or derelict. When a sultan built an imperial mosque, it quickly became the centre of a new quarter. Residences and workshops were soon built nearby.

Each imperial mosque had a *külliye*, or collection of public-service institutions, clustered around it. These might include a hospital, insane asylum, orphanage, soup kitchen, hospice for travellers, religious school, library, baths and a cemetery in which the mosque's imperial patron, his family and other notables could be buried. The *külliye* of the Süleymaniye is particularly elaborate, and includes all of these institutions. Those are the impressive buildings you see surrounding the mosque.

Unfortunately, most visitors enter the mosque precincts by a side door. Though this is the most convenient entrance, coming from Beyazıt, the effect of entering from the north-west side and seeing the four towering minarets and the enormous, billowing domes is better.

Inside, the mosque is breathtaking in its size and pleasing in its simplicity. There is little in the way of decoration, except for some very fine İznik tiles in the *mihrab* (prayer niche), gorgeous stained glass windows done by one İbrahim the Drunkard, and four massive columns, one from Baalbek, one from Alexandria and two from Byzantine palaces in İstanbul. The painted arabesques on the

Süleymaniye Mosque

dome are 19th-century additions, recently renewed.

At the south-east wall of the mosque is the cemetery. Ask for the caretaker (*bekçi*, BEHK-chee) so you can see the tombs (*türbeler*, tewr-beh-LEHR) of Süleyman and his wife Haseki Hürrem Sultan (known in the west as Roxelana), and of his architect, the great Mimar Sinan (MEE-mahr see-NAHN). The tombs are high points of rich, high Ottoman decoration. The İznik tiles in Hürrem's tomb are particularly fine.

Aqueduct of Valens Walk along Süleymaniye Caddesi, which goes south-west from the mosque, and turn right on Kovacılar Caddesi. You can see remnants of the high Aqueduct of Valens (Bozdoğan Kemeri) on the left side of the street. It's not really certain that the aqueduct was

constructed by the emperor Valens (364-378), though we do know it was repaired in 1019, and by several sultans in later times. After the reign of Süleyman the Magnificent, parts of it collapsed.

Şehzade Camii On the south side of the aqueduct is the Şehzade Camii, the Mosque of the Prince. Süleyman had it built in 1544-1548 as a memorial to his son Mehmet, who died in 1543. It was the first important work of Mimar Sinan. Among the many important people buried in tile-encrusted *türbes* here are Prince Mehmet, his brothers and sisters, and Süleyman's Grand Vezirs Rüstem Paşa and İbrahim Paşa.

Municipal Museum If you have a few minutes spare, walk west on Şehzadebaşı Caddesi. The dusty modern building on the left is İstanbul's City Hall, or Belediye Sarayı. Turn right and pass under the aqueduct, then take your life in your hands and cross Atatürk Bulvarı. Just on the other side of the street is the former *medrese* (religious school) of Gazanfer Ağa (1599), now the Belediye Müzesi or Municipal Museum. It has an odd and eclectic assortment of city memorabilia which you might find interesting.

EMİNÖNÜ

No doubt you've already seen Eminönü. The view of the Galata Bridge, crowded with ferries and dominated by the Yeni Cami (YEHN-nee jahm-mee, 'New Mosque'), also called the Pigeon Mosque because of the ever-present flocks of birds, is a favourite for advertisements and magazine articles about İstanbul. The Yeni Cami sits comfortably and serenely in the midst of bustling Eminönü as the traffic, both vehicular and pedestrian, swirls around it. Any visitors to İstanbul find themselves passing through Eminönü time after time.

In a way, Eminönü is the inner city's transportation hub. Not only do the Bosphorus ferries dock here, not only does all Galata Bridge traffic pass through, but Sirkeci railway station is just around the corner.

Galata Bridge

The dusty bridge which has rested here for many decades may not be very impressive at first glance, but it was once a true microcosm of İstanbul, full of little unexpected surprises. As of this writing the old bridge is being taken away and a new, modern bridge is being constructed. The old bridge will be preserved in the park near Seraglio Point.

Though the new bridge will be stationary, the old bridge floated on pontoons. This was so that the central section could be removed to allow larger ships to enter the Golden Horn and reach its shipyards. The central section, unlatched and driven by small motors, was floated out and to the side each morning at 4.30 am. For a half-hour ships steamed out, then for another half-hour ships steamed in. At 5.30 the central section was floated back into place.

Underneath the bridge are small fish restaurants which get their provisions directly from the fishmongers who approach the bridge in boats. Itinerant pedlars sell fishing tackle so you can try your luck in the murky waters. There's even a teahouse where you can get tea, Turkish coffee, soft drinks or a bubbling *nargile* (NAHR-gee-leh, waterpipe).

In Byzantine times the Golden Horn provided a perfect natural harbour for the city's commerce. Suppliers of fresh vegetables and fruits, grain and staple goods set up shop in the harbour. Today their successors still perform the same services, in the same place: west of the Galata Bridge in Eminönü are İstanbul's Haller (hahl-LEHR, from the French *halle*) – wholesale vegetable, fruit and fish markets.

Even more picturesque and interesting is the retail market district which surrounds the Mısır Çarşısı (MUH-suhr chahr-shuh-suh, the Egyptian or Spice Bazaar). But before wandering into the maze of market streets, take a look inside the Mosque of the Valide Sultan (1663), the Yeni Cami.

Yeni Cami

This imperial mosque was begun in 1597, commissioned by Valide Sultan Safiye, the Queen Mother (of Sultan Mehmet III, 1595-1603). The site was earlier occupied by a community of Karaite Jews, radical dissenters from orthodox Judaism. When the Valide Sultan decided to build her grand mosque here, the community was moved to Hasköy, a district further up the Golden Horn which still bears traces of the Karaite presence.

The Valide Sultan lost her august position when her son the sultan died, and the mosque had to be completed (1663) six sultans later by Valide Sultan Turhan Hatice, mother of Sultan Mehmet IV (1648-1687).

In plan, the Yeni Cami is much like the Sultan Ahmet (Blue) mosque and the Süleymaniye, with a large forecourt and a square sanctuary surmounted by a series of half-domes crowned by a grand dome. The interior is richly decorated with gold, coloured tiles and carved marble. The mosque and its tiles are 'late', past the period when Ottoman architecture was at its peak. The tilemakers of İznik were turning out slightly inferior products by the late 1600s. Compare these tiles to the ones in the Rüstem Paşa Camii (described below), which are from the high period of İznik tilework.

Mısır Çarşısı (Egyptian Bazaar)

A century or two ago, this fascinating place was twice as fascinating. Its merchants sold such things as cinnamon, gunpowder, rabbit fat, pine gum, peach pit powder, sesame seeds, sarsaparilla root, aloe, saffron, licorice root, donkey's milk and parsley seeds, all to be used as folk remedies.

Gunpowder, for instance, was prescribed as a remedy for haemorrhoids: you'd boil a little gunpowder with the juice of a whole lemon, strain off the liquid, dry the powder and swallow it the next morning with a little water, on an empty stomach. It was also supposed to be a good cure for pimples when mixed with a little crushed garlic. Whatever its values as a pharmaceutical, it was finally banned from the market because the shops in which it was sold kept blowing up.

The market was constructed in the 1660s as part of the Yeni Cami complex, the rents from the shops going to support upkeep of the mosque and its charitable activities. These included a school, baths, hospital and public fountains.

Enter the market through the big armoured doors which open onto Eminönü square; they're open every day but Sunday. Just inside the doors, to the left, is the little stairway which leads up to the Pandeli restaurant (see the Places to Eat section). Strolling through the market, you can still see numerous shops which sell *baharat* (bah-hah-RAHT, spices), and even a few which specialise in the old-time remedies. Some of the hottest items are bee pollen and royal jelly, used to restore virility. You'll also see shops selling nuts, candied fruits, chocolate and other snacks. Try some figs (*incir*, een-JEER) or Turkish Delight (*lokum* low-KOOM). Fruit pressed into sheets and dried (looks like leather) is called *pestil* (pehs-TEEL); often made from apricots (*kayısı*) or mulberries (*dut*), it's delicious and relatively cheap. Buy 50 grams (*elli gram*) or 100 grams (*yüz gram*) to start.

When you come to the crossroads within the market, you have a choice. I'd suggest you turn left, see the rest of the market, then return to the crossroads and take the street to the right.

Turning left will reveal the rest of the market. Many of the shops on this street no longer sell spices or baskets, but instead are packed with toys, clothing and various household goods. You may see a shop which specialises in the white outfits little boys wear on the day of their circumcision (*sünnet*). The white suit is supplemented with a pillbox hat and a red sash which bears the word *Maşallah* (MAH-shah-lah, 'What wonders God has willed!'). When you see a little kid in such an outfit, you'll know that today he's going to get his. He will probably be riding around in the midst of musicians and merrymakers, for a boy's circumcision (at age eight to 10 or so) is his coming of age and an excellent excuse for a tremendous party.

Turn left again at the first opportunity, and you'll leave the bazaar and enter its busy courtyard, backed by the Yeni Cami. This is the city's major market for flowers, plants, seeds and songbirds.

There's a WC to your left, down the stairs (fee: 20TL, US$0.03). To the right, across the courtyard, is the **tomb** *(türbe)* of Valide Sultan Turhan Hatice, founder of the Yeni Cami. Buried with her are no fewer than six sultans, including her son Mehmet IV, plus dozens of imperial princes and princesses.

Now, back at that crossroads within the bazaar, take the right turning and exit through another set of armoured doors. Just outside the doors is another crossroads of bustling market streets. You can always smell coffee here, because right across the intersection is the shop of Kurukahveci Mehmet Efendi. Clerks wrap customer's parcels with lightning speed (they take great pride in this), and there always seems to be a line waiting to make a purchase. To the right, down toward the Golden Horn, is a small fish market with a few butchers' shops thrown in for good measure. Up to the left, the shops and street pedlars sell mostly household and kitchen items.

Head out the bazaar doors and straight across the intersection. This is **Hasırcılar Caddesi**, Street of the Mat Makers. Shops along it sell fresh fruits, spices, nuts, condiments, knives and other cutlery, coffee, tea, cocoa, hardware and similar retail necessities. The colours,

smells, sights and sounds make this one of the liveliest and most interesting streets in the city.

A few short blocks along Hasırcılar Caddesi, on the right-hand side, you'll come to the **Rüstem Paşa Camii**. Keep your eyes peeled – it's easy to miss as it is not at street level. All you'll see is a tidy stone doorway and a flight of steps leading up; there is also a small marble fountain and plaque. This mosque is used heavily by the merchants and artisans of the bazaar. As with most mosques, you should not visit during prayer-time, so if the müezzin has just given the call to prayer, come back in half an hour.

At the top of the steps is an open space, and the mosque's colonnaded porch.

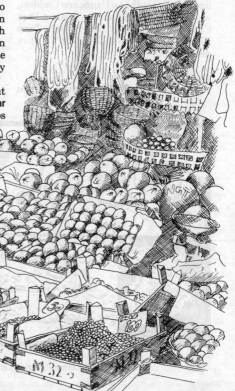

You'll notice at once the panels of dazzling İznik faience set into the mosque's facade. The interior is covered in similarly gorgeous tiles, so take off your shoes (women should also cover heads and shoulders), and venture inside. Particularly beautiful, the mosque was built by Sinan, the greatest Ottoman architect, for Rüstem Paşa, son-in-law and Grand Vezir of Süleyman the Magnificent. Ottoman power, glory, architecture and tilework were all at their zenith when the mosque was built (1561). You won't forget this one.

After your visit to the mosque, you might want to spend some more time wandering the streets of this fascinating market quarter. If you need a goal, head up the hill (south) on Uzunçarşı Caddesi, which begins right near the Rüstem Paşa Camii and ends at the Kapalı Çarşı (Grand Bazaar; see that section for more details).

The Outer City

From early times the heart of this ancient city has been near the tip of Seraglio Point. As the city grew over the centuries, its boundaries moved westward. That process continues.

There are several impressive points of interest farther out, and if you have at least four days to tour the city you should be able to see all the centre's essential sights and still have time for these. They include the mosque of Mehmet the Conqueror, the Kariye Camii (Church of the Holy Saviour in Chora) famous for its Byzantine mosaics, the Palace of Constantine Porphyrogenetus (Tekfur Saray), several other mosques, the mammoth City Walls, the Fortress of the Seven Towers and the village of Eyüp, up the Golden Horn. On your way back downtown, you can stop at the Ecumenical Orthodox Patriarchate and also at a curious Bulgarian church made of cast iron.

A detour to Yedikule, The Fortress of the Seven Towers, is described at the end of this section.

Murakka (17th Century), Turkish & Islamic Arts Museum, İstanbul

Fatih Camii The Mosque of the Conqueror or Fatih Camii is just west of the Aqueduct of Valens, on Fevzi Paşa Caddesi. You can get a dolmuş from Aksaray or Taksim to the City Hall near the Aqueduct (ask for the Belediye Sarayı behl-eh-DEE-yeh sar-rah-yuh) and walk five blocks; or you can catch any bus that has 'Fatih' or 'Edirnekapı' listed on its itinerary board. Buses and trolleybuses going to Edirnekapı pass frequently through Sultanahmet Square.

When Mehmet the Conqueror entered Constantinople in 1453, he found a once-great city depopulated and shrunken in size within the walls. Large tracts of urban land had reverted to grass and shrubs, and many buildings were in ruins. He sought to repopulate the city with groups from the various nations of his empire, sometimes commanding that they move to İstanbul. A prime method of repopulating a district was to commission the construction of an imperial mosque there. The mosque would become the nucleus of a city quarter, first providing work for construction crews and the merchants and pedlars who served them, then providing a focus of religious and social life. The mosque's *külliye* or complex of charitable buildings such as a hospital, orphanage, soup kitchen, library, bath, insane asylum, etc, would also encourage people to move to the quarter.

The Mosque of the Conqueror was the first great imperial mosque to be built in İstanbul following the conquest. For its location, Fatih Sultan Mehmet (Mehmet the Conqueror) chose the hilltop site of the ruined Church of the Apostles. The mosque complex, finished in 1470, was enormous, and included in its *külliye* 15 charitable establishments – religious schools, a hospice for travellers, a caravanserai, etc. But the mosque you see is not the one he built. The original mosque stood for 300 years before toppling in an earthquake (1766). It was rebuilt, but to a completely different plan. The exterior of the mosque still bears some of the original decoration; the interior is not all that impressive.

While you're here, be sure to visit the *türbe* (tomb) of Mehmet the Conqueror behind the mosque. His wife Gülbahar, whose *türbe* is next to the sultan's, is rumoured to have been a French princess.

When you're finished at the mosque, go back to Fevzi Paşa Caddesi and catch a bus or dolmuş headed north-west toward Edirnekapı. Get off the bus just before the massive city walls. You'll see the **Mihrimah Camii**, a mosque built by Süleyman the Magnificent's favourite daughter, Mihrimah, in the 1560s. The architect was Sinan, and the mosque marks a departure from his usual style. The inevitable earthquakes worked their destruction, and the building has been restored several times, the latest being around 1900. Mihrimah married Rüstem Paşa, Süleyman's brilliant and powerful Grand Vezir (you saw his little tile-covered mosque down by the Mısır Çarşısı). You can visit her tomb, and his too, on the south-east side of the mosque.

Take a look at the **city walls** (you can hardly help it!). You'll get a closer look, and even a climb up top, in a little while.

Cross the road from the Mihrimah Camii and, still inside the walls, head north toward the Golden Horn. You'll see signs, and children pointing the way, to the Kariye Camii.

Kariye Camii Mosaics If we translate the original name for this building, it comes out 'Church of the Holy Saviour Outside the Walls' or 'in the Country', because the original church on this site was indeed outside the walls built by Constantine the Great. But just as London's Church of St Martin-in-the-Fields is hardly surrounded by bucolic scenery these days, the Church of the Holy Saviour was soon engulfed by Byzantine urban sprawl. It was enclosed within the walls built by the Emperor Theodosius II in 413, less than 100 years after Constantine. So the Holy Saviour-in-the-Country has been 'in the country' for about 80 years, and 'in the city' for 1550 years. The evolution of the church has not ended with its whereabouts: for four centuries it served as a mosque, coming to rest as a museum.

The building you see is not the original church-outside-the-walls. Rather, this one was built in the late 1000s, with lots of repairs and restructuring in the following centuries. Virtually all of the interior decoration – the famous mosaics and the less renowned but equally striking mural paintings – dates from about 1320. Between 1948 and 1959 the decoration was carefully restored under the auspices of the Byzantine Society of America.

The mosaics are breathtaking. There is a definite order to the arrangement of the pictures. The first ones are those of the dedication, to Christ and to the Virgin Mary. Then come the offertory ones: Theodore Metochites, builder of the church, offering it to Christ. The two small domes of the Inner Narthex have portraits of all Christ's ancestors back to Adam. A series outlines the Virgin Mary's

life, and another Christ's early years. Yet another series concentrates on Christ's ministry. There are lots of saints and martyrs everywhere.

In the nave are three mosaics: of Christ, of the Virgin as Teacher, and of the Dormition of the Virgin (turn around to see this one – it's over the main door you just entered). By the way, the baby in the painting is actually Mary's soul, being held by Jesus, while her body lies 'asleep' on its bier.

South of the nave is the Pareeclesion, a side chapel also used for the tombs of the church's founder and his relatives, close friends and associates. The frescoes, appropriately, deal with the theme of death and resurrection. The striking painting in the apse shows Christ

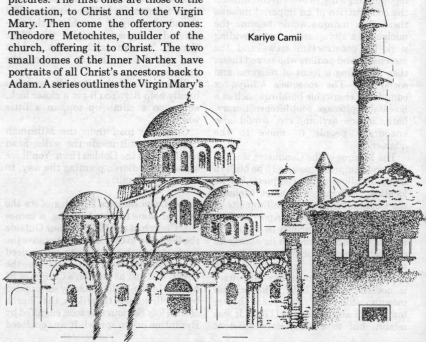

Kariye Camii

Top: Village family in Karatay
Left: Istanbul craftsman at work on a coffee pot
Right: Entry-way niche in Avanos

Top: Cotton pickers near Side
Left: Back streets of Antalya
Right: A Çayci (tea waiter) in his filigree vest

breaking down the gates of hell and raising Adam and Eve, with saints and kings in attendance.

Kariye Muhallebicisi Just across from the Kariye Museum is the Kariye Muhallebicisi or pudding shop, an old İstanbul structure restored, along with other buildings in the neighbourhood, by the Turkish Touring & Automobile Club. *Muhallebi* is a bland rose-water jelly served alone as a sweet. You can have some here, or another sweet or beverage, on the patio or on the ground floor. The upper floor has been arranged as a traditional Ottoman salon.

Tekfur Saray From Kariye, head west to the city walls, then north again, and you'll soon come to the Palace of Constantine Porphyrogenetus, the Tekfur Saray (tehk-FOOR sar-rah-yee). Though the building is only a shell these days, it is remarkably preserved for a Byzantine palace built in the 1300s. Sacred buildings often survive the ravages of time because they continue to be used, even though they may be converted for use in another religion. But secular buildings are often torn down and used as quarries for building materials once their owners die. The Byzantine palaces which once crowded Sultanahmet Square are all gone; so is the great Palace of Blachernae, which adjoined the Tekfur Saray. Only this one remains.

The caretaker will usually haul out a ladder for you, and you can climb up onto the walls for a view of the palace, the walls and the entire city. A small tip (250TL, US$0.35) is proper once you descend.

The City Walls Since being built in the 400s, the city walls have been breached by hostile forces only twice. The first time was in the 1200s, when Byzantium's 'allies', the armies of the Fourth Crusade, broke through and pillaged the town, deposing the emperor and setting up a king of their own. The second time was in

1453 under Mehmet the Conqueror. Even though Mehmet was ultimately successful, he was continually frustrated during the siege as the walls withstood admirably even the heaviest bombardments by the largest cannon in existence at the time. The walls were kept defensible and in good repair until about a century ago, when the development of mighty naval guns made such expense pointless: if İstanbul was going to fall, it would fall to ships firing from the Bosphorus, not to soldiers advancing on the land walls.

For a look at the most spectacular of the defenses in the walls, see Yedikule (Fortress of the Seven Towers), below.

By now you've seen the high points in this part of the city. If you've still got time and stamina, take your bearings for these places while you're still up on the walls: outside the walls, on the Golden Horn (which looks anything but golden from this vantage point), is the suburb of Eyüp, with a famous mosque and coffeehouse. Inside the walls, near the Golden Horn but back toward the centre, is the Rum Patrikhanesi, the seat of the Ecumenical Patriarch of the Orthodox Church. You can't see it, but you'll notice the prominent cupola of a Greek school near it.

Eyüp This suburb, once a village outside the walls, is named for the standard-bearer of the Prophet Muhammad. Eyüp Ensari (Ayoub in Arabic, Job in English) fell in battle here while carrying the banner of Islam during the Arab assault and siege of the city in 674-678. Eyüp had been a friend of the Prophet and a revered member of Islam's early leadership. His tomb and the **Eyüp Sultan Camii** are very sacred places for most Muslims, almost on a rank with Mecca, Medina and Jerusalem. Ironically, the tomb even came to be venerated by the Byzantines after the Arab armies withdrew.

When Mehmet the Conqueror besieged the city in 1453, the tomb was no doubt known to him, and he undertook to build a grander and more fitting structure to commemorate it. But a legend persists that the tomb had been lost, and was miraculously rediscovered by Mehmet's Şeyh-ül-İslam (Supreme Islamic Judge). Perhaps both are true. If the tomb was known to Mehmet Fatih and his leadership, but not generally known by the common soldiers, it could be used for inspiration: have it miraculously 'rediscovered', and the army would take it as a good omen for the holy war in which they were engaged.

Whatever the truth, the tomb has been a very holy place ever since the Conquest. Mehmet had a mosque built here within five years after the Conquest, and succeeding sultans came to it to be girded with the Sword of Osman, a coronation-like ceremony signifying their supremacy. It was levelled by an earthquake in 1766, and a new mosque was built on the site by Sultan Selim III in 1800. The baroque style of the pretty mosque, the tiles, marble, calligraphy and other decoration lavished on it, make this a fine place to see. Be careful to observe the Islamic proprieties when visiting: decent clothing (no shorts), and modest dresses for women, who should also have head, shoulders and arms covered.

As the Eyüp Sultan Camii is such a sacred place, many important people wanted to be buried in its precincts. Many others, particularly the Valide Sultan Mihrişah, mother of Selim III, built important charitable institutions such as schools, baths and soup kitchens.

Pierre Loti Café Up the hill to the north of the mosque is a café where 'Pierre Loti' (Louis Marie Julien Viaud, 1850-1923) used to sit and admire the city. Loti pursued a distinguished career in the French navy, and at the same time became his country's most celebrated novelist. Though a hard-headed mariner, he was also an inspired and incurable romantic who fell in love with the graceful and mysterious way of life he discovered in Ottoman İstanbul. Loti set up housekeeping in Eyüp for several years and had a love affair, fraught with peril, with a married Turkish woman whom he called Aziyadé, the title of his most romantic and successful novel. He was transferred back to France, and forced to leave his mistress and his beloved İstanbul, but he decorated his French home in Ottoman style and begged Aziyadé to flee and join him. Instead, her infidelity was discovered and she 'disappeared'.

Loti's romantic novels about the daily life of İstanbul under the last sultans introduced millions of European readers to Turkish customs and habits, and helped to counteract the politically inspired Turkophobia then spreading through Europe.

Loti loved the city, the decadent grandeur of the empire, and the fascinating late-medieval customs of a society in decline. When he sat in this café, under a shady grapevine, sipping some çay or Turkish coffee, he saw a Golden Horn busy with caiques, schooners and a few steam vessels. The water in the Golden Horn was still clean enough for boys to swim in, and the vicinity of the café was all pastureland. Not only that, but the café owner would have charged him the going rate for his refreshment.

Today it's all different: you pay many times the going rate for a drink, the Golden Horn is not fit to swim in, and buildings crowd the once-bucolic café. Still, there is the view. Loti fans will want to come here; others may enjoy the view, but not stay for tea. If you do stay, by all means find out the price of a drink before you sit down and order.

Back to the Centre

There is still ferry service on the Golden Horn, and it will take you from the dock at Eyüp Sultan, not far from the mosque, down to the Galata Bridge at Eminönü. You'll pass shipyards, warehouses, rundown residential and industrial quarters, a government drydock, naval buildings and the cast-iron Bulgarian church. Boats are not frequent, however, and you may instead find yourself going by bus or taxi.

You can get a bus or dolmuş from Eyüp along the shore of the Golden Horn or up along the walls and into the city that way. Taking the shore road allows you to stop at the Orthodox Patriarchate, the Mosque of Sultan Selim and the Bulgarian church, all very interesting sights.

The neighbourhoods along the Golden Horn are picturesque, though pretty run-down; they're not dangerous, just dilapidated.

Balat

The quarter called Balat used to hold a large portion of the city's Jewish population. Spanish Jews driven from their country by the judges of the Spanish Inquisition found refuge in the Ottoman Empire in the late 1400s and early 1500s. As the sultan recognized, they were a boon to his empire: they brought news of the latest western advances in medicine, clock-making, ballistics and other means of warfare. The refugees from the Inquisition set up the first printing presses in Turkey, almost 500 years ago. Like all other religious 'nations' within the empire, they were under a supreme religious leader, the Chief Rabbi, who oversaw their adherence to Biblical law and who was responsible to the sultan for their good conduct.

Though you can still find a few traces of Jewish life in this quarter, such as inscriptions in Hebrew over doorways, most of the city's Jewish residents have long since moved to more attractive quarters or emigrated to Europe or Israel. There is still a newspaper published in Ladino Spanish, the language brought by the immigrants in Renaissance times and preserved here in İstanbul.

Church of St Stephen

The Church of St Stephen of the Bulgars, between Balat and Fener on the Golden Horn, is made completely of cast iron. The building is unusual, and its history even more so.

During the 19th century the spirit of ethnic nationalism swept through the Ottoman Empire. Each of the many ethnic groups in the Ottoman Empire wanted to rule its own affairs. Groups identified themselves on the bases of language, religion and racial heritage. This sometimes led to problems, as with the Bulgarians.

The Bulgars, originally a Turkic-speaking people, came from the Volga in about 680 AD and overwhelmed the Slavic peoples living in what is today Bulgaria. They adopted the Slavic language and customs, and founded an empire which threatened the power of Byzantium. In the 800s they were converted to Christianity.

The head of the Orthodox church in the Ottoman Empire was an ethnic Greek; in order to retain as much power as possible, the patriarch was opposed to any ethnic divisions within the Orthodox church. He put pressure on the sultan not to allow the Bulgarians, Macedonians and Rumanians to establish their own groups.

The pressures of nationalism became too great, and the sultan was finally forced to recognize some sort of autonomy for the Bulgars. What he did was establish not a Bulgarian patriarchate, but an 'exarchate'. The Bulgarian Exarch would be 'less important' than, but independent of, the Greek Orthodox patriarch. In this way the Bulgarians would get their desired ethnic recognition, and would get out from under the dominance of the Greeks.

St Stephen's is the Bulgarian Exarch's church; the former exarchate head-quarters is directly across the street, and is still the office of St Stephen's clergy. The Gothic church was cast in Vienna, shipped down the Danube on 100 barges, and assembled here in 1871. A duplicate church, erected in Vienna, was destroyed by aerial bombing during WW II. The Viennese cast-iron church factory produced no other products, so far as we know.

A number of years ago St Stephen's was repaired and repainted. The first coat, of course, was metal primer. The whole procedure seemed to fit in well, what with a shipyard on the opposite shore of the Golden Horn.

The priest or sacristan will let you into the church enclosure so you can enjoy the pretty garden, tap a coin on the church wall to verify that it's metal, and admire the interior. Most of the interior decoration is of cast iron as well. The priest or sacristan will expect a tip.

Fener

Next quarter along the Golden Horn is Fener (fehn-EHR, Phanari in Greek: lantern or lighthouse), where the Ecumenical Patriarch has his seat. To find the Patriarchate (Patrikhane, paht-TREEK-hah-neh), you'll have to head inland from the Fener ferry dock on the Golden Horn, and ask. People will point the way.

Ecumenical Patriarchate The Ecumenical Patriarch is a ceremonial head of the Orthodox churches, though most of the churches – in Greece, Cyprus, the Soviet Union and other countries – have their own patriarchs or archbishops who are independent of İstanbul. Nevertheless, the 'sentimental' importance of the patriarchate, here in the city which saw the great era of Byzantine and Orthodox influence, is very great.

These days the patriarch is a Turkish citizen. He is nominated by the church and appointed by the Turkish government to be an official in the Directorate of Religious Affairs. In this capacity he is the religious leader of the country's Orthodox citizens.

Assuming you don't have any business with the patriarchate, your reason for visiting is to look at the **Church of St George**, within the patriarchate compound. Like the rest of the buildings here, it is a modest place, built in 1720. The ornate patriarchal throne may date from the last years of Byzantium. The patriarchate itself has been in this spot since about 1600. In 1941 a disastrous fire destroyed many of the buildings, but spared the church.

Selimiye Camii

Only a few blocks south-east of the patriarchate is the mosque of Yavuz Selim (Sultan Selim I, 1512-1520), on a hilltop overlooking the Golden Horn. Sultan Selim 'the Grim' laid the foundations of Ottoman greatness for his son and successor, Süleyman the Magnificent. Though he ruled for a very short time, Selim virtually doubled the empire's territory, solidified its institutions and filled its treasury. He came to power by deposing his father, Beyazit II (1481-1512), who died 'mysteriously' soon thereafter. To avoid any threat to his power, and thus the sort of disastrous civil war which had torn the empire apart in the days before Mehmet the Conqueror, Selim had all his brothers put to death, and in the eight years of his reign he had eight Grand Vezirs beheaded. So 'Grim' is indeed the word.

But all of this force was in the interests of empire-building, at which he was a master. He doubled the empire's extent during his short reign, conquering part of Persia, and all of Syria and Egypt. He took from Egypt's decadent, defeated Abbasid rulers the title Caliph of Islam, which was borne by his successors until 1924. In his spare time he liked to write poetry in Persian, the literary language of the time. When he died, the empire was well on the way to becoming the most powerful and brilliant in the world.

The mosque was built mostly during the reign of Selim's son Süleyman. It is especially pretty, with lots of fine, very early İznik tiles (the yellow colour is a clue to their 'earliness') and a shallow dome similar to that of Sancta Sophia. Selim's *türbe* behind the mosque is also very fine. Among the others buried nearby are several children of Süleyman the Magnificent; and Sultan Abdül Mecit (1839-1861).

To the Galata Bridge

You can walk back down the hill to the Fener ferryboat dock and catch a ferry down to the bridge. They aren't all that frequent, so check the schedule first. Otherwise, catch a bus or dolmuş along the waterfront street, Abdülezel Paşa Caddesi.

Yedikule

The Fortress of the Seven Towers (Yedikule) is a long way from most other sights of interest in İstanbul, and involves a special trip. Situated where the great city walls meet the Sea of Marmara, it's accessible by city bus ('Yedikule') from Eminönü, Sultanahmet and Divan Yolu. The ride takes almost a half-hour. If you arrived in İstanbul by train from Europe, or if you rode in from the airport along the seashore, you've already had a glance of Yedikule towering over the southern approaches to the city.

Theodosius I built a triumphal arch here in the late 300s. When the next Theodosius (408-450) built his great land walls, he incorporated the arch. Four of the fortress's seven towers were built as part of the Emperor Theodosius's walls; the other three, inside the walls, were added by Mehmet the Conqueror. Under the Byzantines, the triumphal arch became known as the **Golden Gate**, and was used for triumphal state processions into and out of the city. For a time, its gates were indeed plated with gold. The doorway was sealed in the late Byzantine period.

In Ottoman times the fortress was used for defense, as a repository for the imperial treasury, as a prison and as a

place of execution. Diplomatic practice in Renaissance times included chucking into loathsome prisons the ambassadors of countries with which yours didn't get along. For foreign ambassadors to the Sublime Porte, Yedikule was that prison. It was also here that Sultan Osman II, a 17-year-old youth, was executed in 1622 during a revolt of the Janissary corps.

The best view of the city walls and of the fortress is from the **Tower of Sultan Ahmet III**, near the gate in the city wall.

Beyond the fortress are the city's leather-tanning industries. Even in medieval times, the tanners were required to work outside the city walls because their work generated such terrible odours.

Right down at the shoreline, where the land walls meet the Sea of Marmara, is the **Marble Tower**, once part of a small Byzantine imperial seaside villa.

BEYOĞLU

Beyoğlu (BEY-oh-loo) is fascinating because it holds the evidence of the Ottoman Empire's frantic attempts to modernize and reform itself, and the evidence of the European powers' attempts to undermine and subvert it. The Ottomans were struggling for their very existence as a state; the Europeans were struggling for domination of the entire Middle East, and especially its oil (already important at that time), holy places and sea lanes through the Suez Canal to India.

New ideas walked into Ottoman daily life down the streets of Pera (which with Galata comprises Beyoğlu). Europeans brought new fashions, machines, arts and manners, and rules for the diplomatic game, and the Europeans lived in Pera. The Old City across the Golden Horn was content to sit tight and continue living in the Middle Ages with its oriental bazaars, great mosques and palaces, narrow streets and traditional values. But Pera was to have telephones, underground trains, tramways, electric light and

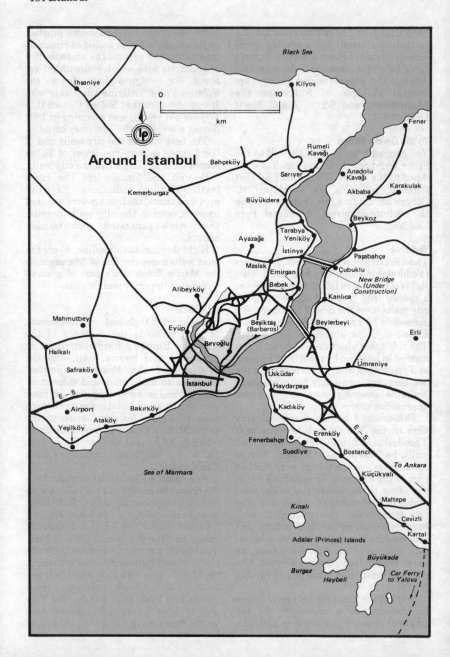

Around İstanbul

modern municipal government. Even the sultans got into the act. From the reign of Abdülmecit (1839-1861) onward, no sultan lived in Mehmet the Conqueror's palace at Topkapı. Rather, they built opulent European-style palaces in Pera and along the shores of the Bosphorus to the north.

The easiest way to tour Beyoğlu is to start from its busy nerve-center: Taksim Square. You can get a dolmuş directly to Taksim from Aksaray or Sirkeci; buses to Taksim are even more plentiful.

History

Often called the New City, Beyoğlu is 'new' just in a relative sense. There was a settlement on the northern shore of the Golden Horn, near Karaköy Square, before the birth of Jesus. By the time of Theodosius II (408-450), it was large enough to become an official suburb of Constantinople. Theodosius built a fortress here, no doubt to complete the defense system of his great land walls, and called it Galata (gah-LAH-tah), as the suburb was then the home of many Galatians. (The Galatians, by the way, were Gauls who invaded Asia Minor from the west after 300 BC, and settled near Ankara.) During the height of the Byzantine Empire Galata became a favourite place for foreign trading companies to set up business. To this day, it still harbours the offices of many non-Muslim businesspeople and foreign representatives.

The word 'new' actually applies more to Pera, the quarter above Galata, running along the crest of the hill from the Galata Tower to Taksim Square. This was built up only in later Ottoman times. Together, Galata and Pera make up Beyoğlu.

In the 19th century, the European powers were waiting eagerly for the 'Sick Man of Europe' (the decadent Ottoman Empire) to collapse so that they could grab territory and spheres of influence. All the great colonial powers – the British, Russian, Austro-Hungarian and German empires, France and the kingdom of Italy – maintained lavish embassies and tried to cajole and pressure the Sublime Porte into concessions of territory, trade and influence. The embassy buildings, lavish as ever, still stand in Pera. Ironically, most of the great empires which built them collapsed along with that of the Ottomans. Only the British and French survived to grab any of the spoils. Their occupation of Middle Eastern countries under League of Nations 'mandates' has given us the Middle East we have today.

Taksim Square

The name could mean 'my taxi' in Turkish, but it doesn't; after a look at the square, you may wonder why not. Rather, it is named after the *taksim* (tahk-SEEM), or distribution point, in the city's water-conduit system. The main water line from the Belgrade Forest, north of the city, was laid to this point by Sultan Mahmut I (1730-1754) in 1732, and the branch lines lead from the *taksim* to all parts of the city. You'll get a glance at the *taksim* in a moment.

First thing you'll notice in the elongated 'square' is the **Atatürk Cultural Palace (Atatürk Kültür Sarayı)**, sometimes called the Opera House, the large building at the eastern end. In the summertime, during the İstanbul International Festival, tickets for the various concerts are on sale in the ticket kiosks here, and numerous performances are staged in its various halls.

The grassy mall stretching from the Cultural Palace to the traffic circle holds a knife-shaped **monument** to war veterans. To the south is the luxury Etap Marmara Hotel. To the north is the **Taksim Gezi Yeri or promenade**, with the İstanbul Sheraton at the northern end of it.

In the midst of the roundabout, swirling with traffic, is the **Cumhuriyet ve İstiklal Abidesi, Monument to the Republic & Independence**, one of the earliest monuments erected during the time of the Republic. It was done by an Italian sculptor in 1928. Atatürk, his assistant and successor İsmet İnönü and other revolutionary leaders are prominent.

From the roundabout, Cumhuriyet Caddesi (Republic Avenue) leads north past several sidewalk cafés and restaurants, banks, travel agencies, airline offices, nightclubs and the İstanbul Hilton Hotel to the districts called Harbiye and Şişli.

Askeri Müzesi (Military Museum)

A km north of Taksim is the Askeri Müzesi or Military Museum. The small museum, with its exhibits of Ottoman battle dress and relics, is interesting enough. But the best reason to go is for a little concert by the Mehter, or Ottoman military band. The Mehter, according to historians, was the first true military band in the world. Its purpose was not to make pretty music for dancing, but to precede the conquering Ottoman *pashas* into vanquished towns, impressing upon the defeated populace that everything was going to be different now. They would march in with a steady, measured pace, turning all together to face the left side of the line of march, then the right side. With tall Janissary headdresses, fierce moustaches, brilliant instruments and even kettledrums, they did their job admirably.

The museum is open from 9 am to 5 pm, closed Monday and Tuesday. The Mehter performs each afternoon that the museum is open (if the band is not on tour somewhere) at 3 pm. Check this time at a Tourism Information Office to be sure; there's an office in the İstanbul Hilton Hotel arcade, on the way to the Military Museum.

To reach the museum, walk north out of Taksim Square along Cumhuriyet Caddesi and past the Hilton entrance. Just past the Hilton on the right side of Cumhuriyet are the studios of TRT, the Turkish Radio & Television corporation, in a building called **Radyo Evi (Radio House)**. Just past

Radyo Evi, turn right. The road curves to the left and passes the **Spor ve Sergi Sarayı (Sports & Exhibition Hall)**; the Askeri Müzesi is next, on the left-hand side.

South of Taksim

To the south, two streets meet just before the roundabout. Sıraselviler Caddesi goes south and İstiklal Caddesi goes south-west. The famous **taksim** is to the south-west of the roundabout, just to the right of İstiklal Caddesi. It is a little octagonal building of stone. You'll also notice a wall with fountains and a pool, a little public celebration of the city's water system.

Nestled in the small triangle formed by the two mentioned streets, rising above the shops and restaurants which hide its foundations, is the Aya Triada Kilisesi, the Greek Orthodox **Church of the Holy Trinity**. If it's open, as it is often during the day, you can visit: take either street out of Taksim Square, and look for the first possibility to turn toward the church.

Now head down İstiklal Caddesi for a look at the vestiges of 19th-century Ottoman life.

İstiklal Caddesi

Stretching between Taksim and Tünel squares, İstiklal Caddesi (ees-teek-LAHL, Independence Avenue) was once known as the Grand Rue de Pera. It was the street with all the smart shops, several large embassies and churches, many impressive office buildings and a scattering of tea shops and restaurants. Some vignettes of this glory still survive, though İstiklal is now heavy with traffic and its buildings are cracked and dusty. The smart shops and classy offices have mostly moved farther north. As you stroll along İstiklal, try to imagine it during its heyday a century ago: frock-coated merchants and Ottoman officials, European officers in colourful uniforms, women with parasols, and even some lightly-veiled Turkish women.

Just out of Taksim Square, the first

building you'll come to on your right is the former French plague hospital (1719), for years used as the **French Consulate-General** in İstanbul. There's a **French library** here as well.

İstiklal Caddesi is packed with little restaurants and snack shops, bank branches, clothing stores, itinerant pedlars, shoppers and strollers. If you have the time, take a few detours down the narrow side streets. Any one will reveal glimpses of Beyoğlu life. The street names alone are fascinating: Büyükparmakkapı Sokak, 'The Street of the Gate of the Thumb'; Sakızağacı Sokak, 'The Street of the Pine-Gum Tree'; Kuloğlu Sokak, 'The Street of the Slave's Son'.

This used to be the cinema centre of İstanbul. With the advent of television, the cinemas found it necessary to appeal to baser appetites, which is what many of them do now. Baser appetites are also satisfied by going up some of the stairways which lead from the back streets. Though I wouldn't recommend doing a lot of wandering along narrow, dark streets here late at night, the area is perfectly safe during the day and early evening.

A few streets before coming to Galatasaray Square, look on the left for Suterazisi Sokak. Turn into this street, and at its end you'll find the **Tarihi Galatasaray Hamami or Historical Galatasaray Turkish Bath**. The bath is one of the city's best, with lots of marble decoration, comfy little cubicles for resting and sipping tea after the bath, pretty fountains and even shoeshine service. However, the staff is very hungry for tips. If you go, you'll enjoy it more if you don't go alone; best of all, go with a Turkish friend. The women's part of the bath, by the way, is not nearly so elegant as the men's.

Galatasaray Square Halfway along the length of İstiklal Caddesi is Galatasaray (gahl-AH-tah-sah-rah-yee), named for the imperial lycee you can see behind the huge gates on your left. This is the country's most prestigious school, established in its present form by Sultan Abdül Aziz in 1868, who wanted a place where Ottoman youth could hear lectures in both Turkish and French. Across İstiklal from the school is a branch of the PTT (post office).

Çiçek Pasajı Before coming into the square, you'll notice on your right a small street with some flower-sellers' stalls. This is İstanbul's renowned Çiçek Pasajı (chee-CHEHK pah-sah-zhuh), or 'Flower Passage'. Besides the flowers, there is a charming market called the Balık Pazar, literally the 'fish market', although meats, fruits, vegetables, condiments and kitchen items are sold as well. You can do a lot of interesting exploring here.

Turn right from İstiklal into the flower-lined street, and then right again into a courtyard. On the lintel of the doorway into the courtyard you can see the legend 'Cite de Pera', for this was at one time the municipal headquarters of the 'modern' European-style city. The building has been recently restored. For years the courtyard has held a dozen little restaurant-taverns. In good weather beer barrels are rolled out onto the pavement, marble slabs are balanced on top, little stools are put around, and they are filled with enthusiastic revellers as soon as they hit the ground. This place is lively and interesting any time of day, but particularly in the early evening.

Pick a good place, pull up a stool and order a mug of *bira: beyaz* (bey-AHZ) is lager, *siyah* (see-YAH) is dark beer. For something stronger, say *Bir kadeh rakı* (BEER kah-deh rah-KUH), 'A shot of rakı'. As for food, it's delicious and not very expensive. Printed menus, even if you can find them, mean little here. If you already know a few Turkish dishes you like, order them. Otherwise, the waiter will lead you to the kitchen so you can see what's cooking.

During your supper, strolling musicians will come through (you needn't pay unless you want to, or unless you signal to them that you want a song). Other vendors will pass by with assorted delicacies and treats. A small fight may break out, but will be quickly settled. You may be toasted by the entire multitude. At least three nearby revellers will want to know where you come from; when you tell them, the inevitable response is *Çok iyi*, 'Very good!' The Çiçek Pasajı is perhaps the soul of İstanbul, and you shouldn't miss an evening here.

Balık Pazar Walk out of the courtyard to the flower stalls, turn right, then look for a little passage off to the left. This is the Avrupa Pasajı, the 'European Passage', a small gallery with marble paving and little shops selling this and that. In Pera's heyday it was undoubtedly very elegant.

Further up the market street, another little street leads off to the left, down to the British Consulate-General (more of that in a moment). Continuing on the same street, though, just past this junction on your right is the entrance to an **Armenian church**. You can visit if the doors are open; a sacristan will greet you, and will watch to see if you drop a small donation into the box.

Unless you want to continue down the slope among the fishmongers, turn back and then down the little street to the British consulate. You will notice small stands where skewered mussels (*midye*, MEED-yeh) are frying in hot oil, and others where *kokoreç* (koh-koh-RETCH, lamb intestines packed with more lamb intestines) is being grilled over charcoal. I recommend the mussels, but get a skewer that's been freshly cooked, or at least re-cooked.

At the end of the market street you emerge into the light. Right in front of you is Meşrutiyet Caddesi, which makes its way down to the Pera Palas Oteli (see below) and the American Consulate-General. On the corner here are the huge gates to the **British Consulate-General**, an Italian palazzo designed by Sir Charles Barry and built in 1845. Sir Charles did the Houses of Parliament as well.

Walk past the British consulate along Meşrutiyet Caddesi. Watch for an iron gate and a small passage on the left, leading into a little courtyard with a derelict lamp-post in the center. Enter the courtyard, turn right up the stairs, and you'll discover the Greek Orthodox **Church of Panaya Isodyon**. It's quiet and very tidy, hidden away in the midst of other buildings. The doors are open to visitors most of the day.

When you've seen the church, go down the stairs *behind* it (not the stairs you came up). Several little streets here are lined with tiny shops, many bearing their Greek proprietors' names. Turn right, and just past the church property on the right-hand side you will see the entrance to the **Yeni Rejans Lokantası or New Regency Restaurant**. Founded, as legend would have it, by three White Russian dancing girls who fled the Russian Revolution, the restaurant is still operated by their Russian-speaking descendants. This area of Beyoğlu was a favourite with Russian émigrés after the revolution. The Yeni Rejans, by the look of it, was a cabaret complete with orchestra loft and grand piano. Lunch and dinner are still served. The food is good, though you pay a certain amount for the seedy nostalgia.

Out the restaurant door, down the steps, turn right, then left along the narrow alley called Olivo Çikmazı, which brings you back to İstiklal Caddesi.

Back on İstiklal Across İstiklal, notice the large Italian Gothic church behind a fence. The Franciscan **Church of San Antonio di Padua** was founded here in 1725; the brick building dates from 1913.

Cross over to the church, turn right, and head down İstiklal once more. After the church you will pass Eskiçiçekçi Sokak on the left, then Nuriziya Sokak.

The third street, a little cul-de-sac, ends at the gates of the **Palais de France**, once the French embassy to the Ottoman sultan. The grounds of the palais are extensive. The buildings include the chapel of St Louis of the French, founded here in 1581, though the present chapel building dates from the 1830s. You can get a better look at the palais and grounds another way: read on.

A few steps along İstiklal brings you to the pretty **Netherlands Consulate-General** (1855), built by the former architect to the Russian tsar. The first embassy building here dated from 1612.

Past the Dutch consulate, turn left down the hill on Postacılar Sokak. You'll see the **Dutch Chapel** on the left side of the street. If it's open, take a look inside. The chapel is now the home of the Union Church of İstanbul, a multinational Protestant congregation that holds services in English.

The narrow street jogs right, bringing you face-to-face with the former **Spanish embassy**. The little chapel, founded in 1670, is still in use though the embassy is not.

The street then jogs left and changes names to become Tomtom Kaptan Sokak. At the foot of the slope, on the right, is the **Palazzo di Venezia**, once the Venetian embassy, now the Italian consulate. Venice was one of the great Mediterranean maritime powers during Renaissance times, and when Venetian and Ottoman fleets were not madly trading with one another, they were locked in ferocious combat.

To the left across the open space is a side gate to the Palais de France. Peek through the gates for another, better view of the old French embassy grounds. Then you've got to slog back up that hill to İstiklal Caddesi.

Continuing along İstiklal, the **Church of St Mary Draperis** (1678, 1789) is behind an iron fence and down a flight of steps. It's rarely open to visitors. Past the church, still on the left-hand side, is the grand

Soviet Consulate-General, once the imperial Russian embassy. It is still a busy place as the Soviet Union has a common border with Turkey, and dozens of Soviet ships pass through the Bosphorus and the Dardanelles each day.

Now take a detour: turn right off of İstiklal Caddesi along Asmalı Mescit Sokak, a narrow, typical Beyoğlu street which holds some fusty antique shops, food shops, suspect hotels and little eateries. The street intersects Meşrutiyet Caddesi. To the left of the intersection is the American library and cultural center, and just beyond it the pretty marble mansion which was first the American embassy, now the **American Consulate-General**. To the right of the intersection is the grand old Pera Palas Oteli (peh-RAH pah-LAHS), the Pera Palace.

Pera Palas Oteli The Pera Palas was built in the 1890s by Georges Nagelmackers, the Belgian entrepreneur who founded the Compagnie International des Wagons-Lits et Grands Express Europeens (1868). Nagelmackers, who had succeeded in linking Paris and Constantinople by luxury train, found that once he got his passengers to the Ottoman capital there was no suitable place for them to stay. So he built the hotel here in the section today called Tepebaşı.

It's a grand place, with huge public rooms, a sympathetic bar, a good dining room and a birdcage elevator. Once you've taken a turn through the hotel, head back to İstiklal Caddesi.

Near Tünel Meydanı When you reach İstiklal, go straight across it and down the hill on Kumbaracı Yokuşu to reach the **Crimean Memorial Church**. The Anglican church was built as a memorial to English troops of the Crimean War, and designed by C E Street. Lord Stratford de Redcliffe, the very influential British ambassador of the time, was instrumental in the church's foundation. The building is not often open to visitors.

Back on İstiklal, you will notice three good **bookstores** on the left-hand side. The *ABC Kitabevi* has Turkish and foreign-language books; *Haşet (Hachette)* has books, magazines and newspapers in French, English and Turkish; the *Alman Kitabevi* specialises in German books.

Next along the avenue, on your left, is the **Royal Swedish Consulate**, once the Swedish embassy, and after that the Four Seasons Restaurant. The road curves to the right; the open space here is known as Tünel Meydanı, Tunnel Square.

Tünel

You now have a chance to take a peek at İstanbul's underground railway. Built by French engineers over a century ago (1875), the Tünel provided a means by which the 'modern' citizens of Pera and Galata could negotiate the steep hillside without undue exertion. Up to a few decades ago, the cars were of dark wood with numerous coats of bright lacquer. Signs said, 'It is requested that cigarettes not be smoked'. A modernisation program swept away the quaint Swiss-chalet lower station and replaced it with a concrete bunker, modern rubber-tired French trains and signs that say 'No Smoking'.

The fare is 80TL (US$0.11). Trains run as frequently as necessary during rush hours, about every five or 10 minutes other times. Though you may want to use the Tünel later to ascend the hill, right now you should stay on foot. There's a lot to see as you descend slowly toward Karaköy: a whirling dervish convent, the Galata Tower and fascinating glimpses of Beyoğlu daily life.

Whirling Dervish Convent Though the main road (İstiklal) bears right as you come into Tünel Square, you should continue walking straight on. The surface turns to paving stones, the street narrows and takes the name of Galip Dede Caddesi, and on your left you'll notice the doorway into the Galata Mevlevi Tekkesi.

The Whirling Dervishes, or Mevlevi, took their name from the great Sufi mystic and poet, Jelaleddin Rumi (1207-1273). Rumi was called Mevlana or 'Our Leader' by his disciples. Sufis (Muslim mystics) seek mystical communion with God through various means. For Mevlana, it was through a *sema* or ceremony involving chants, prayers, music and a whirling dance. The whirling induced a trance-like state which made it easier for the mystic to 'get close to God'. The dervish order, founded in Konya during the 1200s, flourished throughout the Ottoman Empire and survives in Konya even today. The Galata Mevlevihane (whirling dervish hall) was open to foreign, non-Muslim visitors, who could witness the *sema*. The dervishes stressed the unity of mankind before God regardless of creed or belief.

Though the dervishes no longer whirl here, you can visit their *tekke* any day except Monday from 9 am to 5 pm; on Sunday and holidays the 200TL (US$0.28) admission charge is one-half that much. The dervish orders were banned in the early days of the republic. Though a few still survive unofficially, the hall is now called the Museum of Divan Literature and holds exhibits of *hattat* (Arabic calligraphy).

The Turks are passionate gardeners, as you'll see when you enter the grounds. In the midst of the city is this oasis of flowers and shady nooks, where you can sit and have a glass of tea. Notice the tomb of the sheik by the entrance passage, and also the *şadırvan* (ablutions fountain).

The modest frame *tekke* was restored in 1967-1972, but the first building here was erected by a high officer in the court of Sultan Beyazıt II in 1491. Its first *şeyh* (sheik, or leader) was Şeyh Muhammed Şemai Sultan Divani, a grandson of the great Mevlana. The building burned in 1766 but was repaired that same year by Sultan Mustafa III.

As you approach the building, notice the little graveyard on the left. The stones are very beautiful with their graceful

Arabic lettering. The shapes on top of them are of hats of the deceased; each hat denotes a different religious rank.

Inside the *tekke*, the central area was where the dervishes whirled. In the galleries above, visitors could sit and watch. Separate areas were set aside for the orchestra and for female visitors (behind the lattices). Don't neglect the exhibits of calligraphy, writing instruments and other paraphernalia associated with this highly developed Ottoman art.

Galata

Leaving the Whirling Dervish Convent, turn left down Galip Dede Caddesi. The hillside is covered with winding streets, little passageways, alleys of stairs and European-style houses built mostly in the 19th century. There are some older houses, a glimpse of what life was like for the European émigrés who came to live here and make their fortunes centuries ago. A few minutes' walk along Galip Dede will bring you to Beyoğlu's oldest landmark, the Galata Tower.

Galata Tower The Galata Tower (Galata Kulesi) was the highpoint in the Genoese fortifications of Galata. The tower, rebuilt many times, is ancient. Today it holds an observatory and a restaurant/nightclub. The tower is open to visitors from 10 am to 6 pm every day, for a fee of 800TL (US$1.12). In the evening the restaurant, bar and nightclub swing into action.

Daily life in the vicinity of the tower is a fascinating sight. There are woodworking shops, turners' lathes, workshops making veneer and other materials for interior decoration, a few dusty antique stores. This neighbourhood is also one of the last inhabited by the city's Spanish-speaking Jewish population. There's a synagogue named **Neve Shalom** only a block northeast of the Galata Tower. This was the site of a horrible massacre by Palestinian terrorists during the summer of 1986.

From the Galata Tower, continue downhill on the street called Yüksek Kaldırım to reach Karaköy, once the heart of the Genoese city of Galata.

Karaköy

In order to avoid 'contamination' of their way of life, both the later Byzantine emperors and the Ottoman sultans relegated European traders to Galata. Under the late Byzantines, Genoese traders got such a hold on the town that it was virtually a little Genoa. Though Galata still harbours many shipping and commercial offices, and some large banks, it is also busy with small traders. As you approach the Galata Bridge from Karaköy, the busy ferryboat docks and also the docks for Mediterranean cruise ships are to your left. To your right are a few fishmongers' stands and a warren of little streets filled with hardware stores and plumbing-supply houses. Scattered throughout this neighbourhood are Greek and Armenian churches and schools and a large synagogue, reminders of the time when virtually all of the empire's businesspeople were non-Muslims.

At the far end of the square from the Galata Bridge, right at the lower end of Yüksek Kaldırım, Voyvoda Caddesi (also called Bankalar Caddesi) leads up a slope to the right toward Şişhane Square. This street was the banking centre during the days of the empire, and many merchant banks still have headquarters or branches here. The biggest building was that of the Ottoman Bank, now a branch of the Turkish Republic's Central Bank.

Karaköy has busy bus stops, dolmuş queues and the lower station of the Tünel. To find the Tünel station descend into the hubbub of the square from Yüksek Kaldırım, and keep to the right. Don't go down the stairs into the pedestrian underpass (subway); instead squeeze through the narrow passage to the right of the stairway, and then turn right into Tersane Caddesi. The Tünel is a few steps along, on the right, in what looks like a concrete bunker.

Sultan Muhammad II (1451-1481)

Sultan Bayazid I (1389-1403)

THE BOSPHORUS

The strait which connects the Black Sea and the Marmara, 32 km long, 500 to 3000 metres wide, 50 to 120 metres (average 60 metres) deep, has determined the history not only of İstanbul, but even of the empires governed from this city. In earlier centuries it was one of the city's strongest defenses. Until the age of armoured gunboats, the city was never seriously threatened from the sea.

In Turkish, the strait is the Boğaziçi, from *boğaz*, throat or strait, and *iç*, inside or interior: within the strait.

The Bosphorus provides a convenient boundary for geographers. As it was a military bottleneck, armies marching from the east tended to stop on the eastern side, and those from the west on the western. So the western side was always more like Europe, the eastern more like Asia. Though the modern Turks think of themselves as Europeans, it is still common to say that Europe ends and Asia begins at the Bosphorus.

Except for the few occasions when the Bosphorus has frozen solid, crossing it has always meant going by boat – until 1973. Late in that year, the Bosphorus

Bridge, fourth longest in the world, was opened to travellers. For the first time in history there was a firm physical link across the straits from Europe to Asia. (Interestingly, there had been a plan for a bridge during the late years of the Ottoman Empire, but nothing came of it.) Traffic was so heavy over the new bridge that it paid for itself in less than a decade.

History

Greek legend recounts that Zeus, unfaithful to his wife Hera in an affair with Io, tried to make up for it by turning his erstwhile lover into a cow. Hera, for good measure, provided a horsefly to sting Io on the rump and drive her across the strait. In ancient Greek, *bous* is cow, and *poros* is crossing place, giving us Bosphorus: the place where the cow crossed.

From the earliest times it has been a maritime road to adventure. It is thought that Ulysses' travels brought him through the Bosphorus. Xenophon, in his *Anabasis*, wrote the history of the ill-fated Greek army of the Ten Thousand who, badly defeated by the Persians, retreated through Anatolia. The end of their tribulations came when they reached the beautiful waters of the Bosphorus.

Byzas, founder of Byzantium, explored these waters before the time of Jesus. Mehmet the Conqueror built two mighty fortresses at the strait's narrowest point so he could close it off to allies of the Byzantines. And each spring, enormous Ottoman armies would take several days to cross the Bosphorus on their way to campaigns in Asia. At the end of WW I, the defeated Ottoman capital cowered under the guns of Allied frigates anchored in the strait. And when the republic was proclaimed, the last Ottoman sultan snuck down to the Bosphorus, boarded a launch, and sailed away to exile on a British man-o'-war.

Touring the Bosphorus

You could spend several days exploring the sights of the Bosphorus. It holds five Ottoman palaces, four castles, the mammoth suburb of Üsküdar, and dozens of interesting little towns. But if you're pressed for time, you can see the main points in a day.

The essential feature of any Bosphorus tour is a cruise along the strait. You just can't appreciate its grandeur and beauty completely if you're in a bus or car. On the other hand, it's time-consuming to take a ferryboat to a certain dock, debark, visit a palace or castle, and return to the dock to wait for the next boat, so a trip combining travel by both land and sea is best. I recommend that you begin your explorations with a ferry cruise up the strait. This will give you a glimpse of everything, and allow you to decide which sites you'd like to visit and see in more detail. Below is a description of the cruise, followed by detailed information on the more important sites.

A Bosphorus Cruise

Though tour agencies and luxury hotels have private boats for cruises on the Bosphorus, it's considerably cheaper and much more fun to go the authentic way, on one of the orange-and-white ferries of the Denizyolları (Turkish Maritime Lines). Special Bosphorus cruise trips are operated twice daily on summer weekdays and Saturday, and five times on summer Sundays and holidays. The cost for the 2½-hour cruise from Eminönü to Anadolu Kavağı, or vice-versa, is 750TL (US$1.05). If you can't afford the time for the whole trip, you can get off at any of the nine stops en route (six on the European side, three on the Asian). Prices are printed on all tickets. Save your ticket to show the ticket-taker when you leave the ferry at your destination.

Reading the Ferry Schedule The special cruise ferries are called Boğaziçi Özel Gezi Seferleri. Look for this heading on the schedules, which are posted in the waiting area of each ferry dock. Times will be close to the following, but check to be sure: Eminönü departure at 10.25 am and 1.35 pm; Anadolu Kavağı departure at 3 and 5.10 pm. On Sundays and holidays, departure times from Eminönü are 9.45, 10.45, 11.45 am; 1.45 and 4.45 pm. From Anadolu Kavağı, Sunday departures are at 1.15, 3.15, 5.15, 6.15 and 7.10 pm.

By tradition, European ports of call are printed on the schedules in black, Asian ports in red.

If you visit in the cooler months when the special ferries aren't running, look at the schedule for the heading 'Boğaz'a Gidiş' ('To the Bosphorus'), and also 'Boğaz'dan Geliş' ('From the Bosphorus') for long-distance boats that make good substitutes. Heaviest travel will naturally be down the Bosphorus in the morning rush-hour, and up the Bosphorus in the evening.

These special cruise ferries are popular, and they fill up quickly, early and often. It's a good idea to get to the dock well ahead of departure (say, a half hour or even more), locate the boat, board and seize a seat. Keep the sun in mind when you choose your place; you may want some shade as you head north.

Heading Out As you steam out from the mouth of the Golden Horn, **Galata** will be on your left and **Seraglio Point** on your right with **Topkapı Palace** rising above it. Down at the water's edge is an **Ottoman Shipyard** *(tersane)*. For sights on the Asian shore, refer to the Üsküdar & Beylerbeyi section, below.

Soon you'll be gliding past the incredible facade and sea-fence of **Dolmabahçe Palace** on the European side. After that, the main square of Beşiktaş, or **Barbaros Hayrettin Paşa**, comes into view. Barbaros Bulvarı, a wide highway, cuts a swath up the hill westward. To its right (north) is the green expanse of **Yıldız Park**. At the waterline is the burned-out hulk of **Çirağan Palace**, which is being restored and converted into a luxury hotel. See the later European Shore section for more detail.

The handsome Neo-Renaissance mosque nestled at the foot of the Bosphorus Bridge's European pylons is the **Ortaköy Camii**. Though it has hardly anything to do with Turkish architecture, it's very attractive and well sited. Within the mosque hang several masterful examples of Arabic calligraphy executed by Sultan Abdülmecit, an accomplished calligrapher who had the mosque built in 1854.

Above the town you'll notice the New England 19th-century architecture of the **Bosphorus University (Boğaziçi Üniversitesi)**, on a hilltop above the town of Bebek. Founded as Robert College in the mid-19th century by the American Board of Foreign Missions, the college had an important influence on the modernisation of political, social, economic and scientific thought in Turkey. Though donated by the Board to the Turkish Republic a decade ago, instruction is still in both English and Turkish.

Robert College survives as a special school to prepare bright students for university, having joined forces with the American College for Girls in nearby Arnavutköy.

Just north of Bebek on the European shore is **Rumeli Hisar** (roo-mehl-LEE hee-sahr), the Fortress of Europe. Here at the narrowest part of the Bosphorus, Mehmet the Conqueror had this fortress built in a mere four months (1452), in preparation for his planned siege of Byzantine Constantinople. In concert with Anadolu

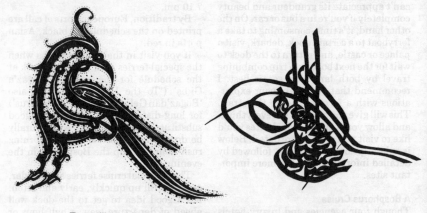

Two calligraphic versions of the **Basmallah** – the phrase 'Bismillah al-rahman al-rahim': In the name of God the Compassionate the Merciful.

Hisar on the Asian shore just opposite, the cannon of Rumeli Hisar controlled all traffic on the Bosphorus, and cut the city off from resupply by sea from the north. Built just for use in the conquest of the city, the mighty citadel served as a glorified toll booth for a while, and was then more or less abandoned. It has been restored and is now used for folk dancing, drama and other performances in the summertime, particularly during the İstanbul International Festival.

Across the strait from Rumeli Hisar is the **Fortress of Asia, Anadolu Hisar** (ahn-nah-doh-LOO hee-sahr). This small castle had been built by Sultan Beyazıt I in 1391. It was repaired and strengthened by Mehmet the Conqueror in preparation for the great siege. These days a picturesque village snuggles around its foundations.

Each spring a Tulip Festival takes place in **Emirgan**, a well-to-do suburb of İstanbul on the European side. North of Emirgan, at İstinye, is a cove with a drydock. A ring ferry service runs from İstinye to Beykoz and Paşabahçe on the Asian shore. Across on the Asian shore lies **Kanlıca**, a town famous for its yoghurt. The mosque in the town square dates from 1560.

On a point jutting out from the European shore is **Yeniköy**, first settled in classical times. This place later became a favourite summer resort, and preserves that distinction by being the site of the modern Yeniköy Carlton Hotel. Just north of the hotel is the lavish 19th-century Ottoman *yalı* or **seaside villa** of one Sait Halim Paşa. Not too many of these luxurious villas survive. All were made of wood. Modern economics (and desire for modern conveniences) have caused many to be torn down. Fire has destroyed many others.

Across from Yeniköy are the Asian towns of **Paşabahçe** and **Beykoz**. Much of Turkey's best glassware is produced at the famous Paşabahçe factory – you'll see the name as a brand. In Beykoz, legend

says that one of Jason's Argonauts, Pollux by name, had a boxing match with the local king, Amicus. Pollux was the son of Leda (she of the swan); Amicus was a son of Poseidon. Pollux won.

Originally called Therapeia for its healthful climate, the little cove of **Tarabya** has been a favourite summer watering-place for İstanbul's well-to-do for centuries. Now there is a big hotel here, the Grand Tarabya (Büyük Tarabya Oteli). Little restaurants, specialising in fish, ring the cove. North of the village are some of the old summer embassies of foreign powers. When the heat and fear of disease increased in the warm months, foreign ambassadors and their staffs would retire to palatial residences, complete with lush gardens, on this shore. The region for such embassy residences extended north to the next village, Büyükdere.

The quaint, pretty town of **Sarıyer** is a logical place to end your cruise up the Bosphorus (or to begin your cruise down). Sarıyer has several good fish restaurants, an interesting little marketplace, and good transportation down the Bosphorus or north to the Black Sea coast at Kilyos.

The far northern port of call for the ferryboats is **Rumeli Kavağı**. From here northward is a military zone. The sleepy little town gets most of its excitement from the arrival and departure of ferries. There is a little public beach named Altınkum (ahl-TUHN-koom) near the village.

Perched above the village of **Anadolu Kavağı** on the Asian side are the ruins of a Genoese castle. As the straits are narrow here, it was a good choice for a defensive site to control traffic. Two more fortresses, put up by Sultan Murat IV, are north of here. But Anadolu Kavağı is the final stop on the special cruise ferry route, and the land to the north is in a military zone.

From Sarıyer you can get a bus or dolmuş to **Kilyos**, on the Black Sea coast. There are some little pensions, hotels and guest houses here, open during the summer for beach fanciers. If you go to Kilyos for swimming, keep in mind that the waters of the Black Sea are fairly chilly. More important, there is a deadly undertow on many beaches. Swim only in protected areas or where there is an attentive lifeguard. And don't swim alone.

European Shore

If you've cruised up the Bosphorus on a ferry, catch any bus or dolmuş headed south. To be safe, mention the name of your destination, Rumeli Hisar for example, when you board.

Coming from downtown to visit the sights along the Bosphorus, your best bet is to take a bus or dolmuş to reach Dolmabahçe, one km down the hill from Taksim Square. From Taksim, the walk is short and pleasant with views of the Bosphorus and the palace. Walk toward the Cultural Palace. As you stand facing it, the tree-lined, divided street on your right is İnönü Caddesi, formerly called Gümüşsuyu Caddesi. It leads directly to Dolmabahçe. On the right-hand side of İnönü Caddesi, just out of Taksim, you'll see ranks of dolmuşes. Routes are mostly long ones up the European Bosphorus shore, but you may find one going to Beşiktaş/Barbaros Hayrettin Paşa. Take this one to Dolmabahçe if you need to ride.

Coming from other parts of the city, catch a bus that goes via Eminönü and Karaköy to B Hayrettin Paşa. Any bus heading out of Karaköy along the Bosphorus shore road will take you to Dolmabahçe. Get off at the Kabataş stop. Just north of the stop you will see the Dolmabahçe Camii (mosque), and beyond it the palace.

Dolmabahçe Palace For centuries the *Padişah* (Ottoman sultan) had been the envy of all other monarchs in the world. Cultured, urbane, sensitive, courageous; controller of vast territories, great wealth and invincible armies and navies, he was the Grand Turk. The principalities, city-states and small kingdoms of Europe, Africa and the Near East cowered before him, and all stood in fear of a Turkish conquest. Indeed, the Turks conquered all of North Africa, parts of southern Italy, and eastern Europe to the gates of Vienna. The opulent palace of Dolmabahçe might be seen as an apt expression of this Ottoman glory. But it's not.

Dolmabahçe was built between 1843 and 1856, when the homeland of the once-mighty Padişah had become 'the Sick Man of Europe'. His many peoples, aroused by a wave of European nationalism, were in revolt; his wealth was mostly mortgaged to, or under the control of, European interests; his armies, while still considerable, were obsolescent and disorganized. The European, western, Christian way of life had triumphed over the Asian, eastern, Muslim one. Attempting to turn the tide, 19th-century sultans 'went European', modernizing the army and civil service, granting autonomy to subject peoples, and adopting – sometimes wholesale – European ways of doing things.

The name Dolmabahçe, 'filled-in garden', dates from the reign of Sultan Ahmet I (1607-1617), when a little cove here was filled in and an imperial pleasure kiosk built on it. Other wooden buildings followed, but all burned to the ground in 1814. Sultan Abdülmecit, whose architect was an Armenian named Balyan, wanted a 'European-style' marble palace. What he got is partly European, partly oriental, and certainly sumptuous.

When you arrive, look for the ornate **clock tower** between Dolmabahçe Camii and the palace. The gate near the clock tower is the one you enter. The palace is open from 9 am to noon and from 1.30 to 4.30 pm, closed Monday and Thursday. Entry costs 1000TL (US$1.40); the ISIC may not be accepted for free entry. There is a camera fee, but you should check your camera rather than pay the fee as the palace interior is too dark to photograph, even with fast film, and flash and tripod are not allowed. Rather, take your photos from the small garden near the clock tower. You must take a tour here; it lasts between 60 and 90 minutes. Make sure the tour leader will be speaking a language you understand.

The palace gardens are very pretty. High-stepping guards by the main gate add a martial note. The fence along the Bosphorus, and the palace facade, go on for almost half a km. Inside, you'll see opulent public and private rooms, a harem with steel doors, lots of stuff like Sevres vases and Bohemian chandeliers, and also a staircase with a crystal balustrade.

One room was used by Sultan Abdül Aziz (1861-1876), an enormously fat fellow who needed an enormously large bed. You will see just how large. The magnificent throne room, used in 1877 for the first meeting of the Ottoman Chamber of Deputies, has a chandelier that weighs over 4000 kg. The place is awesome.

Don't set your watch by any of the palace clocks, however. They are all stopped at the same time: 9.05 am. On the morning of 10 November 1938, Kemal Atatürk died in Dolmabahçe. You will be shown the small bedroom which he used during his last days. Each year on 10 November, at 9.05 am, Turkey – the entire country – comes to a dead halt in commemoration of the Republic's founder.

After you've boggled your mind at Dolmabahçe, go back to the vicinity of the clock tower and turn right, heading north along the palace wall, down an avenue lined with poplars. Soon on your right you'll come to the **Kuşluk ve Sanat Galerisi or Aviary & Art Gallery**, open from 9.30 am to 4 pm for 200TL (US$0.28), closed Monday and Thursday. Only mad palace-lovers need spend the money, however, because there is not a lot to see.

This section of the palace was the aviary, its bird-house and cages now restored. The art gallery, lined with paintings by 19th and 20th-century Ottoman artists (many of them from the nobility), is actually an old passageway leading from one part of the palace to another. That accounts for its extraordinary shape, a single corridor over 100 metres long.

Barbaros Hayrettin Paşa When you've finished at the aviary and gallery, turn right (north) again and walk for five minutes to the suburb of Barbaros Hayrettin Paşa. It's not a long walk if you're willing, but the heavy traffic in this corridor between two walls is noisy and smelly. When you emerge from the walls, you'll be in the suburb now officially named Barbaros Hayrettin Paşa, which used to be named Beşiktaş. Most people still call it by that name.

Naval Museum The Deniz Müzesi, or Naval Museum, is on the Bosphorus shore just south of the flyover in Beşiktaş/Barbaros. Among its exhibits are an outdoor display of cannon (including Selim the Grim's 23-tonne monster) and a statue of Barbaros Hayrettin Paşa (1483-1546), the famous Turkish admiral known also as Barbarossa who conquered North Africa for Süleyman the Magnificent. The admiral's *türbe* (tomb), designed by Sinan, is close by.

There are two parts to the museum, one entered from the main road, the other from the Bosphorus shore. You must pay an admission fee for each part. The museum is open from 9.30 am to 5 pm, closed Monday and Tuesday. Admission costs 250TL (US$0.35) in each part.

Though the Ottoman Empire is most remembered for its conquests on land, its maritime power was equally impressive. During the reign of Süleyman the Magnificent (1520-1566), the eastern Mediterranean was virtually an Ottoman lake. The sultan's navies cut a swath in the Indian Ocean as well. Sea power was instrumental in the conquests of the Aegean coasts and islands, Egypt and North Africa. Discipline, well-organized supply and good ship design contributed to Ottoman victories. But the navy, like the army and the government, lagged behind the west in modernisation during the later centuries. The great battle which broke the spell of Ottoman naval invincibility was fought in 1571 at Lepanto, in the Gulf of Patras off the Greek coast. (Cervantes fought on the Christian side, and was badly wounded.) Though the Turkish fleet was destroyed, the sultan quickly produced another, partly with the help of rich Greek shipowners who were his subjects.

In the Bosphorus section of the museum, you enter beneath a replica of Piri Reis's famous medieval map of the New World, on the wall above the door. Inside, be sure to see the sleek, swift imperial barges, in which the sultan would shoot up and down the Bosphorus from palace to palace (in those days the roads were not very smooth or fast). Over 30 metres in length but only two metres wide, with 13 banks of oars, the barges were obviously the rocket boats of their day. The ones with latticework screens were for the imperial ladies. There's also a war galley with 24 pairs of oars.

You may also be curious to see a copy of the Map of Piri Reis, an early Ottoman map (1513) which purports to show the coasts and continents of the New World. It's assumed that Piri Reis ('Captain Piri') got hold of Columbus's work for his map. The original map is in Topkapı; colourful copies are on sale here in the museum.

Çırağan Palace From the Naval Museum and the flyover in Beşiktaş/Barbaros, you can walk north for 10 minutes, or catch a bus or dolmuş heading north along the shore, to reach the entrance to Yıldız Park (bus stop Galatasaray Lisesi). Before you reach the entrance, you'll be passing Çırağan Palace on your right; the ruined

palace is hidden from the road by a high wall, though you can get a glimpse of it through its battered gates.

Unsatisfied with the architectural exertions of his predecessor at Dolmabahçe, Sultan Abdül Aziz (1861-1876) had to build his own palace. He built Çırağan on the Bosphorus shore only a km north of Dolmabahçe, replacing an earlier wooden palace. The architect was the self-same Balyan as for Dolmabahçe. The sultan didn't get to live here much, however. Instead, it served as a detention place for his successor, Sultan Murat V, who was deposed before he had even reigned a year. Later the palace housed the Ottoman Chamber of Deputies & Senate (1909), but in 1910 it was destroyed by fire under suspicious circumstances. Plans for rebuilding it as a luxury hotel have taken on some momentum but it will some time before there will be any noticeable changes in the place.

Yıldız Palace & Park Sultan Abdülhamid II (1876-1909), who succeeded Murat V, also had to build his own palace. He added considerably to the structures built by earlier sultans in Yıldız Park, on the hillside above Çırağan. Today the kiosks and summer palaces, as well as the park itself, have been restored by the Turkish Touring & Automobile Club, and several now serve as delightful restaurants and tea houses.

The park is open from 9 am to 6 pm every day; admission costs 20TL (US$0.03) for pedestrians, 200TL (US$0.28) for cars (including taxis). The park began life as the imperial reserve for Çırağan Palace, but when Abdülhamid built the Şale Köşkü, the park served that palace. Under Abdülhamid, the park was planted with exotic and valuable trees, shrubs and flowers, and was provided with manicured paths and a superior electric lighting and drainage system. The sultan could reach Çırağan Palace by a private bridge over the roadway from the park. If you come to the park by taxi, you might as well have it take you up the steep slope to the Şale Köşkü. You can visit the other kiosks on the walk down.

As you toil up the hill along the road, near the top of the slope to the left you'll see the **Çadır Köşkü**. This pretty, ornate little kiosk was built between 1865 and 1870 as a place for the sultan to enjoy the view, rest from a walk, and have a cup of tea or coffee. It serves the same purpose today for visitors. Only drinks are served (no food), but you can enjoy them on the marble terrace overlooking the Bosphorus, and afterwards walk around the artificial 'lake', complete with island.

To the right (north) as you are hiking up the road from the gate, you will notice two greenhouses and another kiosk. These are the **Kış Bahçesi** (Winter Garden), the **Yeşil Sera** (Green Nursery), and the **Malta Köşkü** (tel 160-2752). The Malta Kiosk, restored in 1979, is now a café serving refreshments, alcoholic drinks and light meals. The view here is the best in the park, much better than that at the Çadır Köşkü. If you sit down to a plate of grilled lamb and then finish up with something sweet, your bill will add up to 2000TL or 2500TL (US$2.80 to US$3.50).

Also to the right are the **Yıldız Porcelain Factories** (Yıldız Porselen Fabrikası), constructed to manufacture dinner services for the palace. They still operate.

At the very top of the hill, enclosed by a separate, lofty wall, is the **Şale Köşkü or Chalet Kiosk**, a 'guest house' put up in 1882 and expanded in 1898 by Abdülhamid for use by Kaiser Wilhelm II of Germany during a state visit. I expect the Kaiser had enough space to move in, as the 'chalet' has 64 rooms. After his imperial guest departed, the sultan became quite attached to his 'rustic' creation, and decided to live here himself, forsaking the more lavish but less well-defended palaces on the Bosphorus shore. Abdülhamid was paranoid, and for good

reason. Fate determined that his fears would come true. He was deposed, departed this wooden palace in April 1909, and boarded a special train which took him to a life of house arrest in Salonika.

As though this were not enough dolorous history for the place, the last sultan of the Ottoman Empire, Mehmet V (Vahideddin), lived here until, at 6 am on 11 November 1922, he and his First Chamberlain, bandmaster, doctor, two secretaries, valet, barber and two eunuchs, accompanied by trunks full of jewels, gold and antiques, boarded two British Red Cross ambulances for the secret journey to the naval dockyard at Tophane, where they would board the British battleship HMS *Malaya* for a trip into exile, ending the Ottoman Empire forever. On the way to the quay one of the tyres on the sultan's ambulance went flat; while it was being changed, the Shadow of God on Earth quaked, fearing that he might be discovered.

In the Republican era, the Şale Köşkü has served as a guest house for visiting heads of state, including Charles de Gaulle, Pope Paul VI, Nikolai Ceausescu and the Empress Soraya. You must pay a separate admission fee of 500TL (US$0.70) to see the Chalet Kiosk, which is open from 9.30 am to 4 pm daily; closed Monday.

The gravel walkways along which you approach the palace are said to have been ordered by Abdülhamid as a security measure. It's impossible for anyone to walk on them without making a lot of noise. As you enter the palace, a guide will approach you to give you the tour, which is required. The guide will tell you that all of the carpets in the palace are from the imperial factory at Hereke, east of İstanbul.

The first section you visit was the original chalet, built in 1882. The first room on the tour was used by Abdülhamid's mother for her religious devotions, the second was her guest reception room, with a very fine mosaic tabletop. Then comes a women's resting-room, and afterwards a tea-room furnished with furniture having a gold star on a blue background, which reminds one that this was the 'star' *(yıldız)* palace.

In 1898 the chalet was expanded, and the older section became the harem (with steel doors), while the new section was the *selamlık*, or reception area. In the *selamlık* are a bathroom with tiles from the Yıldız Porcelain Factories, and several reception rooms, one of which has furniture made by Abdülhamid himself, an accomplished woodworker. The grand hall of the *selamlık* is vast, its floor covered by a 7½-tonne Hereke carpet woven just for this room. So huge is the rug that it had to be brought in through the far (north) wall before the building was finished and the wall was closed.

Other buildings at Yıldız include the **Merasim Köşkü or Ceremonial Kiosk** and barracks, now used by İstanbul University. Part of the Merasim Kiosk has been restored and opened as a gallery. It's reached from Barbaros Bulvarı, the road along the south side of the park, not from within the park itself.

Onward After seeing Yıldız, you can take a bus or dolmuş north to Bebek and Rumeli Hisar (see below), or return to Beşiktaş/Barbaros to catch a shuttle ferry over to Üsküdar, on the Asian side, in order to continue your sightseeing. The ferries operate every 15 or 20 minutes in each direction, from 6 am to midnight. There are equally frequent boats between Üsküdar and Eminönü. Ferries to Eminönü may bear the sign 'Köprü' or 'bridge', meaning, of course, the Galata Bridge.

If you'd like to pick up the special Bosphorus cruise ferry from Barbaros, catch it heading north at 10.40 am or 1.50 pm (on Sunday and holidays at 10 and 11 am, noon, and 2 at 5 pm). The cruise ferry does not call at Üsküdar.

Rumeli Hisar This impressive fortress was built under duress. To speed its completion in line with his impatience to conquer Constantinople, Mehmet the Conqueror ordered each of his 17 vezirs to take responsibility for one of the 17 towers. If the tower's construction was not completed on schedule, the vezir would pay with his life. As far as we know, the work was done on time.

Rumeli Hisar is open from 9.30 am to 5 pm daily; closed Monday. Admission costs 200TL (US$0.28), half-price on Sundays and holidays.

Asian Shore

The best and most pleasant means of transport is a ferryboat from Eminönü (Dock No 2). They run every 20 minutes between 6 am and midnight, even more frequently during rush hours. A similar, frequent ferry service operates between Üsküdar and Beşiktaş/Barbaros Hayrettin Paşa. There are also city buses and dolmuşes departing Taksim Square for Üsküdar. The ferryboats are much faster and infinitely more fun, though.

If you take the ferry to Üsküdar, you'll notice **Leander's Tower**, called the Kız Kulesi (Maiden's Tower) in Turkish. The tower was a toll booth and defense point in ancient times; the Bosphorus could be closed off by means of a chain stretching from here to Seraglio Point. The tower has really nothing to do with Leander, who was no maiden, and who swam not the Bosphorus but the Hellespont (Dardanelles), 340 km from here. The tower is subject to the usual legends: oracle says maiden will die by snakebite, concerned father puts maiden in snake-proof tower, fruit-vendor comes by in boat, sells basket of fruit (complete with snake) to maiden, maiden gets hers, etc. The legend seems to crop up wherever there are offshore towers, and maidens. Anyway, it's a pretty tower, and an İstanbul landmark.

Another landmark for travellers is the German-style **Haydarpaşa İstasyonu**,

İstanbul's terminus for Asian trains. During the late 19th century, when Kaiser Wilhelm was trying to charm the sultan into economic and military cooperation, he gave him the station as a little gift.

You will also notice the large **Selimiye Barracks (Selimiye Kışlası)**, a square building with towers at the corners. It dates from the early 19th century, when Selim III and Mahmut II reorganized the Ottoman armed forces along European lines. Not far away is the **Selimiye Mosque** (1805). During the Crimean War (1853-56), when England and France fought on the Ottoman side against the Russian Empire, the Selimiye served as a military hospital as well. It was here that the English nurse Florence Nightingale, horrified at the conditions suffered by those wounded in action, established, with 38 companion nurses, the first model military hospital with modern standards of discipline, order, sanitation and care. In effect, her work at the Selimiye established the norms of modern nursing, and turned nursing into a skilled, respected profession.

That other highly ornamented building, very storybook Ottoman, was formerly a harem for aging palace ladies. It's now a school.

Üsküdar Üsküdar (ER-sker-dahr) is the Turkish form of the name Scutari. Legend has it that the first ancient colonists established themselves at Chalcedon, the modern Kadıköy, south of Üsküdar. Byzas, bearing the oracle's message to 'Found a colony opposite the blind', thought the Chalcedonites blind to the advantages of Seraglio Point as a townsite, and founded his town on the European shore. Still, people have lived on this, the Asian shore, longer than they've lived on the other.

Today Üsküdar is a busy 'bedroom' community for İstanbul, and you will enjoy an hour's browse through its streets, markets and mosques. You

should definitely see the Çinili Cami, with its brilliant tiles, and the attractive little palace of Beylerbeyi.

Hop off the ferry in Üsküdar. The **main square** is right before you. North of the square, near the ferry landing, is the **Mihrimah Camii** (1547), built by Sinan for a daughter of Süleyman the Magnificent. To the south of the square is the **Yeni Valide Camii**, or Mosque of the New Queen Mother (1710), built by Sultan Ahmet III for his mother. It resembles the Rüstem Paşa mosque near the Spice Bazaar in Eminönü. Having been built late in the period of classical Ottoman architecture, it is not as fine as earlier works.

West of the square, overlooking the harbour, is the **Şemsi Paşa Camii** (1580), designed by Sinan.

Walk out of the busy square along the main road, called Hakimiyeti Milliye Caddesi, or Popular Sovereignty Avenue. (After six centuries of monarchy, the idea of democracy, of the people ruling, is enough to inspire street names.) Watch on the left for Tavukçu Bakkal Sokak, and turn into it. When you reach Çavuşdere Caddesi, turn right and walk less than a km to the little **Tiled Mosque** (Çinili Cami, chee-nee-LEE jahm-mee).

The mosque doesn't look like too much from the outside: just a shady little neighbourhood mosque with the usual collection of bearded old men sitting around. Inside, it is brilliant with İznik faience (tin-glazed earthenware). It is the work of Mahpeyker Kösem (1640), wife of Sultan Ahmet I (1603-1617) and mother of sultans Murat IV (1623-1640) and Ibrahim (1640-1648).

From the European shore of the Bosphorus, you may have noticed a hill or two behind Üsküdar, and a television transmission tower. The hills are **Büyük Çamlıca** (bew-YEWK chahm-luh-jah, Big Pine Hill) and **Küçük Çamlıca** (kew-CHEWK, Little Pine Hill). Büyük Çamlıca, especially, has for years been a special picnic place for İstanbullus. You can get there from the main square in Üsküdar on an Ümraniye bus or dolmuş. Get off at Kısıklı. You can walk to the top on Büyük Çamlıca Caddesi or take a taxi; if it's a busy time (weekend or holiday), take a dolmuş.

Beylerbeyi Palace Catch a bus or dolmuş north along the shore road from Üsküdar's main square to reach Beylerbeyi, just north of the Asian pylons of the Bosphorus Bridge. Get off at the Çayırbaşı stop. Beylerbeyi Palace is open from 9 am to 5 pm, closed Monday; small admission fee.

Every emperor needs some little place to get away to, and Beylerbeyi was the place for Abdül Aziz (1861-1876). Mahmut II had built a wooden palace here, but Abdül Aziz wanted stone and marble, so he ordered Serkis Balyan to get to work on Beylerbeyi. The architect came up with an Ottoman gem, complete with fountain in the entrance hall, and two little tent-like kiosks in the sea wall.

One room is panelled in wonderful marquetry (woodwork), all done by the sultan himself. Woodwork was not just a hobby. Under the laws of Islam, every man should have an honest skill with which to make a living. Being a soldier was a duty and an honour, not a living. So was being king. Thus every sultan had to develop a skill by which, theoretically, he could earn his living. Frequently the sultans chose calligraphy; Abdül Aziz chose woodwork.

Abdül Aziz spent a lot of time here. But so did other monarchs and royal guests, for this was, in effect, the sultan's guest quarters. Empress Eugenie of France stayed here for a long visit in 1869. Other royal guests included Nasruddin, Shah of Persia; Nicholas, Grand Duke of Russia; and Nicholas, King of Montenegro. Its last imperial 'guest' was none other than the former sultan, Abdülhamid II, who was brought here to spend the remainder of his life (1913 to 1918), having spent the four years since his deposition (1909) in Ottoman Salonika. He had the dubious pleasure of gazing across the Bosphorus at Yıldız, and watching crumble before his eyes the great empire which he had ruled for over 30 years.

Küçüksu Kasrı If Beylerbeyi was a sultan's favourite getaway spot, Küçüksu was for picnics and 'rustic' parties. The Büyük Göksu and Küçük Göksu (Great Heavenly Stream and Lesser Heavenly Stream) were two brooks which descended from the Asian hills into the Bosphorus. Between them was a flat, fertile delta, grassy and shady, just perfect for picnics. The Ottoman upper classes used to get away from the hot city for picnics and rowing here. Foreign residents, referring to the place as 'The Sweet Waters of Asia', would often join them.

Take a bus or dolmuş along the shore road north from Beylerbeyi to reach Küçüksu. The tiny palace here, actually an ornate lodge, was restored and opened to the public in 1983, having been closed for decades. Sultan Abdülmecit was responsible for building this little place in 1856. Earlier sultans had wooden kiosks here. Hours are 9 am to 5 pm, closed Monday.

Onward If you can get to the ferry dock in Çengelköy, the next village north of Beylerbeyi, by 10.55 am (except Sunday and holidays), you can catch the special Bosphorus cruise ferry heading north. Otherwise, there are ferries which run on a ring route from İstinye on the European side to Beykoz and Paşabahçe on the Asian. Another ring operates from Sarıyer and Rumeli Kavağı in Europe to Anadolu Kavağı in Asia. These rings run about every hour. Check the schedules.

If the timing's right, you might want to take a bus or dolmuş north all the way to Anadolu Kavağı and catch the Bosphorus cruise ferry as it heads back down toward the city. It departs Anadolu Kavağı at 3 and 5.10 pm (1.15, 3.15, 5.15, 6.15 and 7.10 pm on Sunday and holidays).

THE PRINCES' ISLANDS

The Turks call these islands, which lie about 20 km south-east of the city in the Sea of Marmara, the Kızıl Adalar, 'Red Islands'. Most İstanbullus get along with 'Adalar' (The Islands) however, as there are no other islands nearby.

It's convenient to have islands near a big city. They serve all sorts of useful purposes. In Byzantine times, so the story goes, refractory princes, deposed monarchs and others who were a threat to the powers-that-be were interned here. A Greek Orthodox monastery and seminary turned out Orthodox priests until only a decade or two ago.

Under the Ottomans, stray dogs were rounded up from the city's streets and shipped out to Köpek Adası (Dog Island), where they were released. After that, their fate was up to God. (Muslim belief holds that animals, too, have immortal souls, and that it is not the business of men to take animal lives needlessly; that is, to kill dogs just to get them off city streets.) From one of the islands, copper was mined. Another was used as a self-contained rabbit farm: bunnies were released on the deserted island to breed, and the 'crop' gathered at leisure.

In the 19th century the empire's business community of Greeks, Jews and Armenians began to favour the islands as summer resorts. The population was most heavily Greek up to the end of the empire. Many of the pretty Victorian holiday villas and hotels survive, and make the larger islands, Büyükada and Heybeliada, charming places.

If you have the time and want a leisurely, relaxing outing with no heavy sightseeing or scheduling, by all means cruise out to the islands. The ferry steams out of the Bosphorus, with good views all around. To the right is a magnificent panorama of Topkapı Palace, Sancta Sophia and the Blue Mosque; to the left, Üsküdar, Haydarpaşa and Kadıköy. Along the southern coast of Asia are more suburbs of İstanbul, some of them

industrial. Before coming to the bigger islands, you'll pass the small ones named **Kınalı** and **Burgaz**. Heybeli is next. Finally, you debark at Büyükada.

If you don't have the time for this excursion, you still have a chance for a look: if you're heading off to İznik and Bursa, you'll probably take a ferry from Kabataş to Yalova. It will pass, and probably call at, both Heybeli and Büyükada.

Büyükada

The first thing you will notice about this delightful place is that cars are not allowed. Except for the necessary police, fire and sanitation vehicles, transportation is by bicycle, horse-drawn carriage and foot. It's wonderful!

Something you may not notice, but that you should be aware of, is that there is no fresh water in the islands; it must be tanked in from the mainland.

Walk from the ferry to the clock tower and the main street. The business district, with some fairly expensive restaurants, is to the left. For a stroll up the hill and through the lovely old houses, bear right. If you need a goal for your wanderings, head for the Greek Monastery of St George, in the 'saddle' between Büyükada's two main hills.

Horse-drawn carriage tours of the island are available. You can take either the 'long tour' (*büyük tur*) for about 5000TL (US$7), or the 'short tour' (*küçük tur*) which gives you a look mostly at the town, not the shores or hills, for 3500TL (US$4.90).

Heybeliada

Called Heybeli for short, this small island holds the Turkish Naval Academy. The presidential yacht is often anchored off the academy landing. Within the academy grounds is the grave of Sir Edward Barton (died 1598), ambassador of Queen Elizabeth I to the Sublime Porte.

Getting There

Ferries depart from both Sirkeci (Dock No 5) and Kabataş, but it's Kabataş which has the express ferries. By express, the trip to Heybeli takes 50 minutes; by normal boat it's about one hour, 20 minutes. Büyükada is an additional 15 minutes' trip beyond Heybeli. Perhaps the best plan for you is to take a boat all the way to Büyükada, see that island, shuttle back to Heybeli, see that one, and then catch a returning ferry to İstanbul.

The summer schedules are heavily in favour of commuters, with frequent morning boats from the islands and frequent evening boats from the city. But you'll have no trouble getting a convenient boat if you check the schedules ahead of time. The few morning boats from the city to the islands fill up quickly, and though you'll almost certainly get aboard, you may have to stand the whole way unless you board the boat and seize a seat at least half an hour before departure time.

Here are some convenient times (subject to change, so check): from Sirkeci, normal ferries depart at 6.50 am, 10.50 am, 12.50 pm and 2.50 pm. From Kabataş (near Dolmabahçe), the one morning express ferry departs at 9.45 am. There are many afternoon and evening boats, but these don't leave you much time for sightseeing.

Return trips depart Büyükada at 1.40, 2.40 and 6.40 pm, express to Kabataş; and at 4, 6 and 7.30 pm (plus three more late evening boats), normal to Sirkeci. Departures from Heybeli are 15 minutes later in each case.

Between the islands of Büyükada and Heybeliada there are fairly frequent ferries on the 15-minute trip.

Besides the Denizyolları ferries, there is now a private hydrofoil *(deniz otobüsü)* service from Kabataş to the islands. The trip takes only 22 minutes but costs 1000TL (US$1.40), whereas the regular ferries cost less than 500TL (US$0.70).

PLACES TO STAY

İstanbul is well provided with hotels in all categories, particularly in the budget and moderate ranges. Hotel clusters in various areas of the city make it easy to find the room you want at an affordable price. If the first hotel you look at is full, there will be another one around the corner, or even right next door.

As everywhere in Turkey, you should inspect the hotel room before you register. It may be better or worse than the lobby or facade. Also, one room may be better than another. If you don't like what you see, you can look at something else; just ask, *Başka var mı* (BASH-kah VAHR-muh, 'Are there others?').

The letter and number in parentheses after the hotel's name indicate its official Turkish government rating: HL is Hotel, Luxury; H2 is Hotel, 2nd class, etc. There are five official classes from HL down to H4; below that, the hotel may be rated by the city government. The Hilton and Sheraton are HL; a hotel rated H4 would typically be a modern, respectable little place with quite small but tidy rooms equipped with private showers, a lift, central heat and at least one or two staff members who know a foreign language.

Generally speaking, the best selection of budget-to-moderate rooms is in the quarter named Laleli, and there are some of these near the Topkapı bus station as well. The lowest-priced hotels and hostels are near Sultanahmet and İstanbul University, or near Sirkeci Railway station. The moderate-to-luxury places are around Taksim Square in Beyoğlu. Camping areas are in the beach section named Florya.

Places to Stay – bottom end

You can find a hotel for less than 7000TL (US$10) double in the Sultanahmet area, Sirkeci Railway Station area, Laleli, or Topkapi bus station area.

Sultanahmet The Blue Mosque is officially the Mosque of Sultan Ahmet I (Sultan

Ahmet Camii). It gave the square and the quarter its name, contracted to Sultanahmet.

Around the Hippodrome are grouped the premier sights of İstanbul: Topkapı Palace, Sancta Sophia, the Blue Mosque, the 'Cistern Basilica' and the Hippodrome, so when you stay here the sights are mere steps from your hotel door.

The favourite in this area is the *Hotel Klodfarer* (tel 528-4850 or 528-4851), Klodfarer Caddesi 22, off Divan Yolu facing the Binbirdirek Underground Cistern. Old fashioned and dark but friendly, it has a cheap restaurant and rooms with bath for 5000TL (US$7) single, 7000TL (US$10) double, 10,500TL (US$14.70) triple.

You'll notice several hotels right on Divan Yolu facing the Hippodrome – *Hotel Güngör, Hotel Stop, Sultan Turist Oteli*, etc. While these do have similarly low prices, they are extremely noisy. Keep this in mind if you check in.

The *Yücelt Y Hostel* (tel 522-4790), Caferiye Sokak 6, Sultanahmet, is literally across the street from the front door of Sancta Sophia. Many years ago it was affiliated with the YMCA. Though the affiliation ended long ago, it keeps a 'Y' in its name to draw the clientele. The Yücelt is where most backpackers head when they arrive in İstanbul, because it has all the things a good tourist hostel should have: double rooms without baths for 4400TL (US$6.16), with bath for 5500TL (US$7.70), three-bed rooms for 1750TL (US$2.45) per person, and dormitory beds for 1250TL (US$1.75) each. It has an inexpensive cafeteria, laundry room, bulletin board, public showers and Turkish bath. The location couldn't be better.

In the summer (July and August), several university dormitories open their doors to foreign students. These tend to be extremely basic and cheap. They're not for all tastes, but if you want to look into one, ask for the latest information from the Tourism Information Office in Sultanahmet, right at the northern end of the Hippodrome next to the bus stop on Divan Yolu.

Sirkeci Railway Station Hotels near Sirkeci tend to be noisy, run-down or off-colour, with a few exceptions. Walk out of the station's main (west) door, turn left, then left again onto Muradiye-Hüdavendigar Caddesi. A block up on the right you'll see Orhaniye Caddesi going up a gentle slope.

The *Küçük Karadeniz Oteli* (tel 522-6300), Orhaniye Caddesi 12, Sirkeci, is new, modern, fairly quiet and presentable, with 20 rooms, each with hot and cold water (but not private baths) priced at 5500TL (US$7.70) double. Walk up one flight, then there's an elevator.

Hotel İpek Palas (tel 520-9724), Orhaniye Caddesi 9, is all the way up at the end of Orhaniye Caddesi, on the right. In the '30s and '40s this 'Silk Palace' was probably a place where traders and business travellers put up for the night. It's seen a lot of use, but the rooms are big, the location fairly good and quiet, and the prices good: 7000TL (US$10) for a double with a bath, slightly less for a room without.

The İpek Palas is at the intersection of Orhaniye Caddesi and İbni Kemal Caddesi. On the latter street are a half-dozen other hotels, all fairly quiet, all pretty cheap. *Hotel Fahri* (tel 522-4785 or 520-5686), İbni Kemal Caddesi 14-16, is modern, clean, not fancy but suitable, and charges 5000TL (US$7) single, 7000TL (US$10) double for rooms with shower. It's quiet because the street in front of it is used as an unofficial car park.

At the western end of İbni Kemal Caddesi, near where it meets Ankara Caddesi, is a small side street called Serdar Sokak. On it is the *Hotel Duru Palas* (tel 522-2170 or 522-0456), Serdar Sokak 28, which is often busy with Yugoslavian tour groups. Rooms are priced at 4500TL (US$6.30) single,

5500TL (US$7.70). You can speak Serbo-Croatian here, should you have a mind to.

Laleli (LAA-leh-LEE) is just east of Aksaray, just west of İstanbul University and north of Ordu Caddesi. It's a pleasant residential and hotel district with relatively quiet, shady, narrow streets. Several dozen little hotels sit cheek-by-jowl, and a new place seems to open each year. To the north lies the district named Şehzadebaşı (sheh-ZAH-deh-bosh-uh). It's really all one area, but some hotels will have Laleli in their address, others Şehzadebaşı.

Hotels in this area will rent you a clean, quiet double room with a private shower for about US$6 per night single, US$9 or US$10 double. Off-season, or if you intend to stay for more than just a few days, you can haggle for a reduction. Most will grant it quickly.

Tour groups from a number of European countries use some of the hotels in high summer, as the area is quiet yet convenient. Thus you may find some of them full, and others may be able to rent you a room only until another group arrives.

Start your explorations by walking up Harikzadeler Sokak from Ordu Caddesi. This will take you past several inexpensive hotels, and into the heart of Laleli.

The little hotels along Harikzadeler Sokak tend to be the cheaper ones. *Hotel Oran* (H4, tel 528-5813 or 527-0572), Harikzadeler Sokak 40, has 22 rooms with shower for 4200TL (US$6) single, 7000TL (US$10) double; it may be filled with tour groups.

Hotel Neşet (tel 526-7412 or 522-4474), Harikzadeler Sokak 23 across the street from the Hotel Oran, is very similar though a few liras cheaper; staff are very friendly.

Hotel Ayda (tel 526-7867), Harikzadeler Sokak 11, is less expensive still: double rooms with shower are priced at 6000TL (US$8.40).

The *Ömür Hotel* (tel 526-3030 or 520-9728), at the intersection of Zeynep Kâmil Sokak and Harikzadeler Sokak, has quite suitable rooms for 4250TL (US$5.95) single, 6250TL (US$8.75) double, with private shower.

Hotel Sırmalı (tel 520 7642), just off Harikzadeler at Zeynep Kâmil Sokak 45, two steps from the Hotel Ömür, is a popular place for foreign backpackers. A bit older than most of the above, it charges 4000TL (US$5.60) single, 6000TL (US$8.40) double for room with shower.

Aksaray Across Ordu Caddesi from Laleli, to the south, are dozens of other small hotels. In recent years this area has become popular with tourists, students and job-seekers from Iran and the Arab countries south and east of Turkey. Some of the hotels are used to Europeans, but most cater to Middle Eastern tourists.

The *İstanbul Youth Hostel* (tel 521-2455 or 523-6019) is here, however, at Cerrahpaşa Caddesi, Müezzin Sokak 2, in the Eskişehir Öretim ve Eğitim Vakfı building. Price for a bed is 1500TL (US$2.10) with a Youth Hostel card, 2000TL (US$2.80) with a student card, 2500TL (US$3.50) without any card. Rooms have four or six beds each. On the top floor there's a kitchen you can use. The hostel season is July through September. To find this place, ask for Cerrahpaşa Caddesi (jeh-RAH-pah-shah), which is on the west side of Aksaray square, and take the second turning to the left, Müezzin Sokak.

Topkapı Bus Station When you arrive at İstanbul's chaotic Topkapı international bus station, you may just want to make your way to the nearest cheap hotel. That's the *Hotel Ulubat* (tel 585-4694, 5), Kalburcu Çeşme Sokak 10. Simple but very suitable rooms with bath cost 5000TL (US$7) single, 7250TL (US$10.15) double. The hotel has a restaurant and car park. To find it, go through the Topkapı (Cannon Gate) on Millet Caddesi,

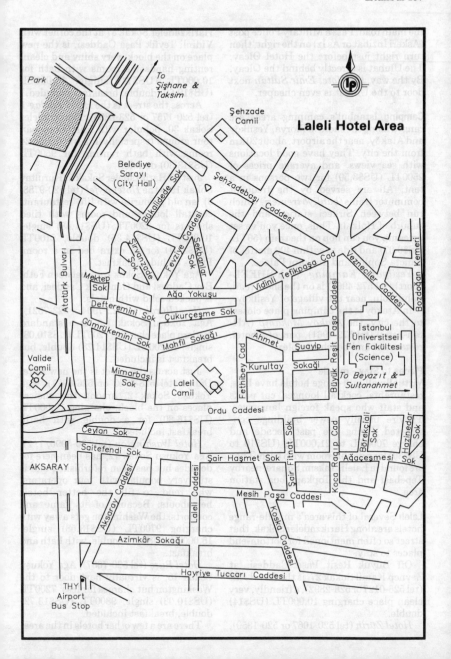

Laleli Hotel Area

the main road. Pass a Military Police post (Askeri İnzibat or As İz) on the right, then turn right just before the Hotel Olcay. The Ulubat is directly behind the Olcay. By the way, the *Hotel Emir Sultan* next door to the Ulubat is even cheaper.

Camping İstanbul's camping areas are ranged along the shore in Florya, Yeşilköy and Ataköy, near the airport, about 20 km from the city. They have good locations with sea views, and average prices of 2500TL (US$3.50) for two persons in a tent. All are served by the frequent commuter trains *(banliyö trenleri)* which run between Sirkeci station and the suburb of Halkalı. Thus, once you've set up camp you can hop on the train (50TL, US$0.07) and ride to within 400 metres of Sancta Sophia and Topkapı Palace.

Yeşilyurt Kamping (yeh-SHEEL-yoort) (tel 572-4961) is on the shore road, Sahil Yolu, near the village of Yeşilköy.

In Ataköy is the camping place closest to the city, the *Ataköy Mokamp* (AH-tah-keuy) (tel 572-4961), part of a hotel, restaurant and beach complex.

Places to Stay - middle
Virtually all mid-range hotels have lifts, restaurants, cocktail lounges, car parks and staff who speak foreign languages. They're usually newer buildings constructed during the past decade and charge 7000TL to 21,000TL (US$10 to US$30) for a double room with bath. They are found in Laleli, Taksim Square, nearby Tepebaşı and the Topkapı bus station area.

Laleli Several of this area's middle-range hotels are along Harikzadeler Sokak, that street so often mentioned for bottom-end places to stay.

Off Büyük Reşit Paşa Caddesi, at Zeynep Kamil Sokak 27, is the *Hotel Kul* (tel 526-0127 or 528-2892), a friendly, very clean place charging 10,000TL (US$14) double.

Hotel Zürih (tel 520-1067 or 520-1359),

Harikzadeler Sokak 37 at the corner with Vidinli Tevfik Paşa Caddesi, is the new place on the block, very shiny and clean, renting handsome rooms with bath for 10,000TL (US$14) single, 14,000TL (US$19.60) double, breakfast included.

Across the street is the *Hotel Pilolag-1* (tel 520-1757 or 523-6896), Harikzadeler Sokak 30, popular with East European tour groups (especially Poles). It has 24 rooms with bath renting for 9500TL (US$13.30) double.

Just off Harikzadeler Sokak at Kurultay Sokak 19 is the *Hotel Eyfel* (tel 520-9788, 9), an old favourite with lift, restaurant, cocktail lounge and rooms with tiled showers for 8200TL (US$11.48) single, 10,250TL (US$14.35) double, 2100TL (US$2.94) for an extra bed in a room. Prices include breakfast.

Ağa Yokuşu Sokak runs between Fethi Bey Caddesi and Gençtürk Caddesi, and is packed solid with hotels.

Hotel Burak (tel 522-7904 or 523-7521), Ağa Yokuşu Sokak 1-3, is a standard modern place charging 7200TL (US$10.08) single, 10,200TL (US$14.28) double, but breakfast is included.

Just across the street is the new *Hotel Diana* (tel 528-0760 or 526-6921), Ağa Yokuşu Sokak 2, among the choicer places on the block, charging 12,000TL (US$16.80) for a double with bath, breakfast included.

Hotel Washington (tel 520-5990, 1, 2), Ağa Yokuşu Sokak 12, has been here for decades but has been refurbished and is still very popular with tour operators, who tend to fill the better hotels hereabouts. Because of its fame and comforts, the Washington gets away with charging 9700TL (US$13.58) single, 15,000TL (US$21) double, with bath and breakfast.

Hotel Burç (tel 520-7667), Ağa Yokuşu Sokak 18, is virtually next door to the Washington but charges far less: 7200TL (US$10.08) single, 9800TL (US$13.72) double, breakfast included.

There are a few other hotels in the area,

several lying just a few steps off Ağa Yokuşu Sokak.

One of the nicer places is *Hotel Barın* (H3, tel 522-8426 or 526-4440), Fevziye Caddesi 25, Şehzadebaşı, a newer place with 30 rooms. All have showers, some have tubs. Prices are 9250TL (US$12.95) single, 13,000TL (US$18.20) double, bath and breakfast included.

Despite its name, you should have no trouble finding the *Hotel La Miraj* (tel 511-2445, 6, 7), Fethi Bey Caddesi 28, an older building but well kept up and restored, charging 7000TL (US$10) single, 11,000TL (US$15.40) double for largish rooms with bath, breakfast included.

Hotel Doru (H3, tel 526-5905 or 527-6928), Gençtürk Caddesi 44, Laleli, a few steps down the street from the aforementioned hotels, is yet another with 25 similar (if small), clean, modern rooms at similar prices.

Taksim Though the city has changed greatly in a century, Beyoğlu is still, generally speaking, the centre of European-style living. The airline offices, foreign banks and luxury hotels are all here. The Etap Marmara (formerly the Inter-Continental) hotel is right in Taksim; the Sheraton is a block away, the Hilton two blocks. All these places charge US$100 to US$150 for a double room – international rates.

There are several smaller hotels near Taksim which charge more reasonable rates, but even these suffer from price inflation due to location. They all charge a bit more because they're in the shadow of the Big Boys. A hotel room that costs 9500TL (US$13.30) at a nice little place in Laleli will cost 17,000TL (US$23.80) near Taksim.

Before looking for a hotel room near Taksim, ask yourself 'Why?' Laleli hotels are more convenient to the major tourist attractions of the Old City, and cheaper. The answer might be that you like the comforts. Taksim hotels tend to have

hotter water, more English-speaking staff, little things like note-paper in the rooms. Some of the moderately-priced hotels have rooms with views of the Bosphorus, and you definitely pay a premium for these (but that view is marvellous). There is also status: Laleli is middle class, Taksim is upper.

There are two old favourites with tourists in Taksim. *Hotel Keban* (keh-BAHN) (H2, tel 143-3310, 1, 2, 3), Sıraselviler Caddesi 51, Taksim, is just out of Taksim Square near İstiklal Caddesi. Look for the MAKSİM theatre – that's at the beginning of Sıraselviler Caddesi, and the hotel is just a few doors down from it. The Keban has 87 rooms with bath or shower, plus elevators, air-conditioning, barber shop, restaurant, even little refrigerators in some of the rooms. For all this posh stuff you pay 12,000TL (US$16.80) single, 14,700TL (US$20.58) double.

The *Dilson Hotel* (DEEL-sohn) (H2, tel 143-2032), Sıraselviler Caddesi 49, Taksim, a few steps down from the Keban, is very similar. Its 90 rooms are priced at 13,500TL (US$18.90) single, 18,800TL (US$26.32) double; family rooms available.

Walk down Sıraselviler Caddesi out of Taksim, and turn left at a sign reading *Plaza Hotel* (tel 145-3273, 4) just before the Alman Hastanesi (German Hospital). The hotel, hidden away on quiet Aslanyatağı Sokak 19/21 ('Street of the Lion's Bed'!), has some marvellous views of the Bosphorus, and older rooms and facilities kept clean and priced at 8000TL (US$11.20) single, 12,000TL (US$16.80) double for a room with bath, or 1000TL to 1500TL (US$1.40 to US$2.10) less for a room without private bath. Go here if you want that Bosphorus view.

Up near the Hilton, on Cumhuriyet Caddesi, is the *Hotel Konak* (tel 148-4744, 5), Nisbet Sokak 9, a hotel several decades old which benefits from an experienced staff and an upscale location. Rooms with bath are priced at 22,000TL

(US$30.80) single, 28,000TL (US$39.20) double, 33,000TL (US$46.20) triple, breakfast included.

Tepebaşı Between Galatasaray Square and Tünel Square, west of İstiklal Caddesi, is the district called Tepebaşı (TEH-peh-bah-shuh), which was the first luxury hotel district in the city. The main road through Tepebaşı is Meşrutiyet Caddesi, where one finds the British and American consulates-general, the Pera Palas Hotel and the Etap İstanbul Hotel, so if you stay here, you're in good company. The best way to get here is by taxi, or failing that, by dolmuş from Taksim; you may have to use a dolmuş that goes past Tepebaşı (say, to Aksaray), and pay the full fare. You can catch a bus along Tarlabaşı Caddesi (TAHR-la-bash-uh) just out of Taksim near the Air France office. Coming from Karaköy, take the Tünel to the top station and walk the several blocks to the hotels.

Down the hill a few steps from the Pera Palas and behind the American Consulate-General is the comfortable, modern *Otel Bale* (tel 150-4912), Refik Saydam Caddesi, the most modern hotel in the area after the Etap İstanbul. Some rooms have views of the Golden Horn, all have baths, and prices are 12,000TL (US$16.80) single, 15,500TL (US$21.70) double.

Just behind the towering Etap İstanbul Hotel is the older and more modest *Yenişehir Palas* (tel 149-8810, 1, 2), Meşrutiyet Caddesi. It is a hotel of eight floors, little in the way of views, and moderate prices of 10,000TL (US$14) single, 13,000TL (US$18.20) double with bath. It's a popular place with Greek tourists.

The *Büyük Londra Oteli* (tel 149-1025 or 145-0670), Meşrutiyet Caddesi 117, dates from the same era as the Pera Palas, has much smaller rooms and bathrooms, and is a bit the worse for wear, but it does preserve some of the *fin de siècle* glory (in the public rooms at least) at an eminently affordable price. A room with shower here

costs 8800TL (US$12.32) with one double bed, 17,500TL (US$24.50) with two beds.

Facing the entrance to the Pera Palas Hotel is the *Hotel Sedir* (tel 149-9589), Meşrutiyet Caddesi 189, which has rooms with bath for 9800TL (US$13.72) double, a lift and a handy location, but the rooms on the front are unbearably noisy; get one at the back.

Topkapı Bus Station Right next to the Hotel Ulubat described in the 'bottom end' section is the *Hotel Olcay* (OHL-jahyee) (tel 585-3220, 1, 2), Millet Caddesi 187, a bright and modern place with smooth service, a large restaurant and very comfortable rooms priced at 17,000TL (US$23.80) double with bath. Next door is the *Otel Şehrazat*, under construction at this writing, but it may be finished by the time you arrive.

Places to Stay - top end
The centre of the posh hotel district is certainly Taksim Square, but there are several important exceptions to this rule. In Sultanahmet is the phenomenally successful Yeşil Ev, formerly called the Konak, and near it several similar restored Ottoman houses. In Tepebaşı is the famous Pera Palas Hotel, built for the passengers on the original Orient Express. And up the Bosphorus at Çubuklu is the Hidiv Kasrı, the former mansion of the khedives of Egypt, now converted into a fabulous villa hotel. Here you can sleep in the bed of King Faruk if you like.

There are many plans for new luxury hotels in İstanbul, including the conversion of a palatial Ottoman barracks building into a Regent Hotel, and the restoration of the ruined Çırağan Palace into a small, exclusive hotel. At the moment, most of the rooms are in fairly modern buildings made to international standards.

Taksim The *Etap Marmara Hotel* (tel 144-8850), Taksim Square, was built as

Top: The Mosque of Sultan Ahmet III (Blue Mosque), İstanbul
Left: The Grand Bazaar (Kürkçüler Çarşısı), İstanbul
Right: A hazy view of the Golden Horn

Top: Sancta Sophia, İstanbul
Bottom: A spice merchant in the Egyptian Bazaar

an Inter-Continental. Many rooms have fabulous Bosphorus views; the rest overlook Taksim, its park and the city. Prices are US$90 to US$110 single, US$100 to US$135 double, plus 15% service.

The *İstanbul Sheraton Hotel* (tel 148-9000), Taksim Park, also provides wonderful views and a good location for slightly higher prices.

A bit farther from Taksim along Cumhuriyet Caddesi, the *İstanbul Hilton Hotel* (tel 146-7050), Cumhuriyet Caddesi, is set in its own spacious park with tennis courts and swimming pool, and gives one the feeling of staying at a private club, albeit a very large club. Though the oldest luxury hotel in the city, the Hilton has been carefully kept up to date, and a big new addition is under construction.

There is a middle ground for those who want some of the comforts of a luxury hotel but don't want to pay 'international' prices. A few steps out of Taksim Square along the western side of Cumhuriyet Caddesi is the office of Air France, and to the left of the office is the beginning of Şehit Muhtar Caddesi. Walk along this street for two short blocks and you'll come to the *Otel Eresin* (tel 150-3367 or 150-4476), Topçu Caddesi 34, a new seven-floor, 60-room hotel with bathtubs, television sets and little refrigerators in all the rooms. The street is quiet and the price is 35,000TL (US$50) double.

The *Divan Oteli* (dee-VAHN) (HL, tel 146-4020), is on Cumhuriyet Caddesi, across from the Sheraton and a block from the Hilton. Founded by Vehbi Koç, Turkey's millionaire industrialist, it was meant as a suitable place for his friends and associates in the days before the big international chain hotels arrived. It is very comfortable, but smaller (96 rooms) than the 400-room-plus Hilton or Sheraton. The dining room has a reputation for being among the best restaurants in the city and is reasonably priced compared with the 'international' places. All the comforts and services of a luxury hotel are

here; the staff are friendly, expert and accommodating. Rooms cost US$60 single, US$75 double, taxes and services included.

Tepebaşı The *Etap İstanbul Oteli* (H1, tel 144 8880), Meşrutiyet Caddesi, Tepebaşı, is across the street from the Pera Palas and a few steps from the American Consulate, in Beyoğlu. Don't confuse it with its sister hotel, the Etap Marmara, which is in Taksim Square. The Etap İstanbul has all the modern conveniences; a good enough location; a splendid view of the Golden Horn, the Old City and the Bosphorus from many of its rooms; and room prices similar to the Divan Oteli. If you take a room with a less spectacular view, you save money. The view from the rooftop swimming pool is the best of all. For the price, this is the best hotel in the city, and it's often booked solid.

When Georges Nagelmackers began his renowned Compagnie Internationale des Wagons-Lits et Grands Express Europeens in the 1880s, he had a problem. When his pampered passengers debarked in Constantinople the luxury ended, for there was no suitable place for them to stay. So he built a place in Pera (Beyoğlu) and called it the Pera Palace. It opened in the 1890s, advertised as having ' . . . a thoroughly healthy situation, being high up and isolated on all four sides', and 'overlooking the Golden Horn and the whole panorama of Stamboul'.

Though it is no longer 'isolated on all four sides', the Pera Palas Oteli (PEH-ra pa-LAHS) (H1, tel 145 2230), Meşrutiyet Caddesi 98-100, Tepebaşı (TEP-eh-bash-uh), is still open and thriving. It fills up regularly with tourists looking to relive the great age of Constantinople, and with groups brought in by travel agents. It is a worthy place.

It used to be fairly cheap, too, but the management has discovered what foreigners will pay for nostalgia (a lot), and has upped the prices to breathtaking heights. The Pera Palas has 120 rooms with high ceilings, period (more or less) furnishings and bathrooms to match. Some rooms have views of the Golden Horn. Nostalgia is your main consolation here, as you pay luxury-class prices but do not really receive luxury services such as air-conditioning and sound-proofing. Rooms with bath and buffet breakfast are currently priced at US$75 to US$95 single, US$85 to US$115 double. Rooms on the lower floors can be very noisy, and west-facing rooms can get quite hot from the setting sun in summer.

Sultanahmet The Turkish Touring & Automobile Club has been restoring historic buildings throughout the city, including an Ottoman mansion very near Sancta Sophia and the Blue Mosque. This is the *Yeşil Ev* (tel 528-6764 or 511-1150, 1), formerly called the Konak but this caused confusion with the Hotel Konak on Cumhuriyet Caddesi. The house is simply lovely, a graceful old Ottoman place perfectly restored (virtually rebuilt) and furnished in period pieces and antiques with exquisite taste. It is very difficult to get a reservation here, but if you do, you'll pay US$75 single, US$90 to US$100 double, US$115 to US$125 for the Pasha's Room. Breakfast, service and tax are included in the rates.

Not far from the Yeşil Ev, against the walls of Topkapı Palace, is a row of Ottoman houses which have also been rebuilt and refitted by the Touring Club as lodgings for travellers, at similar prices. Inquire at the Yeşil Ev for details on the Ayasofya Pansiyonları.

Bosphorus Having ruled Egypt for centuries, the Ottomans lost control to an adventurer named Muhammad Ali, who took over the government of Egypt and defied the sultan in İstanbul to dislodge him. The sultan, unable to do so, gave him quasi-independence and had to be satisfied with reigning over Egypt rather than ruling. The ruling was left to Muhammad Ali and his line, and the ruler of Egypt was styled *hidiv*, 'khedive' (not 'king', as that would be unbearably independent). The khedives of Egypt kept up the pretense of Ottoman suzerainty by paying tribute to İstanbul.

The Egyptian royal family, who looked upon themselves as Turkish and spoke Turkish rather than Arabic as the court language, often spent their summers in a traditional *yalı*, or wooden mansion on the Bosphorus shore. In 1906, Khedive Abbas Hilmi built himself a palatial villa on the most dramatic promontory on the Bosphorus, a place commanding a magnificent view. The Hidiv Kasrı (hee-DEEV kahss-ruh) (tel 331-2651), set in its own large park, is in pure, delicious Art Nouveau style, with a circular entry hall complete with fountain. A semi-circular facade looks west across the Bosphorus. The ground floor is now the restaurant; the upper floor, the master bedroom.

There is room for only 50 guests in the hotel, but every single one has an unforgettable stay. Rooms with bath are priced from US$42 to US$62 for a double on the top (servants') floor, through US$100 for a large bedroom as used by the royal family, to US$200 for the Hidiv'in Dairesi, the Khedive's Suite. You'll need a taxi to reach the hotel. Çubuklu is about a 30 to 45-minute drive north of the city centre.

PLACES TO EAT

In İstanbul you will eat some very tasty food, no matter if you eat in a simple workingman's cafeteria or in a luxury restaurant. Good food has been a Turkish passion for centuries. In fact, the fearsome Janissary corps, the sultan's shock troops, were organized along the lines of a kitchen staff. They had a habit of signalling revolt by overturning the cauldrons which held their dinner of *pilav*. The message from these elite troops to their sovereign might be phrased, 'If you call this food, we have confidence in neither your taste buds nor your leadership'.

İstanbul's restaurants are literally everywhere. Price, by the way, has little to do with quality in Turkish restaurants. In the posh places you will get slightly finer food, elegant presentation and highly polished European-style service. But in the moderate, inexpensive and even very cheap places, the food will be savoury and delicious.

Little neighbourhood places, mostly 'ready-food' (hazır yemek) restaurants, kebapçıs and pidecis, will charge between 400TL (US$0.56) for a simple main-course lunch to perhaps 800TL to 2100TL (US$1.12 to US$3) for a several-course budget tuck-in.

In slightly nicer places with white tablecloths and attentive waiters, if you order something more expensive such as a nice portion of meat or fish, wine or beer, dessert, etc, expect to pay 3500TL (US$5) to a top of 7000TL (US$10) per person. Above that you're definitely in the top end, but even so, a meal costing more than 14,000TL (US$20) per person is a rarity in Turkey except in the big world-class hotels.

Mid-range restaurants are found everywhere. Bottom-end places exist in all areas except Tepebaşı, Tünel and the Bosphorus. Top-end restaurants are mostly in Beyoğlu (Taksim, Tepebaşı, Tünel, Karaköy) and along the Bosphorus shores.

Places to Eat – bottom end
Sultanahmet Several little restaurants are open along Divan Yolu, the main street which goes from Sultanahmet Square up the hill toward the university and the Grand Bazaar.

Perhaps the most popular place on Divan Yolu is the Vitamin Restaurant (VEE-tah-meen) (tel 526-5086) at Divan Yolu 16, opposite the Hippodrome, a bright and modern hazır yemek eatery with all sorts of savoury dishes displayed in the street-side windows. Choose a meal such as taze fasulye (green string beans), kabak dolması (stuffed marrow/squash),

flat pide bread and fruit juice, and the meal will cost 1300TL (US$1.82).

Just up the slope on Divan Yolu is the Çınar Restaurant, an old standby which looks fancier than its prices really are. For only slightly more than at the afore-mentioned place you can enjoy two floors of tables with white cloths, waiter service and tasty food.

Behind the Blue Mosque on Torun Sokak is a little place called Hacı Bekir Oğulları Lahmacun, Kebap ve Pide Salonu, which has these advantages: it is quiet and serves lahmacun (the Arabic 'pizza') and pide (the Turkish pizza) for only 300TL to 650TL (US$0.42 to US$0.91), as well as the heartier, more costly kebaps. To find it, walk from the Hippodrome with the Blue Mosque on your right-hand side.

For refreshments and snacks, the Derviş Aile Çay Bahçesi (Dervish Family Tea Garden), Kabasakal Caddesi 2/1 near the Yeşil Ev Hotel, has tea for 100TL (US$0.14), coffee for 250TL (US$0.35), small sandwiches (sandviç) or grilled sandwiches called tost for 200TL (US$0.28). Try a peynirli tost, a cheese sandwich mashed in a vice-like sandwich cooker.

Across Divan Yolu from the Hippodrome is the famous Pudding Shop, where the drop-out generation of the 1960s kept alive and happy on various nutritious, tasty, inexpensive puddings such as sütlaç (SEWT-latch), a milk-and-rice pudding; or its even tastier baked version, fırın sütlaç (FUH-ruhn SEWT-latch), served cold. Today the Pudding Shop serves all sorts of meals. Prices are higher and food quality not the same as in the hippy heyday. The traffic on busy Divan Yolu out front is objectionable.

Tourists frequent many of the other little restaurants along Divan Yolu. Although prices aren't bad here, you can do even better by walking up Divan Yolu (west) and turning right onto one of the little side streets. Wander around back in the neighbourhood for a few blocks and you'll come across several small restaurants which don't get many tourists. The food is equally good, the prices definitely working-class. They tend to be open all the time, so if it's very crowded at lunch come back in an hour.

Sirkeci & Eminönü There are lots of good small restaurants in the Sirkeci area. Leave the station by the main (west) door. The busy street before you is Ankara Caddesi. Turn left (south), cross busy Muradiye Caddesi, and walk up the slope on Ankara Caddesi, turning into the second or third little street on the left. This will bring you to İbni Kemal Caddesi, one of those areas of workshops and offices with a half-dozen eateries, all delightfully low in price.

For example, the *Kardeşler Anadolu Lokantası*, on İbni Kemal Caddesi at the corner with Hocapaşa Caddesi opposite the little mosque, served me a meal of *mercimek çorbası* (lentil soup), *biber dolma* (green pimiento/pepper stuffed with rice and lamb), bread and spring water for 600TL (US$0.84).

There are many other cheap little restaurants within a few steps of that one, including the *Hoca Paşa Pidecisi*, serving fresh pizza for very little, and the *Bozkurt Döner Kebap Salonu* for the delicious lamb grilled on a vertical spit. If you want something to finish off your meal, buy fresh fruit from a vendor and wash it at the tap by the mosque.

Facing the plaza in Eminönü, to the right of the Denizcilik Bankası, to the left of the Yeni Cami (Pigeon Mosque), is a tiny stand which bears the name *Vefa Bozacısı*. *Boza* (BOH-zah) is a thick, slightly tangy slightly sweet, fairly bland fermented grain drink made from millet. Usually sold in winter, it is hearty and nutritious. That's all they serve here; glasses of boza, except in summer when they may switch to *sıra* (SHUH-rah), a tangy unfermented white grape juice.

Karaköy has some little restaurants, but it is much more famous for *börek* and *baklava*. A *börekçi* (bur-REK-CHEE) makes various sorts of flaky pastries filled with cheese and chopped parsley. Each type of *börek* has its own name. *Su böreği* (SOO bur-reh-yee, 'water pastry') is a thick, noodle-like affair with sprinklings of white sheep's-milk cheese and chopped parsley. Ask for 200 grams (ee-KEE yewz gram), and the clerk will cut out a square, chop it into manageable bites, and hand it to you on a plastic plate with a fork. It will cost perhaps 250TL (US$0.35).

Other sorts of *börek* are the more familiar flaky pastries with filling, like *sosisli börek* (soh-sees-LEE), wrapped around a sausage; or *peynirli*, stuffed with cheese. In Karaköy's many *börekçi* shops they're cheap, fresh and good.

The *baklava* places are also good. The *baklava* comes with all sorts of stuffings. Prices are marked per kg and per portion (usually 150 grams, though you can order as little or as much as you like for a portion). Stuffings include pistachios (ask for *şam fıstıklı*, SHAHM fuhs-tuhk-luh); walnuts (*cevizli*, jeh-veez-LEE); even clotted cream (*kaymaklı*, kah-ee-mahk-LUH). İstanbul's most famous *baklavacı* is *Güllüoğlu* (GEWL-loo-oh-loo), in a shop on the street level of the big parking garage across from the Yolcu Salonu (International Maritime Passenger Terminal), 100 metres from the Galata Bridge.

Grand Bazaar On the map of the Grand Bazaar, you will notice a half-dozen little restaurants marked. With one exception, these are tiny, basic places where bazaar workers eat, or from which prepared meals are taken to their workshops on trays.

Some of these little places rarely see a foreign tourist, some are used to them. All will welcome you and make extra efforts to please. The ones that are used to foreigners, where the menus may be in English and where the waiter will know at least a few words of a foreign language, are grouped on Koltuk Kazazlar Sokak and Kahvehane Sokak. The most prominent one is the *Sevim Lokantası*. Take a seat in the little dining room, or sit at a table set out in one of the little streets, order two or three plates of food, and the bill won't exceed 2200TL (US\$3.08) – probably less.

Another place is the *Rumeli 2 Restaurant* at Perdahçılar Sokak 60, corner of Takkeciler. Don't let its tiny entrance fool you, as the dining room is larger and there is another dining room upstairs. Choose one of the ready-food items or order *döner kebap*. I had a *çerkez kebabı* (chehr-KEHZ, Circassian) of peas, aubergine/eggplant, lamb, potatoes, tomatoes and peppers/pimientos in a rich sauce, plus *bulgur pilav* (cracked-wheat pilaf) with beans, *ayran* and bread for 1200TL (US\$1.68).

Grand Bazaar Cafés You will no doubt pass the *Şark Kahvesi* (SHARK kah-veh-see, the Oriental Café), at the end of Fesçiler Caddesi. Always filled with locals and tourists, it can be difficult to find a seat in. But this is the real bazaar, and a cup of Turkish coffee, soft drink or glass of *çay* (CHA-ee) will cost only about 150TL to 350TL (US\$0.21 to US\$0.49).

In fine weather, head out of the bazaar and next door to the Beyazıt Camii (Mosque of Beyazıt, between the bazaar and the university gates). You can go through the Sahaflar Çarşısı, the Old Book Bazaar. On the east side of the mosque is a lovely tea garden, a plaza filled with tables, most of them shady. Waiters in traditional coffee-house costumes circulate through the sea of tables carrying trays filled with the pretty little glasses of tea. Signal to the waiter when you see him with a tray and you'll get your tea right away; or order and have your drink brought to you. As this garden is patronised by university students, the drinks are not expensive.

Laleli & Aksaray Laleli is a good place to look for low-priced eats because İstanbul University is close by. You'll see several places stuffed with students, good food and low prices. Down the slope in Aksaray are dozens of little restaurants, neighbourhood places catering not to tourists, but to a local clientele.

A favourite in this district has the daunting name of *Hacıbozanoğulları*. It's a *kebapçı* at the corner of Ordu Caddesi and Laleli Caddesi, on the south side of Ordu Caddesi, across from the Laleli Camii (mosque). Though it's somewhat fancied up, prices are still very moderate as this is a working-class district. A *porsyon* (pohr-SYOHN, portion) of *kebap* is 100 grammes and costs only about 350TL (US\$0.49); you may want to order a *duble porsyon*, or double portion. With your *kebap* you may get *yufka*, the paper-thin unleavened peasant flat bread; or *pide*, the thicker, leavened flat bread. For a drink, try *ayran*, a healthful and refreshing mix of yoghurt and spring water. Hacıbozanoğulları (that's ha-JUH-bo-ZAHN-oh-ool-lahr-uh) also has a separate pastry shop, called a *baklavacı* (BAHK-lah-vah-juh, 'baklava-maker'). Besides this many-layered pastry stuffed with nuts and honey, the shop features other Turkish sweets.

Kebap restaurants abound in the little side streets off Ordu Caddesi. For instance, the *Gaziantep Emek Saray Kebapçısı* at Gençtürk Caddesi 6, just a few steps north from Ordu Caddesi, will serve you a portion of *Urfa kebap* (OOR-fah, roast ground lamb with spices and onions) plus a glass of *ayran* (a drink of spring water mixed with yogurt) for only 800TL (US\$1.12). When you order your *kebaps* here, specify whether you want them *acısız* (ah-juh-SUHZ, without hot pepper) or *acılı* (ah-juh-LUH, with hot pepper). The restaurant's specialty is *çiğ köfte* (CHEE kerf-teh), uncooked ground lamb with spices.

Another place to find a good meal is at the *Kardeşler Restaurant*, Ordu Caddesi

202, at the corner of Büyük Reşit Paşa Caddesi, across that street from the lofty portal of the university's Chemistry (Kimya) Faculty. Though a ready-food restaurant, it's fixed up with touches of brass and marble, and is quite attractive. Expect to spend 1400TL to 2000TL (US$1.96 to US$2.80) for a full meal.

There are cheaper places. Facing the Chemistry Faculty on Büyük Reşit Paşa Caddesi are the Şar Lokantası at No 62, a tidy little ready-food cafeteria; and the Altuğ Köfte Salonu at the corner with Kurultay Sokak, serving simple meals based on köfte. At either place, lunch for 700TL to 1000TL (US$1 to US$1.40) is a simple matter.

Taksim Taksim has dozens of restaurants. The variety is equally vast, making it one of the best areas in the city to find good and inexpensive food. As Turkish dishes are so varied and their names so incomprehensible, you might want to start off at the Selvi Kafeterya, Sıraselviler Caddesi 40, across from the Dilson and Keban hotels. This big, bright, plain place has the standard cafeteria line, tin trays, steam tables and low prices. They're not as low as they might be, however; this is Taksim. Don't over-eat with your eyes. Three selections, plus that good Turkish bread, is plenty for anyone; two will usually suffice. You can always go back. Fill up at lunch or dinner for 1350TL to 1700TL (US$1.96 to US$2.47).

İstiklal Caddesi, Beyoğlu's main street, runs (one way to traffic) from Tünel Square to Taksim. At the beginning of İstiklal you'll see the Antep Restaurant at No 3 and the Pehlivan Restaurant at No 5, side by side. These, too, are cafeterias where you can choose three dishes and a drink and end up paying less than 1500TL (US$2.18).

Continuing along, İstiklal takes you past the Fıçı Restaurant, a place with waiter service, and a Bursa kebap restaurant, then numerous little büfe places, good for a cheap, quick snack. In many of these you must buy a fiş (FEESH), or receipt, from the cashier for the total of your purchases before you order. If you're not sure what things cost, ignore the system, ask for (or point to) what you want, and the cook will shout the total to the cashier. They are very tolerant of foreigners.

Perhaps the best and most plentiful food for the lowest price is to be found at the Ada Lokantası, at No 25 on a narrow side street called Büyükparmakkapı Sokak (the 'Street of the Thumb Gate') going south from İstiklal; it's the third little street on the left as you come from Taksim. A bright, fairly large restaurant, it has lots of ready-food choices on which you can fill up easily for 700TL to 1500TL (US$0.98 to US$2.10).

Tepebaşı & Tünel From Galatasaray, Meşrutiyet Caddesi leads north, then west, then south, roughly parallel to İstiklal Caddesi. Several restaurants are of interest on these two streets, most of them in the middle range; there's not a lot of good, cheap eating to be had. For a light lunch or snack, go to the pideci behind and to the left of the Etap İstanbul Hotel, where you can get a pide with butter and cheese for 450TL (US$0.65).

Places to Eat – middle

Topkapı Palace Everyone who visits Topkapı Palace has a problem: since it can take almost a whole day to see the palace properly (including the Harem), where do you eat lunch? There is a restaurant in the palace, all the way at the far end from the main entrance. Tables are both inside and outside under an awning. The outside tables have marvellous views of the Bosphorus and the Asian shore.

Because the restaurant has a captive audience of tourists (not locals, who might complain), food and service are not quite what they should be, though the restaurant is always crowded at lunchtime. The trick is to arrive by 11.30 am to beat the lunch rush, or to come later in the afternoon. For a meal of soup, shish kebab, salad and drink with tax and tip included, figure to pay about 3000TL to 4500TL (US\$4.20 to US\$6.30).

If it's just a nice seat and a cool drink you're looking for, go to the café just below the restaurant, where there are even better views.

Sirkeci & Eminönü Go out the station door, turn left, then left again onto Muradiye Caddesi. The first street to the right is Orhaniye (described in the hotel section). Across the street from the Küçük Karadeniz Oteli is the Şehir Lokantası (sheh-HEER), with white tablecloths, waiter service, fancier surroundings and prices of 2500TL to 4000TL (US\$3.50 to US\$5.60) for a full meal.

In the same range, perhaps a bit more expensive, is the Borsa Lokantası, behind the İnterbank Uluslararası building. Open only for lunch from 11.30 am to 4.30 pm, Monday through Saturday, it serves the local business community in some style and comfort.

Karaköy & Galata Bridge The Yolcu Salonu contains two of İstanbul's best restaurants. As headquarters for Turkish Maritime Lines, the Yolcu Salonu had to have a showplace seafood restaurant. In fact, it has two. Enter on the building's right (west) end and go to either the Liman Lokantası or the Liman Kafeteryası. Both are open from noon to 4 pm (lunch only) every day.

The Kafeterya is a less elegant, less expensive version of the restaurant. You pay a set price (about 4000TL, US\$5.60) and help yourself to the various courses at the steam tables.

Upstairs in the Liman Lokantası, a spacious, simple, somewhat old-fashioned dining room overlooks the mouth of the Golden Horn and the Old City. (If there's a cruise ship tied up at the Yolcu Salonu dock, the ship will block the view.)

Service is very polite and refined, fish is the speciality, and a full, elegant, delicious lunch from soup to baklava and coffee, with wine, will cost between 6000TL and 9000TL (US\$8.40 to US\$12.60).

With the new Galata Bridge under construction, I can't say what the dining situation will be here, but little fishing smacks used to tie up to the Galata Bridge to sell their daily catch. This has been going on for a century, and was the reason numerous little fish restaurants grew up under the bridge. They used to charge almost nothing for the freshest fish you'd ever eaten. Today you must be careful to ask prices in advance, for menus rarely carry them – they change daily, with the bounty of the catch.

These places are not at all fancy, with their formica tables and fluorescent lights. But the fish can be very good and the prices reasonable, about 3750TL to 4500TL (US\$5.25 to US\$6.30) for a full meal with wine or beer; be sure to ask prices in advance, though.

Grand Bazaar At the Havuzlu Lokantası prices are in the moderate range. The food is about the same as at the bottom-end places mentioned in this area, but you get a lofty dining room made of several bazaar streets (walled off for the purpose long ago), a few tables set out in front of the entrance by a little stone pool (Havuzlu means 'with pool'; I suspect it was a deep well centuries ago). Waiter service is much more polite and unhurried. If you want to escape the activity of the bazaar into a haven of quiet and calm, spend a little more (2750TL to 4500TL, US\$3.85 to US\$6.30) and go to the Havuzlu. It's next to the PTT (peh-teh-TEH, the post office). Follow the yellow-and-black signs and ask for the PTT or the restaurant.

Kumkapı In Byzantine times, the harbour called Kontoscalion was located due south of Laleli. The gate into the city from that port came to be called Kumkapı (KOOM-kah-puh, Sand Gate) by the Turks. The harbour has been filled in and the gate is long gone, but the district is still filled with fishermen who moor their boats in a more modern version of the old harbour, then pass beneath the railway to reach their homes in one of İstanbul's most colourful and delightful neighbourhoods. Where there are fishermen, there are fish restaurants, and Kumkapı is famous for them. Before the mid-1970s fish was the poor person's protein throughout the world. Since that time demand has exceeded supply, and a fish dinner, even in a modest restaurant, has become something of a luxury. You should, however, stroll around Kumkapı one evening, choose a likely place for dinner, and expect to part with 5500TL to 7000TL (US$7.70 to US$10).

Kumkapı has at least two dozen seafood restaurants, many operated by Greeks and Armenians. The best one, according to an İstanbul friend of mine, is *Kemal*. Among the favourite things to order is *kılıç şiş*, or swordfish shish kebab, chunks of fresh swordfish skewered and grilled over charcoal, but there are fish soups and stews, fish poached with vegetables *(buğlama)*, pan-fried fish and pickled fish.

Typical of Kumkapı's seafood eateries is the *Minas Restaurant* (MEE-nahss) (tel 522-9646) at Samsa Sokak 7, facing the little square. It has white tablecloths, airy windows with lacy curtains, and on one wall a cartoon of a vengeful giant fish about to dine on an embarrassed and frightened fellow lying, fishlike, on a plate. Minas is not one of the cheaper places; you can dine for less money elsewhere. If you're not in the mood for seafood but would like to explore Kumkapı in any case, come for a meat kebab and you'll spend a mere 2000TL (US$2.80) or so.

You can get to Kumkapı by one of three methods. From Laleli, Beyazıt or the Grand Bazaar, walk. Just opposite the

Beyazıt Camii (mosque) in Beyazıt Square, on the south side of Yeniçeriler Caddesi, is the beginning of Tiyatro Caddesi. Follow this street south for 10 short blocks (for the last block, it veers to the left), and you'll find yourself in Kumkapı's main square.

You can also take a taxi, but it may be a bit expensive as the driver might choose to cruise all the way around the old city in order to enter this congested district from the sea side; figure on 1200TL (US$1.75) from Sultanahmet.

Perhaps the most enjoyable way to go is by train from Sirkeci Station. Enter the station, bear to the right and buy a ticket at one of the kiosks marked 'Banliyö' (that's the French *banlieue* in Turkish guise) for 70TL (US$0.10), and board any of the electric commuter trains on the right-hand platforms. Most will be for Halkalı, but in fact any train will do, as they all pass Kumkapı. The train will round Seraglio Point, giving you some marvellous views of the Sea of Marmara and Topkapı Palace, and stop briefly at Cankurtaran station before pulling into Kumkapı station. Leave the train and the station, and walk down the most prominent street, which is Ördekli Bakkal Sokak, the 'Street of the Grocer with a Duck'. You'll pass the *Gönül Pastanesi* on the left, a good place for a sweet after dinner. Then you're in Kumkapı, with its market, Orthodox church, itinerant vendors of delicious fresh almonds *(taze badem)* and stuffed mussels *(midye tavası)*, shops selling fishing tackle and wellingtons, and many, many restaurants. The main square of the quarter is just at the far end of Ördekli Bakkal Sokak.

By the way, the next station on the rail line after Kumkapı is Aksaray (Yenikapı). You can use the train to come and go from that district, as well.

Taksim & Galatasaray The *Hacı Baba Restaurant* (ha-JUH bah-bah) (tel 144-1886) at İstiklal Caddesi 49 deserves

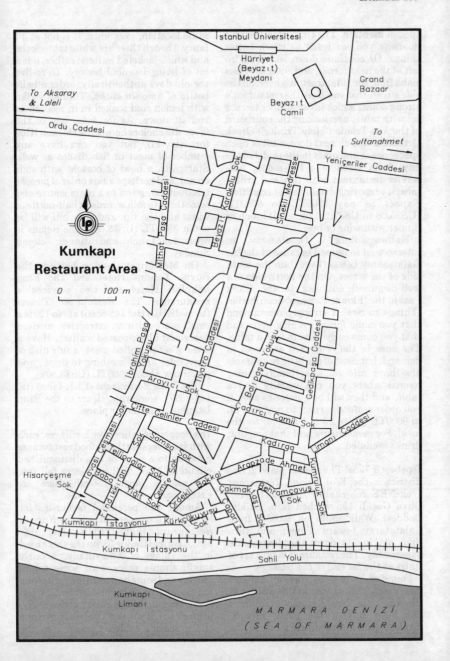

İstanbul Üniversitesi

Hürriyet
(Beyazıt)
Meydanı

Grand
Bazaar

Beyazıt
Camii

To Aksaray
& Laleli

Ordu Caddesi

To
Sultanahmet

Yeniçeriler Caddesi

**Kumkapı
Restaurant Area**

0   100 m

Sinekli Medrese

Beyazıt Karakolu Sok

Mithat Paşa Caddesi

Gedikpaşa Caddesi

Balıpaşa Yokuşu

Tiyatro Caddesi

İbrahim Paşa Yokuşu

Arayıcı Sok

Çadırcı Camii Sok

Çifte Gelinler Caddesi

Kadırga

Limanı Caddesi

Samsa Sok

Aragözade Ahmet

Kumruluk Sok

Tavası Çeşmesi Sok

Telliodalar Sok

Cemre Sok

Behramçavuş Sok

Hisarçeşme
Sok

Hıtkıhan

İğdit Sok

Baba Sok

Ordekli Bakkal

Çakmak Taşı Sok

Çopariz Sok

Kumkapı İstasyonu

Kürkçükuyusu Sok

Kumkapı İstasyonu

Sahil Yolu

Kumkapı
Limanı

MARMARA DENİZİ
(SEA OF MARMARA)

special mention. The tiny, unimpressive doorway you see leads to much better things. Or continue down İstiklal, turn left at the next corner, and enter the Hacı Baba from the side street. It's here, on the side street, that you'll see the restaurant's strong point: a nice little outdoor terrace set with tables overlooking the courtyard of the Aya Triada ('Holy Trinity') Greek Orthodox church next door, a bit of open space, peace and quiet in the midst of the city. Hacı Baba is a full-menu, full-service restaurant with fish and grilled meats, preparing dishes and specialities. Expect to pay 3500TL to 5000TL (US$5.08 to US$7.25) for a full lunch or dinner with wine or beer.

Halfway along is Galatasaray, an intersection so named because of the big Galatasaray Lisesi (Lycée) on the south side of the street. On the north side is a well-disguised entrance to the Çiçek Pasajı, the 'Flower Passage' described in 'Things to See'. I strongly recommend that you come for an evening here, and that you come early so as to find a table. The ones in the courtyard are most in demand, but most of the little restaurants also have *aile salonus* (family dining rooms) where you can usually find a table, and they will be quieter as well. If you order seafood, expect to pay 4500TL to 6000TL (US$6.53 to US$8.70) for the meal. For meat, figure half that amount, drinks included.

Tepebaşı & Tünel The special place in this district is the *Yeni Rejans Restaurant* (yeh-NEE reh-zhahnss) (tel 144-1610), Olivo Geçidi 15, reached from İstiklal Caddesi. Walk south on İstiklal from Galatasaray toward Tünel, and turn right at No 244 down the dingy little passageway. The restaurant is up a set of stairs at the far end of the passage.

Founded in 1930 by Russian emigrés (there were many living in this district at the time), the 'New Regency' restaurant has been serving the same French-inspired Russian-modified food, in the same location, ever since. It is not at all fancy, though there are white tablecloths and white-jacketed waiters; rather, it is a bit of living İstanbul history. To re-live the old days authentically, order a half-bottle of *limonlu votka*, Turkish vodka with lemon rind soaked in it, as soon as you sit down. As for food, one of the favourite choices here is the chicken Kiev (or Kievski), but you can have any number of meat or fish dishes as well. Start with a bowl of borscht with sour cream, and perhaps a side order of *piroçki* (croquettes), go on to a main course and something to follow, order a half-bottle of wine, add the tip, and your bill will be about 3500TL (US$5.08). The Rejans is open for lunch and dinner; closed Sunday.

On Meşrutiyet Caddesi between the Büyük Londra Hotel and the Etap İstanbul Hotel are two serviceable restaurants. The *Restaurant Tuncel* (toon-JEHL) (tel 145-5566) at No 129 is a small place with an attractive, modern decor and black-coated waiters. Have a meal of soup, grilled meat, a side dish of vegetables and something to drink, and you'll pay about 2500TL (US$3.50).

The *İrfan Restaurant* (EER-fahn) (tel 144-2597), somewhat closer to the Etap İstanbul, is a similar place.

The Bosphorus is lined with villages, each with its several little seafood restaurants catering to a more or less distinguished clientele. Most of these places fall into the middle range, though there are exceptions.

Among the perennial favourites for locals and foreigners alike is the *Kaptan Restaurant* (kahp-TAHN) (tel 165-8487), Birinci Cadde 53, on the shore road in the village of Arnavutköy. A fairly small, simple place with some tables indoors and some on a terrace overlooking the Bosphorus, it is crowded by 7.30 pm every evening of the week; arrive early, before 7 pm, if you want to be assured one of the seaside tables. Choose from the salads and side dishes in the cold cases, select a fish to be grilled, order a bottle of cold white wine, and you're in for an unforgettable experience. I recently dined at the Kaptan with two friends; we ordered fish, fried potatoes, aubergine/eggplant salad, white cheese, *böreks* and grapes, all washed down with copious amounts of *rakı*, and the total bill for the three of us came to 12,000TL (US$16.80).

Close by, within one km to the north in the town of Bebek, is a similar but slightly trendier place, the *Yeni Bebek Restaurant* (yeh-NEE beh-BEHK) (tel 163-3447), next to the Hotel Bebek on the shore road.

Places to Eat - top end

Sirkeci & Eminönü The *Mısır Çarşısı* (MUH-suhr char-shuh-suh, 'Egyptian Market') is also called the spice bazaar because of the many spice shops within. A famous old restaurant here has been going for decades.

Quite a while ago, a man named Pandeli opened a modest little restaurant down by the wholesale vegetable and fish markets on the Golden Horn. After gaining a citywide reputation, he moved to the guardroom over the main entrance (facing Galata Bridge) of the Mısır Çarşısı. The small guardroom chambers are covered in beautiful faience, and some of the tables have views out onto the square of Eminönü and the bridge, or inward to the bazaar's main street.

Pandeli Usta ('Chef Pandeli') long ago went to that great kitchen in the sky, but his restaurant (tel 522-5534) remains. It still serves only lunch and you'll enjoy the fresh fish, the specialty, or the grilled meats. I had an absolutely delicious *beğendi kebap* here (shish kebab on top of warm, buttery aubergine/eggplant puree). Plan to spend 5000TL to 7000TL (US$7 to US$10) for a full meal based on meat, somewhat more for fish.

Tepebaşı & Tünel Popular with the diplomatic set at lunchtime is the *Dört*

Mevsim or *Four Seasons Restaurant* (DEWRT mehv-seem) (tel 145-8941). It's at İstiklal 509, very near Tünel. Founded and operated by an international couple (he's Turkish, she's English), it is well located to draw diners from the Swedish, Soviet, Dutch, British and American consulates. Lunch is served from noon to 3 pm, dinner from 6 pm to midnight; closed Sunday. If you order the fixed menu *(tabldot)* at lunch, you might pay 3500TL (US$4.90), drink and tip included. Ordering from the regular menu at dinner can drive your bill up to 7000TL (US$10), but it will be money well spent.

The Bosphorus İstanbul's old standard for excellent dining is the *Abdullah Lokantası* (tel 163-6406) in the Bosphorus hills above the town of Emirgân. Founded a century ago, it was located for most of that time on İstiklal Caddesi, but moved to the outskirts several decades ago in order to achieve a more bucolic setting, and to be right in the midst of its own vegetable gardens. Much of what you are served springs from the land within a few hundred metres of the restaurant.

The cuisine at Abdullah is Turkish with continental influences. Thus, you can expect the menu to include grilled lamb, but also sturgeon; *börek* but also caviar. It's a good place to try some of the more unusual Turkish dishes such as *mantı*, a lamb ravioli in a light yogurt sauce. You can expect to pay 8000TL to 10,000TL (US$11.20 to US$14) per person for a fine dinner here.

The dining room is a modernish, stylized chalet at Koru Caddesi 11, which you must reach by taxi. The ride from the city centre might take 20 to 40 minutes. The restaurant is open for lunch (noon to 3 pm) and dinner (8 pm to midnight) every day. Call for reservations.

ENTERTAINMENT

The name 'İstanbul' often conjures up thoughts of mysterious intrigues in dusky streets, dens in which sultry belly-dancers do what they do, and who knows what else? As with most aged stereotypes, the reality is somewhat different.

İstanbul International Festival The most prominent entertainment event in İstanbul is the İstanbul International Festival, which begins in late June and continues through the first half of July. World-class performers – soloists, orchestras, dance companies, etc – give recitals and performances in numerous concert halls, historic buildings and palaces. The highlight is Mozart's 'Abduction from the Seraglio' performed in Topkapı Palace, with the Sultan's private Gate of Felicity as backdrop. Don't miss it. Check at the box offices in the Atatürk Cultural Centre (Taksim) for schedules, ticket prices and availability.

Another good bet during the festival, and on other warm summer evenings as well, is a performance of drama or folk dance given in Rumeli Hisar, up the Bosphorus. Several years ago, I saw a fine English company do Shakespeare's 'A Midsummer Night's Dream' here. The performance was excellent, the setting simply spectacular.

There is another open-air theatre (Açık Hava Tiyatrosu) just north of the İstanbul Hilton Hotel, off Cumhuriyet Caddesi.

Folklore Turks are enthusiastic folklore fans, and many are still close enough in tradition to their regional dances to jump in and dance along at a performance. It's usually pretty easy to find a dance performance. University groups, good amateur companies and professionals all schedule performances throughout the year. The Turkish Folklore Association usually has something going on. For current offerings, ask at a Tourist Information Office or at one of the larger hotels.

High Culture There are symphony, opera and ballet seasons, and occasional tour performances by the likes of Jean-Pierre Rampal or Paul Badura-Skoda. Many but not all of these performances are given in the Atatürk Cultural Centre in Taksim Square. The box offices there will have schedules.

Theatre The Turks are enthusiastic theatre-goers, and as a people they seem to have a special genius for dramatic art. The problem, of course, is language. If you're a true theatre-buff you might well enjoy a performance of a familiar classic, provided you know the play well enough to follow the action without benefit of dialogue.

Cinema İstiklal Caddesi used to be the centre of İstanbul's cinema (*sinema*, SEE-neh-mah) district, with many foreign films being shown. The advent of television changed all that, and now some of İstiklal's cinemas screen the racier movies, plus the much-beloved Turkish melodramas. Many first-run feature films do make it to İstanbul, however, and you will be able to enjoy them at bargain prices in certain cinemas. Some are along Cumhuriyet Caddesi between Taksim and Harbiye. Others are in the section called Nişantaşı (nee-SHAHN-tah-shuh): head north on Cumhuriyet past the Hilton to Harbiye, and bear right on Valikonağı Caddesi. The cinemas are along this street in the first few blocks.

You may need some words on your cinema outing. Look on the cinema posters for the words 'Renkli' and 'Türkçe' or 'Orijinal' (ohr-zhee-NAHL). If you see 'Renkli Orijinal', that means the film is in colour and in the original language with Turkish subtitles. But if you see 'Renkli Türkçe', the film is in colour but has been dubbed in Turkish, in which case you may understand nothing.

There are three general seating areas, and you pay according to which you choose: *koltuk* (kohl-TOOK), on the floor in the mid-section to the rear; *birinci* (beer-EEN-jee), on the floor near the screen; and *balkon* (bahl-KOHN), in the balcony where the young lovers congregate. If you're going to the cinema to watch the film, ask for *koltuk*.

When possible, buy your tickets a few hours in advance. Tickets cost 300TL to 550TL (US$0.42 to US$0.77). Also, the usher will expect a small tip for showing you to your seat.

Nightclubs Belly-dancers do still perform in Turkey, of course. Many of the nightclubs along Cumhuriyet Caddesi between Taksim and the Hilton feature belly-dancers, folk dance troupes, singers and bands. The usual arrangement is that you pay one price and get dinner and the show; drinks are extra. With Turkish prices being what they are, the price is not all that unreasonable at the independent clubs, perhaps 10,000TL (US$14) per person. At the large hotels, which also have belly-dancers in their nightclubs, the cost may be twice as high.

The trick is to get a good, legitimate club. The *Kervansaray*, on the north side of the Hilton, has been catering to both Turks and tourists for years. This is not the cheapest, but it's reasonable and the show is good. Actually, it may be among the cheaper ones when you remember that at the sleazy ones you may tussle over the bill. İstiklal Caddesi and the side streets running from it have many clubs where you can watch the show (more or less), meet ladies of the night and get suckered into paying big money for their drinks.

Gazinos Turkish gazinos have nothing to do with gambling. Rather, they are open-air nightclubs popular in the summertime. (Some have been built up and operate in winter to the point that they are actually nightclubs with a gazino heritage.) The best of these are along the European shore of the Bosphorus. You won't find much belly-dancing here. The shows are mostly Turkish popular singers. Dinner and drinks are served. If the name of the place has the word *aile* (ah-yee-LEH, 'wife' or 'family') in it, as in *Bebek Aile Gazinosu*, it means the proprietor wants to appeal to a respectable, mixed crowd and avoid all-male or heavy-drinking audiences.

Dinner on the Bosphorus For my money, the most enjoyable thing you can do in İstanbul at night is have a long, leisurely seafood dinner at a little restaurant overlooking the Bosphorus. As Turks very often have the same idea, there are lots of little restaurants to choose from. Most, it must be stated, are in the moderate price range, not extremely cheap. A fish dinner with wine might cost 4500TL to 7000TL (US$6.30 to US$9.80) per person.

Among the Bosphorus villages with a good selection of restaurants are **Arnavutköy, Bebek** and **Tarabya**, all on the European side. The Asian coast has its share of little places as well. See 'Places to Eat' for some details.

Night Cruise About the cheapest yet most enjoyable nighttime activity is to take a Bosphorus ferry somewhere. It doesn't really matter where, as long as you don't end up on the southern coast of the Sea of Marmara or out in the Princes' Islands. Catch one over to Üsküdar or any town up the Bosphorus, and enjoy the view, the twinkling lights, the fishing boats bobbing in the waves, the powerful searchlights of the ferries sweeping the sea lanes. Have a nice glass of tea (a waiter will bring it round regularly). Get off anywhere, and take a bus or dolmuş home if you can't catch a ferry back directly.

Perhaps the easiest ferry to catch for this purpose is the Eminönü-Üsküdar. Just go to Eminönü's Dock No 2, buy a ticket to Üsküdar, and walk aboard. (If you want a ticket there and back, say *Üsküdar, gidiş dönüş* (EW-skew-dahr, gee-DEESH dur-NEWSH). From Üsküdar, just come back; or wait for one of the frequent ferries to Beşiktaş/

Barbaros Hayrettin Paşa. From Barbaros you can catch a bus or dolmuş back to your part of town. There are dolmuş ranks right outside the ferry dock.

A fail-safe evening ferry ride is the one to Haydarpaşa or Kadıköy, from Karaköy's Dock No 7 or 8. These two Asian suburbs are the only destinations for ferries from these docks, so you can't end up way off somewhere. Return boats bring you back to Karaköy. Each way, the voyage takes 20 minutes and costs 90TL (US$0.13).

Turkish Bath Actually, you're not confined to bathing only in the evenings, but it does feel wonderful after a tiring day. Two baths attract foreigners. First is the Cağaloğlu Hamamı (jaa-AHL-oh-loo) (tel 522-2424), on Yerebatan/Hilaliahmer Caddesi at Babiâli Caddesi, just 200 metres from Sancta Sophia near Cağaloğlu Meydanı (square). Built over three centuries ago, it boasts that King Edward VIII, Kaiser Wilhelm II, Franz Liszt and Florence Nightingale have all enjoyed its pleasures. Any day between 7 am and midnight (7 am to 8 pm for women) descend the stairs and enter the bath.

The other bath is the Tarihi Galatasaray Hamamı (tel 144-1412) at the end of Suterazi Sokak, a little street going south-east from İstiklal Caddesi, just north of Galatasaray. Look for the sign on İstiklal Caddesi, which points the way. This is a beautiful old bath filled with gleaming marble.

The procedure is this: you will be shown to a cubicle where you can undress, store your clothes and wrap around you the cloth that's provided. An attendant will lead you through the cool room and the warm room to the hot room, where you sit and sweat for a while, relaxing and loosening up. You can have a massage here. Haggle with a masseur or masseuse on a price before beginning.

When you are half-asleep and soft as putty from the steamy heat, you have a choice. The cheapest bath is the one you do yourself, having brought your own soap, shampoo and towel. But the true experience is to have an attendant wash you, providing all the necessaries. You'll be led to the warm room, doused with warm water, then lathered with a sudsy swab. Next, the attendant will scrub your skin with a coarse cloth mitten loosening dirt you didn't ever expect that you had. Next comes a shampoo, another dousing with warm water, then one with cool water.

When the scrubbing is over, head for the cool room, there to be swathed in Turkish towels, then led back to your cubicle for a rest or a nap. You can order tea, coffee, a soft drink or a bottle of beer. For a nap, tell the attendant when to wake you.

Bath etiquette requires that men remain clothed with the bath-wrap at all times. During the bathing, you wash your private parts yourself, without removing the modesty wrap. In the women's section modesty is less in evidence, depilatory is more in evidence.

The price for the entire experience can range from about 1500TL (US$2.10) if you bring your own soap, shampoo and towel, and bathe yourself; through 3000TL to 4500TL (US$4.20 to US$6.30) for an assisted bath; to 6500TL (US$9.10) for the deluxe service. Tips will be expected all around, and I've included them in these estimates. Don't let yourself be pressured into tipping heavily; tip on a Turkish scale, not a foreign one.

After you're all done, you'll be utterly refreshed, squeaky clean, and almost unable to walk due to the wonderful relaxation of muscles, mind and spirit.

GETTING THERE & AWAY

All roads lead to İstanbul. As the country's foremost transportation hub, the question is not how to get there (see the Getting There chapter), but how to negotiate this sprawling urban mass when you arrive. Here is the information you may need on arrival.

Air After many years of waiting, the new, modern terminal building is open at Atatürk Havaalanı (Atatürk Airport), formerly known as Yeşilköy Airport. The Ministry of Culture & Tourism (Kütür ve Turizm Bakanlığı) maintains an information office in the arrivals terminal and will be happy to help with questions or problems. There is also a hotel reservation desk in the arrivals terminal, but some readers of this guide have written to say that they always recommend the same expensive, inconvenient hotel to everyone, regardless of their preference. This may change, so check anyway.

Before you pass through customs, avail yourself of the opportunity to buy duty-free goods at decent prices, with no transcontinental carrying problems. See the Getting Around section below for airport transport details.

For examples of airfares from İstanbul to other Turkish cities, see the Getting Around chapter.

Rail All trains from Europe terminate at Sirkeci (SEER-keh-jee) Station, right next to Eminönü in the shadow of Topkapı Palace. The station has its own small Tourism Information Office.

The main (west) station door of Sirkeci now is a modern structure. But take a look on the north side of the station, facing the Bosphorus: this more ornate facade was the original front of the station, more in keeping with the romantic ideas of what the terminus for the Orient Express should look like.

Right outside the station door and across the street (use the overhead walkway) you can catch a bus or dolmuş going to Sultanahmet, Beyazıt, Laleli and Aksaray.

If you're headed for Taksim, go out the station door and turn right. Over by the little refreshments kiosk is the stop for the dolmuş to Taksim. The dolmuş operates only until the late afternoon, however. If there is no dolmuş, walk a bit farther toward the sea and you'll see the

Eminönü bus ranks to your left. Catch a bus to Taksim from here.

Departures: the train for Athens and cities in Europe departs Sirkeci station, on the European side of the Bosphorus, at 8.40 pm each evening, arriving at the Turkish frontier about 6.20 am the following morning.

To continue a train journey deeper into Turkey (meaning Anatolia), you must get to Haydarpaşa Station on the Asian side. The best way is by ferryboat from Karaköy. Cross the Galata Bridge from Eminönü to Karaköy (by bus, dolmuş or taxi if your luggage is heavy), go to the prominent ferry dock, buy a token, go through the turnstile and look for the illuminated sign saying Haydarpaşa. Some ferries stop both at Haydarpaşa and Kadıköy; but you should be careful not to get a ferry that goes *only* to Kadıköy. If in doubt, just say *Haydarpaşa' ya mü?* ('To Haydarpaşa?') to anyone while pointing at the boat. By the way, don't let anyone suggest that you take a taxi to Haydarpaşa. Ferries are scheduled to depart Kadıköy and arrive at Haydarpaşa in time for the departure of all major trains. The ferry is cheap, convenient, pleasant and speedy. A taxi would be expensive and slow.

Ferries depart Kadıköy for Haydarpaşa every 15 to 30 minutes; the special ferries, timed in sync with departure times of the major expresses, leave Karaköy about a half-hour before express train departure. Fare is 90TL (US$0.13).

The major trains departing Haydarpaşa for Ankara are: Boğaziçi Ekspresi, 9.15 am, arriving in Ankara at 7 pm; Mavi Tren I, the first Blue Train, departing at 1.30 pm, arriving at Ankara at 9 pm; Doğu Ekspresi, departing at 11.40 pm, arriving in Ankara at 9.57 am the following day, then continuing to Erzurum and Kars; Anadolu Ekspresi, departing at 9.05 pm, arriving at 8.05 am the next day; Ankara Ekspresi, an all-sleeping-car train, departing at 9.40 pm, arriving at 8.30 am the following day; and the Mavi Tren II, departing at 10.50 pm, arriving the following morning at 7.30 am. The fare from İstanbul to Ankara is 2100TL (US$2.94) on an express train, 3200TL (US$4.48) on a Mavi Tren.

Bus Coming from Europe, your bus will drop you at the Topkapı Otogar, right outside the city walls next to the Topkapı (TOHP-kahp-uh), or Cannon Gate. This is nowhere near Topkapı Palace, which lies seven km to the east, on the Bosphorus. It seems that two gates, at very different places in the city walls, had cannons associated with them.

Though a new, modern bus terminal is in the works, the Topkapı Otogar at this writing is nothing but a bewildering chaos of little bus offices, snack stands, taxi shills, mud, dust, noise and air pollution. The better bus lines such as Bosfor Turizm and Varan will provide a *servis arabası* (sehr-VEES ah-rah-bah-suh) or minibus to take you from the bus station into the city. Both Bosfor Turizm and Varan have their main ticket offices near Taksim Square, so that's where the minibus will end up. But if you ask to be dropped in Aksaray or Laleli, the driver will doubtless oblige.

Coming from Edirne, you get off the bus at Topkapı bus station and, if your bus company doesn't have a *servis arabası*, you'll have to make your own way into the city. Taxi drivers will be waiting to buttonhole you as you alight. You might want one if your bags are heavy. Otherwise, make your way out of the bus station and across to the Cannon Gate itself. Just inside the gate (on the other side of the walls from the bus station) is a city bus stop, from which you can catch a bus or a dolmuş to Aksaray. If Aksaray or Laleli is not your final destination, you must change in Aksaray for a bus or dolmuş to Sultanahmet, Eminönü or Taksim.

There is also a bus station on the eastern shore of the Bosphorus at Harem, though you will have little use for it.

Many buses entering and leaving the city make a stop at Harem to serve residents of the Asian suburbs.

Bus Ticket Offices Bus company ticket offices are found clustered in Laleli on Ordu Caddesi, and near Sirkeci Railway Station on Muradiye Caddesi.

In Taksim, try the offices of the Pamukkale company (tel 145-2946) at Mete Caddesi 16, to the left (north) of the Atatürk Cultural Centre. Pamukkale has routes to many points in Turkey, as well as to Europe.

Two more offices near Taksim are to the right (south) of the Cultural Centre, down the hill a block along İnönü Caddesi, on the left-hand side of the road. Varan (tel 149-1903 or 144-8457) is at İnönü Caddesi 29/B; its routes include those to Ankara, Athens, Çanakkale, Dornbirn, Edirne, Innsbruck, İzmir, Salzburg, Strasbourg and Zurich, and to the more popular holiday destinations in Turkey. Kamil Koç is represented by Arama Turizm (tel 145-2795), İnönü Caddesi 31, where you can also buy tickets for the TCDD (Turkish State Railways). It will save you much time and trouble to buy your tickets at a downtown office rather than have to go all the way out to Topkapı Otogar.

Here are some examples of bus fares from İstanbul to: Ankara, 2000TL to 3000TL (US$2.80 to US$4.20); Antalya, 3800TL (US$5.32); Bodrum, 4800TL (US$6.72); Bursa, 1400TL (US$1.96); Denizli (for Pamukkale) 3300TL (US$4.62); Fethiye, 5400TL (US$7.56); İzmir, 2750TL (US$3.85); Kuşadası (or Selçuk/ Ephesus), 3500TL (US$4.90); Marmaris, 4800TL (US$6.72); Side, 4500TL (US$6.30).

Sea Passenger ships dock at Karaköy, near the Yolcu Salonu (YOHL-joo sahl-ohn-oo, International Passenger Terminal) on Rıhtım Caddesi. The Ministry of Culture & Tourism has an office in the Yolcu Salonu, near the front doors.

The international dock is next to the Karaköy ferryboat dock and only 100 metres from Galata Bridge. Bus and dolmuş routes to Taksim pass right in front of the Yolcu Salonu; for those to destinations in the Old City such as Sultanahmet, Laleli and Aksaray, go to the western side of Karaköy Square itself, right at the end of the Galata Bridge. You'll have to find the pedestrian underpass to get to the dolmuş and bus stops.

Some domestic-line ships dock at Kabataş (KA-ba-tash), about two km north of Karaköy on the Bosphorus shore, very near Dolmabahçe Palace and Mosque. As you leave the dock at Kabataş, buses and dolmuşes heading left will be going to Karaköy and the Old City; those travelling right will be going to Taksim or up the Bosphorus shore.

Road The E5 from Europe brings you to Atatürk Airport and a bypass heading north and east to cross the Bosphorus Bridge. If you're headed for Aksaray, don't take the bypass, but rather head straight on and you'll end up at Topkapı, the Cannon Gate. Continue straight on through the gate, along Millet Caddesi, and you will end up in Aksaray Square. For Laleli, continue straight through the square and turn left just before the big university buildings on the left. For Taksim, use the flyover in Aksaray Square to turn left and head up Atatürk Bulvarı. Cross the Atatürk Bridge over the Golden Horn, push onward up and up the hill, bear right after passing the Turkish Airlines terminal (on the right), and you'll join İstiklal Caddesi at Tünel Square. İstiklal Caddesi ends in Taksim Square.

If you're a bit more daring, leave the expressway at the airport, following signs for Yeşilköy or Ataköy. You can make your way to the shore of the Sea of Marmara and drive into the city along the water's edge. You'll pass the city walls near Yedikule, the Fortress of the Seven

Towers and the Marble Tower, which has one foot in the water. The city's southern wall will be on your left as you drive. Across the Bosphorus, the view of Üsküdar, Haydarpaşa and Kadıköy is impressive. You can turn left onto Mustafa Kemal Caddesi for Aksaray and Laleli; or continue on around Seraglio Point to Sirkeci, Eminönü and the Galata Bridge.

GETTING AROUND
Transport within İstanbul moves slowly. The medieval street patterns do not receive automobiles well, let alone buses. Several conflagrations in the 19th century cleared large areas of the city and allowed new avenues to be opened. Were it not for these providential disasters, traffic would be even slower.

A subway system has been in the planning for years, but the costs, astronomical in any case, increase dramatically when İstanbul's hilly terrain and water bodies are taken into account. Then there are the Byzantine ruins: every time a Byzantine structure is discovered, construction must be halted and the archaeologists brought in for weeks, perhaps months of study.

Airport Transport The fastest way to get into town from the airport is by taxi, but this may cost as much as 5000TL (US$7), depending upon what part of the city you're headed for. A far cheaper alternative is the USAŞ (OO-sahsh) airport bus for 550TL (US$0.77), which departs the domestic terminal and goes into the city, stopping in Aksaray (near Laleli) before ending its run at the Turkish Airlines terminal in Şişhane Square, near the Galata Tower and Tepebaşı in Beyoğlu. Buses leave every 20 or 30 minutes from 5.30 to 9 am, every hour from 9 am to 2 pm, and every 20 or 30 minutes from 2 pm to midnight. The journey, depending upon the traffic, may take between 25 and 45 minutes. Free shuttle buses leave the airport's international terminal for the domestic terminal every 10 minutes throughout the day.

For the return trip to the airport, catch the USAŞ bus at the Şişhane terminal. You must be at the airport for check-in *at least* 20 minutes before departure time for domestic flights, and it's not a bad idea to be there earlier, 30 or 40 minutes before departure time. For international flights, be at the airport at least 50 minutes before take-off or, better yet, 75 minutes before take-off. Remember, there are three security checks, customs, check-in and immigration procedures to pass through before you board, and if the aircraft is a wide-body, the officials will have to process about 400 passengers before boarding is completed.

Bus İstanbul's red-and-beige city buses run most everywhere. Fares are 100TL (US$0.14) per ride, or 60TL (US$0.08) for students. If the bus is blue-and-white, it's a privately owned Özel Halk Otobüsü (people's bus). Fares on these are sometimes a few liras cheaper. Both operate according to directives from the city government.

Fares are paid on a ticket system (see the Getting Around chapter). The route name and number appear on the front of the bus; also on the front, or on the curb side, is a list of stops along the route.

Some buses fill to capacity right at the departure point, leaving no room for passengers waiting along the route. It's frustrating to wait five or 10 minutes for a bus, only to have it pass right by due to wall-to-wall flesh inside. Even if the driver does stop, is it worth it to jam in? If you're jammed in the middle of the bus when your stop comes, you may not be able to get off. (What you do in this situation is let the driver, and other passengers, know you must get out by saying, *İnecek var!* (een-eh-JEK vahr), 'I must get out!').

Dolmuş The dolmuş and minibus system is preferable to the city buses for several reasons. As a car or minibus has a set number of seats, they are rarely over-crowded, like a bus. It's against the law to carry more than the designated number of passengers. Also, they tend to be faster. Finally, they tend to run on short routes between the major squares, so the tourist unfamiliar with İstanbul's topography can be sure of ending up at the chosen destination.

Fares are only slightly more expensive than the buses on short routes, somewhat more expensive on the longer routes; but it is on the longer routes that one appreciates the comfort more.

Major dolmuş termini of use to tourists are: Taksim, Karaköy, Eminönü, Sirkeci and Beyazıt. Sultanahmet, near the majority of İstanbul's most important sights, is not well-served by dolmuş except from Aksaray and Beyazıt. Coming from Galata Bridge, Eminönü and Sirkeci, they tend to pass a few blocks west of Sultanahmet. But a few blocks out is better than walking all they way, so ask for Cağaloğlu (ja-AHL-oh-loo) and you'll be close.

At these major dolmuş termini, look for the rows of cars and lines of people being matched up. If there's no sign indicating your destination, look in the cars' front windows, or ask just by saying the name of your destination.

Here are some rules of dolmuş etiquette. If your stop comes before the final destination, you may do some shuffling to ensure that you are sitting right by the door and not way in the back. Also, a woman is expected to choose a side seat, not a middle seat between two men, for her own comfort and 'protection'. If a man and a woman passenger get into the front of a car, for instance, the man should get in first and sit by the driver (contrary to everything his mother taught him about letting the lady go first), so that the woman is between 'her' man and the door. This is not a gesture against women, but rather the opposite, to show respect for her honour.

The fare might be written on the destination sign, whether it's on a signpost or in the car window. If it's not, watch what other people pay, or ask, or hand over a bill large enough to cover the fare but small enough not to anger the driver, who will never have enough change and will not want a large bill. Collection of fares will begin after the car starts off, and the driver will juggle and change money as he drives. This thrilling practice costs no extra. Should there be any doubt about fares or problem in payment (rare), you can always settle up at the last stop.

To signal the driver that you want to get out, say *İnecek var* (een-eh-JEHK vahr, 'I must get out'). Other useful words are *durun* (DOOR-oon, 'stop') and *burada* (BOO-rah-dah, 'here').

Tünel İstanbul's little underground train, the Tünel (teu-NEHL), runs between Karaköy and the southern end of İstiklal Caddesi called Tünel Meydanı (Tünel Square). Built by French engineers over a century ago, the Tünel allowed European merchants to get from their offices in Galata to their homes in Pera without hiking up the steep hill. The lovely old cars of lacquered wood have been replaced by shiny Paris Metro-type cars with quiet rubber wheels. The fare is 80TL (US$0.11).

There are only two stations on the line, the upper and lower, so there's no getting lost. Buy a token, enter through the turnstile and board the train. They run every five or 10 minutes from early morning until about 10 pm.

Ferryboat Without doubt the nicest way to go any considerable distance in İstanbul is by ferryboat. You will (and should) use the ferries whenever possible. The alternatives are bus and dolmuş along the coastal roads or across the Bosphorus Bridge. These can be faster, but they will also be less comfortable and sometimes more expensive. Most ferry rides cost

about the same as a bus ticket. In February 1987 the city was scheduled to take delivery of its first hydrofoils.

The mouth of the Golden Horn by the Galata Bridge is a seething maelstrom of the sleek white ferries at rush hour. At other times of day, the number of ferries (dozens) and the number of docks (10) can lead to confusion, but a few bits of information will make it all come clear.

First of all, each dock serves a certain route, though a few routes may overlap. At each dock is a framed copy of the timetable or *tarife* (tah-ree-FEH) outlining the service. It's only in Turkish, so I'll give you the necessary translations. Each route (*hat* or *hattı*) is designated by the names of the principal stops. Please note that the tarife has two completely different parts, one for weekdays *(normal günleri)* and Saturday *(Cumartesi)*, and another for Sunday *(Pazar)* and holidays *(Bayram günleri)*. Make sure you're looking at the proper part.

The ferry you're most likely to use is the 'Special Touristic Excursion' (Eminönü-Kavaklar Boğaziçi Özel Gezi Seferleri) up the Bosphorus. These depart Eminönü at about 10.30 am and 1.30 pm each day of the year (with more trips in summer), and go all the way to Rumeli Kavağı and Anadolu Kavağı at the Black Sea mouth of the Bosphorus. The entire trip takes about 2½ hours one way and costs 750TL (US$1.05). You may want to go only as far as Sarıyer, about two hours' ride, then take a dolmuş back down, stopping at various sights along the way. These boats fill up early, so buy your ticket and walk aboard at least 30 minutes prior to departure in order to get a seat.

Otherwise, if you just want to take a little ride around Seraglio Point (good for photos of Topkapı Palace, Sancta Sophia and the Blue Mosque) and across the Bosphorus, catch any boat from Docks 7 or 8 in Karaköy. The trip over to Haydarpaşa or Kadıköy and back will take about an hour. For more details, see the Rail section.

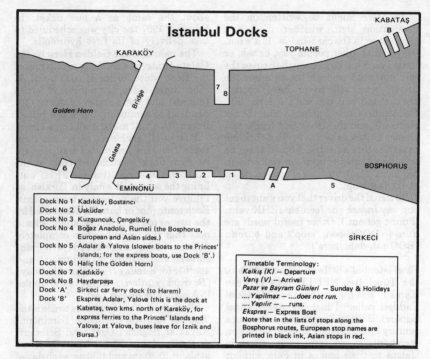

İstanbul Docks

KABATAŞ
B

KARAKÖY

TOPHANE

Golden Horn

Galata Bridge

7 8

6

BOSPHORUS

EMİNÖNÜ

4 3 2 1

A 5

SİRKECİ

Dock No 1   Kadıköy, Bostancı
Dock No 2   Üsküdar
Dock No 3   Kuzguncuk, Çengelköy
Dock No 4   Boğaz Anadolu, Rumeli (the Bosphorus, European and Asian sides.)
Dock No 5   Adalar & Yalova (slower boats to the Princes' Islands; for the express boats, use Dock 'B'.)
Dock No 6   Haliç (the Golden Horn)
Dock No 7   Kadıköy
Dock No 8   Haydarpaşa
Dock 'A'   Sirkeci car ferry dock (to Harem)
Dock 'B'   Ekspres Adalar, Yalova (this is the dock at Kabataş, two kms. north of Karaköy, for express ferries to the Princes' Islands and Yalova; at Yalova, buses leave for İznik and Bursa.)

Timetable Terminology:
Kalkış (K) — Departure
Varış (V) — Arrival
Pazar ve Bayram Günleri — Sunday & Holidays
.... *Yapılmaz* — ....does not run.
.... *Yapılır* — ....runs.
Ekspres — Express Boat
Note that in the lists of stops along the Bosphorus routes, European stop names are printed in black ink, Asian stops in red.

Taxi Unlike in the bad old days, İstanbul's hordes of taxi drivers now all have digital fare meters, and they seem to use them all the time with very few exceptions. Taxis are plentiful, and it is usually not difficult to find one. The base (drop) rate is 250TL (US$0.35); a trip between Aksaray and Sultanahmet costs about 500TL (US$0.70); between Taksim and Karaköy about 700TL (US$1); between Taksim and Sultanahmet about 1300TL (US$1.82).

On Foot With an overburdened public transport system, walking can often be faster and more rewarding. The street scenes are never dull, and the views from one hill to the next are often extraordinary. While walking, watch out for broken pavement, bits of pipe sticking a few cm out of the pavement, and all manner of other obstacles. Don't expect any car driver to stop for you in any situation. In Turkey, the automobile seems to have the right of way virtually everywhere, and drivers get very annoyed at pedestrians who assert ridiculous and specious rights. It is obvious, isn't it? The automobile, being such a marvellous and expensive machine, should go wherever its driver is capable of taking it, without hindrance from mere pedestrians. This, at least, is the common belief.

Near İstanbul

Thrace

The land to the north of the Aegean Sea was called Thrace by the Romans. Today this ancient Roman province is divided among Turkey, Bulgaria and Greece, with Turkey holding the easternmost part. Turkish Thrace (Trakya) is not large or particularly exciting except for its major city, Edirne.

EDİRNE

A glance at the map seems to tell you all about Edirne (eh-DEER-neh): it's the first town you come to if you're travelling overland from Europe to Turkey, it's a way-station on the road to İstanbul. It wouldn't be surprising if this had been Edirne's role throughout history, even in the old days when the town was called Adrianople. But there's more to Edirne than this. Because of its history, it holds several of the finest examples from the greatest periods of Turkish mosque architecture, and if you have the chance you should take time for a visit.

If you're coming from İstanbul, you can make the trip to Edirne and back to İstanbul in a day, though a longish one. Get an early morning bus, plan to have lunch and see the sights, and catch a return bus in the late afternoon.

History

This town was indeed built as a defense post for the larger city on the Bosphorus. The Roman emperor Hadrian founded it in the 2nd century as Hadrianopolis, a name which was later shortened by Europeans to Adrianople, then again by the Turks to Edirne.

The Ottoman Empire grew from the seed of a Turkish emirate in north-western Anatolia. By the mid-1300s, the emirate of the Ottomans with its capital at Bursa had become very powerful, but not powerful enough to threaten the mighty walls of Constantinople. Bent on more conquest, the Ottoman armies crossed the Dardanelles into Thrace, skirting the great capital. Capturing Adrianople in 1363, they made it their new capital and base of operations for military campaigns in Europe.

For almost 100 years, this was the city from which the Ottoman sultan would set out on his campaigns to Europe and Asia. When the time was finally ripe for the final conquest of the Byzantine Empire, Mehmet the Conqueror set out from Edirne on the road to Constantinople. Even after the great city was captured, Edirne played an important role in Ottoman life and society, for it was still a forward post on the route to conquest in Europe.

When the Ottoman Empire fell apart after WW I, the Allies had decided to grant all of Thrace to the Greek kingdom. Constantinople was to become an international city. In the summer of 1920, Greek armies occupied Edirne. But Atatürk's republican armies were ultimately victorious, and the Treaty of Lausanne left Edirne and Eastern Thrace to the Turks. Edirne returned to its role as 'the town on the way to İstanbul'.

Orientation

The centre of town is Hürriyet Meydanı (Freedom Square), at the intersection of the two main streets, Saraçlar/Saraçhane Caddesi and Talat Paşa Caddesi. Just west of the square is the Üçşerefeli Cami. North along Talat Paşa Caddesi will bring you to Edirne's masterpiece, the Selimiye Camii. On the way to the Selimiye, you'll pass the Eski Cami. South of Hürriyet Square is the Ali Paşa Çarşısı, Edirne's covered bazaar.

Information

There is a Tourism Information Office (tel (1811) 1518) near Hürriyet Meydanı on Talat Paşa Caddesi; there's another at the Kapıkule border post.

Things to See

The principal reason to stop in Edirne is to see mosques, so start out from Hürriyet Meydanı and go the few steps to the Üçşerefeli Cami.

Üçşerefeli Cami The name means 'mosque with three galleries (balconies)'. Actually it's one of the mosque's four minarets which has the three balconies. The minarets, built at different times, are all different and wonderfully various.

Enter at the far end of the courtyard rather than through a side gate. That way you can enjoy the full effect of the architect's genius. The courtyard at the Üçşerefeli (EWCH-sheh-reh-feh-LEE) with its şadırvan (ablutions fountain) was a prototype for the courtyards of the Ottoman mosques to be built in later centuries.

The mosque was constructed in the mid-1400s and finished by 1447. It exemplifies a transition from the Seljuk Turkish type of architecture of Konya and Bursa to a truly Ottoman style, which would be perfected later in İstanbul. The Seljuks were greatly influenced by the Persian and Indian styles prevalent in their empire to the east. The Ottomans learned a great deal from the Byzantines, and for the Byzantines Sancta Sophia was the purest expression of their ideal. Sancta Sophia's outstanding characteristic is its wide, expansive dome covering a great open space. After the Ottomans took Constantinople in 1453, the transition accelerated, as you will see.

In the Seljuk style, smaller domes are mounted on square rooms. But here at the Üçşerefeli, the wide (24 metres) dome is mounted on a hexagonal drum and supported by two walls and two pillars.

Keep this transitional style in mind as you visit Edirne's other mosques, which are either earlier or later in style.

Across the street from the mosque is a *hamam* (hah-MAHM), or **Turkish bath**, built in the late 1500s and still in use. Designed by the great Mimar Sinan for Grand Vezir Sokullu Mehmet Paşa, it is actually two *hamams* in one: one for men, one for women. (At most Turkish baths there is only one system of bathing rooms, used by men and women on different days.)

Eski Cami Now head back to Hürriyet Meydanı, and walk north-east on Talat Paşa Caddesi to the Eski Cami (ehs-KEE jah-mee), or Old Mosque. On your way you'll pass the *bedesten*, another covered market, this one dating from the early 1400s. Behind it to the east is the Rüstem Paşa Hanı, a grand caravanserai 100 years younger than the *bedesten*.

The Eski Cami (1414) exemplifies one of two principal mosque styles used by the Ottomans in their earlier capital, Bursa. Like Bursa's great Ulu Cami, the Eski Cami has rows of arches and pillars supporting a series of small domes. Inside, there's a marvellous *mihrab* (prayer niche) and huge calligraphic inscriptions on the walls. The columns at the front of the mosque were lifted from some Roman building, a common practice over the centuries.

Selimiye Camii Up the hill past the Eski Cami stands the great Selimiye (seh-LEE-mee-yeh), the finest work of the great Ottoman architect Sinan – or so the architect himself considered it. Though smaller than Sinan's tremendous Süleymaniye in İstanbul, the Selimiye is wonderfully harmonious and elegant. Crowning its small hill, it can be seen from a good distance across the rolling Thracian steppeland, and makes an impressive sight.

The Selimiye was constructed for Sultan Selim II (1566-1574) and finished just after the sultan's death. Sinan's genius guided him in designing a broad and lofty dome, and supporting it by means of pillars, arches and external buttresses. He did it so well that the interior is very spacious, and the walls can be filled with windows because they don't have to bear all of the weight. The result is a wide, airy, light space for prayer, similar to that of the Süleymaniye.

Part of the Selimiye's excellent effect comes from its four slender, very tall (71 metres) minarets. The fluted drums of the minarets add to the sense of height. You'll notice that each is *üçşerefeli*, or built with three balconies: Sinan's respectful acknowledgement, perhaps, to his predecessor who designed Edirne's Üçşerefeli Cami.

As you might expect, the interior furnishings of the Selimiye are exquisite, from the delicately carved marble *mimber* (pulpit) to the outstanding İznik faience in and around the *mihrab* (prayer niche).

The Selimiye had its share of supporting buildings – religious schools, libraries, etc. However, all that survive are a *medrese* (theological seminary) and a gallery of shops, called the Arasta, beneath the mosque. The shops have been restored and are still in use; rents are dedicated to the upkeep of the mosque, as they have been for over 400 years.

Beyazıt II Camii Edirne's last great imperial mosque is that of Sultan Beyazıt II (1481-1512), on the far side (northwest) of the Tunca River. From Hürriyet Meydanı, the pleasant walk to the mosque will take you about 15 or 20 minutes, and another 15 or 20 for the return. Walk along Saraçhane Caddesi beside the Üçşerefeli Cami (on your right), and turn left immediately after its Turkish bath, the one built by Sinan. Walk one block and bear right at the ornate little fountain. This street is Horozlu Bayır Caddesi; it changes names

later to İmaret Caddesi, but it will take you right to the bridge (1488) across the Tunca to Sultan Beyazıt's mosque.

The Beyazıt complex (1484-88) was fully restored in the late 1970s, so it now looks good as new. The architect of the complex, a fellow named Hayrettin, didn't have the genius of Mimar Sinan, but did a very creditable job nonetheless.

The mosque lies between the Üçşerefeli and the Selimiye in style, sliding back a bit rather than advancing: its large prayer hall has one large dome, more like the mosques in Bursa, but it has a courtyard and *sadırvan* like the Üçşerefeli Cami. Though it's certainly of a high standard, it can't compare with the Selimiye, which was built less than a century later.

The mosque's *külliye* (complex of service buildings) is extensive, including a *tabhane* (hostel for travellers), *medrese* (theological seminary), *imaret* (soup kitchen) and *darüşşifa* (hospital).

Eski Saray & Sarayiçi *Saray* means 'palace' in Turkish. Upriver (east) from the Sultan Beyazıt II mosque complex are the ruins of the Eski Saray, or Old Palace. Begun by Sultan Beyazıt II in 1450, the Old Palace once rivalled İstanbul's Topkapı in luxury and size. Today, little is left of it: a few bits of the kitchen buildings. But it's a pleasant walk along the river, less than a half-hour, to reach Eski Saray from the Beyazıt mosque, and if the day is nice you might want to do it. From the Eski Saray, Saraçhane Köprüsü (bridge) will take you back across the Tunca; Saraçhane Caddesi then leads directly back to Hürriyet Meydanı.

East of Eski Saray, across a branch of the Tunca (there's a bridge called Fatih Sultan Köprüsü), is Sarayiçi ('within the palace'). This scrub-covered island, once the sultans' hunting preserve, is now the site of the famous annual Kırkpınar Oiled Wrestling Matches (Tarihi Kırkpınar Yağlı Güreş Festivali – 'yah-LUH gew-RESH', oiled wrestling). In late May and early June, huge wrestlers clad only in leather knickers and slathered with olive oil take part in freestyle matches. An early sultan is said to have invented the sport to keep his troops in shape. Whatever the origin, a *pehlivan* (wrestler) at the Kırkpınar matches is something to behold. Folk-dancing exhibitions are organized as part of the wrestling festivities.

If you've made it all the way to Sarayiçi, look for the Kanuni Köprüsü (bridge) to get you back to the south bank of the Tunca. Bear right coming off the bridge, and the road will lead you to Saraçhane Caddesi, and eventually to Hürriyet Meydanı.

The Old Town While you're here, don't neglect to take a stroll through the old town of Edirne to discover some scenes of Turkish daily life. The Old Town, called Kale İçi ('within the fortress') by the locals, was the original medieval town, with streets laid out on a grid plan. Some fragments of Byzantine city walls are still visible at the edges of the grid, down by the Tunca River. The Old Town is bounded by Saraçlar Caddesi and Talat Paşa Caddesi, basically the area behind and to the west of the Ali Paşa Çarşısı.

Places to Stay
It's relatively easy to find inexpensive pensions and rooming houses in Edirne, as this is the first stop within Turkey on the route from Europe. Travellers who know the route will often push on through northern Greece or Bulgaria in order to get into Turkey so they can enjoy the lower prices and better food. Edirne is their first night's stay in the country.

However, this route is heavily travelled by Turkish workers on their way to and from Europe, and by international lorry-drivers heading to or from Iran and the Arabic countries. So your companions in the inexpensive hostelries may be mostly bachelors. Also, many places will be filled by crowds at holiday time.

Places to Stay – bottom end
You don't really need to spend a night here in order to absorb all the sights, as mentioned above. But should you want to stay, the Tourism Office (tel 1518) in Hürriyet Meydanı can help you locate a room for the night. They're especially good on the cheap little pensions and *otels* such as the *Konak* or *Nil*, where a double room without bath costs about 2500TL (US$3.50).

Places to Stay – middle
Edirne's old standard hotel is the *Kervan Oteli* (tel (1811) 1382 or 1355) on Talat Paşa Caddesi, Kadirhane Sokak 134. They have a private garage for guests' cars, a good restaurant (in which you are required to take breakfast) and rooms priced at 8800TL (US$12.32) single, 10,200TL (US$14.28) double.

Another long-running favourite is the *Sultan Oteli* (tel (1811) 1372 or 2156), Talat Paşa Caddesi 170, Edirne 22100, a larger (80-room) place with prices of 6900TL (US$9.66) single, 11,400TL (US$15.96) double, with bath. The Sultan has a restaurant as well.

Places to Eat
The hotels have the priciest dining rooms in town, but there are plenty of alternatives. A short stroll along Saraçlar Caddesi or in the Old Town will reveal any number of tiny hole-in-the-wall *hazır yemek* (ready-food) restaurants, perhaps just bearing the word *lokanta*. For grilled meat rissoles, locate a *köfteci*. A filling lunch at any such place can be had for 1100TL (US$1.54) or less.

Getting There & Away
Border Posts There are two frontier crossing-points on the outskirts of Edirne. From Bulgaria on the E5, you come to the busy border post of Kapıkule. After the formalities, you enter the town by crossing the Tunca at the Gazi Mihal bridge (1420) and passing some fragments of Byzantine city walls.

From Greece, the major road goes to Pazarkule, south of the town on the Maritsa (Meriç, mehr-EECH) River, to a border post originally meant to serve the rail line. The frontier, as determined at the Treaty of Lausanne, left the Turkish rail line passing through Greece on its way to Edirne! A bypass line was built in the 1970s, though.

From Pazarkule, or from the nearby railway station, you will probably have to take a taxi into town, though you may be lucky and find a dolmuş, which is cheaper.

Rail You may be coming to Turkey by train, in which case you will probably be ready for a break. Except for the luxurious tour-group re-creation of the Orient Express (Paris-İstanbul, single, US$5000), train service is slow and tedious. The international train can take another six to 10 hours to reach İstanbul. Get off. Don't miss Edirne.

Rail service between Edirne and İstanbul is not convenient. Trains leave İstanbul at 3.40 and 8.50 pm, arriving at the Kapıkule border station at 10.28 pm and 2.20 am respectively. From Edirne, trains depart for İstanbul at 4.25 and 8.05 am, arriving at 10.10 am and 2.45 pm. Tickets cost 1000TL (US$1.40) single, with a 10% discount for students. You'd be better off taking the bus.

Bus Buses operate very frequently throughout the day – about every 20 minutes or so – and take only four hours; tickets cost between 1000TL and 1200TL (US$1.40 and US$1.68). In Edirne, they operate out of the city's Otobüs Garajı on the outskirts of town. Take a city bus or dolmuş from the Eski Cami to get to the Otobüs Garajı. In İstanbul, the terminus is the Topkapı Otogar, the big bus station just outside the city walls at Topkapı gate, on the E5 highway (also called the Londra Asfaltı).

Road The E5 highway between Europe and İstanbul follows very closely the ancient road which connected Rome and Constantinople. It follows the river valleys past Niš and Sofia, flows comfortably between the mountain ranges of the Stara and Rhodopi to Plovdiv, and cruises along the Maritsa riverbank into Edirne. After Edirne, the road heads out into the rolling, steppe-like terrain of eastern Thrace toward İstanbul, 225 km further along. The city stands alone on the gently undulating plain, snuggled into a bend of the Tunca (TOON-jah) River.

Onward If you've come from İstanbul, it might make sense to head due south from Edirne directly to the Dardanelles and Troy. But buses do not run frequently on this route, and by doing this you miss the ferry cruise across the Sea of Marmara as well as the delightful cities of İznik, ancient Nicaea, and Bursa, the first Ottoman capital. So if you've got the time, head back to İstanbul and catch a ferryboat to Yalova, first stop on your explorations of the south Marmara shore.

İznik, Bursa & the South Marmara Shore

The southern shore of the Sea of Marmara is a land of small villages surrounded by olive groves, fruit orchards, sunflower fields, rolling hills and rich bottom-land. During the Ottoman Empire the choice olives for the sultan's table came from here, as did snow to cool his drinks from the slopes of Bursa's Uludağ (the Bithynian Mt Olympus). The region's few cities are of moderate size and significant interest to visitors.

You can enjoy this region and its sights in only two days: catch an early ferry from İstanbul to Yalova, make a quick tour of İznik (the ancient city of Nicaea), and spend the night in Bursa. After seeing the sights of Bursa the next morning, catch a bus westward to Çanakkale. You'll reach that town on the Dardanelles in time for a late supper.

If you have another day, you can truly enjoy the Marmara's southern shore. Plan to spend most of your extra time in Bursa, where the mosques and museums are particularly fine (this was the Ottomans' first capital city, before Edirne and İstanbul). You can even bask in hot mineral baths at Çekirge, a spa suburb of Bursa, and take the cablecar to the top of Uludağ, snow-capped for most of the year (skiing in winter).

If you must, you can rocket down to Bursa just for the day. But this means a lot of travel time for only a few hours' sightseeing, and the city really deserves an overnight stay.

On your way to Bursa, you will probably pass through the Sea of Marmara port of Yalova.

YALOVA

This small town (pronounced 'YAHL-oh-vah', population 55,000) is a farming and transportation centre. The highway between the industrial cities of Bursa and İzmit (not to be confused with İznik) passes near here, as does the ferryboat/bus link between Bursa and İstanbul. It's a pleasant enough small town, with a few small, modest hotels and restaurants, most within two blocks of the ferry dock. Everything else you'd need is here as well, including banks, chemists/drugstores, etc. The market area is a short stroll straight off the wharf.

Other than these few amusements, there's nothing to detain you in Yalova. You can plan to head for the spa at Termal, the ancient city of İznik or booming Bursa without delay.

Getting There

To reach Yalova, Termal, İznik and Bursa from İstanbul, most people choose the express ferryboats across the Sea of Marmara. An alternative method, involving less expense but more time and bother, is to take the car ferry from Kartal. If you miss the express ferry, consider taking the car ferry which, though a bit slower, leaves more often.

Express Ferryboat The best and most enjoyable way to get to Bursa is by express ferryboat across the Sea of Marmara. The ferries depart Kabataş dock just south of Dolmabahçe Monday through Saturday at 9 am (non-stop), 9.45 am (two stops), 2.15, 6.30 and 7.40 pm. On Sunday and holidays, departures are at 8.30 am (two stops), 9.30 am and noon (non-stop), 2.15 pm (two stops), 5.45 pm (non-stop) and 9 pm (two stops). A single ticket on a non-stop voyage costs 1300TL (US$1.82), half that amount on a voyage which stops at Heybeliada and Büyükada in the Princes' Islands. These are summer schedules; there is less service in winter. There may now be faster hydrofoils on this route in which case the schedules will have changed drastically.

Departures from Yalova for the return to İstanbul are Monday through Saturday at 6, 8.30 (except Saturday) and 11.30 am; and at 1.30, 5 and 8.50 pm. On Sunday and holidays, boats leave Yalova for Kabataş at 6.20 and 11.15 am (two stops), 1 pm (non-stop) and 8.20 pm (two stops); this last boat docks at Sirkeci rather than at Kabataş. Two boats on Sunday afternoon, at 3 and 6.15 pm, go only to Büyükada, not to İstanbul. There are only three boats per day in each direction in the wintertime.

The voyage takes about two hours, depending on stops. Board the boat *at least* a half-hour before departure time (45 minutes or an hour is not too early in summer) if you want to be assured of a seat.

Car Ferry Whether you have a car or not, you can take a car ferry as part of your travel to Yalova. Take a ferry (90TL, US$0.13) from Karaköy to Haydarpaşa railway station, then take any *banliyö* (suburban) train (50TL, US$0.07) as far as Kartal. The trains begin at 6 am and run every 20 minutes; the journey from Haydarpaşa to Kartal takes about 40 minutes. Leave the train at the Kartal station and walk downhill to the shore and left to the car ferry dock. Purchase a ticket (400TL, US$0.56 single), then board one of the ferries which depart every hour on the hour (except 2 and 4 am). The voyage takes 1¼ hours and lands you right in Yalova.

Return car ferry voyages from Yalova are at the same times and prices as those from Kartal. The trains operate until around midnight.

Getting Away

Debark from the ferryboat, and as you walk from the wharf you will see a traffic circle centred on an enormous statue of Atatürk. Just off the dock, look to the left. You'll see rows of buses and minibuses. Approach them, and a man will approach you to find out where you're going. Say 'İznik' (EEZ-neek) or 'Bursa' (BOOR-sah) as the case may be, and he'll lead you to a waiting minibus. Be certain that your bus is going to İznik, not İzmit, which is a different city entirely. Climb in and have a seat. In a few minutes the bus will be full, and will set off. The fare is 600TL (US$0.84) to İznik, 650TL (US$0.91) to Bursa, and it will be collected en route.

Yalova city bus No 4 (Taşköprü-Termal) will take you to Termal for 90TL (US$0.13); a Termal dolmuş charges 150TL (US$0.21). Both leave from a lot only a block from the ferry dock. Coming off the ferry, walk to the traffic circle with the statue and turn right, walk a block and the lot is on the left.

TERMAL

Twelve km west of Yalova, off the road to Çınarcık, is Termal (tehr-MAHL), a spa. The baths here take advantage of hot, mineral-rich waters that spring from the earth and were first exploited in Roman

times. The Ottomans used the baths since the 1500s, and Abdülhamid II repaired and refurbished them in 1900 to celebrate the 25th anniversary of his accession to the throne. He had the work done in the wonderfully gaudy Ottoman Baroque style. Atatürk added a simple but comfortable spa hotel, where time seems to stand still: at luncheon you may still hear a violin-and-piano duo play a lilting rendition of 'Santa Lucia', as though the great Turkish leader were resting and taking the waters here, as he did in the 1930s. You can come just to stroll through the shady gardens and have a look at the facilities, or you can come to bathe or stay the night.

Things to See

The gardens and greenery at Termal are worth the trip. But then there are the baths. At the Valide Banyo you get a locker for your clothes, then take a shower and enter a pool. An admission charge of 550TL (US$0.77) gets you 1½ hours of bathing. Soap and shampoo cost 55TL (US$0.08) more. The Sultan Banyo is even grander and much pricier at 1750TL (US$2.45) single, 2200TL (US$3.08) double; you can rent a swimsuit here. The Kurşunlu Banyo features an open-air pool for 850TL (US$1.19), an enclosed pool and sauna for 1000TL (US$1.40), and small private cubicles for 850TL (US$1.19) single, 1150TL (US$1.61) double.

Atatürk had a small house or *köşk* here, which you can visit.

Places to Stay – top end

Though fairly simple as befits a health resort, the hotels here are extremely nice, but both are in the upper price range. The *Turban Yalova Termal Hotel* (tel (1931) 4905) and the *Çınar Oteli* (same telephone) charge 17,200TL to 19,825TL (US$24.08 to US$27.76) single, 22,500TL to 26,200TL (US$31.50 to US$36.68) double, the price depending upon whether the room is on the front or the back of the hotel; breakfast is included in these high summer season prices. Off-season rates are 25% to 30% lower, but do not include breakfast.

Places to Eat

Termal has several restaurants and cafés, but all are fairly pricey. A cup of Nescafé, for example, costs 550TL (US$0.77).

İZNİK

The road from Yalova to İznik (population 16,000) runs along fertile green hills punctuated by tall, spiky cypress trees, passing peach orchards, cornfields and vineyards. The journey of 60 km takes about 1½ hours.

As you approach İznik you may notice fruit-packing plants among the orchards. You will certainly have admired the vast İznik Gölü, or İznik Lake. Watch for the great Byzantine city walls: the road passes through the old İstanbul Kapısı (İstanbul Gate) and then becomes Atatürk Caddesi, and goes to the ruined Church of Sancta Sophia (now a museum) in the very centre of town. The bus station is a few blocks south-east of the church.

History

This ancient city may well have been founded around 1000 BC. We know for sure that it was revitalized by one of Alexander the Great's generals in 316 BC. Another of the generals, Lysimachus, soon got hold of it and named it for his wife Nikaea. It became the capital city of the province of Bithynia.

Nicaea lost some of its prominence with the founding of Nicomedia (today's İzmit) in 264 BC, and by 74 BC the entire area had been incorporated into the Roman Empire.

Nicaea flourished under Rome. The emperors built a new system of walls, plus temples, theatres and baths. But invasions of the Goths and the Persians brought ruin by 300 AD.

Ecumenical Councils With the rise of Constantinople, Nicaea took on a new importance as well. In 325, the First Ecumenical Council was held here for the purpose of condemning the heresy of Arianism. During the great Justinian's reign, Nicaea was grandly refurbished and embellished with new buildings and defenses. They served the city well a few centuries later when the Arabs invaded. Like Constantinople, Nicaea never fell to its Arab besiegers.

In 787 yet another Ecumenical Council, the seventh, was held in Nicaea's Sancta Sophia Church. The deliberations solved the problem of iconoclasm: henceforth it would be church policy not to destroy icons. Theologians who saw icons as 'images', prohibited by the Bible, were dismayed. But Byzantine artists were delighted, and went to work on their art with even more vigour.

Though the city never fell to the Arabs, it did fall to the Crusaders, just like Constantinople. During the period from 1204 to 1261 when a Latin king sat on the throne of Byzantium, the true Byzantine emperor, Theodore Lascaris, reigned over the 'Empire of Nicaea'. When the Crusaders cleared out, Lascaris moved his court back to the traditional capital.

The Turks The Seljuk Turks had a flourishing empire in Central Anatolia before 1250, and various tribes of nomadic warriors had circulated near the walls of Nicaea during those times. In fact, Turkish soldiers had served as mercenaries in the interminable battles which raged among rival claimants to the Byzantine throne. At one point, a Byzantine battle over Nicaea ended with a Turkish emir as its ruler!

It was Orhan (1326-1361), son of Osman and first true sultan of the Ottoman Empire, who conquered İznik on 2 March 1331. The city soon had the honour of harbouring the first Ottoman college. Proussa (Bursa) had fallen to the Ottomans on 6 April 1326, and became

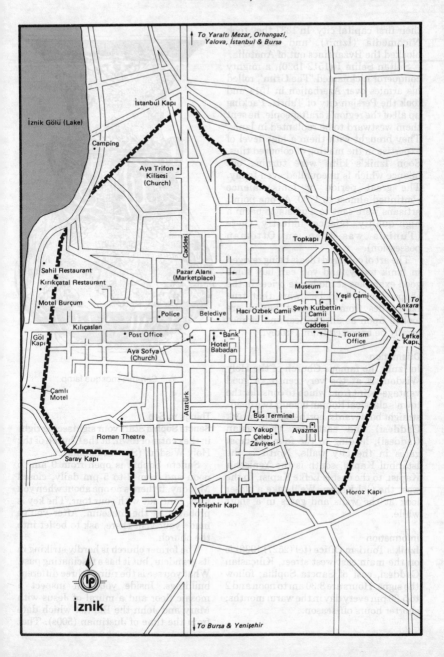

İznik

their first capital city. In 1337 they took Nicomedia (İzmit), and effectively blocked the Byzantines out of Anatolia.

Sultan Selim I (1512-1520), a mighty conqueror nicknamed 'The Grim', rolled his armies over Azerbaijan in 1514 and took the Persian city of Tabriz. Packing up all of the region's craftspeople, he sent them westward to be replanted in İznik. They brought with them a high level of expertise in the making of coloured tiles. Soon İznik's kilns were turning out faience which is unequalled even today. The great period of İznik faience continued almost to 1700. At one point, artisans were sent to Tunisia to begin a high-quality faience industry there (Tunisia was then an Ottoman possession).

The art of coloured tiles is being revived in İznik today, and you can buy some good examples at moderate prices in the shops. You should be aware that true İznik tiles from the great period are looked upon as antiquities, and cannot legally be exported from Turkey.

Orientation

In İznik the famous Church of the Holy Wisdom is at the very centre, a good vantage-point from which to consider the town's classical Roman layout: two dead-straight boulevards, north-south (Atatürk Caddesi) and east-west (Kılıçaslan Caddesi), leading to the four principal gates in the city walls. North is the İstanbul Kapısı, south is the Yenişehir Kapısı, to the east is Lefke Kapısı, to the west the Göl Kapısı. We'll take a closer look at the walls and gates in a short while.

Information

İznik's Tourism Office (tel (2527) 1933) is on the main east-west street, Kılıçaslan Caddesi, east of Sancta Sophia; follow the signs. Hours are 8.30 am to noon and 2 to 5.30 pm every day in the warm months; shorter hours off-season.

Ceramic mosque lamp

Things to See

Sancta Sophia Start your sightseeing right in the centre of town, at the Church of the Holy Wisdom (Sancta Sophia).

Sancta Sophia is open from 9 am to noon and from 2 to 5 pm daily, closed Monday. If there's no one about when you visit, continue with your tour. The key is probably at the museum. After you've made your visit there, ask to be let into the church.

The former church is hardly striking in its grandeur, but it has a fascinating past. What you see is the ruin of three different buildings. Inside you can inspect a mosaic floor and a mural of Jesus with Mary and John the Baptist which date from the time of Justinian (500s). That original church was destroyed by earthquake in 1065 but later rebuilt. Mosaics were set into the walls at that time. With the Ottoman conquest (1331), the church became a mosque. A fire in the 1500s ruined everything, but reconstruction was carried out under the expert eye of Mimar Sinan, who added İznik tiles to the decoration.

The Main Street Now walk east toward Lefke Gate, along İznik's main street, Kılıçaslan Caddesi. On the left is the **Belediye Sarayı (Town Hall)**, with a sign out front that reads 'Our motto is, Clean City, Green City'. It really is a very pleasant, quiet, peaceful and agreeable place with its big poplars shading the commercial district from the summer sun.

A bit farther along on the left is the **Hacı Özbek Camii**, one of the town's oldest mosques, dating from 1332.

A short detour along the street opposite the Hacı Özbek Camii, to the south, will bring you to the **Süleyman Paşa Medresesi**. Founded by Sultan Orhan shortly after he captured Nicaea, it has the distinction of being the very first college (actually a theological seminary) founded by a member of the Ottoman dynasty.

Back on the main street, you will come to the Tourism Office on the right-hand side. Soon, to the left, you can see the tile-covered minaret of the Yeşil Cami (Green Mosque).

Yeşil Cami Built in the year that Columbus discovered America (1492), the Yeşil Cami has Seljuk Turkish proportions influenced more by Persia (the Seljuk homeland) than by İstanbul. The green-glazed bricks of the minaret foreshadowed the tile industry that arose a few decades after the mosque's construction. Sultan Selim, impatient to see a tile industry of his own, simply relocated a large number of artisans from Tabriz.

Museum Across the road from the Yeşil Cami is the Nilüfer Hatun İmareti, or Soup Kitchen of Lady Nilüfer (1388), now set up as the town's museum. Hours are 9 am to noon and 1.30 to 5 pm, closed Monday. Admission fee is 200TL (US$0.28), half-price on weekends (for Sancta Sophia, you must pay the same amount again).

I'll wager that Lady Nilüfer would be pleased to see her pious gift in its present state. Though intended as a place where the poor could come for free food, it now dispenses culture to the masses. The front court is filled with marble statuary, bits of cornice and column, and similar archaeological flotsam and jetsam. In the lofty, cool halls are exhibits of İznik faience, Ottoman weaponry, embroidery and calligraphy. Many of the little signs are in French and English, but you'll need to know the word *yüzyıl* – 'century', as in 'XVI Yüzyıl', '16th century'.

While at the museum, inquire about a visit to the **Byzantine tomb** (Yeraltı Mezar or Katakom) on the outskirts of town. You must have a museum official accompany you with the key; there is a small charge for admission, and the official should receive a small tip. Also, you will have to haggle with a taxi-driver for a return-trip price. But once these arrangements have been made, you're in for a treat. The little tomb, discovered by accident in the 1960s, has delightful Byzantine murals covering walls and ceiling. There is another tomb nearby, but it's not really worth the bother or expense to see.

Across the road to the south of the museum is the **Şeyh Kutbettin Camii** (1492), now in ruins. Sometimes the caretaker will let you climb the stairs in the minaret, up to the stork's nest, for a look at the view.

City Walls Go back to Kılıçaslan Caddesi and continue east to the **Lefke Kapısı or Lefke Gate**. This charming old monument is actually three gates in a row, all dating from Byzantine times. The middle one has an inscription which tells us it was built by the Proconsul Plancius Varus in 123 AD. It's possible to clamber up to the top of the gate and the walls here, a good vantage-point for inspection of the ancient walls.

Outside the gate is an **aqueduct**, still very much in use, and the **tomb** of Çandarlı Halil Hayrettin Paşa (late 1300s), with the graves of many lesser mortals nearby.

Lefke, by the way, is now called Osmaneli. In Byzantine times it was a city of considerable size, though Osmaneli is just a small town.

Re-enter the city through the Lefke Gate, and turn left. Follow the walls south and west to the **Yenişehir Kapısı**. On the way you will pass near the ruined **Church of the Koimesis**, which dates from about 800. It's not much to look at, but it is famous as the burial-place of the Byzantine Emperor Theodore I Lascaris. When the Crusaders took Constantinople in 1204, Lascaris fled to Nicaea and established his court here. He never made it back to his beloved capital. By the way, it was Lascaris who built the outer ring of walls, supported by over 100 towers and protected by a wide moat. No doubt he didn't trust the Crusaders, having lost one city to them.

Near the church is an Ayazma *(aghiasma)* or **sacred fountain**.

After admiring the Yenişehir Kapısı, start toward the centre along Atatürk Caddesi. Halfway to Sancta Sophia, a road on the left leads to the ruins of a **Roman theatre** (Roma Tiyatrosu). Nearby is the **Saray Kapısı or Palace Gate** in the city walls. Sultan Orhan had a palace hereabouts in the 1300s.

The Lake Make your way to the lakeshore, where there's a bathing beach (the water tends to be chilly), tea houses and little restaurants. This is the place to rest your feet, have an ice cream, soft drink or glass of tea, and ponder the history of battles which raged around this city. It is

obviously much better off as a sleepy fruit-growing centre.

Places to Stay – bottom end

İznik has a few modest hostelries good for a one-night stay. In the centre, just across the street from the Belediye Sarayı, is the plain *Hotel Babacan* (tel (2527) 1211) at Kılıçaslan Caddesi 104. Thirty of the rooms come with washbasins, and are priced at 2750TL (US$3.85) single, 3850TL (US$5.39) double. With private shower, the prices are 3300TL (US$4.62) and 4950TL (US$6.93), respectively.

Camping Both of the places described below have basic camping areas.

Places to Stay – middle

Motel Burcum (tel (2527) 1011) has tidy rooms, some with views of the lake, for 7020TL (US$9.83) double, breakfast included.

The tidy *Çamlık Motel* (CHAHM-luhk) (tel (2527) 1631) at the southern end of the lakefront road, has nice rooms and a pretty restaurant, at prices similar to those at the Burcum.

Places to Eat

The lakeside restaurants are the most pleasant for a light meal, if the weather is fine. A snack of white cheese *(beyaz peyni)*, bread and a bottle of beer will cost less than 650TL (US$0.91). Of the restaurants along the lakeshore, the *Dostlar* (tel 1585) is perhaps the busiest; it's near the Motel Burcum.

You'll find a greater selection of hot dishes along the main street in the centre, though, and prices will be lower. Near the Belediye Sarayı, look for the *Köşk* and *Çiçek* restaurants, facing one another across the main street. The Çiçek serves no alcohol; the Köşk (tel 1843) perhaps has the edge in terms of attractiveness.

Another choice near the Town Hall is the *İnegöl*. It specializes in İnegöl *köftesi*, rich grilled rissoles of ground lamb in the style used in the nearby town of İnegöl.

Top: İstanbul as seen from the Süleymaniye minaret
Bottom: Dolmabahçe Palace

Top: The rooftops of the Covered Bazaar
Bottom: Fishing skiffs on the Bosphorus at sunset

Ceramic dish

There is also a *pastahane* (pastry-shop) hereabouts, the *Saray Pastanesi*, good for breakfast or a snack.

Shopping
Coloured tiles, of course, are the natural souvenir from İznik. Several small shops along the main street sell these. There is also embroidered work, a local cottage industry.

Getting Away
Bursa has a much better selection of hotels and restaurants than does İznik. Unless you are unusually interested in İznik, take one of the hourly buses from İznik's bus station to Bursa. Don't wait until too late in the day, however, as the last bus heads out at 6 or 7 pm on the 1½-hour trip. A ticket costs 650TL (US$0.91).

BURSA
Bursa (population 900,000, altitude 155 metres) has a special place in the hearts of the Turks. It was the first capital city of the enormous Ottoman Empire, and in a real sense the birthplace of modern Turkish culture. The city has its pretty parts, despite its industrial might.

History
Called Prusa by the Byzantines, Bursa is a very old and important city. It was founded, according to legend, by Prusias, king of Bithynia, before 200 BC; there may have been an even older settlement on the site. It soon came under the sway of Eumenes II of Pergamum, and thereafter under direct Roman control.

Bursa grew to importance in the early centuries of Christianity, when the thermal baths at Çekirge were first developed on a large scale and when a silk trade was founded here. The importation of silkworms and the establishment of looms began an industry which survives to this day. It was Justinian (527-565) who really put Bursa on the map. Besides favouring the silk trade, he built a palace for himself and bathhouses in Çekirge.

With the decline of Byzantium, Bursa's location near Istanbul drew the interest of would-be conquerors, including the Arab armies (circa 700 AD) and the Seljuk Turks. The Seljuks, having conquered much of Anatolia by 1075, took Bursa with ease that same year, and planted the seeds of the great Ottoman empire to come.

With the arrival of the First Crusade in 1097, Bursa reverted to Christian hands, though it was to be conquered and reconquered by both sides for the next 100 years. When the rapacious armies of the Fourth Crusade sacked Constantinople in 1204, the Byzantine emperor fled to İznik and set up his capital there. He succeeded in controlling the hinterland of İznik, including Bursa, until moving back to Constantinople in 1261.

Ever since the Turkish migration into Anatolia during the 11th and 12th centuries, small principalities had risen here and there around Turkish military leaders. A *gazi* (warrior chieftain or 'Hero of the Faith') would rally a group of

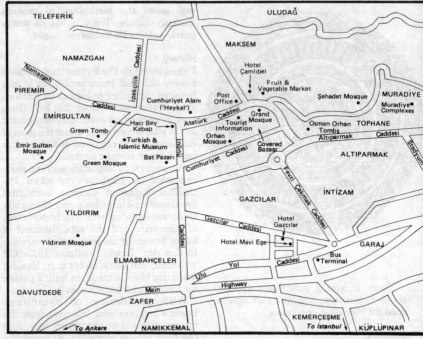

followers, gain control of a territory, govern it and seek to expand its borders. One such prince was Ertuğrul Gazi (died 1281), who formed a small state near Bursa. Under his son Osman Gazi (1281-1326) the small state grew to a nascent empire and took Osman's name (*Osmanlı*, 'Ottoman'). Bursa was laid siege to by Osman's forces in 1317 and finally yielded on 6 April 1326. It immediately became the Ottoman capital.

After Osman had expanded and enriched his principality, he was succeeded by Orhan Gazi (1326-1361) who, from his base at Bursa, expanded the empire to include everything from Ankara in Central Anatolia to Thrace in Europe. The Byzantine capital at Constantinople was thus surrounded, and the Byzantine Empire had only about a century to live. Orhan took the title of *sultan* (lord), struck the first

Ottoman coinage, and near the end of his reign was able to dictate to the Byzantine emperors. One of them, John VI Cantacuzene, was Orhan's close ally and later even his father-in-law (Orhan married the Princess Theodora).

Even though the Ottoman capital would be moved to Edirne (Adrianople) in 1402, Bursa remained an important, even revered, Ottoman city throughout the long history of the empire. Both Osman and Orhan were buried in Bursa, and their tombs are still proud and important monuments in Turkish history.

With the founding of the Turkish Republic, Bursa's industrial development began in earnest. What really brought the boom was the automobile assembly plants, set up in the 1960s and 1970s. Large factories here assemble Renaults, Fiats (called Murat) and a Turkish car called the Anadol. Also, Bursa has always

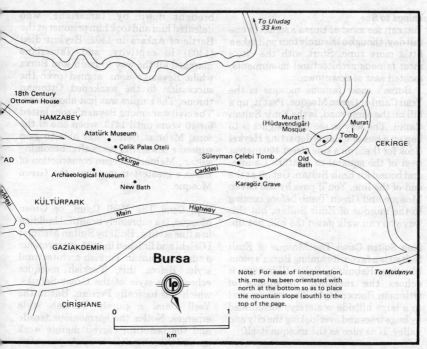

To Uludag
33 km

18th Century
Ottoman House

HAMZABEY

Atatürk Museum

• Çelik Palas Oteli

Çekirge

Archaeological Museum

AD

New Bath

KÜLTÜRPARK

Süleyman Çelebi Tomb

Çekirge Caddesi

Karagöz Grave

Murat !
(Hüdavendigâr)
Mosque

Murat
Tomb

Old
Bath

ÇEKIRGE

Main

Highway

GAZİAKDEMİR

ÇİRİŞHANE

Bursa

0   1
km

Note: For ease of interpretation,
this map has been orientated with
north at the bottom so as to place
the mountain slope (south) to the
top of the page.

To Mudanya

been noted for its fruits, and it was logical that a large fruit juice and soft drink industry should be centred here. Tourism is also important.

Orientation

Bursa clings to the slopes of Uludağ and spills down into the fertile valley below. The major boulevards are Uluyol and Atatürk Caddesi, which run across the slope, not up and down it.

Bursa's main plaza is Cumhuriyet Alanı (joom-hoor-ee-YEHT ah-lahn-uh, 'Republic Plaza'), where you will see an equestrian statue of Atatürk. Most people refer to the plaza as Heykel (hey-KEHL, statue), and that's what you will see written on a little plastic sign in the windscreens of dolmuşes waiting just outside the bus station. Hop in a dolmuş to get up the hill to Heykel.

Bursa's main street, Atatürk Caddesi,

runs west from Heykel to the Ulu Cami (oo-LOO jah-mee, Great Mosque), a distance of perhaps half a km. This is the downtown business section, the centre of Bursa. The westward continuation of Atatürk Caddesi becomes Cemal Nadir Caddesi, then Altıparmak Caddesi, then Çekirge Caddesi. It leads to the spa suburb of Çekirge, about a 10-minute ride.

From Heykel and Atatürk Caddesi you can get dolmuşes and buses to all other parts of the city, including hotel and sightseeing areas.

Information

The Tourism Information Office (tel (241) 12 359) is at Atatürk Caddesi 82, right in the centre of the city near the Ulu Cami. The staff are helpful, and some speak English. There is also a small booth in the Şehir Garajı (bus station).

Things to See

You can see most of Bursa's sights in one full day, though a leisurely tour will take a little more time. Start with the city's most famous architectural monuments, located east of downtown.

Bursa's most famous mosque is the Yeşil Cami or Green Mosque. Past it, up a hill on the same road, is the Emir Sultan Camii. The way to see these sights is to hop on a bus or dolmuş departing Heykel (look for them on a side street 100 metres west of the square) or Atatürk Caddesi and bound for Emir Sultan. Get off at the end of the line. You'll pass by the Green Mosque and Green Tomb before coming to the mosque of Emir Sultan, but this way you can walk *down* the hill, not up.

Emir Sultan Camii The Mosque of Emir Sultan is a favourite among Bursa's pious Muslims. Rebuilt by Selim III in 1805, it echoes the romantic decadence of Ottoman Rococo style. The setting next to a large hillside cemetery, surrounded by huge trees and overlooking the city and valley, is as nice as the mosque itself.

Yıldırım Beyazıt Camii Gazing across the valley from the Emir Sultan Camii, you'll see the two domes of the Yıldırım Beyazıt Camii, the Mosque of Beyazıt the Thunderbolt. It is earlier (1391) than Bursa's famous Yeşil Cami, and takes part in the same architectural evolution (see below). You can walk through the city to this mosque if you like, but go see the Yeşil Cami first.

Next to the Yıldırım Beyazıt Camii is its *medrese*, once a theological seminary, now a public health centre. Here also is the tomb of the mosque's founder, Sultan Beyazıt I, and of his son İsa. This peaceful spot gives one no sense of the turbulent times which brought Beyazıt to his death.

Yıldırım Beyazıt (1389-1402) led his Ottoman armies into Yugoslavia and Hungary, and captured even more of Anatolia for the Ottomans. But he was brought down by Tamerlane, who defeated him and took him prisoner at the Battle of Ankara in 1402. Beyazıt died (1403) in captivity, and Tamerlane marched all the way to İzmir and Bursa while Beyazıt's sons argued over the succession to the weakened Ottoman throne. The empire was just about dead. The civil war among Beyazıt's sons lasted for 10 years until 1413, when one of the sons, Mehmet Çelebi, was able to gain supreme power. Six years after becoming sultan, Mehmet I began construction of Bursa's greatest monument, the Green Mosque.

Yeşil Cami The Yeşil Cami, or Green Mosque, is a supremely beautiful building in a fine setting. Built by Sultan Mehmet I Çelebi and finished in 1424, it represents a turning-point in Turkish architectural style. Before this, Turkish mosques echoed the style of the Great Seljuks, which was basically Persian. But in the Yeşil Cami a purely Turkish style emerges. Notice the harmonious facade and the beautiful carved marble work around the central doorway. As you enter, you will pass beneath the sultan's private apartments into a domed central hall. The rooms to the left and right, if not being used for prayer, were used by high court officials for transacting government business. The room straight ahead, with the 15-metre-high *mihrab* (prayer niche), is the main prayer room. Greenish-blue tiles on the interior walls gave the mosque its name.

Much of Bursa, including the Green Mosque, was destroyed in an earthquake in 1855. But the mosque was restored, authentically, by 1864.

At some point during your visit a caretaker is likely to approach you and, with a conspiratorial wink, signal you to follow him up a narrow stairway to the *Hünkâr mahfili*, or sultan's loge, above the main door. The loge is sumptuously tiled and decorated. This is where the sultan actually lived (or at least it was one of his residences), with his harem and household staff in less plush quarters on either side. The caretaker will not take large groups up to the *mahfil*; he'll choose single travellers or couples. He'll expect a tip.

Yeşil Türbe Walk around the Green Mosque, noticing the slender minarets rising from bulbous bases, across the road and up the steps to the Yeşil Türbe, or Green Tomb. It's not green, of course. The blue exterior tiles were put on during restoration work in the 1800s; the lavish use of tiles inside is original work, however. No need to remove your shoes to enter here. The tomb is open 8.30 am to noon, 1 to 5.30 pm, for free.

The most prominent tomb is that of the Green Mosque's founder, Mehmet Çelebi (1413-1421). Others include those of his children. The huge tiled *mihrab* here is very impressive. Take a walk around the outside of the tomb for a look at the tiled calligraphy above several windows.

After seeing the mosque and the tomb, you might want to take a rest and have something to drink at one of the cafés on the east side of the mosque. They have wonderful views of the valley.

Museum Down the road a few steps from the Green Mosque is its *medrese*, now used as the Bursa Etnoğrafya Müzesi, Bursa Ethnographic Museum. The building is in the Seljuk style for religious schools, and the museum collection contains many local craft items. The museum is open from 8.30 am to noon and 1 to 5.30 pm, closed Monday; admission costs 200TL (US$0.28), half-price on Sunday and holidays.

Bat Pazarı From the plaza at Heykel, walk down the hill on İnönü Caddesi until you come to a small mosque set partly in the roadway. The section to your right – a warren of little streets – is the Bat Pazarı, or Goose Market. The one thing you won't find here today are geese, but

you will find ironmongers' shops and pedlars of old clothes, carpets, rope, utensils, potions and just about everything else. This market section is lively and colourful, perfect for photographing. When you snap a shot of the blacksmith at his forge, chances are he will ask you to send him a copy. It's only fair; you should try to do so.

Bedesten After an hour's stroll through the Bat Pazarı, head back to İnönü Caddesi and ask someone to point out the Bedesten (BEH-deh-stehn), the Covered Bazaar. Cross İnönü Caddesi and head into the side streets, following their directions.

The Bedesten was originally built in the late 1300s by Yıldırım Beyazıt, but the earthquake of 1855 brought it down. The reconstructed Bedesten retains the look and feel of the original, though it is obviously much tidier. This is not a tourist trap; most of the shoppers are local people. As you wander around, look for the **Eski Aynalı Çarşı**, which was once a Turkish bath; the domed ceiling with many small lights shows this.

In the Eski Aynalı Çarşı is a shop called Karagöz, run by a man named Şinasi Çelikkol. Şinasi specializes in quality goods (copper and brass, carpets and *kilims*, knitted gloves and embroidery, old jewellery, etc) at fair prices, as did his father before him. This is the place to find the delightful Karagöz shadow-play puppets. Cut from flat, dried camel leather, painted in bright colours and oiled to make them translucent, the puppets are an authentic Turkish craft item. The Karagöz shadow play originated in Bursa.

The raising of silkworms is a cottage industry in Bursa. Each April, villagers buy silkworm grubs from their co-operatives, take them home and raise them on mulberry leaves. After a month the worms spin their cocoons and are soon ready for the trip to the **Koza Han or Silk Cocoon Building**, just outside the bazaar's eastern entrance, which is lively with cocoon dealers in June and also in September when there is a second harvest. When you visit, you may well see huge sacks of the precious little white cocoons being haggled over by some of the 14,000 villagers who engage in the trade. In the centre of the Koza Han courtyard is a small mosque *(mescit)* constructed by Yıldırım Beyazıt in 1493, restored by the guild of silk traders in 1948 and again in 1985 by the Aga Khan. The product of all this industry, silk cloth *(ipek*, ee-PEHK*)*, is for sale in the Covered Bazaar.

Another place you ought to visit in the Bedesten is the **Emirhan**, a caravanserai used by many of Bursa's silk brokers, as it has been for centuries. Ask directions by saying *Emirhan nerede?* (eh-MEER-hahn neh-reh-deh, 'Where's the Emirhan?'). There's a lovely fountain in the centre of the courtyard, and a tea garden for refreshment. Camels from the silk caravans used to be corralled in the courtyard, while goods were stored in the ground-floor rooms and drovers and merchants slept and did business in the rooms above.

Ulu Cami Next to the Bedesten is Bursa's Great Mosque, the Ulu Cami. This one is completely Seljuk in style, a big rectangular building with immense portals and a forest of supporting columns inside. The roof is a mass of 20 small domes. A *şadırvan* (ablutions fountain) is right within the mosque. It was Yıldırım Beyazıt who put up the money for the building in 1396. Notice the fine work in the *mimber* (pulpit) and the preacher's chair; also the calligraphy on the walls.

Legend has it that one of the men working on construction of the mosque was a hump-back called Karagöz (Black-eye). He and his straight-man Hacivat indulged in such humorous antics that the other workmen abandoned their tasks to watch. This infuriated the sultan, who had the two miscreants put to death. Their comic routines (many of them

bawdy) live on in the Karagöz shadow-puppet theatre, a Bursa tradition that later spread throughout the Ottoman lands. The puppets are manipulated behind a white cloth onto which their coloured shadows are cast by a light behind them.

Hisar From the Ulu Cami, walk west and up a ramp-like street to the section known as Hisar (fortress). Coming by bus or dolmuş from Heykel, get a vehicle labelled 'Muradiye'.

The main street here is Pınarbaşı Caddesi. This section is among the oldest in Bursa, once enclosed by stone ramparts and walls. Some picturesque old frame houses and neighbourhood quarters survive here.

In a little park near the edge of the cliff, overlooking the boulevard (Cemal Nadir Caddesi) and the valley, are the **tombs of sultans Osman and Orhan**, founders of the Ottoman Empire. The originals were destroyed in the earthquake of 1855 and rebuilt in Ottoman Baroque style by Sultan Abdül Aziz in 1868. The tomb of Orhan Gazi was built on the foundations of a small Byzantine church, and you can see some remnants of the church's floor. The park here is nice, as is the view of the city.

Muradiye The Mosque of Sultan Murat II (1421-1451) is further west and up the slope from the tombs. With a shady park in front and a quiet cemetery behind, the place is pretty and peaceful. The mosque proper dates from 1426 and follows the style of the Yeşil Cami.

Beside the mosque are a dozen **tombs** dating from the 1400s and 1500s, including those of Sultan Murat himself. Tomb-visiting may not be high on your list of priorities but you should see the beautiful decoration, especially in the **Murat II Türbesi, Cem Türbesi** and **Mustafa Şehzade Türbesi**.

Across the park from the mosque is an **old Ottoman house** (the sign says '17. Y.Y.

Ev', or '17th-Century House'). Now a museum, it gives you a fascinating glimpse into the daily life of the Ottoman nobility in the 1600s. Carpets and furnishings are all authentic. Don't miss this one. It's open 8.30 am to noon, 1 to 5 pm, closed Monday, with a small admission charge of 100TL (US\$0.14), half-price on Sunday and holidays.

Kültür Parkı Bursa's Cultural Park (kewl-TEWR pahr-kuh) is laid out to the north of the Muradiye complex, down the hill some distance. You can reach it from Heykel by any bus or dolmuş going to Çekirge. Besides a pleasant stroll, the Kültür Parkı is good for lunch in one of its shady outdoor restaurants (see 'Places to Eat').

The park also holds the **Bursa Arkeoloji Müzesi or Bursa Archaeological Museum**. Bursa's history goes to the time of Hannibal (200 BC), and Roman artefacts are preserved here. The collection is nice but not at all exceptional. If you've seen another good Turkish collection, this is more of the same. Find the bus stop named 'Arkeoloji Müzesi', enter the park by the gate nearby, and visit the museum from 8.30 am to noon, 1 to 5.30 pm, any day but Monday; admission costs 500TL (US\$0.70), half-price on Sunday and holidays.

Çekirge & The Baths The warm, mineral-rich waters which spring from the slopes of Uludağ have been famous for their curative powers since ancient times. Today the ailing and the infirm come here for several weeks at a time, taking a daily soak or two in the tub, spending the rest of the time chatting, reading or dining. Most stay in hotels which have their own bathing facilities. There are independent baths (*kaplıca*) as well, some of historical importance.

The Yeni Kaplıca is a bath built in 1522 by Sultan Süleyman the Magnificent's Grand Vezir, Rüstem Paşa, on the site of a much older one built by Justinian. The

Kükürtlü bath is noted for its high sulphur content. At the Kaynarca ('Boiling') bath, it's the extreme heat of the water that is outstanding. Other baths are the Kara Mustafa and the Eski Kaplıca.

Bathing arrangements vary. Some have private steam rooms, some have rows of tubs, some have a common steam room and pool, some have several of these all under one roof. Bathing fees are low, though tips to the staff can run up the final tab somewhat. Baths will be crowded on Friday, the Muslim sabbath, as local people clean up for the holy day.

The standard Turkish bath has three rooms, as did the ancient Roman bath. The first is cool, the second warm, the third hot. After a soak in the hot room, you retire to the warm one for a wash, then to the cool one for a towelling. A nap followed by a glass of tea comes next, if you have the time.

Places to Stay

Though there are a few hotels downtown, many of Bursa's best lodgings in terms of both quality and prices are in the western suburb of Çekirge. Hotels atop Uludağ are mentioned in the section (below) describing the mountain.

Places to Stay – bottom end

You can find a very cheap room in Bursa near the bus station, in the centre, or in Çekirge, but you must choose carefully. Hotels near the Şehir Garajı tend to be outrageously noisy and not well kept; noise is a problem in the downtown section as well.

I strongly recommend that you look for lodgings away from the bus station. If you must stay here, at least find a quiet place. Walk out the front door of the Şehir Garajı, and cross Uluyol. There are several hotels here, but they are noisy and expensive. Turn left, then right, and walk along this small street to the *Mavi Ege Oteli* (mah-VEE eh-GEH) (tel

(241) 48 420), Fırın Sokak 1. The 'Blue Aegean' is very plain and simple, but quieter than most, and charges 2000TL (US\$2.80) single, 2800TL (US\$3.92) double, 3200TL (US\$4.42) triple for a room with washbasin.

For much better accommodation, continue walking along the small street to Gazcılar Caddesi. Turn left and you'll see the *Gazcılar Oteli* (GAHZ-juh-LAHR) (tel (241) 49 477), Gazcılar Caddesi 156. Neat and clean, the Gazcılar has central heat and rooms with or without private shower. Without, prices are 3300TL (US\$4.62) single, 4700TL (US\$6.58) double; with shower, rates are 4500TL (US\$6.30) single, 6200TL (US\$8.68) double.

In the midst of downtown, the choice place is the *Otel Çamlıbel* (CHAHM-luh-behl) (tel (241) 12 565 or 25 565), İnebey Caddesi 71, an old and well-worn place with these advantages: quiet location, rooms with constant hot water and good cross-ventilation, a lift and a few parking places in front of the hotel. Rates are very good, at 3300TL (US\$4.62) single, 4700TL (US\$6.58) double, 6000TL (US\$8.40) triple without private shower; or 4500TL (US\$6.30) single, 6200TL (US\$8.68) double and 7500TL (US\$10.50) triple with private shower. Breakfast is served in the hotel. To find the Çamlıbel, walk one block west from the PTT on Atatürk Caddesi (it's across from the Ulu Cami), pass the Türkiye Emlak Kredi Bankası, and turn left. This is İnebey Caddesi. Walk two blocks up the hill on İnebey, and the hotel is on the right-hand side.

There are several other smaller, even plainer hotels in this area. Also on İnebey Caddesi is the *Yeni Ankara Oteli*, a half-block up from Atatürk Caddesi, with very basic rooms without bath for 2800TL (US\$3.92) double. Past it, up the hill a few more steps and to the right, is the *Küçük Çamlıbel Oteli* (tel (241) 28 496), an equally basic and cheap place just around the corner from a pretty little

neighbourhood fruit-and-vegetable market.

Most Çekirge hotels have their own facilities for 'taking the waters', since that's the reason people come to Çekirge. You may find that the bathtub or shower in your hotel room runs only mineral water, or there may be separate private or public bathing-rooms in the basement of the hotel. One day's dip in the mineral waters is no great thrill. The benefits are acquired over a term of weeks, and are therapeutic. All the same, you may find that a soak in a private tub is included in the price of the room, even in the very cheapest hotels, so take advantage of it.

For all of the Çekirge hotels, get a bus or dolmuş from Heykel or along Atatürk Caddesi, and get out at the bus stop mentioned.

In Çekirge, my choices are the *Huzur Oteli* (hoo-ZOOR) (tel (241) 68 021), Birinci Murat Camii Bitişiği, on the east side of the Hüdavendigâr mosque, more or less behind the Ada Palas hotel near the entrance to Çekirge. The Huzur has it all: tidiness, quiet, friendly staff and mineral baths included in the rates of 3850TL (US\$5.39) double, 4730TL (US\$6.62) triple.

Slightly more expensive are the rooms at the *Yeşil Yayla Oteli* (yeh-SHEEL YAHY-lah) (tel (241) 68 026), up at the far end of the village past the military hospital, behind the Yıldız Otel. For a simple bathless room here one person pays 3250TL (US\$4.55) single, 4400TL (US\$6.16) double; the fee for a bath is included in the rates.

Places to Stay – middle

In downtown Bursa noise is a big problem, but it's minimized at the *Hotel Dikmen* (deek-MEHN) (tel (241) 14 995, 6, 7), Fevzi Çakmak Caddesi 78 (the street is also called Maksem Caddesi; it leads ultimately to Uludağ). The Dikmen is popular with tour groups, but if there's a room, you can rent it for 9622TL (US\$13.47) single with shower, 12,585TL

(US$17.62) double with shower, 13,325TL (US$18.66) double with bath. The hotel is about 50 metres up the hill on the street that begins beside the main PTT (across from the Ulu Cami).

Just across Fevzi Çakmak Caddesi from the PTT, on Atatürk Caddesi, you'll find the *Hotel Artıç* (ahr-TUCH) (tel (241) 19 500, 1), Postane Yanı, Ulucami Karşısı 123. Noise can be a problem here but the location is supremely convenient, and prices aren't bad at 6600TL (US$9.24) single, 9350TL (US$13.09) double.

Places to Stay - top end

In Çekirge, the *Termal Hotel Gönlü Ferah* (GEWN-lew feh-RAH) (tel (241) 62 700, 1) in the very centre of the village, is among the more deluxe. Some rooms have wonderful views over the valley. Rates are 26,860TL (US$37.60) double on the street side, 30,500TL (US$42.70) double on the panoramic side, breakfast included. Next door, the *Hotel Dilmen* (DEEL-mehn) (tel (241) 21 701, 2) is about the same price for similar rooms.

The *Yıldız Otel* (yuhl-DUHZ) (tel (241) 66 605, 6, 7) at the upper end of the village, used to be a small and exceedingly modest place but is now deluxe, proud and expensive. Lavish refurbishing has produced a hotel with all the comforts. Prices are 21,450TL (US$30.03) double, with breakfast. A half km farther along the road, on the outskirts of Çekirge, is its sister establishment, the new and modern *Büyük Yıldız Otel* (same phone), with the finest views of the valley, a wonderfully quiet location, and a price of 30,650TL (US$42.91) double, breakfast included.

Places to Eat

Bursa's culinary specialties include fresh fruit (especially peaches in season), candied chestnuts (*kestane şekeri*) and two types of roast meat. *Bursa kebap* or *İskender kebap* is the most famous, made from *döner kebap* laid on a bed of fresh *pide* bread and topped with savoury

tomato sauce and browned butter. When I'm in Bursa, I have this every single day. The other specialty is *İnegöl köftesi*, a type of very rich grilled rissole (ground meat patty) which is actually the specialty of the nearby town called İnegöl. You will see several restaurants which specialize in these dishes exclusively, called *Bursa kebapçısı* or *İnegöl köftecisi*.

Most of Bursa's eateries are quite inexpensive and would suit a bottom-end budget, while the food is good enough for the top end. The exceptions are in Çekirge, where the marvelous views ratchet up the prices.

Bursa Kebapçıs My favourite Bursa *kebapçı* is *Hacı Bey* (hah-JUH bey) (tel 16 440) on Ünlü Cade, a small street just east of Heykel (ask in the plaza for 'hah-JUH bey BOOR-sah keh-bahp-chuh-suh'). Just a few steps down the street, on the right, you'll recognise it by the *döner* turning in the window. Simple but neat and tidy, the restaurant serves *Bursa kebap* in one, 1½ and two-portion sizes called *bir porsyon, bir buçuk porsyon* and *duble* (BEER pohr-syohn; BEER boo-CHOOK; DOOB-leh). A single portion with yoghurt (*yoğurtlu*) and a dab of smoky aubergine puree on the side, plus a bottle of mineral water or a glass of *şıra* (grape juice), and Turkish coffee, tip included, will cost about 1650TL (US$2.31). Remember - after your *kebap* is served, don't begin eating until the waiter brings the tomato sauce and browned butter.

Hacı Bey has two other restaurant locations as well, one in the Kültür Parkı and another on the road to the Yeşil Camii, a half-block from the Ethnography Museum; but I think the original location is the best.

Bursa kebap was invented in a small restaurant now called *Kebabcı İskenderoğlu* ('İskender's Son') at Atatürk Caddesi 60 in the centre of town; another location is just a few steps past the Hacı Bey on Ünlü Cadde, marked by a sign,

'İskender İskenderoğlu.' This is also a good choice for the famous *kebap*.

İnegöl Köfteci For *İnegöl köftesi*, try the *İnegöl Köftecisi*, on a little side street by Atatürk Caddesi 48. On your second visit you might try the *köfte* made with onions or cheese as a variation on the basic stuff. A full lunch need cost only 1200TL (US$1.68).

Another good *köfteci* is the *Özömür*, on the western side of the Ulu Cami.

Hazır Yemek Those marvellously cheap and tasty meals you sampled in İstanbul are readily available in Bursa's many *hazır yemek lokantası*. Look for ready-food restaurants down side streets near Heykel. Also, the *Şehir Lokantası* (sheh-HEER) (tel 26 203) at İnebey Caddesi 85, a half-block up from Atatürk Caddesi, is near the Çamlıbel and Yeni Ankara hotels. Simple, clean and attractive, it serves filling ready-food meals for less than 1300TL (US$1.82).

Kültür Parkı Strolling around the Cultural Park is pleasant, and having a meal here is more so. The *Selçuk Restaurant* is good, quiet, shady and inexpensive. I paid 1900TL (US$2.66) for a full lunch here, beverage and tip included. The *Yusuf Restaurant* also looks good, but I couldn't find out; I sat at a table for a quarter-hour but no waiter approached.

Çekirge Çekirge has several good restaurants which are especially pleasant because they have delightful views of the green river valley. Both the *Çardak* and the *Papağan* are near the Ada Palas hotel in the center of Çekirge. A full meal of soup, mixed grill of lamb, salad, dessert, wine or beer, tax and tip might cost 4000TL (US$5.60). But ask prices and check your bill; also, beware the tremulous organ music.

Shopping
I've already mentioned those Bursa

exclusives, silk cloth (especially scarves), hand-knitted woollen mittens, gloves and socks, Karagöz shadow puppets and candied chestnuts. If you're in the market for English-language books, try the *ABC Kitabevi* (that's ah-beh-JEH KEE-tah-beh-vee) (tel 10 893), at Altıparmak Caddesi 69/A, several hundred metres west of the Ulu Cami on the road to Çekirge.

Getting There & Away
The best way to reach Bursa is by ferry and bus. Though there is limited air service, there is no rail service.

Air Bursa has air service from İstanbul via Sönmez Holding Hava Yolları (tel (241) 10 099, in İstanbul tel 573-9323 or 149-8510 or 146-8084), with one daily flight in each direction (except Sunday).

Bus You will probably arrive in Bursa by bus or minibus from the ferryboat dock at Yalova, or from İznik. These services come into Bursa's Otogar (bus station), sometimes called the Şehir Garajı. For local transport, see under 'Getting Around'.

When the time comes to leave Bursa, go to the Şehir Garajı. Buses, minibuses and dolmuşes leave frequently for İznik (650TL, US$0.91) and for the İstanbul ferryboats at Yalova (650TL, US$0.91). If you plan to catch a boat at Yalova, get a bus that departs at least 90 minutes before scheduled ferryboat departure. If you miss the express ferryboat you can always take the car ferry. See the Yalova section for details.

For other destinations, buy your ticket in advance to ensure a good seat and departure time. The bus trip to Ankara (2400TL to 2800TL, US$3.36 to US$3.92) takes seven hours; to İzmir (2200TL, US$3.08), 7½ hours; to Çanakkale (for Troy and Gallipoli, 2000TL to 2400TL, US$2.80 to US$3.36), six hours.

Getting Around

Out the front door of the Otogar is a big street named Uluyol (oo-LOO-yohl, 'Great Road') or Ulu Caddesi. Here you will find dolmuşes, taxis and city buses. For the city buses, you will need to buy a ticket (70TL, US$0.10) *before* you board the bus. Look for the ticket kiosk.

You will be looking for transport to the centre of town and its hotels, or the hotels at Çekirge. To reach Heykel, walk out the front door of the bus station, cross Uluyol, and look for the rank of cars filling up with people; most of these dolmuşes go to Heykel (100TL, US$0.14). To get to the Ulu Cami from the bus station, go out the front door, turn right, walk to the big intersection, cross the avenue, and catch a bus or dolmuş heading up the slope. Most will pass the Ulu Cami (ask for OOloo JAH-mee).

The fastest way to travel between Heykel and Çekirge is by dolmuş; they run frequently and charge according to how far you travel. Also, city bus No 1 travels the entire 'tourist route', from the Emir Sultan Camii at the eastern end of town, through Heykel and along Atatürk Caddesi, past the Kültür Parkı and the Turkish baths to Çekirge.

ULUDAĞ

Bursa's Mt Olympus dominates the city. There were numerous mountains named Olympus in the ancient world. This was the one in the Kingdom of Bithynia, later the Roman province of Mysia.

The gods no longer live atop Uludağ, but there is a cable car *(teleferik)*, a selection of hotels, a National Park, cool forests and often snow. Even if you don't plan to hike to the summit (three hours each way from the hotel zone) or to go skiing (winter only), you might want to take the cable car up for the view and the cool, fresh air.

Things to See

Cable Car For a summer visit to Uludağ, getting there is most of the fun. Take a

Bursa city bus *(Teleferik)*, a dolmuş (from about 100 metres west of the statue) or a taxi to the lower terminus, called Teleferuç (tel 13 635), a 15-minute ride away at the eastern edge of town. In summer when crowds abound, the cars depart when full or at least every 30 to 45 minutes, weather and winds permitting. The trip to the top takes about 30 minutes each way and costs 900TL (US$1.26) one way; twice that for the round trip.

The cable car stops at an intermediate point named Kadıyayla, from whence you continue upward to the terminus at Sarıalan (sah-RUH-ah-lahn, altitude 1635 metres). From Sarıalan, there is a smaller cable car, called *tele-kabin*, which runs to Çobankaya (1100TL, US$1.54, round trip), but it's not worth the time or money.

At Sarıalan there are a few snack and refreshment stands, a National Park camping area (full at all times, it seems) and the occasional dolmuş to the hotel zone *(Oteller Mevkii)*, six km farther up the mountain slope. That's all there is to do, except enjoy the scenery.

Dolmuş You can take a dolmuş from Bursa's bus station to the hotel zone on Uludağ, but it costs somewhat more than the cable car. On the winding, 22-km trip you'll have to stop (11 km) and pay an entry fee for the National Park of 200TL (US$0.28) per person, 500TL (US$0.70) for a car and driver. The hotel zone is 11 km farther up from the National Park entrance. Almost half of the entire 22 km is on rough granite-block pavement.

Places to Stay

A dozen inns are scattered about the mountaintop. All are meant for skiers, so they close for much of the year. A few stay open all the time, though they have little business in summer unless they can schedule a commercial meeting.

The best place to stay, no matter what the price, is the *Otel Beceren* (BEH-jeh-REHN) (tel (2418) 1111). The hotel

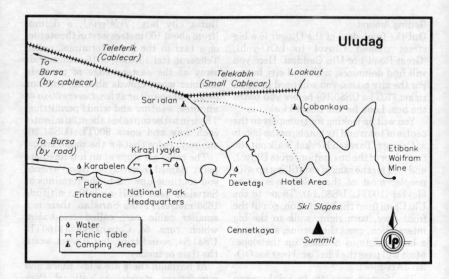

consists of two buildings, one of which closes in summer, the other staying open. For 15,000TL (US$21) double you get a room with bath, plus breakfast; the room has a television and six channels of video programming. For 25,000TL (US$35) two people can have a room and all three meals.

Among the other hotels, the *Büyük Otel* (bew-YEWK) (tel (2418) 1216, 7, 8) is a traditional favourite, an older place with small rooms with showers or baths renting for 20,000TL (US$28) double, breakfast and dinner included. The status address atop the mountain is the *Grand Hotel Yazıcı* (YAH-zuh-juh) (tel (2418) 1050), where a lot of the status is in the lobby, the minds of the staff and the prices: 19,000TL (US$26.60) single, 30,000TL (US$42) double, for a room with shower and no television or meals.

Çanakkale, Gallipoli & Troy

A tremendous amount of world commerce travels by sea. Since commerce means wealth and wealth means power, the people who control the sea have enormous commercial – not to mention military – power. The best place for a small group of people to control an awful lot of sea is at a strait.

The story of the Çanakkale Boğazı (cha-NAH-kah-leh boh-ah-zuh), or Dardanelles, is one of people battling each other for control of this narrow passage which unites the Mediterranean and Aegean seas with the Marmara and Black seas. In ancient times it was the Achaeans attacking the Trojans; in modern times the Anzacs facing Atatürk at Gallipoli. The name 'Dardanelles' comes from Dardanus, ruler of a very early city-state at Çanakkale, who controlled the straits.

The story of the Dardanelles is not all war and commerce; romance, too, has been central to its mythical associations:

legends says that the goddess Helle fell from a golden-winged ram into the water here, giving the straits the name of Hellespont. And the lovesick Leander, separated from his beloved Hero, swam to her through the fierce currents each night, until one night he didn't make it. 'Swimming the Hellespont' is a challenge for amateur and professional swimmers to this day.

The height of romance is the story of two ancient peoples battling over the love and honour of Helen, most beautiful woman in the world. Historians now tell us that Helen was just a pawn in the fierce commercial and military rivalries between Achaea and Troy. Still, no one says she wasn't beautiful, or that the Trojan horse didn't actually fool the Trojans and lead to their defeat by the Achaeans.

The area of the straits holds these attractions: the town of Çanakkale (population 45,000), a fast-growing agricultural centre on the south-east shore of the straits; the fortifications, ancient and modern, which guarded the straits; the battlefields of Gallipoli on the north-west side of the straits; and the excavated ruins of ancient Troy 32 km to the south. For a week in mid-August, the Çanakkale Festival fills the hotels in town. Arrive early in the day and start your search for a hotel room at once, if you plan to be here around 10 to 18 August.

Orientation

In Çanakkale, everything you need is within two blocks of the ferry docks and the clock tower, except for the Otogar and the Archaeological Museum. To get from the Otogar to the centre of town by the clock tower and car ferry docks, leave the bus station by the front doors, turn left, walk to the first turning to the right, and follow signs straight to the Feribot (ferryboat!). Just before you come to the docks you'll see the vaguely Teutonic clock tower (Saat Kulesi, sah-AHT koo-leh-see) on your left.

Information

The town's Tourism Information Office (tel (1961) 1187) is in a little booth near the quay, between the clock tower and the ferry docks.

Things to See

You can easily walk to Çanakkale's interesting sights. In the broad main street at the centre of the town is a **monument** constructed of old WW I cannons. The words on the plaque translate as 'Turkish soldiers used these cannons on 18 March 1915 to ensure the impassability of the Çanakkale strait'. To reach the **market** area, walk behind the clock tower and turn into one of the streets on the left-hand side.

Military Zone There is an interesting **Military & Naval Museum** (Askerî ve Deniz Müzesi, ahs-kehr-EE veh deh-NEEZ mew-zeh-see) in the Military Zone at the southern end of the quay, open from 9 am to noon and 1.30 to 5 pm, free admission. It's supposedly closed on Monday and Thursday but I visited on a Thursday with no problem. The nice lawns and gardens are open for strolling until 10 pm. Start from the ferry docks and walk along the quay to the zone and its fortress. If you walk inland, the zone is two blocks beyond the Hotel Konak.

Within the zone you'll see a mock-up of the old **minelayer** *Nusrat*, which had a heroic role in the Gallipoli campaign. The day before the Allied fleet was to steam through the straits, Allied minesweepers proclaimed the water cleared. At night the *Nusrat* went out, picked up loose mines and relaid them, helping to keep the Allies from penetrating the straits the next day.

There's also a small **museum** with memorabilia of Atatürk and the battles of Gallipoli.

The impressive **fortress**, built by Mehmet the Conqueror in the mid-1400s, is still considered active in the defense of the straits, so it is forbidden to climb to

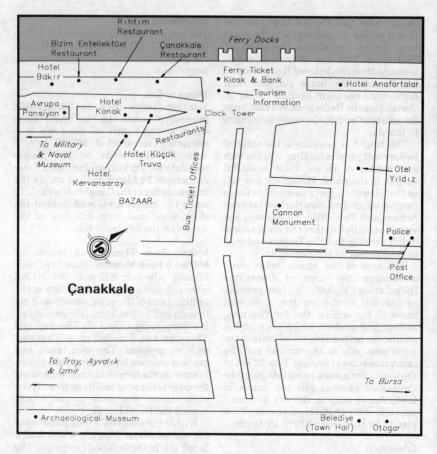

the top of the walls or keep. But you're free to examine the wonderful old cannons left from various wars, many made in French, English or German foundries. The keep is a gallery for changing exhibits.

Archaeological Museum Çanakkale's brand-new Archaeological Museum (Arkeoloji Müzesi, ahr-keh-yohl-oh-JEE mew-zeh-see) is on the southern outskirts of town, about one km from the clock tower, on the road to Troy. Hours are 10 am to 5 pm; closed Monday. You pay 500TL (US$0.70)

for admission, half-price on Sunday and holidays. City buses (İntepe, Güzelyalı) and dolmuşes (same destinations) run by the museum from the centre of town.

The museum is arranged chronologically, starting with prehistoric fossils and continuing through Bronze Age and later artefacts. Perhaps the most interesting exhibits are those from Troy, labelled (in Turkish and English) by 'city', that is, Troy I, Troy II, etc; and the exhibits from Dardanos, the ancient town near Çanakkale. It's a nice collection, pleasantly displayed. Don't miss the glass case of bone pins and small implements near the exit.

Gallipoli

The slender peninsula which forms the north-western side of the straits, across the water from Çanakkale, is called Gelibolu (geh-LEE-boh-loo) in Turkish. The **fortress** on the Gallipoli side of the strait, visible from Çanakkale, is called Kilitbahir, 'Lock on the Sea'. It was built by Mehmet the Conqueror as an aid to cutting off supplies and reinforcements to Constantinople, which Mehmet held under siege in the 1450s. Many foreign naval forces have tried, over the centuries, to force any such 'lock' put on the Dardanelles. Most have had İstanbul as their goal, and most have failed.

On the hillside by Kilitbahir, clearly visible from the far shore, are gigantic letters spelling out the first few words of a poem by Necmettin Halil Onan.

Dur yolcu! Bilmeden gelip bastığın
u toprak bir battığı yerdir
gil de kulak ver, bu sessiz yığın
ir vatan kalbinin attığı yerdir.

Traveller, halt! The soil you tread
Once witnessed the end of an era.
Listen! In this quiet mound
There once beat the heart of a nation.

The poem refers to the battles of Gallipoli in WW I. With the intention of capturing the Ottoman capital and the road to eastern Europe, Winston Churchill, First Lord of the Admiralty, organized a naval assault on the straits. A strong Franco-British fleet tried first to force the straits in March 1915 but failed. Then in April, British, Australian and New Zealand troops were landed on Gallipoli, and French troops near Çanakkale. After nine months of disastrous defeats the Allied forces were withdrawn.

The Turkish success at Gallipoli was due in part to disorganization in the Allied ranks, and partly due to reinforcements under the command of General

Liman von Sanders. But a crucial element in the defeat was that the Allied troops happened to land in a sector where they faced Lieutenant-Colonel Mustafa Kemal (Atatürk). Though a relatively minor officer, he had General von Sanders' confidence. He read the Allied battle plan correctly when his commanders did not, and stalled the invasion in bitter fighting which wiped out his division. Though suffering from malaria, he commanded in full view of his troops and of the enemy, and miraculously escaped death several times. At one point a piece of shrapnel tore through the breast pocket of his uniform but was stopped by his pocket watch (now in the Çanakkale Military & Naval Museum). His brilliant performance made him a folk hero and paved the way for his promotion to general.

The Gallipoli campaign lasted for nine months until January 1916, and resulted in huge numbers of casualties on both sides. You can visit Turkish, British and French monuments to the war dead at Seddülbahir, as well as Australian and New Zealander cemeteries at Arıburnu.

Troy-Anzac Tours, near the clock tower in Çanakkale, organise three-hour tours of the battlefields which include car, driver and guide for about 11,500TL (US$16.10) per person. It's best to have a car and guide, as the battlefields are spread out and a guide can fill in the exciting details of the battles.

Troy

The approach to Troy (Truva, TROO-vah) is across low, rolling countryside of grain fields, with here and there a small village. This is the Troad of ancient times, all but lost to legend until a German-born California businessman and amateur archaeologist named Heinrich Schliemann (1822-1890) rediscovered it in 1871. The poetry of Homer was at that time assumed to be based on legend, not history, but Schliemann got permission from the Ottoman government to excavate

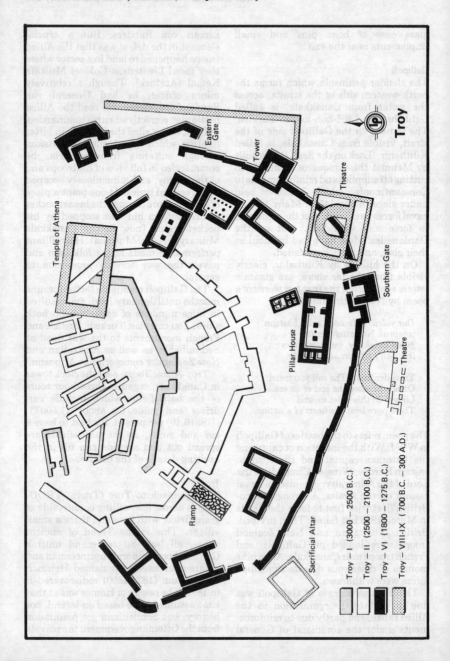

here at his own expense. He uncovered four superimposed ancient towns and went on to make notable excavations at other Homeric sites.

History The first people to live here were of the Early Bronze Age. The cities called Troy I to Troy V (3000-1800 BC) were of similar culture, but with Troy VI (1800-1275 BC) the town took on a new character, with a new population of Indo-European stock related to the Mycenaeans. The town doubled in size and carried on a prosperous trade with Mycenae. It also held the key, as defender of the straits, to the prosperous trade with Greek colonies on the Black Sea. Troy VI is the city of Priam which engaged in the Trojan War. A bad earthquake brought down the walls in 1275 and hastened the Achaean victory.

The heroic Troy was followed by Troy VII (1275-1100 BC). The Achaeans may have burned the city in 1240; an invading Balkan people moved in around 1190 BC, and Troy sank into a torpor for four centuries. It was revived as a Greek city (Troy VIII, 700-300 BC), and then as a Roman one (Troy IX, 300 BC-300 AD). At one point Constantine the Great thought of building his new eastern Roman capital here, but he chose Byzantium instead. As a Byzantine town, Troy didn't amount to much.

Now for Troy's history according to Homer. In the *Iliad*, this is the town of Ilium. The battle took place in the 1200s BC, with Agamemnon, Achilles, Odysseus (Ulysses), Patroclus and Nestor on the Achaean (Greek) side, and Priam with his sons Hector and Paris on the Trojan side. Homer alludes to no commercial rivalries as cause for the war. Rather, he says that Paris kidnapped the beautiful Helen from her husband Menelaus, king of Sparta, and the king asked the Achaeans to help him get her back.

The war went on for a decade, in which time Hector killed Patroclus, and

Achilles killed Hector. When the time came for Paris to kill Achilles, he was up to the task. Paris knew that Achilles' mother had dipped her son in the River Styx, holding him by his heel, and had thus protected Achilles from wounds anywhere that the water had touched. So Paris shot Achilles in the heel.

Even this carnage didn't end the war, so Odysseus came up with the idea of the wooden horse filled with soldiers. That's the way Homer reported it.

One theory has it that the earthquake of 1275 BC gave the Achaeans the break they needed, bringing down Troy's formidable walls and allowing them to battle their way into the city. In gratitude to Poseidon, The Earth-Shaker, they built a monumental wooden statue of Poseidon's horse. Thus there may well have been a real Trojan horse, even though Homer's account is less than fully historical.

The last people to live here were Turkish soldiers and their families, subjects of the Emir of Karası in the 1300s. After them, the town disappeared until Schliemann arrived.

Touring the Ruins Today at Troy you'll find a parking area, a replica of the wooden Trojan horse (children can climb up inside and peer out the windows), and Troy itself. The excavations by Schliemann and others have revealed nine ancient cities, one on top of another, going back to 3000 BC. Though there are few thrilling sights here (and some visitors say it's not worth the trip), Troy is interesting because of the Troad's beauty, great antiquity and semi-legendary character. Just half a km before the archaeological site is the village of **Tevfikiye**, with drink stands, simple restaurants, souvenir shops, replicas of the Trojan treasure, etc. There are a few primitive camping areas as well.

The identifiable structures at Troy are well marked. Notice especially the walls from various periods, the **Bouleterion or**

Council Chamber built about Homer's time (700s BC) and the **Temple of Athena** from Troy VIII, rebuilt by the Romans. Also, don't miss the beautiful views of the Troad, particularly over toward the straits. On a clear day you can see the Gallipoli war memorials on the far shore, and ships passing through the Dardanelles. And you can almost imagine the Achaean fleet beached on the Troad's shores, ready to begin a battle that would be remembered over 3000 years later.

Places to Stay

Çanakkale has a good if small selection of hotels in all price ranges. There is also a comfortable motel in a quiet forest setting on the road to Troy.

Places to Stay - bottom end

The downtown hotels are clustered near the clock tower. Best of the cheap hotels is the *Hotel Konak* (koh-NAHK) (tel (1961) 1150), just behind the clock tower, which boasts central heat, constant hot water and prices of 3080TL (US$4.31) double without private shower, or 4840TL (US$6.78) double with private shower. If the Konak is full, try the funky old brick *Hotel Kervansaray* directly opposite, which has a delightful garden with a fountain, cooking facilities you can use and rooms for 1000TL (US$1.40) single, 1600TL (US$2.24) double.

For a clean, friendly family pension, the place to go is the *Avrupa Pansiyon* (ahv-ROO-pah) (tel (1961) 4084), Matbaa Sokak 8, past the Hotel Konak a bit farther from the clock tower. It's quiet here, as the pension is on a block-long street. As it is family-run, it's clean. The basic charge for a bed is 2000TL (US$2.80) per person, or 5000TL (US$7) for two if breakfast is included.

The *Küçük Truva Oteli* (kew-CHEWK TROO-vah) (tel (1961) 1552), very near the Konak, has rates of 1600TL (US$2.24) single, 2800TL (US$3.92) double, without shower. The hotel has fly screens *(sineklik)* on its windows, but these do not keep the bedbugs out. The nearby *Hotel Efes* (eh-FEHS) (tel (1961) 3256) is a similar place.

Places to Stay - middle

Best is the 35-room *Hotel Bakır* (bah-KUHR) (tel (1961) 2908, 4088, 9), Rıhtım Caddesi, also called Yalı Caddesi, No 12, very near the clock tower, where a modern double room with bath and view of the straits, breakfast included, costs 8750TL (US$12.25) single, 13,650TL (US$19.11) double, 17,300TL (US$24.22) triple. The 66-room *Truva Oteli* (TROO-vah) (tel 1024), Kayserili Ahmet Paşa Caddesi, is several blocks from the centre but charges about the same as the Bakır.

Just a block from the ferry docks is the new *Otel Yıldız* (yuhl-DUHZ) (tel (1961) 1793 or 1069), Kızılay Sokak 20, on a quiet side street. It is a bright, new, clean place renting rooms with private shower for 6000TL (US$8.40) with a double bed, 9000TL (US$12.60) with twin beds. To find the hotel, get to the front door of the Hotel Anafartalar (see below), walk out that door and head straight down the side street, and you'll see it.

Places to Stay - top end

You can't miss the new *Otel Anafartalar* (ah-nah-fahr-tah-LAHR) (tel (1961) 4454, 5, 6), İskele Meydanı, on the north side of the ferry docks. The front rooms in this seven-floor structure have nice views of the water and cost only 11,300TL (US$15.82) single, 13,000TL (US$18.20) double. The hotel has a pleasant restaurant on its roof.

Only someone with a car would be interested in the motels on the outskirts. Look first at the *Tusan Truva Motel* (TOO-sahn TROO-vah) (tel (1961) 4987), located in a quiet pine forest at the end of a road. Most rooms have views of the straits, and the establishment has more the ambience of a small, quiet retreat than of a highway motel. Rooms with bath are priced at 13,300TL (US$18.62) double with shower, 14,800TL

(US$20.72) double with bath. To find the motel, leave Çanakkale by the road to Troy (Truva), drive about 14 km, and take the turning for Güzelyalı, then follow the motel's signs. The motel is 2.3 km from the turning.

Places to Eat

Çanakkale has inexpensive eateries all through town, but the most enjoyable are those right along the quay, to the left of the car ferry docks as you face the water. *Restaurant Boğaz* (boh-AHZ) is big and lively. The *Rıhtım* is one of long standing, and the *Bizim Entellektüel Restaurant* (Our Intellectuals' Restaurant!) has the most amusing name, but the *Çanakkale* is thought to have the better food. These, and others, set out tables along the promenade on summer evenings. The *Efes Pilsen* beer garden encourages consumption of the local pilsener but serves food as well. At the *Yalova Liman Restaurant* the attraction is a 3rd-floor patio with a fine view of the straits and of Kilitbahir fortress on the opposite shore. A meal of an appetizer, fried or grilled fish, salad and a bottle of beer might cost 2200TL (US$3.08).

For even cheaper fare, head inland along the main street or by the clock tower until you see a *köfteci* or *pideci* shop. At a *pideci*, fresh flat *pide* (PEE-deh) bread is topped with such things as whole eggs, cheese or ground lamb, dabbed with butter, then baked. It's filling, delicious and very cheap. Price depends on the toppings. Ask for your pide *yumurtalı* (yoo-moor-tah-LUH, with egg) or *peynirli* (pey-neer-LEE, with cheese), or *kıymalı* (kuy-mah-LUH, with ground lamb).

A meal of soup, *pide* or *köfte*, bread and a soft drink should cost about 650TL (US$0.91).

Getting There & Away

Bus Çanakkale has a central bus station (Otogar) with 13 buses a day to Bursa (5½ hours, 2400TL, US$3.36) which continue to Ankara; numerous buses to İstanbul (5½ hours, 2400TL, US$3.36); and at least 15 buses a day to İzmir (1500TL, US$2.10) via Ayvacık, Ayvalık and Bergama. For Edirne, there are two direct buses per day; otherwise, you must take a bus to Keşan and change for another bus to Edirne. By the way, you can buy bus tickets at the Otogar, or at the bus company offices on the main street in the centre of town, near the ferry docks.

At the Otogar you will also find dolmuşes or minibuses heading for Truva (Troy) every 30 to 60 minutes in high summer. Troy is less than an hour away; the fare is 300TL (US$0.84) each way. If you are here in winter, early spring or late

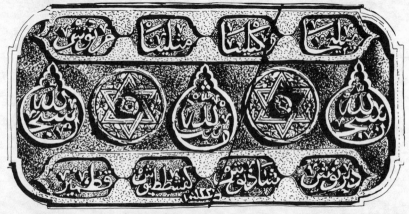

fall, the dolmuşes may not be running all the way to Troy, but only as far as the village of Tevfikiye, and you may have to walk the last half km to the archaeological zone. Otherwise it's a tour by taxi.

If you plan to visit Troy and then head south, you should try to buy a ticket on a southbound bus a day in advance, let the ticket seller know you want to be picked up at Troy, then be out on the main highway in plenty of time to catch the bus. Without a ticket you can hitch out to the highway from Troy and hope a bus will come by, and that it will have vacant seats. This often works, though it entails some waiting and some uncertainty as to availability of seats.

Ferryboat Two services run across the straits. The northern one is between the towns of Gelibolu and Lâpseki. Ferries leave Gelibolu at 1, 6, 7, 8, 9 and 10 am; noon; and 2, 4, 5, 6, 7, 8, 9, 10 and 11 pm. From Lapseki, ferries are at 2, 6, 7, 8, 9, 10 and 11 am; 1, 3, 5, 6, 7, 8, 9 and 10 pm; and midnight.

The southern car ferry service runs between Çanakkale and the town of Eceabat (eh-jeh-AH-baht) near the battlefields of Gallipoli. Between 6 am and 11 pm, boats run in each direction every hour on the hour; also at midnight and 2 am from Eceabat; and 1 and 3 am from Çanakkale.

Passengers as well as cars are carried on the boats at fares of 90TL (US$0.13) per person, 1200TL (US$1.68) and up for a car and driver. The crossing from Çanakkale to Eceabat takes about 25 minutes in good weather. Because of the schedules, over-and-back thus takes 1½ hours.

You can shorten this time by climbing aboard a *motor* (moh-TOHR, motorboat). These small craft ply between Çanakkale's docks and the village of Kilitbahir, at the foot of the fortress on the opposite shore. The voyage over takes 15 to 20 minutes in a motorboat, which will leave as soon as it has a sufficient number of passengers.

Aegean Turkey

The Aegean coast is a beautiful procession of golden wheat fields, fig and olive orchards, fishing villages and holiday resort towns. Assos (Behramkale) is an out-of-the-way village built on an ancient city, yet undiscovered by the tourist hordes. Ayvalık is a pleasant fishing and resort town with good beaches, good seafood restaurants, and beautiful panoramas of pine forest and Aegean islands. At Bergama, the ancient Pergamum, you should see the impressive ruins of the Acropolis and the Asclepion, an early medical centre. Many visitors make their base in İzmir and go north to Bergama or east to Sardis for the day.

South of İzmir the main attractions are the many Ionian cities, including Ephesus, the best-preserved classical city in the world, and also Priene, Miletus, Didyma, Labranda, Aphrodisias, Hierapolis and several others. A bonus is the spa at Pamukkale.

At the southern end of the Aegean coast is the beautiful little resort and yachting port of Bodrum, with its Crusader castle, just across the water from the Greek island of Kos.

Here's what you'll find on the coastal highway (E24), heading south from Troy.

The North Aegean

ASSOS (BEHRAMKALE)

It's 73 km from Çanakkale to Ayvacık (AHY-vah-juhk, not to be confused with nearby Ayvalık), a ride of less than two hours. Turn at Ayvacık for Behramkale, called Assos in ancient times. Then, 19 km from the highway you'll come to the village and the ruins in a gorgeous setting overlooking the Aegean and the nearby island of Lesvos (Midilli, MEE-dee-lee in

Turkish). The main part of the village and the ruins is perched atop a hill, but down the far (sea) side of the hill a tiny cluster of little stone buildings clings to the cliff in an incredibly romantic, not to mention unlikely, setting. It's a picture-postcard sight, and a perfect place to spend a few days' mindless relaxation with the occasional swim.

History

Assos was founded in the 700s BC by colonists from Lesvos. Aristotle stayed here for three years, and St Paul visited briefly. In its long history, Assos has flourished as a port, agricultural town and centre for Platonic learning. Today the main part of the village atop the hill is just a Turkish farming village. The tiny port settlement on the seaside is crammed if a few dozen foreigners show up.

Things to See

There's a fine Ottoman **hump-back bridge**, built in the 1300s, to the left of the road as you approach the village. When you get to a fork in the road, go left up to the village proper, or right to see the massive city walls, necropolis and port hamlet.

Acropolis Taking the village road, you wind up to a small square with a few shops and a small restaurant or two. Continue upward on the road, and you'll come to a small square with a tea house and a bust of Atatürk; at the very top of the hill you will get a spectacular view, and perhaps meet some village girls crocheting lace and importuning you to buy some.

You also get a look at the **Murad Hüdavendigâr Camii** (1359-1389). This early mosque is very simple, a dome on squinches set atop a square box of a room. The *mihrab* is nothing special. The Ottomans had not yet conquered Constan-

Aegean Turkey

tinople and begun to elaborate on the theme of Sancta Sophia at the time this mosque was built. Curious, though, is the lintel above the entrance, which bears Greek crosses and inscriptions. It probably was left over from a Byzantine church.

The principal sight atop the hill used to be the **Temple of Athena**, but there is hardly anything left to see. The temple exists these days mostly in guidebooks rather than on earth.

Port Hamlet By taking the right fork of the entry road, you'll reach the impressive

city walls and the **necropolis** or cemetery. Just 2½ km past the fork, on a block-paved road which winds down the cliffside, is the port hamlet, the most picturesque spot in Assos. Here's where you can find a place to stay and the better places to eat.

Places to Stay

At this writing there are only three small hotels and a few little camping places in the hamlet, but I'm sure more little lodging-places will open soon.

Places to Stay – bottom end
The cheap places are the *Hotel Yıldız* (yuhl-DUHZ) (tel 18) and the *Motel Assos*, where double rooms with shower go for 6000TL (US$8.40).

Places to Stay – middle
Hotel Behram (BEHH-rahm) (tel 16) will rent you quite a nice room for 17000TL (US$23.80) double, breakfast and dinner included.

Places to Eat
Each of the hotels has its own restaurant perched at quay-side beneath a shade of reeds. The Hotel Behram's is the most expensive, with meals for 2500TL to 4000TL (US$3.50 to US$5.60); there's also the very basic *Sahil Lokantası* to the right by the Jandarma post. The Sahil is the cheapest place in town, but in fact everything is at city prices, as it all must be transported from Ayvacık or beyond.

Getting There & Away
This is not easy, unless you have your own car. Though the occasional dolmuş runs from Ayvacık, you had better depend on hitching. Leave Ayvalık or Çanakkale early in the day, get to Ayvacık as soon as possible, then hang out on the road to Assos.

Back on the highway, heading south, you will come round the Bay of Edremit. At the eastern end of the bay are the holiday resorts of **Akçay** and **Ören**, with moderately priced hotels and motels.

AYVALIK
Across a narrow strait from the Greek island of Lesvos, Ayvalık (EYE-vah-luhk) is a beach resort, fishing town, olive oil and soap-making centre, and terminus for boats to and from Lesvos. The coast here is cloaked in pine forests and olive orchards, the shore sprinkled with 23 islands.

Orientation
The town of Ayvalık is small and manageable, with some inconveniences: the Otogar is 1½ km north of the centre, the Tourist Office one km to the south. Three km farther to the south are the areas called Çamlık and Orta Çamlık, with a scattering of pensions popular with Turkish vacationers. Eight km south of the centre is Sarmısaklı Plaj (SAHR-muh-SAHK-luh plahzh, Garlic Beach), a nice if not spectacular beach lined with hotels, motels and a few pensions.

Information
The Tourism Information Office (tel (6631) 2122), is a km south of the main square around the curve of the bay, opposite the yacht harbour.

Things to See
Ayvalık is about 350 years old. It was inhabited by Ottoman Greeks until after WW I and repopulated with Greek-speaking Turks from Crete. A few locals still speak some Greek, and most of the town's mosques are converted Orthodox churches. You can take a look in one of these curiosities as you stroll around town.

Boats depart the harbour for **Ali Bey Adası**, an island just across the bay where there are pleasant little seaside restaurants. A causeway links the island to the mainland, so you can go by taxi, but this isn't nearly so much fun as the boat, nor as cheap.

Among the standard tourist activities are daytime and evening boat tours among the dozens of islands that fill the bay. The average tour is priced at 1200TL (US$1.68), or 5000TL (US$7) with a meal.

Another goal for excursions is **Şeytan Sofrası** (shey-TAHN soh-frah-suh, Devil's Dinnertable), a hilltop south of the town from which the view is magnificent. There's a snack stand. As no bus or dolmuş runs here regularly, you'll have to take a taxi.

City buses run through the centre of town and south to Sarmısaklı beach.

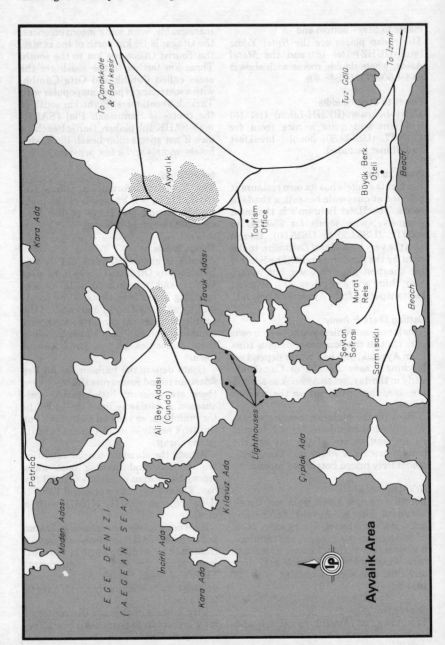

Ayvalık Area

EGE DENIZI
(AEGEAN SEA)

To Çanakkale
& Balıkesir

To İzmir

Tuz Gölü

Beach

Büyük Berk Oteli

Ayvalık

Tourism Office

Tavuk Adası

Murat Reis

Şeytan Sofrası

Sarımsaklı

Beach

Kara Ada

Patrica

Ali Bey Adası (Cunda)

Lighthouses

Çıplak Ada

Maden Adası

İncirli Ada

Kılavuz Ada

Kara Ada

Places to Stay

There are numerous beach resort hotels, motels and camping areas on Sarmısaklı Plaj, several km south of the centre. You'll also see many pensions, camping areas and little hotels along the road to Sarmısaklı, at Çamlık and Orta Çamlık. The hotels downtown are convenient, simple and very cheap.

Places to Stay – bottom end

There's the *Motel Kıyı* (tel (6631) 1438) at 18 Gümrük Meydanı, where rooms without private bath cost 3300TL (US$4.62) single, 5500TL (US$7.70) double, 6600TL (US$9.24) triple. The motel (actually a tiny hotel) is just off the main square by the harbour, out along the quay in the warren of little streets. The front rooms have nice water views.

El Otel (tel (6631) 2217) is a block off the main street near the main square, at Safa Caddesi 3, overlooking the intersection with Talat Paşa Caddesi which leads to a church-like mosque. It is very clean and correct, run by God-fearing types who will rent you a room with washbasin for 1650TL (US$2.31) single, 2750TL (US$3.85) double, 3300TL (US$4.62) triple.

Not far from the El Otel is the *Canlı Balık Oteli* (tel (6631) 2292), next door to the Canlı Balık Restaurant at 20 Gümrük Caddesi. Prices are the same as at the El, but rooms may be quieter.

The *İpek Oteli* (tel (6631) 1201) is about 200 metres south of the main square, a half-block off the main road, hidden somewhat by a larger building. Lots of fluorescent lighting here, and bare but bright corridors leading to simple but clean rooms with washbasin renting for 5000TL (US$7) double. The owner is enthusiastic.

Places to Stay – middle

The resort hotels in Ayvalık are nice and not expensive. One is near Çamlık on the way to Şeytan Sofrası, the others are on Sarmısaklı beach. Yet another moderately priced hotel is under construction near the main square of the town.

The *Murat Reis Oteli* (moo-RAHT reh-eess) (tel (6631) 1680 or 2788), Sarmısaklı Mevkii, is set apart in its own pine grove with its own beach, which gives it an air of splendid isolation and tranquillity. Double rooms with bath cost 20,350TL (US$28.49) with breakfast, 27,000TL (US$37.80) with breakfast and dinner, or 33,550TL (US$46.97) for two with all meals included. In the busy summer season, if the hotel is close to full, you will probably have to pay the full-board price.

Down on Sarmısaklı beach, a mere 50 metres from the water, are numerous hotels, the nicest of which includes the *Otel Ankara* (tel (6631) 1195), with 57 rooms with bath priced at 12,000TL (US$16.80) single, 15,900TL (US$22.26) double, breakfast included. If they require you to take all meals, you will pay a total of 29,000TL (US$40.60) for room and meals. The hotel has a card-and-game room, bar, café and terrace restaurant.

Very nearby is the *Büyük Berk Oteli* (tel (6631) 2311), a modern building with lots of services including a swimming pool, discotheque, playground for children, billiard and table-tennis room, and facilities for various water sports. The 112 guest rooms have balconies, bathrooms, telephones and prices of 24,500TL (US$34.30), breakfast and dinner included.

On my last visit to Ayvalık, the *Önen Oteli* was under construction a block north of the main square, on the main street. It may well be open and ready to receive customers by the time you arrive.

Places to Eat

Right on the main square are numerous tea houses, with a view of the harbour.

The tiny streets just north of the harbour, around the agencies selling tickets to Lesvos, have several small,

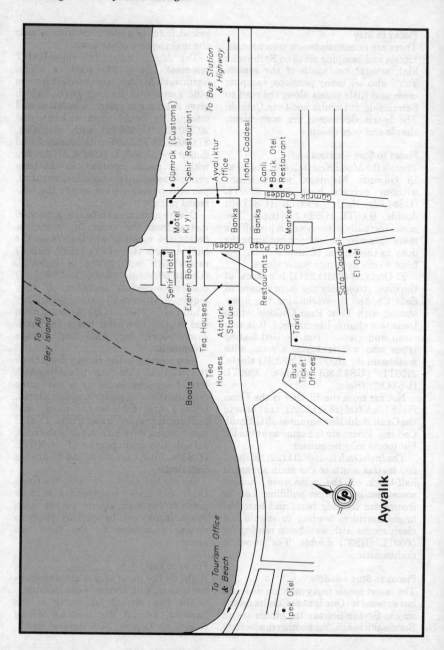

simple restaurants with good food and low prices. Try looking on the street which starts between the Tariş Bankası and the Yapı ve Kredi Bankası. You'll find the *İmbat Restaurant*, specializing in *döner kebap* and Bursa (İskender) *kebap*, and several other *kebapçıs*. Nearby are the *Ayvalık Restaurant, Anadolu Pide ve Kebap Salonu* and *Sultan Pasta Salonu*, this last one good for biscuits or pastries and tea.

The full-service restaurant in the area is the *Sahil Restaurant* (tel 1418), on the Customs-House Square (Gümrük Meydanı) near the Motel Kıyı. With both indoor and outdoor dining areas, the Sahil serves in all weather. Seafood is the specialty. A full dinner, beverage and tip included, costs 2000TL to 3000TL (US$2.80 to US$4.20), the latter figure being for seafood.

Getting There & Away

Bus Ayvalık is served by the frequent bus service running up and down the Aegean coast between Çanakkale and İzmir, but you may have to hitch-hike in from the highway. See the Getting Around section below.

When it comes time to leave Ayvalık, you should know that you can buy bus tickets at offices in the main square. The Sebat company runs 10 buses per day to İzmir (800TL, US$1.12), six or seven per day to Bergama (400TL, US$0.56). The Dikici company has 10 buses per day to Bursa (4½ hours, 2000TL, US$2.80), some continuing to İstanbul, others to Eskişehir and Ankara.

It's less than 40 km from Ayvalık to Bergama. Surprisingly, there is not always easy transport between the two. You'll find it easiest to get a bus or dolmuş in the morning and early afternoon, more difficult in late afternoon, and impossible in the evening.

Boats to Lesvos For information about boats to Lesvos, ask at one of the several agencies in the warren of little streets

north and west of the main square. One agent is Ahmed Cemil Erener, who can sell you a ticket to Lesvos and on to Piraeus or Haifa. (On Lesvos the agent is Dimitrios Koraka, on Yunani Antonios Picolos.) Next door is Eresos-Tur, Ali Barış Erener, agent; there's also Ayvalık Tur (tel (6631) 2740).

Greek and Turkish boats share the trade, and make daily trips in summer (roughly from late May-early June through September). Thus you can leave from Ayvalık on any day at 9 am with the Turkish boat, or 5 pm with the Greek boat. From Lesvos the weekday times are 8.30 am for the Greek boat and 1.30 pm for the Turkish boat. On weekends the times are different: Saturday at 5.30 am, Sunday at 6 pm from Ayvalık; Saturday at 9 am, Sunday at 8 or 9 pm from Lesvos for the Turkish boat. Off-season, boats operate about once or twice a week, but may halt completely in bad winter weather.

Cost of a single trip is US$15, a return trip US$25. Usually you must buy your ticket and surrender your passport for paperwork a day in advance of the voyage, whether you are departing from Turkey or from Greece.

Getting Around

Buses along the highway will drop you at the northern turning for Ayvalık, exactly five km from the centre, unless the bus company specifically designates Ayvalık Otogar as a stop. From the highway you must hitch-hike into town. If you are dropped in town, it will be at the Şehirlerarası Otobüs Garajı (Intercity Bus Garage), which is 1½ km (15 or 20 minutes' walk) north of the main square. City buses marked 'Ayvalık Belediyesi' run all the way through the town from north to south, and will carry you from the bus station to the main square, south to the Tourist Office, and farther south to Çamlık, Orta Çamlık and Sarmısaklı.

BERGAMA (Pergamum)

Modern Bergama (BEHR-gah-mah, population 60,000) is an agricultural market town in the midst of a well-watered plain. There has been a town here since Trojan times, but Pergamum's heyday was during the period after Alexander the Great and before Roman domination of all Asia Minor. At that time, Pergamum was one of the richest and most powerful small kingdoms in the Middle East. Its ruins are very impressive.

History

Pergamum owes its prosperity to Lysimachus and to his downfall. Lysimachus, one of Alexander the Great's generals, controlled much of the Aegean region when Alexander's far-flung empire fell apart after his death in 323 BC. In the battles over the spoils Lysimachus captured a great treasure, which he secured in Pergamum before going off to fight Seleucus for control of all Asia Minor. But Lysimachus lost and was slain (281 BC), so Philetarus, the commander he had posted at Pergamum to protect the treasure, set himself up as governor.

Philetarus was a eunuch but he was succeeded by his nephew Eumenes I (263-241 BC), and Eumenes was followed by his adopted son Attalus I (241-197 BC). Attalus took the title of king, expanded his power and made an alliance with Rome. He was succeeded by his son Eumenes II, and that's when the fun began.

Eumenes II (197-159 BC) was the man who really built Pergamum. Rich and powerful, he added the library and the Altar of Zeus to the hilltop city, and built the 'middle city' on terraces halfway down the hill. The already-famous medical centre of the Asclepion was expanded and beautified as well.

The Pergamum of Eumenes II is remembered most of all for its library. Said to have held more than 200,000 volumes, it was a symbol of Pergamum's social and cultural climb. Eumenes was a mad book-collector. His library came to challenge the world's greatest in Alexandria (700,000 books). The Egyptians were afraid Pergamum and its library would attract famous scholars away from Alexandria, so they cut off the supply of papyrus from the Nile. Eumenes set his scientists to work, and they came up with *pergamen* (Latin for 'parchment'), a writing-surface made from animal hides rather than pressed papyrus reeds.

The Egyptians were to have their revenge, however. When Eumenes died, he was succeeded by his brother Attalus II (159-138 BC). Things went pretty well under him, but under Eumenes' son Attalus III (138-133 BC) the kingdom was falling to pieces. Attalus III had no heir so he willed his kingdom to Rome. The Kingdom of Pergamum became the Roman province of Asia in 129 BC.

In the early years of the Christian era the great library at Alexandria was damaged by fire. Marc Antony, out of devotion to Cleopatra, pillaged the library at Pergamum for books to replace those of the Egyptian queen.

Orientation

Bergama's layout is pretty easy to figure out. Everything you'll need is between the bus station to the west and the market to the east, including hotels, restaurants and the Archaeology Museum. The two principal archaeological sites are out of town, several km in each case. The 'centre of town', for our purposes, is the Archaeology Museum on the main street, Cumhuriyet Caddesi, which to the east becomes Hükümet Caddesi.

Information

Bergama's Tourism Information Office (tel (5411) 1862 or 1848) is two km west of the centre of town, on the main road out to the highway, at the turning for the Asclepion.

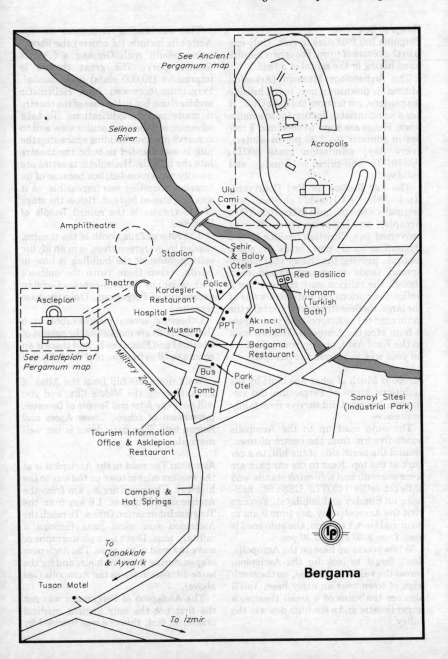

Bergama

Things to See

Bergama has four sites to visit. Only one is in the centre of town; the others require some hiking or the rental of a taxi.

The **Archaeology Museum** (Arkeoloji Müzesi) is downtown next to the hillside tea gardens, not far from the Park Oteli. It has a substantial collection for so small a town. Hours are 9 am to noon and 1 to 7 pm in summer (to 5.30 pm in winter), every day; admission costs 500TL (US$0.70), half-price on Sunday and holidays.

The **Red Basilica** (or Red Courtyard, Kızıl Avlu, KUH-zuhl ahv-loo) was originally a temple built in the 100s AD to Serapis, an Egyptian god. It was converted to a Christian basilica by the Byzantines and now holds a small mosque, proving the theory that sacred ground tends to remain sacred even though the religion may change. You'll notice the curious red flat-brick walls of the large, roofless structure if you take the main road to the Acropolis; or you can see it from atop the Acropolis. You can walk to the Kızıl Avlu, or stop your taxi there on your way to or from the Acropolis.

Acropolis Much of what was built by the ambitious kings of Pergamum did not survive, but what did survive is certainly impressive.

The auto road up to the Acropolis winds five km from the centre of town, around the north side of the hill, to a car park at the top. Next to the car park are some souvenir and soft-drink stands, and a ticket-seller (400TL, US$0.56, half-price on Sunday and holidays). You can visit the Acropolis any day from 9 am to noon and from 1 to 7 pm; the auto road is open from 8.30 am to 5.30 pm.

While you're up here on the Acropolis, don't forget to look for the Asclepion, across the valley to the west, on the north edge of town near an army base. You'll also see the ruins of a small theatre, a larger theatre and a stadium down in the valley.

The outstanding structures on the Acropolis include (of course) the **library**, being rebuilt with German aid to its former glory. The great **theatre** is impressive (10,000 seats) and unusual. Pergamum borrowed from Hellenistic architecture, but in the case of the theatre it made major modifications. To take advantage of the spectacular view and to conserve precious building space atop the hill, it was decided to build the theatre into the hillside. Hellenistic theatres are usually more rounded, but because of its location, rounding was impossible, so it was heightened instead. Below the stage of the theatre is the ruined **Temple of Dionysus**.

The **Altar of Zeus**, south of the theatre, shaded by evergreen trees, is in an idyllic setting. Most of the building is now in Berlin, taken there (with the sultan's permission) by the 19th-century German excavators of Pergamum. Only the base remains.

Otherwise, several piles of rubble atop the Acropolis are marked as the **palaces** of Attalus I and Eumenes II, and there is an **agora** as well as fragments of the defensive **walls**.

Walk down the hill from the Altar of Zeus, through the **Middle City**, and you will pass the **Altar and Temple of Demeter, gymnasium or school, Lower Agora** and **Roman bath**. The path down is not well marked.

Asclepion The road to the Asclepion is at the western edge of town on the way to the highway. The ruins are 3½ km from the Archaeology Museum, 1.6 km from the Tourism Information Office. To reach the Asclepion you must pass through a military zone. Don't take photographs or leave the road in the zone. The Asclepion is open during the same hours and for the same admission fee as the Acropolis (see above).

The Asclepion of Pergamum was not the first nor the only ancient medical centre. In fact, this one was founded by

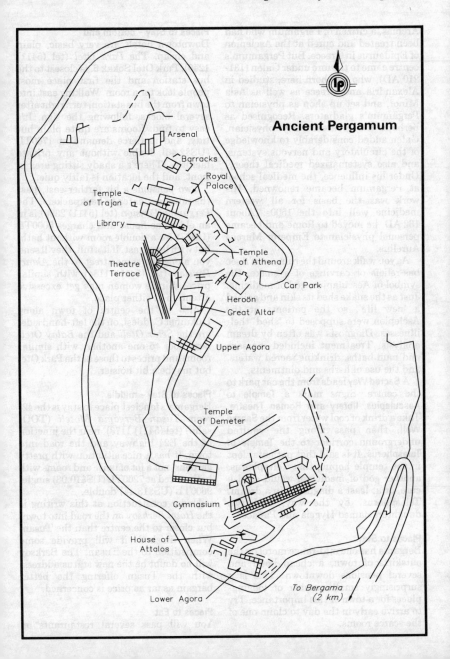

Ancient Pergamum

Arsenal

Barracks

Royal Palace

Temple of Trajan

Library

Temple of Athena

Theatre Terrace

Car Park

Heroön

Great Altar

Upper Agora

Temple of Demeter

Gymnasium

House of Attalos

Lower Agora

To Bergama
(2 km)

Archias, a citizen of Pergamum who had been treated and cured at the Asclepion of Epidaurus in Greece. But Pergamum's centre came to the fore under Galen (131-210 AD), who was born here, studied in Alexandria and Greece as well as Asia Minor, and set up shop as physician to Pergamum's gladiators. Recognised as perhaps the greatest early physician, Galen added considerably to knowledge of the circulatory and nervous systems, and also systematized medical theory. Under his influence, the medical school at Pergamum became renowned. His work was the basis for all western medicine well into the 1500s. About 162 AD, he moved to Rome and became personal physician to Emperor Marcus Aurelius.

As you walk around the ruins, you'll see bas-reliefs or carvings of a snake, the symbol of Aesculapius, god of medicine. Just as the snake shed its skin and gained a 'new life', so the patients at the Asclepion were supposed to 'shed' their illnesses. Diagnosis was often by dream analysis. Treatment included massage and mud baths, drinking sacred waters, and the use of herbs and ointments.

A **Sacred Way** leads from the car park to the centre. Signs mark a **Temple to Aesculapius, library** and **Roman Theatre**. Take a drink of cool water from the **Sacred Well**, then pass along the vaulted underground corridor to the **Temple of Telesphorus**. It is said that patients slept in the temple hoping that Telesphorus, another god of medicine, would send a cure, or at least a diagnosis, in a dream. Telesphorus, by the way, had two daughters named Hygeia and Panacea.

Places to Stay

Bergama has one mid-range motel on the outskirts of town, a cheap hotel and several pensions downtown. This is a surprisingly small number of lodging-places for a town of this importance. Try to arrive early in the day to claim one of the scarce rooms.

Places to Stay – bottom end

Downtown hotels are very basic, plain and cheap. The *Park Otel* (tel (5411) 1246), Park Otel Sokak 6, is closest to the bus station and the first place most people look for a room. Walking east into town from the bus station, turn right after several blocks, following the sign. It's easy to find. Rooms are quite plain but tidy, and in fierce demand at 1760TL (US$2.46) double without any private facilities. There's a shady sitting area in front, and the location is fairly quiet.

Two pensions a bit farther east, past the museum, cater to backpackers. The *Pergamon Pension* (tel (5411) 2395) is in an old stone house and charges 5000TL (US$7) for a double room without bath, but with breakfast. If it's full, they'll send you along the same street to the *Akıncı Pension* (tel (5411) 1184) with similar prices. Single women may get excessive attention at either place.

Also in the centre of town along Hükümet Caddesi, on the left-hand side, are the *Şehir Oteli* and the *Balay Oteli* next door to one another, with similar rooms and prices to those at the Park Otel but maybe a bit noisier.

Places to Stay – middle

Bergama's fanciest place to stay is the 42-room *Tusan Bergama Moteli* (TOO-sahn) (tel (5411) 1173), near the junction of the E24 highway and the road into town. It has a nice situation with pretty gardens, not a lot of noise and rooms with bath priced at 7200TL (US$10.08) single, 9600TL (US$13.44) double.

Under construction at this writing is the *Hotel Berksoy* on the road into town, but closer to the centre than the Tusan. When finished, it will provide some competition to the Tusan. The Berksoy will no doubt be the new status address, with the Tusan offering the better bargain as far as price is concerned.

Places to Eat

You will pass several restaurants on

Top: The walls of Ancient Troy
Left: A latter-day Trojan Horse in Troy
Right: The minaret of the Green Mosque in İznik

Top: A burst cannon and a commemorative mural in Çanakkale (Dardenelles)
Bottom: A caravanserai courtyard in Bursa

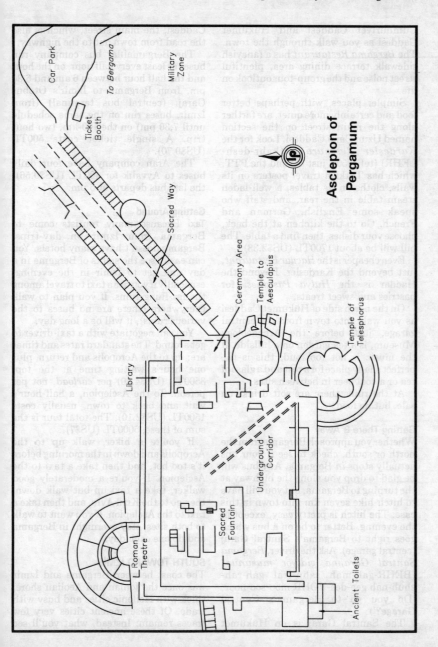

Asclepion of Pergamum

Car Park

Ticket Booth

To Bergama

Military Zone

Sacred Way

Ceremony Area

Temple to Aesculapius

Temple of Telesphorus

Library

Underground Corridor

Sacred Fountain

Roman Theatre

Ancient Toilets

Cumhuriyet Caddesi and Hükümet Caddesi as you walk through the town. The *Bergama Restaurant* has a fancyish sidewalk terrace dining area, plentiful street noise and the group-tour outlook on life.

Simpler places, with perhaps better food and certainly more quiet, are farther along the main street on the section named Uzun Çarşı Caddesi. Look for the *Kardeşler Restaurant* (kahr-desh-LEHR) (tel 1050), just beyond the PTT, which has Turkish travel posters on its walls, cloths on its tables, a well-laden steam table in the rear, and staff who speak some English, German and French. Go to the kitchen at the back, choose your dishes, then find a table. The bill will be about 1700TL (US$2.38).

Even cheaper is the *Hacılar Restaurant*, just beyond the Kardeşler. Beyond the Hacılar is the *Hülya Pastanesi* for pastries and sweet treats.

On the north side of Hükümet Caddesi as you walk into town from the central garage, just before the Archaeology Museum, is a tea garden on a hillside. If the music is not too loud, this is the perfect shady place for a rest and a glass of tea or a cool beer in between sites.

At the ruins there are soft drinks on sale, but no food.

Getting There & Away

Whether you approach Bergama from the north or south, check to see if your bus actually stops *in* Bergama. Any bus will be glad to drop you along the highway at the turning to Bergama, but you will have to hitch-hike seven km into town in this case. The hitch is pretty easy, except in the evening. Better to be on a bus which goes right to Bergama's Santral Garaj (central garage). Ask the driver, *Bergama Santral Garajına gidiyor musunuz?* (BEHR-gah-mah sahn-tral gah-rah-zhuh-nah gee-dee-YOHR moo-soo-nooz, 'Do you go to Bergama's Central Garage?')

The Santral Garaj is on Hükümet Caddesi, the main street, which is also the road from town out to the highway.

The Bergamalılar bus company run buses at least every half hour, on the hour and the half hour between 6 am and 6.30 pm, from Bergama to İzmir's Otobüs Garajı (central bus terminal) (from İzmir, buses run on the same schedule until 7.30 pm) on the 100-km, two-hour trip. A single ticket costs 500TL (US$0.70).

The Aran company have four daily buses to Ayvalık for 400TL (US$0.56); the last bus departs at 5 pm.

Getting Around

Taxi Because many tourists come to Bergama from İzmir on day-trips, Bergama doesn't have many hotels. You can easily see the sights of Bergama in a day and get to İzmir in the evening, especially if you use a taxi to travel among the far-flung ruins. If you plan to walk everywhere (there are no buses to the various ruins), it will be a long day.

You can negotiate with a taxi-driver to get around. The standard rates and times are: up to the Acropolis and return, plus one hour's waiting time at the top, 3500TL (US$4.90) per *carload*, not per person. To the Asclepion, a half-hour's wait and back to town, usually costs 1500TL (US$2.10). The total tour is the sum of these, 5000TL (US$7).

If you're a hiker, walk up to the Acropolis and down in the morning before it's too hot, and then take a taxi to the Asclepion. If you're a moderately good walker, take a taxi up but walk down, then go to the Kızıl Avlu, and then take a taxi to the Asclepion. If you want to walk to both sites, stay overnight in Bergama and do one each day.

SOUTH TOWARD İZMİR

The coast between Bergama and İzmir was once the Ionian and Aeolian shore, thick with Hellenic cities and busy with trade. Of these ancient cities very few traces remain. Instead, what you'll see are farming towns and villages, plus the occasional beach resort.

Due west of Bergama is **Dikili**, four km west of the E24 highway, on the seacoast. A new wharf capable of serving ocean liners is bringing cruise ships to Dikili; the passengers then bus to Bergama to see the ruins. There are a few small, inexpensive hotels and some nice waterfront restaurants.

Twenty km south of Dikili along a side road is **Çandarlı**, a farming village with a little restored Genoese fortress of the 1300s and a pension or two.

North of Menemen, a road leads west to **Foça** and **Yenifoça**. Foça is the ancient Phocaea, a town founded before 600 BC (nothing remains). At Yenifoça there's a Club Med holiday village (*tatil köyü*).

Menemen

Menemen (MEHN-eh-mehn), 33 km north of İzmir, is famous for a reactionary riot which took place in 1930. Atatürk's cultural reforms such as abolishing religious law, separating religion from the state and recognising the equality of women were not received well by religious conservatives. A band of fanatical dervishes staged a riot in Menemen's town square. When a young army officer named Mustafa Fehmi Kubilay attempted to quell the disturbance, he was shot and beheaded by the dervishes. The government took immediate action to quash the fanatics' revolt, and proclaimed Kubilay a republican hero. The statue here honours the young officer.

Manisa

A road goes east 30 km to Manisa (mah-NEES-ah, population 130,000, altitude 74 metres), the ancient town of Magnesia ad Sipylus. It is a modern little city with an ancient past. An early king here was Tantalus, from whom we get the word 'tantalise'. The early, great Ottoman sultans favoured it as a residence, and for a while the province of Manisa was the training-ground for crown princes.

During the War of Independence, retreating Greek soldiers wreaked terrible destruction on Manisa. After they passed through, Manisa's 18,000 historic buildings had been reduced to only 500.

Near the end of April each year, Manisa has a special festival celebrating Powergum (*kuvvet macunu*, kew-VEHT mah-joo-noo). Manisa Powergum, a local concoction made from who-knows-what, is distributed. It is supposed to restore health, youth and potency.

Things to See As you might expect, there are several old mosques, among them the **Muradiye** (1586) with nice tilework, a small museum and near it the tomb of Saruhan Bey; the **Sultan Camii** (1572) with some gaudy painting but a nice *hamam* (Turkish bath) next door; and, perched on the steep hillside above the town, the **Ulu Cami** (1366), ravaged by the ages, and not as impressive as the view from the tea house next to it. Other mosques in town are the **Hatuniye** (1490) and the **İlyas Bey** (1363).

Places to Stay Manisa has one nice hotel, the *Hotel Arma* (tel (5511) 1980) on Doğu Caddesi, with a willing and helpful staff, restaurant and bar, 42 clean and presentable rooms, a lift and prices of 8400TL (US$11.76) single, 12,000TL (US$16.80) double.

Into İzmir

If you approach İzmir from Menemen along the E24, you will pass a road at Çiğli (CHEE-lee) to İzmir's airport (*havaalanı*, hah-VAH-ah-lahn-uh). İzmir's new airport is abuilding at Cumaovası, south of the city. Shortly afterward, the highway passes the suburb of Karşıyaka (KAHR-shuh-YAH-kah), then curves around the end of the bay to the Otobüs Garajı.

Coming from Manisa, the road passes through the suburb of Bornova, once the residence of wealthy Levantine businesspeople. Some of their mansions still stand, most now converted to public use such as municipal offices and schools. There's a university here. İzmir city buses run from Bornova to the centre of İzmir.

İZMİR

İzmir (EEZ-meer, population 2,000,000) is Turkey's third-largest city and its major port on the Aegean. It's got a different feeling about it, something Mediterranean, something more than just being a large and prosperous Turkish city. The setting is certainly dramatic, for İzmir rings a great bay and is backed to the east and south by mountains. Most of the city is quite modern and well laid-out, with broad boulevards radiating from a series of hubs. The streets are lined with stucco-and-glass apartment and office blocks, and dotted with shady sidewalk cafés, though here and there the red tile roof and bull's-eye window of a 19th-century warehouse hide in the shadow of an office tower. When you see an old mosque in İzmir it comes as a surprise, as though it doesn't really fit in.

You may enjoy a short stay in İzmir, with its palm-lined waterfront promenade. The city can be explored and enjoyed in a fairly short time because there's not a whole lot to see; most of the remains from its long and eventful history have been swept away by war, fire and earthquake. You can also use İzmir as a base for excursions to a few nearby points: Sardis, for instance. But in most cases you will be ready to move on in a day, perhaps two. Otherwise, you may find it to be just a big, busy, somewhat noisy and impersonal Turkish city, and you may want to move on pretty soon.

History

İzmir owes its special atmosphere, indeed its entire appearance, to an eventful and turbulent history. What you see today is new because it has risen on the ashes of Ottoman İzmir since 1923, when a Greek invasion and a disastrous fire razed most of the city. Before that year, İzmir was Smyrna, the most western and cosmopolitan of Turkish cities, with more Christian and Jewish citizens than Muslim, and with thousands of foreign diplomats, traders, merchants and seamen. Its connections with Greece and Europe were close and continuous. To the Turks it was 'Infidel Smyrna'.

İzmir's commercial connections with Europe began in 1535, but the city is far, far older than that. The first settlement that we know of, at Bayraklı near the eastern end of the bay, was by Aeolians in the 10th century BC, but there were probably people here as far back as 3000 BC. The city's name comes from the goddess Myrina, prevalent deity before the coming of the Aeolians, who worshipped Nemesis in addition to Myrina. Famous early citizens of Smyrna included the poet Homer, the founder of western literature, who lived before 700 BC.

The city began its history of war and destruction early, for the Aeolians were overcome by the Ionians, and they in turn were conquered by the Lydians, whose capital was at Sardis. Around 600 BC, the Lydians destroyed the city and it lay in ruins until the coming of Alexander the Great.

Alexander (356-323 BC) re-founded Smyrna on Mt Pagus, now called Kadifekale, in the centre of the modern city. He erected the fortress that you can still see crowning the hill, and made many other improvements.

Smyrna's luck changed during the struggles over the spoils of Alexander's empire. The city sided with Pergamum, the Aegean power-to-be. Later it welcomed Roman rule and benefited greatly from it. When an earthquake destroyed the city in 178 AD, Emperor Marcus Aurelius sent money and men to aid in reconstruction. Under Byzantium, the later Roman Empire, it became one of the busiest ports along the coast.

As Byzantium's power declined, various armies marched in, and often out again, including the Arabs, Seljuk Turks,

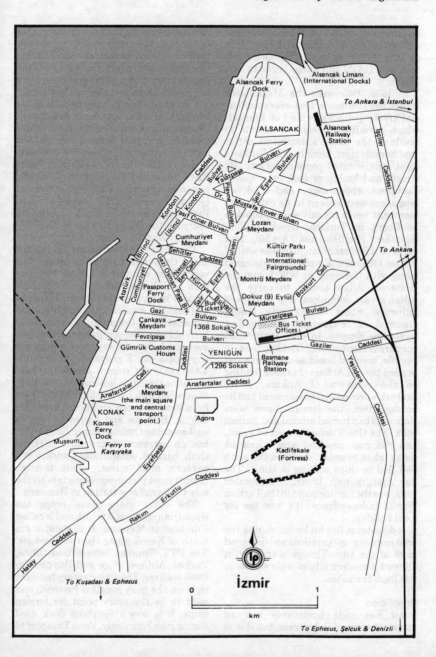

Alsancak Limanı
(International Docks)

Alsancak Ferry
Dock

To Ankara & İstanbul

ALSANCAK

Alsancak Railway
Station

İşçiler Caddesi

Bulvarı

Talatpaşa Bulvarı

Kordon Caddesi

Dr. Pleyne Bulvarı

Mustafa Enver Bulvarı

Şair Eşref Bulvarı

Yaşı Cınar Bulvarı
(İkinci) Kordon

Cumhuriyet
Meydanı

Lozan
Meydanı

To Ankara

(Birinci) Kordon

Gazi Osman Paşa Blv.

Şehitler Caddesi

Necati Bey Cad.

Hürriyet Bulvarı

Şair Eşref

Bozkurt Cad.

Kültür Parkı
(İzmir
International
Fairgrounds)

Montrö Meydanı

Atatürk Cumhuriyet

Pasaport
Ferry Dock

Gazi Bulvarı

Çankaya
Meydanı

Dokuz (9) Eylül
Meydanı

Bus
Tickets

Mürselpaşa Bulvarı

Gaziler Caddesi

Yeşildere Caddesi

1368 Sokak

Bus Ticket
Offices

Fevzipaşa

Gümrük Customs
House

Bulvarı

Anafartalar Cad.

Caddesi

YENİGÜN
1296 Sokak

Basmane
Railway
Station

Konak
Meydanı
(the main square
and central
transport point.)

Anafartalar Caddesi

KONAK

Agora

Museum

Konak
Ferry Dock

Ferry to
Karşıyaka

Eğretpaşa

Caddesi

Erkutlu Caddesi

Kadifekale
(Fortress)

Hatay Caddesi

Rakım Caddesi

To Kuşadası & Ephesus

İzmir

0   1
km

To Ephesus, Şelcuk & Denizli

Genoese and Crusaders. When Tamerlane arrived in 1402 he destroyed the city, true to form, but after he left, the Ottomans took over (1415) and things began to look better.

In 1535, Süleyman the Magnificent signed the Ottomans' first-ever commercial treaty (with François I of France), which permitted foreign merchants to reside in the sultan's dominions. After that humble start, İzmir became Turkey's most sophisticated commercial city. Its streets and buildings took on a quasi-European appearance, and a dozen languages were spoken in its cafés. Any merchant worth his salt was expected to be fluent in Turkish, Greek, Italian, German, English and Arabic, and perhaps a few other languages as well.

The Ottoman Empire was defeated along with Germany in WW I, and the victorious Allies sought to carve the sultan's vast dominions into spheres of influence. Some Greeks have always dreamed of re-creating the long-lost Byzantine Empire. In 1920, with Allied encouragement, the Greeks took a gamble, invaded İzmir, seized Bursa and headed toward Ankara. In fierce fighting on the outskirts of Ankara, where Atatürk's provisional government had its headquarters, the foreign forces were stopped, then turned around and pushed back. The Greek defeat turned to a rout, and the once-powerful army, half its ranks taken prisoner, scorched the earth and fled to ships waiting in İzmir. The day Atatürk took İzmir, 9 September 1922, was the turning point in the Turkish War of Independence. It's now the big local holiday.

A disastrous fire broke out during the final mopping-up operations and destroyed most of the city. Though a tragedy, it allowed a modern city of wide streets to rise from the ashes.

Orientation

İzmir has wide boulevards and an apparent sense of orderliness, but it is in fact somewhat difficult to negotiate. This is because the numerous roundabouts/traffic circles, with their streets radiating like spokes from a hub, don't give you the sense of direction a street grid does. Here are some tips on getting your bearings.

First of all, the city's two main avenues run parallel to the waterfront, downtown. The waterfront street is officially Atatürk Caddesi, and that is what you will see given in written addresses. But everyone in town calls it the Birinci Kordon (beer-EEN-jee kohr-DOHN, First Cordon); just inland from it is Cumhuriyet Bulvarı (joom-hoor-ee-YEHT bool-vahr-uh, Republic Boulevard), which is called by everyone the İkinci Kordon (ee-KEEN-jee), or Second Cordon.

The city's two main plazas are located along these two parallel avenues. The very centre of town is Konak Meydanı (koh-NAHK mey-dah-nuh, Government House Plaza), or simply Konak. Here you will find the municipality buildings, the Ottoman clock tower (İzmir's symbol), a little old tiled mosque, pedestrian bridges over the busy roadway, and a dock for ferryboats to Karşıyaka (kahr-shuh-YAH-kah), the suburb across the bay. Konak is the city's bus and dolmuş hub, so you can pick up a vehicle to any part from here. You can also board buses for Selçuk, Ephesus and Kuşadası here as well as at the Otobüs Garajı. Konak also has an entrance to the çarşı (CHAR-shuh, bazaar). Anafartalar Caddesi, the bazaar's main street, winds through İzmir's most picturesque quarters all the way to the railway station at Basmane.

The other main plaza holds the equestrian statue of Atatürk and is called Cumhuriyet Meydanı. It is about a km north of Konak along the two Kordons. The PTT, Tourism Information Office, Turkish Airlines office and Büyük Efes Oteli are here. The 19th-century building right on the quay is called **Pasaport**, and used to be the entry point for foreign ships. It is now a ferryboat dock used during rush hours only. From Pasaport to

Konak along the Birinci Kordon is an active shipping centre for local commerce, with colourful *kayık* (kah-YUK) boats moored along its length. The offices of the Denizyolları (Turkish Maritime Lines) are here as well.

The section called Çankaya (CHAN-kah-yah) is two long blocks inland, south-east of Cumhuriyet Meydanı.

Another İzmir landmark is the Kültür Parkı (kewl-TEWR), site of the annual İzmir International Fair, an amusement and industry show extravaganza which takes place from about 26 August to 15 September each year. Hotel space is very hard to find during the fair. When it's not fair time the grounds provide a pleasant, shady place to walk, sit and rest, with some amusements.

Finally, the hill directly behind the main part of town is crowned by Kadifekale (kah-dee-FEH-kah-leh, Velvet Fortress), a bastion built by Alexander the Great when he moved the city here.

Information

The Tourism Information Office (tel (51) 14 21 47) is next to the Büyük Efes Oteli, in the row of offices which includes the Turkish Airlines office.

Things to See

Compared to most Turkish towns, İzmir does not have a large number of antiquities.

As you make your way around town, you will certainly see the **equestrian statue** of Atatürk in Cumhuriyet Meydanı. It symbolizes Atatürk's leadership as he began the counter-offensive from Ankara, with the aim of reaching the Aegean.

A few blocks north of Cumhuriyet Meydanı is the South-Eastern Head-quarters of **NATO**, in a building with a long row of flags in front. Here and there along the Birinci Kordon you can see the few old stone houses which survived the Great Fire of 1922.

Agora The marketplace built on the

orders of Alexander was ruined in an earthquake (178 AD), but there is much remaining from the Agora as it was rebuilt by Marcus Aurelius just after the quake. A few columns, vaulted chambers and statues mark this conspicuously open spot in the midst of the crowded city. To reach it, walk up Eşrefpaşa Caddesi from Fevzipaşa Caddesi to 816 Sokak, on the left. This street leads to the Agora, which is open from 8.30 am to 5.30 pm daily.

Bazaar İzmir's bazaar, already mentioned, is large and fascinating. A half-day's explorations along Anafartalar Caddesi is a must. You can pick up this street easily from Eşrefpaşa Caddesi, after your visit to the Agora, or enter the street from Basmane or Konak.

Culture Park The Kültür Parkı is pleasant, and you can dodge in here any time of day for a quiet walk or picnic away from the city bustle.

Kadifekale The time to ride up the mountain is an hour before sunset. Catch a dolmuş in Konak (it may say only 'K Kale' on the sign) and allow 15 or 20 minutes for the ride. The view on all sides is spectacular. Look inside the walls, and even climb up on them if you like. Just at sunset, the muezzins will give the call to prayer from İzmir's minarets. A wave of sound rolls across the city as the lights twinkle on.

Near the gate in the walls are a few little terrace tea houses where you can have a seat and a tea, soft drink or beer.

Archaeology Museum İzmir's new Archaeology Museum is in the southern part of town, near the road up to Kadifekale. For details of hours and transport, contact the Tourism Information Office next to the Büyük Efes Oteli.

Places to Stay

İzmir has lots and lots of good, very cheap

places to stay, and several nice expensive places. The mid-range establishments, unfortunately, often suffer from street noise so you must choose your room carefully. The magic word for low prices is Basmane; there are several middle-range places near that railway station as well. The top-end places tend to be on the waterfront near Cumhuriyet Meydanı.

Places to Stay – bottom end

The quarter named Yenigün, bounded by Fevzipaşa Bulvarı, Basmane Meydanı, Anafartalar Caddesi and Eşrefpaşa Caddesi, and right next to Basmane, İzmir's main railway station, is a low-budget traveller's dream-come-true. Several streets are entirely lined with clean, very cheap, safe places to stay.

Walk out the front door of Basmane Railway Station, turn left, fight your way across the flood of traffic and walk up the shady street. The best plan is to walk out the door of the railway station, turn left, cross the road, turn right then left almost immediately, keeping the little mosque on your left: this is Anafartalar Caddesi. It turns right after a block or so and becomes the main street of the Yenigün section, and (with twists and turns) goes all the way to Konak. But for now, take the first street on your right, which is 1296 Sokak. (All these directions sound complicated, but in fact you're just across the road from the railway station.)

Now, 1296 Sokak is nothing but small hotels, some in new buildings, others in grand old İzmir houses with coloured glass, fancy woodwork and mosaic floors. Though there is some spread in prices, most tend to charge between 700TL and 1200TL (US$0.98 and US$1.68) per bed in a room with washbasin only, or about 3000TL (US$4.20) per bed in a room with private shower.

A few steps along 1296 Sokak, on the left-hand side, is the *Yıldız Palas Oteli* (yuhl-DUHZ pah-lahss) (tel (51) 25 15 18), 1296 Sokak No 50, an *aile* (family) hotel where single men are not particularly welcome, but couples and women travellers are the norm. Bright, clean and airy, it is quite simple, but so are its prices: 1400TL (US$1.96) for a double without running water, 2250TL (US$3.15) for a double with washbasin and telephone.

Slightly farther along 1296 Sokak, look left down a side street and you'll see the *Otel Gümüş Palas* (gerr-MERSH pah-lahss) (tel (51) 13 41 53), 1299 Sokak No 12, a more modern place (but hardly ultra-modern) where a double with washbasin costs 2300TL (US$3.22). The Gümüş Palas is owned by the same people who own the *Otel Yeşil Palas* nearby on 1296 Sokak, which offers rooms without running water for 1600TL (US$2.24).

These suggestions are only the tip of the iceberg. In the unlikely event that you don't find what you want on 1296 Sokak, look on the parallel 1294 Sokak, between 1296 and Fevzi Paşa Bulvarı.

Should you want a slightly better class of hotels, head for a different area equally near Basmane station, packed with hotels and with good restaurants as well. Go out the station door and straight down the right-hand side of Fevzi Paşa Bulvarı to the Hotel Hisar. Turn right and you will be on 1368 Sokak, which is lined with little hotels charging about 4250TL to 5000TL (US$5.95 to US$7) for a double room with private shower.

The *Otel Özcan* (ERZ-jahn) (tel (51) 13 50 52), 1368 Sokak No 3, is typical, being an older building with clean, quiet rooms renting for 4250TL (US$5.95) double without private shower, or 4850TL (US$6.79) with. Try also the *Yeni Park Oteli* (tel (51) 13 52 31) and the *Bilen Palas* (tel (51) 13 92 46). Walk along 1368 Sokak, and at the end on 1369 Sokak are several more: the *Otel Akgün* (tel (51) 13 55 63) and the *Otel Oba* (tel (51) 13 54 74), just to name two. Most of these hotels give you a choice between rooms with shower and rooms without, and most are very quiet, even in this noisy city.

Places to Stay – middle

Basmane Of the moderately priced hotels in the Basmane area, the most popular is the *Otel Billûr* (bee-LYOOR) (tel (51) 13 62 50), Basmane Meydanı 783, facing the railway station. The rooms are fine and the prices not bad (12,155TL, US$17.02 single, or 17,160TL, US$24.04 double, with bath, breakfast included), but many of the rooms facing the street will be noisy, so be sure to look at and listen to the room before you rent it.

Hotel Nil (NEEL) (tel (51) 13 52 28 or 13 56 20), Fevzi Paşa Bulvarı 155, is just a block or so along the boulevard from the railway station, on the right-hand side. Though the façade and entrance have been modernized, most of the hotel is actually older, which accounts for its relatively low prices: 3250TL (US$4.55) single, 6500TL (US$9.10) double, with shower. There's a lift. Right next door, the *Hotel Hisar* is under construction as of this writing. When completed, it will no doubt charge something like 20,000TL (US$28) for a brand-new double room.

Rooms are a bit cheaper at the *Babadan Oteli* (BAH-bah-dahn) (tel (51) 13 96 40, 3), in the section named Çanakya, 2½ long blocks from the waterfront and about the same distance from Basmane, at Gazi Osman Paşa Bulvarı 50 and Fevzipaşa Bulvarı. Readers' reaction to the Babadan has been both good and not so good. Try to get the penthouse room, which is well away from the street noise.

Cumhuriyet Meydanı *Hotel Anba* (AHN-bah) (tel (51) 14 43 80, 4), Cumhuriyet Bulvarı 124, is on the İkinci Kordon just a block south of Cumhuriyet Meydanı and the Büyük Efes; air-conditioned, bath-equipped rooms in this status location cost 14,700TL (US$20.58) single, 26,100TL (US$36.54) double, breakfast included.

The *Kilim Oteli* (kee-LEEM) (tel (51) 14 53 40), right in front of the Anba on Atatürk Bulvarı (Birinci Kordon) charges a bit more for the sea-view rooms.

The *Kısmet Oteli* (kuss-MEHT) (tel (51) 21 70 50, 2), behind the Büyük Efes at 1377 Sokak No 9, is comfortable and air conditioned, and charges 14,300TL (US$20.02) for a single room with bath, 20,700TL (US$28.98) for a double.

Places to Stay – top end

İzmir's best is the 296-room *Büyük Efes Oteli* (bew-YEWK eh– FEHS) (tel (51) 14 43 00, 29), the Grand Ephesus Hotel on Cumhuriyet Meydanı. Though not as luxurious as a Hilton or Sheraton, it is comfortable and has these advantages: pretty, private gardens with a swimming pool, good dining room and patio restaurant, nightclub and some rooms with a view of the bay. Rates vary with the seasons and with the location of the room within the hotel (rooms with sea views and pool views are most expensive, those with street views are cheapest). July through October is high season, with rooms renting for US$52 to US$70 single, US$65 to US$79 double. March through June, prices are US$46 to US$61 single, US$60 to US$70 double. Winter prices are a few dollars cheaper.

The 128-room *Etap İzmir* (eh-TAHP) (tel (51) 14 42 90, 9) is just around the corner, across from the PTT, at Cumhuriyet Bulvarı 138. Part of the worldwide French chain, its rooms cost US$52 single, US$65 double, US$81 triple in high summer, with reductions offered at other times of year.

Behind the Büyük Efes Oteli, at Necatibey Bulvarı 1379 Sokak No 55, stands the bright and modern, almost plush, *Otel Karaca* (KAH-rah-jah) (tel (51) 14 44 45 or 14 44 26), equivalent in comfort to the Büyük Efes but without the status address and sea views. Prices are comfortably lower, at 21,750TL to 26,220TL (US$30.45 to US$36.71) single, 31,800TL to 34,600TL (US$44.52 to US$48.44) double, breakfast included. The higher-priced double rooms have television sets and little refrigerators.

Places to Eat – bottom end

The lowest-priced meals are to be found in the same areas as the lowest-priced hotels. Some of the most delightful are along Anafartalar Caddesi in the bazaar. Start from the Basmane end, and *hazır yemek lokantas, kebapçıs* and *köftecis* will appear all along the way as you wander. A few will have one or two small tables outside.

Check out *Osman'in Yeri*, Anafartalar 806, which serves alcoholic beverages and therefore may have a bit heavier atmosphere, but at least you can get a beer with lunch. A few steps farther on is the *Güneydoğu Lokantası*, bright, clean and cheap. The *Güneydoğu Firin* (bakery) is right next door, with windows full of fresh breads, rolls, buns and biscuits.

Just before you come to a little open square with a mosque, look for the *Ege Lezzet Lokantası* and the *Kısmet Aile Içkisiz Lokantası*, facing one another across Anafartalar Caddesi. Both front windows are filled by steam tables holding hearty *pilav*, stew and vegetable dishes. Lunch for 1000TL (US$1.40) is a simple matter. No alcohol is served at these two.

For slightly nicer restaurants, go to that section with slightly better hotels on 1368 Sokak, described in Places to Stay. The *Zeybek Mangal Restaurant* (tel 13 52 31), 1368 Sokak No 6A, specializes in *döner kebap* and has pleasant sidewalk tables. A portion of *döner* and something to drink costs 1800TL (US$2.52).

The *Güzel İzmir Restaurant* (tel 14 05 01), 1368 Sokak 8B, virtually next door to the Zeybek Mangal, has more ready food dishes, sidewalk tables and similar prices.

Places to Eat – mid-range

Birinci Kordon For medium-priced meals, the city's most interesting section is the waterfront north of Cumhuriyet Meydanı. Many of the restaurants here, along the Birinci Kordon, have sidewalk tables, views of the harbour activity, lots of good *meze* (appetizers) and fresh fish prepared various ways.

The *Deniz Restaurant*, on the street level of the İzmir Palas Hotel, looks expensive and charges only 1250TL (US$1.75) for *şiş kebap*, 1800TL (US$2.52) for *bonfile*, a small filet beefsteak. Thus, you should be able to dine well for just over twice those amounts.

Up past the NATO building are numerous sidewalk cafés where young people come to sip drinks, talk, flirt and have something to eat. Prices are even lower here, with a serving of the ubiquitous *şiş kebap* going for only 750TL (US$1.05). The *Sirena* at Atatürk Caddesi 194 is one such place, the *Hitit* another.

South of Cumhuriyet Meydanı there used to be several little restaurants overlooking the water, but development and construction have wiped out a number of them, and the others are being threatened. Still, as long as it exists, the *Mangal* will serve you a fine seafood dinner for 4500TL to 5500TL (US$6.30 to US$7.70).

Konak A special place for sweets is the *Ali Galip Pastanesi* (ah-LEE gah-LEEP), just a few steps along Anafartalar Caddesi from Konak, on the right-hand side. This is one of the city's oldest and best confectioners, justly famed for its *baklava, helva* and other treats.

Getting There & Away

Air Turkish Airlines (tel (51) 14 12 20, 1) serves İzmir with four to six daily flights from İstanbul, one daily flight from Ankara. They also run a Sunday flight between İzmir and Antalya in summer, and one non-stop flight per week to Athens, Köln, Frankfurt, Hamburg, Milano, Munich, Paris and Zurich. Three direct flights per week connect London (Heathrow) and İzmir.

İstanbul Airlines also flies between İstanbul and İzmir.

Rail Arrival by rail is easy. All inter-city trains come into Basmane Garı, from whence there are buses and dolmuşes to other sections, and numerous hotels close by.

Trains departing Basmane include the three daily *mototrens* to Denizli at 8.10 am, 3.30 pm and 6 pm; this is the best train to take for Selçuk, Ephesus and Kuşadası. A single ticket as far as Selçuk costs 300TL (US$0.42), or 250TL (US$0.35) for a student.

You can also get to Selçuk on the daily *mototren* to Söke, departing İzmir at 6.45 pm and costing 450TL (US$0.63) single, 400TL (US$0.56) student.

For Ankara, the Ege Ekspresi departs at 7.35 am; the İzmir Ekspresi, hauling sleeping cars and a restaurant car, at 5.45 pm. A single 1st-class ticket on either express to Ankara costs 2600TL (US$3.64), 2nd class is 1900TL (US$2.66), a student pays 1700TL (US$2.38). The most luxurious train on this run is the Mavi Tren, departing at 7.35 pm; a single ticket costs 3300TL (US$4.62), or 5600TL (US$7.84) return.

To Bandırma on the Sea of Marmara coast, the Marmara Ekspresi departs İzmir at 6.35 am; a ticket costs 1150TL (US$1.61).

İzmir's other railway depot, at Alsancak (AHL-sahn-jahk), at the northern end of the city near the international passenger ship docks, is for commuter and suburban lines. There is one daily *yolcu* train to Denizli via Selçuk departing at 8.20 am, but it takes over 2½ hours to do this short stretch, arriving at 10.58 am.

Bus Buses arrive at İzmir's Otobüs Garajı (oh-toh-BEWS gah-rah-zhuh, Bus Garage), sometimes called the Yeni Garaj (yeh-NEE, new), a mammoth establishment north-east of the city's centre.

If you've come on a premium line such as Varan, there may be a *servis arabası* (sehr-VEES ah-rah-bah-suh, service car), a minibus shuttle, to take you into town at no extra charge. Otherwise, taxis,

dolmuşes and city buses (No 50, 'Yeni Garaj') are available just outside the terminal grounds. For the more expensive and moderate hotels, get something to Konak (koh-NAHK) but get out at Cumhuriyet Meydanı. For inexpensive hotels get something to Basmane (bahs-mah-NEH), the railway station.

To buy bus tickets downtown without having to drag yourself all the way out to the Otobüs Garajı, go to 9 Eylül Meydanı (doh-KOOZ ey-LEWL), just a few steps from Basmane station. Here, at the beginning of Gazi Bulvarı, are numerous bus ticket offices, including those for Aydın, Dadaş, Hakikî Koç, İzmir Seyahat, Kâmil Koç, Karadeveci, Kent, Kontaş, Vantur and others. You should be able to buy a ticket to any point in the country from here.

For buses to Bergama, just go to the Otobüs Garajı and catch the next bus out; they run frequently. For Selçuk, go to the southern part of Konak, where there is a stop for buses heading south to Selçuk, Ephesus and Kuşadası. This is easier than getting out to the Otobüs Garajı. If you're headed for Sardis, just go out to the Otobüs Garajı and catch the next bus for Salihli (sah-LEEHH-lee), the large town just beyond Sardis. A single ticket will cost about 200TL (US$0.28).

Boat If you are lucky enough to arrive in İzmir by sea, the city will present itself to you wonderfully as you glide by, and your ship will come into the Yeni Liman (yeh-NEE lee-mahn, New Harbour), also called Alsancak Limanı (AHL-sahn-jahk lee-mah-nuh, Alsancak Harbour), at the northern tip of the city's central section. The harbour is about equidistant from the Otobüs Garajı and the centre of the city, Konak. For transport, turn left as you leave the dock area and walk the block to Alsancak railway station, from which buses, dolmuşes and taxis will take you downtown.

Getting Around

Airport Transport Although a new airport is under construction at Cumaovası, south of the city, as of this writing you will touch down at Çiğli Havaalanı (CHEE-lee hah-VAH-ah-lah-nuh, Çiğli Airport) (tel (51) 29 14 14), a 30-minute bus ride north from the city centre. Turkish Airlines buses will trundle you into town for 550TL (US$0.77), right to the airline's office at the Büyük Efes Oteli.

To return to the airport at the end of your stay, take the same bus, 90 minutes prior to any domestic-flight departure, 120 minutes prior to an international departure.

City Transport Transport on arrival in the city is covered directly above. Within the city, blue and silver city buses (80TL, US$0.11) lumber along the major thoroughfares, but dolmuşes are much faster. Dolmuşes in İzmir tend to be Fiat taxis. One of these running between Alsancak station and Konak via Cumhuriyet Meydanı charges 100TL (US$0.14).

SARDİS

The phrase 'rich as Croesus' made its way into language early, in the 6th century BC to be precise. Croesus was the king of Lydia, and Sardis was its capital city. It was here that one of humankind's most popular and valuable inventions appeared: coinage. No doubt the Greeks thought Croesus (560-546 BC) rich because he could store so much wealth in such a small place. Rather than having vast estates and far-ranging herds of livestock, Croesus kept his wealth in his pockets, and they were deep pockets at that.

History

For all his wealth, Croesus was defeated and captured by Cyrus and his Persians, after which he leapt onto a funeral pyre. Even Croesus couldn't take it with him.

The Lydian kingdom had dominated much of the Aegean area before the Persians came. Besides being the king-dom's wealthy capital, Sardis was a great trading centre as well, obviously because coinage facilitated trade.

After the Persians, Alexander the Great took the city in 334 BC and embellished it even more. The inevitable earthquake brought its fine buildings down in 17 AD, but the Romans rebuilt.

Orientation

There are actually two small villages at Sardis, nestled in a valley rich in vineyards (for sultanas, not wine grapes), olive groves, melon fields and tobacco fields. **Sartmustafa** (SART-MOOS-tah-fah) is the village on the highway, with a few tea houses and grocery shops. **Sartmahmut** (SART-mah-MOOT) is north of the highway, clustered around the railway station. The station is precisely one km north of the highway.

During the day the farmers come into town, park their tractors in front of the tea houses, sit down for a few glasses and discuss the crops. In early August the harvest is in progress, and little stands by the roadside, attended by children, sell huge bunches of luscious, crisp, sweet sultanas to passers-by.

The tea houses in town are where you wait to catch a bus back to İzmir.

Things to See

The ruins of Sardis are scattered throughout the valley which lies beneath the striking ragged mountain range to the south. Two concentrations of ruins are of interest.

Gymnasium & Synagogue Just east of the village (away from İzmir), on the north side of the highway, lies the most extensive part of the ruins, open virtually all the time during daylight hours, every day, for 400TL (US$0.56), half-price on Sunday and holidays.

Buy your ticket at the little booth, then enter the ruins along the Marble Way past rows of Byzantine-era shops, noting the elaborate drainage system, with pipes buried in the stone walls. Some of the shops have been identified from inscriptions. There's a *lokanta* (restaurant), Jacob's Paint Shop, an office, a hardware shop, the shop of Sabbatios and the shop of Jacob, an elder of the synagogue. At the end of the Marble Way is an inscription on the marble paving-stones honouring Prince Germanicus, done in either 17 or 43 AD.

Turn left from the Marble Way and enter the synagogue, impressive because of its size and beautiful decoration. It has lots of nice mosaic paving, and coloured stone on its walls. A modern plaque lists donors to the Sardis American Excavation Fund, who supported the excavations carried out during the period from 1965 to 1973.

The striking façade to the right of the synagogue is that of the gymnasium. Note especially the finely chiselled inscriptions in Greek, and the serpentine fluting on the columns. Behind the façade is a swimming pool and rest area.

Temple of Artemis South of the village (take the road beside the tea house) just over one km is the Temple of Artemis, a once-magnificent building which was actually never completed. Today only two columns stand untoppled, but the temple's plan is clearly visible and quite impressive. Next to the temple is an **altar** used since ancient times, refurbished by Alexander the Great and later by the Romans. Clinging to the south-eastern corner of the temple is a small brick **Byzantine church**. From archaic times through the Hellenistic, Roman and Byzantine periods this was a sacred spot, no matter what the religion.

You are supposed to pay the same amount again to enter the ruins here, but that depends upon the guard and whether he's around or not.

Getting There
Sardis is 90 km east of İzmir along the Ankara road. In high summer, start out early so you're not tramping the ruins in the heat of the day, which can be oppressive.

Rail There are several daily trains from Basmane which stop here; they are slower than the buses.

Bus Buses depart frequently from İzmir's Otobüs Garajı on the 1½-hour trip. You needn't buy a ticket in advance, just go out to the bus station and buy a ticket for the next bus to Salihli (200TL, US$0.28). Tell them you want to get out at Sart.

Dolmuş minibuses run between Sartmustafa and Manisa for 400TL (US$0.56) per ride.

Tours Alternatively, local travel agencies in İzmir operate full-day tours to Sardis and Manisa for about US$16, lunch included.

ÇEŞME

The name of this village and resort area due west of İzmir means 'fountain' or 'spring' (*çeşme*, CHESH-meh). From the village, it's only about 10 km across the water to the Greek island of Chios. The ferries to the Greek islands are the main reason people go to Çeşme, though the area is popular with weekend-trippers from İzmir.

Orientation

Though Çeşme itself is a pleasant enough little seaside village, the land to the east of it is rolling steppe, a foretaste of Anatolia and Central Asia, though this barrenness subsides as one approaches İzmir, giving way to wheat fields, lush orchards, olive groves and tobacco fields. East of Çeşme 23 km is the pretty Uzunkuyu Piknik Yeri, a roadside picnic area in a pine forest. One passes the official city limits of İzmir a full 30 km west of Konak Meydanı (50 km east of Çeşme).

Six km east of Çeşme is Ilıca, a seaside

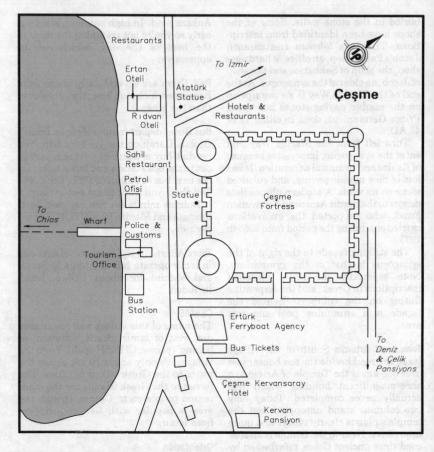

Restaurants

Ertan
Oteli

Atatürk
Statue

To İzmir

Çeşme

Rıdvan
Oteli

Hotels &
Restaurants

Sahil
Restaurant

Petrol
Ofisi

Statue

Çeşme
Fortress

To
Chios

Wharf

Police &
Customs

Tourism
Office

Bus
Station

Ertürk
Ferryboat Agency

Bus Tickets

To
Deniz
& Çelik
Pansiyons

Çeşme Kervansaray
Hotel

Kervan
Pansiyon

resort town with lots of hotels in all price ranges, from family pensions to the big Turban Çeşme Oteli. Dolmuşes run between Ilıca and Çeşme frequently (100TL, US$0.14), but unless you want to spend time at the beach you're better off staying in Çeşme proper.

In Çeşme everything you need is very near the main square, with its inevitable statue of Atatürk on the waterfront. The Tourism Information Office, Customs House (Gümrük), ferry boat ticket offices, bus ticket offices, restaurants and hotels are all here, or within two blocks.

Information

The Tourism Information Office (tel (5492) 1653) is down by the dock at İskele Meydanı No 8.

Things to See

The old fortress in the centre of town was built by the Genoese but repaired by Beyazıt, son of Sultan Mehmet the Conqueror, to defend the coast from attack by the Knights of St John, based on Rhodes, and from pirates. It now holds the museum and is called the **Çeşme Kalesi ve Müzesi** (Çeşme Fortress and

Museum), open every day from 10 am to noon and from 1 to 5.30 pm, for 400TL (US$0.56). The entrance is up the hill on the right-hand side as you face the fort from the main square. Seeing the fortress is about the most fun you'll have in Çeşme.

Facing the main square, with its back to the fortress, is a **statue** of Cezayirli Gazi Hasan Paşa (1714-1790), together with a lion who symbolizes his temperament. As a boy he was captured in a battle on the Iranian border, sold into slavery by the Ottoman army and bought by a Turkish tradesman who raised him with his own sons. Having joined the Janissary corps at 25, he began a brilliant military, naval and political career which included fierce battles with the Russian fleet off Çeşme. He retired an extremely wealthy man, having served as the sultan's Grand Vezir and having built public monuments, fountains and mosques on Lesvos, Limnos, Chios, Kos and Rhodos (all were Ottoman islands at the time).

In the evening the people of Çeşme still observe the custom of dressing up and coming down to the main square for a stroll, a glass of tea, a bit of conversation and some people-watching. That's night-life in Çeşme, and it's pleasant enough.

Places to Stay

Çeşme has several inexpensive pensions and hotels, a moderately priced hotel (and more being built), a restored caravanserai and a luxury resort. All charge more than normal, yet the upper-range lodgings are often booked solid by tour agencies in the summer season. The lodging situation in Çeşme is thus not particularly good in any respect.

Places to Stay - bottom end

The best cheap lodgings are at the several little pensions in private homes. Walk up the hill along the walls of the fortress and follow the signs to reach the *Deniz Pansiyon* (deh-NEEZ) (tel (5492) 6122), or the nearby *Çelik Pansiyon* (cheh-

LEEK) (tel (5492) 6153) ... 3850TL (US$5.39) single, ... double for a room without ... The *Kervan Pansiyon* (tel (5492) 6662), just south of the main square and the docks, charges the same, but will allow you to roll out your sleeping bag on the roof for 1000TL (US$1.40).

There are several small, fairly noisy and severely plain hotels along the main shopping street, which heads inland toward İzmir. The *Ege Oteli* (EH-geh) (tel (5492) 6586) charges 4500TL (US$6.30) for a noisy double without bath; the nearby *İmren Oteli* (eem-REHN) is the same.

Places to Stay - middle

Right on the shore, facing the main square, is the *Ertan Oteli* (ehr-TAHN) (tel (5492) 6795, 6), Cumhuriyet Meydanı 12, with 60 rooms with bath, some of them facing the sea, priced at 18,500TL (US$25.90) single, 20,300TL (US$28.42) double. This is a bit expensive for what you get, but demand is high in Çeşme, rooms are scarce and the Ertan is often filled with tour groups.

Next door to the Ertan, the *Rıdvan Oteli* is under construction. When finished (as it might be by the time you arrive), it will bring some welcome competition to the Çeşme hotel scene.

Places to Stay - top end

The *Çeşme Kervansaray* (kehr-VAHN-sah-rah-yee) (tel (5492) 6490, 1, 2), at the southern end of the main square, was built in 1528 during the reign of Süleyman the Magnificent. Recently restored by the same company that operates the Golden Dolphin resort, it is now a beautiful hotel decorated with a mixture of modern and traditional Turkish styles. Rates for room with bath, breakfast included, in the summer season (mid-June through mid-September) are 20,000TL (US$28) single, 27,000TL (US$37.80) double, 37,000TL (US$51.80) for a suite; off season, rates are about 20% lower. A table d'hote meal

...priced at 4000TL (US$5.60). For reservations in İzmir, call (51) 14 17 20.

Outside of Çeşme village proper is the luxury *Golden Dolphin Holiday Village* (Altın Yunus Tatilköyü) (tel (5492) 1250), a complete resort with facilities for all water sports, a yacht harbour and luxury accommodation.

Places to Eat

Except for meals in the more expensive hotels, Çeşme's restaurants are all fairly cheap, but some are cheaper than others. For the lowest-priced meal, walk inland from the main square on the main street to the *Hasan Abi Lokantası*, on the right (east) side. Tiny, un-beautiful, crowded and always busy, 'Big Brother Hasan' (that's the name) serves *kebaps* and ready-food dishes throughout the day. I had *salçalı kebap*, a stew in a rich sauce, *pilav*, a glass of the yogurt drink *ayran*, bread and water for 840TL (US$1.18).

Down on the waterfront the *Sahil Restaurant*, across the main square from the Ertan Oteli, is perhaps the most popular eatery, with lots of outdoor tables, some facing the square, others the sea. The bill of fare includes a lot of seafood, and full meals run 2000TL to 2500TL (US$2.80 to US$3.50), more if you order fish. They serve an early breakfast but it's a bit expensive at 750TL (US$1.05) for the same bread, honey, tea, cheese and olives that you get inland for 500TL (US$0.70).

For a local taste treat, try the *sakızlı dondurma* (sah-kuhz-LUH dohn-doormah), ice cream flavoured with pine resin, the same stuff they put in Greek *retsina* wine. It tastes like you think it's going to taste, there's no mystery or discovery involved. If you like retsina, you may like this weird incarnation of the flavour. And if you hate retsina . . . .

Getting There & Away

Bus It's simple. Çeşme is almost a suburb of İzmir, and Çeşme Turizm buses and minibuses make the run into the big city every 15 minutes or so from 6 am to 6 pm, for 600TL (US$0.84) single.

Chios Ferry The reason you've come to Çeşme is the ferry between this town and the Greek island of Chios. Boats run on Thursday during the winter months, weather and customers permitting; Sunday and Thursday in early May; Tuesday, Thursday and Sunday from mid-May till mid-July, and from mid-September through October. In high summer there are daily boats (except Monday) from mid-July through mid-September.

At other times, extra boats may run if there is sufficient traffic. Most of these boats depart in the morning at 9.30 or 10, but a few depart at 4 pm.

Single fare between Çeşme and Chios is US$18, same-day return trip costs US$20, a return-trip ticket valid for one year costs US$30. Children four to 12 years old get a 50% reduction.

Motorcycles, cars, even caravans and minibuses can be carried on some of the ferries. The fare for an auto is between US$40 and US$60.

The Thursday boat can also serve as a day trip to Chios; you leave Çeşme in the morning, spend the better part of the day on Chios, and return to Çeşme in the evening.

For details, reservations and tickets, contact the Ertürk Travel Agency (EHR-tewrk) (tel (5492) 6768 or 6876) in Çeşme's main square at Cumhuriyet Meydanı 11/A, near the fortress and across from the docks. It's a good idea to buy your ticket at least a day in advance, if possible.

By the way, the Ertürk people usually have information about onward connections from Chios to Piraeus (daily, except Saturday, at 8 pm), to Athens by air, and to Samos, Lesvos and Thessaloniki by boat, as well as multiple connections to other Greek islands.

Ephesus

It's often said that Turkey has more ancient cities and classical ruins than does Greece. Well, it's true, and the Aegean coast holds a great number of sites, including Ephesus, the grandest and best-preserved of them all.

Even if you are not fascinated by archaeology, there's great pleasure in riding through a countryside rich in fields of tobacco, passing orchards of fig trees, tramping among verdant fields bright with sunflowers, resting in little village tea houses, and strolling along marble streets which once witnessed the passing of the men who practically invented architecture, philosophy, mathematics and science. And when it gets hot, there's always the beach.

History

This was Ionia. About 1000 BC, colonists from Greece arrived on these shores, fleeing an invasion by the Dorians. The Ionian culture flourished, and its cities exported these cultural refinements back to Greece.

The history of Ionia is much the same as that of İzmir, with the original Ionian league of cities being conquered by the Lydians of Sardis, then the Persians, then Alexander. They prospered until their harbours silted up, or until the predominance of İzmir siphoned off their local trade.

Ephesus (Efes, EFF-ess) was a great trading and religious city, centre for the cult of Cybele, Anatolian fertility goddess. The Ionians replaced Cybele with Artemis and built a fabulous temple in her honour. When the Romans took over and made this the province of Asia, Artemis became Diana and Ephesus became the Roman provincial capital. Its Temple of Diana was counted among the Seven Wonders of the World.

As a large and busy Roman town with ships and caravans coming from all over,
it had an important Christian congregation very early. St Paul visited Ephesus and later wrote the most profound of his epistles to the Ephesians.

Ephesus was renowned for its wealth and beauty even before it was pillaged by Gothic invaders in 262 AD, and it was still an important enough place in 431 AD that a church council was held here. There is a lot of the city's glory left for you to see. As for the other Ionian ports, sometimes a sleepy Turkish village rose among the ruins, sometimes not. Today several of those once-sleepy villages are bustling seaside resort towns.

Orientation

The region around Ephesus is rich in attractions. The city itself is an archaeological zone, but only four km away is the Turkish town of Selçuk (population 20,000), where you catch buses and dolmuşes, have meals and find pensions to sleep for the night. On a hilltop about 10 km south of Selçuk is Meryemana, the House of the Virgin Mary. About seven km from Selçuk, past Ephesus, is the Aegean coast and Pamucak beach, a long, wide swath of sand backed by some beach-shack eateries and a small motel.

Farther south along the coast, 20 km from Selçuk, is Kuşadası (population 30,000), a resort town and port for Aegean cruise ships doing the Greek islands route. Kuşadası is also where you can catch a ferryboat to Samos. Inland 15 km from Kuşadası and about 35 km due south of Selçuk is the farming town of Söke (population 50,000), a pleasant enough place, but really of interest as a transportation point on the way to three nearby archaeological sites of great importance: Priene, Miletus and Didyma.

It is easy to spend at least three days seeing the sights in this region. Plan a day for Selçuk and Ephesus, another for Priene, Miletus and Didyma, and a third for Kuşadası and the beach. If you have more time, plan to make your base in Kuşadası.

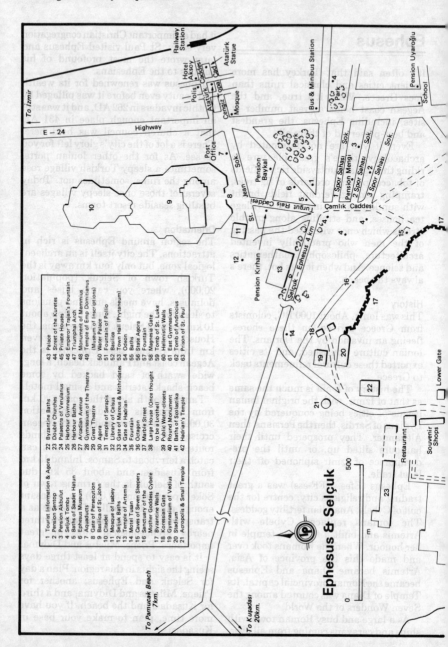

Ephesus & Selçuk

1 Tourist Information & Agora	22 Byzantine Baths
2 Pension Sentop	23 Double Churches
3 Pension Akbulut	24 Palaestra of Verulanus
4 Selçuk Tombs	25 Harbour Gymnasium
5 Baths of Saadet Hatun	26 Harbour Baths
6 Ephesus Museum	27 Arcadian Avenue
7 Aquaducts	28 Gymnasium of the Theatre
8 Gate of Persecution	29 Great Theatre
9 Basilica of St. John	30 Agora
10 Citadel	31 Temple of Serapis
11 Baths of Isabey	32 Library of Celsus
12 Selçuk Baths	33 Gate of Mazeus & Mithridates
13 Temple of Artemis	34 Gate of Hadrian
14 Motel Tusan	35 Baths
15 Caves of Seven Sleepers	36 Octagon
16 Sanctuary of the	37 Marble Street
Mother Goddess Cybele	38 Large House (Once thought
17 Byzantine Walls	to be a brothel)
18 Koressian Gate	39 Public Water-closets
19 Gymnasium of Vedius	40 Round Monument
20 Stadium	41 Baths of Scolastika
21 Acropolis & Small Temple	42 Hadrian's Temple
43 Palace	
44 Street of the Kuretes	
45 Private Houses	
46 Emperor Trajan's Fountain	
47 Triumphal Arch	
48 Monument of Memmius	
49 Temple of Emp Domitianus	
(Museum of Inscriptions)	
50 Water Palace	
51 Fountain of Pollio	
52 Basilica	
53 Council Hall (Prytaneum)	
54 Odeon	
55 Baths	
56 State Agora	
57 Fountain	
58 Magnesia Gate	
59 Tomb of St. Luke	
60 Hellenistic Walls	
61 East Gymnasium	
62 Tomb of Androcius	
63 Prison of St. Paul	

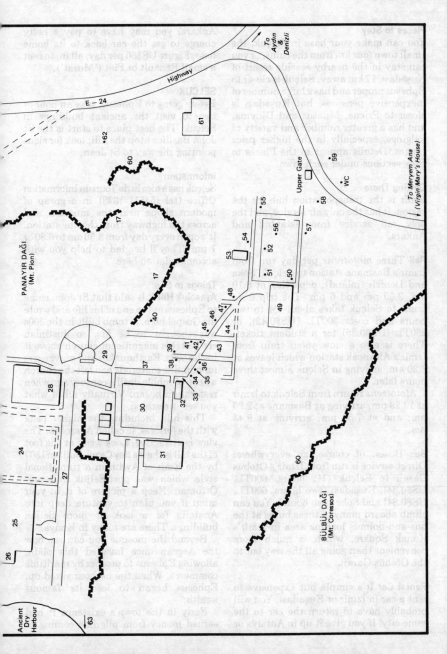

Places to Stay

You can make your base in Selçuk, the small town four km from the ruins, or you can stay in the nearby seaside resort of Kuşadası, 17 km away. Selçuk is closer to Ephesus proper and has a large number of inexpensive pensions, but Kuşadası is closer to Priene, Miletus and Didyma, and has a greater number and variety of lodgings, especially in the higher price ranges. Details appear in the Places to Stay sections under each town.

Getting There

İzmir is the transportation hub for the region. It has the only air service, and the only rail service from İstanbul and Ankara.

Rail Three *mototrens* per day run from İzmir's Basmane station to Selçuk, Söke and Denizli (inland), departing at 8.10 am, 3.30 pm and 6 pm. The trip from İzmir to Selçuk takes about 1½ to two hours and costs 300TL (US$0.42), or 250TL (US$0.35) for a student ticket. There is also a slow *yolcu* train from İzmir's Alsancak station which leaves at 8.20 am, arriving in Selçuk almost three hours later.

Mototrens return from Selçuk to İzmir at 12.29 pm, arriving at Basmane at 2.20 pm; and at 7.53 pm, arriving at 9.43 pm.

Bus Buses, of course, go everywhere. Direct service is run from İzmir's Otobüs Garajı to Selçuk (1½ hours, 600TL, US$0.84), Kuşadası (two hours, 600TL, US$0.84) and Söke (two hours). You can climb aboard many of these buses at the bus-and-dolmuş loading area in İzmir's Konak Square, which is much more convenient than going all the way out to the Otobüs Garajı.

Rental Car It's simple but expensive to rent a car in İzmir or Kuşadası. You will probably have to return the car to the same city. If you give it up in Antalya or Ankara, you may have to pay a hefty charge to get the car back to its home base. Figure US$50 per day, all in, to rent a small Renault or Fiat ('Murat').

SELÇUK

Before going to Ephesus, take an hour or two to visit the ancient buildings in Selçuk. The best place to start is the St John Basilica atop the hill; look for signs pointing the way to St Jean.

Information

Selçuk has a nice little Tourism Information Office (tel (5451) 1328) in a group of modern shops near the museum and across the highway from the bus station. It's open every day from 8.30 am to 6.30 or 7 pm. They'll be glad to help you with accommodation here.

Things to See

Ayasoluk Hill It is said that St John came to Ephesus at the end of his life and wrote his Gospel here. A tomb built in the 300s was thought to be his, so Justinian erected this magnificent church above it in the 500s. Earthquakes and scavengers for building materials had left the church a heap of rubble until a century ago when restoration began. Virtually all of what you see is restored.

This hill, including the higher peak with the fortress, is called Ayasoluk. The view is attractive. Look west: at the foot of the hill is the İsa Bey Camii, built in 1307 by the Emir of Aydın in a transitional style which was post-Seljuk and pre-Ottoman. Keep a picture of it in your mind if you plan to venture deep into Anatolia for a look at more Seljuk buildings. There are many in Konya.

Beyond the mosque you can see how the Aegean once invaded this plain, allowing Ephesus to prosper by maritime commerce. When the harbour silted up, Ephesus began to lose its famous wealth.

Early in the town's existence it had earned money from pilgrims coming to pay homage to Cybele/Artemis. The many-breasted Anatolian fertility goddess had a fabulous temple, the **Artemision**, to the south-west of the St John Basilica. A sign marks the spot today, and you can see the outline of the foundation, but that's all. When you visit the huge temple at Didyma you can get an idea what the great temple looked like, as the one at Didyma is thought to be very similar. But the cult of the fertility goddess has now moved from Ephesus to men's magazines.

By the way, the **citadel** atop the hill to the north of the St John Basilica was originally constructed by the Byzantines in the 500s, rebuilt by the Seljuks and restored in modern times. A small Seljuk mosque and a ruined church are inside.

Other Sites Selçuk has some **tombs** and a little **mosque** dating from the Seljuk period; these are near the bus station. Also, on the streets between the highway and the railway station you can see the remains of a Byzantine **aqueduct**, now a favourite nesting-place for a large population of storks.

Ephesus Museum Don't miss the beautiful museum in the centre of Selçuk. The collection is a significant one, and its statuary, mosaics and artefacts are attractively displayed. Among the prime attractions in this rich collection are several marble statues of Cybele/Artemis, with rows of breasts and elaborate headdresses, and several effigies of Priapus, the phallic god. There are also good mosaics and frescoes. The museum is open every day from 9.30 am to 6.30 pm; admission costs 500TL (US$0.70), half-price on Sunday and holidays.

Places to Stay – bottom end
Selçuk has numerous small pensions, a complete list of which is painted on a signboard in front of the Tourism Information Office. Rooms in these modest, friendly and very cheap places cost 1650TL (US$2.31) single, 3300TL

(US$4.62) double without bath; or 3500TL (US$4.90) single, 7000TL (US$9.80) double with private shower.

Try the *Pension Baykal* (bye-KAHL) (tel (5451) 1908), next to the museum; or the *Pension Kırhan* (KURR-hahn), tel (5451) 2257), just up the street from the Baykal, more or less behind the museum – this one has a pretty little front garden with citrus trees. The *Pension Mengi* (MEHN-gee) (tel (5451) 1056) is a tidy two-storey suburban-type structure, more modern. The *Pension Akbulut* (AHK-boo-loot) (tel (5451) 1139) is similar, with marvellous jasmine and rose bushes in front. The *Hülya Pansiyon*, five minutes' walk back along the highway toward İzmir, is another good one.

As for hotels, there's the *Hotel Aksoy* (AHK-soy) (tel (5451) 1040) Namık Kemal Caddesi 17, between the main highway and the railway station. The 21 rooms cost 3850TL (US$5.39) double with shower. Across the street is the newer *Ürkmez Otel* (ewrk-MEHZ) (tel (5451) 1312), Namık Kemal Caddesi 18, with willing staff, some rooms with balconies, all rooms with shower, and a price of 5000TL (US$7) double.

Camping The *Tusan Efes Moteli*, the closest lodging to the ruins of Ephesus, has the prime site for camping. Here you're the only a few minutes' walk from the ruins, and also within walking distance of Selçuk. Dolmuşes to Kuşadası pass right by the motel.

Places to Stay – middle
Selçuk's poshest lodgings are at the *Tusan Efes Moteli* (tel (5451) 1060) at the turning from the Selçuk-Kuşadası road into the ruins of Ephesus. The location is excellent, a 10-minute walk from the archaeological zone entrance. The 12 rooms cost 9800TL (US$13.72) double, with shower.

Places to Eat – bottom end

The place to look for an inexpensive meal is Cengiz Topal Caddesi (jehn-GEEZ toh-PAHL), between the highway and the railway station. It has numerous restaurants, including several with pleasant outdoor tables by the street. A full meal of two courses plus bread, beverage and tip need cost only 1000TL (US$1.40). For variety, try the *Girne Köftecisi* (GEER-neh) or the *Lezzet Lokantası* (leh-ZEHT). By the railway station there are some shady tea gardens where you can sit, sip tea and watch the storks atop the aqueduct. Two popular places opposite the Hotel Aksoy are the *Turan Köfteci* and the *Ephesus Pub*. English is more readily spoken here, and is also seen on the menus.

Places to Eat – mid-range

For nicer surroundings, head for the *Villa Restaurant* (tel 1299 or 1331), at the beginning of the shady road to Ephesus. Vines and lattices shade the tables here. In summer there is a wooden rig out front which holds a large barrel-like churn for *ayran*, as the best of this yogurt-and-spring water drink is churned *(yayık ayran)*, not simply mixed. Prices for meals are not high here, as meat dishes range from 700TL to 950TL (US$0.98 to US$1.33). Try *çöp şiş* (churp sheesh), delicate small morsels of lamb grilled on little wooden skewers.

Getting Around

There's a small bus and dolmuş station right in the centre, on the highway opposite the turning for Kuşadası, from which you can get minibuses to Ephesus, Kuşadası and Söke.

It's a good idea to do your travelling early in the day. Minibus service from Selçuk to Kuşadası, for instance, stops at around 6 or 7 pm. After that time, you pay for a taxi unless you can find enough fellow travellers to hire a whole minibus or car and share the cost. Should you find yourself in this predicament, look for taxis lurking near the museum in Selçuk. Sometimes there's a driver who lives in Kuşadası, on his way home, looking for some fares so he doesn't travel empty. He'll be amenable to bargaining.

Minibus drivers at the Selçuk bus station will organize a tour to Priene, Miletus and Didyma, lasting from 10 am to 7.30 pm, including lunch and a few hours' swimming time at Altınkum Beach for 6000TL (US$8.40) per person.

EPHESUS

Half a day will do you for sightseeing at Ephesus, though you can easily spend a full day if you go into detail. In high summer it gets very hot here. Best to start your tramping early in the morning, then retire to a shady restaurant for lunch and to your hotel or the beach for a siesta. By the way, there is not much reason to take a guided tour of Ephesus. Transport to the site is frequent, fast and cheap; explanations of the major buildings are given below; and if you want to hear a guide's spiel, just tag along with one of the dozens of group tours.

I like to walk the four km from Selçuk to Ephesus, but only in morning or evening. The walk takes about 45 minutes. But as you'll be doing a lot of walking to get around the large archaeological site, you might want to ride. Dolmuşes headed from Selçuk to Kuşadası will drop you at the Tusan Efes Moteli, from which it's a 10-minute walk to the entrance of the archaeological zone.

Things to See

As you walk in from the highway, you will see a road to the left. This leads (after a 10-minute walk) to the **Grotto of the Seven Sleepers**, on the north-east side of Mt Pion. A legend says that seven persecuted Christian youths fled from Ephesus in the 3rd century and took refuge in this cave. Agents of the Emperor Decius, a terror to Christians, found the cave and sealed it. Two centuries later an earthquake broke down the wall, awakening the sleepers, and they ambled back to town for a meal. Finding that all of their old friends were long dead, they concluded that they had undergone a sort of resurrection. Ephesus was by this time a Christian city. When they died they were buried in the cave, and a cult following developed. The grotto is actually a fairly elaborate Byzantine-era **necropolis** with scores of tombs cut into the rock.

Back on the Ephesus entry road you pass the **Gymnasium of Vedius** (100s AD) on your left, which had exercise fields, baths, latrines, covered exercise rooms, a swimming pool and a ceremonial hall. Just south of it is the **Stadium**, dating from about the same period. Most of its finely cut stones were taken by the Byzantines to build the citadel and walls of Ayasoluk. This 'quarrying' of pre-cut building stone from older, often earthquake-ruined structures continued through the entire history of Ephesus.

The road comes over a low rise and descends to the parking lot, where there are a few tea houses, restaurants and souvenir shops. To the right (west) of the road are the ruins of the **Church of the Virgin Mary**, also called the Double Church.

Pay the 1000TL (US$1.40) admission fee and enter the archaeological zone. As you walk down a lane bordered by evergreen trees, a few colossal remains of the **Harbour Gymnasium** are off to the right (west). Then you come to the marble-paved **Arcadian Way**. This was the grandest street in Ephesus. Constructed with water and sewer lines beneath the paving, installed with street lighting along the colonnades, lined with shops and finished with triumphal columns, it was and still is a grand sight. The builder was the Byzantine emperor Arcadius (395-408). At the far (western) end was the harbour of Ephesus, long since silted up. Near the western (harbour) end of the street is a **Nymphaeum**, or fountain and pool.

At the east end of the Arcadian Way is the **Great Theatre**, still used for performances. Its design is Hellenistic; construction was begun in 41 AD and finished in 117. It could – and can – hold almost 25,000 spectators. During the Selçuk Ephesus Festival of Culture & Art, held in the first week of May, performances are given in this dramatic setting.

When you visit the theatre, no doubt someone will be standing on the orchestra floor, speaking to someone who is seated high up in the *cavea* (auditorium), to demonstrate the fine acoustics of the place.

Behind the Great Theatre is **Mt Pion**, which bears a few traces of the ruined city walls.

From the theatre, continue along the marble-paved **Sacred Way**, also called the Marble Way. Note the remains of the city's elaborate water and sewer systems. The large open space to the right, once surrounded by a colonnade and shops, was the **Agora** (3 BC) or marketplace, heart of Ephesus' business life.

At the end of the Sacred Way, Curetes Way heads east up a slope. This corner was 'downtown Ephesus'. The beautiful **Library of Celsus** is here, carefully restored with the aid of the German Archaeological Institute.

Across the street is an elaborate building with rich mosaics and several fountains. It was once thought to be the **brothel**, but some say it was just a grand private residence. In the maze of ruined walls you'll come upon a **spring** served by a hand pump from which, with a little effort, you can coax the most deliciously refreshing cool water.

As you head up Curetes Way, a passage on the left leads to the **Public Latrines**, their design demonstrating their function unmistakably. These posh premises were for men only. The women's were elsewhere.

On the right side of Curetes Way, the hillside is covered in **private houses**. Most of these were small, as houses in classical times were mostly for sleeping and dressing. Bathing, amusements, socializing and business were all conducted in public places. The houses are still being excavated and restored. A few of the ones along the street belonged to wealthy families, and have elaborate decoration.

You can't miss the impressive **Temple of Hadrian**, on the left. It's in Corinthian style, with beautiful reliefs in the porch and a head of Medusa to keep out evil spirits. The temple was finished in 138 AD. Across the street is an elaborate house from the same period.

Further along Curetes Way, on the left, is the **Fountain of Trajan**, who was Roman emperor from 98 to 117 AD.

To the right is a side street leading to a colossal temple dedicated to the Emperor Domitian (81-96 AD), which now serves as the **Museum of Inscriptions**.

Up the hill on the left (north) are the very ruined remains of the **Prytaneum**, a municipal hall; and the **Temple of Hestia Boulaea**, in which the perpetual flame was guarded. Finally you come to the pretty little marble **Odeum**, a small theatre used for lectures, musical performances and meetings of the town council. There is another entrance to the archaeological zone here, near the Odeum at the Upper Gate, on the road which leads to Meryemana (mehr-YEHM-ah-nah), the House of the Virgin Mary, also called Panaya Kapulu. You will need a taxi to go the five km to Meryemana.

MERYEMANA

Legend has it that the Virgin Mary, accompanied by St Paul, came to Ephesus at the end of her life. A woman named Catherine Emmerich (1774-1824) had visions of Mary and of her surroundings. When clergy from İzmir followed the detailed descriptions, they discovered the foundations of an old house; a tomb, also described by Emmerich, was not found. In 1967 Pope Paul VI visited the site, where a chapel now stands, and confirmed the authenticity of the legend. A small traditional service celebrated on 15 August each year in honour of Mary's Assumption into heaven by Orthodox and Muslim clergy is now the major event here. To Muslims, Mary is Meryemana, Mother Mary, who bore İsa Peygamber, the Prophet Jesus.

The view from the hilltop is wonderful. A small restaurant can provide refreshments.

PAMUCAK

About nine km west of Selçuk, by a right turn off the Kuşadası road, lies Pamucak (PAH-moo-jahk) beach, an absolutely gorgeous, long wide crescent of dark sand. Until my last visit there had been very little development at Pamucak for years, but now a new road is being built and hotel construction will no doubt follow. There is already one motel here. Other visitors to Pamucak simply camp on the beach, whether in a tent, a caravan or under the stars. Shacks thrown together in a few hours serve as restaurants. It's all a bit chaotic at the moment, with no organisation and a growing number of inhabitants, but the beach is marvellous and the water inviting.

Transport to Pamucak tends to be by luck and thumb. If enough people gather at Selçuk's bus station looking for a dolmuş to Pamucak, drivers will run one. Otherwise, it's hitching and hiking.

Places to Stay

As of this writing there is only one small motel, the 36-room *Motel Pamucak*, where singles with shower rent for 2000TL to 3150TL (US\$2.80 to US\$4.41), doubles with shower 4000TL to 5300TL (US\$5.60 to US\$7.42), triples with shower 6000TL (US\$8.40). They have a camping area as well.

KUŞADASI

Twenty km from Selçuk, down on the Aegean coast, is Kuşadası (koo-SHAH-dah-suh, Bird Island, population 30,000), a seaside resort town and base for excursions to the ancient cities of Ephesus, Priene, Miletus and Didyma, and even inland to Aphrodisias.

Many Aegean cruise ships on Greek Islands tours stop at Kuşadası so that their passengers can take a tour to Ephesus and haggle for trinkets in Kuşadası's shops. The town's appearance, not to mention its economy, has been affected by this cruise business, of course. But Kuşadası is still a mixture of hotels and pensions for Turks and foreigners on holiday, of shops for the cruise people, and of businesses serving the farmers, beekeepers and fishermen who make up much of the town's population.

Coming into Kuşadası from Selçuk and Ephesus is a wonderful experience, for the road winds through fields and hills, past olive orchards and a few little houses, then around a turn and down the cliffs, with a splendid view of the Aegean.

Kuşadası gets its name from a small island, now connected to the mainland by a causeway, called Güvercin Adası (gew-vehr-JEEN ah-dah-suh, Pigeon Island). You can recognise it by the small stone fort, now a supper club, which is the tiny island's most prominent feature. As for downtown landmarks, the biggest is the Öküz Mehmet Paşa Kervansarayı, an Ottoman caravanserai which is now a hotel called the Club Caravanserail, operated by Club Méditerranée. It's at the intersection of the two main streets.

Orientation

The waterfront road is named Atatürk Bulvarı. During high summer, a horse-drawn buggy rolls along this street carrying people from the centre to the northern beach. The main street heading from the wharf into town is officially named Barbaros Hayreddin Caddesi, but many locals still call it by its former name of Tayyare Caddesi; the street changes names to become Kahramanlar Caddesi as it progresses inland past the police station, which is in a little stone tower

that was once part of the town's defensive walls. The bus and dolmuş station is north on Kahramanlar Caddesi, near the prominent mosque named the Hanım Camii, about one km from the sea.

Information

The Tourism Information Office (tel (6361) 1103), is down by the wharf where the cruise ships dock, about 100 metres in front of the Club Caravanserail.

Things to Do

Besides a stroll through the Kervansaray and out to Güvercin Adası, and a short ride to the beaches, the thing to do is take dolmuşes to the nearby ruined cities (see below). While you're in Kuşadası, however, you might want to shop for onyx, meerschaum, leather clothing and accessories, copper, brass, carpets and jewellery. Don't shop while the cruise ships are in port, however.

Places to Stay

Prices for rooms in Kuşadası are highest in July and August, about 20% lower in June and September, and up to 50% lower in other months. Rates quoted below are the high summer rates.

With one exception, the more luxurious hotels are on the outskirts of town, as are the camping areas (see above). In the centre are small, attractive, moderately priced hotels and very cheap pensions.

Places to Stay – bottom end

Cheap rooms can be very nice or pretty basic. Most will have a washbasin, few will have private bath. The price for a double room ranges from 4400TL to 6600TL (US$6.16 to US$9.24). Many of the cheap establishments are in the same area: walk up Barbaros Caddesi, turn right toward the Akdeniz Hotel, and take *Arslanlar Caddesi*, the road on the right side of the hotel, which will take you up past a half-dozen pensions and inexpensive hotels. Look for the *Hotel Rose* (tel (6361) 1111); the *Hotel Ada* (no phone);

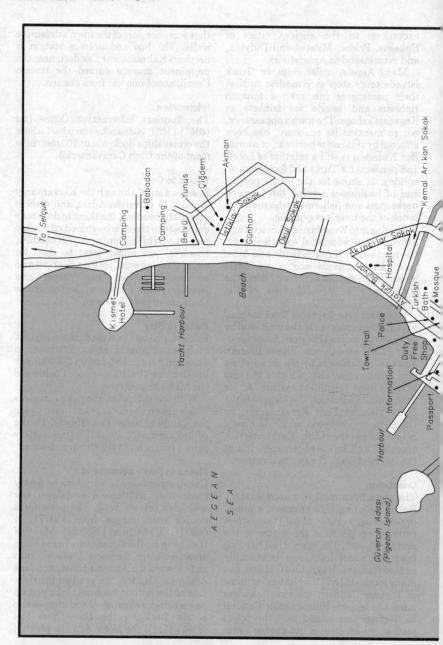

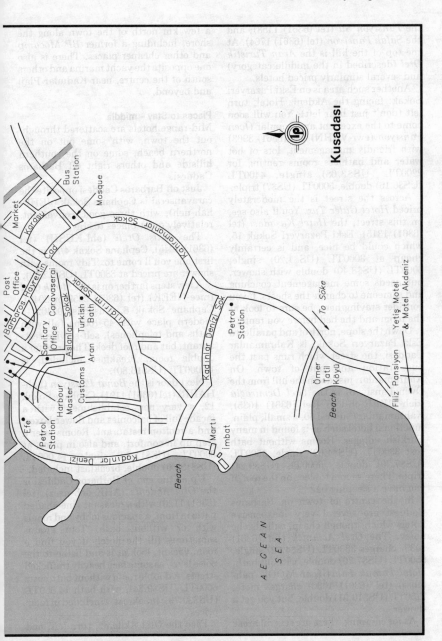

Kusadası

the *Pansiyon Su* (tel (6361) 1453); and the *Şafak Pansiyon* (tel (6361) 1764). At the top of the hill is the *Aran Turistik Otel* (described in the middle category) and several similarly priced hotels.

Another such area is on Eski Pazaryeri Sokak: facing the Akdeniz Hotel, turn left (don't just bear left). You will soon come to the excellent and popular *Öven Pansiyon* (ewr-VEHN) (tel (6361) 3963) with friendly management, lots of hot water and bathless rooms renting for 2200TL (US$3.08) single, 4400TL (US$6.16) double, 5000TL (US$7) triple.

Across the street is the moderately priced *Hotel Güler Tur*. You'll also see, on this street, the *Hotel Kuşadası* (tel (6361) 1315), Eski Pazaryeri Sokak 15, which could be nice, and is certainly cheap at 3000TL (US$4.20) single, 6000TL (US$8.40) double with shower, but needs some management coaching and someone to change the sheets. If you consider staying here, be sure to look at the room and the bed before you rent.

Down the slope, north of and parallel to Eski Pazaryeri Sokak, is Kahramanlar Caddesi, the street which runs past the bus station and out of town. On Kahramanlar, just down the hill from the Öven Pansiyon, is the *Otel Demiroglu* (deh-MEER-oh-loo) (tel (6361) 1035), Kahramanlar Caddesi 60, a small, plain, functional hotel such as is found in many Turkish villages. Rooms without bath cost 3300TL (US$4.62) single, 5500TL (US$7.70) double, 6600TL (US$9.24) triple. There's room to sleep on the roof, if you have a sleeping bag.

In the centre of town on Barbaros Caddesi are several very inexpensive hotels which, though cheap, will also be noisy. The *Otel Atlantik* (tel (6361) 1039) charges 3300TL (US$4.62) single, 5500TL (US$7.70) double, without bath. *Hotel Pamuk Palas* (pah-MOOK pah-lahss) (tel (6361) 1080) charges more, 7150TL (US$10.01) double, but you get a shower.

As for camping, there are several areas

a few km north of the town along the shore, including a former *BP Mocamp* and other cheaper places. There is also one opposite the yacht marina and others south of the centre, near Kadınlar Plajı and beyond.

Places to Stay – middle

Mid-range hotels are scattered throughout the town, with some out on the northern beach, some on the southern hillside and others right off Barbaros Caddesi.

Just off Barbaros Caddesi opposite the caravanserai is Cephane Sokak (JEHP-hah-neh), with three good, convenient, relatively quiet places to stay.

The *Alkış Oteli* (ahl-KUSH) (tel (6361) 1245), Cephane Sokak 4/A, is the first one you'll come to. Tidy rooms with shower are priced at 8800TL (US$12.32).

A few steps farther on is the *Minik Otel* (mee-NEEK) (tel (6361) 2359 or 2043), Cephane Sokak 8, Kuşadası 09402, a modern place with 45 rooms (all with baths and telephones), self-service restaurant, bar and roof deck. The price for a double room, breakfast included, is 12,000TL (US$16.80).

Next door is the *Bahar Pansiyon* (bah-HAHR) (tel (6361) 1191), Cephane Sokak 12, a very new establishment with a façade full of balconies and flower-boxes, and a rooftop restaurant. Rooms offer a step up in comfort, and also in price, at 8000TL (US$11.20) single, 14,000TL (US$19.60) double, breakfast included.

Up at the end of Barbaros Caddesi is the *Otel Akdeniz* (AHK-deh-neez) (tel (6361) 1120) with a pleasant vine-shaded patio in front, a spacious lobby and rooms with or without bath. Tour groups sometimes fill the hotel. If you find a room vacant, look at it and listen to the noise level, as some face heavily trafficked streets. A double room without bath costs 6600TL (US$9.24), with bath 14,850TL (US$20.79); breakfast is included in room prices.

Face the Otel Akdeniz, turn left, and

walk down Eski Pazaryeri Sokak to find the *Güler Tur Otel* (gew-LEHR toor) (tel (6361) 2996), Eski Pazaryeri Sokak 26, a newish hotel with friendly management who always seem to be reading newspapers. The rooms are plain but tidy and fairly quiet, with lowish prices of 5000TL (US$7) single, 8000TL (US$11.20) double, with bath.

At the top of Arslanlar Caddesi, which mounts the slope next to the Otel Akdeniz, is the *Aran Turistik Otel* (ah-RAHN too-rees-TEEK) (tel (6361) 1076 or 1325), Kaya Aldoğan Caddesi 4. Its 22 rooms have showers with solar-heated water and are priced at 6900TL (US$9.66) single, 11,350TL (US$15.89) double, breakfast included. Some rooms and the roof terrace have marvellous views and it's quiet up here, but it is also a long climb up the hillside on a hot day.

While you're up on the hillside, head west toward the sea until you come to the *Hotel Stella* (tel (6361) 1632 or 3787), PO Box 110, a tidy, airy place with fabulous views of the town and the harbour, friendly and personable management, and bright, modern rooms priced at 18,600TL (US$26.04) double with shower, breakfast included.

Less charming but also less expensive is the *Hotel Pamuk Palas* (pah-MOOK pah-lahss) (tel (6631) 3191), near the bus station (not to be confused with its plainer sister hotel downtown on Barbaros Caddesi). New and shiny, with its own swimming pool and another for children, it charges 15,000TL (US$21) for a double room with shower, breakfast included.

North of the centre about one km is another group of moderately priced lodgings, either on the waterfront street or west of it a block or two. Most can be found by following their signs.

The *Günhan Hotel* (GEWN-hahn) (tel (6361) 1050) faces the sea at Atatürk Bulvarı 52, Kuşadası 09400, and charges 8800TL (US$12.32) double, 12,375TL (US$17.33) triple with bath, breakfast included.

Nearby is a group of other good places, including the *Çidem Pansiyon* (chee-DEHM) (tel (6361) 1895), next to the Yunus Pansiyon at İstiklal Caddesi 9, a clean and cheerful place with single rooms for US$9 with washbasin or US$13.50 with shower, and doubles for US$11 with washbasin, US$16 with shower.

The 18-room *Posacı Turistik Pansiyon* (POHSS-ah-juh) (tel (6361) 1151), Leylak Sokak 5, back inland from the shore road a few blocks, has tidy rooms for US$11.50 single, US$17 double, without bath, but with breakfast.

The nearby *Hotel Akman* (AHK-mahn) (tel (6361) 1501), İstiklal Caddesi 13, Kuşadası 09401, is a neat and modern little place open from March through November, used by Teutonic tour groups. Some of them have bathtubs, and all of them are priced at US$22 for a single, US$31 for a double, and this price includes breakfast.

Places to Stay – top end

Kuşadası's poshest place to stay is the refurbished Ottoman caravanserai, now a hotel operated by the Club Mediterranée called the *Club Caravansérail* (tel (6361) 2457 or 2423). It's in the centre of town at the seaside end of Barbaros Caddesi. Rooms are attractive if small and folksy-simple, the courtyard is lush, the ambience superb. A double costs US$36.62, with room, breakfast, tax and service included, but you're usually required to buy 'half-pension' (breakfast and dinner), which brings the daily tab up to US$53.75. If you don't stay here, at least come for a meal (expensive), a drink or a free look around.

Hotel Efe (EH-feh) (tel (6361) 3660, 1, 2), PO Box 49, Güvercin Ada Caddesi 37, is the dramatic step-fronted structure facing the cruise ship dock near Güvercin Adası. The rooms have excellent views, balconies with flowers, private baths and prices of 25,300TL (US$35.42) double, breakfast included.

The *Tusan Oteli* (TOO-sahn) (tel
(6361) 1094 or 2080), north of town on the
beach, charges less, and has well-used but
quiet rooms with direct access to its own
beach as well as plenty of equipment for
water sports.

On Kadınlar Plajı south of town are
other hotels priced at US$25 to US$35
double. These include the *İmbat Oteli*
(EEM-baht) (tel (6361) 2000, 1, 2) at the
high end, and the *Martı Oteli* (mahr-
TUH) (tel (6361) 1198, 1031), lower in
price. Unless you have a car or plan to
spend most of your time on the beach, it's
more fun to be in town.

Places to Eat

Restaurant prices stretch across the full
range in this resort-and-farming town. As
you get away from the sea, prices drop
dramatically and quality stays high.

Places to Eat – bottom end

Go up Barbaros Caddesi past the little
police station in the stone tower, continue
on Kahramanlar Caddesi, and prices
drop even more. The *Konya Restoran*
and *Nazilli Pideci* are places where you
can fill up for 800TL to 1500TL (US$1.12
to US$2.10).

As usual, the very cheapest eateries are
next to the market (*pazar*, pah-ZAHR),
which is north off Kahramanlar Caddesi
one block, next to the bus station. Little
restaurants here such as the *Kısmet* equal
or undercut those on Kahramanlar as far
as price is concerned.

For a cheap *kebapçı*, find the Hotel
Alkış (see above); facing it across the
street is the *Öz Urfa Kebapçısı* (tel
3244).

Places to Eat – mid-range

The *Çatı* on Barbaros Caddesi is on the
roof of a building, has a fine view of town
life and costs 3500TL to 4500TL (US$4.90
to US$6.30) for a full fish dinner with
wine. But it's actually more pleasant to
sit at one of the fish restaurants next to
the wharf. This is the town's prime dining

location, so a full fish dinner with wine at
the *Toros Canlı Balık* (tel 1144), *Kâzım
Usta'nın Yeri* (tel 1226) or *Diba* (tel 1063)
may cost 5000TL to 6500TL (US$7 to
US$9.10) per person. Perhaps the best
prices, with equally good food, are at the
Çam Restaurant (tel 1051).

Places to Eat – top end

Most expensive is definitely the *Club
Caravanserail*, where a meal can easily
set you back 8000TL to 10,000TL
(US$11.20 to US$14).

Getting Around

Buses of the Elbirlik company run
between İzmir and Kuşadası 10 times or
more daily in each direction from about
7 am to 6 or 7 pm, charging 600TL
(US$0.84) for the two-hour trip. Dolmuşes
buzz off from Kuşadası to Ephesus and
Selçuk every 30 minutes, on the hour and
half-hour, charging 300TL (US$0.42) for
the ride. There are dolmuşes to Söke as
well; this is what you take if your ultimate
destination is Priene, Miletus or Didyma.
Catch another dolmuş in Söke (see
below).

Dolmuşes for Kadınlar Plajı, south of
town, depart from Barbaros Caddesi next
to the Club Caravanserail.

Boats to Samos Any travel agency in
Kuşadası will sell you a ticket for a boat to
Samos. You can go over for the day and
return in the evening, or go there to stay.
Boats depart each port, Samos and
Kuşadası, at 8.30 am and 5 pm daily in
high summer; about four times weekly in
spring and autumn. Service is usually
suspended in winter except for special
excursions. The trip costs US$25 one way,
US$30 return. In most cases, you must
surrender your passport for immigration
processing the evening before you travel;
same thing happens if you're coming from
Samos to Kuşadası.

PRİENE, MİLETUS & DİDYMA

South of Kuşadası lie the ruins of three

very ancient and important settlements well worth a day trip. Priene occupies a dramatic position overlooking the plain of the Meander River. Miletus preserves a great theatre, and Didyma's Temple of Apollo is among the world's most impressive religious structures.

Priene

As you approach the archaeological zone, you'll come to a shady rest-spot in a romantic setting: water cascades from an old aqueduct next to the *Prien Şelale Restaurant*, where you can get a cool drink or hot tea, make a telephone call or have a meal. This is where you recover from your tramp through the ruins. A motto painted on one of their trash receptacles reads, 'Tourists want a smiling face and pleasant speech'.

The site at Priene is open from 9 am to 6 pm daily for 400TL (US$0.56), half price on Sunday and holidays.

Priene was important around 300 BC because it was where the League of Ionian Cities held its congresses and festivals. Otherwise, the city was smaller and less important than nearby Miletus, which means that its Hellenistic buildings were not buried by Roman buildings. What you see in Priene is mostly what one saw in the city over 2000 years ago.

The setting is dramatic, with steep Mt Mykale rising behind the town, and the broad flood plain of the River Meander (Menderes) spread out at its feet.

Priene was a planned town, with its streets laid out in a grid (the grid system originated in Miletus). Of the buildings which remain, you should see the **Bouleterion** (City Council meeting place); **Temple of Athena**, designed by Pythius of Halicarnassus and looked upon as the epitome of an Ionian temple; **Temple of Demeter**; **theatre**; ruins of a **Byzantine church**; and **gymnasium** and **stadium**. As you gaze across the river's flood plain, you will see why the name of this river came to signify a river which twists and turns (meanders) across its flood plain.

Miletus

Miletus' **Great Theatre** rises to greet you as you approach the flood plain's southern boundary and turn left, riding through swampy cotton fields to reach the archaeological zone. It is the most significant building remaining of this once-grand city, which was an important commercial and governmental centre from about 700 BC till 700 AD. After that time the harbour filled with silt, and Miletus' commerce dwindled. The 15,000-seat theatre was originally a Hellenistic building, but the Romans reconstructed it extensively during the 1st century AD. It's still in very good condition, and very impressive to explore.

The ticket booth in front of the theatre will sell you a ticket from 9 am to 6 pm, any day, for 400TL (US$0.56), half price on Sunday. The site is open, at least unofficially, until dusk. You will have to buy a separate ticket for the little **museum**, which is about a km south of the theatre. Across the road from the ticket booth is a small restaurant where you can get snacks and beverages, and drink them in a shady grove.

A hundred metres south of the ticket booth is a **Seljuk caravanserai**, currently under restoration, to be opened as a souvenir bazaar.

Climb to the top of the theatre for a view of the entire site, with several groups of ruins scattered about, among them a **stadium**; two **agoras**, northern and southern; the **Baths of Faustine**, constructed upon the order of Emperor Marcus Aurelius's wife; and a **bouleterion** or city council meeting-place.

To the south of the main group of ruins, nearer to the museum, is the **İlyas Bey Camii** (1404), a mosque dating from the Emirate period. After the Seljuks but before the Ottomans, this region was the Emirate of Menteşe. The mosque's doorway, and inside it the *mihrab*, are nice, but perhaps nicest of all is the ambience of the place. A small gem of a building when new, it is now partly in

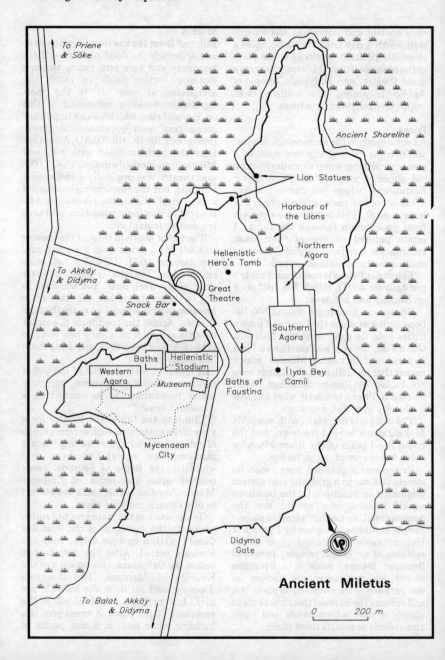

Ancient Shoreline

Lion Statues

Harbour of
the Lions

Northern
Agora

Hellenistic
Hero's Tomb

To Priene
& Söke

To Akköy
& Didyma

Great
Theatre

Snack Bar

Southern
Agora

İlyas Bey
Camii

Baths

Hellenistic
Stadium

Western
Agora

Museum

Baths of
Faustina

Mycenaean
City

Didyma
Gate

To Balat, Akköy
& Didyma

Ancient Miletus

0   200 m

ruins, its roof a favourite nesting-place for storks. Grass and weeds grow in the courtyard, and a romantic, ageless melancholy surrounds the place.

From Miletus, head south again to Akköy (seven km) and Didim (14 km farther). Transportation may be infrequent in these parts, and it may take some time to reach Akköy by hitch-hiking. South of Akköy there is more traffic, however, and most of it goes past Didyma to Altınkum Beach.

Didyma

Called Didim in Turkish, this was the site of a stupendous temple to Apollo, where lived an oracle as important as the one at Delphi. The temple and the oracle were important since very early times, but the great temple you see is the one started in the late 300s AD. It replaced the original temple which was destroyed in 494 BC by the Persians, and later construction was done by Alexander the Great.

The Temple of Apollo was never finished, though its oracle and its priests were hard at work until Christianity became the state religion of the Byzantines and they put an end to all such pagan practices. Fourteen hundred years of operation is a pretty good record, however.

When you approach Didyma today, you come into the Turkish village of Yenihisar (yeh-NEE-hee-SAHR). A few tea houses and restaurants across the road from the temple provide drinks and meals. Admission hours and times are as at Priene and Miletus.

Ancient Didyma was not a town, but the home of a god. People did not live here, only priests. I assume that the priests, sitting on the temple treasure (which was considerable) had a pretty good life. The priestly family here, which specialized in oracular temple management, originally came from Delphi.

The temple porch held 120 huge columns, the bases of which are richly carved. Behind the porch is a great

doorway at which the oracular poems were written and presented to petitioners. Beyond the doorway is the *cella* or court, where the oracle sat and prophesied after drinking from the sacred spring. We can only speculate on what that water contained to make someone capable of prophesies. The *cella* is reached today by a covered ramp on the right side of the porch.

In the temple grounds are fragments of its rich decoration, including a striking head of Medusa (she of the snakes for hair). There used to be a road lined with statuary which led to a small harbour. The statues stood there for 23 centuries, but were then (1858) taken to the British Museum.

Altınkum Beach

Five km south of Didyma is Altınkum Beach (AHL-tuhn-koom, Golden Sand), with little restaurants, pensions and hotels. It's nice, but not as nice or as convenient for transport as Kuşadası.

Getting Around

If you start early in the morning from Kuşadası or Selçuk, you can get to all three of these sites by dolmuş, returning to your base at night. If you have a car, you can see all three on your own and be back by mid-afternoon.

Tours of these sites can save you time and uncertainty; one that covers these three sites, including lunch and a swim at Altınkum Beach, will cost about 6000TL (US$8.40).

If you want to do it yourself, begin by catching a dolmuş from Kuşadası (15 km, 300TL, US$0.42) or Selçuk (35 km) to Söke, then another onward to Priene.

When you're done at Priene, wait for a passing dolmuş or hitch-hike across the flat flood plain to Miletus (22 km). The dolmuş may bear a sign saying 'Balat' (the village next to Miletus) or 'Akköy', a larger village beyond Balat.

From Miletus, catch something to Akköy or, if you can, something going all the way to Didim or Altınkum. For the return trip from Didyma or Altınkum get a dolmuş to Söke, and change for another to your base. If you do it all by dolmuş the fares will total about 1800TL (US$2.52).

SÖKE

The modern bus and dolmuş station in this transport town is divided into separate bus and dolmuş sections. From the bus side of the station, Söke Belediyesi buses depart for İzmir every hour on the half-hour until 4 pm for 700TL (US$0.98). Others head east to Denizli and Pamukkale, south to Bodrum and to Muğla (for Marmaris).

The dolmuş side of the station serves vehicles going to Güllübahçe (the village next to Priene, 14 km, 200TL, US$0.28); Balat (the village near Miletus, 35 km, 500TL, US$0.70); Davutlar (300TL, US$0.42); Milâs, on the way to Bodrum (82 km, 500TL, US$0.70); Didim, otherwise known as Didyma (56 km, 500TL, US$0.70); Aydın, on the way to Aphrodisias, Denizli and Pamukkale (55 km, 480TL, US$0.67); Altınkum, the beach (61 km, 500TL, US$0.70); and Güzelçamlı, where there is a National Park (Milli Park).

Aphrodisias & Pamukkale

At the spa named Pamukkale (pah-MOO-kah-leh, Cotton Fortress), 220 km due east of Kuşadası, hot mineral waters burst from the earth to run through a ruined Hellenistic city before cascading over a cliff. The cascades of solidified calcium from the waters form snowy white *travertines*, waterfalls of white stone, which give the spa its name. Nearby are the ruins of Laodicea, one of the Seven Churches of Asia.

On the way to Pamukkale you can make several detours to significant

archaeological sites, including the hilltop city of Nyssa about 100 km east of Kuşadası. About 150 km east of Kuşadası is Aphrodisias, one of Turkey's most complete and elaborate archaeological sites, with several buildings exceptionally well preserved.

From Denizli, the city near Pamukkale, you can catch a bus onward to Ankara, Konya or Antalya, but you'll miss the lovely Aegean Coast if you do. Only those pressed for time and anxious to see Central Anatolia should consider such a shortcut. Everyone else should plan to visit Pamukkale as a one or two-night side trip from Selçuk or Kuşadası before continuing down the coast to Bodrum, Marmaris, Fethiye and Antalya.

As you begin your trip you may pass through the ruins of Magnesia ad Meander, which lie on the road between Söke and Ortaklar. This ancient city is not really worth a stop, but the fragments of wall easily visible from the road are certainly impressive.

From Ortaklar to the provincial capital of Aydın (ahy-DUHN, population 100,000, altitude 64 metres) is 33 km. Aydın is a farming town with little to detain you.

Getting There

Bus and train services are good on the route from İzmir through Selçuk, Aydın and Nazilli to Denizli. There is no air service.

From Kuşadası, get a direct bus to Denizli or a dolmuş to Selçuk, Söke or Ortaklar, and transfer to a bus or train; at Ortaklar you wait on the road for a bus. If you plan to take the side trip to Aphrodisias, hop on a bus or train and go as far as Nazilli; otherwise, go all the way to Denizli.

See also the Getting There sections under each town.

NYSSA

Heading east from Aydın 31 km brings you to the town of Sultanhisar and, three km to the north, the site of ancient Nyssa, set on a hilltop amid olive groves. You'll have to walk or hitch to the site, as there is no public transport. When you reach the ruins you'll find a water fountain, public toilets, a guard and no admission fee. The guard will show you around the site if you wish. Offer a tip at the end of the tour.

The major ruins here are of the **theatre**, next to the parking area, which has olive trees growing from its tiers of seats, and a long **tunnel** beneath the road. A five-minute walk up the hill along the road and through a field brings you to the **bouleterion or council chamber**, which has some nice fragments of sculpture.

What you will remember about Nyssa, however, is the peacefulness and bucolic beauty of its site, very different from tourist centres such as Ephesus.

Fourteen km east of Nyssa and Sultanhisar is Nazilli (NAH-zee-lee, population 95,000), the transfer point for a trip to Aphrodisias.

APHRODISIAS

The city's name quickly brings to mind 'aphrodisiac'. Both words come from the Greek name for the goddess of love, Aphrodite, called Venus by the Romans. Aphrodite was many things to many people. As Aphrodite Urania she was the goddess of pure, spiritual love; as Aphrodite Pandemos she was the goddess of sensual love, married to Hephaestus but lover also of Ares, Hermes, Dionysus and Adonis. She got around. Her children included Harmonia, Eros, Hermaphroditus, Aeneas and Priapus, the phallic god. All in all, she was the compleat goddess of fertility, fornication and fun.

You come to Aphrodisias from Nazilli (52 km) by way of the town of Karacasu (KAH-rah-jah-soo, population 6000), surrounded by tobacco fields, fig trees and fruit orchards.

The site and museum at Aphrodisias, 13½ km past Karacasu, are open from 9 am to 6.30 pm for 400TL (US$0.56), half-price on Sunday and holidays. One ticket gets you into both the site and the museum. No photography is permitted in the museum, and you are also prohibited from photographing excavations in progress here.

History

The temple at Aphrodisias was famous and a favourite goal of pilgrimages for over 1000 years, beginning in the 700s BC. The city prospered. (How could it not, with such a popular goddess? Just think what worship entailed!) But under the Byzantines the city changed substantially: the steamy Temple of Aphrodite was transformed into a chaste Christian church, and ancient buildings were pulled down to provide building stones for defensive walls (circa 350 AD). The town, diminished from its former glory, was attacked by Tamerlane on his Anatolian rampage (1402), and never recovered.

Ruins lay abandoned and mostly buried until French, Italian, American and Turkish archaeologists began to resurrect them. What they found was a city that held a surprisingly well-preserved stadium, odeum and theatre. The National Geographic Society (USA) supported some of the excavation and restoration. Articles on Aphrodisias are in the August '67, June '72 and October '81 issues of their magazine.

Things to See

Museum On the way to the ruins is a tidy modern museum with a good collection of pieces from the ruins. Check your camera at the door. During Roman times there was a school for sculptors here, which accounts in part for the rich collection. Beds of high-grade marble are nearby. Note especially the 'cult statue of Aphrodite, second century' and the 'cuirassed statue of an emperor or high official, second century'.

Ruins Unfortunately the site is not yet well marked, so it can be confusing to get around, even with our handy map.

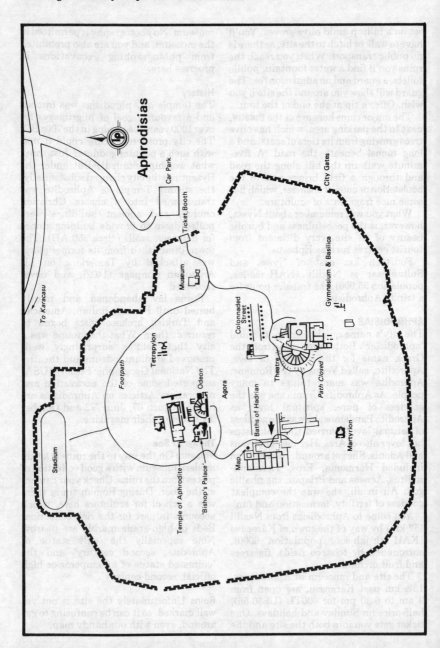

The dazzling white marble **theatre** is beautiful, and virtually complete. Behind it, the **odeum** is more or less the same, in miniature. During your walk around you'll discover the elaborate but well-ruined **Baths of Hadrian** (circa 200 AD) and the remains of the **Temple of Aphrodite**. The temple was completely rebuilt when it was converted into a basilica church (circa 500 AD), so it's difficult to picture the place in which orgies to Aphrodite were held. Behind the temple is a **monumental gateway** which led to a sacred enclosure.

The **stadium** is wonderfully preserved, and most of its 20,000 seats are usable. Mow the grass in the field, post a ticket-seller, and one could hold chariot races this very afternoon.

Places to Stay

A half-km before coming to the ruins you'll spot *Chez Mestan*, a big house with an airy, shady front porch. You can stay the night here in a simple but clean room decorated with Turkish crafts and equipped with a private hand-held 'telephone' shower for 5000TL (US$7) double, less if they're not busy or if you're good at haggling. Meals on the front porch are priced about 2000TL (US$2.80). It's a simple place, run by villagers, but it's all there is here.

In the town of Karacasu, there is an *otel* on the upper floor of the bus station building where you can sleep for a mere 1200TL (US$1.68) per person, but it is only that, a place to sleep, and really for emergencies.

Places to Eat

Besides *Chez Mestan*, you can get simple meals in Karacasu at the *Afrodit Restaurant* a block up hill from the bus station, and at the *Öztekin* on the main street.

Getting There

Bus There are a few direct buses a day between Karacasu and İzmir (1200TL,

US$1.68) and Selçuk (1000TL, US$1.40). If you don't get one of these, take a bus from İzmir, Selçuk, Ortaklar, Aydın or Denizli to Nazilli, and from there a dolmuş to Geyre (GEHY-reh), a village 52 km from Nazilli and right next to the ruins. If you can't find a dolmuş to Geyre, take one to Karacasu, 45 km from Nazilli, and take a dolmuş (250TL, US$0.35), hitch a ride or hire a taxi in Karacasu (3000TL, US$4.20 one way; 5000TL, US$7 return) for the final 12½ km to Geyre and the ruins.

Nazilli (population 95,000) is the local transportation hub, with buses to and from İzmir and Selçuk about every 45 minutes or less in the morning and afternoon, but infrequent in the evening. Fares from Nazilli are 900TL (US$1.26) to Selçuk, 1200TL (US$1.68) to İzmir, 500TL (US$0.70) to Denizli, 2900TL (US$4.06) to Antalya, 3200TL (US$4.48) to Konya, 3800TL (US$5.32) to Ankara, and 5000TL (US$7) to İstanbul.

Car For those driving, Aphrodisias is 52 km from Nazilli, 101 km from Denizli and 38 km off the E24 highway.

DENİZLİ

Denizli (deh-NEEZ-lee, population 185,000, altitude 354 metres) is a prosperous and bustling agricultural city with some light industry as well. It has a number of hotels and restaurants in all price ranges, but little else of direct interest to the tourist.

Denizli's Tourism Information Office (tel (621) 13 393) is in the railway station (Denizli Gar) on the main highway only one block from the bus station, very near the traffic roundabout by which one goes to Pamukkale 19 km to the north.

Delikli Çınar Meydanı, the city's main square, is two km from the railway station and the bus station.

Places to Stay – bottom end

If all accommodation at Pamukkale is full, you can easily and pleasantly stay in

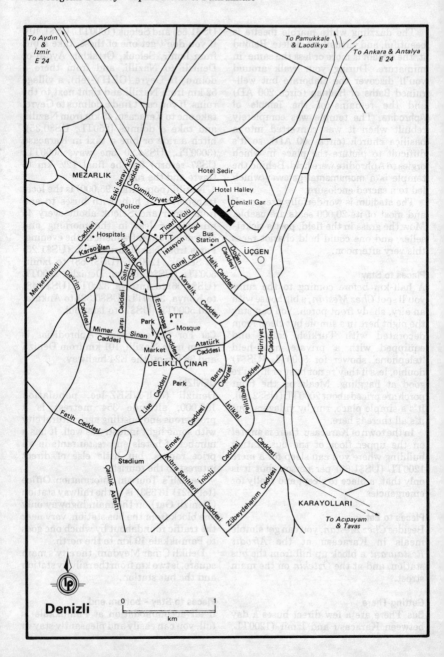

To Aydın
&
İzmir
E 24

To Pamukkale
& Laodikya

To Ankara & Antalya
E 24

MEZARLIK

Eski Saray Köy Caddesi

Cumhuriyet Cad

Police

Hotel Sedir

Hotel Halley

Denizli Gar

Ticari Yolu

PTT

İstasyon Cad

Bus
Station

ÜÇGEN

Hospitals

Karaoğlan Cad

Hastane Cad

Saltık Cad

Garaj Cad

Doğan Cad

Halk Caddesi

Merkezefendi

Devrim Caddesi

Çarşı Caddesi

Kayalık Caddesi

Enverpaşa Caddesi

Park

Mimar
Sinan
Caddesi

Market

PTT

Mosque

Atatürk
Caddesi

DELİKLİ ÇINAR

Barış Caddesi

Hürriyet Caddesi

Park

Lise Caddesi

Fatih Caddesi

Emek Caddesi

Stadium

Kıbrıs Şehitleri Caddesi

İnönü Caddesi

Pelitlibağ Caddesi

İstiklal Caddesi

KARAYOLLARI

To Acıpayam
& Tavas

Zübeydehanım Caddesi

IP

Denizli

0   1
km

Denizli. Walk up İstasyon Caddesi from the railway station and turn right onto Cumhuriyet Caddesi. One block along this street at No 13, beyond the Halley Oteli, is the *Otel Sedir* (seh-DEER) (tel (621) 16 998), an older but still very presentable hotel with a lift and rooms renting for 3300TL to 4500TL (US$4.62 to US$6.30) single, 5000TL to 6500TL (US$7 to US$9.10) double; the higher prices are for rooms with private shower. Bathless triples go for 7500TL (US$10.50); breakfast costs 600TL (US$0.84).

Places to Stay – middle

The modern, comfortable *Halley Oteli* (HAHL-ley, named for the comet) (tel (621) 19 544 or 21 843) is on İstasyon Caddesi (Denizli 20100), one very long block up the hill from the railway station. It is the nearest hotel to the bus and railway stations, however, and charges a moderate 12,200TL (US$17) single, 16,500TL (US$23.10) double with bath. An extra bed costs 5000TL (US$7).

Just a step or two off Delikli Çınar Meydanı is the *Kuyumcu Oteli* (koo-YOOM-joo) (tel (621) 13 749 or 13 750) with virtually identical prices.

Places to Eat

If you're staying in the Kuyumcu Oteli in Delikli Çınar Meydanı, there's a restaurant a few steps away. The *Sevimli Kardeşler Döner Kebap Salonu* (tel 14 700) will serve you a portion of *döner kebap*, soft drink and slice of watermelon (in season) for about 900TL (US$1.26).

Denizli's bus station has an inexpensive restaurant called the *Doyuran Kafeterya* (DOY-oo-rahn, 'filling-up'), serving *kıymalı pide* (flat bread topped with ground lamb) for 280TL (US$0.39). I recommend this because they bake the bread and make up the *pide* fresh to your order.

Getting There

Rail Three trains a day ply between Denizli and İzmir. A slow *yolcu* train departs Denizli at 5.27 am (arriving Basmane at 10.40 am); two express trains depart at 7.55 am (arriving Basmane at 2.20 pm) and 3.35 pm (arriving 9.40 pm).

There is also a daily night train hauling couchettes between Denizli and İstanbul called the Pamukkale Ekspresi, which departs Denizli at 6.05 pm and arrives at Haydarpaşa at 9.40 am the next morning.

Tickets go on sale an hour before departure. First-class fares from Denizli are 650TL (US$0.91) to Selçuk, 900TL (US$1.26) to Basmane (İzmir) and 2200TL (US$3.08) to Haydarpaşa (İstanbul). Second-class fares are 27% cheaper; student fares are 41% cheaper.

When you arrive at the railway station (Denizli Gar), walk out the front door, go out to the highway, cross over, turn left and walk one block to the Santral Garajı (bus station), where you can catch a dolmuş or bus to Pamukkale.

Bus There are frequent buses between İzmir and the Denizli Belediyesi Oto Santral Garajı, the Denizli Municipal Central Bus Station; these buses take a route via Selçuk, Ortaklar, Aydın and Nazilli.

For your onward journey, you can catch a bus in Denizli for Ankara (6½ hours, 3000TL, US$4.62), İzmir (four hours, 1500TL, US$2.31), Kuşadası (3½ hours, 1500TL, US$2.31), Konya (6½ hours, 2500TL, US$3.85) and Antalya (five hours, US$3.08); and also to Bodrum, Marmaris, Adana, Trabzon, Diyarbakır and Erzurum.

PAMUKKALE

As you approach Pamukkale from Denizli, the gleaming travertines form a white scar on the side of the ridge. As you come closer, the road winds through the midst of them up to the plateau. It's an unlikely landscape, beautiful and yet somehow unsettling. The travertines form shallow **pools** supported by stalactites of white and black, and filled with the warm, calcium-rich mineral waters.

Beneath the travertines in the valley is the village of Pamukkale Köyü, filled with little pensions charging low rates. On the plateau above are several motels lining the ridge, a municipal bathing establishment with various swimming pools and bath houses, and the ruined city of Hierapolis. An overnight stay here is recommended for several reasons. The site is beautiful, the waters deliciously warm and inviting, the accommodation good and the ruins – especially the restored theatre – worth visiting.

Today at Pamukkale you'll find a Tourism Information Office, a PTT and a First Aid station.

Things to Do & See

Swimming Virtually all the lodgings have a place where you can swim. If you want to try some different ones, you can usually do so by paying a small day-use fee. The pool at the Pamukkale Motel, with its submerged fragments of fluted marble columns, is the most charming, and a day pass only costs 400TL (US$0.56). Similarly cheap rates are charged at the Belediye Turistik Tesisleri, the municipal baths, but these, though bigger, are hardly as picturesque. Don't have a bathing suit? You can rent one for the day at the Belediye. By the way, *umumi havuzlar* (350TL, US$0.49 for two hours' swimming) are the large public pools; *özel aile havuzu* is a private family pool (1050TL, US$1.47 per hour).

Signs at the edges of the travertines forbid anyone to enter or wade in these natural pools, but everyone seems to ignore the signs.

Hierapolis After you've sampled the warm mineral waters, tour the ruins of Hierapolis. It was a cure centre founded about 190 BC by Eumenes II, king of Pergamum, which prospered under the Romans and even more under the Byzantines. It had a large Jewish community and therefore an early Christian church. Earthquakes did their worst a few times, and after the one in 1334 the people decided it was actually an unhealthy spot to live, and moved on.

The ancient city's **mineral baths**, parts of which are now the **Pamukkale Museum**, are next to the modern motels, closest to the Pamukkale Motel. The museum is open from 9 am to noon and from 1.30 to 5 pm for 400TL (US$0.56), half-price on Sunday and holidays.

Walking toward the prominent theatre, you pass a ruined **Byzantine church** and a **Temple of Apollo**. As at Didyma and Delphi, the temple had an oracle attended by eunuch priests. But the source of inspiration was a **spring** which gave off toxic vapours so the priests took it easy on the heavy breathing.

The **theatre** dates from Roman times and, appropriately, has been restored exquisitely by Italian stonecutters. The plan is to hold performances here, and you may find some scheduled.

For a health spa, it has a surprisingly large **necropolis** or cemetery, extending several km to the north.

Karahayıt Five km to the north of Pamukkale is the village of Karahayıt (KAH-rah-hah-yuht), which has no spectacular travertines but boasts healthful mineral waters nonetheless. The waters of Karahayıt leave clay-red deposits. You can get cured (and stained red) at any of several small family pensions, camping places or motels here, patronized mostly by ageing locals in search of the Fountain of Youth. The dolmuş from Denizli to Pamukkale usually continues as far as Karahayıt.

Places to Stay

On weekends you may find the pensions and motels at Pamukkale full up, and may have to seek lodgings in Denizli. But the point of a trip to Pamukkale is to sleep at Pamukkale, so plan to come during the week, or very early in the day on Friday or Saturday.

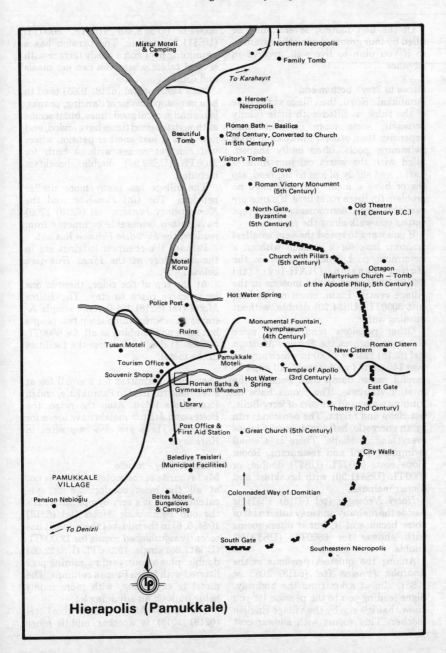

Hierapolis (Pamukkale)

Mistur Moteli & Camping

Northern Necropolis

To Karahayıt

Family Tomb

Heroes' Necropolis

Beautiful Tomb

Roman Bath – Basilica
(2nd Century, Converted to Church in 5th Century)

Visitor's Tomb

Grove

Roman Victory Monument
(5th Century)

North-Gate, Byzantine
(5th Century)

Old Theatre
(1st Century B.C.)

Motel Koru

Hot Water Spring

Church with Pillars
(5th Century)

Octagon
(Martyrium Church – Tomb of the Apostle Philip, 5th Century)

Police Post

Monumental Fountain, 'Nymphaeum'
(4th Century)

New Cistern

Roman Cistern

Tusan Moteli

Ruins

Tourism Office

Souvenir Shops

Pamukkale Moteli

Hot Water Spring

Temple of Apollo
(3rd Century)

Roman Baths & Gymnasium (Museum)

Library

East Gate

Theatre (2nd Century)

Post Office & First Aid Station

Great Church (5th Century)

Belediye Tesisleri
(Municipal Facilities)

City Walls

PAMUKKALE VILLAGE

Colonnaded Way of Domitian

Pension Nebioğlu

Beltes Moteli, Bungalows & Camping

To Denizli

South Gate

Southeastern Necropolis

Of the best motels, several may be filled by tour groups during the summer, so if you plan to live well, reserve in advance.

Places to Stay – bottom end

Pamukkale Köyü, the village at the base of the ridge, is filled with little family pensions, some more elaborate and expensive than others. Many have little swimming pools, often oddly shaped, filled with the warm calcium mineral water, and shady places to sit, read, sip tea or have a meal. You will have no problem finding a room here, if rooms are available, as pension owners will intercept you as you walk along the road.

If you want to spend the very smallest amount, look for a pension without a swimming pool. Such a place is the *Halley Pension* (HAH-ley) (tel (6218) 1204), next to the mosque in the village centre. Plain, clean rooms here cost 3000TL (US$4.20) double, without running water.

Other pensions tend to be more elaborate, such as the *Pension Mustafa* (tel (6218) 1240 or 1096) in which anyone over 140 cm (4 foot 6 inches) tall must be careful not to bump their head on the interior staircase. The rooms have no running water and are sort of jerry-built, but clean and bright. The pension is run by an energetic, hefty matron who keeps everything in shape. There is a small swimming pool and restaurant. Room alone costs 5000TL (US$7) double, or 8000TL (US$11.20) with breakfast and dinner included.

Hotel Nebioglu (tel (6218) 1031) is beside the highway and may suffer a bit of noise because of it, but it offers rooms with shower for 6600TL (US$9.24) double.

Among the quietest pensions is the *Anatolia Pension* (tel (6218) 1052 or 1085), almost a km from the highway. Signs leading you to the pension let you know that it's run by the village English teacher. Tidy rooms with shower cost

6000TL (US$8.40) single, 8000TL (US$11.20) double. The pension has a swimming pool and a shady terrace with several tables where you can get meals and drinks.

Ali's Pension (tel (6218) 1065) used to be a non-stop fun fair of dancing, pranks, jokes and general good times, but it seems as though the good times have ended, and now Ali's is just another pension where you can get rooms without bath for 7100TL (US$9.94) double, breakfast included.

The village has many more similar pensions. The *Gül Pansiyon* and the *Kervansaray Pension* (tel (6218) 1209) have gotten favourable comments from readers; the *Paradise Pension* has not.

Perhaps the cheapest lodgings are in the dormitory at the *Pizza Hut* (see below).

At the top of the ridge, there is one inexpensive place to stay. The *Beltes Motel* (tel (6218) 1014) rents simple A-frame structures which sleep two people but have no plumbing at all, for 6600TL (US$9.24) double. You use the facilities in the motel.

Camping is permitted for a small fee at sites along the road to Pamukkale, and in Pamukkale Köyü. Atop the ridge, the *Beltes* and *Mistur* motels have areas for camping. There are also campsites in Karahayıt.

Places to Stay – middle

My favourite of the motels up here is not at all the most comfortable or eye-catching, but it's very sympathetic. It's the odd *Pamukkale Motel* (tel (6218) 1024, 5, 6) in the midst of the ruins. It has recently refurbished rooms for 12,000TL (US$17.65) single, 15,000TL (US$22.06) double, plus a courtyard swimming pool littered with fallen Roman columns. The motel is expanding, with more rooms being built on an adjoining lot.

The *Mistur Motel* (MEES-toor) (tel (6218) 1013) is another middle-range choice. It is at the northern end of 'motel row', slightly away from things; its plumbing could be better; its odd beehive rooms produce unnerving echoes (you will scare yourself silly if you snore); but it's not bad for all that. Single rooms with bath are priced at 12,500TL (US$18.38), doubles at 18,000TL (US$26.47), breakfast included. They have camping facilities with some shade as well.

Places to Stay – top end

The big 130-room *Motel Koru* (kohr-OO) (tel (6218) 1020), with a big, beautiful swimming pool, good restaurant and pleasant gardens, is perhaps the nicest place here. Rates are 20,000TL (US$29.41) single, 23,400TL (US$32.76) double.

The *Tusan Moteli* (tel (6218) 1010, 1) was the first very comfortable motel here, and still commands the premium prices of 18,400TL (US$25.76) single, 23,000TL (US$32.20) double. The Tusan is off by itself a bit, away from the crowds, yet still very close to the ruins of Hierapolis.

At the *Beltes Motel* (BEHL-tess) (tel (6218) 1014, 5, 6, 7) you can have your own individual section of swimming pool right off your room, with a magnificent view of the valley. With one of the finest situations on the ridge, the Beltes can get away with renting rooms only with breakfast and dinner included, at 32,000TL to 35,000TL (US$44.80 to US$49) double; the more expensive rooms have the private pools.

Places to Eat – bottom end

As with lodgings, so with meals. The inexpensive places (and they're not all that cheap for what you get) are at the bottom of the ridge in Pamukkale Köyü. Most of the pensions serve meals, and the best deal may be to take a room with half-pension (breakfast and dinner) included.

The famous *Pizza Hut* was built to resemble one in Australia, in which its owner worked for several years. But don't expect a shiny plastic fast-food place; this one's far more Turkish village-y, with prices to match, and excellent fresh pizza. The upper deck gives you a view with your meal. I should mention that the pizza place is becoming something of a pick-up joint, though.

In the village square by the mosque is the *Büfe Karavan*, a few tables set out as an annex to a shop, where I once waited 45 minutes to get breakfast. (I never got it; some other tourists were willing to pick up where I had left off.) If you can get served, dishes like *köfte* cost 400TL (US$0.56); meats are slightly more, but beans *(taze fasulye)* and the spicy egg-and-tomato dish called *menemen* cost only 300TL (US$0.42).

Atop the ridge there is a *pideci* and a café selling soft drinks, with tables overlooking the travertines, but at resort prices somewhat higher than those in the valley.

Places to Eat – mid-range

For a special treat I'd dine at the *Motel Koru*, where a moderately priced dinner of, say, soup, mixed grill and beverage might cost 2000TL (US$2.80). But in fact all of the motels have very suitable dining rooms, at similar prices.

Getting There

Municipal buses (Denizli Belediyesi) make the half-hour trip every 45 minutes or so, more frequently on Saturday and Sunday, for 150TL (US$0.23); dolmuşes go more frequently, and faster, and charge 200TL (US$0.31). If you arrive in the evening the dolmuşes and buses may have ceased to run, and you may have to take a taxi, which will cost about 3800TL (US$5.85).

LAODİKYA

Four km north of the Üçgen, the large traffic roundabout near Denizli's bus station, is the turning (left) for the site of Laodicea (Laodikya, LAH-oh-DEEK-yah); the turning is marked by the standard yellow sign with black lettering used to indicate archaeological remains.

From the turning, the site is three km west of the Denizli-Pamukkale road.

Laodicea was a prosperous commercial city located at the junction of two major trade routes running north-south and east-west. Famed for its black wool, banking and medicines, it had a large Jewish community and a prominent Christian congregation. Cicero lived here a few years before he was put to death at the request of Marc Antony.

Though the city was a big one, as you see by the ruins spread over a large area, there is not much of interest left for the casual tourist. The **stadium** is visible, but most of the cut stones were purloined for construction of the railway. One of the **two theatres** is in better shape, with many of its upper tiers of seats remaining, though the bottom ones have collapsed. Unless you have a car or are interested in church history, you can bypass Laodicea.

The South Aegean

The south-western corner of Anatolia is mountainous and somewhat isolated. In ancient times this was the Kingdom of Caria, with its own people and customs, who later took on a veneer of Hellenic civilisation. Later, Christian anchorites (hermits) sought out the mountains and lake islands of Caria to be alone, and to escape the invading Arab armies. Ottoman sultans used the mountainous region to exile political troublemakers in Bodrum, secure in the belief that they could raise no turmoil from such a remote spot.

Today the region is not at all forbidding, though still remote enough so that development has not ruined the beautiful scenery or polluted the air.

Your goal is Bodrum, the charming seacoast town in which sleek yachts are anchored in twin bays beneath the walls of a medieval Crusader castle. Along the way are a number of ancient cities and temples worth stopping at.

SÖKE TO BODRUM

About 35 km south of Söke there is a turning, on the right, for Akköy, Miletus and Didyma, described above in the section on Kuşadası. Soon afterwards, the highway skirts the southern shore of Lake Bafa (Bafa Gölü, BAH-fah gurlew). The lake was once a gulf of the Aegean Sea. Along the shore are a few isolated little restaurants and tea houses.

Latmos

Sixteen km off the highway along a rough road are the ruins of Latmos/Heraclea, near the village of Kapıkırı. If you have a car, it's worth the detour to see the city walls, necropolis, Temple of Athena, agora, bouleterion and theatre. There's also a shrine thought to be dedicated to Endymion, the legendary shepherd-boy. As the story goes, Endymion was asleep on Mt Latmos (Beşparmak Dağı, 1500 metres) when Selene, the moon goddess, fell in love with him. She gave him dreams so wonderful that Endymion begged Zeus to allow him to sleep forever.

This area, ringed by mountains, was one of refuge for Christian hermits during the Arab invasions of the 700s AD. Ruins of monasteries can be seen here and there, including one on a little island in the lake.

Euromos

About 15 km past the lake, keep your eyes open for the extremely picturesque **Temple of Euromos**, on the left-hand side of the road. The Corinthian colonnades set in green olive groves seem too good to be true, like a Hollywood idea for a classical setting. Once there was a town here, but now only the temple remains.

There are no facilities whatsoever at Euromos. The temple is open to visit for free. About 12 km past the temple is Milâs, but before it, the road to Labranda.

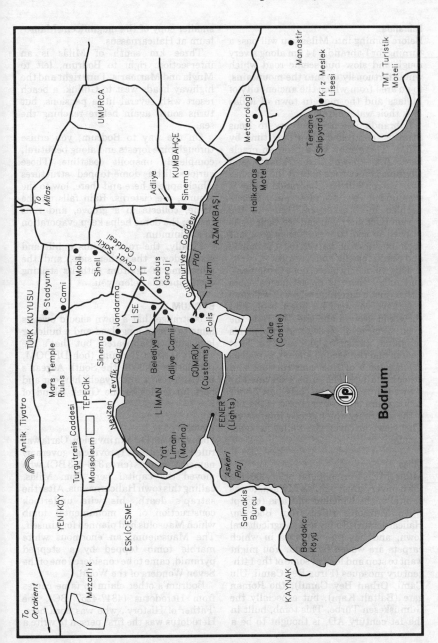

Labranda

Before coming into Milâs you will pass a turning for Labranda, 14 km along a very rough and slow but scenic road which winds tortuously up into the mountains, to an area from which the ancient city of Mylasa and the modern town of Milâs took their water supplies.

Labranda was a sanctuary to Zeus Stratius, controlled for a long time by Milâs. There may have been an oracle here. It's known that festivals and Olympic games were held at the site. Set into a steep hillside, Labranda today is surrounded by fragrant pine forests peopled by bee-keepers. Late in the season (October) you can see their tents pitched in cool groves as they go about their business of harvesting the honey and rendering the honeycombs.

This was a holy place, not a settlement, and today there is no settlement here either, just a caretaker who will welcome you, have you sign his guest book, and show you around the site. There is the great Temple of Zeus, and two men's religious gathering-places, the **First Andron** and the **Second Andron**, as well as a large **tomb** of fine construction, and other buildings. The ruins, excavated by a Swedish team in the early part of our century, are interesting, but it is the site of the sanctuary which is most impressive. The view out over the valley is spectacular.

Milâs

Milâs (MEE-lahs, population 35,000) is a town of very great age. As Mylasa, it was capital of the Kingdom of Caria (except when Mausolus ruled from Bodrum/Halicarnassus). Today it is an agricultural town, and has many homes in which carpets are woven by hand. You might want to stop and look at some of the 14th-century mosques (Firuz Bey Camii, Ulu Cami, Orhan Bey Camii), the Roman gate (Baltalı Kapı), but especially the Gümüşkesen Türbe. This tomb, built in the 1st century AD, is thought to be a smaller copy of the magnificent Mausoleum at Halicarnassus.

Three km south of Milâs is an intersection: right to Bodrum, left to Muğla and Marmaris. Turn right and the highway heads west to Güllük, a beach resort with several little pensions, but turns south again before reaching the sea.

On the way to Bodrum, you cruise through pine forests and along beautiful, completely unspoilt coastline. Those curious little dome-topped structures which appear here and there, low to the ground, are cisterns. Rain falls on the dome, collects in a groove, and runs inside; the dome helps keep evaporation to a minimum.

Finally, the road climbs a hill and starts down the other side, and the panorama of Bodrum with its striking castle spreads before you.

BODRUM

It is strange that a town should owe its fame to a man long dead and a building long since disappeared, but that's the way it is with Bodrum (boh-DROOM, population 14,000), the South Aegean's prettiest resort town, yacht harbour and port for ferries to the Greek island of Kos.

History

Following the Persian invasion, Caria was ruled by a satrap (provincial governor) named Mausolus (circa 376-353 BC), who moved the capital here from Milâs, calling this town Halicarnassus. After the satrap's death, his wife undertook construction of a monumental tomb which Mausolus had planned for himself. The Mausoleum, an enormous white marble tomb topped by a stepped pyramid, came to be considered one of the Seven Wonders of the World.

Bodrum's other claim to fame comes from Herodotus (484?-425? BC), the 'Father of History', who was born here. Herodotus was the first person to write a

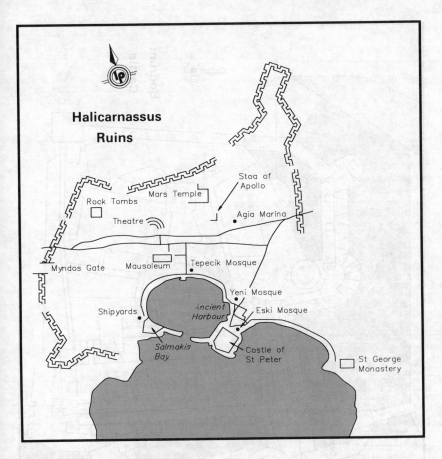

Halicarnassus Ruins

Rock Tombs
Mars Temple
Stoa of Apollo
Theatre
Agia Marina
Myndos Gate
Mausoleum
Tepecik Mosque
Yeni Mosque
Ancient Harbour
Eski Mosque
Shipyards
Salmakis Bay
Castle of St Peter
St George Monastery

comprehensive 'world history', and all other histories in our civilisation owe him a debt.

Orientation
The bus station is only a block inland from the water, and only three blocks from the castle. Between the bus station and the castle is the market district. Walk from the bus station toward the castle, and you arrive quickly at the Adliye Camii (AHD-lee-yeh jah-mee, Court-house Mosque). Turn right, and you'll be heading west on Neyzen Tevfik Caddesi

toward the Yat Limanı (Yacht Marina); turn left and you will go through a section of market, then pass dozens of hotels and pensions in all price ranges. The array of lodgings continues all the way around the bay, and then along the shore of another bay farther on.

Information
The Tourism Information Office (tel (6141) 1091) is in 12 (Oniki) Eylül Meydanı, the plaza beneath the castle walls, with yachts moored alongside (most local people call the plaza İskele

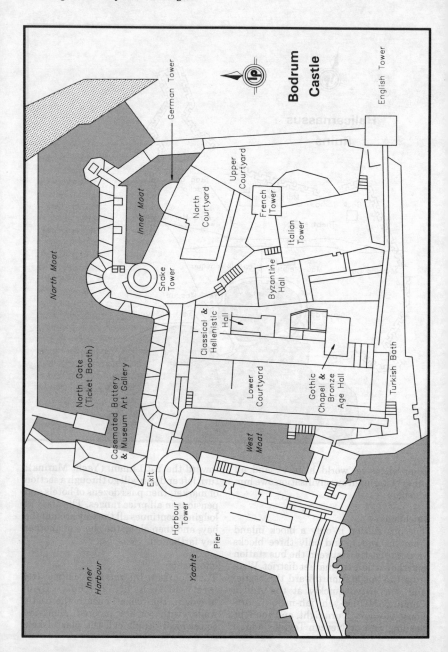

Bodrum Castle

English Tower

German Tower

Inner Moat

North Moat

North Courtyard

Upper Courtyard

French Tower

Italian Tower

Byzantine Hall

Snake Tower

Classical & Hellenistic Hall

North Gate (Ticket Booth)

Casemated Battery & Museum Art Gallery

Lower Courtyard

Gothic Chapel & Bronze Age Hall

Turkish Bath

Exit

West Moat

Harbour Tower

Pier

Yachts

Inner Harbour

Meydanı, ees-KEHL-eh). Summer hours are Monday through Friday 8 am to 8 pm, Saturday 9 to noon and 3.30 to 7.30 pm, closed Sunday.

The Bodrum Festival is held annually during the first week in September. Lodgings may be crowded then.

Things to See

Herodotus and the Mausoleum are long gone, but Bodrum has many other attractions. Most striking is the fairytale Crusaders' castle in the middle of town, guarding twin bays now crowded with yachts. Palm-lined streets ring the bays, and white sugar-cube houses are scattered on the hillside. Yachting, boating, swimming, snorkelling and scuba diving are prime Bodrum activities. So is just hanging out and enjoying life. Bodrum's economy is now dedicated to tourism, though in winter there is a bounteous citrus crop (especially tangerines), and you will still see a few sponge fishermen's boats. For diversion, you can take boat or jeep trips to nearby secluded beaches and villages, or over to the Greek island of Kos.

Castle of St Peter The castle, of course, is first on anyone's list. When Tamerlane invaded Anatolia in 1402, the Knights Hospitaller of St John of Rhodes took the opportunity to capture Bodrum. They built the Castle of St Peter, and it defended Bodrum all the way through WW I. It is now Bodrum's Museum of Underwater Archaeology and open-air theatre. Hours are 8.30 am to noon and 3 to 7 pm every day from June through mid-September; 8 am to noon and 1 to 5 pm in winter. Admission costs 400TL (US$0.56).

Perhaps the best plan is to head straight for the French Tower, the castle's highest point. After enjoying the view, descend through the museum exhibit rooms.

As you find your way up into the castle, you'll pass several coats-of-arms carved in marble and mounted in the walls. Many of the stones in these walls came from the ruined Mausoleum. As always, the question which the knights put to themselves was this: with all this lovely cut stone from some old fellow's tomb, why bother to cut our own?

Many of the museum's exhibits are the result of underwater archaeology. Numerous ancient coastal cargo ships have been found sunk off Bodrum, and divers have recovered many artefacts. Construction is underway on an exhibit which will include an ancient ship raised from the bottom of the Aegean off Bodrum.

Within the French Tower is the Sub-Mycenaean Archaic Age Hall, with the very oldest finds. The Italian Tower holds the Hellenistic Hall and the Classical Hall. Then, in descending order, you come to the Medieval Hall, the Hall of Coins and Jewellery, a collection of tombstones (outdoors), and the Snake Tower with a collection of ancient amphorae. Finally, there is a Bronze Age Hall.

Mausoleum Though archaeological excavations now mark the spot where this Wonder of the World once stood, you might like to pay a visit. It's located inland from Neyzen Tevfik Caddesi. Turn inland near the little white mosque on the shore, then left onto the road to Turgut Reis and Gümüşlük.

Touring the Peninsula The Bodrum peninsula has several little towns and villages which you can visit. Some have fragments of ancient ruins, others have small beaches. There are no really splendid beaches easily accessible on the peninsula, but there are at least several serviceable ones.

The beach at **Gümbet**, backed by lots of hotels and pensions, with more being built, is only a 10-minute ride from town; or you can walk. It has numerous restaurants to provide sustenance.

You can ride in a dolmuş to **Turgut Reis,**

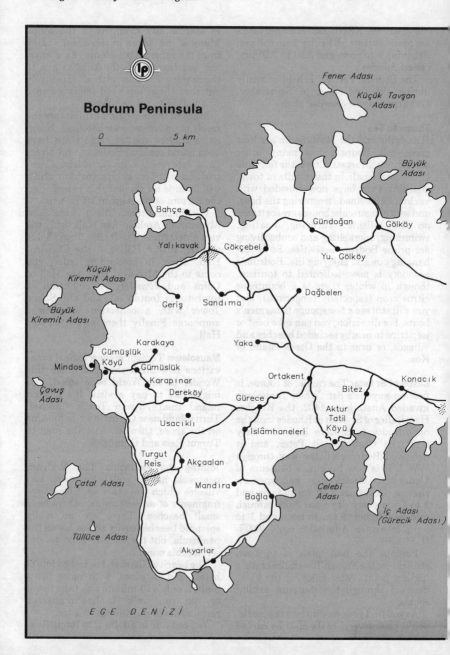

EGE DENİZİ

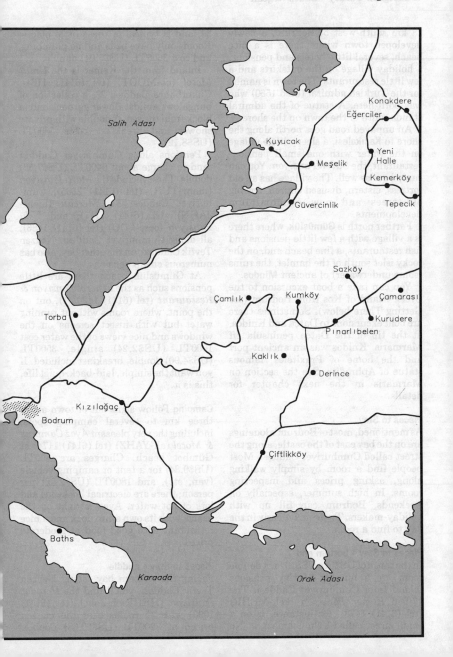

18 km south-west of Bodrum, a newly developed town where there is a nice beach, several little hotels and pensions, a holiday village on the outskirts and a few little restaurants. The town is named for the Turkish admiral (died 1560) who was born here. A statue of the admiral stands south of the town on the shore.

An unpaved road goes north along the shore to **Kadıkalesi**, a sleepy little village on the water with one small pension-restaurant, the *Süzen Pansiyon*. You can camp here as well. The village has an old fortress, cistern, disused church, few big old trees and new condominium developments.

Farther north is **Gümüşlük**, where there is a village with a few little pensions and fish restaurants, a fine beach and, on the rocky islet south of the hamlet, the ruins (some underwater) of ancient **Mindos**.

You can take a boat excursion to the Greek island of Kos from Bodrum (see Getting There below). Sometimes there are boat excursions to Datça and Knidos, at the tip of the Datça peninsula off Marmaris. Knidos was an ancient port and the home of Praxiteles' famous statue of Aphrodite. See the section on Marmaris in the next chapter for details.

Places to Stay

As mentioned, most of Bodrum's lodgings are on the bay east of the castle, along the street called Cumhuriyet Caddesi. Most people find a room by simply walking along, asking prices and inspecting rooms. In high summer, especially on weekends, Bodrum can fill up with holiday-makers. Try to arrive early in the day to find a room.

Places to Stay – bottom end

In the range of US$5 to US$10 for a double room are a number of tiny pensions inland from Cumhuriyet Caddesi. The 17-bed *Kemer Pansiyon* (keh-MEHR) (tel (6141) 1473), for instance, is on a small street called Uslu Çıkmazı, at No

30, and is typical of these little places. Rooms only have beds and no plumbing, and cost 3600TL (US$5.04) double.

Inland from the Kemer is the *Umut Motel* (oo-MOOT) (tel (6141) 1164), Çukurbahçe Caddesi 23, a collection of bungalows amidst flower gardens only a block from the sea. A double with private shower and breakfast costs 5800TL (US$8.12).

Pensions along Cumhuriyet Caddesi tend to charge about 5400TL (US$7.56) double. These include the *Martı Pansiyon* (mahr-TUH) (tel (6141) 2605), Cumhuriyet Caddesi 84; *Mercan* (mehr-JAHN) (tel (6141) 1111); and *Uslu Pansiyon* (ooss-LOO) (tel (6141) 1486), all along Cumhuriyet Caddesi. Neyzen Tevfik Caddesi, on the other bay, also has numerous cheap pensions.

At Gümüşlük beach there are little pensions such as the *Fenerci Pansiyon & Restaurant* (tel (6141) 1420/51), out on the point, where rooms without running water but with insect screens on the windows and nice views of the water cost 1600TL (US$2.24) single, 3500TL (US$4.90) double, breakfast included. If you want the simple, laid-back, quiet life, this is it.

Camping Follow signs out of town about three km to several camping spots, including the very pleasant *Ayaz Camping & Motel* (ah-YAHZ) (tel (6141) 1174) at Gümbet beach. Charges are 600TL (US$0.84) for a tent or camping vehicle (van, etc), and 1800TL (US$2.52) per person; there are electrical hook-ups and lots of hot water. Ayaz is right on the beach, with its own swim dock and a nice restaurant with good food at moderate prices.

Places to Stay – middle

Facing the western bay, along Neyzen Tevfik Caddesi, you'll find the *Herodot Pansiyon* (HEHR-oh-doht) (tel (6141) 1093) with 15 rooms near the marina priced at 7200TL (US$10.08) double:

quiet and tidy, but often full up. Also on Neyzen Tevfik Caddesi, at No 164/1, is *Seçkin Konaklar* (sech-KEEN koh-nahk-lahr) (tel (6141) 1351) with four multi-bed rooms priced at 11,000TL (US$15.40) double, and also 12 apartments capable of housing four to six people, priced about 3500TL to 4000TL (US$4.90 to US$5.60) per person; this is a good choice for families or small groups.

Along Cumhuriyet Caddesi you'll see the *Artemis Pansiyon* (AHR-teh-mees) (tel (6141) 2530), a 22-room place facing the bay and charging 9600TL (US$13.44) double, breakfast included.

The *Baraz Oteli* (bah-RAHZ) (tel 57, 714), Cumhuriyet Caddesi 58, is normal and standard, with 24 modern, clean doubles priced at 12,500TL (US$17.50). Get one with a sea view.

Walk all the way out Cumhuriyet Caddesi to the area called Kumbahçe (KOOM-bahh-cheh) to find the *Feslegen Pansiyon* (fehs-leh-EHN) (tel (6141) 2910) at Papatya Sokak 18/1; any one of the 13 double rooms costs 9500TL (US$13.30).

At the *Murat Villa* (moo-RAHT) (tel (6141) 1710), Koyular Sokak 3 off Cumhuriyet Caddesi, one of the 14 rooms costs only 8800TL (US$12.32); same price at the *Evin Pansiyon* (eh-VEEN), tel (6141) 1312), Ortanca Sokak 7.

Out at Gümbet beach, the *Ayaz Camping & Motel* (tel (6141) 1174) has rooms for rent as well as camping places. Double rooms are priced at 9800TL (US$13.72) per person, in a room with private shower, breakfast and dinner included.

Also here at Gümbet, atop the hill and commanding fantastic views, is the *Esentepe Motel* (eh-SEHN-teh-peh) (tel (6141) 2045, 6) where a new, modern double with shower costs 9000TL (US$12.60). Next door, the *Kıvanç Motel* (kuh-VAHNCH) (tel (6141) 2043, 4) has similar accommodation, prices and fantastic views.

Places to Stay - top end

Top of the line in Bodrum is a motel on the outskirts, in the section named Akçabük, two km to the east of the centre. It's the *TMT Motel* (TEH-meh-TEH) (tel (6141) 1423 or 1440), a large place (171 rooms) set in nice gardens by the beach, with its own swimming pools and tennis courts. Modern rooms with sea views cost 25,500TL (US$35.70) double, breakfast and dinner included.

The chic-est place in Bodrum may or may not be for you: it's the *Halikarnas Motel* (ha-lee-kahr-NAHS) (tel (6141) 1073), well around the eastern bay at Cumhuriyet Caddesi, Kumbahçe Mahallesi. It is 'stylish', with a disco-club for the glitter set that booms and thrums till all hours. The mod customers pay 20,000TL to 30,000TL (US$28 to US$42) for one of the 28 double rooms.

Places to Eat

You will have no trouble finding places to eat, but you may encounter a good deal of mediocre food. Many of the restaurants are seasonal, with part-time staff. In general, these are the pseudo-fancy ones, tarted up with pretentious decoration; avoid them. The centre of town has the best places; the further east along Cumhuriyet Caddesi you go, the more tawdry the restaurants become.

Places to Eat - bottom end

For cheaper food, look for the little eateries in the grid of market streets. The *Kardeşler* (kahr-desh-LEHR) and the *Yıldız* (yuhl-DUHZ), near the Türkiye İş Bankası have ready food, outdoor tables, usually a television set and low prices. The *Ender Pastanesi* (ehn-DEHR pahs-tah-neh-see) serves breakfast, and pastries the rest of the day.

For very cheap eats, buy a *dönerli sandviç* (dur-nehr-LEE sahn-dveech, sandwich with roast lamb). You may also want to try the ice cream. The filling of the cone is a great show, done with a long-handled paddle.

Places to Eat – mid-range

Bodrum's most prominent restaurants are those by the sea in the centre of the town, not far from the castle. These are also the more expensive ones. For a good fish dinner with wine and a sea view, at the *Körfez Restaurant* (kewr-FEHZ) for example, you might pay 4000TL to 5500TL (US$5.60 to US$7.70) per person. One of the best fish to try is *trança* (TRAHN-chah), a tuna of about 10 kg, cut into chunks and grilled over charcoal. Ask for *trança şiş* (SHEESH). Always ask the price of fish, and choose those in season. When in doubt, ask *Mevsimli mi?* (mehv-seem-LEE mee, Is it in season?).

Out along the western bay is the *Mauzolos Restaurant*, where two of us had two *meze* (appetizer) plates, a perfectly grilled fish, salad, bottle of wine and after-dinner coffee for 13,000TL (US$18.20), tip included.

Getting There

Bodrum is 270 km (four hours) south of İzmir, 150 km south of Kuşadası along a good, fast road through lovely country.

There is no rail service south of Söke. The nearest airports to Bodrum are at İzmir and Dalaman (near Fethiye), though Muğla may get an airport soon.

Bus Three companies operate buses along the route from İzmir: Koç, Karadeveci and Pamukkale. Catch a bus in İzmir, Selçuk, Söke or Milâs. There are frequent buses between Bodrum and İzmir (four hours), Ankara (14 hours) and İstanbul (15 hours).

The Pamukkale company operate two minibuses daily in each direction on the route Bodrum-Muğla-Marmaris; it's a three-hour trip.

Boats to Kos Boats run in the morning on Monday, Wednesday and Friday in summer, and on other days if demand warrants. Make reservations and buy tickets (US$21 for the single trip over) at least a day in advance at the Denizyolları Acentalığı (deh-NEEZ-yoh-lahr-uh ah-jehn-tah-luh, Maritime Lines Agency) in the plaza just beneath the castle walls, by the dock.

Mediterranean Turkey

The southern coast of Turkey is delightful: a succession of scenic roads, sympathetic villages and picturesque ancient ruins. Only a few decades ago one had to explore parts of this coast with a rugged vehicle, pack animal or boat. New highway construction has changed all that, and now you can ride easily from Marmaris, where the Aegean meets the Mediterranean, to Antakya on the Syrian border, enjoying the countryside rather than battling it.

For all its natural beauty, the coast is unspoilt. It looks as though the government will attempt to keep it that way, limiting touristic development to holiday village enclaves. For the moment, congratulate yourself on being one of the early visitors to this pristine area. In years to come, you'll be able to boast that you knew it before it was overrun.

The most idyllic way to explore the coast is by private yacht – not as outrageous as it sounds. While yachts chartered in the Greek islands may charge over US$100 per person per day, you can charter a beautiful wooden yacht in Turkey for as little as US$25 to US$50 per person per day, meals included. The meals, made by the crew, will include fish and octopus pulled fresh from the blue waters, and herbs gathered along the shore. There's more information on yacht chartering in the Marmaris section.

You can spend as much or as little time as you like on the coast. Towns such as Marmaris, Kalkan, Kaş, Side and Alanya are perfect for all-summer idylls lasting from spring to autumn, days in which you swim, sun, dine on seafood, dance and cruise to islands and secluded coves. The Greek island of Rhodes is close enough for a day trip from Marmaris. Those without a lot of time can see the coast from Marmaris as far as Alanya pretty well in a week. In this chapter I'll describe the towns and sights along the coast, from west to east.

Getting There

Air The airport at Dalaman near Fethiye is new and used mostly for charter flights from abroad, though Turkish Airlines does operate daily flights linking Dalaman with İstanbul and Ankara in summer. For detailed information on land transport from Dalaman to other points on the Mediterranean coast, see below under Dalaman.

Otherwise, the south coast's airports are at Antalya and Adana. For details, see the sections under either town.

Rail There is no rail service south of Söke, Denizli and Isparta; trains do run from Ankara to Adana and Mersin, however. See the sections on Ankara and Adana for details.

Bus Your coastal explorations will be by bus, car or hired yacht. With the yacht and car you can make progress as you like. With the bus you must be aware that traffic is sparse along the coast. There may be only a few buses a day between points. As with most parts of Turkey, service dwindles and disappears in late afternoon or early evening, so do your travelling early in the day, and relax in the evening. With fewer buses it's all the more important to buy your reserved-seat tickets a day or so in advance.

From Bodrum The trip from Bodrum takes you back to Milâs, then up into the mountains through the towns of Yatağan and Muğla. The land is rich and heavily cultivated, with vast fields of sunflowers and frequent colonies of beehives. Thirty km from Marmaris the road descends by switchbacks into a fertile valley. It then turns right and crosses the valley floor through a magnificent double lane of great eucalyptus trees over two km in length. At the other side, the road narrows and ascends into the hills again before coming down into Marmaris.

MARMARİS

The once-quaint fishing village called Marmaris (MAHR-mahr-ees, population 10,000) has in recent years become a busy holiday resort. This is partly due to the boat connection with Rhodes; partly to local enthusiasm, because it's now the 'in' place for Turkey's rich and famous, who are followed in their choice of holiday places by *hoi polloi*.

Why Turkey's movie stars and magnates chose Marmaris is something of a mystery. It is not as cosmopolitan as Kuşadası, it does not have a fine castle as at Bodrum, nor does it have impressive ruins as at Side. The choice may have something to do with the yachting trade, as Marmaris has a fine little marina in its centre and is one of Turkey's busiest yacht chartering ports. And Marmaris does have two luxurious 'holiday village' resorts.

Besides the throngs of middle-class locals and the occasional newsworthy Turk, the streets and shores of Marmaris host a varied collection of international tourists and yachtsmen, from Saudi princes to university students. There are also day-trippers from Rhodes who, ignoring the dire warnings of Greeks that Turkey is expensive, unfriendly and dangerous, come over to find just the opposite. But Marmaris is also local village people – some farmers and fishermen, others waiters and shopkeepers. It is not a flashy resort. If it's idyllic little fishing towns you're looking for, take only a brief look at Marmaris, then rush on to Datça (see below).

Orientation

Except for its shoreline development, Marmaris is a small village, and a few minutes' stroll will show you the layout.

The very heart of town is the little plaza next to the ferry boat dock, where you'll find the customs house, tourism office, currency exchange booths, many small hotels and the market district. The Türkiye Halk Bankası exchange booth at the wharf is usually open on summer evenings and weekends when other banking facilities are closed.

The waterfront road is officially named Atatürk Caddesi, though most locals refer to it as Kordon Caddesi. A landmark here is the equestrian statue of Atatürk on Kordon Caddesi. Plaques on the plinth bear the sayings *Türk Ögün Çalış Güven* (Turk! Be Proud. Work. Trust.) and *Ne Mutlu Türküm Diyene* (What joy to him who says, 'I am a Turk'). Both sayings were meant to dispel the Ottoman inferiority complex.

Information

The Tourism Information Office (tel (6121) 1035) is at İskele Meydanı 39 by the yacht harbour, the wharf for boats to Greece and the market – in short, right at the centre. Though it nominally closes at 6.30 pm, it often stays open later during the summer months.

Things to See

Marmaris has a little ruined **fortress**, not at all prominent, on the hill just above the yacht harbour, but it holds little to see.

Do look at the **menzilhane**, an Ottoman 'pony express' way-station which now serves as a shopping centre for souvenirs, and has been somewhat ruined by the commercialism. It's just behind the tourism office. Look for the Ottoman Turkish inscription in Arabic letters, on a plaque on the doorway, which records that the *menzilhane* was built by Sultan Süleyman the Magnificent in 1545.

Daytime occupations in Marmaris usually have to do with beaches and boats. The better beaches are near the fancy hotels, and still others can be reached by boat from near the tourism office. See below about excursion boats.

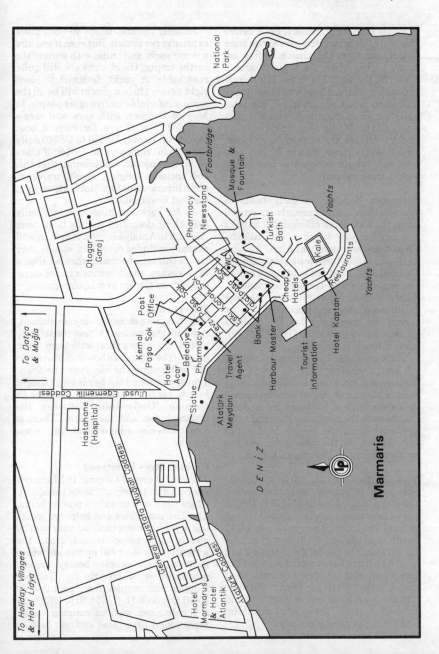

Marmaris

DENİZ

To Datca
& Muğla

To Holiday Villages
& Hotel Lidya

National
Park

Footbridge

Mosque &
Fountain

Turkish
Bath

Kale

Yachts

Yachts

Restaurants

Hotel Kaptan

Cheap
Hotels

Tourist
Information

Harbour Master

Bank

Travel
Agent

Atatürk
Meydanı

Statue

Belediye

Pharmacy

Kemal
Paşa Sok

Post
Office

Hotel
Acar

Pharmacy

Newsstand

YKM

Otogar
Garaj

Hastahane
(Hospital)

Ulusal Egemenlik Caddesi

General Mustafa Muğlalı Caddesi

Atatürk Caddesi

Hotel
Marmarus
& Hotel
Atlantik Caddesi

If you shop for souvenirs, do it before the boats full of day-trippers arrive from Rhodes, or after they leave. Prices are much higher when the trippers are in town. By the way, Marmaris is a honey-producing centre. Those who know honey will want to sample several of the local varieties, most famous of which is *çam balı* (CHAHM bah-luh, pine-scented honey). Others are *akasya balı* (locust tree flower), *çiçek* (flower honey) and *oğul balı* (virgin honey, the first honey from a fresh swarm).

Excursions Besides the daily boats to Rhodes, there are numerous boats ranged along the waterfront offering day tours of the harbour, its beaches and islands. Departures are usually at 9 am. About a half-hour before then, walk along Kordon Caddesi, check out the boats, and talk to the captains about the *gezi* (excursion): where it goes, what it costs, whether lunch is included, and if so, what's on the menu. An average price for a day's pleasure outing is about 1000TL (US$1.40), more if lunch is included.

There are longer, more serious excursions by boat, including trips to Datça and Knidos, well out along the hilly peninsula west of Marmaris. Ask at a travel agency or haggle with a boatman for a day's excursion to the coves, beaches and ruins scattered along the peninsula. For full information on the peninsula, see the sections below on Datça and Knidos.

Yacht Charters You can charter a comfortable yacht in Turkey, and out of season the cost can be as low as US$25 to US$50 per person daily, meals included (booze extra). The larger the yacht (up to 12 berths) and the earlier (in spring) or later (in autumn) the cruise, the cheaper it will be. An 11-berth yacht rented for a week in late April, without crew or meals, need cost a mere US$18 per person per day. The same yacht in July or August would be twice as much. If you want a captain, add US$5 per person per day.

Smaller boats tend to be more expensive per person. But even if you hire a larger yacht and cruise with some of the berths empty, the charges are still quite reasonable. A yacht designed to sleep eight people (10 in a pinch) will be all the more comfortable for five or six people. In May or October, with crew and meals included, the charge for such a boat would still be only US$50 to US$60 daily per person, compared to US$40 if there were eight people. Considering that this cost includes lodging, meals, transport and a luxurious, unforgettable experience, the cost is unbeatable.

As for yachting itineraries, virtually everything described in this book from Bodrum to Antalya is open to you, as well as many secluded coves and islands. Any trip in this area becomes what is called a Blue Voyage, which means a cruise along the ancient Carian and Lycian coasts.

Places to Stay
The cheapest places are very convenient, right in the centre. A few moderately priced hotels are a short walk from town. Most of the expensive hotels in Marmaris are well around the bay from the town. Transport around the bay is easy though: in summer the municipality operates an open-air 'trailer-train' between the distant hotels and the centre. There is sometimes also a launch running across the bay.

Places to Stay – bottom end
The very cheapest lodgings in Marmaris are called *ev pansiyon* (home pensions), where you rent a room in a private home. The Tourism Office can help you locate one of these, or you can find your own by merely proceeding inland from the waterfront for 50 or 100 metres anywhere in town. This simple, homey accommodation is where thrifty Turkish families and couples stay, paying only 3000TL to 5000TL (US$4.20 to US$7) for a double room without running water. Some rooms have three and four beds.

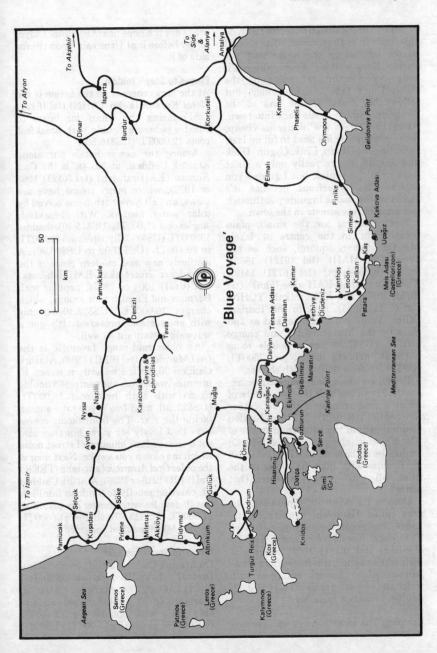

If the rooming situation seems tight, do this: walk from the tourism office around to the left, along the water past the yachts. Keep walking. Eventually you'll see a wooden footbridge heading off to the right. Don't take the footbridge, but follow the street, at the end of the footbridge, which heads back into town. Along this street are numerous cheap, quiet pensions which tend to fill up last, including the *Okşan, Ufuk, Uygun, Dilek* and *Işıksal*. You're really only a short walk from the centre, but I guided you around the waterfront because it's virtually impossible to guide you through the maze of tiny streets in the town.

Next cheapest are the small, plain hotels right in the centre at İskele Meydanı (wharf square), such as the *Sema* (seh-MAH) (tel (6121) 1595); *İmbat* (EEM-baht) (tel (6121) 1413); *Karaaslan* (kah-RAH-ahss-lahn) (tel (6121) 1867); and *Kalyon* (kahl-YOHN) (tel (6121) 1085), next to the Tourism Office. These hotels are ranked as 2nd class by the Municipality, and charge 5500TL (US$7.70) for a double room without private bath, or 7500TL (US$10.50) for a double with shower.

Better, and marginally more expensive, are the Municipality's 1st-class hotels, of which a good example is the *Hotel Acar* (ah-JAHR) (tel (6121) 1117) on Kordon Caddesi behind the equestrian statue of Atatürk, which charges 7000TL (US$9.80) for doubles at the back, 8000TL (US$11.20) for doubles with little balconies at the front, all with private showers (hot water).

Despite its expensive reputation, the area called Uzunyalı, near the Hotel Lidya, has some inexpensive pensions. The *Motel Küçükevler* (kew-CHEWK-ehv-lehr) (tel (6121) 1856) offers nice little whitewashed, tile-roofed bungalows surrounded by flowers, equipped with toilet and shower, for 6800TL (US$9.52) double, breakfast included.

Camping The most convenient camping

areas are the ones near the Hotel Lidya, either before it at Uzunyalı, or on the far side of it.

Places to Stay – middle
At the very centre of all the action is the *Hotel Kaptan* (kahp-TAHN) (tel (6121) 1251) facing the wharf for boats to Rhodes, where a double with breakfast costs 12,000TL (US$16.80).

Among the newer hotels out along Atatürk Caddesi, at No 48, is the *Otel Karaca* (KAH-rah-jah) (tel (6121) 1663 or 1992), where many rooms have sea views, and all have bathrooms served by solar water heaters. With breakfast, singles cost 11,000TL (US$15.40), doubles 15,400TL (US$21.56); triples are 19,300TL to 26,400TL (US$27.02 to US$36.96). A similarly new and modern place is the *Karadeniz Hotel* (kah-RAH-deh-neez) (tel (6121) 1064 or 2837), popular with German and Finnish tour groups, which charges 16,000TL (US$22.40) double with shower and breakfast. It's got a sidewalk restaurant as well.

An older mid-range favourite is the *Otel Marmaris* (tel (6121) 1308), Atatürk Caddesi 30, on the waterfront street, 15 minutes' walk from the centre; 63 double rooms with bath here cost 18,000TL (US$25.20), a bit less if you take a room facing the rear. The front-facing rooms have that lovely sea view, but they also get a tremendous amount of street noise which may keep you awake. Next door is the older *Otel Atlantik* (aht-lahn-TEEK) (tel (6121) 1218 or 1236), Atatürk Caddesi 34, catering mostly to Turkish families; the 40 doubles with shower are priced at 17,000TL (US$23.80), singles at 8500TL (US$11.90), breakfast included.

Places to Stay – top end
On Atatürk Caddesi is the new and shiny *Otel 47* (oh-TEHL kirk-yeh-DEE) (tel (6121) 1700 or 2730), Atatürk Caddesi 10, Marmaris 48700, a polished and comfortable place with doubles for 23,400TL (US$32.76), singles for 15,000TL (US$21),

breakfast included. Nearby and cheaper is the *Otel Yavuz* (yah-VOOZ) (tel (6121) 2937, 8, P K 125), with doubles-cum-bath for 20,000TL (US$28), breakfast included. The Yavuz is like many of its neighbours, but can also boast a tiny rooftop swimming pool.

Other hotels are out along the western shores of the bay. The grand dame here is the *Hotel Lidya* (LEED-yah) (tel (6121) 2940, 1, 2), a comfortable if not posh place of 220 rooms around the bay from the town in Uzunyalı. Lodgings include rooms looking onto the sea or the gardens, suites, motel-style rooms and apartments. Prices range from 18,000TL to 23,000TL (US$25.20 to US$32.20) double for rooms, twice as much for an apartment, from mid-June through mid-September. Reductions off-season are about 35%.

Two 'holiday villages' charge more than the Lidya. The *Turban Marmaris Tatil Köyü* (TOOR-bahn) (tel (6121) 1843), a 250-room place funded by the government, charges only slightly more, but requires that you take breakfast and dinner with your room. The posh *Martı Tatil Köyü* (mahr-TUH) (tel (6121) 1930) is considerably more expensive, its 213 rooms costing 30,000TL (US$42) double.

Places to Eat - bottom end

As always, for less expensive fare head into the market area and look for a *pideci*. Besides these Turkish pizza places there are small and cheap restaurants. The *Ayyıldız Lokantası* (AHY-yuhl-duhz) (tel 2158) has tables set outside beneath the market awnings. A meal of *döner kebap, bulgur pilav* (cracked wheat pilaf), salad and drink costs 1100TL (US$1.54). Across the street from the Ayyıldız is the similar *Emre*. The *Şadırvan* (SHAH-duhr-vahn) on İsmet Paşa Sokak is even cheaper and very popular.

If you must eat out on the waterfront, look for a *pideci* or restaurant which is full of Turks, as it will have the lower prices. The cheapest places tend to be those located between the Tourism Office and the Acar Pide restaurant.

Places to Eat - mid-range

Downtown restaurants near the yacht harbour have pleasant outdoor dining areas and moderate prices. The *Birtat* (BEER-taht, 'one taste') (tel 1076) is well established, with a good reputation, but in fact the best strategy is to stroll along the waterfront and look for a restaurant which is busy and popular.

Places to Eat - top end

Expensive meals are those served in the top hotels and holiday villages, and even these are not outrageous in price for what you get. In any case, the food will be similar to that in moderately priced places. What you pay extra for is atmosphere, location, live music, floor shows, exotic liquor, etc.

Getting There

Marmaris is somewhat remote, but that's part of its charm. Transport by bus is not inconvenient, in any case.

Air The airport at Dalaman is about 100 km from Marmaris. Buses from the municipality of Marmaris (Marmaris Belediyesi) are usually on hand to transport passengers directly to and from Marmaris for 1000TL (US$1.40) per person. A taxi from the airport to Marmaris will charge about 17,000TL (US$23.80). See the section on Dalaman for more details.

Bus As of this writing, Marmaris has no Otogar. Bus company ticket offices are concentrated on the waterfront street near the equestrian statue of Atatürk. In the summer months bus traffic is furiously active, with dozens of the huge growling machines rolling in and out of town all day long; but in winter service drops off to that required by a small farming town.

Direct buses run 30 times daily from

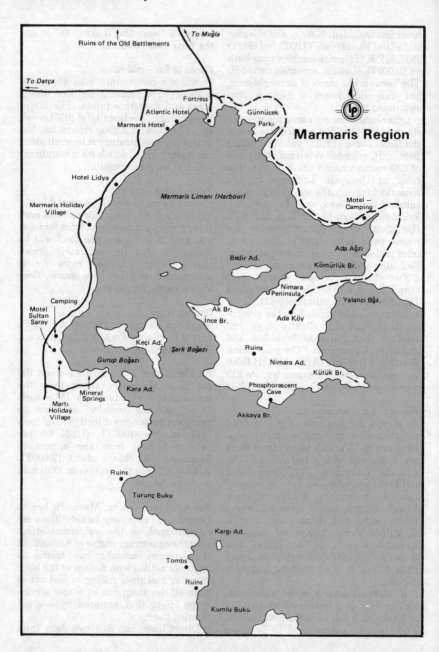

To Muğla

Ruins of the Old Battlements

To Datça

Fortress

Atlantic Hotel

Marmaris Hotel

Günnücek Parkı

Marmaris Region

Hotel Lidya

Marmaris Limanı (Harbour)

Motel — Camping

Marmaris Holiday Village

Bedir Ad.

Ada Ağzı

Kömürlük Br.

Camping

Nimara Peninsula

Yalancı Bğz.

Motel Sultan Saray

Ak Br.

İnce Br.

Ada Köy

Keçi Ad.

Şark Boğazı

Ruins

Gurup Boğazı

Nimara Ad.

Kütük Br.

Mineral Springs

Kara Ad.

Phosphorescent Cave

Martı Holiday Village

Akkaya Br.

Ruins

Turunç Buku

Kargı Ad.

Tombs

Ruins

Kumlu Buku

Izmir to Marmaris, a six-hour journey costing 2000TL (US$2.80). To İstanbul there are 13 buses charging 5500TL to 6600TL (US$7.70 to US$9.24), depending upon the company. There are the same number of daily buses to Ankara, at a fare of 4500TL to 4800TL (US$6.30 to US$6.72).

Nine buses a day run (and return) from Bodrum to Marmaris via Muğla, a three-hour, 160-km trip costing 1500TL (US$2.10).

Twenty-two buses a day make the trip each way between Marmaris and Fethiye. The distance is 160 km, the time about two or three hours, the price 1500TL (US$2.10).

If your goal is nearby Datça, there are nine daily buses charging 700TL (US$0.98) for a mountainous, winding 75-km trip of less than two hours.

Boats to Rhodes Boats to and from Rhodes run daily except Sunday in high summer, with Greek and Turkish boats sharing the service. If traffic is heavy, they may put on a Sunday boat. Buy your ticket (US$15 single trip, US$20 same-day return, US$27 open-date return) at least a day in advance if you can.

The Road Eastward

Leaving Marmaris and heading north, the road climbs into mountains with beautiful panoramas, and fertile valleys in between. At the end of the long rows of eucalyptus trees is a highway junction at which you can turn right, toward Köyceğiz and Fethiye. Along the way are fields of cotton and tobacco, and orchards of fruits and nuts, as well as cool pine forests. At places named Kadırga and Günlük are forest picnic areas.

Near Köyceğiz, a local agricultural centre, is the town of Dalyan, with an archaeological site named Caunus, worth a side-trip. See below.

DATÇA

A narrow, mountainous finger of land points westward from Marmaris, stretching 100 km to touch the edge of the Aegean. About 75 km west of Marmaris through pine forests and past gorgeous vistas lies the pleasant and relatively undiscovered village of Datça. Another 35 km brings you to the hamlet and ruins of Knidos, the ancient city of Praxiteles.

Leaving Marmaris for the trip along the peninsula takes you up into the mountains. At the 22-km mark is Çubucak Dinlenme Yeri, a rest area, camping place and park operated by the Directorate of Forests. There's also a small motel, the Fırat, here.

After 70 km you reach Reşadiye, where a road goes off to the left for Datça while the main road continues westward to Knidos.

Orientation

Datça is essentially a one-street town. The road into Datça passes near the hospital, past the gendarmerie, through a commercial district of shops selling scented honey and spices, and past several small tea houses and restaurants, to reach the main plaza with its marketplace and bus area. The street then mounts a hill, curves to the left down the other side, scoots across an isthmus, and ends on a hill at the end of a short peninsula. This whole distance is about one km.

Information

Datça's Tourism Information Office (tel (6145) 1163) is next to the main square. Lists of accommodation are posted in its windows.

Things to See

There is nothing to see in Datça but the town itself, which is small, charming and quiet. To the east is a long beach, and to the south is another one on the cove. Datça is a place to relax and hang out. For exciting sights you must take an excursion to Knidos.

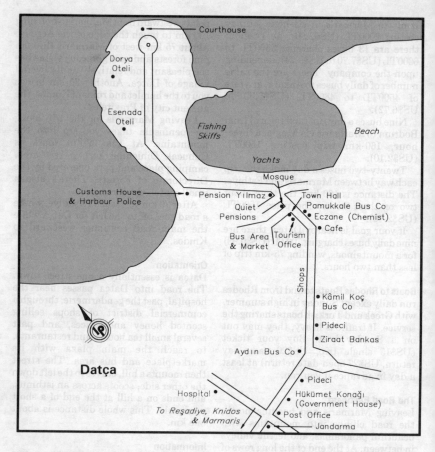

Datça

Knidos At Knidos, 35 km west of Datça at the very tip of the peninsula, are ruins of a prosperous port town dating from about 400 BC. The Dorians who founded it were smart: the winds change as one rounds the peninsula, and ships in ancient times often had to wait at Knidos for good winds. This happened to the ship carrying St Paul to Rome for trial.

Knidos, being rich, commissioned the great Praxiteles to make a large statue of Aphrodite. It was housed in a temple in view of the sea. The statue, said to be the sculptor's masterpiece, has been lost.

The trip to Knidos, as of this writing, must be made by private car, taxi (about 13,000TL, US$18.20 for a day-trip) or boat. There is not really any minibus service. A *feribot* (ferryboat) departs Datça each morning in summer at 9 am for a day-trip to Knidos, returning at 5 pm and charging 3000TL (US$4.20) per person.

About five km from Datça the road reverts to a stabilized dirt surface which becomes rougher as you near Knidos.

Knidos is a large archaeological site with ruins scattered along the three km at

Top: A driveway to a former mansion in İzmir
Bottom: An antique and carpet shop in Side, Antalya

Top: Ancient columns litter a swimming pool, Pamukkale
Left: Rock tombs at Demre
Right: Distinctive Ottoman gravestone

the end of the peninsula. It is also dramatic, with steep hillsides terraced and planted with groves of olive, almond and fruit trees, and is peopled by goatherds and the occasional wild boar. All this surrounds two picture-perfect bays in which a handful of yachts rest at anchor. Few of the buildings are in recognisable shape, but you can appreciate easily the importance of the town by exploring the site. The *bekçi* (BEHK-chee, guardian) will show you around the site if you like, for a small tip.

Other than the ruins, Knidos consists of a tiny *jandarma* post with a telephone for emergencies, four little makeshift restaurants (the Bora and the Knidos were most popular on my last visit), a repository for artefacts found on the site (no entry), and the *Bora Pansiyon* (no phone), which will put you up for 1500TL (US$2.10) per person in a room without running water if space is available; or you can camp nearby and use the Bora facilities for a small fee. You can swim in the bays from wooden piers, but the beaches are out of town several km. The nearest PTT is in Çeşme Köyü, the last village you passed through on the road to Knidos.

Places to Stay – bottom end

Datça has about 50 small pensions, with a total of perhaps 400 or 500 beds costing about 1000TL (US$1.40) apiece. A list of the pensions is on display at the Tourism Office. Among the quieter pensions are the *Bora* (tel (6145) 1327); *Karaoğlu* (kah-RAH-oh-loo) (tel (6145) 1079); *Huzur* (hoo-ZOOR) (tel (6145) 1052); *Sadık* (sah-DUHK) (tel (6145) 1196); and *Çağla* (CHAH-lah) (tel (6145) 1084). The *Pansiyon Yılmaz* (yuhl-MAHZ) is actually much fancier, a proto-hotel, with higher prices.

If you prefer a small, cheap hotel to a pension, try the *Esenada Oteli* (eh-SEHN-ah-dah) (tel (6145) 1014), almost at the end of the main street, out on the little peninsula. Though it's right next door to the town's only fancy hotel and has pleasant gardens, the Esenada charges only 3000TL (US$4.20) double, 3750TL (US$5.25) triple in rooms without running water. The showers have hot water. If no one's around, ask for assistance in the Çimen Kardeşler clothing shop next door.

At the main square facing the bus area is the *Deniz Motel* (deh-NEEZ) (tel (6145) 1038), actually a little hotel charging 3000TL (US$4.20) for a double room without water.

Camping There's camping in the district called Ilıca, on the eastern bay.

Places to Stay – top end

Datça's premier place to stay is the *Dorya Motel* (DOHR-yah) (tel (6145) 1036) at the end of the main street, out on the little peninsula. The Dorya has fine gardens of bougainvillea, eucalyptus and grassy lawn, a patio restaurant, a discotheque, and fine panoramas from its hilltop perch. The rate for two is 22,500TL (US$31.50) for room and breakfast, 30,000TL (US$42) if you want breakfast and dinner.

Places to Eat

Except for the expensive dining room at the Dorya Motel, Datça's restaurants tend to charge 700TL (US$0.98) for the standard *komple kahvaltı* Turkish breakfast, and 1200TL to 2100TL (US$1.68 to US$2.94) for a full lunch or dinner with a meat course. The *Taraca* doesn't look like much from the street, but enter it and you'll find a nice terrace with very good views of the harbour. The *Liman*, on the upper floor, has similarly fine views. The *Köşem* has bits of sculpture in front, a few outdoor tables and slightly lower prices.

Getting There

Bus Datça is served by the Pamukkale, Kâmil Koç and Aydın companies, which together run about 14 buses from Datça to Marmaris (700TL to 800TL, US$0.98 to

US$1.12), eight buses to Muğla (3½ hours, 1350TL, US$1.89), seven buses to İzmir (eight hours, 3000TL, US$4.20) and one or two direct buses daily to İstanbul and Ankara.

Boat There are often boat excursions to Datça from Marmaris, and sometimes you can buy a single (one-way) ticket.

There are scheduled ferryboat services between Bodrum and Datça during the summer months, organized by Karya Tour Yachting & Travel Agency (tel (6141) 1759 or 1914), Karantina Caddesi 13, Bodrum. Daily departures are at 8.30 am from Bodrum, 5 pm from Datça, with these exceptions: on Friday there is a second boat which leaves Bodrum at 5.30 pm; on Saturday the boat departs Bodrum at 6 pm and departs Datça at 8 am; on Sunday boats depart Datça at 7.30 am and 5 pm. The single fare is 5000TL (US$7), or 7000TL (US$9.80) for a return-trip ticket.

DALYAN (Caunus)

About 70 km east of Marmaris, at a place called Yuvarlak Çay, signs point south (right) to 'The Graves of Likya' and 'The Ruins of Caunus', 14 km down a side road. (Coming by bus, get out at Ortaca and catch a dolmuş, 150TL, US$0.21, to Dalyan.) The road brings you to the settlement, a small farming and fishing town with a sideline in tourism, through lush cotton and vegetable farms, along the winding course of a stream.

Things to See

On the town's tidy quay is where you haggle with boatmen for a cruise to the ruins of Caunus.

Some of the Lycian tombs, cut high in the rock face on the opposite side of the stream (Dalyan Çayı), are visible from the dock. Walk one km along the road past the village for a better view, or hire a boat and see them from the river.

The trip to the ruins takes two or three hours. To rent the entire boat (which can take about a dozen people) costs 6000TL (US$8.40) total. With enough people to share, the price per person is thus very low.

Caunus was an important Carian city by 400 BC. Right on the border with the kingdom of Lycia, its culture shared aspects of both kingdoms. The **tombs**, for instance, are in Lycian style (you'll see many more of them at Fethiye, Kaş, and other points east). Though of good size, Caunus suffered from endemic malaria.

Besides the tombs, the **theatre** is very well preserved; parts of an **acropolis** and other structures are near the theatre. Those curious wooden structures in the river are **fishing weirs** *(dalyan)*. No doubt the ancient Caunians benefited from such an industry as well.

Places to Stay

Dalyan's accommodation is very simple and cheap, though a new and fancier hotel is being built on the outskirts of town. Pensions charge about 1000TL (US$1.40) per bed.

The *Göl Motel* (say 'Girl') (tel (6114) 1447, 8, 9, +62), across from the quay and next to the market, is the nicest place in town and charges only 2000TL (US$2.80) for a double with shower! It has triples as well. Near it is the *İmren Pansiyon* (eem-REHN), which will also let you camp on its grounds. The *Koç Pansiyon* (KOHCH) faces the market-place.

The road through the town continues for just over one km before ending at the riverbank. Along the way are many small home pensions such as the *Çiğdem, Sahil, Gözde, Aktaş, Kaunos, Ada* and *Huzur*, all marked by signs. At the very end of the road there is also a small pension and restaurant.

Places to Eat

The *Sahil Lokantası* (sah-HEEL, shore) is not on the shore but near the mosque, beneath a shady tree. It is very plain and simple, and the hard-working cook serves

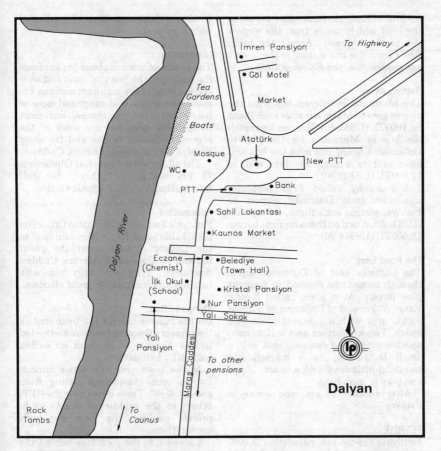

Dalyan

To Highway

İmren Pansiyon

Göl Motel

Market

Tea
Gardens

Boats

Atatürk

Mosque

WC

New PTT

Bank

PTT

Sahil Lokantası

Kaunos Market

Eczane
(Chemist)

Belediye
(Town Hall)

İlk Okul
(School)

Kristal Pansiyon

Nur Pansiyon

Yalı Sokak

Yalı
Pansiyon

To other
pensions

Rock
Tombs

To
Caunus

Dalyan River

Maraş Caddesi

---

up good food at rock-bottom prices. I had *salçalı köfte* (ground lamb meatballs in a rich sauce), *pilav*, bread, mineral soda and the yogurt drink *ayran* for a total of 620TL (US$0.87).

A big step up in class is the *Denizatı Restaurant* (deh-NEEZ-ah-tuh, seahorse) on the riverbank, which prides itself on serving the best fish in town at prices that are very low when measured against those of Marmaris.

DALAMAN

This agricultural town (population 15,000) was quite sleepy until the regional airport was built on the neighbouring river delta. Now the town stirs whenever a jet arrives, but otherwise slumbers as in the past. Most visitors pass right through, as they should.

Orientation

It is 5½ km from the airport to the town, and another five km from the town to the east-west highway. The town itself has one main street, about a half-km long, with banks, shops and simple restaurants. The bus station, served by the Pamukkale,

Aydın and Köseoğlu companies, is next to the road which passes from the airport out to the highway. Across the main street from the bus station is the town's one modest inn, the *Belediye Oteli*.

Getting Away

The Marmaris Belediyesi bus from the airport goes to Marmaris after each flight for 1000TL (US$1.40). You can also catch the bus in Marmaris for the trip to Dalaman. Should you miss the bus and have to hire a taxi, the fare will be 17,000TL (US$23.80).

A company called Fetur operates minibuses from Dalaman airport to Fethiye, serving each flight, for 1000TL (US$1.40). A taxi on the same run charges 13,500TL (US$18.90).

The Road East

The highway east of Dalaman winds through mountains cloaked in fragrant pine forests. At a place called Küçük Kargı, 33 km east of Dalaman, is a forest picnic area with a camping-place and beach. Two km farther east is Katrancı, another picnic and camping spot with a small restaurant, on a marvellously beautiful little cove with a beach. If you can plan it, stop here.

After another 18 km, you arrive in Fethiye.

FETHİYE

Fethiye (FEH-tee-yeh, population 25,000) is a very, very old town with few old buildings. An earthquake in 1958 levelled the town, leaving only a few buildings standing. Of these few, most were tombs from the time when Fethiye was called Telmessos (400 BC), but that's good since one of the things Fethiye is famous for is tombs.

The bay of Fethiye is an excellent harbour, well protected from storms. Beaches are good here, and even better at Ölüdeniz, one of Turkey's newly discovered seaside hot spots. You may want to stop in Fethiye, spend an afternoon or two at

Ölüdeniz, climb up to the rock tombs and then head east.

Orientation

The centre of town is about 3½ km from the highway; the bus station is just over one km west of the highway, and one km east of the centre. Mid-range and top-end hotels are near the centre, but most inexpensive pensions are west of the centre. Dolmuşes run to and fro along Fethiye's main street, Atatürk Caddesi.

The all-important beach at Ölüdeniz is 15 km south of Fethiye. For full information see the Ölüdeniz section.

Information

Fethiye's Tourism Information Office (tel (6151) 1051) is at İskele Meydanı next to the Dedeoğlu Hotel, near the yacht harbour at the end of Atatürk Caddesi downtown. They will help you with lodgings and inexpensive yacht charters.

Things to See

On the hillside behind the town, notice the ruins of a **Crusader fortress** constructed by the Knights of St John on earlier (400 BC?) foundations.

In the town you will notice curious Lycian stone **sarcophagi** dating from about 450 BC. There is one near the PTT, others in the middle of streets or in private gardens; the town was built around them.

Carved into the rock face behind the town is the **Tomb of Amyntas** (350 BC), in the Doric style. Other, smaller tombs are near it. Walk up or take a taxi for a look at the tomb, and the fine views of the town.

Fethiye's **museum** *(müze)* is closed as of this writing for refurbishing, but should be open again by the time you arrive.

Excursions Hotels and travel agencies in town will want you to sign up for the 12-island tour, a boat trip around Fethiye Bay which takes most of a day and costs between 2000TL and 2500TL (US$2.80 and US$3.50) per person.

North-east of the centre is Çalış, a long swath of beach with some little hotels and pensions, now somewhat ignored by the crowds racing to Ölüdeniz.

You can arrange to take a boat or minibus tour to some of the archaeological sites and beaches along the nearby coasts. Standard tours are those which go west to Günlük, Pınarbaşı, Dalyan and Caunus, and east to Letoön, Kalkan, Kaş, Patara and Xanthos. For details on the latter sites, see below.

The old city of Karmylassos near the village of Kaya is reached by a road which climbs the hillside behind Fethiye to the south, passing the Crusader castle ruins and offering wonderful views. The shore at Karmylassos is protected by Gemile Island, so the swimming is good, warm and safe, though there's not a lot of sandy beach. On Gemile are unexcavated ruins of an ancient city with a large necropolis. This is a favourite anchorage for yachts embarked on a Blue Voyage.

Places to Stay

Fethiye has a good selection of lodgings, but you must choose among three areas. For a night or two, stay right in the town. For a beach holiday of three days or more, stay at Ölüdeniz.

Places to Stay - bottom end

Fethiye has 15 small downtown hotels and almost 100 small pensions, so you're sure to find suitable cheap lodgings.

If you want a downtown hotel, try the tidy, modern little *Hotel Kaya* (KAH-yah) (tel (6151) 1161 or 2469), Cumhuriyet Caddesi 6, a block inland from the main road on a narrow market street. Graced with a wonderful jasmine vine on its facade, the Kaya charges 6000TL (US$8.40) double, 4000TL (US$5.60) for rooms with private shower.

The fancy-looking *Otel Ulvi* (OOL-vee) (tel (6151) 1650), Atatürk Caddesi a half-block east of the statue of Atatürk, charges 6600TL (US$9.24) for a double with shower but watch out for noise.

For real savings, find a pension. There are lots of them in Fethiye, left from the time before Ölüdeniz was discovered and developed. In those halcyon days, Turks on beach holiday would stay in Fethiye's homes, bringing delightful income to the town's matrons. Since Ölüdeniz the trade has dropped off but the pensions remain, and they're better bargains than ever. The Tourism Office will help you find one, or you can simply walk up the hill behind the Hotel Likya, along Karagözler Caddesi, and look for the little 'pansiyon' signs. The houses are all about the same, as are the rates: about 1500TL to 2000TL (US$2.10 to US$2.80) per bed in rooms without running water; the price of a cold shower is included in the charge. Soap and towels are not normally provided, so bring your own.

Places to Stay - middle

Cheapest is perhaps the *Kordon Oteli* (kohr-DOHN) (tel (6151) 1834), Atatürk Caddesi 8, where Atatürk Caddesi (the main street) curves to the left in the centre of town. A double with shower costs 7700TL (US$10.78), breakfast included.

Of all the hotels in town, highest marks for service and friendliness go to the experienced staff at the *Otel Dedeoglu* (deh-DEH-oh-loo) (tel (6151) 4010), İskele Meydanı, next to the Tourism Office. The 41 rooms with sea view and private bathrooms are priced at 8800TL (US$12.32) single, 13,200TL (US$18.48) double, breakfast included.

A few steps westward is the newer *Hotel Prenses* (PRENN-sess) (tel (6151) 1305), which charges slightly more for its rooms, but which has a long way to go in order to equal the comfort and congeniality of its older neighbour.

Places to Stay - top end

Fethiye's best is the *Hotel Likya* (LEEK-yah) (tel (6151) 1169 or 1690), down by the yacht marina past the Tourism Office. Its 16 tidy rooms open onto the sea and

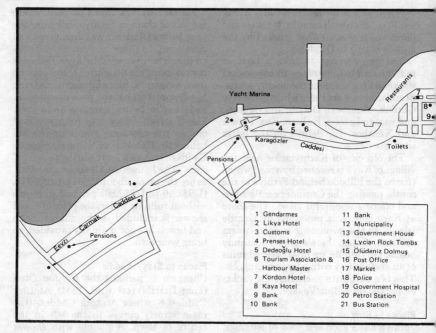

1 Gendarmes
2 Likya Hotel
3 Customs
4 Prenses Hotel
5 Dedeoğlu Hotel
6 Tourism Association &
  Harbour Master
7 Kordon Hotel
8 Kaya Hotel
9 Bank
10 Bank
11 Bank
12 Municipality
13 Government House
14 Lycian Rock Tombs
15 Ölüdeniz Dolmuş
16 Post Office
17 Market
18 Police
19 Government Hospital
20 Petrol Station
21 Bus Station

pleasant gardens, and cost 19,000TL (US$26.60) double, breakfast included. The rooms are equal to those of other places in town; you are paying somewhat more for the nice gardens and the swimming pool.

Places to Eat

In recent years Fethiye has seen numerous quayside restaurants set up for business along its waterfront, and these are perhaps the most pleasant places to have breakfast or an evening meal. The quayside restaurants, however, tend to be more expensive than the ones which crowd the narrow market streets, lending it an air of carnival.

Places to Eat – bottom end

Among the least expensive of the restaurants on Çarşı Caddesi, the market street, are the *Lezzet* and the *Tuna Merkez*. Otherwise, there's the *Doyum*

(doh-YOOM, fill-up) on Atatürk Caddesi a half-block east of the Atatürk statue. Its auspicious name is also its claim to fame, as one can easily fill up on decent food for less than 1500TL (US$2.10).

A very popular spot on my last visit was *Pizza 74* (tel 1869), next door to the Kordon Oteli. Sidewalk tables were filled with locals and visitors sipping cold beer from frosty mugs and munching *pide* and *döner kebap*. Pizzas are served, yes, but this place is really no different from any other little Turkish restaurant. The beer and food are good and cheap (*pides* cost 200TL to 300TL, US$0.28 to US$0.42), and the view of the sunset is good as well.

Places to Eat – mid-range

For local colour, the most pleasant place to dine is the *Yacht Restaurant*, facing the yacht harbour just by the Hotel Likya. It's not fancy, with fluorescent

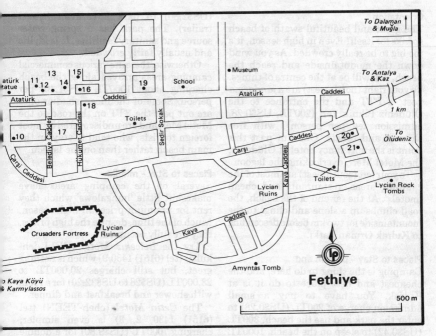

Fethiye

0   500 m

lights and a noisy television set, but the outdoor tables are very pleasant, the service polite, the food quite good. A fish dinner might cost 3000TL or 3500TL (US$4.20 to US$4.90), drinks included.

For fancier meals, dine in the Dedeoğlu and Likya hotels.

Getting There & Away
For Ölüdeniz, catch a dolmuş on Atatürk Caddesi near Çarşı Caddesi for the 15-km ride (250TL, US$0.35).

From Fethiye's bus station, six buses depart daily for İzmir, one for Denizli and one each for İstanbul and Ankara.

For points east of Fethiye such as Kaş, Pınara, Xanthos, etc, use the minibuses operated by Sunny Boy Turizm, which run along this route several times per day.

ÖLÜDENİZ
Ölüdeniz is not dead like its Biblical

namesake. Rather, it is a very sheltered lagoon not at all visible from the open sea. The scene, as you come down from the hills, is absolutely beautiful: in the distance is open sea, in the foreground a peaceful lagoon bordered by forest, in the middle a long sand spit of perfect beach. Yachts stand at anchor in the blue water, or glide gracefully along the hidden channel out to sea.

The development of Ölüdeniz has been somewhat haphazard, with a jumble of makeshift camping areas and rentable shacks beginning 100 metres inland from the shore. The bright spots in the development are the parks operated by the Directorate of Forests, which include the excellent section of beach on the sand spit called the Ölüdeniz Piknik Yeri, and Kıdrak Orman Parkı, the forest park at the south-eastern end of the bay.

Orientation

The great and beautiful swath of beach speaks for itself! Even in high season, it's too big to be really crowded. As you wind down the mountainside and reach the beach, you will be at the centre of things. To your right (north-west) are a *jandarma* post, a PTT and the entrance to the Ölüdeniz Piknik Yeri (200TL, US$0.28, admission fee per person), with free showers and toilets. One km past this point is the only fancy hotel at Ölüdeniz, the Motel Meri, overlooking the lagoon.

To your left (south-east) are most of the camping areas, restaurants and cheap 'motels'. At the far end of the beach, the road climbs up a slope and clings to the mountainside for two km before descending to Kıdrak Orman Parkı.

Places to Stay - bottom end

Camping is the thing to do here, and the cheapest and best place to do it is at Kıdrak. You have to pay a small admission charge of 200TL (US$0.28) to enter the park and use the beach, 300TL (US$0.42) to sleep on the beach, 1000TL (US$1.40) to pitch a tent, 2000TL

Ölüdeniz

1 Motel Meri
2 Çavuş Campsite
3 Post Office
4 Entry to pay beach (Piknik Yeri)
5 Jandarma
6 Çetin Campsite
7 Deniz Campsite
8 Derya Campsite
9 Belcekız Campsite

To Fethiye

To Kıdrak

(US$2.80) to park a caravan (travel trailer). The park has a spring water source and sanitary facilities. It is idyllic and usually fairly crowded.

Otherwise, there are various commercial camping areas arrayed along the beach charging about 1000TL (US$1.40) per person. Some of the nicer, shadier ones are out past the PTT on the road to the Motel Meri and are undiscovered by most foreign tourists, who tend to stay on the main beach rather than on the lagoon.

Places to Stay - middle

Several of the camping areas have makeshift little 'bungalows' which they rent for premium prices in high season. Much of the time, despite the high prices, they are fully occupied.

Try the *Belcekız Motel* (BELL-jeh-kuhz) (tel (6151) 1430/9) which is nothing great, but still charges 20,000TL to 23,000TL (US$28 to US$32.20) for a room with shower and breakfast and dinner.

The *Çetin Motel* (cheh-TEEN) (tel (6151) 1430, 2, 3) is even simpler, charging 7000TL (US$9.80) for a double room without private shower, 10,000TL (US$14) for one with shower, breakfast included. In high season, chances are good that all of the rooms with shower will be reserved long before you arrive.

Places to Stay - top end

The *Meri Motel* (meh-REE) (tel (6151) 1430, 1) has 75 rooms scattered down a steep hillside amidst pretty gardens. The views from many of the rooms are very fine; the rooms are a bit musty, but this place has a lock on the market here, so the price for a double with bath, breakfast and dinner included, is 36,000TL (US$50.40). The motel has its own beach and seaside restaurant. For reservations in Fethiye, call (6151) 1025.

Places to Eat

All of the restaurants at Ölüdeniz charge resort prices, so a portion of *döner kebap* which might cost 600TL (US$0.84) in

Fethiye costs 1000TL (US$1.40) here. The quality of restaurant food and service changes constantly. On my last visit, the *Han Restaurant* at Han Camping was the cheapest and most popular beachfront spot. You can save a bit of money by walking inland along the road to the *Pirate's Inn Restaurant & Bar* which is cheaper because of its distance from the beach (100 metres).

FETHIYE TO KAŞ

This portion of the Lycian coast, sometimes called the Lycian Peninsula,

because it extends well south into the Mediterranean, is littered with the remains of ancient cities. If you have your own car, you can visit as many as you like by making a few short detours. Without a car, you can still make your way to a few of them. The easiest to reach is Xanthos, one of the best. The distance from Fethiye to Kaş is 108 km.

Leave Fethiye on Atatürk Caddesi. A few km along, near the town of Kemer, the road forks. Take the right fork to 'Kaş-Antalya'; the left fork to 'Korkuteli-Antalya' is the inland route.

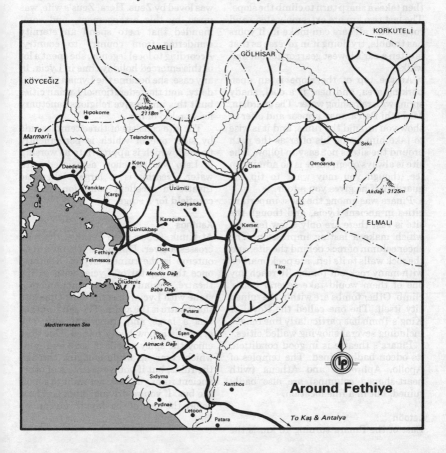

Around Fethiye

The road takes you up into fragrant evergreen forests and down to fertile valleys. Herds of sheep and goats (a few cattle) skitter along the roadway near the villages. The road is curvy and somewhat slow. Farm tractors pulling trailers can slow you down as well.

Pınara

East of Fethiye 37 km is the turning (right) for Pınara, which lies up in the mountains. The road winds through tobacco and maize fields and along irrigation channels for over three km, then takes a sharp turn to climb the slope. The last two km are extremely steep and rough. Not all cars can make it. If yours has trouble, try doing it in reverse as that is often a car's lowest gear; or get out and walk.

At the top of the slope is an open parking area, and near it a cool, shady spring with refreshing water. The guardian, Mr Fethi Parça, may appear and offer to show you around the ruins, and it is wise to take him up on his offer as the path around the site is not easy to follow. The site is always open; there is no admission fee, though you may want to tip the guardian if he gives you a tour.

Pınara was among the most important cities in ancient Lycia, and though the site is vast there are only a few features which make a lasting impression. The sheer column of rock behind the site, and the rock walls to its left, are pock-marked with many rock-cut tombs. To reach any one of them would take several hours' climb. Other tombs are within the ruined city itself. The one called the Royal or King's Tomb has particularly fine reliefs, including several showing walled cities.

Pınara's theatre is in good condition, its odeon badly ruined. The temples of Apollo, Aphrodite and Athena (with heart-shaped columns) are also badly ruined, but in a fine location.

Letoön

East of the Pınara turning 16 km is the road to Letoön, near the village of Kumluova. Turn right off the highway, go 3.2 km to a 'T', turn left, go 100 metres, then turn right (this turn is easy to miss), and proceed one km to the site. If you miss the second turn, you'll end up in the village, which has a very plain hotel, the *Otel Yıldız*, on the main square near the bust of Atatürk. When you get to the site, a man selling soft drinks and admission tickets (250TL, US$0.35) will greet you.

The Letoön takes its name and importance from a large and impressive shrine to Leto, who according to legend was loved by Zeus. Hera, Zeus's wife, was upset by this arrangement, and commanded that Leto spend an eternity wandering from country to country. According to local legends, she spent a lot of this enforced holiday time in Lycia. In any case, she became the Lycian national deity, and the federation of Lycian cities built this impressive religious sanctuary for worship of her.

The site consists of three temples side by side, one of which is permanently flooded, which is appropriate as worship of Leto was somehow associated with water. Nearby is a large Hellenistic theatre in excellent condition, with a cornfield for a stage.

Xanthos

At Kınık, 63 km from Fethiye, the road crosses a river. Up to the left on a rock outcrop is the ruined city of Xanthos, once the capital of Lycia, with a fine theatre, Lycian tomb and monumental stone with Lycian inscriptions. Opposite the theatre is the agora. Though Xanthos was a large and important city, the acropolis is now badly ruined. One does enjoy the spicy smells of sage and mint which come up while trudging through the ruins, but if you've seen lots of other ancient ruins you may not want to get off the bus. If you're driving, stop. Get here before the heat of the day, if you can.

Patara

Heading east again, seven km brings you to the turning for Patara. The ruins here are of some interest, and they come with a bonus in the form of a wonderful white sand beach some 50 metres wide and 20 km long, populated by a mere handful of people. As of this writing there are no public transport services, but they will no doubt come.

Look for the Patara turning in the village of Ovaköy, where you can find a meal in a simple eatery and you may be able to find a taxi to take you the five km to the ruins; the beach is one km past the ruins. At the end of the road, by the beach, is a little restaurant where you can buy snacks and drinks.

The Ruins The ruins at Patara include a **triumphal arch** at the entrance to the site and just past it a **necropolis** with a **Lycian tomb**. Next are the **baths** and a much later **basilica**. You'll approach a car park attended by a guardian, but there is no fee for visiting the ruins.

The **theatre** is of good size, and striking because it is half-covered by wind-driven sand, which seems intent on making a dune out of it. Climb to the top of the theatre for a good view of the whole site.

Several other baths, two temples and a Corinthian temple by the lake are also here, though the swampy ground may make them difficult to approach. Across the lake is a **granary**.

Places to Stay The lodging situation at Patara is complicated because this is an archaeological zone, which means it is public property; and camping is not allowed due to the danger of theft of antiquities. But there are still a few inexpensive little lodgings, including the *Golden Pansiyon* with 15 rooms – six with private shower, nine without – and a restaurant on the roof. The charge for a double room with shower is 4000TL (US$5.60).

Kalkan

About 11 km east of the Patara turning, or 81 km east of Fethiye, the highway skirts Kalkan (kahl-KAHN), an old village with a new interest in tourism. New installations include a yacht marina in the serene, unspoilt bay and several hotels as well as inexpensive pensions. Kalkan is one of those idyllic villages which offer nothing to do, and everything to enjoy.

Orientation Kalkan is built on a hillside sloping down to the bay, and you will find yourself trekking up and down it all day. Coming in from the highway, the road descends past the Belediye (town hall), then takes a switchback turn by the Ziraat Bankası (bank) to pass the Orman Genel Müdürlüğü (Directorate of Forests) office and the PTT before entering the main shopping area. The Kalkan Han hotel is here. though most other little hotels and pensions are on terraces below the shopping area, all the way down to the harbour's edge.

Places to Stay As the selection of accommodation is limited, and because Kalkan is visited exclusively by tourists, prices for lodgings tend to be higher than normal, but are still very affordable.

Cheapest are the pensions rated 2nd class by the town, the *Akın Pansiyon* (ah-KUHN) (tel Kalkan 25) and the *Dalkıran* (DAHL-kuh-rahn), charging 4500TL (US$6.30) for a double without private shower. First-class pensions such as the *Ay Pansiyon* (AHY) (tel Kalkan 58) provide double rooms with showers for 6000TL (US$8.40) per night; the Ay is family-run.

Among the hotels, the best is the *Kalkan Han* (kahl-KAHN) (tel Kalkan 151), an old village house wonderfully restored and now equipped with 16 guest rooms, each with private bath, for 17,000TL (US$23.80). Guests have a telex at their disposal.

The *Patara Pansiyon* (PAH-tah-rah)

(tel Kalkan 76) is run by two men who have modernized the building completely with honey-coloured pine and white stucco. Price for a double with shower, breakfast included, is 10,000TL (US$14).

Places to Eat Dining has yet to approach the level of an art in Kalkan, but you can have a very pleasant and not overly expensive dinner down on the waterfront at the *Yakamoz, Pala'nin Yeri, Kalamaki, Lipsos* or *Köşe*. On the terrace above are the *Kalkan* and the *Doy Doy*, with more panoramic views. Least expensive fare is at the top of the town in the *Köşk Restaurant* (KURSHK) (tel 46), not far from the PTT in the market street; they're more serious about doing good cooking here. The *İmren* nearby is the cheapest, but it's small, dark and cramped.

Kalkan to Kaş

At 87 km from Fethiye is Kaputaş (or Kapıtaş), a striking mountain gorge crossed by a small highway bridge. The marble plaque on the east side of the bridge, embedded in the rock wall, commemorates four road workers who were killed during the dangerous construction of this part of the highway. Below the bridge is a perfect little sandy cove, reachable by a long flight of stairs.

A short distance past Kaputaş, 20 km before Kaş, is the Blue Cave (Mavi Mağara), beneath the highway, marked by a sign. You may see boats approaching, bringing tourists for a glimpse of this Turkish Capri. You can climb down from the road for a look and a swim if you like.

KAŞ

Fishing boats and a few yachts in the harbour, a town square with tea houses and restaurants in which one can hear a half-dozen languages spoken, inexpensive pensions and hotels, classical ruins scattered about: this is Kaş (KAHSH, population 5000), the quintessential

Turkish seaside village. But Kaş has been discovered by the vanguard of foreign travellers and by some Turkish vacationers, so you won't have it all to yourself. The town has awoken to its tourism potential, and the main street is now hung with little signs admonishing local people to do their best: 'The Tourist is our guest!', and 'Let's all treat the Tourist well!'

Kaş is not popular because of its beaches – small, not sandy but pebbly, and a good distance out of town. But Kaş can be used as a base for boat trips to several fascinating spots along the coast.

Orientation

Life centres on the town square by the harbour, with its tea houses, restaurants, mosque, police station and shops. Come down the hill into the town from the highway, and turn left to the town square; if you turn right, you will go to the ancient theatre along Hastane Caddesi. The theatre is about all that's left of ancient Antiphellus, which was the Lycian town. On the sheer rock mountain wall above the town are a number of Lycian rock tombs. They're illuminated at night.

Information

The Tourism Information Office (tel (3226) 1238), is on the main square. They speak English, and have numerous handouts on local lodgings and sights.

Things to See

Though boat excursions are the popular sport here, there are several significant things to see in the town itself.

On Foot Walk up the hill on the street to the left of the Tourist Office to reach the **Monument Tomb**, a Lycian sarcophagus mounted on a high base. It is said that Kaş was once littered with such sarcophagi, but that over the years most were broken apart to provide building materials. This one, on its lofty perch, survived very well.

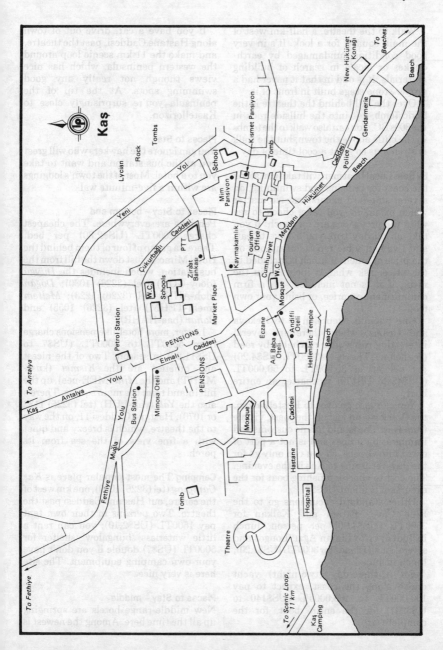

Kaş

To Beaches

To Beaches

Beach

New Hükümet Konağı

Gendarmerie

Police

Beach

Caddesi

Hükümet

Tomb

Kısmet Pansiyon

Tombs

Lycian Rock

School

Mim Pansiyon

Yol

Meydanı

Kaymakamlık

Tourism Office

Cumhuriyet

Mosque

W.C.

Yeni

Caddesi

Çukurbağ

PTT

Ziraat Bankası

W.C.

Schools

Market Place

Eczane

Andifli Oteli

Ali Baba Oteli

Hellenistic Temple

Beach

Petrol Station

PENSIONS

Elmalı

Caddesi

PENSIONS

Mimosa Oteli

Bus Station

Mosque

Hastane Caddesi

To Antalya

Kaş Antalya Yolu

Muğla Yolu

Fethiye Yolu

Tomb

Theatre

Hospital

To Fethiye

To Scenic Loop.
11 km

Kaş Camping

Walk to the **theatre**, a half-km west of the main square, for a look. It's in very good condition, undamaged by earthquakes or locals in search of building materials. It is odd in that it never had a proper stone stage built in front of it.

Over the hill behind the theatre is the **Doric Tomb**, cut into the hillside rock in the 300s BC. You can also walk to the tombs in the cliffs above the town, but the walk is strenuous so go at a cool time of day.

By Boat Local boatmen will take you along the coast for cruising and swimming, on several standard excursions. No matter which excursion you take, check to see what the provisions are for lunch. If you take an all-day trip, you'll have to eat, and I've had some reports of rip-offs on the price of lunch. If lunch is included in the price, ask what is included in the meal; if it is not included, get a firm commitment on price, or bring your own food.

One popular excursion is to Kekova and Üçağız, where there are several interesting ruins, also reachable by road (see below). The cost is 3000TL (US$4.20) per person, or 30,000TL to 50,000TL (US$42 to US$70) to charter an entire boat.

You can also go over to Kastellorizon, the Greek island just off the coast, visible from Kaş. The island has no customs and immigration offices and is not a port of entry into Greece, so you can only go for the day, returning to Kaş in the evening. The cost to charter a fishing boat for the excursion is about US$50.

Other standard excursions go to the Blue Cave, Patara and Kalkan for 3500TL (US$4.90) per person, lunch included; or to Liman Ağzı, Longos and several small islands for 3000TL (US$4.20), lunch included.

For a three-day (two-night) yacht cruise along the coast, expect to pay 100,000TL to 165,000TL (US$140 to US$231) for the entire boat, for the complete trip.

If you have a car, drive out of town along Hastane Caddesi, past the theatre, and make the 11-km scenic loop around the western peninsula, which has nice views though not really any good swimming spots. At the tip of the peninsula you're surprisingly close to Kastellorizon.

Places to Stay
You can ignore the hawkers who will greet you at the bus station and want to take you to a hotel. Most of the town's lodgings are within a five-minute walk.

Places to Stay – bottom end
Pensions are everywhere. The cheapest charge 2000TL (US$2.80) per bed. There's a group of four of them behind the Hotel Mimosa, just down the hill from the bus station, which includes the *Duygu* (dooy-GOO) (tel (3226) 1080); *Doğan* (doh-AHN) (tel (3226) 1223); *Meltem* (mehl-TEHM) (tel (3226) 1055) and *Bahar* (baa-HAHR).

Larger, more hotel-like pensions charge from 5000TL to 8000TL (US$7 to US$11.20) in season. Two of the nicest and quietest are the *Kısmet* (kuss-MEHT) and the *Mini* (MEE-nee), up the hill inland from the main square. There's also the *Yalı* (yah-LUH) (tel (3226) 1132 or 1070), Hastane Caddesi 11, on the way to the theatre, which is breezy and quiet with a fine view of the sea from its porch.

Camping The most popular place is *Kaş Camping* (tel (3226) 1050), one km west of the centre, out Hastane Caddesi past the theatre. Two persons in their own tent pay 1500TL (US$2.10); you can rent a little waterless 'bungalow' shelter for 5000TL (US$7) double if you don't have your own camping equipment. The site here is very nice.

Places to Stay – middle
New middle-range hotels are springing up all the time here. Among the newest is

the *Hotel Mimosa* (mee-MOH-sah) (tel (3226) 1272 or 1368), Elmalı Caddesi, just down the hill a few steps from the bus station. Opened in August 1986, it charges 16,500TL (US$23.10) double for the first three nights, 15,000TL (US$21) per night thereafter. Rooms are small but tidy, and each has a little balcony and a shower. The restaurant on the second level has a good view.

Just down the hill is the *Oriental Hotel* (tel (3226) 1445), Elmalı Caddesi 10, the next choice, charging 15,000TL (US$21) for a double with bath and breakfast.

At the beginning of Hastane Caddesi, the road to the theatre, is the *Ali Baba Otel* (ah-LEE bah-bah) (tel (3226) 1126), a modern building in which a room with bath costs 6500TL (US$9.10) single, 8000TL (US$11.20) double, in season.

Places to Eat

Prices for restaurant dishes are established and fixed by the municipal authorities, so all of the various restaurants in a given class should charge exactly the same for any item you order. Restaurant quality varies with the seasons and the patronage, and nothing is certain, but here are some tips.

Local people tend to choose the *Derya Restaurant* (DEHR-yah) (tel 1093), beside the Kaymakamlık (KAHY-mah-KAHM-luhk, county government house) on the main square. The restaurant takes its English name ('Shady') from its awnings and shade trees. Try to pick a quiet table, as this place is sometimes chaotic. Many dishes are set out for you to choose from, which simplifies ordering somewhat. A basic meal of *şiş kebap*, salad and a beer costs less than 2000TL (US$2.80).

Other restaurants are at the eastern edge of the square near the Belediye (beh-leh-DEE-yah, Municipality); look for the *Mercan* (mehr-JAHN), which has a nice waterfront location.

The *Çınar*, on the main square next to the Tourism Office, is among the simplest

and cheapest restaurants in town. For snacks, pastries and puddings, the *Noel Baba Pastanesi* (Father Christmas) on the main square is the favourite, and the best for people-watching when its outdoor tables are in shade. I paid 300TL (US$0.42) for an éclair and a cup of Turkish coffee.

Among the prominent restaurants on the main square is the *Eriş*, with shady pseudo-rustic tables in front. Prices are not bad and better food can be found, but the candlelight dining atmosphere is tempting.

Getting There & Away

Most of the buses in and out of Kaş are handled by the Aydın Turizm company, but there is competition, so shop around for good ticket prices. In summer there are eight daily buses to Fethiye (1000TL, US$1.40), two of them going directly to Ölüdeniz. Four buses run to Marmaris (five hours, 2500TL, US$3.50), three to Bodrum (3000TL, US$4.20), four to Antalya (five hours, 1300TL, US$1.82), two to Denizli for Pamukkale, one to Aydın, whence you can easily get a bus or minibus to Denizli (nine or 10 hours, 3000TL, US$4.20), and two night buses to İzmir via Selçuk (Ephesus).

Eastward

From Kaş you climb into the mountains again. You may want to stop to take photos near the top of the hill overlooking the town.

KEKOVA

Sixteen km east of Kaş you will see signs for a turning (south, right) to Üçağız, Kekova, Teimuse (Simena). A 30-minute drive of 19 km along this dirt road, rough at times, will bring you to the village of Kale Üçağız, in an area of ancient ruined cities, some of them partly submerged in the Mediterranean's waters. This area is regularly visited by day-trippers on boats from Kaş, and by yachts, but is virtually undiscovered by travellers wanting to stay overnight. For a short time it remains an unspoilt Turkish fishing and farming village hidden away behind the mountains, living on fish, carob beans and fruit orchards, unsullied by the rest of the world.

The setting of the village is absolutely idyllic, on a bay amidst islands and peninsulas. The old village houses are of the local stone, often whitewashed. The largest building in town is the modern Ilk Okul (Primary School). Cows and chickens wander the streets, villagers heft sacks of carob beans down to the town wharf, fishermen repair their nets on the quay as sailboats glide through the harbour. Üçağız, at this writing, is for real, not yet Disney-fied by the force of investment and advertisement.

Orientation

The village you enter is Üçağız (Three Mouths, that is, entrances to the harbour), the ancient Teimiussa. Across the water to the east is Kale, a village on the site of the ancient city of Simena. South of the villages is a larger harbour called Ölüdeniz (not to be confused with the famous beach spot near Fethiye), and south of that the channel entrance, shielded from the Mediterranean's sometime fury by a long island named Kekova.

Things to See

Though Üçağız is where you will make your base, Kale is where you will go by motorboat to see the ruins of ancient Simena and the medieval **castle**. Within the castle is a little **theatre** cut into the rock. Near the castle are ruins of several temples and public baths, and the city walls are visible on the outskirts. It's a deliciously pretty spot. Boats from Üçağız will take you on a tour of the area lasting one to 1½ hours; the price to charter an entire boat is about 4000TL (US$5.60).

Places to Stay

There are only small pensions in Üçağız, charging 1000TL (US$1.40) for a bed. The Koç and the Likya are two of these.

Places to Eat

Most of the food and all of the drinks served in the village's simple restaurants must be brought in by boat from Kaş or even farther away, so prices are higher than you would expect, but still quite cheap. On the waterfront are a half-dozen little eateries, including the Kordon, Liman, Yazır, Koç and Kekova, all charging about 1100TL (US$1.54) for a simple meal of şiş kebap, pilav and soft drink. The Adanalı, inland a bit, is more expensive.

There are a few simple shops in the village at which you can buy basic food supplies.

Getting There

There is no regular or daily road transport to Üçağız as of this writing, though there will no doubt be minibus service from Kaş in the near future, as tourism develops here. For the moment, though, travellers without their own car must come by motorboat or yacht from Kaş or from Demre. Motorboats can be chartered at Demre's western beach, called Çayağzı, for 10,000TL (US$14); often it is possible to buy one place in the boat for a single journey (one way) for 1000TL (US$1.40).

DEMRE (MYRA)

The road descends from the mountains to a very fertile river delta, much of it covered in greenhouses. At Demre (DEHM-reh), also called Kale, 37 km east of Kaş, is the Church of St Nicholas. It is said that the legend of Father Christmas (Santa Claus) began here when a 4th-century Christian bishop gave anonymous gifts to village girls who had no dowry. He would drop bags of coins down the chimneys of their houses, and the 'gift from heaven' would allow them to marry. This is perhaps why he is the patron saint of virgins; he went on to add sailors and children, pawnbrokers and Holy Russia to his conquests. His fame grew, and in 1087 a raiding party from the Italian city of Bari stole his mortal remains from the church. In medieval Europe, relics were hot items. (They missed a few bones, which are now in the Antalya museum.)

Orientation

Demre is spread all over the valley. At the centre are the famous church, several small pensions and restaurants, shops and bus ticket offices. The best hotel is one km south of the centre, near the shore. Four km west of the centre is Çayağzı beach, with several places to camp (for free) and several which charge a small amount. The impressive rock tombs and ruins of ancient Myra are about two km north of the centre.

Things to See

The church has been restored and offers a rare chance to see what a 5th-century Byzantine church looked like. A symposium on St Nicholas is held here each year in December. Admission costs 250TL (US$0.35), half-price on weekends.

A few km inland from the church are the ruins of Myra, with a striking honeycomb of **rock-hewn tombs** and a **Roman theatre**. They're worth a look. Taxi drivers in town will offer to take you on a tour, but it's not really necessary. The walk from the main square takes only about 20 minutes, and the site is pretty much self-explanatory.

Places to Stay

The *Myra Pension* near the main square is the cheapest, but the *Kıyak Otel* (kuh-YAHK) (tel 2092, 3) is much nicer and charges only 2200TL (US$3.08) for a double room with private shower and one large bed, 2750TL (US$3.85) for a double with two beds. Its only disadvantage is that it is a 10-minute walk (one km) south of the main square, at the junction with the coastal highway.

On the road to the rock tombs are the *Noel Pansiyon* and the *Palmiye Pansiyon*, charging 1500TL (US$2.10) per person, breakfast included.

FİNİKE

Thirty km along the twisting mountain road brings you to Finike (FEE-nee-keh, population 7000), the ancient Phoenicus, now a sleepy fishing port and way-station on the burgeoning tourist route. Most of the tourists are Turks, those who have built ramshackle dwellings on the magnificent beach to the east of the town.

Places to Stay

Finike has only a few very modest hotels, the best of which is the *Hotel Sedir* (seh-DEER) (tel (3225) 1183, 1256), Cumhuriyet Caddesi 37, where a double room with shower costs 3500TL (US$4.90). The *Köşk*, behind the Sedir, is older and perhaps noisier, but has sea views. There are also some very cheap pensions; you'll notice the *Kale Pension*, a large white building overlooking the docks.

Places to Eat

As for restaurants, the *Fish Restaurant*, which bears a giant sign with its name, catches most of the tourists, though townfolk prefer the *Lezzet Lokantası* or the slightly nicer *Deniz Restaurant*, right around the corner from the Hotel Sedir.

HEADING EAST

As you leave Finike the highway skirts a sand-and-pebble beach which runs for about 15 km. Signs at intervals read 'Plaj Sahası Halka Açıktır', which means 'The Beach Area is Open to the Public'.

Upon leaving the long beach, the road passes through the town of Kumluca, full of farmers, and then winds back up into the mountains. You may see crews of wood-cutters, a reclusive people called Tahtacılar who hold to their own unique culture and traditions.

About 28 km from Finike there is an especially good panorama. Three km later you enter Beydağları Sahil Milli Parkı, the Bey Mountains Coastal National Park. Another six km and you get splendid views of the mountains.

Phaselis

At 55 km from Finike (13 to Kemer) is a turning for Phaselis, a Lycian city on the shore. The sign on the highway indicates that the archaeological site is one km from the turning, but that is the distance only to the entrance of the area; the distance to the ruins themselves is two km.

The site is open from 8 am to 6 pm daily, for free admission. Near the entry to the site is a small modern building where you can buy soft drinks, snacks and souvenirs, use the WC, and visit a small one-room museum.

About one km past the building, shaded by soughing pines, are the ruins of Phaselis, arranged around three small perfect bays, each with its own small beach. Among the ruins there is not a lot to see, and it is all from Roman and Byzantine times, but the setting is incomparably romantic. You will want to have a look at the aqueduct, but that's about all.

Prominent signs read 'No Picnicking in the Ruins!', and point the way to a designated picnic area. Turkish visitors largely ignore the signs, and picnic where they like.

If you have no picnic supplies, you can eat at one of several small restaurants. The *Mola* and the *Rosengarten* are on the highway two km west of the village of Tekirova, not far from Phaselis. The centre of the village is actually 1.4 km off the highway, and in it you will find the *Ölmez Aile Pansion* (erl-MEHZ, no phone), plain but clean, charging 2000TL (US$2.80) per person, only a half-km from a vast and empty pebble beach. Feel free to camp here if you have your own equipment.

Olympos

Not far east of Phaselis is the turning for Olympos, another Lycian city. By walking 1½ hours from Olympos you can see the Chimaera, a perpetual flame issuing from a hole in the rock. Ruins of a temple to Hephaistos (Vulcan) are at the site.

Kemer

Kemer (keh-MEHR), 42 km south-west of Antalya, is a burgeoning beach holiday resort being built under government supervision. Accommodation is in all price ranges, so you should be able to find whatever you like once the hotels are completed. Laid out by a city planner, it is meant to attract groups on package tours.

ANTALYA

Antalya (ahn-TAHL-yah, population 300,000, altitude 38 metres) is the chief city of Turkey's eastern Mediterranean coast. Agriculture, light industry and tourism have made Antalya boom during the past few decades, and this attractive Mediterranean city is still growing.

Though Antalya is well worth a visit, one doesn't normally come here for a beach vacation because the city's beaches are out of town. Rather, people come to see the large museum packed with the archaeological and ethnographic wealth of this deeply historical coast; to see the Old Town and its cosy harbour, which date back several centuries before Christ; and to use this pleasant city as a base for excursions to the dramatic ruins nearby at Termessos, Perge and Aspendos.

History

Antalya is not as old as many other cities which once lined this coast, but it is still prospering while the older cities are dead. Founded by Attalus II of Pergamum in the 100s BC, the city was named Attaleia for its founder. When the Pergamene kingdom was willed to Rome, Attaleia became a Roman city. Emperor Hadrian visited here in 130 AD, and a triumphal arch (Hadriyanüs Kapısı) was built in his honour.

The Byzantines took over from the Romans. In 1207 the Seljuk Turks based in Konya took the city from the Byzantines and gave Antalya a new version of its name, and also its symbol, the Yivli Minare (Grooved Minaret). After the Mongols broke Seljuk power, Antalya was held for a while by the Turkish Hamidoğulları emirs. It was taken by the Ottomans in 1391.

During WW I the Allies made plans to divide up the Ottoman Empire, and at the end of the war they parcelled it out. Italy got Antalya in 1918, but by 1921 Atatürk's armies had put an end to all such foreign holdings in Anatolia.

Though always a busy port (trade to Crete, Cyprus and Egypt), Antalya has grown rapidly since the 1960s and is now Turkey's 15th largest city.

Orientation

The city now sprawls well beyond its ancient limits. A *çevre yolu* (ring road or bypass) carries long-distance traffic around the city. To the west is Konyaaltı Plajı, a pebble beach several km long, now partly sullied by industrial development. To the east are the sandy bathing beaches, especially Lara Plajı, which has its own hotels, motels and pensions.

In the centre, the main streets have been renamed in recent years, which leads to some confusion since maps and street signs may bear the new names but citizens may use the old names. The street which has the bus terminal is officially called Kâzım Özalp Caddesi, but you may also hear Şarampol, the old name. Cumhuriyet Caddesi, the main thoroughfare, used to be called Hastane Caddesi; Ali Çetinkaya Caddesi is the eastern continuation of Cumhuriyet Caddesi. Atatürk Caddesi goes from Cumhuriyet/Ali Çetinkaya down to the large Karaali Parkı.

Antalya's landmark and symbol is the Yivli Minare, the Grooved Minaret, built in the early 1200s during Seljuk rule. It is on Cumhuriyet Caddesi, next to the plaza which bears the equestrian statue of Atatürk (a very dramatic one), and at the top of the Old Town. Across the avenue from the statue of Atatürk is a currency exchange place that stays open until 8 pm in the summer and charges no commission.

The Old Town is called Kaleiçi (kah-LEH-ee-chee, within the fortress) or Eski Antalya (ehs-KEE, old).

There are two bus stations, the Oto Garajı, which is the central station for the long-distance inter-city buses; and the Doğu Garajı or Eastern Garage, a parking area in the eastern part of town from which minibuses depart for villages and points as far east as Manavgat and Side.

Information

The Tourism Information Office (tel (311) 11747 or 15271) is at Cumhuriyet Caddesi 73, several blocks west of the Yivli Minare.

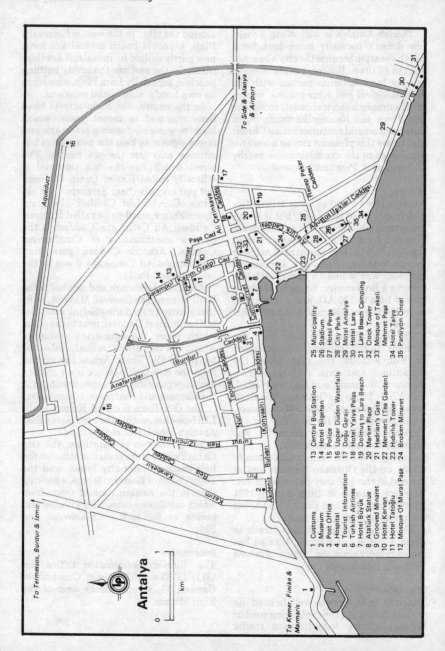

Things to See

You can hire one of those romantic old horse-drawn carriages *(fayton)* for a short tour of the main sights in town for about 1000TL (US$1.40).

Start your sightseeing at the **Yivli Minare** (YEEV-lee mee-NAH-reh). The handsome and unique minaret was erected by the Seljuk Sultan Alaeddin Keykubat I in the early 1200s, next to a church which the sultan had converted to a mosque. There is an old stone clock tower in the plaza just above it. The view from the plaza, taking in the Old Town, the bay and the distant ragged summits of the Beydağları (Bey Mountains) is spectacular. Tea houses behind the Büyük Otel offer the opportunity to enjoy the view at leisure.

The Old Town (Kaleiçi)

Go down the street at the eastern end of the plaza which descends into the Old Town. Note another old clock tower at the beginning of the street. Just below this is the **Ali Paşa Camii**, the Mosque of Ali Pasha, another Seljuk structure with beautiful Arabic inscriptions above the doors and windows.

Wander down to the harbour, now used for yachts. The harbour had been Antalya's lifeline since the 200s BC, through the Roman, Byzantine, Seljuk and Ottoman empires, up till very recently when a new port was constructed on the outskirts.

The Old Town has been declared a historic zone and is slated for restoration, which will take some time though the port area is already completed. The quaint, twisted streets and picturesque Ottoman houses are certainly charming. East of the harbour you might come across the **Kesik Minare**, or Broken Minaret. Its mosque was once a 5th-century church.

Bazaar

Antalya's tidy bazaar *(çarşı)* is north of Cumhuriyet Caddesi, between Kazım Özalp and Atatürk Caddesis. Don't go in the heat of the afternoon, as many of the shops will be closed.

Hadrian's Gate & Karaali Park

Down Atatürk Caddesi is Hadriyanüs Kapısı, Hadrian's Gate, erected during the reign of that Roman emperor (117-138). The monumental marble arch, which now leads to the Old Town, makes a shady little park in the midst of the city.

Farther along Atatürk Caddesi toward the sea is Karaali Parkı, a large, attractive, flower-filled park good for a stroll and for views of the sea. Sunset is the time most Turks go; it's the prettiest time. An old stone tower here, the Hıdırlık Kulesi, was once a lighthouse and a bastion in the city walls.

Antalya Museum

Antalya's large and rich museum (Antalya Müzesi) is at the western edge of town, two km from the Yivli Minare, reachable by bus along Cumhuriyet Caddesi. Ask the driver: *Müzeye gider mi?*, mew-ZEH-yeh gee-DEHR mee, 'Does this go to the museum?'. The collections include fascinating glimpses into the popular life of the region, with crafts and costume displays as well as a wealth of ancient artefacts. Hours are 9 am to noon and 1.30 to 6 pm, closed Monday; admission costs 500TL (US$0.70), half-price on Sunday.

The exhibits, most of them labelled in English as well as Turkish, start with fossils, proceed chronologically through the Stone and Bronze ages (in which Turkey is especially rich in artefacts), and continue through the Mycenaean, Classic and Hellenistic periods. The Gods Gallery has statues of 15 classical gods from Aphrodite to Zeus, some of them very fine. Among the exceptionally good smaller objects are jewellery, vases, glass items and statuettes. The Tomb Room is quite good as well.

The museum has a small collection of Christian art, including a room for icons which also contains a few of the bones of St Nicholas. There are also several sections of mosaic pavement.

The collection continues through Seljuk and Ottoman times, with costumes, armour, calligraphy (Hattat), implements, faience, musical instruments, carpets and saddlebags. The ethnographic exhibits are fascinating, including a fully furnished nomad's tent, a room with carpet loom from a village home and several rooms from a typical Ottoman household.

A shady patio has tables where you can sit and have a cool drink or hot tea.

Places to Stay - bottom end

Undoubtedly the nicest place to stay is one of the little pensions in Kaleiçi, the Old Town. Some are in modern buildings, others in historical houses; some are very comfortable, even fancy, while others are quite spartan.

Among the best of the pensions is the *Hadriyanus Pansiyon* (tel (311) 12313), Kılınçarslan Mahallesi, Zeytin Çıkmazı, an old house very nicely fixed up, fronting on a walled garden. The owners are very friendly and charge 7500TL (US$10.50) for a double room without running water.

The *Tunay Aile Pansiyonu* (TOO-nahy) (tel (311) 24677), Selçuk Mahallesi, Mermerli Sokak 7, is a nice old house with a roof terrace and waterless double rooms renting for 3000TL (US$4.20).

Other pensions in Kaleiçi, which you can find easily by following their signs, are the *Harika Pansiyon* (HAH-ree-KAH) (tel (311) 24677) next to the Tunay at Selçuk Mahallesi, Mermerli Sokak 11, charging 5000TL (US$7) double; and the *Anatolia Pension*, tel (311) 26358), Kılınçarslan Mahallesi, Hesapçı Geçidi 3, next to the Hadriyanus Pansiyon, the somewhat lackadaisical management charging 4000TL (US$5.60) for a waterless double.

Should you want a hotel room with private shower, about the cheapest is the *Otel Asya* (AHSS-yah) (tel (311) 12632), Atatürk Caddesi, 1251 Sokak 7, behind the better-known Yayla Palas Hotel (described below). The Asya is no beauty but it's central and cheap, with a friendly

manager and shower-equipped rooms priced at 2400TL (US$3.36) single, 3750TL (US$5.25) double. The Asya is only a half-block from the intersection of Cumhuriyet Caddesi and Atatürk Caddesi, and is thus very near the cheap restaurants on Eski Sebzeciler İçi Sokak.

Near the Oto Garajı is the congenial and very cheap *Sima Pension* (SEE-mah, no phone), Balbey Mahallesi, 426 Sokak 13, a five-minute walk. The price for a clean dorm bed is 1000TL (US$1.40), for space on the roof, 500TL. The lady of the house, Mrs Kurt, cooks delicious vegetarian food.

Another place near the bus station is the quaint and funky old *Süngül Oteli* (seun-GURL) (tel (311) 11408), Tahıl Pazarı, Badik Muhtar Sokak 3, behind the prominent Kervan Oteli on Şarampol Caddesi. A real traditional old Turkish marketplace hotel in a stone building freshly painted, the Süngül charges 1800TL (US$2.52) for a waterless double room, 250TL (US$0.35) for a hot shower. Also, the *Otel Tatoglu* (TAHT-oh-loo) (tel (311) 12119) on Şarampol/ Kâzım Özalp Caddesi 91, is near the bus terminal, has 36 rooms and costs 5000TL (US$7) double with shower. To reach either of these hotels, walk out the front gate of the Oto Garajı and turn left.

Near the Yivli Minare is the *Ülker Pansiyon* (eurl-KEHR) (tel (311) 29636), Posta Sokak 6, behind the THY cargo building, which is directly across Cumhuriyet Caddesi from the dramatic statue of Atatürk. The pension, which charges 2000TL (US$2.80) per person in waterless rooms, might best be described as new, neat, tidy, spartan, central and cheap.

Places to Stay - middle

Best of the mid-range hotels (US$10 to US$20 double) is the *Yayla Palas* (YAHY-lah pah-lahs) (tel (311) 11913, 4), Ali Çetinkaya Caddesi 14, not far from the corner of Atatürk Caddesi. Though an older hotel, it is well kept, with an

accommodating staff; doubles cost 19,800TL (US$27.70), singles are 15,000TL (US$21).

The *Büyük Otel* (bew-YEWK) (tel (311) 11499), Cumhuriyet Caddesi 57, is in the centre next to the plaza with the equestrian statue of Atatürk and the Yivli Minare (Grooved Minaret). It was once Antalya's premier hotel, but is fairly modest for all that. Doubles now cost 15,000TL (US$21), breakfast included. The location and views are excellent.

Near the Oto Garajı, visible from its centre in fact, is the *Hotel Bilgehan* (BEEL-geh-hahn) (tel (311) 15184 or 25324) on Şarampol Caddesi (walk out the front gate of the Oto Garajı and turn right), a modernish, comfortable, undistinguished place charging 18,000TL (US$25.20) for a double with bath and breakfast.

Not far away at Şarampol 138 is the *Kervan Oteli* (kehr-VAHN) (tel (311) 12044), which is slightly less comfortable and charges a bit less: 16,500TL (US$23.10) for a double with bath and breakfast.

Places to Stay – top end
The best is the *Talya Oteli* (TAHL-yah)

(tel (311) 15600), Fevzi Çakmak Caddesi, a bright and modern 150-room palace overlooking the sea. For the price of 77,000TL to 100,000TL (US$107.80 to US$140) double you get a modern, air-conditioned room, swimming pool, tennis court, restaurant, bar and nightclub, hairdressers and exercise room.

Prices are considerably lower at the *Turban Adalya Oteli* (TOOR-bahn ah-DAHL-yah) (tel (311) 18066), an old building with a sense of history, now beautifully restored. It is down by the old harbour in the Old Town, and an air-conditioned double costs 51,500TL (US$72.10) in the high summer season, breakfast included.

Places to Eat – bottom end
Those in search of low-cost meals should go to the intersection of Cumhuriyet and Atatürk Caddesis and find the little street (parallel to Atatürk Caddesi) called Eski Sebzeciler İçi Sokak. The name means 'The Old Inner Street of the Greengrocers' Market', and it is now lined with little restaurants and pastry-shops, many of which have outdoor tables. Most of the food is *kebaps*, including Antalya's specialty, *tandır kebap* (tahn-DUHR), mutton baked in an earthenware pot buried in a firepit; it's rich and flavourful, but pretty greasy. If there's fish, have it. Other inexpensive restaurants can be found along Kazım Özalp/Şarampol Caddesi.

Places to Eat – mid-range
For moderately priced meals, try the *Parlak Restaurant* across Cumhuriyet Caddesi from the Yivli Minare; also the *Şehir Restaurant*, directly behind the Antalya Restaurant, reachable by a passage which goes through the building. The Antalya has a view from its rooftop terrace and music in the evenings.

The *Oda Restaurant* is on the top (6th) floor of the Antalya Ticaret ve Sanayii Odası (Antalya Chamber of Commerce & Industry) building, which is one block

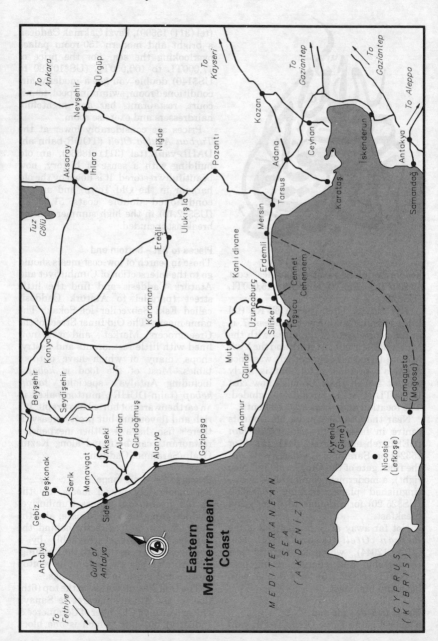

along Şarampol Caddesi from the Yivli Minare, on the left-hand side. At lunchtime, take the lift to the 5th floor and then climb the stairs to the 6th to partake of the *tabldot* (table d'hôte), set-price lunch. Four courses cost about 660TL (US$0.92), and the view is magnificent!

Down by the Old Harbour are numerous patio restaurants such as the *Ahtapot*, with prices marked on a signboard and meals of meat or fowl for 2500TL to 3000TL (US$3.50 to US$4.20), of fish for about 1000TL (US$1.40) more.

Places to Eat – top end
The top restaurant is in the *Talya Oteli*, of course, and it's very good. In fine weather tables are set out on the terrace overlooking the sea.

Getting There & Away
Air Turkish Airlines has non-stop flights to Amman, Jordan (three per week), Ankara (several daily), İstanbul (several daily, 50 minutes, 32,000TL, US$44.80), İzmir (one non-stop per week), Lefkoşe (Nicosia, Cyprus, one non-stop weekly) and London, England (one non-stop weekly). Many European and Middle Eastern cities are served by direct flights via İstanbul or Ankara.

İstanbul Airlines also serves Antalya from its home city of İstanbul.

Bus Because Antalya is such a popular tourist and commercial city, bus transport there is frequent and convenient from all points in Turkey. Antalya's Oto Garajı is on Kâzım Özalp/Şarampol Caddesi, several blocks north of Cumhuriyet Caddesi and the Yivli Minare.

There are about a dozen buses a day to Alanya (two hours, 700TL, US$0.98), stopping at Manavgat (for Side, 1½ hours). Other direct buses go to Adana (12 hours, 4000TL, US$5.60), Ankara (2200TL, US$3.08), Denizli for Pamukkale (5½ hours, 2000TL, US$2.80), Fethiye (six hours, 2300TL, US$3.22), Kaş (five hours, 1300TL, US$1.82), Konya (seven

hours), Marmaris (eight hours) and Ürgüp (11 hours, 4000TL, US$5.60). The best-quality bus companies such as Kâmil Koç and Varan may charge somewhat more for tickets to these destinations.

For minibuses to places east of Antalya such as Perge, Aspendos, Manavgat and Side, go to the Doğu Garajı, which is not a building but a parking lot and staging area for the minibus traffic. You can take a dolmuş (D Garajı) between the Oto Garajı and the Doğu Garajı for 60TL (US$0.08). The minibus to Lara Plaj (80TL, US$0.11) leaves from here.

SİDE
Cleopatra and Marc Antony chose Side (SEE-deh, population 1500) as the spot for a romantic tryst, and today lots of Turkish couples follow their example. Side has everything: a km of fine sand beach on either side, good Hellenistic ruins, an excellent little museum and a Turkish village.

It is perhaps too good. In recent years Side has been overrun by tourists in the summer months. During the season even moving down the streets can be difficult. In spring and autumn the town is delightful, however; and the swimming is still excellent.

The government has a grand scheme for Side. For a decade it has battled in the courts for the right to limit development and to regulate it according to a master plan for the entire region. This includes the preservation of traditional Turkish stone village houses, restoration of the classical ruins and construction of new hotels away from the historic zone.

History
Ancient Side's great wealth was built on piracy and slavery. Many of its great buildings were raised with the profits of such dastardly activities. But slavery flourished only under the Greeks, and was stopped when the city came under Roman control.

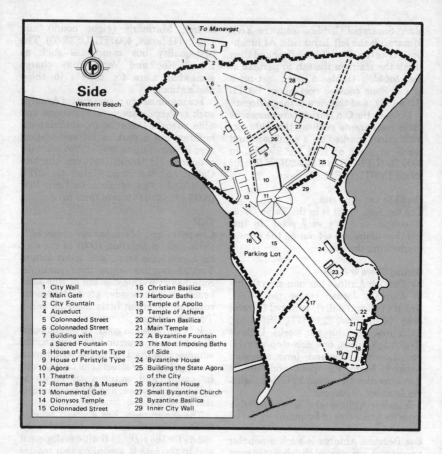

To Manavgat

Side

Western Beach

Parking Lot

1 City Wall
2 Main Gate
3 City Fountain
4 Aqueduct
5 Colonnaded Street
6 Colonnaded Street
7 Building with
   a Sacred Fountain
8 House of Peristyle Type
9 House of Peristyle Type
10 Agora
11 Theatre
12 Roman Baths & Museum
13 Monumental Gate
14 Dionysos Temple
15 Colonnaded Street

16 Christian Basilica
17 Harbour Baths
18 Temple of Apollo
19 Temple of Athena
20 Christian Basilica
21 Main Temple
22 A Byzantine Fountain
23 The Most Imposing Baths
   of Side
24 Byzantine House
25 Building the State Agora
   of the City
26 Byzantine House
27 Small Byzantine Church
28 Byzantine Basilica
29 Inner City Wall

No one knows where Side got its name, though it probably means 'pomegranate' in some ancient Anatolian language. The site was colonized by Aeolians about 600 BC, but by the time Alexander the Great swept through, the inhabitants had abandoned much of their Greek culture and language.

After the period of piracy and slave-trading, Side turned to legitimate commerce, and still prospered. Under the Byzantines it was still large enough to rate a bishop. But the Arab raids of the 600s AD diminished the town, which was

dead within two centuries. In the late 1800s the Ottomans revived it as a town.

Orientation

Side is several km south of the east-west highway. The road to the village is dotted with little hotels and pensions, often bearing signs which read *Boş Oda Var* ('Rooms Available'). The road passes through the archaeological zone and past the museum, beneath an arch and around the theatre before ending at a barrier by a car park. In high season you will not be allowed to drive a car into the village proper. You must pay a fee and park in the car park, which is also Side's bus terminal.

Information

The shiny new Tourism Information Office (tel (3213) 1265) is somewhat inconveniently located on the outskirts of the village, a walk of about one km.

Things to See

Side's impressive ruins are an easy walk from the village. Look first at the **theatre**, one of the largest in Anatolia, with 15,000 seats. Originally constructed during Hellenistic times, it was enlarged under the Romans.

Next to the theatre and across the road from the museum is the **agora**. The **museum** is built on the site of the Roman baths. It has a very fine small collection of statuary and reliefs.

To the east, between these buildings and the **Hellenistic city walls**, lie a Byzantine basilica and some foundations of Byzantine houses. Down at the edge of the eastern beach is another agora.

At the very southern tip of the point of land upon which Side lies are two temples, the **Temple of Athena** and **Temple of Apollo**, which date from the 100s AD. Who knows that Cleopatra and Marc Antony didn't meet at exactly this spot? Though they met (42 BC) before these great columns were erected, might they not have sat in earlier marble temples to enjoy one of Side's spectacular sunsets? Wandering among these marble remains at dusk is one of the finest things to do here.

Places to Stay

You may have difficulty finding a room in high summer. If you visit then, arrive early in the day. Before mid-June and after mid-September you should have no problem finding the lodgings you want. Prices are lower in this off-season as well.

Places to Stay – bottom end

In the village proper, little pensions abound. There are dozens to choose from, and your choice will be dictated by availability as much as price.

My favourite is the *Hermes Pansiyon* (HEHR-mess), run by Mrs Ayşe Güzel and her daughter Perihan. Ask in the main square as there may be no sign on the pension. The pension is an old Side house, nothing fancy, but with rooms facing a garden. Only two rooms have plumbing, but all can use a common kitchen and enjoy the scent of the jasmine vine in the shady garden. The beach is close by, as is the main square.

Near the Hermes are the *Şen Pansiyon* (Shen) and the *Huzur Pansiyon* (hoo-ZOOR). A nice one near the eastern beach is the *Martı* (mahr-TUH). Some readers of this book have enjoyed the *Çiğdem*. As you comb the town for good lodgings, look for little signs which say *Boş Oda Var* ('Rooms Available'). Prices depend on season and facilities, but range from 4000TL to 7500TL (US$5.60 to US$10.50) double, without private bath.

Places to Stay – middle

In the village, the *Köseoğlu Otel* (kurr-SEH-oh-loo) (tel (3213) 0303) is a glorified pension, with bare modern rooms priced at 10,000TL (US$14) double with private bath and breakfast.

Side has a few comfortable motels on its western beach, among which the best is the *Motel Side* (tel (3213) 1022). Close to the village, attractive, with a pretty patio restaurant, the motel charges 22,000TL (US$30.80) for a double room, breakfast and dinner included.

Other motels along the western beach include the *Subaşı Motel* (SOO-bah-shuh) (tel (3213) 1215 or 1047), near the turning from the main road into the village. The location here is good, as it's only a 15-minute walk to the village. Two people pay 12,000TL (US$16.80) for a double room with bath and breakfast; some rooms have water views.

The *Motel Turtel* (TOOR-tehl) (tel (3211) 2225, 6) is a fairly lavish spread with motel rooms renting for 16,000TL (US$22.40) double with breakfast; bungalows are slightly more.

Places to Stay – top end

Well out along the western beach are the *Sırma Holiday Apartments* (tel (3211) 2220), a huge complex of condominium and rental apartments and hotel rooms, row after row of them. Prices are 35,700TL (US$49.98) single, 47,200TL (US$66.08) double for a luxurious hotel room, or about 60,700TL (US$84.98) for an apartment for two people, per day.

Places to Eat

When looking for a pension, ask about cooking facilities. Most have them, and this allows you to save substantial amounts of money. At the motels you may be required to buy at least two meals a day, so the food problem is solved that way whether you like it or not.

The restaurants in town, good and not-so-good, tend to be expensive for what you get, except for *Enişte'nin Yeri*, which has reasonably good food at the lowest prices. Service may be inexperienced here, but so may it be in the higher-priced places. The shady terrace is very nice, even with the fluorescent lights.

The *İlgi Restaurant* (eel-GEE) on the main street has an upper-level terrace, a full menu of *kebaps* and ready dishes, and a specialty, *Side kebap*, which is ground lamb stuffed with nuts and served with flat *pide* bread. Another specialty is *İlgi kebap*, a small beef filet steak stuffed with mild yellow *kaşar* cheese, pistachios, peanuts and lamb's liver, then grilled.

The *Nergiz Tea Garden & Cocktail Place*, at the beach end of the main street, is nice for breakfast (500TL, US$0.70) or a cool *rakı* (600TL, US$0.84) in the evening.

Among the most pleasant of the fish restaurants is the *Afrodit Restaurant*, at the beach end of the main street. It's also among the more expensive places, but even so, a seafood dinner need cost no more than 6000TL (US$8.40).

Ask your pension *hanım* (lady) for tips on other current restaurant favourites.

Getting There

Side, 75 km east of Antalya, is so popular as a resort that it has its own direct bus service to Ankara, İzmir and İstanbul. The numerous buses which run along the coast between Antalya and Alanya will drop you in Side or in Manavgat, the town on the highway. From Manavgat, dolmuşes travel the few km down to the shore frequently.

You may find it best to take a dolmuş from Side to the highway junction or to Manavgat, to catch the bus to Alanya.

AROUND ANTALYA

You can, if you like, use Antalya as a base for excursions to Olympos and Phaselis, Termessos, Perge, Aspendos and Side. But you might find it easier to visit Olympos and Phaselis on your way to or from Kaş, and Perge and Aspendos on your way to Side. Using the small towns of Kaş and Side as a base is both delightful and less expensive.

With your own car, you can stop at Termessos on your way north or west to Ankara, İstanbul or İzmir. Otherwise, Termessos is the one city you must visit using Antalya as your base.

Travel agencies in Antalya operate tours to all of these sites. For instance, a half-day tour to the Düden Waterfalls (Düden Şelalesi) and Termessos costs 5000TL (US$7) per person and is perhaps a bit rushed – there's a lot to see at Termessos. A full-day tour to Perge, Aspendos and Side costs 9000TL (US$12.60). Or you can organize your own transport. If you can scrape together a party of four or five people, you can negotiate with a taxi driver for a private excursion. The private taxi method is especially useful for getting to Termessos.

Termessos

High in a rugged mountain valley 34 km inland from Antalya lies Termessos (tehr-MEH-sohs), a Pisidian city of warlike, spartan people. They lived in their impregnable fortress city and guarded their independence fiercely. Alexander the Great did not attack them, and the Romans accepted them as allies, not as a subject people.

Start early in the day, as you will have to walk and climb a good deal to see the ruins. Though it's cooler up in the mountains than at the shore, the sun is still quite hot. Do this visit in the morning, and spend the afternoon at the beach.

Leave Antalya by the E24 highway toward Burdur and Isparta, turning after about 12 km onto the road for Korkuteli. Signs mark the entrance to Termessos Milli Parkı (National Park). Entry to the park costs 250TL (US$0.35) for a car, 100TL (US$0.14) per person. A half-mile into the park is a small museum with photographs and artefacts from the ruins, plus displays touching on the botany and zoology of the park. Near the museum are camping and picnic sites. Continue another 8½ km up the rough dirt road to the ruins.

The road winds up through several gates in the city walls to the agora, the largest flat space in this steep valley. From here you must explore the ruins on foot.

At the agora are the remains of a small **Temple of Hadrian**, now little more than a doorway. Head up the path to the city gate, the theatre (best-preserved building here), gymnasium, a Corinthian temple and the upper city walls.

Your goal is the **necropolis** at the very top of the valley, three km up from the agora. It's a hike, but the necropolis is a fantastic sight and the mountain vistas are breathtaking. As you toil upward you'll notice a wire running alongside the path. It goes to a fire tower at the top of the valley, where a man sits, drinks tea, smokes cigarettes, reads newspapers and keeps a lookout for fires. He has to carry up from the agora all the water he uses.

The necropolis *(mezarlık)* is really something, a vast field of huge stone sarcophagi tumbled about by earthquakes and grave-robbers. The scene is reminiscent of medieval paintings portraying the Judgment Day, when all tombs are to be cast open.

Perge

Perge (PEHR-geh), 15 km east of Antalya near the town of Aksu (take a minibus from the Doğu Garajı), is one of those very ancient towns. Greek colonists came here after the Trojan War and probably displaced even older inhabitants. The city prospered under Alexander the Great and the Romans, but dwindled under the Byzantines. The substantial remains of a great theatre, stadium, huge Hellenistic and Roman gates, and an impressive colonnaded street are worth seeing. The acropolis, on a rise behind the other ruins, has nothing much to see. For a fine view of the site, climb to the top of the theatre.

A visit to Perge can be included in the trip eastward to Aspendos and Side. Leave early in the morning. Ride the 13 km east from Antalya to Aksu and the turning for Perge, then two km north to the ruins.

Aspendos (Belkis)

The land east of Antalya was called Pamphylia in ancient times. The Taurus Mountains (Toros Dağları) form a beautiful backdrop to the fertile coast, rich with fields of cotton and vegetables. Irrigation troughs of concrete radiate like spiderwebs through the lush agricultural land.

Aspendos (ahs-PEHN-dohs) lies 47 km east of Antalya in the Pamphylian plain. Go as far as the Köprüçayı stream, and notice the old Seljuk humpback bridge. Turn left (north) along the western bank of the stream, following the signs to Aspendos. The great theatre is less than

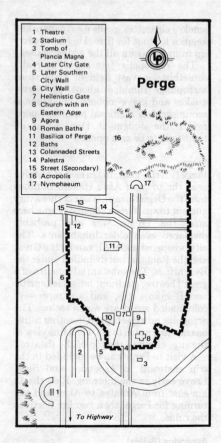

Perge

1 Theatre
2 Stadium
3 Tomb of Plancia Magna
4 Later City Gate
5 Later Southern City Wall
6 City Wall
7 Hellenistic Gate
8 Church with an Eastern Apse
9 Agora
10 Roman Baths
11 Basilica of Perge
12 Baths
13 Colonnaded Streets
14 Palestra
15 Street (Secondary)
16 Acropolis
17 Nymphaeum

To Highway

four km from the highway. Hours for the site are 8 am to 7 pm daily; admission costs 400TL (US\$0.56), half-price on Sunday.

What you see here remains from Roman times, though the history of the settlement goes well back to the Hittite Empire (800 BC). In 468 the Greeks and Persians fought a great battle here (the Greeks won, but not for long). Under the Romans, during the reign of Marcus Aurelius (161-180 AD), Aspendos got its theatre.

There are many fine Hellenistic and

Roman theatres in Anatolia, but the one at Aspendos is the finest of all. Built by the Romans, maintained by the Byzantines and Seljuks, it was restored after a visit by Atatürk. A plaque by the entrance states that when he saw the theatre, Atatürk declared that it should be restored and used again for performances and sports.

Purists may question the authenticity of the restorations, but more than any other, the theatre at Aspendos allows the modern visitor to see and feel a true classical theatre: its acoustics, its lighting by day and night, and how the audiences moved in and out. Don't miss it.

Other ruins of a stadium, agora and basilica offer little to look at. Note, however, the arches and several towers of a long aqueduct out in the fields.

EASTWARD TO ALANYA

The journey from Manavgat to Alanya is 60 km and takes about an hour. About 12 km east of Manavgat a highway heads north, up to the Anatolian plateau, to Konya via **Akseki**, twisting its way through an endless expanse of mountains. Though the road appears to be far shorter than that via Antalya or Silifke, in fact it winds so much that it takes at least as long. However, the scenery is spectacular, and it is an area rarely seen by tourists.

The coastal highway (E24) skirts good sandy beach virtually the whole way to Alanya. Here and there a modern motel or government rest camp has been built to exploit the holiday potential. On the landward side you see the occasional bit of aqueduct or the foundations of some old caravanserai or baths. Thirteen km before Alanya, notice the Şarapsa Hanı, a Seljuk caravanserai. Another one, the Alarahan, is accessible (30 km) by a side road heading north.

ALANYA

The Seljuk Turks built a powerful empire, the Sultanate of Rum (ROOM,

Rome), which thrived from 1071 to 1243. Its capital was in Konya, but its prime port was Alanya.

Alanya (ah-LAHN-yah, population 36,000), like Side, occupies a point of land flanked by two great sweeping beaches. A pleasant, small agricultural and tourist town, Alanya has an easy pace, friendly people (many of whom wear the traditional baggy *şalvar* trousers) and the added attraction of significant Seljuk archaeological remains. It's a delightful place to spend several days before heading east to Silifke or north to Konya.

Orientation
The bus station (Otogar) is on the E24 highway (Atatürk Caddesi) three km west of the centre. It is served by city buses, which will take you into town every half-hour for 100TL (US$0.14). You can buy bus tickets in the town, though, at the open lot from which dolmuşes leave.

Information
The Tourism Office (tel (3231) 1246) is at the north-western foot of the promontory, near the Alanya Müzesi and Damlataş cave. Buses to the top of the promontory depart from the office every hour.

Things to See
Head for the Seljuk sights early in the day, as Alanya gets very hot. Walk down to the harbour for a look at the **Red Tower** (Kızıl Kule, KUH-zuhl koo-leh), constructed in 1226 in the reign of the Seljuk Sultan Alaeddin Keykubad I by a Syrian Arab architect. The five-storey octagonal tower, now restored to its former glory, was the key to Alanya's harbour defenses. Past it, out toward the sea, a path leads to the old Seljuk **Tersane** or shipyard (1228).

Alanya's most exciting historical site is of course the **Fortress** (Kale, KAH-leh) atop the promontory, reachable by city bus (100TL, US$0.14) from the Tourism Office; a bus leaves every hour. Otherwise it's a very hot hour's walk (three km) or a

taxi (2500TL, US$3.50); with your own car, you can drive right up to the fort.

The ancient city was enclosed by the rambling wall (1226) which makes its way all around the peninsula. At the top is the **Ehmedek Kalesi**, the inner fortress. From the İç Kale (EECH-kah-leh, inner fort or keep) you get a dazzling view of the peninsula, walls, town and great expanses of beautiful coast backed by the blue Taurus Mountains.

You can hire a boat for an hour's coastal tour around the promontory, during which you'll approach several caves, including those called the **Lovers' Grotto** (Aşıklar Mağarası, ah-shuk-LAHR mah-ah-rah-suh), **Pirates' Cave** (Korsanlar Mağarası, kohr-sahn-LAHR), **Phosphorescent Cave** (Fosforlu, fohs-fohr-LOO) and **Cave of Dripping Stones** (Damlataş, DAHM-lah tahsh), as well as **Cleopatra's Beach** on the west side of the promontory. To hire the entire boat for such a tour costs 4000TL (US$5.60); a boat can take seven or eight passengers. By the way, Damlataş is accessible on foot at the western side of the promontory, not far from the Tourism Office.

Alanya has a tidy little **museum** (Alanya Müzesi) on the west side of the peninsula, near the Tourism Office on the way to Damlataş cave, open daily 9 am to noon and 1.30 to 6.30 pm; admission costs 200TL (US$0.28), half-price on Sunday. Exhibits span the ages from Old Bronze through Greek and Roman to Ottoman. Don't miss the Ethnology Room at the back, with a fine assortment of *kilims* (woven mats), *cicims* (embroidered mats), Turkish carpets, inlaid work of wood and copper, gold and silver, and beautifully written and illuminated religious books.

Places to Stay
The most comfortable and luxurious lodgings are well out on the eastern beach, but they're inconvenient if you want to stroll in town. Downtown hotels are moderately priced or quite cheap.

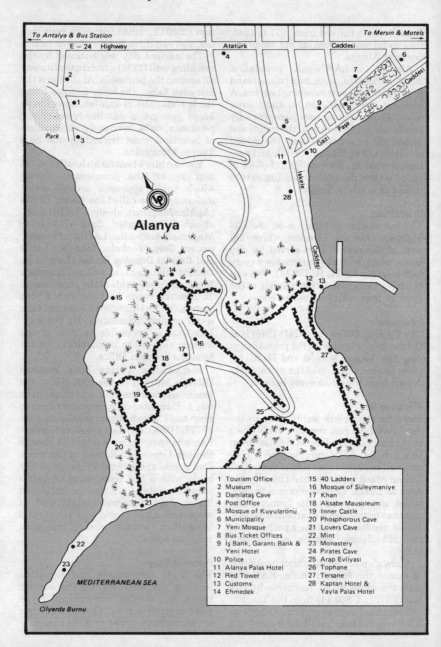

Alanya

To Antalya & Bus Station

To Mersin & Motels

E – 24 Highway

Atatürk

Caddesi

Park

Gazi Paşa Caddesi

İskele Caddesi

MEDITERRANEAN SEA

Cilyarda Burnu

1 Tourism Office	15 40 Ladders
2 Museum	16 Mosque of Süleymaniye
3 Damlataş Cave	17 Khan
4 Post Office	18 Aksabe Mausoleum
5 Mosque of Kuyularönü	19 Inner Castle
6 Municipality	20 Phosphorous Cave
7 Yeni Mosque	21 Lovers Cave
8 Bus Ticket Offices	22 Mint
9 İş Bank, Garantı Bank &	23 Monastery
Yeni Hotel	24 Pirates Cave
10 Police	25 Arap Evliyası
11 Alanya Palas Hotel	26 Tophane
12 Red Tower	27 Tersane
13 Customs	28 Kaptan Hotel &
14 Ehmedek	Yayla Palas Hotel

Top: Slicing döner to make *Bursa Kebabı*
Bottom: Turkey's first republican parliament building in Ankara

Top: The Library of Celsus, Ephesus
Bottom: Angelic figure in high relief, Ephesus

Places to Stay - bottom end

Small hotels and pensions in the town rent rooms for as little as 3000TL (US$4.20) double. The *Yayla Palas* (YAHY-lah pah-LAHS) (tel (3231) 1017 or 3544), a converted house at İskele Caddesi 48, has waterless rooms for 4000TL (US$5.60). At the nearby *Baba Hotel* (BAH-bah) (tel (3231) 1032), İskele Caddesi 8, doubles without bath cost 4000TL (US$5.60), or 5000TL (US$7) with bath. The neighbouring *Alanya Palas* (tel (3231) 1016), charges a mere 2250TL (US$3.15) single, 3000TL (US$4.20) double, or 4000TL (US$5.60) for a double with shower.

The very tidy *Hotel Kent* (tel (3231) 2754), İskele Caddesi 12, is a cut above its neighbours, and charges a bit more for a double with bath: 7000TL (US$9.80). My favourite, however, is the *Hotel Günaydın* (gur-nahy-DUHN) (tel (3231) 1943), Kültür Caddesi 30, a long block inland from the competition in a quiet location. Prices for a tidy room with shower are 4000TL (US$5.60) single, 6000TL (US$8.40) double.

Camping Look for camping areas along the beach both east and west of town, especially east.

Places to Stay - top end

I prefer hotels in the centre of the town, as they allow you to walk easily to restaurants and attractions. If you prefer them too, head for the *Kaptan Otel* (kahp-TAHN) (tel (3231) 2000 or 1094), İskele Caddesi 62, very near the Red Tower. The modern 45-room hotel faces the harbour, town and beach; air-conditioned singles cost 22,500TL (US$31.50), doubles are 29,700TL (US$41.58).

Alanya's most comfortable rooms are at the 99-room *Club Alantur* (ah-LAHN-toor) (tel (3231) 1224 or 1924), also sometimes called the Alantur Motel. It is six km east of the centre, a lavish (for Alanya) layout with lawns and gardens,

sea views and a swimming pool. Air-conditioned doubles cost 50,000TL (US$70).

Places to Eat

Though Alanya has several inexpensive *hazır yemek* restaurants, you should have at least a few meals at one of the little waterfront restaurants along Gazi Paşa Caddesi in the centre. Walk along the street and you'll see the *Şirin, Yönet, Havuzbaşı* and *Mahperi*. Sitting here and having a full lunch or dinner will cost about 2500TL (US$3.50).

In the market streets off Gazi Paşa Caddesi are several even cheaper restaurants, including a very inexpensive *pide* and *kebap* place, the *Konya Etli Pide ve Kebap Salonu*. Here the price for a tuck-in drops to 1600TL (US$2.24).

While you're here, try a few of the local fish: *levrek* (sea bass), *barbunya* (red mullet) or *kuzu balığı* ('muttonfish').

An unusual treat is the local ice cream, made with flavours such as *şeftali* (peach), *kavun* (melon), *dut* (mulberry) and *sakız* (pine resin).

Getting There & Away

There are 10 buses daily to and from Antalya (800TL, US$1.12), seven to Adana (2500TL, US$3.50) via Silifke and Mersin (2300TL, US$3.22), five to Ankara (2800TL, US$3.92) via Konya (10 hours, 2000TL, US$2.80) or Nevşehir (12 hours, 4000TL, US$5.60), two to İzmir (11½ hours), two to İstanbul (3800TL, US$5.32) and one via Kaş (six hours, 2000TL, US$2.80) to Marmaris.

Traffic is very sparse eastward around the 'bulge' of Anamur. Few buses originate in Alanya, so you must depend on passing buses to have empty seats, which they sometimes don't have, so make your departure arrangements as far in advance as possible. Also keep in mind that the road eastward is mountainous and curvy, and takes a good deal longer to traverse than you might think from looking at the map.

Boats to Cyprus You can make arrangements in Alanya to catch a ferryboat to northern Cyprus. Boats leave from Taşucu, just west of Silifke, 262 km east of Alanya. At Alanya's Otogar you can make a boat reservation and also buy a ticket for the very early morning bus from Alanya to the ferry docks. For more information on these boats, see the section on Silifke.

ALANYA TO SİLİFKE

From Alanya, you will probably want to head north to Konya, Cappadocia and Ankara. The eastern Mediterranean coast has a few sights of interest, but the cities of Mersin, Tarsus, Adana and İskenderun have very little to hold your interest. Agriculture, commerce and shipping, not the tourist trade, are what keep them going. But should you be heading east along the coast, here are some details.

From Alanya to Silifke is 270 km along a twisty road cut into the cliffs which rise steeply from the sea. Every now and then the road passes through the fertile delta of a stream, planted with bananas or figs. Views of the sea and stretches of cool evergreen forest are nice, but there's little else to look at until Anamur.

Anamur

Anamur (AH-nah-moor, population 24,000) has a few small hotels and restaurants in the town off the main road, and numerous camping places near the beach. Down by the sea is the Marmure Kalesi, a fortress built by the emirs of Karahan in 1240. About 12 km later are the ruins of another fortress, the Softa Kalesi.

The highway finally comes down from the cliffside to the Cilician Plain, the fertile littoral at the foot of the Taurus Mountains which stretches from Silifke to Adana.

SİLİFKE

Silifke (see-LEEF-keh, population 42,000) is the ancient Seleucia, founded by Seleucus I Nicator in the 290s BC. Seleucus was one of Alexander the Great's most able generals, and founder of the Seleucid dynasty which ruled ancient Syria after Alexander's death.

Silifke's other claim to fame is as the place where Emperor Frederick I Barbarossa (1125-1190), while leading his troops on the Third Crusade, drowned as he crossed the river.

A striking castle dominates the town from a Taurus hillside, and seems to promise good sightseeing. But to many people Silifke is just a place to catch the boat to Cyprus or a bus to Mersin, Adana or Konya.

Orientation

The bus terminal is near the junction of highways to Alanya, Mersin and Konya. From the bus terminal into the centre of the town is exactly one km; at the half-km mark you pass the Temple of Jupiter.

The town is divided by the Göksu River, called in ancient times the Calycadnus. Most of the services you'll want are on the southern bank of the river, along with the bus station. Exceptions are the Tourism Office and the dolmuş to Uzuncaburç, which are on the river's northern bank.

Information

Silifke's Tourism Information Office (tel (7591) 1151) is at Atatürk Caddesi 1/2, on the traffic roundabout just at the northern end of the bridge across the river. The staff speak some English, and have lots of interesting materials on Silifke and its history.

Things to See

The **Archaeological Museum** is not far from the bus terminal, and includes a large number of Hellenistic coins and several mosaics, among many other exhibits from the area's deep and eventful past. The **fortress** *(kale)* on the hill dates from medieval times. Perhaps

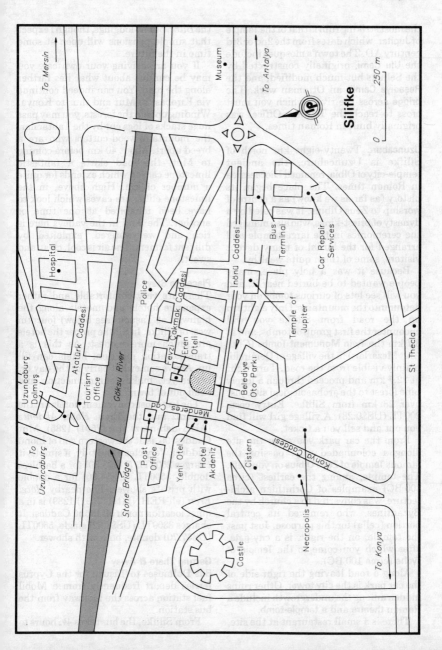

Silifke

To Mersin

To Antalya

0   250 m

Museum

To Konya

To Antalya

Bus Terminal

İnönü Caddesi

Temple of Jupiter

Car Repair Services

Police

St Thecla

Hospital

Atatürk Caddesi

Göksu River

Fevzi Çakmak Caddesi

Eren Oteli

Belediye Oto Parkı

Uzuncaburç Dolmuş

Tourism Office

Post Office

Stone Bridge

Menderes Cad

Yeni Otel

Hotel Akdeniz

Konyol Caddesi

Cistern

Necropolis

Castle

To Uzuncaburç

To Konya

the most striking ruin is that of the **Temple of Jupiter**, which dates from the 2nd or 3rd century AD. The town's mosques include the **Ulu Cami**, originally constructed by the Seljuks but much modified, and the **Reşadiye Camii**, an Ottoman work. The **bridge** across the river, which you must cross to reach the Tourism Office, was originally built in Roman times.

Uzuncaburç Twenty-eight km north of Silifke is Uzuncaburç, the ancient temple-city of Olbia, renamed Diocaesarea in Roman times. The place began its history (as far as we know) as a centre of worship to Zeus Olbius. It was ruled by a dynasty of priest-kings, who also managed the ceremonies in the large temple and arranged for the burial of many devout visitors, some of them quite wealthy.

Because it was a holy place, many people wanted to be buried near it, and you will see lots of curious **tombs** on your detour into the mountains. Only eight km up the road from Silifke you will encounter the first group of tombs, and at 8.7 km the **Twin Monument Tombs** (Çifte Anıt Mezarları) in the village of Demircili, plainly visible from the road. Turn right at 22.7 km and proceed through a lovely pine forest to the archaeological site, just over 28 km from Silifke. Entry costs 200TL (US$0.28). A village girl will find you out and sell you a ticket.

From the car park you enter the site along a colonnaded way, passing the famous **Temple of Zeus Olbius** on your left. The temple, among the earliest (circa 300 BC) examples of Corinthian architecture, was converted to a church by the Byzantines, who removed its central portion (cella) for this purpose. Just past the temple, on the right, is a **city gate**, after which you come to the **Temple of Tyche** (circa 100 BC).

Along a road leaving the right side of the car park is the **city tower**. Other ruins hidden among the undergrowth include a Roman **theatre** and a **temple-tomb**.

There is a small restaurant at the site,

the *Burç*, but no lodgings, though I expect that simple pensions will open at some time in the future.

If you are driving your own car, you may be curious about what lies farther along the road. You can indeed continue via Kırobası to Mut and thus to Konya. Winding up into the forests, you may pass huge stacks of logs cut by the Tahtacılar, the mountain wood-cutters who are a breed apart. About 40 km before coming to Mut, the road skirts a fantastic limestone **canyon** which extends for quite a number of km. High above, in the limestone cliffs, are caves which look to have been inhabited at one time or another. The land in the valleys here is rich and well-watered, exploited by diligent farmers. The air is cool, clean and sweet.

Places to Stay

There are very comfortable and rather expensive hotels and motels along the highway at Taşucu (see below) four km west of Silifke. In Silifke proper the hotels are much more modest. As this is a transportation junction, hotels can fill up. Arrive somewhat early in the day or, better yet, make your connection and head out of town.

The two most convenient hotels are the Akdeniz and the Eren. *Hotel Akdeniz* (AHK-deh-neez) (tel (7591) 1285), Mut Caddesi 96, is at the western end of İnönü Caddesi. Very clean and tidy, if simple, it charges 2500TL (US$3.50) for a bathless double, 3500TL (US$4.90) for a double with private shower. The nearby *Hotel Eren* (eh-REHN) (tel (7591) 1289) is in a quiet location north off İnönü Caddesi. It charges 3300TL (US$4.62) single, 5500TL (US$7.70) double, both with shower.

Getting There & Away

Bus Dolmuşes to Taşucu for the Cyprus ferries depart frequently from a Mobil fuel station across the highway from the bus station.

From Silifke, the bus takes 4½ hours to

Konya (2000TL, US$2.80), two hours to Adana (1000TL, US$1.40), 1¼ hours to Mersin, 6½ to Alanya (2500TL, US$3.50), eight hours to Antalya (3000TL, US$4.20), eight hours to Ankara (3000TL, US$4.20). To Narlıkuyu (see below), the fare is 200TL (US$0.28).

Dolmuşes north to Uzuncaburç depart from near the Tourism Office at 11 am and noon daily.

The highway east from Silifke to Adana is well-travelled by bus traffic. The buses of the Silifke Koop company depart for Adana every 15 minutes throughout the morning and afternoon, and will stop to pick you up on the road, should you be visiting one of the many archaeological sites east of town.

Boats to Cyprus Passenger boats to Kyrenia (Girne, Turkish Republic of Northern Cyprus) depart from Taşucu, four km west of Silifke. See above for dolmuş information.

In Taşucu there's a Tourism Information Office (tel (7593) 1234) by the boat dock at Atatürk Caddesi, Gümrük Meydanı 18/A. There's also a cheap and friendly little hotel across the street from the ticket office, and the absurdly cheap *Meltem Lokantası* nearby.

You can also make your arrangements and buy tickets for the boats in Silifke's bus terminal. Look for the signs for the Uğur company's Deniz Otobüsü (deh-NEEZ oh-toh-bew-sew, 'sea bus', hydrofoil). The hydrofoil departs Monday, Wednesday and Friday at 10 am on the two-hour trip. A single ticket costs US$23, twice that amount to go and return.

For the regular boat, tickets cost less, but the trip is longer. The Ertürk company (tel (7593) 1033 or 1325 and Girne (581) 52308), operates boats on Tuesday, Thursday and Saturday at 10 am on the six-hour trip. Return trips from Girne to Taşucu are made on Wednesday, Friday and Saturday. A single ticket costs US$18; to go and return

costs US$29. The Ertürk boat carries cars as well as passengers. Note that Turkish Maritime Lines operates big, modern car ferries to Cyprus from Mersin (see below).

SILIFKE TO ADANA

The distance from Silifke to Adana is 153 km; from Silifke to Mersin, 85 km. The buses of the Silifke Koop company run along the coast here about every 15 minutes, and you can use them to shuttle among the various sights described below.

Twenty km east of Silifke you'll notice a romantic castle about 200 metres offshore, and another one (in ruins) right on the shore. This is the **Maiden's Castle** (Kız Kalesi, KUHZ kah-leh-see), to which many legends are attached. Historically, the castles were built by the Byzantines and later used by the Armenian kings. The castles and good beach are served by a few small restaurants, some pensions, camping areas and a motel or two.

Inland from the Kız Kalesi, a road winds two km to the **Caves of Heaven and Hell** (Cennet ve Cehennem). This limestone coast is riddled with caverns, but the Cennet (jeh-NEHT) is among the most impressive. Little soft drink and snack stands cluster at the top. Walk down a long path of many steps to reach the cavern mouth. Along the way, notice the strips of cloth and paper tied to twigs and tree branches by those who have come to this 'mystical' place in search of cures. The bits of cloth and paper are reminders to a saint or spirit that a supplicant has asked for intercession. At the mouth of the cave are the ruins of a small Byzantine church. The cave is not lighted, so the immense mouth is about as far as you can go. Near Cennet is Cehennem (jeh-HEHN-nehm), or Hell, a deep gorge entered by a ladder.

The village of **Narlıkuyu**, on the seashore at the turning for Cennet ve Cehennem, has a few seaside restaurants, a little shop for snacks and necessities, a water pump, a little pension and the remains of a Roman bath (300s AD) with a nice mosaic of the Three Graces, Aglaia, Thalia and Euphrosyne. Entry to the museum which protects the mosaic costs 200TL (US$0.28).

Only 8½ km east of Kız Kalesi, at a place called Kumkuyu (KOOM-kooyoo), is a turning to **Kanlıdivane**, the ruins of ancient Elaiussa-Sebaste-Kanytelis, which lie three km off the highway. The ancient city occupies a vast site around limestone caverns. As you ride the four km up into the hills, the ruins become thicker. The main part of the old city has many buildings, mostly in great ruin. The necropolis, with its tombs built as little temples, is interesting. If you have camping equipment, you can make camp at Kumkuyu.

Back on the highway, you see unmarked ruins at various points along the roadside, testifying to the long and confused history of the area. It served as a pathway between the Anatolian plateau and Syria.

Just before Mersin, at a place called Mezikli, is a turning on the right (south) to **Viranşehir**, the ancient Soles or Pompeiopolis. Two km down the road is a row of Corinthian columns standing in a field. In the distance is part of an aqueduct, both dating from the 200s AD.

MERSİN (İCEL)

Mersin (mehr-SEEN), population 350,000), also called İçel (ee-CHEHL), is a modern city, built only a few decades ago to give Anatolia a large port conveniently close to Adana and its agriculturally rich hinterland. It has several good hotels in each price range, and can serve as an emergency stop on your way through.

Information

The Tourism Information Office (tel (741) 11265 or 12710) is down near the docks, east of the park, at Yenimahalle, İnönü Bulvarı, Liman Giriş Sahası. Near the office is the stop for buses going out to Viranşehir.

Places to Stay – bottom end

There is a cheap, clean and convenient hotel near the bus station. As you walk out of the bus station, the centre of town is to your right; but turn left and walk 1½ blocks to the *Otel Murat* (moo-RAHT) (tel (741) 24681), Zeytinli Bahçe Caddesi 208, the closest presentable hotel to the Otogar, which will rent you a double room without private bath for 3000TL (US$4.20).

Downtown, several small hotels are at the centre of the action. *Hotel Kent* (tel (741) 11655), İstiklal Caddesi 51 near Kuvayi Milliye Caddesi, charges 3200TL (US$4.48) for a double with shower. The *Erden Palas Oteli* (ehr-DEHN pahlahss) (tel (741) 11329), Cami Şerifi Mahallesi, 3 Sokak 19, is just off Uray Caddesi east of Kuvayi Milliye Caddesi (follow the narrow street between the little square mosque and the Türkiye Vakıflar Bankası). Quiet except for the amplified call of the muezzin, it charges a mere 2200TL (US$3.08) for a double. The *Büyük Otel* (beur-YEURK) (tel (741) 12606), on Kuvayi Milliye Caddesi only one block north of the deluxe Mersin Oteli, is a place of last resort, charging 2800TL (US$3.92) double.

Places to Stay – middle

The *Otel Ege* (EH-geh) (tel (741) 21419), İstiklal Caddesi, 33 Sokak 24, is new, bright, folksy and fairly quiet. Decorated with lots of Turkish crafts, it charges 11,000TL (US$15.40) single, 14,000TL (US$19.60) double.

Rooms are cheaper but still good at the *Hosta Otel* (HOHS-tah) (tel (741) 14760), Fasih Kayabalı Caddesi 4, Yeni Hal Civarı, near the wholesale vegetable markets just a few blocks from the Mersin Oteli. A single with shower is a mere 5000TL (US$7), a double 7000TL (US$9.80).

Mersin

0   200
approx. m.

To Tarsus & Adana

Railway Station

Commercial Port

100 Yıl Parkı

Harbour

Atatürk Parkı

Water Sports

Stadium

Deresi

Müftü

To Silifke, Antalya & Konya

1 Tourism Information
2 Mersin Hotel
3 Otogar
4 Municipality
5 State Hospital
6 Government Hall
7 Directory General
   of Customs
8 Post Office
9 Turkish Airlines
10 Turkish Maritime Lines
   Agency
11 Police
12 WC
13 Hotels
14 Restaurants
15 Churches
16 Banks
17 Auto Park
18 Social Security Hospital
19 Private Hospital
20 Amusement Places
21 Directory of Health
22 Italian Consulate
23 Swedish Consulate
24 Turkish Federated State
   of Cyprus Office of
   Mersin Representative

Places to Stay - top end

The *Mersin Oteli* (tel (741) 12200), Gümrük Meydanı 112 at the seaward end of Kuvayi Milliye Caddesi, is down on the waterfront; its 116 rooms are the most comfortable in town and go for 25,000TL (US$35) single, 36,000TL (US$50.40) double. Rooms are air-conditioned and equipped with mini-bars; there's a restaurant on the hotel's roof.

Places to Eat

Try the *Ali Baba Restaurant* (tel 20388) on Silifke Caddesi, which is one street inland from Atatürk Caddesi; it's across from the Silifke Garajı. Prices are moderate, English and German are spoken, and seafood is the specialty.

Getting There & Away

Bus From Mersin's Otogar on the northwestern outskirts of town, buses depart for all points, including to Alanya (eight hours, 2500TL, US$3.50), Antalya (10½ hours, 3000TL, US$4.20) and Konya (six hours, 2500TL, US$3.50). The TOK company has very frequent buses to Adana; it's virtually a shuttle service. The Tezcanlar and Silifke Koop companies operate very frequent buses westward to Erdemli, Silifke and intermediate points. A ticket to Silifke costs 500TL (US$0.70).

To get to the centre of Mersin from the Otogar, a taxi is the quickest way. There are city buses, but infrequently; dolmuşes are a better bet but they are not frequent either.

Ferries to Cyprus Turkish Maritime Lines, down at the docks in Mersin, operates the *M/F Yeşilada* on car ferry service to Famagusta (Magosa, mah-GOS-sah), Cyprus and Lattakia (Laskiye), Syria, from Mersin all year. Ferries depart Mersin at 10 pm on Monday, Wednesday and Friday to arrive the next morning at Famagusta at 8 am. The Friday departure arrives in Famagusta on Saturday morning, departs at 11 pm Saturday evening, and arrives in Lattakia at 7 am

Sunday morning, departing for the return trip to Famagusta at noon Sunday.

Fares for the trip between Mersin and Famagusta range from US$26 for a Pullman chair to US$50 per person for a luxury cabin; mid-range cabins rent for US$30 per person. The fare for an auto is US$21. Agents for the ferry service are the Kıbrıs Türk Denizcilik Şirketi Ltd, 3 Bülent Ecevit Bulvarı, Famagusta (tel 65995); and the Lattakia Shipping Agencies Company, Port Said St, PO Box 28, Lattakia (tel 33163 or 34263).

MERSİN TO ADANA

Going east, 27 km brings you to Tarsus, where St Paul was born almost 2000 years ago. There is very little left of old Tarsus, certainly not enough to stop for.

Three km east of Tarsus, the E5 highway heads north through the Cilician Gates, a wide gap in the Taurus Mountains, to Ankara.

ADANA

Turkey's fourth largest city, Adana (AH-dah-nah, population 950,000), is commercial. Its wealth comes from the intensely fertile Çukurova (CHOO-koor-oh-vah), the ancient Cilician Plain formed by the rivers Seyhan and Ceyhan, and by the traffic passing through the Cilician Gates. The city has grown rapidly and chaotically during the last few decades. Though the local people take pride in their city, many look upon it as an overgrown village, an adolescent metropolis.

Adana has one or two sights of touristic interest, but if you are not here on business you will find yourself in and out of town in no time. This is good, as Adana suffers from high humidity in summer and the clammy air doesn't cool off very much, even at night.

Orientation

The Seyhan River skirts the eastern edge of the city; the E5 highway rushes right through the centre from west to east.

Adana's airport (Havaalanı) is several km west of the centre on the E5 highway. The bus station (Otogar) is in the eastern part of town, a 20-minute walk from the centre just north of the E5, on the west bank of the river. The Railway Station (Gar) is at the northern end of Ziya Paşa Bulvarı, several km north of the centre. The main commercial and hotel street is İnönü Caddesi; it will serve as your reference point for everything else in town.

Information

The Tourism Information Office (tel (711) 11323) is at Atatürk Caddesi 13, a block north of İnönü Caddesi, in the centre of town.

Things to See

Adana has a little gem of a museum, the **Adana Ethnography Museum** (Adana Etnoğrafya Müzesi (tel 22417), housed in a former church built by the Crusaders. Nicely restored, the building now houses displays of carpets and *kilims,* weapons, manuscripts, inscriptions and funeral monuments. Hours are 9 am to noon and 1.30 to 5.30 pm, closed Monday; admission costs 200TL (US$0.28), half-price on Sunday. The museum is on a little side street off İnönü Caddesi, just to the left of the Adana Sürmeli Oteli.

Adana's other museum is the **Adana Regional Museum** (Adana Bölge Müzesi) (tel 43856), beside the Otogar on the bank of the Seyhan just north of the E5 highway. Admission costs 400TL (US$0.56), hours are 8.30 am to 12.30 pm and 1.30 to 5.30 pm. It has lots of Roman statuary, as the Cilician Gates were an important transit point even in Roman times.

Have a look at the long Taşköprü, or **Roman Bridge**, built by Hadrian and repaired by Justinian, which marches for 300 metres across the Seyhan. Sullied by lots of modern traffic, it is impressive, though not romantic. The bridge is one long block south of the Regional Museum.

Places to Stay

Adana has lots of hotels in all classes. There are a few cheap emergency hotels near the Otogar, but most of the mid-range and top-end hotels are on İnönü Caddesi, downtown. There are no hotels near the airport or the railway station.

Places to Stay - bottom end

The *Otel Köşk Palas* (KERSHK pahlahss) (tel (711) 37215), at the corner of Türkkuşu Caddesi and Ordu Caddesi one block west of the Otogar, is a big old building on a back street well away from the intense traffic noise, yet conveniently close to the Otogar. The plain rooms contain nothing but beds, which rent for 1500TL (US$2.10) single, 2500TL (US$3.50) double, 3000TL (US$4.20) triple. To find it, leave the Otogar, cross the boulevard (Fuzuli Caddesi), turn left and look for a little sign pointing the way west (right) to the hotel.

The downtown hotels are more congenial and comfortable. They include the little *Mehtap Oteli* (mehh-TAHP) (tel (711) 21954), İnönü Caddesi, 123 Sokak 6, on a tiny street opposite the Adana Sürmeli Oteli. The entrance to the Mehtap is populated with public scribes banging out citizens' petitions to the government. It's quiet here, yet central, and waterless rooms cost only 1000TL (US$1.40) single, 1800TL (US$2.52) double.

The *Öz Otel* (EURZ) (tel (711) 17844), İnönü Caddesi 34, is right on the main street, and thus you must be careful of noise. Doubles without shower go for 2500TL (US$3.50), with shower for 3500TL (US$4.90).

Places to Stay - middle

Two hotels on İnönü Caddesi serve middle-range visitors. The *Otel Duygu* (dooy-GOO) (tel (711) 16741), İnönü Caddesi 14/1, has a lift, a bar, and rooms with private baths and fans for 7500TL (US$10.50) single, 11,000TL (US$15.40) double. Nearby, the *Otel İpek Palas* (ee-PEHK) (tel (711) 18743), İnönü Caddesi

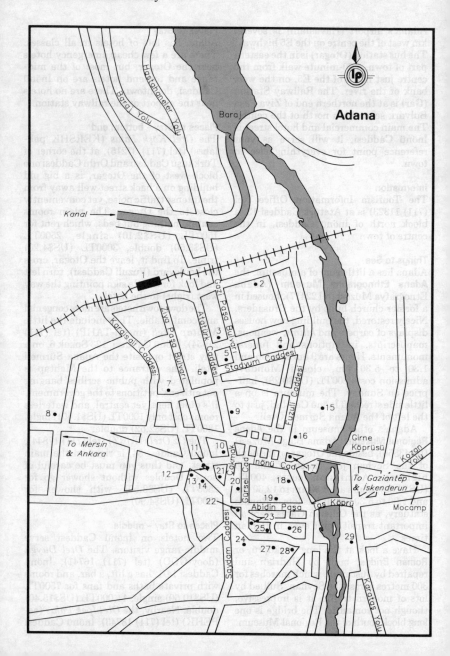

1	Railway Station
2	National Parks Office
3	American Consulate
4	Sports Arena
5	Turkish Airlines Office
6	Atatürk Park
7	Swimming Pool
8	Airport
9	Municipality (Belediye)
10	Tourism Office
11	Adana Sürmeli Hotel
12	Ethnographic Museum
13	Büyük Sürmeli Hotel
14	Koza Hotel
15	Bus Station
16	Museum
17	Cultural Centre
18	Atatürk Museum
19	Central Bank (Merkez Bankası)
20	Church
21	New Mosque (Yeni Cami)
22	Kemeraltı Camii
23	PTT (Post Office)
24	Yağ Camii
25	Clock Tower
26	Ulu Cami
27	Bazaar
28	Government House (Vilayet)
29	Hospital

103, charges just slightly more for similar accommodation.

Places to Stay – top end
The top place, with 116 air-conditioned doubles priced at 50,000TL (US$70), is the *Adana Sürmeli Oteli* (tel (711) 22701), İnönü Caddesi 142. Its sister establishment behind it, the *Büyük Sürmeli Oteli* (bew-YEWK sewr-meh-LEE) (tel (711) 21944), is an older 80-room hotel with very comfortable rooms going for slightly less.

New and recommendable is the posh *Zaimoğlu Oteli* (zah-EEM-oh-loo) (tel (711) 13366), Özler Caddesi 72, between the two aforementioned hotels. Opened in the summer of 1986, the Zaimoğlu charges 16,500TL (US$23.10) single, 22,000TL (US$30.80) double, 30,250TL (US$42.35) for a suite, 41,250TL

(US$57.75) for an apartment, all air-conditioned and bathroom-equipped. These prices might rise soon, however.

Places to Eat
While you're here, and if you like spicy food, try *Adana kebap*, the local specialty. Ground lamb is mixed with hot pepper and wrapped around a flat skewer, then grilled over charcoal. You'll find other Arab-inspired dishes as the Syrian influence is strong.

My favourite place for *Adana kebap*, or indeed for any lunch or dinner, is the *Yeni Onbaşılar Restorant* (yeh-NEE ohn-bah-shuh-LAHR) (tel 14178), on Atatürk Caddesi more or less opposite the Tourism Office. The restaurant is up a flight of stairs in the building called the Özel Sancak İşhanı. The open-air terrace is a fine place to dine in fair weather. The *Adana kebap* is delicious, not too spicy, served on a bed of very thin bread which is used in place of knife and fork. With a salad, water, excellent fresh *pide* bread and a large, cold bottle of Efes beer to counteract the humidity, I paid 1800TL (US$2.52), tip included.

For even cheaper fare, try the *Üç Kardeşler Lokanta ve Kebap Salonu* (EWCH kahr-desh-lehr) (tel 17314), İnönü Caddesi, to the right of the Adana Sürmeli Oteli.

Getting There & Away
As an important transfer point for centuries, Adana is well served by all means of transport.

Air Turkish Airlines (tel (711) 37247 or 43143), Stadyum Caddesi 1, operates twice-daily flights between Adana and İstanbul (1¼ hours), and Adana and Ankara (one hour). There are also three flights weekly in each direction between Adana and Nicosia (Lefkoşe), Cyprus.

İstanbul Airlines links its namesake city with Adana as well.

Rail The façade of the Adana Gar (tel

(711) 33172) is decorated with pretty faience panels. Inside, trains depart six times daily for Mersin (300TL, US$0.42) via Tarsus (200TL, US$0.28), a 75-minute trip. Tickets on the express trains, 1st class, to other points are priced as follows: Ankara, 2100TL (US$2.94); Gaziantep, 1000TL (US$1.40); Haydarpaşa (İstanbul), 3500TL (US$4.90); Kayseri, 1100TL (US$1.54); Mardin, 2100TL (US$2.94); Niğde, 650TL (US$0.91).

Bus Adana's large and modern Otogar is active, as you might imagine, with direct buses to everywhere, including Adıyaman (seven buses per day, six hours, 2200TL, US$3.08; two of these go on to Kâhta for an extra 300TL, US$0.42), Antalya (eight hours, 3000TL, US$4.20), Alanya (seven hours, 2500TL, US$3.50), Diyarbakır (nine hours, 3000TL, US$4.20), Gaziantep (three hours, 1200TL, US$1.68), Halep (Aleppo, Syria, 12 hours, 6000TL, US$8.40), Konya (6½ hours, 2500TL, US$3.50), Malatya (eight hours, 2500TL, US$3.50), Şanlıurfa (six hours, 2000TL, US$2.80) and Van (16 hours, 4500TL, US$6.30).

Getting Around
Airport Transport An airport bus (350TL, US$0.49) trundles you into town from the Şakirpaşa Havaalanı (airport) (tel (711) 12637).

ADANA TO ANTAKYA
The very eastern end of the Turkish Mediterranean coast is at İskenderun and Antakya, in the province of Hatay. On the road are some striking sights. About 45 minutes (35 km) east of Adana is the **Snake Castle** (Yılan Kalesi), a fortress perched on a hilltop two km south of the highway. Built by Armenians and Crusaders in the 12th or 13th centuries, it takes its name from the serpent entwined in the coat-of-arms above the main entrance. If you have the time, feel free to drive up and have a look around.

At a point 72 km east of Adana the highway divides, skirting the **Earth Castle** (Toprakkale), built about the same time as the Snake Castle. The right fork goes to İskenderun and Antakya, the left to Gaziantep and Malatya.

İskenderun
İskenderun (ees-KEHN-deh-roon, population 150,000), 130 km east of Adana, was founded by Alexander the Great, and once bore the name Alexandretta, of which İskenderun is a translation (İskender = Alexander). It was the most important port city on this part of the coast until Mersin was developed (1960s), but has now become less active. It was occupied by the French after WW I, and was included under the French Protectorate of Syria as the Sanjak of Alexandretta.

Past İskenderun the road winds uphill, with a gorge on the right, through the town of Sarımazı to Belen, the town at the head of the gorge. Belen looks to be an old settlement, and indeed it is, as archaeological excavations nearby have unearthed evidence of settlements here since the time of Hammurabi, king of Babylon.

At 147 km from Adana, the road passes over the Belen Pass (Belen Geçidi), altitude 740 metres, and then descends to the fertile Amik Plain, the source of Antakya's prosperity.

ANTAKYA
Antakya (ahn-TAHK-yah, population 200,000), also called Hatay (HAH-tahy), is rather Arabic in its culture and language. Many people speak Arabic as a first language, Turkish as the second. You will soon see that there are two Antakyas, the tidy, modern one on the western bank of the Asi River (the ancient Orontes) which divides the town, and the older, ramshackle, sympathetic, Arabic other one, with many buildings left from the times of the Ottoman Empire and the French Protectorate, on the eastern bank.

History

This is the ancient Antioch, founded by Seleucus I Nicator in 300 BC. Soon it had a population of half a million. Under the Romans it developed an important Christian community (out of its already large Jewish one), which was at one time headed by St Paul.

Persians, Byzantines, Arabs, Armenians and Seljuks all fought for it, and the Crusaders and Saracens battled for it as well. In 1268 the Mamelukes of Egypt took the city and wiped it out. It was never to regain its former glory.

The Ottomans held the city until Muhammad Ali of Egypt captured it in his drive for control of the empire (1831). But the Ottomans, with European help, drove their rebellious vassal back. The French held it as part of their Syrian protectorate until 1939. Atatürk saw WW II approaching, and wanted the city rejoined to the republic as a defensive measure. He began a campaign to reclaim it, which came to fruition by means of a plebiscite shortly after his death.

Orientation

The modern town is on the western bank, with its Tourism Office, PTT, government buildings and museum; the older Ottoman town on the eastern is the place to find the bus station (Santral Garaj), a few blocks north of the centre. Most of the city's hotels are on the eastern bank, along the riverbank promenade; the exception is the new Antakya Hotel, across from the PTT on the western bank.

Information

The provincial Tourism Office (tel (891) 12636) is two km north of the PTT, on the western bank at a traffic roundabout.

Things to See

In the city you can see a Roman bridge built under the reign of Diocletian (200s AD), an aqueduct, the old city walls, several Arab-style mosques (very different from the Turkish) and, most importantly, the **Antakya Museum** (Antakya Müzesi), on the western bank at the southern side of the traffic roundabout by the bridge. The museum is justly famed for its marvellous Roman mosaics. Admission costs 500TL (US$0.70).

On the outskirts of town (two km from the centre) is the **Senpiyer Kilisesi or Church of St Peter**. In this grotto, closed by a wall in Crusader times, it is said that St Peter preached. There is no bus service to Senpiyer; you must take a taxi (1500TL, US$2.10, return trip), or plan to walk the three or four km from town.

Places to Stay – bottom end

Closest to the bus station is the *Şeker Palas Oteli* (sheh-KEHR pah-lahss) (tel (891) 11603), west across the street. It's nothing special but it's the closest, and charges 2200TL (US$3.08) for a waterless double room.

Walk south on İstiklal Caddesi to find the *Hotel İstanbul* (tel (891) 11122), İstiklal Caddesi 14, half-way between the bus station and the bridge, charging the same prices as the Şeker Palas. The hotel's façade is nicer than its rooms.

The *Hotel Kent* (tel (891) 11670), opposite the bridge but back from the riverbank a few metres, has double rooms without bath for 2500TL (US$3.50), with bath for 3000TL (US$4.20).

Places to Stay – middle

On the eastern bank, south of the bridge and inland a bit, is the 28-room *Atahan Oteli* (AH-tah-hahn) (tel (891) 11036 or 11407), Hürriyet Caddesi 28, the nicest in town, charging 8000TL (US$11.20) single, 12,000TL (US$16.80) double.

The less fancy *Divan Hoteli* (dee-VAHN) (tel (891) 11518 or 11735), İstiklal Caddesi 62, just a few steps south of the bus station, is cheaper, with 23 rooms going for 6000TL (US$8.40) single, 7500TL (US$10.50) double, 9300TL (US$13.02) triple.

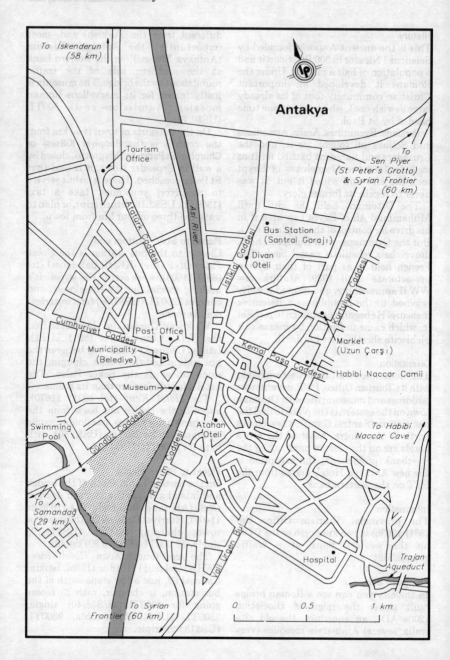

Antakya

To İskenderun
(58 km)

Tourism
Office

Asi River

Atatürk Caddesi

İstiklal Caddesi

To
Sen Piyer
(St Peter's Grotto)
& Syrian Frontier
(60 km)

Bus Station
(Santral Garajı)

Divan
Oteli

Cumhuriyet Caddesi

Post Office

Municipality
(Belediye)

Museum

Swimming
Pool

Gündüz Caddesi

To
Samandağ
(29 km)

Rıhtım Caddesi

Atahan
Oteli

Vali Ürgen Bul.

Kurtuluş Caddesi

Market
(Uzun Çarşı)

Kemal Paşa Caddesi

Habibi Naccar Camii

To Habibi
Naccar Cave

Hospital

Trajan
Aqueduct

To Syrian
Frontier
(60 km)

0   0.5   1 km

There are also several hotels at Harbiye, the ancient suburb of Daphne. In Seleucid and Roman times the city's residents went to Daphne to indulge in the pleasures of picnics and moonlight strolls, and it is still a resort. Two hotels are the *Hidro* (HEE-droh) (tel 6) and the *Çağlıyan* (CHAH-luh-YAHN) (tel 11).

Places to Stay - top end

As of this writing, the big, new *Antakya Hotel* on the western bank across from the PTT is still under construction, but it will undoubtedly be finished and open by the time you arrive. It is only a few steps from the bridge and the museum.

Places to Eat

Except for the hotel restaurants, Antakya's eateries tend to be simple, cheap, and on the eastern bank near the bridge. With most meals you will be offered a plate of pimientos (peppers) and mint, a nice Arabic touch. Also, you will find *hummus* readily available here, something one does not find easily in other parts of Turkey. The spring water served with the meal is the sweetest I have ever tasted.

Getting There & Away

Bus Buses to Adana (2½ hours, 1100TL, US$1.54) depart frequently throughout the day. There are also buses for Gaziantep (four hours, 1000TL, US$1.40) and Şanlıurfa (seven hours, 2500TL, US$3.50). If you don't find a direct bus to Urfa or other points east, change in Gaziantep (buses to Urfa leave Gaziantep every 30 minutes).

Minibuses depart every five minutes or so to the beachfront town of Samandağ (35 minutes, 150TL, US$0.21). Every 10 minutes a minibus departs for İskenderun.

Into Syria You can take a dolmuş for Yayladağ, a crossing point on the Syrian frontier, but direct buses depart Antakya for several Syrian cities, so why not just take a bus directly to your destination? You can easily travel to Aleppo (Halep in Turkish) or Lattakia (Laskiye), but only if you already have a Syrian visa. At last report, they are not issued at the border. You'll have to get one in your home country (preferable) or in Ankara. At the border, you must change the equivalent of US$100 into Syrian currency at the official exchange rate.

Central Anatolia

When nomadic Turkish shepherds moved into Anatolia around the year 1100, they found a land which reminded them of Central Asia: semi-arid, rolling steppeland covered with grass, perfect for their flocks. Mountains and great lakes (some of them salt) broke up the vast expanse of steppe. By the numerous streams, marked with rows of tall, spindly cypresses, the nomads finally established villages.

In spring, Central Anatolia is a sea of wildflowers. Great swaths of vivid colour are splashed across the spare landscape in an annual extravagance born of the spring rains. Days are pleasantly warm, nights chilly. In summer the rain and its lushness disappear, and the Anatolian plateau is hotter and drier, but never humid as on the coasts. As you ride across Anatolia in summer, you will see the dark red of newly ploughed furrows, the straw yellow of grass, grey and green bands of sandstone in a rockface. Winter is cold and rainy, with numerous falls of snow. You shouldn't be surprised at the snow, for the plateau has an average altitude of 1000 metres (3280 feet).

Though Central Anatolia yields a first impression of emptiness, this is deceptive. The armies of a dozen empires have moved back and forth across this 'land bridge' between Europe and Asia; a dozen civilizations have risen and fallen here, including the very earliest established human communities, which date from 7500 BC. Crumbling caravanserais *(han)* scattered along the modern highways testify to rich trade routes which flourished for several millennia.

Today, Central Anatolia is still flourishing. Wheat and other grains, fruits and vegetables (including delicious melons) are grown in the dry soil, and livestock is still a big concern. Ankara, Turkey's capital city, is a sprawling urban mass in the midst of the semi-desert; Konya and Kayseri, fuelled by the wealth of agriculture and light industry, are growing at a remarkable pace. These cities have a modern aspect of wide boulevards, apartment blocks and busy traffic. At the heart of each is an old town, a fortress dating to Roman times, a few foundations going back to the dawn of civilisation.

Ankara

Capital of the Turkish Republic, Ankara (AHN-kah-rah, population three million; altitude 848 metres) was once called Angora. The fine, soft hair *(tiftik)* on Angora goats became an industry which still thrives. But today Ankara's prime concern is government. It is a city of ministries, embassies, universities, medical centres, gardens, vineyards and some light industry. Vast suburbs are scattered on the hillsides which surround the centre; most are filled by country people who have moved here in search of work and a better life. Many have found it.

But Ankara has a problem. The principal fuel for heating is a soft brown coal called lignite which produces thick, particle-filled smoke. During the heating season (15 October to 15 April), the air is badly polluted.

Your stay in Ankara need not be as long as in İstanbul. The city has several significant attractions, but you should be able to tour them all in 1½ to two days.

History

It was the Hittites who named this place Ankuwash before 1200 BC. The town prospered because it was at the intersection of north-south and east-west trade routes. After the Hittites, it was a

Phrygian town, then taken by Alexander, claimed by the Seleucids, and finally occupied by the Galatian tribes of Gaul who invaded Anatolia around 250 BC. Augustus Caesar annexed it to Rome in 25 BC as Ankyra.

The Byzantines held the town for centuries, with intermittent raids by the Persians and Arabs. When the Seljuk Turks came to Anatolia after 1071, they made the town they called Engüriye into a Seljuk city, but held it with difficulty. Ottoman possession of Angora did not begin well, for it was near the town that Sultan Yıldırım Beyazıt was captured by Tamerlane, and the sultan later died in captivity. After the Timurid state collapsed and the Ottoman civil war ended, Angora became merely a quiet town where long-haired goats were raised.

Modern Ankara is a planned city. When Atatürk set up his provisional government here in 1920, it was a small, rather dusty Anatolian town of some 30,000 people, with a strategic position at the heart of the country. After his victory in the War of Independence, Atatürk declared this the new capital of the country (October 1923), and set about developing it. European urban planners were consulted, and the plan resulted in a city of long, wide boulevards, a large forested park with an artificial lake, a cluster of transportation termini, and numerous residential and diplomatic neighbourhoods. From 1919 to 1927, Atatürk did not set foot in the old imperial capital of İstanbul, preferring to work at making Ankara the country's capital city in fact as well as in name.

For republican Turks, İstanbul is their glorious historical city, still the centre of business and finance, but Ankara is their true capital, built on the ashes of the empire with their own blood and sweat. It is modern and forward-looking, and they're proud of it.

Orientation

The main boulevard through the city is, of course, Atatürk Bulvarı, which runs from Ulus in the north all the way to the Presidential Mansion in Çankaya, six km to the south.

The old city of Ankara, dating from the time of Rome and including the Hisar (fortress), is near Ulus Meydanı, called simply Ulus (oo-LOOS), the centre of 'old Ankara'. This is an area with many of Ankara's cheapest hotels, restaurants and markets. The most important museums are near Ulus. You can recognize the square by the large equestrian statue of Atatürk at the south-east corner.

Kızılay (KUH-zuh-lah-yee) is the intersection of Atatürk Bulvarı and Gazi Mustafa Kemal Bulvarı/Ziya Gökalp Caddesi. Officially called Hürriyet Meydanı, everyone knows it by the name Kızılay, the 'Red Crescent' (Turkish 'Red Cross') headquarters which used to be here but was demolished long ago. This is the centre of 'new Ankara', called Yenişehir (yeh-NEE-sheh-heer). It holds several moderate hotel and restaurant choices. There are also bus and airline ticket offices, travel agencies and department stores. On Kocatepe hill in Yenişehir is the Kocatepe Camii, a modern mosque (still being built) in Ottoman style, which is among the largest in the world.

At the southern end of Atatürk Caddesi, in the hills overlooking the city, is Çankaya, the residential neighbourhood which holds the Cumhurbaşkanlığı Köşkü, the Presidential Mansion, plus many of the most important ambassadorial residences. Between Kızılay and Çankaya along Atatürk Bulvarı are most of the city's important embassies and many government ministries, plus the Büyük Millet Meclisi, the Grand National Assembly, parliament of the Turkish Republic.

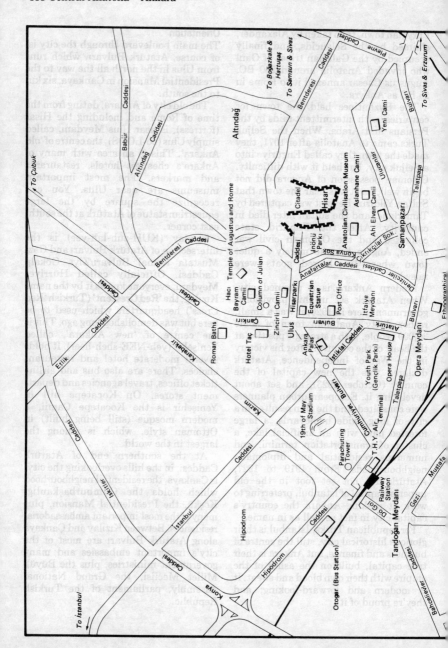

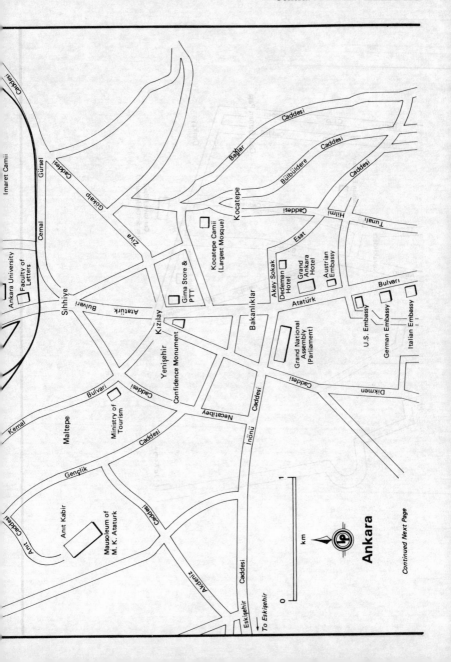

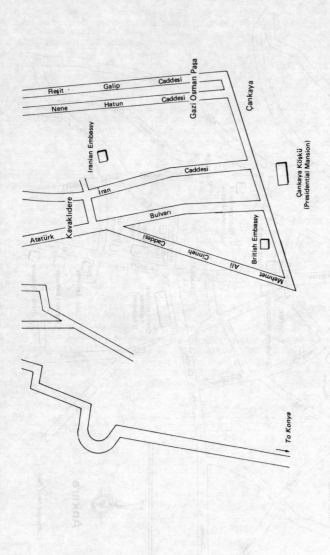

Information

There are Tourism Information Offices at Ankara's Otogar and at Esenboğa Airport. For information downtown, direct your feet and your questions to the Ministry of Culture & Tourism (Kültür ve Turizm Bakanlığı) (tel (4) 229-2930/95), Gazi Mustafa Kemal Bulvarı 33, a 10-minute walk west of Kızılay. The entrance to the information office is actually around on the right side of the Ministry building, on Özveren Sokak.

Things to See

Many of Ankara's important sights are near Ulus, some within an easy walk.

Museum of Anatolian Civilisations First goal of most sightseers is the Hisar (hee-SAHR) or Kale, the citadel atop the hill. Near the Hisar, on the south-western slope of the hill, is the important Museum of Anatolian Civilisations (Anadolu Medeniyetleri Müzesi), also called the Anadolu Uygarlıkları Müzesi, Hitit Müzesi or Arkeoloji Müzesi.

If you're a walker and the day is not too hot, you can climb the hillside to the museum; otherwise, take a taxi. Walk east from Ulus on Hisarparkı Caddesi and turn right into Anafartalar Caddesi, then bear left along Çıkrıkçılar Sokak to reach the museum, which is open from 8.30 am to 12.30 pm and from 1.30 to 5.30 pm, closed Monday; admission costs 500TL (US$0.70), half-price on Sunday. Photographs are permitted (for free) only in the central room of the museum; photography in other rooms must be approved by the director, and a fee of 5000TL (US$7) per exposure must be paid.

The museum building is a restored *bedesten* or covered market built by order of Grand Vezir Mahmut Paşa in 1471, and the adjoining Kurşunlu Han, an Ottoman warehouse. Exhibits are heavily in favour of the earlier Anatolian civilisations such as the Urartu, Hatti, Hittite, Phrygian and Assyrian. Among the more fascinating items are those brought from Çatal Höyük, the earliest known human community. You'll also enjoy the graceful, lively Hittite figures of bulls and stags, and the early water vessels.

As you stroll through the museum's exhibits, you should know that MÖ is the Turkish abbreviation for BC.

Hisar The imposing fortress just up the hill from the museum took its present form in the 800s with the construction of the outer walls by the Byzantine Emperor Michael II. The earlier inner walls date from the 600s. Enter the citadel by the gate called **Parmak Kapısı** (pahr-MAHK kah-puh-suh), and you're in a Turkish village right at the centre of Ankara! The small mosque here, the **Alaettin Camii**, dates originally from the 1100s, but has been much rebuilt. Wander into the village, following any path that will take you higher, and soon you'll arrive at the **Şark Kulesi** (SHARK koo-leh-see, Eastern Tower), from which there's a magnificent view over the entire city, all the way to Yenişehir and Çankaya. The tower at the north, **Ak Kale** (AHK kah-leh, White Fort), also offers fine views.

Come down from the Hisar, exit by the Parmak Kapısı, and you'll be in the **bazaar**. Warehouses here are filled with *tiftik* (Angora goat hair), and merchants busy themselves with its trade. Turn left and walk down through the bazaar area, lined with vegetable stalls, copper and ironmongers' shops, and every variety of household goods shop. Soon you will come to the **Aslanhane Camii** (ahs-LAHN-hah-neh, Lion House), which dates from the 1200s and is very Seljuk in aspect. Go inside for a look.

Continue down the hill on Can Sokak, and turn right into Anafartalar Caddesi for Ulus.

Railway Museum Rail enthusiasts will want to have a look at Atatürk's private white railway coach, on display at the Ankara Railway Station. Enter the station from the street, walk through the main hall and out to the platforms, turn right, and walk along until you come to the coach, on the right. It was constructed in Breslau in 1935 and looks very comfy. You can't go inside the coach, but you can tour the Demiryolları Müzesi (deh-MEER-yoh-lah-ruh mew-zeh-see), the Railway Museum, just past the coach. It's open from 8.30 am to noon and 1 to 5.30 pm, closed Monday. As there are few visitors, it may be locked. Find an official and request, *Müzeyi açarmısınız?* (mew-zeh-YEE ah-CHAR-muh-suh-nuhz, 'Would you open the museum?'). If the time is within the hours given, he should oblige.

Roman Ankara At the north-east corner of the square in Ulus are some buildings; behind them is the first stop on your tour of Roman Ankara. Set in a small park (Hükümet Meydanı), surrounded by the Ankara provincial government house and the Ministry of Finance & Customs, is the Jülyanüs Sütunu (zhewl-YAH-news sew-too-noo), the **Column of Julian**. The Roman Emperor Julian (the Apostate, 361-363), last of the scions of Constantine the Great, visited Ankara in the middle of his short reign, and the column was erected in his honour. Turkish inhabitants later gave it the name Belkız Minaresi, the Queen of Sheba's Minaret.

Walk east from the park, up the hill; turn right, then left to reach Bayram Caddesi and the **Hacı Bayram Camii** (hah-JUH bahy-RAHM), Ankara's most revered mosque, built on the ruins of the **Temple of Augustus and Rome**. Hacı Bayram Veli was a Muslim saint who founded the Bayramiye order of dervishes around the year 1400. Ankara was the centre of the order, and Hacı Bayram Veli is still revered by the city's pious Muslims.

The temple walls that you see were once surrounded by a colonnade. Originally built by the kings of Pergamum for the worship of Cybele, the Anatolian fertility goddess; and Men, the Phrygian phallic god, it was later rededicated to Emperor Augustus. The Byzantines converted it to a church, and the Muslims built a mosque and saint's tomb in its precincts. The gods change, the site stays the same.

From Hacı Bayram, walk north on Çiçek Sokak until it meets Çankırı Caddesi. Across this main road, up the hill on the opposite side, is the fenced enclosure of the **Roman Baths** (Roma Hamamları). The layout of the 3rd-century baths is clearly visible, as is much of the water system. Hours are 8.30 am to 12.30 pm and 1.30 to 5.30 pm; admission costs 200TL (US$0.28). If you're short on money or pressed for time, you can ignore the baths.

Republican Ankara In the 1920s, at the time of the War of Independence, Ankara consisted of the citadel and a few buildings in Ulus. Atatürk's new city grew with Ulus as its centre, and thus many of the buildings here saw the birth and growing-pains of the Turkish Republic. A short tour through a few of the buildings tells a great deal about how a democratic nation-state grew from the ruins of a vast monarchy.

The museums described below are open from 9 am to noon and 1.30 to 5 pm daily except Monday, free of charge.

Kürtülüs Savaşı Müzesi The War of Salvation Museum is on Cumhuriyet Bulvarı at the north-west corner of Ulus. Photographs and displays recount great moments and people in the War of Independence; captions are in Turkish only. This was where the republican Grand National Assembly held its early sessions (earlier called the TBBM Müzesi for Türkiye Büyük Millet Meclisi, Grand National Assembly). Before it was Turkey's first parliament, this building was the Ankara headquarters of the Committee of Union & Progress, the political party which overthrew Sultan

Abdül Hamid in 1909 and attempted to bring democracy to the Ottoman Empire.

Cumhuriyet Müzesi The Republic Museum is on Cumhuriyet Bulvarı, just down the hill from Ulus. This was the second headquarters of the Grand National Assembly, the parliament founded by Atatürk in his drive for a national consensus to resist foreign invasion and occupation of the Anatolian homeland. The early history of the assembly is documented in photographs and documents; all captions are in Turkish only, but you can visit the assembly's meeting-room and get a sense of its modest beginnings. The Grand National Assembly is now housed in a vast and imposing building in Yenişehir.

Across Cumhuriyet Caddesi from the museum is the former **Ankara Palas** hotel, built as the city's first luxury lodging. It has recently been beautifully restored, and now serves as guest quarters for important official visitors.

Gençlik Parkı & Opera House Walk south from Ulus along Atatürk Bulvarı and you'll soon reach the entrance to Gençlik Parkı, the 'Youth Park'. A swamp on this site was converted to an artificial lake on Atatürk's orders, and the park was included in the city's master plan. It has a permanent fun fair with amusements for children and, in the evening, outdoor cafés with musical performances. Single women should find a café with the word *aile* (family) in its name.

Notice the quaint, small Opera House just past the entrance to the park. Atatürk became enamoured of opera during a tour of duty as military attaché in Sofia (1905), and saw to it that his new capital had a suitable hall for performances as well. The opera has a full season, beginning in autumn.

Ethnography Museum The Etnografya Müzesi is perched above Atatürk Bulvarı, to the east of the boulevard and south of

Ulus past Gençlik Parkı. It's an eye-catching white marble Oriental structure (1925) with an equestrian statue of Atatürk in front, reached by walking up Talatpaşa Bulvarı from Atatürk Bulvarı. Recently restored, it has fine collections of Seljuk and Ottoman art, craftwork, musical instruments, weapons, folk costumes, jewellery and household effects. Also on view is a large and elaborately decorated room used by Kemal Atatürk as his office. Hours are 8.30 am to 12.30 pm and 1.30 to 5.30 pm, closed Monday.

Next door to the Ethnography Museum is the **Painting & Sculpture Museum** (Resim ve Heykel Müzesi), in the former headquarters of the Turkish Hearths (Türk Ocağı) movement.

Ulus Markets Walk up the hill on Hisarparkı Caddesi out of Ulus, and turn right at the first traffic signal onto Susam Sokak; a Ziraat Bankası will be on your right. Bear left, then turn left, and on your right will be Ankara's **New Produce Market** (Yeni Haller), a good place for buying supplies or photographing colourful local life.

Behind the New Produce Market, on Konya Caddesi, is the **Vakıf Suluhan Çarşısı**, a restored caravanserai with lots of clothing shops, a café, toilets and a free-standing *mescit* (small mosque) at the centre of its courtyard.

Anıt Kabir Atatürk's mausoleum, called the Anıt Kabir (ah-NUHT-kah-beer, Monumental Tomb), stands atop a small hill in a green park about two km west of Kızılay along Gazi Mustafa Kemal Bulvarı. If you saw Ankara from the Hisar or the terrace of the Ethnography Museum, you've already admired from a distance the rectangular mausoleum with squared columns around its sides, on the hill. A visit to the tomb is essential when you visit Ankara.

Walking along Gazi Mustafa Kemal Bulvarı from Kızılay, you can make a shortcut by turning left onto Maltepe

Sokak. This becomes Erdönmez Sokak and then meets Gençlik Caddesi. Turn right onto Gençlik, then left onto Akdeniz Caddesi, and you'll see the back entrance to the park. You may not be allowed to enter by the pedestrian gate, but past it is the auto exit road, and you can enter there.

Should you take a taxi to the Anıt Kabir's main entrance, from Tandoğan Meydani up Anıt Caddesi, you'll see the mausoleum as it is meant to be approached. Up the steps from the car park you pass between allegorical statues and two square kiosks; the right-hand one holds a model of the tomb and photos of its construction. Then you pass down a long monumental avenue flanked by Hittite stone lions, to the courtyard.

To the right as you enter the courtyard, beneath the western colonnade, is the sarcophagus of İsmet İnönü (1884-1973), Atatürk's close friend and chief of staff, an Ottoman pasha, Republican general (hero of the Battle of İnönü, from which he took his surname), diplomat, prime minister and second president of the republic.

Across the courtyard, on the east side, is a museum which holds memorabilia and personal effects of Atatürk. You can also see his official automobiles, several of which are American-made Lincolns.

As you approach the tomb proper, the high-stepping guards will probably jump to action. Past the colonnade, look to left and right at the gilded inscriptions, which are quotations from Atatürk's speech celebrating the 10th anniversary of the republic (1932). As you enter the tomb past its huge bronze doors, you must remove your hat (if you don't, a guard will remind you that this is correct protocol). The lofty hall is lined in red marble and decorated sparingly with mosaics in timeless Turkish folk designs. At the northern end stands the immense marble sarcophagus, cut from a single piece of stone.

The Anıt Kabir was begun in 1944 and finished in 1953. Its design seeks to capture the spirit of Anatolia: monumental, spare but beautiful. Echoes of several great Anatolian empires, from the Hittites through the Romans and Seljuks, are included in its design. The final effect is modern but somehow timeless.

Çankaya Köşkü One last museum in Ankara is well worth a visit. At the far southern end of Atatürk Bulvarı in Çankaya is the Presidential Mansion. Within the mansion's beautiful gardens is the Çankaya Köşkü, or Çankaya Atatürk Müzesi. This quaint little chalet was Atatürk's country residence, set amid vineyards and evergreens. In the early days of the republic it was a retreat from the town, but now the town reaches up to it, and beyond. Visits to the mansion gardens and grounds and to the museum are permitted on Sunday afternoons from 1.30 to 5.30 pm, and on holidays from 12.30 to 5.30 pm, free of charge. Bring your passport.

Take a bus (No 8 or 13) or taxi to the far southern end of Atatürk Bulvarı, where you will find an entrance to the grounds of the Presidential Mansion. At the guard-house, exchange your passport for an identity badge, leave your camera, and a guide will accompany you to and through the museum.

The house is preserved as Atatürk used it, with decor and furnishings very much of the 1930s. You enter a vestibule, then turn right into a game room, complete with tables for billiards and cards (the British ambassador was a favourite card partner). The next room is a parlour done in green, Atatürk's favourite colour. The large dining room at the back of the house has its own little nook for after-dinner coffee, cigars and brandy.

Upstairs is a formal office, the bedroom and bath, a work room and the library with many books in foreign languages.

Downstairs again, to the left of the vestibule is a reception room for dignitaries.

Places to Stay – bottom end

Ulus holds numerous very inexpensive hotels in its back streets. Most are quiet. The first area to explore is İtfaiye Meydanı, also called Opera Meydanı, across Atatürk Bulvarı from the Opera House. At the far eastern end of the square are several small streets, Sanayi Caddesi, Kosova Caddesi and, next to the PTT, Posta Caddesi, with almost a dozen cheap little places.

The *Otel Devran* (dehv-RAHN) (tel (4) 311-0485, 6) has as its official address Opera Meydanı Tavus Sokak 8, but you'll find it most easily by looking for Gazi Lisesi (a high school) on Sanayi Caddesi, across Atatürk Bulvarı from the Opera House and Gençlik Parkı. It's an older building, well-used, but with those nice touches such as marble staircases, brass trim and little chandeliers. Doubles cost 5600TL (US$7.84) with shower, 6600TL (US$9.24) with bathtub.

The *Otel Akman* (ahk-MAHN) (tel (4) 324-4140, 1), Tavus Sokak 6, is next to the Otel Devran. It's much more modern, has a lift, car park and bar with colour TV, and charges 7700TL (US$10.78) for a double with bath.

The *Erden Hotel* (ehr-DEHN) (tel (4) 311-3738 or 324-3191), Gazi Lisesi Yanı 23, is beside the Gazi Lisesi, a more or less modern building in which double rooms rent for 4400TL (US$6.16) bathless, 5500TL (US$7.70) with bath.

The *Otel Sipahi* (SEE-pah-hee) (tel (4) 324-0235, 6), Kosova Sokak 1 at Azat Sokak, is tidy, friendly and not too noisy, and charges similar prices. The *Sönmez Palas* next door is the same.

Cheaper is the *Otel Ugur Palas* (oo-OOR) (tel (4) 324-1296, 7), Sanayi Caddesi 54, older but clean, with bathless double rooms at 4300TL (US$6.02).

Another grouping of hotels is just a few steps away, near the large post office (PTT) on Atatürk Bulvarı. The *Hotel Zümrüt Palas* (zewm-REWT) (tel (4) 324-5165, 6), Posta Caddesi 16, is a block east of Atatürk Bulvarı, at the corner of Posta and Sanayi caddesis (look for the PTT on Atatürk Bulvarı, and go a block behind it). A clean and tidy place popular with Turkish families, they charge 5000TL (US$7) for a double with washbasin only, 6500TL (US$9.10) for a double bed with shower.

Also near the PTT, on the north side, is the fairly quiet *Otel Oba* (OH-bah) (tel (4) 312-4128), Posta Caddesi 9, with an assortment of rooms. Doubles, bathless, are 4300TL (US$6.02); with shower, 4600TL (US$6.44); with bath, 5600TL (US$7.84).

Cheapest rooms are in the *Sahil Palas Oteli* (sah-HEEL pah-lahss) (tel (4) 310-6935), Hal Sokak 5, next to the Yeni Haller (described in Things to See). Waterless rooms go for only 3000TL (US$4.20).

On the northern side of Ulus, going east off Çankırı Caddesi, is a little street named Beşik Sokak. The *Otel Turan Palas* (too-RAHN pah-lahss) (tel (4) 312-5225), Beşik Sokak 3, is quiet though dark, with bathless doubles for 4000TL (US$5.60). There's hot water for five hours each morning.

A few steps up Beşik Sokak, at its eastern end, is the *Lâle Palas* (lyaa-LEH pah-lahss) (tel (4) 312-5220), Hükümet Meydanı, Telgraf Sokak 5, charging just slightly more for bright, sunny, bathless rooms.

Near Kızılay, the *Otel Ertan* (ehr-TAHN) (tel (4) 118-4084), Selanik Caddesi 70, a half-block south off Meşrutiyet Caddesi, is the best bet. On a quiet street, with a grape arbour and flowers in front, it has rooms with bath for only 4100TL (US$5.74) single, 6400TL (US$8.96) double.

Places to Stay – middle

Convenient to Kızılay is the *Erşan Oteli* (ehr-SHAHN) (tel (4) 118-9875), Meşrutiyet Caddesi 13, a block east of Atatürk Bulvarı. The 64 rooms are nothing special but the location is very convenient; doubles cost 18,150TL

(US$25.41). This is a favourite with businessmen.

The *Otel Gül Palas* (GEWL pah-lahss) (tel (4) 133-3120, 1), Bayındır Sokak 15, is a quiet place on a pedestrian street, with 41 rooms. Over half are equipped with private baths, but the others are inexpensive bathless singles priced at 10,700TL (US$14.98); with bath, a double costs 13,500TL (US$18.90).

Hotel Sultan (sool-TAHN) (tel (4) 131-5980, 1), Bayındır Sokak 35 off Ziya Gökalp Caddesi, is new, modern, quiet and pleasant, with a lift and its own covered car park, and only two blocks from Kızılay. Doubles with bath cost 20,800TL (US$29.12).

A block north of Ulus along Çankırı Caddesi (the northern continuation of Atatürk Bulvarı) is the *Hotel Taç* (TAHCH) (tel (4) 324-3195, 311-1663), Çankırı Caddesi 35, with 35 rooms, over half of them with private bath. A double costs 7700TL (US$10.78) without bath, 8500TL (US$11.90) with. You can walk to many of Ankara's sights from here, but watch out for street noise when selecting a room.

Up the hill from Ulus on Hisarparkı Caddesi, almost to the citadel, is the quiet 53-room *Hotel Hitit* (hee-TEET) (tel (4) 310-8617, 8), Firuzağa Sokak 12. Most of the rooms remain cool in summer and cost 11,000TL (US$15.40).

In the midst of the cheap hotel area of İtfaiye Meydanı is the *Otel Güleryüz* (geur-LEHR-yeurz, Smiling Face) (tel (4) 310-4910), Sanayi Caddesi 37, a new and modern place overlooking the square, with 50 bath-equipped rooms, an enclosed car park, a lift and prices of 12,100TL (US$16.94) double.

There is a hotel next to Ankara's Otogar, the *Terminal Oteli* (TEHR-mee-NAHL) (tel (4) 310-4949), Hipodrom Caddesi 3, fairly dingy but serviceable, and convenient if you're exhausted. Double rooms cost 7700TL (US$10.78) without bath, 9900TL (US$13.86) with bath.

Places to Stay – top end

A Hilton International Hotel is under construction in Ankara, but as of this writing, Ankara's best is the *Büyük Ankara Oteli* (bew-YEWK AHN-kah-rah, the Grand Ankara Hotel) (tel (4) 134-4920). Located near the parliament at Atatürk Bulvarı 183, this 208-room air-conditioned high-rise has all the amenities, including a swimming pool and tennis court, and charges 42,000TL (US$58.80) single, 71,000TL (US$99.40) double.

Less dramatic but equally comfortable is the *Ankara Dedeman Oteli* (DEH-deh-mahn) (tel (4) 213-9690), Büklüm Sokak 1, a block east of Atatürk Bulvarı at Akay Sokak, also near parliament. The Dedeman has 252 air-conditioned rooms and a swimming pool; singles cost 36,000TL (US$50.40), doubles cost 46,000TL (US$64.40).

Only a few steps north of Kızılay, on Atatürk Bulvarı, is the *Hotel Etap Mola* (eh-TAHP MOH-lah) (tel (4) 133-9065), the Ankara representative of the French-run chain. Air-conditioned, comfortable and convenient though not overly fancy, it charges 32,000TL (US$44.80) single, 40,000TL (US$56) double.

Places to Eat – bottom end

Ulus has lots of good, cheap restaurants. North of the square on Çankırı Caddesi are two full-service restaurants with good food, pleasant atmosphere and low prices. The better is perhaps the *Çiçek Lokantası* (chee-CHEK) (tel 311-5997), Çankırı Caddesi 12/A, a half-block north of the square on the right-hand side. Dine on soup, *kebap*, salad and spring water for 1400TL (US$1.96), tip included. There's a pleasant little *havuz* (pool, fountain) here.

Similar is the *Ender Lokantası* (ehn-DEHR) (tel 311-8543), Çankırı Caddesi 10/A, only a few steps from the Çiçek, with white tablecloths and similar prices.

Perhaps the closest restaurant to the Anatolian Civilisations Museum is the *Yavuz Lokantası* (yah-VOOZ) (tel 311-

8508), Konya Sokak 13/F, a clean, airy, bright place with some English-speaking staff, open long hours every day of the week. Good food at low prices (*kebaps* for only 700TL, US$0.98) is the rule. The restaurant is 1½ blocks east off Hisarparkı Caddesi.

On Tavus Sokak near several of the hotels mentioned above is the *Özel Urfa Aile Kebap Salonu*, the 'Authentic Urfa Family Kebab Salon'. Urfa is a city near the Turko-Syrian border, and *Urfa kebap* is *döner* served with sliced onions and spices. You can get *lahmacun* (LAHH-mah-JOON, a soft 'pizza'), *piliç* (pee-LEECH, grilled chicken), *köfte*, salads and desserts such as *tel kadayıf* (TEHL kah-dah-yuhf, shredded wheat in syrup). They make their own *pide* bread here, so it's fresh and delicious. A full meal will be very tasty and cost about 900TL (US$1.26).

Just a few steps up the hill from Ulus, on the left-hand (north) side of Hisarparkı Caddesi, is a building named the Şehir Çarşısı, and at the back of its courtyard, two small *kebap* places, the *Başkent* and the *Misket*. Both have upstairs family dining rooms *(aile salonu)* and both serve that delicious *İskender kebap* from Bursa at about 800TL (US$1.12).

An old favourite *kebap* place is *Hacı Bey*, Devren Sokak 1/B near Tavus Sokak, in this same area. The *kebap* here is Bursa-style, delicious and cheap. A large meal of *kebap*, salad, yogurt and dessert with beverage (no alcohol here) might cost 1800TL (US$2.52).

At the centre of Ulus is the *Akman Boza ve Pasta Salonu*, Atatürk Bulvarı 3, in the courtyard of the large building at the south-east corner of the square. Breakfasts, light lunches (sandwiches, omelets, etc) and pastries are the specialties, consumed at tables beneath umbrellas on the open-air terrace. *Boza*, a fermented millet drink, thick, sweetish and slightly tangy, is a winter favourite.

Near Kızılay are several concentrations of restaurants. On Selanik Caddesi are numerous little eateries, including the *Cihan Kebap* (jee-HAHN) (tel 133-1665), Selanik Caddesi 3/B. This one has chandeliers in the dining room, shaded tables out front by the pedestrian street, and good *kebaps* at prices of 700TL to 800TL (US$0.98 to US$1.12).

Places to Eat – mid-range

The place to look for good moderately priced food near Kızılay is on Bayındır Sokak, to the east of Atatürk Bulvarı. You can't go wrong at the *Körfez Lokantası* (keur-FEHZ) (tel 131-1459), Bayındır Sokak 24, a half-block north of Ziya Gökalp Caddesi. Though there are indoor dining rooms, the terrace is nicer in fine weather. It's simple, pleasant and unpretentious, with many *kebaps* priced under 800TL (US$1.12) and fish dishes for about 2500TL (US$3.50).

Another place for seafood is *Yakamoz I* (YAH-kah-mohz) (tel 134-2913), Bayındır Sokak 14, a tiny place which made its reputation on seafood but now serves as many, or more, *kebaps*.

At the intersection of Tuna Sokak and Bayındır Sokak is the *Piknik Restaurant* (peek-NEEK) (tel 133-0663), a long-time Ankara favourite. It, too, has outdoor tables, and a very long menu. I had *şiş köfte* (skewered ground lamb rissoles, grilled), fried potatoes, yogurt, bread and a large glass *(arjantin)* of draught beer for 1500TL (US$2.10), tip included.

I keep going back to the *Beyaz Saray* on Atatürk Bulvarı at Süleyman Sırrı Sokak, near Sıhhiye Meydanı, though the service is terribly inexpert. Perhaps it's the setting: several interior rooms, and a long terrace set back from the boulevard, high up with a view; this building was once the Turkish Airlines Air Terminal. The food is good and varied; the kitchen is just where you'd suppose a restaurant's lobby to be, so you can choose your salads, *meze*, fish and *kebap* right there, then take a table. Figure 4000TL to 5000TL (US$5.60 to US$7) for a full meal with wine or beer.

Getting There & Away

In Turkey, all roads lead to Ankara. Its role as governmental capital and second-largest city guarantees that transportation will be convenient.

Ankara's Otogar (bus terminal) is one block north-west of the Ankara Garı (railway station). In a wing of the railway station is the THY Hava Terminalı, the Turkish Airlines Air Terminal. The railway station and the bus terminal are separated, appropriately, by the Ministry of Transportation (Ulaştırma Bakanlığı). This whole transportation complex is about 1¼ km from Ulus and three km from Kızılay.

Air Ankara has good international and domestic connections by air. There are non-stop flights between Ankara and the following Turkish cities: Adana (daily, 32,000TL, US$45, 1¼ hours); Antalya (twice or thrice daily in summer, 32,000TL, US$45); Dalaman (twice or thrice daily in summer, 34,000TL, US$47.60); Diyarbakır (daily, 30,000TL, US$42); Elazığ (four times weekly, 25,000TL, US$35); Erzurum (daily, 30,000TL, US$42); İstanbul (six or more flights daily, 30,000TL, US$42); İzmir (daily, 32,000TL, US$44.80); Malatya (five flights weekly, 28,000TL, US$39.20); Merzifon (one or two flights weekly); Samsun (three flights weekly); Trabzon (daily, 30,000TL, US$42); Van (five flights weekly, 30,000TL, US$42).

Flights between Ankara and İstanbul are very frequent, every hour or more, but even so they may fill up. Reserve in advance. Flight time is about an hour. As for İzmir, there is one non-stop flight a day; flight time is about 1¼ hours. If you don't get on this flight, you must fly via İstanbul.

The Turkish Airlines Air Terminal at the railway station has a bank branch for currency exchange, restaurant and bar, and is open daily from 7 am to 8 pm; ticket sales and reservations counters are open between 8.30 am and 7.45 pm, on Sunday from 8.30 am to 5.15 pm. The telephone numbers are: Reservations, 312-6200; Information, 312-4910; Ticket Sales, 312-4900/43. At Esenboğa Havaalanı (airport) the numbers are 324-0650, 1.

Rail Train service is fairly convenient, and very comfortable on the top trains. Any train not named *ekspres* or *mototren* will be very cheap, but fantastically slow. Even if you're out to save money, don't take a slow *yolcu* or *posta* train. You may be on it for days (really!).

The Turkish State Railways (TCDD) has a computerized reservation system, so if you are going to buy a reserved seat, couchette or sleeping-car ticket, go to one of the computer guichets (Bilgisayar Gişe). Tell the agent your preferences: *sigara içilmeyen vagon* is no-smoking car, *gidiş* (gee-DEESH) is single (one-way), *gidiş dönüş* (gee-DEESH deur-NEURSH) is return (round) trip, *talebe* (TAH-leh-BEH) is student fare, *tam* (TAHM) is full fare. Other useful train words are *bugün* (BOO-geurn, today), *yarın* (YAHR-uhn, tomorrow), *hergün* (HEHR-geurn, daily), *bilet* (bee-LEHT, ticket), *yataklı vagon* (yah-tahk-LUH vah-gohn, sleeping car), *kuşet* (koo-SHEHT, couchette).

Cancellation fees for rail tickets are thus: if you cancel a full day before departure, you forfeit 10% of the ticket price; if you cancel on the day of departure, 25%; after departure, 50%.

Ankara-İstanbul Numerous daily express trains run between Ankara and İstanbul. There are three top trains. The Mavi Tren (mah-VEE trehn, Blue Train) is an all-reserved 1st-class (supplement payable) train with club cars and a dining car, Turkey's version of a Trans-Europ-Express. It departs both Ankara and İstanbul at lunchtime on the 7½-hour trip; there is another run at night, departing at 11 pm. For the comfort of a bed, there's the Ankara Ekspresi, an all-sleeping-car train with 1st and 2nd-class berths and a dining car for breakfast only. It departs at 9.40 pm and arrives at 8.30 am.

Two other express trains take a bit longer, but offer similar comfort and convenience at lower prices. The 1st-class Boğaziçi Ekspresi (boh-AHZ-ee-chee, Bosphorus) is a day train with club cars and a dining car which leaves at 8 am and arrives at dinnertime, making the run in about nine hours. The Anadolu Ekspresi (ah-nah-doh-LOO, Anatolia) is a night train with 1st and 2nd-class sleeping cars, club cars and a dining car, which leaves about 9 pm and arrives the next morning about 8 am.

The 'third tier' of express trains are through-trains which stop at Ankara. They are not as dependable or as comfortable as the aforementioned trains, though you may pay as much for a seat. Don't assume these trains will be on time, particularly if you are going from Ankara to İstanbul.

The Toros Ekspresi (TOH-rohs, Taurus) is a morning train to and from İstanbul with sleeping cars and 1st and 2nd-class coaches. If you catch it from Ankara at dinnertime you can ride it to Adana, an overnight trip.

The Doğu Ekspresi (doh-OO, east) and the Mehmetçik Ekspresi go from İstanbul via Ankara, Sivas and Erzurum (3300TL, US$4.62) to Kars; the Vangölü Ekspresi goes from İstanbul to Van, and supposedly on to Tabriz and Tehran, though service to Iran is suspended as of this writing. The İstanbul-Ankara portions of these two trains run together, departing from each city in the evening and arriving the next morning; they haul sleepers, 1st and 2nd-class coaches and diners.

Ankara-İzmir There are three trains, one by day, two by night, at a basic 1st-class fare of 2600TL (US$3.64). The Ege Ekspresi (EH-geh, Aegean) departs about 7.20 am and arrives 13½ hours later, hauling 1st-class coaches and a diner. The İzmir Ekspresi departs just before dinner (6.05 pm) and arrives just after breakfast, hauling 1st and 2nd-class sleepers and coaches, and a dining car. The Mavi Tren departs at 8.05 pm.

Other Trains There are daily express services to and from Kayseri (7½ hours, 1300TL, US$1.82; the bus takes about 4½ hours). The Toros Ekspresi, mentioned above in the İstanbul-Ankara section, will take you from Ankara to Adana (2100TL, US$2.94) and, on Tuesday, Thursday and Sunday, onward to Gaziantep. On Thursday and Sunday the train goes even farther, making its final stop in Halep (Aleppo, Syria).

There are also several daily trains to Zonguldak on the Black Sea coast, most notably the morning Karaelmas Ekspresi and the evening Mavi Tren.

Bus Every city or town of any size has direct buses to Ankara's huge Otogar. From İstanbul, there is a bus to Ankara at least every 15 minutes throughout the day, and late into the night.

As Ankara has many buses to all parts of the country, it is often sufficient to arrive at the Otogar, baggage in hand, and let a barker lead you to a ticket window for your chosen destination (no charge for the lead). However, it might be well to wander through the rows of ticket kiosks to see if there is a more convenient departure time. If you arrive in Ankara by bus, take a few moments to check on schedules to your onward destination. Buy your ticket and at the same time secure your reserved seat, if you can.

Numerous bus companies have offices downtown near Kızılay on Ziya Gökalp Caddesi, Gazi Mustafa Kemal Bulvarı, İzmir Caddesi and Menekşe Sokak. Buying your ticket here will save you a trip to the Otogar.

Fares from Ankara include the following: Adana, 3000TL (US$4.20); Antalya, 3000TL to 4000TL (US$4.20 to US$5.60); Bodrum, 5500TL (US$7.70); Bursa, 2000TL (US$2.80); Diyarbakır, 7000TL

(US$9.80); Gaziantep, 4000TL (US$5.60); İstanbul, 2000TL to 3000TL (US$2.80 to US$4.20); İzmir, 2000TL to 3500TL (US$2.80 to US$4.90); Kayseri, 2000TL (US$2.80); Konya, 1200TL (US$1.68); Samsun, 2500TL (US$3.50); Sivas, 2300TL (US$3.22); Trabzon, 5000TL (US$7).

You can also buy through tickets to Damascus (Şam) for 11,000TL (US$15.40), Tehran for 12,000TL (US$16.80) and other eastern destinations.

Getting Around

Airport Transport The airport is 30 km north of the city. Airport buses (550TL, US$0.77) operated by the USAŞ company depart the Air Terminal in Ankara 1½ hours before domestic flight times, 2¼ hours before international flight times. Minimum check-in time for any flight is 45 minutes.

Bus Ankara is served well and frequently by an extensive bus and minibus network. Some of the important bus routes are: Route 8 (Çankaya) between Ulus and Çankaya runs the entire length of Atatürk Bulvarı; Route 16 (Bahçelievler) and Route 64 (Emek) run between Ulus and the railway station; Route 44 (Terminal) runs past the Otogar, Air Terminal and railway station, then on to Kızılay and Bakanlıklar; Route 63 (Anıttepe) will take you from Ulus to Atatürk's mausoleum, the Anıt Kabir.

City bus tickets cost 100TL (US$0.14) and can be bought from the little ticket kiosks at major bus stops.

If you happen to board an Özel Halk Otobüsü, a privately owned bus, you can buy a ticket right on the bus for 90TL (US$0.13).

Taxi The drop rate is 260TL (US$0.36), and an average trip costs 700TL to 1000TL (US$0.98 to US$1.40). The lower fare would be for a trip from the Otogar or railway station to Ulus; the higher fare, to Kızılay.

BOĞAZKALE/HATTUŞAŞ

Before our own century very little was known about the Hittites, a people who commanded a vast empire in the Middle East, conquered Babylon, and challenged the Egypt of the pharaohs over 3000 years ago. Though their accomplishments were monumental, time has buried Hittite history as effectively as it has buried the Hittites themselves. Only a few references to them, in the Bible and in Egyptian chronicles, remain.

In 1905 excavations began at the site of the Hittite capital near the Turkish village of Boğazkale (also called Boğazköy), 200 km east of Ankara off the highway to Samsun. The digging produced notable works of art, most of which are now preserved in Ankara's Museum of Anatolian Civilisations; also brought to light were the Hittite state archives, written in cuneiform (wedge-shaped characters) on thousands of clay tablets. From these tablets, historians and archaeologists were able to construct a history of the Hittite empire.

The Hittite Cities

The Hittites spoke an Indo-European language. They swept into Anatolia around 2000 BC and conquered the Hatti, from whom they borrowed both their culture and their name. They established themselves here at Hattuşaş, the Hatti capital, and in the course of a millennium enlarged and beautified the city.

Most of the Hittite artefacts are now in Ankara's museum, though there is also a small museum in Boğazkale, open 8 am to noon and 1.30 to 5.30 pm. One 500TL (US$0.70) admission ticket allows you entry to both the ruins and the museum.

The ruins consist of reconstructed foundations, walls and a few rock carvings. The site itself is strange, almost eerie, exciting for its ruggedness and high antiquity rather than for its buildings or reliefs.

Hattuşaş Walk up from the village. Partway up the hill is the **Great Temple of the Storm God**, a vast complex that's almost a town in itself. High above it is the Fortress, which held the royal palace. Both structures date from the 1300s BC. In the walls are several gates, including the **Sphinx Gate**. One of the sphinxes found here is in Berlin; the other is in Istanbul's Museum of the Ancient Orient. Note the tunnel through the wall: it is topped by a corbelled arch (two flat stones leaned against one another). The Hittites did not know how to make a true arch; their neighbours the Chaldaeans and Assyrians, who built mostly of clay, did develop a true arch made of damp mud bricks. The true masonry arch or vault was not fully developed until Roman times, 1400 years later.

Yazılıkaya The Turkish name (yah-zuh-LUH kah-yah) means 'inscribed rock', and that's what you find at this site about three km from Boğazkale. The low reliefs of gods and goddesses indicate that this was the Hittite's holiest religious sanctuary. The Hittites had 1000 gods, but less than 100 are represented here. The shrine dates from very late Hittite times, about the 1200s BC.

Alaca Höyük Another great Hittite city, this one is 20 km north of the Sungurlu-Boğazkale road, or about 28 km from Boğazkale. You can haggle with a taxi driver to take you there and back. As at the other sites, movable monuments have been taken to the museum in Ankara, though there is a small museum on the site, and a few worn sphinxes and low reliefs have been left in place. This is a very old site, settled from about 4000 BC. Time has not been especially kind to it.

Still interested in Hittites? You can visit the very earliest Hittite capital at **Kültepe**, near Kayseri in Cappadocia, but there is even less to see there.

Places to Stay

There are several small hotels in Sungurlu, and also the 25-room *Aşikoğlu Turistik Moteli* (ah-SHUK-oh-loo) (tel 4) in Boğazkale, open from mid-March through November. A very simple but clean double room costs about 5000TL (US$7) – the price goes up and down depending on who's asking, and when. It's also worth noting that the hotel has a restaurant.

Getting There

You can make a day's excursion from Ankara to Boğazkale. Ankara travel agents sell bus tours of the ruins, which are a good way to make your visit. With your own car you can stop at Boğazkale on the way to the Black Sea coast at Samsun.

Going by public bus, leave from Ankara's Otogar on a bus for either Yozgat or Sungurlu. From Yozgat, you can get an organized minibus tour of the ruins which is cheaper than a taxi (see below). A bonus of going via Yozgat is that there are direct buses from Yozgat to Nevşehir, should that be your onward destination.

Sungurlu is a town 175 km east of Ankara. At Sungurlu you must wait for a dolmuş to Boğazkale (perhaps a long wait), or hire a taxi for the trip. The taxi should cost 8000TL (US$11.20) for the entire car, including the trip to Boğazkale (27 km), a tour of the far-flung ruins and return to Sungurlu. This is perhaps a better way to do it, as the ruins are spread out on a sprawling hillside, and you will probably want a taxi tour from Boğazkale (4000TL, US$5.60) anyway; also, taxis there may not be readily available. Considering that you will have to pay about 600TL (US$0.84) per person each way for the dolmuş ride between Sungurlu and Boğazkale, it is thus only slightly more expensive to hire a taxi in Sungurlu.

To see the ruins on foot, plan to walk energetically for three or four hours; it's possible you may even want to spend the night here.

Konya

Standing alone in the midst of the vast Anatolian steppe, Konya (KOHN-yah, altitude 1016 metres, population 550,000) is like some traditional caravan stopping-place. The windswept landscape gives way to little patches of greenery in the city, and when you're in the town you don't feel the loneliness of the plateau.

In recent years Konya has been booming. The bare-looking steppe is in fact good for growing grain, and Konya is the heart of Turkey's very rich 'bread-basket'. Light industry provides jobs for those who are not farmers. Much of the city is new, built within the last 10 years, but the centre is very old. No one knows when the hill at the centre of town, the Alaettin Tepesi, was first settled, but it certainly contains the bones of Bronze Age men and women.

Plan to spend at least one full day in Konya (not a Monday – the museums will be closed!), and preferably two. If your interest in Seljuk history and art takes flame, you could spend another half or full day pleasantly enough. As it takes a good half-day to reach Konya from anywhere, and another half-day to get from Konya to your next destination, you should figure on spending at least two nights in a hotel here.

A point to remember during your visit is that Konya is a fairly conservative place, a favourite with devout Muslims. Take special care not to jar the sensibilities of the pious; look tidy when you enter mosques and the Mevlana Museum. If you visit during the holy month of Ramazan, do not eat or drink in broad public view during daylight hours; this is a politeness to those who are fasting. Another point is that the dervishes do not whirl all the time. They usually only dance during the Mevlana Festival in December.

History

The city has been here for an extremely long time. Neighbouring Çatal Höyük, some 50 km to the south, is thought to be the oldest known human settlement, dating from 7500 BC.

The Hittites called Konya 'Kuwanna' almost 4000 years ago. Over the years, the name has changed slightly; it was Kowania to the Phrygians, Iconium to the Romans, Konya to the Turks.

Under Rome, Iconium was an important provincial town visited on several occasions by the saints Paul and Barnabas, but its early Christian community does not seem to have been very influential.

Konya's heyday was during the 1200s, when it was capital of the Seljuk Sultanate of Rum, the last remnant of an earlier Seljuk empire.

The Seljuk Turks had ruled a powerful state in Iran and Iraq, the Empire of the Great Seljuks, during the 1000s; Omar Khayyam was their most noted poet and mathematician. But Great Seljuk power was fragmented in the early 1100s, and the various parts of the empire set themselves up as independent states. One of these states was the Sultanate of Rum (ROOM, 'Rome'), which encompassed most of Anatolia. Konya was its capital from about 1150 to 1300. In that period, the Seljuk sultans built dozens of fine buildings in an architectural style decidedly Turkish, but with its roots in Persia and Byzantium.

Mevlana The Sultanate of Rum also produced one of the world's great mystic philosophers. Celaleddin Rumi (jeh-LAH-leh-DEEN roo-MEE), founder of the order of whirling dervishes, was called Mevlana (meh-VLAH-nah, Our Guide) by his followers. His poetic and religious work, done mostly in Persian (the literary language of the day), is some of the most beloved and respected in the Islamic world.

Mevlana (1207-1273) was born in

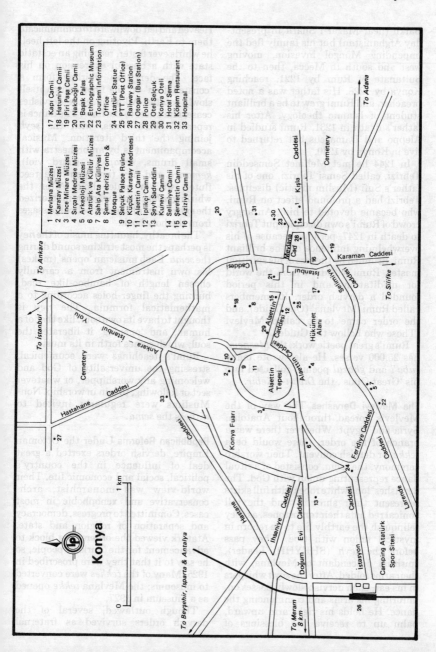

1 Mevlana Müzesi
2 Karatay Müzesi
3 İnce Minare Müzesi
4 Sırçalı Medrese Müzesi
5 Arkeoloji Müzesi
6 Atatürk ve Kültür Müzesi
7 Sahip Ata Külliyesi
8 Şemsi Tebrizi Tomb & Mosque
9 Selçuk Palace Ruins
10 Küçük Karatay Medresesi
11 Alaettin Camii
12 İplikçi Camii
13 Şeyh Sadreddin Kunevi Camii
14 Selimiye Camii
15 Şerefettin Camii
16 Aziziye Camii
17 Kapı Camii
18 Hatuniye Camii
19 Piri Paşa Camii
20 Nakiboğlu Camii
21 Başak Palas
22 Ethnographic Museum
23 Tourism Information Office
24 Atatürk Statue
25 PTT (Post Office)
26 Railway Station
27 Otogar (Bus Station)
28 Police
29 Otel Selçuk
30 Konya Oteli
31 Hotel Sema
32 Köşem Restaurant
33 Hospital

Balkh (near Mazar-i Sharif in present-day Afghanistan) but his family fled the impending Mongol invasion, moving west and south to Mecca, then to the Sultanate of Rum by 1221, reaching Konya by 1228. His father was a noted preacher, and Rumi grew to be a brilliant student of Islamic theology. After his father's death in 1231, Rumi studied in Aleppo and Damascus but returned to live in Konya by 1240.

In 1244 he met Mehmet Şemseddin Tebrizi, called Şemsi Tebrizi, one of his father's Sufi (Muslim mystic) disciples. Tebrizi had a profound effect on Rumi, who became devoted to him. An angry crowd of Rumi's own disciples put Tebrizi to death in 1247, perhaps because of his overwhelming influence on the brilliant Rumi. Stunned by the loss of his spiritual master, Rumi withdrew from the world for meditation, and in this period founded a dervish order. Its members called Rumi 'Mevlana' (Our Guide), and the order came to be called Mevlevi (Those who Follow the Guide).

Rumi's great poetic work, the *Mesnevi*, has 25,000 verses. He also wrote many *ruba'i* and *ghazal* poems, collected into his 'Great Opus', the *Divan-i Kebir*.

The Mevlevi Dervishes The way of the Mevlevis spread throughout Anatolia, Syria and Egypt. Wherever there was a branch of the order, there would be a *tekke*, or dervish convent. Their worship ceremony, the *sema*, consisted of a ritual dance representing union with God. The dervishes' long white robes with full skirts represent their shrouds, and the tall conical red hats their tombstones, as they relinquish the earthly life to be reborn in mystical union with God. They pass before the *şeyh* (SHEYHH, Leader), spiritual descendant of Mevlana, with their arms folded. After the *şeyh* whispers in his ear, each dervish slowly passes on, unfurling his arms and commencing the dance. He holds his right arm upward, palm up to receive the blessings of

Heaven and left downward to communicate them to Earth. Pivoting on the left heel, he whirls ever faster, reaching an ecstatic state with a blissful expression on his face. The dervishes whirling form a 'constellation' on the floor, which itself slowly rotates. All at once the dervishes cease, and kneel to the floor. The dance is repeated three times, with the *şeyh* joining the third iteration. Musical accompaniment is by an orchestra with small drums, *rebap* (a gourd viol), *kemançe* and *ney* (an open-tube reed flute), with a male choir. After the whirling, a *hafiz* (one who has memorized the entire Koran) chants poetical passages from the holy book.

The breathy, haunting music of the *ney* is perhaps the most striking sound during the *sema*. Each musician 'opens' (makes) his own instrument from a carefully chosen length of bamboo-like reed, burning the finger-holes according to a mathematical formula. The *ney* is thought to have its own soul, like that of a human, and 'opening' it liberates the soul, which comes forth in its music.

Rumi's teachings were ecumenical, stressing the universality of God and welcoming any worshipper, of whatever sect or following, to join in worship. Non-Muslims were regularly invited to witness the *sema*.

Republican Reforms Under the Ottoman Empire, dervish orders exerted a great deal of influence in the country's political, social and economic life. Their world-view was monarchist, arch-conservative and xenophobic in most cases. Committed to progress, democracy and separation of religion and state, Atatürk viewed the orders as a block to advancement for the Turkish people, so he saw to it that they were proscribed in 1925. Many of the *tekkes* were converted to museums; the Mevlana *tekke* opened as a museum in 1927.

Though outlawed, several of the dervish orders survived as fraternal religious brotherhoods, stripped of their influence. The whirling dervishes of Konya are now officially a 'cultural association' which preserves a historical tradition. The annual Festival of Mevlana, held in mid-December, is officially encouraged as a popular – not a religious – event. Groups of dervishes are also sent on cultural exchange tours to other countries, performing the *sema* from Leningrad to Los Angeles.

The dervishes are no longer interested in politics, but neither are they truly a 'cultural association'. Young novices are recruited as early as grammar school, and devotion to the principles of the order can still be lifelong. Konya's dervishes whirl today to celebrate a great tradition, but also to worship and to seek mystical union with God as Mevlana taught, and as they have been doing for over 700 years.

Orientation

Though you will want to ride in from the bus and rail terminals, which are each one km from the centre, you can easily walk to most of Konya's attractions once you get downtown. The city's historic axis is Alaettin Caddesi/Mevlana Caddesi, the main street which runs between the hill called Alaettin Tepesi and the Mevlana Museum. Half-way along this street it broadens into Hükümet Alanı, Government Square. By the way, the Mevlana Museum shelters the tomb of Rumi and was the first whirling dervish convent. It's the most important building to visit in Konya.

The distance from the hill to the museum is about one km, a 10 to 15-minute walk.

Information

Konya's Tourism Information Office (tel (331) 11074) is at Mevlana Caddesi 21, across the square from the Mevlana Museum.

Things to See

The centre of Konya is Turkey's best 'outdoor museum' of Seljuk architecture. While the buildings themselves are often starkly simple on the outside, the main portal is always grand and imposing, sometimes huge and wildly baroque in its decoration. The Seljuks built doorways. The interiors are always very harmonious, and often decorated with blue and white tiles. Tiles of other colours are sometimes found, but they rarely have red in them as the fusing of vivid reds on faience was a later, Ottoman accomplishment.

You can walk to all of the buildings described here, but it would be tiring to do so in one day.

Mevlana Museum First place to visit is the Mevlana Museum (Mevlana Müzesi), the former Tekke (Convent) of the Whirling Dervishes, open every day from 9 am to noon and 1.30 to 5.30 pm, closed Monday; admission costs 150TL (US$0.21). Admission tickets are sold until 5.10 pm. At religious holidays, the museum (really a shrine) may be open for longer hours. Women may want to cover their heads and shoulders when they enter.

Enter through a courtyard with ablutions fountain and several tombs, then pass into the Mevlana Türbesi, or tomb of Rumi. The sarcophagi of Rumi and his most illustrious followers are covered in great velvet shrouds heavy with gold embroidery, giving a powerful impression that this is a sacred place.

The tomb dates from Seljuk times; the mosque and room for the *sema* were added later by Ottoman sultans (Mehmet the Conqueror was a Mevlevi adherent, and Süleyman the Magnificent made large charitable donations to the order). Selim I, conqueror of Egypt, donated the Mameluke crystal lamps.

In the rooms adjoining the sepulchral chamber are exhibits of Dervish paraphernalia: musical instruments, vestments, illuminated manuscripts and ethnographic artefacts.

Outside the entrance to the Mevlana

Museum is the **Selimiye Camii**, endowed by Sultan Selim II (1566-1574). Construction on the Ottoman-style mosque was begun during Selim's term as governor of Konya, before his accession to the throne.

The surrounding streets are a lively market district, and you could do some random exploration of the back streets if you have the time.

Alaettin Camii Except for the Mevlana Museum, many of Konya's principal sights are near the Alaettin Tepesi, 'Aladin's Hill'. One, the ancient Alaettin Camii, is right atop the hill.

The Mosque of Alaeddin Keykubat I (or Alaettin), Seljuk Sultan of Rum, is a great rambling building designed by a Damascene architect in the Arab style and finished in 1221. Over the centuries it was embellished, refurbished, ruined and restored. Recent restoration took place as little as a decade ago. Though hardly as harmonious as an Ottoman work of Sinan, it is very sympathetic and impressive. Notice the forest of old columns surmounted with Roman and Byzantine capitals, the fine carved wood *mimber* (pulpit, 1156) and the *mihrab* (prayer niche) of marble. (As of this writing, the mosque is closed for renovations.)

On the north side of the Alaettin Tepesi, the scant ruins of a **Seljuk palace** are protected by a modern concrete shelter.

Büyük Karatay Medresesi Now called the Karatay Museum (Karatay Müzesi, KAH-rah-tah-yee), this Seljuk theological seminary just north of the Alaettin Tepesi houses Konya's outstanding collection of ceramics and tiles. It is open from 8.30 am to noon and from 1.30 to 5.30 pm for 200TL (US$0.28), half-price on Sunday.

The school was constructed in 1251 by the Emir Celaleddin Karatay, a Seljuk diplomat and statesman. It has a magnificent sculpted marble doorway.

Inside, the central dome is a masterpiece of Seljuk blue tilework with gold accents. The Arabic inscription in Kufic style around the bottom of the dome is the first chapter, or *sura*, of the Kuran. The triangles below the dome are decorated with the names of the first four caliphs who succeeded Muhammad; the Arabic letters are highly stylized.

Note especially the curlicue drain for the central pool: its curved shape gave the sound of running water to the quiet room where students were studying, a pleasant background 'noise'.

As for the museum's collection of tiles, they include interesting coloured ones from Seljuk palaces in Konya and Beyşehir. Compare these to the later Ottoman tiles from İznik.

İnce Minare Müzesi Around the Alaettin Tepesi at its west side is the seminary of the Slender Minaret (İnce Minare Medresesi) (een-JEH mee-NAH-reh), now the museum of wood and stone

Büyük Karatay Medresesi

carving. Don't enter the building immediately, for half of what you came to see is the elaborate doorway, with bands of Arabic inscription running up the sides and looping overhead. As this religious school was built in 1258, it may be that the architect was trying to outdo a rival who had designed the Karatay Medresesi only seven years earlier.

The doorway is far more impressive than the small building behind it. The minaret beside the door is what gave the *medrese* its popular name of 'slender minaret', though the greater part of the very tall minaret was knocked off by a lightning bolt less than 100 years ago (having stood here for over 600 years).

The exhibits within the *medrese* show Seljuk motifs used in wood and stone carving, many of them similar to those used in the tile and ceramic work. In Islam, visual representation of creatures with souls (humans and animals) is forbidden as idolatry, but most great Islamic civilisations had artists who ignored the law from time to time. Though most Islamic art is geometrical or otherwise non-representative, you will still see birds (the Seljuk double-headed eagle, for example), men and women, lions and leopards, etc. Though the Ottomans seem to have observed the law more strictly than the Seljuks, there were some lapses. Mehmet the Conqueror, for instance, had his portrait painted by the great Bellini. But as the finished masterpiece was hung in the palace, the mass of people were none the wiser to this 'sacrilege'. (The museum is closed as of this writing for renovation.)

South of the Hill Several other significant Seljuk monuments lie south of the city, in a warren of little streets. If you can find Ressam Sami Sokak, that's the one which will lead you to the following sights.

Not far from the Alaettin Tepesi on Ressam Sami Sokak is another Seljuk *medrese*. Now a museum of funerary monuments, it is the **Sırçalı Medrese**

Müzesi (sirr-chah-LUH). As always, the portal is grand and highly decorated. The tiles on the exterior give the *medrese* its name (*sırçalı* means crystalline). Construction was completed in 1242, sponsored by a Seljuk *vezir* (prime minister). The inscriptions on the gravestones inside are often very fine, done in a variety of Arabic scripts. Symbols of rank – headgear, usually – served to tell the passer-by of the deceased one's important role in life. The museum is closed for renovation as of this writing, but you can still enjoy a view of the marvelous façade.

Konya's small **Archaeological Museum** is a few blocks farther south along Ressam Sami Sokak, on the grounds of the **Sahip Ata Külliyesi**. Museum hours are 8.30 am to noon and 1.30 to 5.30 pm; admission costs 400TL (US$0.56). A *külliye* is a complex of buildings surrounding a mosque. These might include soup kitchens, religious schools, an orphanage or hospital, a library and other charitable works. Sahip Ata was the man who funded the İnce Minare Medresesi. There is also a dervish *tekke* and a *hamam* (Turkish bath). The entire complex was finished in 1283. Note especially the portal to the mosque with its tiled minaret and *mihrab* (prayer niche). Sahip Ata, by the way, was a Seljuk vezir, and obviously very rich.

Not far from the Sahip Ata Külliyesi is the city's small **Ethnography Museum**, open during the same hours as the Archaeological Museum for 400TL (US$0.56).

Other Mosques & Tombs As you wander around town, you will pass other buildings of interest. The **Şemsi Tebrizi Camii**, containing the tomb (1300s) of Rumi's spiritual mentor, is just north of Hükümet Alanı, off Alaettin Caddesi. The **Aziziye Camii** (1874) is a work of Ottoman late Baroque in the bazaar; it's the one which has twin minarets bearing little sheltered balconies. The **İplikçi**

Camii (1202) on the main street is perhaps Konya's oldest mosque. The **Şerefettin Camii** was constructed in 1636. Near the PTT on Hükümet Caddesi is the **Hacı Hasan Camii**.

The Bazaar Konya's market area is behind the modern PTT building. Walk through the city bus lot, along the east side of the Koli PTT (the parcel branch) and to the left of the shoeshine stand, then straight along Çıkrıkçılar Caddesi. Besides shops selling all manner of things, there are lots of inexpensive eateries here.

Meram If you have a spare morning or afternoon, take an excursion (less than 10 km) to Meram, a pleasant, shady suburb west of the city. It's been a getaway destination for Konya city-dwellers for at least 1000 years. Minibuses depart the market area not far from the Mevlana Museum for the 15-minute trip to Meram. The fare is 60TL (US$0.08).

Çatal Höyük You can drive or arrange a taxi excursion to Çatal Höyük, the world's oldest human settlement, 50 km south-east of Konya, but there is little to see except the setting. The prehistoric artefacts have been removed to museums.

Places to Stay – bottom end

Being a God-fearing sort of town, Konya has lots of very inexpensive, very clean, very proper little hotels. The cheap lodging situation here is better than in most other Turkish cities. You get a lot for very little money.

On a quiet street near the Mevlana Museum is the *Otel Köşk* (KEURSHK) (tel (331) 20671), Bostan Çelebi Sokak 13, a tidy and convenient place which charges a mere 2500TL (US$3.50) for a bathless double, 3500TL (US$4.90) with bath. The nearby *Otel Tur* (TOOR) (tel (331) 19825), Eşârizade Sokak 13, has only waterless triple rooms which go for 4500TL (US$6.30), but it's modern and clean.

The *Otel Selimiye* (seh-LEEM-ee-yeh) (tel (331) 20014), Mevlana Caddesi 17, a half-block from the Tourism Office, is very clean and tidy and charges an exceptionally low 1400TL (US$1.96) single, 2500TL (US$3.50) for a waterless room.

An excellent choice is the *Hotel Ulusan* (OO-loo-sahn) (tel (331) 15004), Kurşuncular Sokak 2, behind the PTT (follow the little signs). Clean, tidy and quiet, it charges only 2500TL (US$3.50) in a waterless double room.

Near the Alaettin Tepesi is the *Otel Kanarya* (kah-NAHR-yah) (tel (331) 11575), Alaettin Caddesi, Emirpervane Sokak 4 (turn off the main street by the Anadolu Bankası). This is a homey place with three-bedded, waterless rooms going for 3300TL (US$4.62) triple. Nice!

Kara Hüyüklü Sokak is a little street running south from Alaettin Caddesi, and on it are no less than five small, cheap, clean hotels charging about 2500TL (US$3.50) for a waterless double room. Look for the *Otel Roma, Pak Otel, Otel Nur, Bulvar Oteli* and *Yeni Doğan Oteli,* all within one block of one another.

For a good deal more comfort at a negligibly higher price, head for the *Saray Oteli* (sah-RAHY) (tel (331) 19990), Mevlana Caddesi 15, very near the Tourism Office and the Mevlana Museum, on the main street. A single with private shower here costs 3300TL (US$4.62), a double 5500TL (US$7.70).

The *Şeref Palas Oteli*, around the corner from the much more expensive Başak Palas in Hükümet Alanı, is very clean and nice and charges only 2500TL (US$3.50) double without shower, 3000TL (US$4.20) with.

Camping You can camp at the *Şehir Stadı*, the sports complex just east of the railway station on İstasyon Caddesi.

Places to Stay – middle

Conveniently located next to the Otogar

(bus terminal) are two good middle-range hotels.

The *Özkaymak Park Oteli* (EURZ-kahy-mahk) (tel (331) 33770, 2), has 90 clean and comfortable rooms with bath going for 13,000TL (US$18.20) single, 20,000TL (US$28) double; it's generally regarded as the town's best place to stay and is thus popular with tour groups.

Hotel Sema 2 (tel (331) 32557 or 30138), with 33 rooms priced at 6000TL (US$8.40) for a double without bath, or 10,000TL (US$14) for a double with bath, is the second choice. A bathless single here goes for 4000TL (US$5.60).

The other moderately priced hotels are downtown. The *Konya Otel* (tel (331) 19212 or 16677), just behind the Tourism Office and very near the Mevlana Museum, is a fine choice. At this quiet, older hotel the desk clerk will quote you prices of 9000TL (US$12.60) single, 14,000TL (US$19.60) double for a room with bath, but he's amenable to haggling, which should bring the price down.

The *Başak Palas* (bah-SHAHK pah-LAHS) (tel (331) 11338, 9), at Hükümet Alanı 3 facing the provincial government house, midway along Alaettin Caddesi, is an older place with 40 rooms, kept brightly painted. Bathless singles cost 4500TL (US$6.30), doubles with bath cost 10,000TL (US$14).

Places to Eat

Konya's specialty is *fırın kebap* (fuh-RUHN keh-bahp, oven roast), a rich joint of mutton roasted in an oven *(fırın)*. It is not normally prepared to order, so you must trust to luck for a taste of it. If you see it offered, give it a try.

The *Çatal Lokantası* (chah-TAHL) (tel 14439) is just behind the Tourism Office, near the Mevlana Museum. This is a simple, tidy *kebap* place (no booze) next to the Konya Otel, with good food at low prices. Expect to pay 1400TL (US$1.96) for a full lunch or dinner.

Even cheaper fare is available on Çıkrıkçılar Caddesi in the bazaar, behind the PTT (see under Things to See). At No 19 is the *Şambaba Börekçi*, serving *pide* (called *etli ekmek*, bread with meat) for only 300TL (US$0.42). There are several other such places as well.

For a more upscale meal, try the popular *Şifa Lokantası* (shee-FAH) (tel 20519), Mevlana Caddesi 30, only a short stroll from the Mevlana Museum. It's a modern if simple dining room with tablecloths on the tables and full meals for 1500TL to 2000TL (US$2.10 to US$2.80).

The *Kent Restaurant* on Alaettin Caddesi near the Alaettin Tepesi has good chicken and *İskender kebap*.

Getting There & Away

Konya has no airport, so access is by road or rail.

Rail There is no direct rail link across the steppe between Konya and Ankara. Bus is the best way to make this journey.

Between İstanbul and Konya you can ride the Meram Ekspresi (mehr-AHM), which departs either city in the morning and arrives in the evening, with 1st-class coaches and a dining car. The journey takes about 12½ hours. The only other train takes almost 19 hours to make the trip.

City buses (60TL, US$0.08) connect the İstasyon (railway station) with the centre of town, running at least every half-hour. If you take a taxi from the İstasyon to Hükümet Alanı, it will cost about 650TL (US$0.91).

Bus Konya has a modern bus terminal one km or so from the centre. To travel from the bus terminal into town there are municipal buses and more convenient minibuses (Konak-Otogar, 60TL, US$0.08) waiting at a rank near the Park Oteli, just outside the bus terminal. Climb in, and you'll quickly be transported to Hükümet Meydanı at the very centre of things on Alaettin Caddesi.

Konya is 262 km (three or four hours)

south of Ankara (800TL to 1500TL, US$1.12 to US$2.10), 226 km (3½ hours) south-west of Nevşehir in Cappadocia (1500TL, US$2.10; there are also direct buses to Ürgüp and Avanos), and 218 km (four hours) north-west of Silifke (1500TL, US$2.10). It's about 300 km from Side (2300TL, US$3.22) and Alanya (nine or 10 hours, 2500TL, US$3.50), a long trip of seven hours because of the slow ascent to the plateau. To get from Konya to Antalya, Side or Alanya, you might find that you have to switch buses in Beyşehir (BEHY-sheh-heer). To Adana the trip takes six hours and costs 2000TL (US$2.80). The trip to Bursa takes 8½ hours and costs 2500TL (US$3.50).

Bus service to and from Ankara is frequent and convenient. Service between Konya and Cappadocia may involve a change of vehicles in Aksaray. If you can't find a direct bus or minibus, take something to Aksaray and then ask directions to the ticket office for the onward journey. The phrase is *Nevşehir'e giden otobüs nereden kalkar?* (NEHV-sheh-heer-eh gee-dehn oto-beurss NEH-reh-dehn kahl-KAHR, 'From where does the Nevşehir bus depart?') Going to Konya, you must ask *Konya'ya giden otobüs nereden kalkar?* (KOHN-yah-YAH .... 'From where does the bus to Konya depart?') People in Aksaray are used to foreigners passing through, and will gladly and quickly point the way.

Along the highway between Konya and Aksaray (95 km from Konya, 45 from Aksaray) you'll pass the Sultan Hanı, a Seljuk caravanserai. Keep an eye open for it.

Cappadocia

The region between Ankara and Malatya, between the Black Sea and the Taurus Mountains, with its centre at Kayseri, was once the heart of the Hittite Empire, later an independent kingdom, then a vast Roman province. Cappadocia is mentioned several times in the Bible.

Today the word survives as a name for one of Turkey's most-visited tourist areas, the moon-like landscape around the town of Ürgüp and the Göreme Valley. You won't find the name on an official road map, so you must know that unofficial Kapadokya is the area between Kayseri to the east of Ürgüp, Aksaray to the west, and Niğde to the south.

For all its apparent barrenness, the mineral-laden volcanic tuff is very fertile, and Cappadocia today is a prime agricultural region with many fruit orchards and vineyards. Little wineries experiment with the excellent grapes, sometimes with very gratifying results. Irrigation schemes should greatly increase the productivity of the region.

Another source of wealth is carpet-making, and while the women in Cappadocian villages toil at their looms, Kayseri is a hotbed of persistent rug-dealers. But Cappadocia's new economic dimension is tourism. People come from all over the world to visit the National Park in the Göreme Valley, to explore the rock-hewn churches and dwellings in surrounding valleys, to gaze on the fairy chimneys, and to plumb the depths of the underground cities at Derinkuyu and Kaymaklı, south of Nevşehir.

The most beautiful and artistically significant valleys are National Parks, protected from development. Further protection and support are provided by a UNESCO preservation campaign similar to the one launched in Egypt to protect that country's antiquities from the waters of the Aswan High Dam.

History

The history of Cappadocia begins with the eruption of two volcanoes, Erciyes Dağı near Kayseri and Melendiz Dağı near Niğde. The eruptions spread a thick layer of hot volcanic ash over the region, and the ash hardened to a soft, porous stone called tuff.

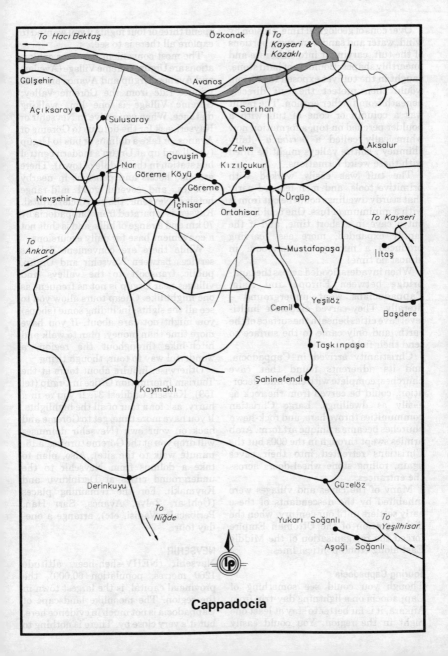

Cappadocia

Over eons of geological time, erosion by wind, water and sand wore away portions of the tuff, carving it into elaborate and unearthly shapes. Boulders of hard stone, caught in the tuff yet exposed to erosion, would then protect the tuff directly beneath from further erosion. The result was a column or cone of tuff with a boulder perched on top, a formation now whimsically called a *peribaca*, 'fairy chimney'. Entire valleys might be filled with these weird formations.

The tuff was easily worked with primitive tools, and men learned early that sturdy dwellings could be cut from it with a minimum of fuss. One could carve out a cave in a short time, and if the family expanded, more easy carving produced a nursery or storeroom in almost no time!

When invaders flooded across the land-bridge between Europe and Asia, Cappadocians went underground – literally. They carved elaborate multi-level cave cities beneath the surface of the earth, and only came to the surface to tend their fields.

Christianity arrived in Cappadocia, and its adherents found that cave churches, complete with elaborate decoration, could be carved from the rock as easily as dwellings. Large Christian communities throve here, and rock-hewn churches became a unique art form. Arab armies swept through in the 600s but the Christians retreated into their caves again, rolling stone wheel-doors across the entrances.

Many of the caves and villages were inhabited by the descendants of these early settlers until our century, when the disintegration of the Ottoman Empire forced the reorganisation of the Middle East along ethno-political lines.

Touring Cappadocia

Though you could see something of Cappadocia on a lightning day-trip from Ankara, it is far better to stay at least one night in the region. You could easily spend three or four nights if you wanted to explore all there is to see.

The most convenient bases for explorations are Ürgüp, Göreme Village (Avcılar) and Avanos. Ürgüp and Avanos are a 10-minute ride from the Göreme Valley; Göreme Village is one km, walking distance. When you arrive in Nevşehir or Kayseri, ask for the dolmuş to Göreme or Avanos, or take a dolmuş or bus to Ürgüp (you'll end up at Ürgüp's modern central bus station in the middle of town). There are also hotels and pensions in nearby villages, and several good mid-range hotels in Nevşehir, the provincial capital. Kayseri is separated from Cappadocia by 70 km and a range of hills, and is thus not a convenient base for daily excursions.

While there are convenient dolmuş services between Nevşehir and Ürgüp, public transport to the valleys and villages near Ürgüp is not as frequent as one might like. Cheap tours allow you to see all the sights, including some (shops) you might not care about. If you have more time than money, plan to walk and hitch-hike throughout the region, a wonderful way to tour, though tiring.

Otherwise, inquire about tours at the Tourism Information Office in Ürgüp (tel 159), Kayseri Caddesi 37. If you're in a hurry, ask for a tour of all the highlights. If you have more time, get to Göreme and back on your own (Nevşehir dolmuşes will drop you at the Göreme turning, a 15-minute walk to the site). Also, plan to take a dolmuş from Nevşehir to the underground cities at Derinkuyu and Kaymaklı. For the remaining places (Üçhisar, Zelve, Avanos, Sarı Han, Peribacalar Vadisi, etc), arrange a one-day tour.

NEVŞEHİR

Nevşehir (NEHV-sheh-heer, altitude 1260 metres, population 60,000), the provincial capital, is the largest town in the region. The moonlike landscape of Cappadocia is not much in evidence here, but it's very close by. There is nothing to see in Nevşehir proper; it is a transfer point, and a base for visiting the underground cities at Kaymaklı and Derinkuyu.

Orientation
Buses will drop you in a large square north of the centre. Walk downhill along the highway, which is also the city's main street, called Atatürk Bulvarı, to reach the business district of banks, shops, restaurants and hotels. At the major intersection in the centre of town, minibus dolmuşes depart for nearby towns and villages.

Information
The Tourism Information Office (tel (4851) 1137) is at Lale Caddesi 22. There is a convenient little information booth at the bus station, open 8.30 am to noon and 1 to 5.30 pm.

Things to See
Göreme and Zelve, near Ürgüp, are where the beauty is. But for sheer fascination and mystery, the places to see are the **underground cities** at Kaymaklı, 20 km south of Nevşehir along the road to Niğde, and at Derinkuyu, 10 km farther south. Board a Niğde minibus at the central intersection in Nevşehir; they depart every 30 minutes or so and charge 400TL (US$0.56) for the ride. Kaymaklı has four underground levels, Derinkuyu eight; Derinkuyu is less touristy as well.

The countryside here is one vast, flat steppe, without enchanting fairy chimneys or sensuously carved valleys. Yet the stone is the same soft volcanic tuff, and it allowed early residents to develop the real estate cheaply. At **Kaymaklı**, an unprepossessing farming village of white houses and unpaved streets, an unimpressive little cave in a low mound leads down into a vast maze of tunnels and rooms. To find the entrance, look for signs saying 'Buried City in Kaymaklı', which indicate a left (east) turn, or ask for the Yeraltı Şehri (YEHR-ahl-tuh shehh-ree, Underground

City). The entrance is one block from the highway, and is open from 9 am to noon and from 1.30 to 6.30 pm; admission costs 400TL (US$0.56), half-price on weekends. Parking at the site costs 100TL (US$0.14).

A guide clicks on the electric lights and leads the way into the cool depths, and the feeling is one of entering a huge and very complex Swiss cheese. Holes here, holes there, 'windows' from room to room, paths going this way and that, more levels of rooms above and below. Without the guide and the electric wires, it would be fearfully difficult to find the way out again. If you wander off along another passage, separated from the group by only a few feet, you can hear what they say, you can converse with them, but you can't find your way back to them! Suddenly a foot comes into view, and you realize that they're on the next level, almost above your head!

The guide points out storage jars for oil, wine and water, communal kitchens blackened by smoke, stables with mangers, incredibly deep wells. Soon you no longer find it impossible to believe that tens of thousands of people could have lived here happily year-round, deep within the earth. It's even suspected that there were underground passages which connected Kaymaklı with its sister city of Derinkuyu, seven km away, though the tunnels have yet to be fully excavated.

Having seen Kaymaklı, you can try to catch a minibus south along the highway to Derinkuyu (deh-REEN-koo-yoo, Deep Well) for a look at another such city. It's more of the same. The sign here says 'Buried City in Derinkuyu'; prices and times are the same as at Kaymaklı.

Places to Stay
You won't want to use Nevşehir as your sightseeing base, but if you have need of lodgings here, they are easy to find and cheap to pay for.

Places to Stay – bottom end
Just above the bus station is the new and

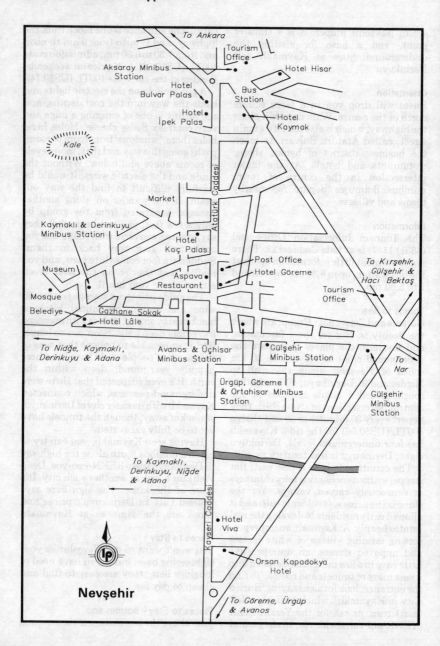

To Ankara

Tourism Office

Aksaray Minibus Station

Hotel Hisar

Hotel Bulvar Palas

Bus Station

Hotel İpek Palas

Hotel Kaymak

Kale

Market

Atatürk Caddesi

Kaymaklı & Derinkuyu Minibus Station

Hotel Koç Palas

Post Office

Hotel Göreme

To Kırşehir, Gülşehir & Hacı Bektaş

Museum

Aspava Restaurant

Tourism Office

Mosque

Belediye

Gazhane Sokak

Hotel Lâle

To Niğde, Kaymaklı, Derinkuyu & Adana

Avanos & Üçhisar Minibus Station

Gülşehir Minibus Station

To Nar

Ürgüp, Göreme & Ortahisar Minibus Station

Gülşehir Minibus Station

To Kaymaklı, Derinkuyu, Niğde & Adana

Kayseri Caddesi

Hotel Viva

Orsan Kapadokya Hotel

Nevşehir

To Göreme, Ürgüp & Avanos

bright *Hotel Hisar* (hee-SAHR) (tel (4851) 3857), Aksaray Caddesi 17, opened in 1986. It looks fancy, what with its posh lobby and lift, but prices at my last visit were only 4400TL (US$6.61) single, 6600TL (US$9.24) double, with shower or bath. Try this first.

Still near the bus station, and even cheaper, is the *Hotel Kaymak* (kahy-MAHK) (tel (4851) 5427), Eski Sanayi Meydanı 11, across the vast bus station lot to the left (south); you'll see its sign. Older, but nice and clean, it has elephant's-feet toilets, but regular bathtubs in the common bathrooms, and charges only 2200TL (US$3.08) single, 3600TL (US$5.04) double for a waterless room.

Walking down the hill on the main street from the bus station, you pass several small hotels which may suffer from street noise. There's the *Bulvar Palas* (bool-VAHR pah-lahss) (tel (4851) 1695 or 5151), Atatürk Bulvarı 101, which rents clean waterless singles for 1200TL (US$1.68), doubles for 2000TL (US$2.80); the triples go for 2700TL (US$3.78), and have washbasins in them. The *İpek Palas Oteli* (ee-PEHK pah-lahss) (tel (4851) 1478), a few doors down to the left, is similar.

A bit farther down the hill is a quieter place, the *Koç Palas Otel* (KOHCH pah-lahss) (tel (4851) 1216), Hükümet Caddesi 1, facing a little square not too far from the bus station. The charge for a waterless double is 2400TL (US$3.36).

Camping There are several camping places along the road to Ürgüp. Rates are generally US$1.50 per person, another US$0.60 to US$1 for tent or caravan.

Follow the signs to Ürgüp, and shortly after leaving Nevşehir you will come to a *Dinler Turizm Mocamp*, behind a BP petrol station. Farther along is the *Koru Mocamp* (tel (4851) 2157), with room for 240 persons and hook-ups of water and electricity for camping vehicles. The *Kervansaray Göreme Mokamp* (tel (4851) 1428), has room for some 600

persons and is more elaborate than most. Rates are a bit higher, about 1500TL (US$2.10) per adult, almost as much for tent or vehicle.

For other camping areas near Göreme, see the Ürgüp section.

Places to Stay – middle

The best place in town is the *Orsan Kapadokya Oteli* (tel (4851) 1035 or 2115) on Kayseri Caddesi, the road east to Ürgüp. The 80 doubles-with-bath rent for 15,000TL (US$21) double; there's a swimming pool. Nearby is the smaller, more modest *Hotel Viva* (VEE-vah) (tel (4851) 1326 or 1760), Kayseri Caddesi 111, popular with tour groups, where the 24 doubles-with-bath are priced at 6000TL (US$8.40).

Right in the centre of Nevşehir, on the main street, the *Hotel Göreme* (GEUR-reh-meh) (tel (4851) 1706) is true to its namesake. Eleven storeys of raw concrete make it look somewhat troglodytic, but it is comfortable with many services; doubles cost 12,000TL (US$16.80). The *Hotel Lale* (LAH-leh) (tel (4851) 1797 or 2905), Gazhane Sokak, is next to the Municipality (Belediye Sarayı), a few short blocks west of the centre. All of its rooms have bath or shower and rent for 4200TL (US$5.88) single, 6100TL (US$8.54) double. This is where the local bureaucrats stay.

Places to Eat

Nevşehir does not have many restaurants, and none of them are fancy. The fanciest meals are in the more expensive hotels. For general purposes, the *Aspava Lokantası* (AHSS-pah-vah) (tel 1057), Atatürk Bulvarı 29 in the centre of town, is a good bet for *kebaps* and *pide*.

Getting There & Away

The bus from Ankara costs 1500TL (US$2.10) and takes four or five hours. To Kayseri there are several daily buses from Nevşehir charging 1000TL (US$1.40), but they take two to three hours, when the minibus costs only 700TL and takes 1½ hours. Look for the minibuses at the main intersection.

The Göreme Turizm company operates an Ürgüp-to-Konya service via Nevşehir, a 2½-hour trip costing 1500TL (US$2.10). An overnight bus from Antalya to Nevşehir or Ürgüp takes 10 or 11 hours and costs 4500TL (US$6.30).

For Ürgüp, catch a bus at the bus station or a minibus from the centre of town. Minibus is also the way to reach Göreme Village (Avcılar) and Avanos. To get to the underground cities at Kaymaklı or Derinkuyu, catch a minibus from the centre; they leave about every half hour.

Heading East

East out of Nevşehir, the rolling terrain is sandy. After a few km the panorama of Cappadocia begins to unfold: distant rock formations become visible as fairy chimneys, and valleys with undulating walls of soft volcanic ash fall away from the road. In the far distance, the gigantic snow-capped peak of the volcano, Erciyes Dağı (Mt Aergius), floats above a layer of cloud.

You will pass the Motel Paris on your left, at the turning for Göreme. The settlement to the right is Ortahisar. Soon afterward, the Turban Ürgüp Moteli will be on your left. Then it's down a long hill (one km) into Ürgüp.

ÜRGÜP

Twenty-three km east of Nevşehir is the village of Ürgüp (EWR-gewp, population 10,000), at the very heart of the Cappadocian wonderland. Life in Ürgüp is divided between farming and tourism, and a hotel might share a stretch of land with a vineyard or alfalfa field. Because of the volcanic soil, sufficient water and abundant sunshine, the town is surrounded by a rich landscape of grain fields, vineyards and clusters of beehives.

Many of the buildings in the town are made of the local tawny limestone with a pronounced grain. Some of the older houses have fine bits of carved stone decoration. Quite a number of Ürgüp's citizens still live or work, at least part of the time, in spaces carved out of the rock. Surrounding villages such as Ortahisar and Üçhisar are similarly troglodytic, peopled by cave-dwellers. At Üçhisar there's a rock-dwelling of a different sort, however. The Hotel Kaya, run by Club Mediterranee, is built partially into the rock, but its guests can hardly be said to live the life of cavepeople.

Ürgüp's main street has a sprinkling of antique and carpet shops, a Tourism Information Office and several restaurants. Though Kayseri is known as the local carpet-making centre, Ürgüp is a better place to buy carpets because the dealers do not hound you here as they do in Kayseri.

Orientation

Ürgüp is a small town, and with the help of the maps in this book, you'll find your way around in no time.

Information

The Tourism Information Office (tel (4868) 1059) is at Kayseri Caddesi 37, on the main street down the hill from the main square.

Things to See

Tours of the sights in the region are offered by several agencies for 2500TL to 3000TL (US$3.50 to US$4.20), and considering the heat of the sun and the difficulties of transport, it's not a bad idea to consider signing up for one. The catch, of course, is that you spend some of your valuable time sitting in shops to which the minibus has brought you. The tour company gets as much as 30% commission on everything you buy in the shops. But the tea is free, and the 'shopping' can actually be just a rest from walking in the sun.

To rent a taxi or minibus on your own to go to, say, Zelve, costs 3000TL (US$4.20);

to Avanos 2000TL (US$2.80). To hire an entire minibus for a full-day tour of all Cappadocia, starting at Ürgüp or Nevşehir, costs 20,000TL to 25,000TL (US$28 to US$35).

Göreme Valley Of all the Cappadocian valleys, Göreme is without doubt the most famous, and rightly so. Approaching it from Ürgüp (eight km), the road winds up over a ridge, then descends into a maze of little valleys, ridges and cones. The rich bottomland at the base of each valley blazes with bright patches of green crops, or is dotted with tidy rows of grapevines. Halfway down the hill is the entrance to the **Göreme Open Air Museum** (Göreme Açık Hava Müzesi), open from 8.30 am to 5.30 pm; admission costs 600TL (US$0.84), half-price on weekends.

It's easy to spend most of a day walking the paths here, climbing stairways or passing through tunnels to reach the various churches. The paintings and frescoes in several **churches** – the Elmalı, Karanlık, Tokalı and Çarıklı – are outstanding. In between churches, the utter improbability of the landscape floods in upon you: the lovely, soft textures in the rock, the fairytale cave dwellings, the spare vegetation growing vigorously from the stark but mineral-rich soil.

Göreme Village The village of Göreme (formerly called Avcılar), 1½ km past the National Park, is small but busy with farm wagons and tractors. An occasional souvenir shop serves the travellers who

wander through. If you take the time to explore Avcılar's winding streets, you will see many buildings – there's even a flour mill! – carved in the rock.

Çavuşin & Zelve From Göreme Village, the Avanos road leads north to Çavuşin, with its Church of John the Baptist near the top of the cliff which rises behind the village. A half-km north of the village, along the road, is the Çavuşin Church (look for the iron stairway).

A side road from Çavuşin heads up another valley five km to Zelve, almost as rich in churches and strange panoramas as Göreme, but much less touristy. If you're walking, a footpath starts from Çavuşin and saves you a few km of walking down to the road junction.

Zelve was a monastic retreat. Hours are the same as at Göreme; admission here costs 400TL (US$0.56). There's a restaurant and tea-garden for refreshments. The entrance is seven km from Avanos.

Peribacalar Vadisi Along the eastern road between Ürgüp and Avanos is the Valley of the Fairy Chimneys (Peribacalari Vadisi). Though many valleys hold collections of strange cones, these are the best formed and most thickly clustered. Most of the rosy rock cones are topped by flattish stones of a darker colour, which have in fact caused the formation of the cones. Being of a harder rock, the dark cap-stones sheltered the cones from the rains which eroded all the surrounding rock.

Other Sights Go to Üçhisar with a camera, and bring a lot of film. The place was almost tailor-made for dramatic and folksy photography. Ortahisar is not as dramatic, but equally folksy.

For a **swim**, the Turban Motel has a pool you can use for an entry fee of 1650TL (US$2.31).

Places to Stay
Though Ürgüp is the most convenient

place to stay if you don't have a car, there are also lodgings along the Ürgüp-Göreme road, in Göreme Village, in Ortahisar and in Üçhisar. For lodgings in Avanos, see the separate section below.

Places to Stay – bottom end

Ürgüp has numerous little *pansiyons* in which you can get a bed in a clean though spartan room for about US$2 per person. The owner (*patron*, pah-TROHN) will be cheerful and helpful. Another bonus is the bath arrangements: you make an appointment for a shower, and a half-hour before the appointed hour the patron builds a fire under the hot water tank. The shower costs an extra 500TL (US$0.70) or so, but you get as much steaming hot water as you like.

The prime area for cheap little pensions and hotels is the quarter called Sivritaş Mahallesi, especially its streets named Santral Sokak and Elgin Sokak. Virtually any *pansiyon* here will be cheap and satisfactory, but my favourite is the *Erciyes Pansiyon* (EHR-jee-yess) (tel (4868) 1206), Santral Sokak No 4. The Erciyes is run by Mr H M Bozan, a retired school-teacher, and his son, who keep it clean and charge 1000TL (US$1.40) per bed in dormitories, 500TL (US$0.70) for a breakfast or a hot shower.

The next street east of Santral Sokak is Elgin Sokak, which holds no fewer than four small *pansiyons* and hotels. Cheapest is the *Otel Villa* (VEE-lah) (tel (4868) 1906), which is clean and tidy inside, though not much to look at from the outside. Doubles without bath rent for 3750TL (US$5.25), with bath for 4500TL (US$6.30). *Hotel Divan* (dee-VAHN) (tel (4868) 1705), Elgin Sokak 4, has its own tiny camping area in the garden, as well as rooms that rent for 2500TL to 3000TL (US$3.50 to US$4.20) single, 3750TL to 4500TL (US$5.25 to US$6.30) double, 4500TL to 6000TL (US$6.30 to US$8.40) triple; the higher prices are for rooms with bath. *Hotel Eyfel* (ey-FEHL) (tel (4868) 1325), Elgin Sokak 8, is the class act on

the street, with a tiny swimming pool. The watering hole raises the prices somewhat, but all of the rooms have private showers, and cost 5000TL (US$7) single, 8000TL (US$11.20) double, 10,000TL (US$14) triple. Campers can pitch their tents at the back of the house. Also on this street is the *Hisar Oteli* (hee-SAHR) (tel (4868) 1261) with double rooms going for 4500TL (US$6.30), with bath. Facing it is the *Hitit Oteli* (hee-TEET) (tel (4868) 1481), charging the same rates for similar accommodation.

The *Pınar Otel* (puh-NAHR) (tel (4868) 1054), Kayseri Caddesi 24, has a garden, camping area and double rooms with bath for 4500TL (US$6.30).

On Dumlupınar Caddesi south of the market are several hotels, most of them not cheap, with the exception of the *Kale Otel* (KAH-leh) (tel (4868) 1069), Dumlupınar Caddesi 26, which is among the town's newer hostelries, and rents rooms for 3000TL (US$4.20) single, 4500TL (US$6.30) double, with shower.

There are a good number of very cheap and congenial pensions in Göreme Village (Avcılar), only one km from the Göreme valley and its churches. Beds in several, including the *SOS* and the *Nazar*, go for 1000TL (US$1.40) per person; in others such as the *Paradise* you get more comfort but pay slightly more money. A number of the pensions here are troglodytic, carved at least in part from the rock. Look at the *Halil Carved Pension* and the *Pansiyon Göreme* as well as the *SOS*.

In Ortahisar, the village opposite the Göreme turning, is the *Hotel Göreme* (tel Ortahisar 5), a very modest place with bathless doubles for 3300TL (US$4.62) single or double, 4200TL (US$5.88) triple. Ortahisar is a 'poor man's' Ürgüp, a farming village with a sleepy ambience except on market day. Stay here if you're adventurous and you want a true non-tourist, living-with-the-locals experience.

Camping Many of the small pensions mentioned above will allow you to pitch

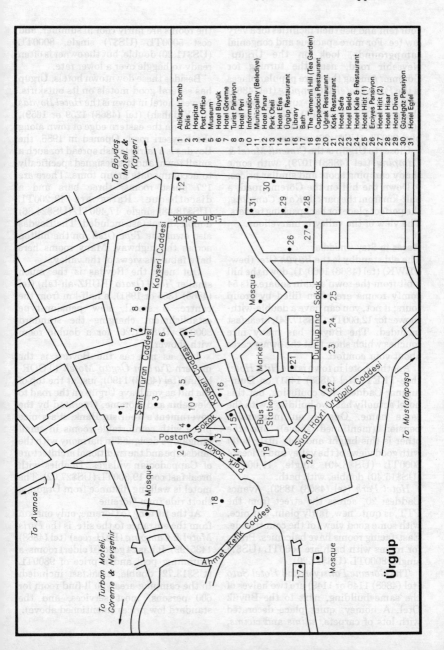

1	Altıkapılı Tomb
2	Polis
3	Hospital
4	Post Office
5	Museum
6	Hotel Büyük
7	Hotel Göreme
8	Turist Pansiyon
9	Hotel Peri
10	Information
11	Municipality (Belediye)
12	Hotel Pınar
13	Park Oteli
14	Hotel Efes
15	Ürgüp Restaurant
16	Library
17	Bath
18	The Temenni Hill (Tea Garden)
19	Cappadocia Restaurant
20	Uğrak Restaurant
21	Köşk Restaurant
22	Hotel Sefa
23	Hotel Belde
24	Hotel Kale & Restaurant
25	Hotel Hitit (1)
26	Erciyes Pansiyon
27	Hotel Hitit (2)
28	Hotel Divan
29	Hotel Hisar
30	Güzelgöz Pansiyon
31	Hotel Egfel

To Boydaş Moteli & Kayseri

Kayseri Caddesi

Şehit Turan Caddesi

Kayseri Caddesi

Lidin Sokak

Mosque

Market

Dumlupınar Sokak

Postane Sokak

Ürgüplü Caddesi

To Mustafapaşa

Bus Station

Suat Hayri

Park Sokak

Postane

To Avanos

Mosque

Mosque

To Turban Moteli, Göreme & Nevşehir

Ahmet Refik Caddesi

Mosque

Ürgüp

your tent and use their facilities for a very low fee. For more spacious and congenial campgrounds, look on the Ürgüp-Nevşehir road, near the turning for Göreme. Among the more popular places is the *Paris Motel & Camping* (tel (4868) 1435/99), just at the turning, which charges 750TL (US$1.05) to pitch a tent, 1050TL (US$1.47) to park a camper-van, plus 900TL (US$1.26) per person.

Closer to Ürgüp is the *Çimenli Motel & Camping* (tel (4868) 1079), with some shady camping spots and similar prices.

Down the hill on the Göreme road, a half-km from the park, is *Kaya Camping*, the perfect place for backpacking tenters. The view of the valley is marvellous.

Places to Stay – middle

The old standby is the *Büyük Otel* (bew-YEWK) (tel (4868) 1060, 1), down the hill a bit from the town's main square. Its 54 comfy rooms are often filled by group tours; if not, you can have a double-with-shower for 12,600TL (US$17.64), breakfast included. The Büyük has many nice touches which show that the owner cares about your comfort.

Another hotel in town is the *Hitit Hotel* (hee-TEET) (tel (4868) 1481) on Dumlupınar Caddesi. It's confusing, but this hotel actually has two buildings with the same name. One is an inexpensive pension (mentioned above), and the other is this bright and tidy little hotel with good views of the valley and prices of 6000TL (US$8.40) single, 11,000TL (US$15.40) double, with bath.

Hotel Park (tel (4868) 1883), Avanos Caddesi 20, across the street from the PTT, is quite new, fairly plain, but nice, with some good views of the countryside. East-facing rooms have balconies. Prices for rooms with bath are 5000TL (US$7) single, 8000TL (US$11.20).

The *Göreme Pansiyon* and *Hotel Şato* (tel (4868) 1146 or 1149) are two halves of the same building, next to the Büyük Otel. A homey, quiet place decorated with lots of carpets, *kilims* and *cicims*,

the rooms are fairly cool in summer, and cost 5000TL (US$7) single, 8000TL (US$11.20) double, but the owner is often ready to haggle over a lower rate.

Besides these downtown hotels, Ürgüp has several good motels on its outskirts. Newest hotel in town is the *Hotel Boydaş* (BOY-dahsh) (tel (4868) 1259 or 1659), PK 11, on the eastern edge of town along the Kayseri road. Opened in 1986, the Boydaş is a fairly lavish spread for such a small town, and it's designed specifically to accommodate group tours. There are 127 guest rooms, three bars and a discotheque. Rates are 13,200TL (US$18.48) single, 17,400TL (US$24.36) double, breakfast included. The Boydaş also owns the *Tepe Oteli*, on the hilltop across the highway. Many rooms here have fabulous views of the valley.

Out near the Boydaş is the much smaller *Hotel Özata* (EURZ-ah-tah) (tel (4868) 1355 or 1981), a half-km from the centre, a small, new pension-type establishment charging the standard 8000TL (US$11.20) for a double room with shower.

Just as nice as the Boydaş is the modern *Turban Ürgüp Moteli* (TOOR-bahn) (tel (4868) 1490), just at the top of the hill as you leave Ürgüp on the road to Nevşehir and Göreme. Operated by the government's Tourism Bank, it's a nice place with comfortable rooms in small bungalows designed in harmony with the landscape and the traditional architecture of Cappadocian villages. Doubles with breakfast cost 19,300TL (US$27.02). The motel is walking distance from Ürgüp, a short ride from Göreme.

At the turning to Göreme, only one km from the entrance to the site, is the *Paris Motel & Camping* (PAH-rees) (tel (4868) 1435/99). It has 24 good (if older) rooms, a swimming pool and a price of 9800TL (US$13.72) double, breakfast included. In the camping area you'll find room for 600 persons, most services, and the standard low prices (mentioned above).

Places to Stay - top end
The tall rock riddled with holes which stands above all else in the valley is Üçhisar (EWCH-hee-sahr, Three Forts), east of Göreme. On the outskirts of the village is the *Kaya Oteli* (KAH-yah) (tel (4851) 1488/7), the area's poshest hostelry, affiliated with Club Med and often busy with tour groups. The hotel's architecture is quite dramatic, as it is perched above a valley of fairy chimneys. Rates are 12,000TL (US$16.80) per person, breakfast included; for 17,000TL (US$23.80) per person you can get bed, breakfast and dinner.

The hotel can be tricky to find. Coming from Nevşehir toward Ürgüp, turn left after eight km (the *third* turning for Üçhisar, not the second!), then look for the hotel on the right after 1.3 km.

Places to Eat - bottom end
Once a culinary wasteland, the dining situation in Cappadocia has improved dramatically during the past few years.

On the main square is the popular *Cappadocia Restaurant* (tel 1029), with a few outdoor tables and many more indoor ones, attentive service, and three-course meals for about 2200TL (US$3.08).

Cheaper restaurants are found on Dumlupınar Caddesi, south of the market. The *Kervan* is one, with a few tiny sidewalk tables and main courses such as *şiş kebap* for only 450TL (US$0.63). The *Köşk* is similar. Even cheaper fare is the *pide* served at the *Kent Etli Pide Salonu*. The *Sefa Restaurant* (seh-FAH) (tel 1182) is at the western end of the street, with prices much like those at the Cappadocia.

On Suat Hayri Ürgüplü Caddesi near the entrance to the bus station is the *Uğrak Restaurant*, with a few outdoor tables on the busy street-corner, and full meals for 1400TL (US$1.96).

In Göreme Village, the *Alaman Restaurant* looks more expensive than it really is.

Places to Eat - middle
The Büyük Otel and the Turban Motel tend to serve table d'hôte meals as they cater to tour groups; try the Büyük first. Their table-d'hôte meal costs 3000TL (US$4.20).

Getting Around
The transport situation for Ürgüp is similar to that at Nevşehir. Indeed, many of the buses departing Nevşehir actually begin their journeys in Ürgüp.

Minibuses connect Ürgüp with neighbouring towns. There is at least one minibus per hour to Nevşehir from 7.30 am to 7.30 pm, operated by the Ürgüp Belediyesi at a fare of 200TL (US$0.28). Minibuses to Kayseri (700TL, US$0.98) are almost as frequent. There are occasional minibuses to Avanos, but few to any of the smaller villages such as Göreme.

Another option is to rent a bicycle or motorbike. Several agencies are in this business, including Angel Tours (tel (4866) 1911) on Kayseri Caddesi in Göreme village. The charge for a day's bicycle rental is 2000TL (US$2.80), for a motorbike (moped) 8000TL (US$11.20).

AVANOS
Four km past Çavuşin on the main road is Avanos (AH-vah-nohs, population 12,000), a town famous for alabaster carving and pottery making. Workshops turn out ashtrays, lamps, chess sets and other souvenirs carved from the colourful translucent stone or moulded from the red clay of the Red River (Kızılırmak), which runs through the town. If you're not staying here overnight, Avanos is a good place to have lunch or at least a *çay* break. Wander around the town a bit, looking in the workshops.

Avanos has banks, a PTT, pensions, restaurants, chemist shops (pharmacies) and other such necessities.

Orientation
Most of the town is on the north bank of

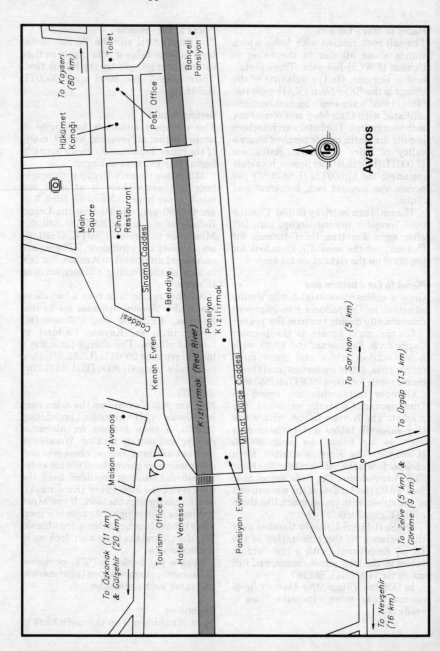

Avanos

To Kayseri (80 km)

Toilet

Bahçeli Pansiyon

Post Office

Hükümet Konağı

Main Square

Cihan Restaurant

Sinama Caddesi

Belediye

Kenan Evren Caddesi

Kızılırmak (Red River)

Pansiyon Kızılırmak

Mithat Dülge Caddesi

Maison d'Avanos

To Özkonak (11 km) & Gülşehir (20 km)

Tourism Office

Hotel Venessa

Pansiyon Evim

To Sarıhan (5 km)

To Ürgüp (13 km)

To Zelve (5 km) & Göreme (9 km)

To Nevşehir (16 km)

the river, but several pensions are on the south. The town is small enough, in any case, that you won't have trouble getting around on foot.

Information

There is a small Tourism Information Office (tel (4861) 1360) next door to the prominent Hotel Venessa, on the traffic roundabout at the northern end of the bridge across the river.

Things to See

Have a look in one of the alabaster or **pottery workshops**. The Poterie d'Erol (tel 1587) on Kenan Evren Caddesi is typical, and Erol, the owner, thoroughly enjoys showing visitors his work. His showroom is a cave behind the shop. He holds classes in pottery-making and carpet-weaving as well.

The **Yellow Caravanserai** (Sarı Han, sah-RUH hahn) is six km east of Avanos along the eastern road back to Ürgüp. (There are three roads between Avanos and Ürgüp; be sure you're on the easternmost, which also passes the Peribacalar Vadisi.) This Seljuk caravanserai looks more ruinous than it is because the finished stones of the walls were taken away for construction of a bridge in Avanos. The elaborate Seljuk portal is still in pretty good shape, however. Inside, the *han* is on the standard plan with a large court where animals were loaded and unloaded, and a great hall where men and animals could escape the rigours of the weather. Above the portal is a *mescit*, or small mosque, which you can reach by climbing to the top of the walls and walking around. A self-appointed guide will no doubt appear to show you around, and perhaps to sell you an admission ticket.

Places to Stay

This town has several good hotels and pensions, and can serve well as a base for your Cappadocian explorations.

Places to Stay – bottom end

Avanos has lots of good, clean, cheap, convenient pensions. Try *La Maison d'Avanos* (tel (4861) 1587), run by Erol of Poterie d'Erol, chief artist in the local bohemian community. Beds in waterless rooms cost 1000TL (US$1.40). Living at Erol's is like bringing the best of the hippie years back to life.

Several of Erol's friends operate the *Sofa Pansiyon* (tel (4861) 1489), Köprübaşı, Venessa Oteli Yanı, four nice old houses joined into one, up the hill from the traffic roundabout near the Venessa Hotel. Several of the 23 rooms are partially built into the rock, and all are quite nicely kept. You can live the troglodytic life here for only 3000TL (US$4.20) per person, breakfast included. The rooftop terrace has a fine view.

Another pension in an old Avanos house is the *Çardak Pansion* (chahr-DAHK) (tel (4861) 1403), with eight rooms, two WCs, two showers and prices of 1500TL to 2000TL (US$2.10 to US$2.80) per person.

For other pensions, explore the cluster on Mithat Dülge Caddesi on the southern bank of the river, near the bridge. The *Evim Pansiyon* (eh-VEEM) (tel (4861) 1614), Mithat Dülge Caddesi 1, is by the bridge but charges more than the others: 2000TL (US$2.80) per bed, 500TL (US$0.70) for a hot bath or shower.

The *Kızılırmak Pansiyon* (KUH-zuh-luhr-mahk) (tel (4861) 1634) is several blocks from the bridge along the river, as is the *Bayer* (tel (4861) 1287).

Places to Stay – middle

By the bridge is the *Hotel Venessa* (tel (4861) 1201), a big, modern place with 73 rooms, each with shower and balcony, priced at 7500TL (US$10.50) single, 11,000TL (US$15.40) double.

The brand-new *Hotel Zelve*, on the main square across from the Hükümet Konağı (Sub-province Government House) is modern and quite suitable, charging 13,000TL (US$18.20) single, 17,000TL

(US$23.80) double, for a room with bath, buffet breakfast included.

Places to Eat

Outside the hotels, there's nothing fancy. The *Cihan Restaurant* (jee-HAHN) (tel 1045) on the main square is a popular ready-food place open for all three meals. Lunch or dinner costs 1400TL (US$1.96).

İHLARA (PERISTREMA)

At the western edge of Cappadocia is the town of Aksaray, on the Konya road. South-east of Aksaray, along a rough road, is İhlara, at the head of the Peristrema gorge. This remote and somewhat forbidding valley was once a favourite retreat of Byzantine monks, and dozens of painted churches, carved from the rock or built from the local stone, have survived. The area, wildly beautiful, is visited by the occasional tour bus, but is otherwise far less touristed than Göreme.

The trip up the gorge, along the course of the Melendiz Suyu stream, is something of a mini-expedition, wilder and more exciting than touring the rock-hewn churches at Göreme. If you've got an adventurous spirit or a car of your own, and haven't had enough of rock churches, you will greatly enjoy a visit here.

If you decide to make this trip, you will probably have to pass through Aksaray and make it your base, though lodging possibilities do exist at the site.

Things to See

The scenery on this trip, especially on the descent into the gorge, is as wonderful as the ancient churches themselves. Plan a full day to see İhlara. If you're coming out from Aksaray, the drive will take some time; if you're taking the minibus, you will have to spend two nights here.

At the south-eastern (upper) end of the gorge, on the rim near İhlara Köyü, is a modern installation with a restaurant, souvenir shop and ticket booth, at which you buy a ticket (400TL, US$0.56) and enter anytime from 8.30 am to 5.30 pm.

You must descend by a very long flight of stairs to the floor of the gorge, and wander for several hours to see the various churches. Pack a picnic or at least take snacks so you won't have to climb back up to the restaurant at the rim of the gorge, and then go down all those steps again.

Signs mark the **churches**. The most interesting, with the best paintings, are the Yılanlı Kilise, Sümbüllü Kilise, Kokar Kilise and Eğritaş Kilisesi. Farther down the valley are the Kırk Dam Altı Kilise, Bahattin Samanlığı Kilisesi, Direkli Kilise and Ala Kilise.

Places to Stay

There is one small pension between the village and the entry to the gorge. The *Vadibaşı Pansiyon* (VAH-dee-bah-shuh) (no phone) is a neat village house charging 2000TL (US$2.80) per person for bed and breakfast. It's ¾ km from the entry at the rim of the gorge, and the same distance into the village. Other pensions are bound to spring up before too long.

Places to Eat

There is only the restaurant at the rim entry to the gorge, which is nice enough but has a limited menu. Though it has a lock on the trade, a full meal still costs only about 2100TL (US$2.94).

Getting There

The rim entry to the gorge is 1½ km from the village of İhlara Köyü, 45 km from Aksaray and 95 km from Nevşehir.

Bus You must take a minibus from Aksaray to İhlara Köyü (300TL, US$0.42). There are normally two daily, departing Aksaray at 3 pm and midnight, and returning from İhlara to the city at 7 and 7.30 am, so catch the 3 pm minibus, find space at the pension (if there's any left), plan to stay two nights, then take a morning minibus back into Aksaray. It's inconvenient now, but transportation and accommodation will no doubt improve as tourism develops.

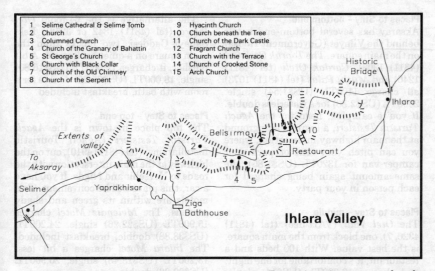

1	Selime Cathedral & Selime Tomb	9	Hyacinth Church
2	Church	10	Church beneath the Tree
3	Columned Church	11	Church of the Dark Castle
4	Church of the Granary of Bahattin	12	Fragrant Church
5	St George's Church	13	Church with the Terrace
6	Church with Black Collar	14	Church of Crooked Stone
7	Church of the Old Chimney	15	Arch Church
8	Church of the Serpent		

Car If you have a car, your visit is made much easier. From the main Aksaray-Nevşehir highway, turn south (right, if you're coming from Aksaray) at a point 11 km east of the intersection of the Ankara-Adana and Aksaray-Nevşehir highways. On my last visit there was no sign marking the turning; it seems to have been removed. After making this turn, go about 23 km to another right turn marked for İhlara Vadisi. The road passes through Selime village, with numerous rock-hewn buildings, and then three km farther on through Yaprakhisar, both villages dramatically surrounded by rock and marked by Göreme-style fairy chimneys. After 13 km you come to İhlara Köyü, where you turn left to reach, after another km or so, the entry point at the rim of the gorge.

It is also possible to come to İhlara from the underground cities of Kyamaklı and Derinkuyu. From Derinkuyu, proceed south toward Niğde, but turn west (right) at the village of Gölcük (signs mark the turning). Drive up into the mountains through Sivrihisar, in a dramatic site, and Güzelyurt, which has its own underground dwellings and a mosque

built in Byzantine times as a church dedicated to the theologian Gregory of Nazianza (born 330 AD). The scenery on this drive is dramatically beautiful. Sixty km after Gölcük, turn left for Selime and the road to İhlara.

AKSARAY

There's nothing to hold your interest in the farming town of Aksaray (AHK-sah-rahy, population 85,000), but it must be your base for visits to İhlara.

Things to See

If you have an evening free, wander into the older part of town to Çerdiğin Caddesi (also called Nevşehir Caddesi), where there are some nice old stone houses and a curious **brick minaret** leaning at a pronounced angle. Built in 1236 by the Seljuks, it is touted by a nearby sign as the 'Turkish Tower of Pisa'.

The **government buildings** on the town's main square have been nicely restored. Just up the hill a short way is the **Ulu Cami**, with a good façade and an interesting *mimber* (pulpit).

Places to Stay – bottom end

Aksaray has several bottom-end hotels behind the Vilayet (Government House) on the main square. The *Toprak Oteli* (tel (4811) 1308), *Çardak Oteli* (tel (4811) 1246) and *Mutlu Palas* (tel (4811) 1073) all charge 1100TL (US$1.54) single, 2000TL (US$2.80) for a waterless double. If you're camping, head for the *Ağaçlı Turistik Tesisleri*, a luxury campground at the main highway intersection, where you can pitch your tent or park your camper-van for 1320TL (US$1.85), the same amount again being charged for each person in your party.

Places to Stay – middle

The *Otel Vadi* (VAH-dee) (tel (4811) 4326, 7), one block from the main square, is the best value. With 100 beds and a restaurant, it's comfortable for one night, and charges 10,000TL (US$14) single, 14,000TL (US$19.60) double.

The alternative is the 64-room *Otel Ihlara* (tel (4811) 1842 or 3252), Eski Sanayi Caddesi, two blocks from the main square on a quiet back street. A bit plusher, it charges 12,000TL (US$16.80) single, 18,000TL (US$25.20) double for a room with bath, breakfast included.

Places to Stay – top end

The top place in town is the *Ağaçlı Turistik Tesisleri* (Ağaçlı Touristic Installations) (tel (4811) 4910), out on the highway at the main intersection with the roads to Nevşehir and Niğde. If you have a car, this place will be convenient. Two motels are within its green and shady gardens. The *Melendiz Motel* charges 15,900TL (US$22.26) single, 24,200TL (US$33.88) double, breakfast included. The *Ihlara Motel* charges a bit less, 13,200TL (US$18.48) single, 20,900TL (US$29.26) double.

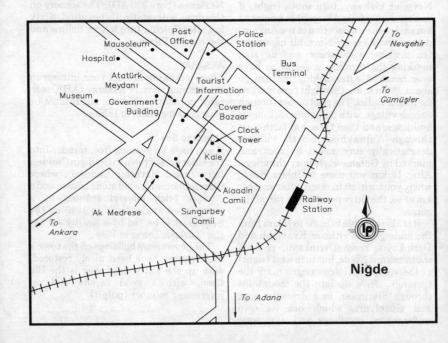

Places to Eat

Outside the better hotels, there are only simple restaurants. The place to look is behind the Vilayet building, near the cheap hotels. Here you'll find the *Zümrüt Restaurant* (zurm-RURT) (tel 2233), *Çardak* (chahr-DAHK) (tel 1926) and *Aksaraylı Restaurant* (AHK-sah-rahy-luh) (tel 3386), all serving tasty if simple meals for under 1500TL (US$2.10).

Getting There

There are direct buses from Ankara, Nevşehir, Niğde and Konya to Aksaray.

NİĞDE

The Seljuks built Niğde (NEE-deh, altitude 1208 metres, population 65,000), and if you are passing through you might want to have a look at the Alaeddin Camii (1223), on the hill with the fortress; the Süngür Bey Camii, restored by the Mongols in 1335; the Ak Medrese (1409), now the town's museum; the Hüdavend Hatun Türbesi (1312), a fine example of a Seljuk tomb; and the Dış Cami, an Ottoman mosque with a carved *mimber* inlaid with mother-of-pearl. The market on Thursdays is lively and colourful.

Should you want to stay, Niğde can offer several small hostelries within a block or two of the main square, including the *Hotel Hisar* (hee-SAHR) (tel 1810) and the *Hotel Anadolu* (ah-NAH-doh-loo) (tel 2949), with rooms at 3100TL (US$4.34) double, with washbasin. For fancier rooms there's the *Merkez Turistik Oteli* (mehr-KEHZ too-rees-TEEK) (tel 1860) in the main square called Atatürk Meydanı, with 50 double rooms costing 16,500TL (US$23.10) double.

KAYSERİ

Once the capital of Cappadocia, Kayseri (KAHY-seh-ree, altitude 1054 metres, population 450,000), in the shadow of Erciyes Dağı (Mt Aergius, 3916 metres) is now a booming farm and textile centre. Beside the sleepy old conservative town surrounding the ancient black citadel, a city of modern boulevards lined with apartment blocks has risen in only a few years. These two aspects of Kayseri aren't completely comfortable together, and something remains of old Kayseri's conservative soul.

In Turkish folklore, the people of Kayseri are the crafty dealers. Though every merchant you meet in the bazaar will not fit this image, you are sure to be persecuted by at least one carpet dealer. Kayseri is at the centre of a region which produces many of Turkey's loveliest carpets, and you may do well shopping here. But if you don't buy, the rug merchant who has been following you for days will be there at the bus station, waving and weeping, as you pull out of town.

If you're passing through on your way to Cappadocia, take a few hours to tour Kayseri, as it has many Seljuk buildings and a nice bazaar. Those heading east might want to see the sights, spend the night, and get an early start the next morning. Besides the sights in town, there are two superb Seljuk caravanserais north-east of the city, off the Sivas road. Taxi drivers in Kayseri will quote you a price for a three or four-hour tour including both of them.

History

This was Hittite country, so its history goes way back. The first Hittite capital, Kanesh, was earlier the chief city of the Hatti. It's located at Kültepe, north-east of Kayseri on the Sivas road. There was probably an early settlement on the site of Kayseri as well, though the earliest traces which have come to light are from Hellenistic times.

Under the Roman emperor Tiberius (14-37 AD) the town received its name, Caesarea, and later became famous as the birthplace of St Basil the Great, one of the early Church Fathers. Its early Christian history was interrupted by the Arab invasions of the 600s and later.

The Seljuks took over in 1084 and held

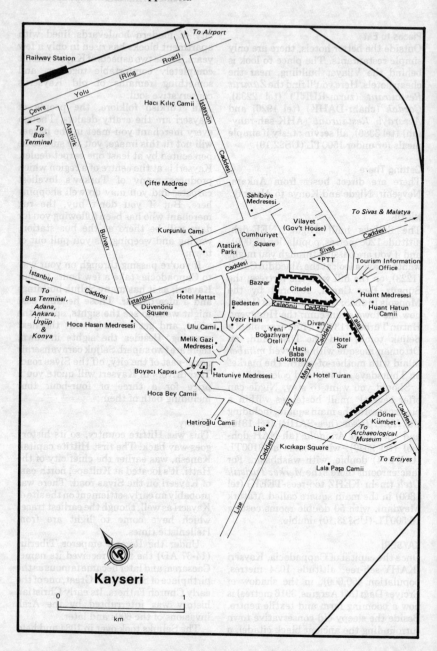

To Airport

Railway Station

(Ring Road)

Yolu

Çevre

Atatürk

Hacı Kılıç Camii

İstasyon

Caddesi

To Bus Terminal

Çifte Medrese

Sahibiye Medresesi

Vilayet (Gov't House)

To Sivas & Malatya

Caddesi

Kurşunlu Camii

Cumhuriyet Square

Atatürk Parkı

Bulvarı

Tourism Information Office

Sivas

PTT

İstanbul

To Bus Terminal, Adana, Ankara, Ürgüp & Konya

Caddesi

İstanbul

Caddesi

Bazaar

Citadel

Huant Medresesi

Huant Hatun Camii

Hotel Hattat

Düvenönü Square

Bedesten

Kaleönü Caddesi

Talas

Hoca Hasan Medresesi

Ulu Cami

Vezir Hanı

Yeni Boğazlıyan Oteli

Divan

Hotel Sur

Melik Gazi Medresesi

Hacı Baba Lokantası

Boyacı Kapısı

Hatuniye Medresesi

Hotel Turan

Mayıs

Hoca Bey Camii

27

Döner Kümbet

Hatiroğlu Camii

Lise

To Archaeological Museum

Kıcıkapı Square

To Erciyes

Caddesi

Lala Paşa Camii

Lise

Kayseri

0   1
km

the city until the Mongols' arrival in 1243, except for a brief period when the Crusaders captured it on their way to the Holy Land. After Kayseri had been part of the Mongol Empire for almost 100 years, its Mongol governor set up his own emirate (1335) which lasted a mere 45 years. It was succeeded by another emirate, that of Kadı Burhaneddin, was then captured by the Ottomans, seized during the Ottoman interregnum by the Karamanid emirs, later taken by the Mamelukes of Egypt, and finally conquered by the Ottomans again in 1515, all in just over 100 years. Those were exciting times in Kayseri.

Orientation

For orientation, use the black-walled citadel at the centre of the old town. The railway station is at the end of İstasyon Caddesi, one km from the citadel. Kayseri's bus terminal is at the western side of the town.

Information

The Tourism Information Office (tel (351) 11190 or 19295) is beside the citadel at Kağnı Pazarı Honat Camii Yanı No 61.

Things to See

Near the Citadel Many of Kayseri's interesting buildings are either found near the citadel, on Cumhuriyet Meydanı or on nearby Düvenönü Meydanı. In this district you will have to spend half your time fighting off the carpet dealers.

The **citadel** *(hisar)*, which now has a market within it, was built by Emperor Justinian in the 500s, and extensively repaired by the Seljuk Sultan Keykavus I around 1224. In 1486, the Ottoman Sultan Mehmet the Conqueror made major repairs. With Erciyes looming over the town, it's not surprising that the citadel should be made of black volcanic stone.

East of the citadel is a complex which includes the **Mosque of Huant Hatun**

(Huant Hatun Camii, 1228), built by the wife of the Seljuk Sultan Alaettin Keykubat, plus the tomb of the lady herself, and bits of a Turkish bath.

Next to the mosque is the **Seminary of Huant Hatun** (Huant Hatun Medresesi, 1237), now Kayseri's Ethnographic Museum (Etnoğrafya Müzesi), open from 8 am to noon and 1 to 5.30 pm; admission costs 200TL (US$0.28). Displays in the historic building include ceramics and faience, weapons, glassware, kitchen utensils, coins, costumes for both men and women, and the interior of a Kayseri household as it was a century ago.

The **Sahibiye Seminary** (Sahibiye Medresesi) is at the north side of Cumhuriyet Meydanı, the large square by the citadel. It dates from 1267 and has an especially beautiful Seljuk portal.

You can spot the Ottoman-style **Lead-Roofed Mosque** (Kurşunlu Cami) by its lead-covered dome, unusual in old Kayseri, north of İstanbul Caddesi and west of Cumhuriyet Meydanı and Atatürk Parkı. Also called the Ahmet Paşa Camii after its founder, it was completed in 1585 to plans that may have been drawn, and were certainly influenced, by the great Sinan.

Two adjoining religious schools, the Gıyasiye and Şifaiye Medreseleri, are sometimes called the Çifte Medrese, the **Twin Seminaries**. They're located in a maze of narrow back streets north of the Kurşunlu Cami. Sultan Gıyaseddin Keyhüsrev I ordered the schools built, and they were finished by 1206. For much of their history they functioned as a combined theological school, medical college and clinic.

North of the Çifte Medrese, near İstasyon Caddesi, is the mosque (1249) of the Seljuk vezir Abdül Gazi, called the **Hacı Kılıç Camii**, with some very fine Seljuk architectural detail, especially in the doorways.

Near Düvenönü Meydanı West of the citadel is Kayseri's tidy, shady **bazaar**, which you should definitely explore, fending off carpet dealers as you go.

Kayseri's **Great Mosque** (Ulu Cami, oo-LOO jah-mee) is near Düvenönü Meydanı. It was begun in 1135 by the Danışmend Turkish emirs and finished by the Seljuks in 1205. There's been a lot of repair and 'restoration' over the centuries, but it's still a good example of early Seljuk style.

South of the Citadel Among Kayseri's other Seljuk archaeological treasures are several *türbes*, or tombs. The **Revolving Tomb** (Döner Kümbet, deur-NEHR kewm-beht) is south-east of the citadel along Talas Caddesi about one km. Though it doesn't (and never did) revolve, its cylindrical shape suggests turning, and as you view its marvellous and elaborate Seljuk decoration (1276), you will at least revolve around it. This was a lady's tomb. Nearby is another, the Sırçalı Kümbet (1300s), which used to be covered in coloured tiles and topped by a pyramidal roof. You may spot other *kümbets* in and near Kayseri.

The city's **Archaeological Museum** is out near the Döner Kümbet, to the east by the railway. The museum houses the finds from Kültepe, site of ancient Kanesh, including the cuneiform tablets which told historians much about the Hittite Empire. Hittite, Hellenistic and Roman statuary, plus exhibits of local ethnography, help to make it worth a visit. Hours are 8 am to noon and 1 to 5.30 pm daily except Monday; admission costs 400TL (US$0.56).

Caravanserais Haggle with a taxi-driver for an excursion to the Sultan Han and Karatay Han, and you will probably end up with a figure of 7000TL to 8000TL (US$9.80 to US$11.20) for the entire car. If time and money are short, bargain for just the Sultan Han. If only money is short, try to find a bus which will drop you at the *han* (start early in the day!), and then trust luck to catch something back to Kayseri.

Head out on the Sivas road. Twenty km from Kayseri there is a left turning to **Kültepe**, site of ancient Kanesh. You may

want to take a quick look at the site of this incredibly old Hittite city (2000 BC), but there's not a lot to see.

The **Sultan Han** is on the highway, 45 km north-east of Kayseri. Besides being a fine example of the Seljuk royal caravan lodging, it has been beautifully restored so it is easy to appreciate the architectural fine points. The *han* was finished in 1236; restoration was carried out only a few decades ago. Don't let the locked gate worry you. Shortly after your car draws up, a boy will come running with the key and a booklet of tickets; admission costs 100TL (US$0.14). Hours are supposedly 9 am to 1 pm and 2 to 5 pm, but in fact it is open whenever the guardian can be found.

Tour the inside, noticing particularly the elegant snake motif on the *mescid* (little mosque) arches. Climb up to the roof if you like, but don't neglect a walk around the exterior as well. Note the lion-faced water spouts on the walls, and the plain towers of varying design.

If time is short, the Sultan Han will do nicely as an introduction to Seljuk Turkish caravanserais. With more time, take your taxi to the **Karatay Han**, in a Turkish village now well off the beaten track. From the Sultan Han, head back toward Kayseri and take the turning south or east to Bünyan. Pass through Bünyan toward Malatya, and about 30 km along there is a road on the right for Elbaşı. Follow this track five km to Elbaşı, and four km beyond to Karatay, also called Karadayı.

The Karatay Han, built in 1240 for the Seljuk vezir Emir Celaleddin Karatay, was once on the main east-west trade route. It was completely restored in the 1960s, and is yet another fine example of high Seljuk art. A visit to the Karatay Han gives you a glimpse into the life of a Turkish village as well.

Climbing Erciyes Mountaineers may like to know that there is a Kayak Evi, or mountain hut of 100 beds, 26 km south of

Kayseri on the mountain road. Leave the city by the road to the airport *(havaalanı)* and the village of Hisarcık (14 km), and continue to Kayak Evi. Even if you don't plan to climb, the outing will give you a look at some spectacular scenery.

Places to Stay – bottom end

Hotel Sur (SOOR) (tel (351) 19545), Cumhuriyet Mahallesi, Talas Caddesi 12, opened only a few years ago and offers good value for money. Doubles cost 2400TL (US$3.36) for one large bed, or 4000TL (US$5.60) for two beds, both with a private shower. The hotel is not far from the citadel, behind the city walls off Talas Caddesi. Walk south-east on Talas Caddesi from the citadel, with a remnant of the city walls on your right. Turn right after passing the wall, then right again, and you'll see the hotel.

A similarly good choice is the *Hotel Kent* (tel (351) 12454), Camikebir Mahallesi, Camikebir Caddesi 2, near Düvenönü Meydanı. Off the square somewhat so you don't get all the noise, it charges 3850TL (US$5.39) for a room with one large bed and a shower, for one or two persons; 4670TL (US$6.54) for a room with two beds and shower; 3740TL (US$5.24) for two beds, no bath.

Hotel Seyhan (SEHY-hahn) (tel (351) 23489), Mimar Sinan Caddesi, Seyhan Sokak 6/D not far from Düvenönü Meydanı, is on a quiet back street, an easy walk from the bazaar and most sights, and charges only 2500TL (US$3.50) for a double room with washbasin.

In the bazaar is the very simple *Yeni Boğazlıyan Oteli* (yeh-NEE boh-AHZ-luh-yahn) (tel (351) 11034), Mevlevi Caddesi 13, a few steps down the street from the Divan Pastanesi. Spartan in its furnishings, but convenient and supremely cheap, it charges only 1200TL (US$1.68) single, 2200TL (US$3.08) double for one of its rooms without private bath.

Places to Stay – middle

Hotel Hattat (hah-TAHT) (tel (351)

19331 or 19829), İstanbul Caddesi 1, is the best in town, with 67 rooms priced at 11,000TL (US$15.40) single, 16,000TL (US$22.40) double, private bath and breakfast included. This is where the businesspeople go.

The older *Hotel Turan* (too-RAHN) (tel (351) 11968) or 12506, Turan Caddesi 8, is classed higher than the Hattat, but rightly charges less for its 70 rooms: 15,000TL (US$21) double, 8800TL (US$12.32) single, both with bath. They're ready to haggle here, and if business is slack you'll pay even less. The hotel has a roof terrace and a Turkish bath.

Next to the bus terminal is an emergency-only lodging, the *Terminal Oteli* (TEHR-mee-NAHL) (tel (351) 15846), İstanbul Caddesi 176, with 21 rooms for 8000TL (US$11.20) double with private shower, 5500TL (US$7.70) double with just a washbasin.

Places to Eat

Kayseri is noted for a few special dishes, among them *pastırma* (from the same root-word as *pastrami*?) – sun-dried beef coated with garlic and savoury spices. It has a very strong flavour, tends to stick in your teeth and despotically rule your breath for hours, but once you acquire the taste you look forward to a return to Kayseri. Shops in the centre will sell it to you for picnics (try 100 grammes); before you buy, ask for a sample (*Bir tat, lütfen*, beer TAHT lewt-fehn, 'A taste, please').

Other Kayseri specialties include *sucuk* (soo-JOOK), a spicy sausage; *salam* (sah-LAHM), Turkish salami; *tulum peynir* (too-LOOM pehy-neer), hard cheese cured in a goatskin; and *bal* (BAHL), honey. Few of these things, with the exception of pastırma, will appear on restaurant menus, so you must buy them in food shops for picnics.

The town's best restaurants are in the top hotels, the Hattat and the Turan. For cheaper, less elegant fare, the *İskender Kebap Salonu*, 27 Mayıs Caddesi 5, is by the citadel, one floor above street level; good *döner kebap*, good view of the busy street, low prices of about 1600TL (US$2.24) for a meal.

The *Kardeşler Lokantası* is south of the İskender along 27 Mayıs Caddesi; it, and the nearby *Cumhuriyet Lokantası*, are equally good choices for dining.

The *Hacı Usta Lokanta ve Kebap Salonu*, Serdar Caddesi 3 & 7, has two locations in the bazaar. To find them, walk from the citadel on 27 Mayıs Caddesi, pass Vatan Caddesi on the right, and then turn right onto Serdar Caddesi. Both these places are very simple, cheap and tasty.

The *Divan Pastanesi* is a good, serviceable pastry shop on 27 Mayıs Caddesi a block south of the citadel, at the corner of Mevlevi Caddesi; try it for breakfast or tea.

Getting There & Away

Air Kayseri is connected with İstanbul by flights two days of the week, with Ankara once a week, by Turkish Airlines (tel (351) 13947), Sahabiye Mahallesi, Yıldırım Caddesi 1. An airport bus (350TL, US$0.49) connects the city with Erkilet airport. Catch the bus an hour before flight departure time, or be at the airport at least 20 – preferably 30 – minutes before scheduled departure time.

Rail There are several daily trains from Ankara and Adana (see the Ankara section for details). You can also take trains eastward to Sivas (3½ hours) and Erzurum (22 hours); the trains are not luxurious. The train between Kayseri and Malatya takes 10 hours, if it's on time; the bus is much quicker. There are not good train connections north to the Black Sea; better to take the train to Sivas, then a bus to Samsun.

To get into town from the railway station, walk out of the station, cross the big avenue and board any bus heading down Atatürk Bulvarı.

Bus Buses run very frequently – at least every hour – between Kayseri and Ankara, a 4½-hour trip. You can also get convenient buses to Adana, Malatya (six hours) and points east. There are several daily dolmuşes to Ürgüp, operating at least every two hours in the morning and afternoon. The fare is 600TL to 700TL (US$0.84 to US$0.98). To Sivas the trip takes under four hours and costs 1300TL (US$1.82).

To get to the citadel from the Otogar, walk out the front door, cross the avenue and board any bus. Or take a dolmuş (60TL) marked 'Terminal-Şehir'. A taxi to the citadel costs about 600TL (US$0.84).

Black Sea Coast

Turkey's Black Sea coast is a unique area of the country, lush and green throughout the year with plentiful rainfall. Dairy farming, fishing and tea production are big industries, and this coast also produces bumper crops of tobacco (tütün), hazelnuts (filberts, fındık) and cherries (kiraz).

History

The coast was colonized in the 700s BC by Milesians and Arcadians, who founded towns at Sinop, Samsun and Trabzon. Later it became the Kingdom of Pontus. Most of Pontus' kings were named Mithridates, but it was Mithridates IV Eupator who gave the Romans a run for their money in 88-84 BC. Mithridates conquered Cappadocia and other Anatolian kingdoms, finally reaching Nicomedia (İzmit), which was an ally of Rome. When Rome came to its defense, Mithridates pushed onward to the Aegean. The Roman response was hampered by civil war at home, but Rome's legions finally drove into Cappadocia and Pontus (83-81 BC), and Mithridates was forced to agree to peace based on pre-war borders.

In 74-64 BC Mithridates was at it again, encouraging his son-in-law Tigranes I of Armenia to seize Cappadocia from the Romans. He tried, but the Romans conquered Pontus in response, driving Mithridates to flee and later to commit suicide. The Romans left a small client kingdom of Pontus at the far eastern end of the coast, based on Trebizond.

The coast was ruled by Byzantium, and Alexius Comnenus, son of Emperor Manuel I, proclaimed himself emperor of Pontus when the Crusaders sacked Constantinople and drove him out in 1204. His descendants ruled this small empire until 1461, when it was taken by Mehmet the Conqueror.

While Alexius was in Trabzon, Samsun was under Seljuk rule. The Seljuks granted trading privileges to the Genoese. But when the Ottomans came, the Genoese burned Samsun to the ground before sailing away.

After WW I, the Ottoman Greek citizens of this region attempted to form a new Pontic state with Allied support. Turkish inhabitants, disarmed by the Allied occupation authorities, were persecuted by Greek guerilla bands which had been allowed to keep their arms. It was fertile ground for a revolt. Mustafa Kemal (Atatürk) used a bureaucratic ruse to escape from the sultan's control in İstanbul, and landed at Samsun on 19 May 1919. He soon moved inland to Amasya, and began to organize what would become the battle for independence.

Touring The Coast

Travelling along the coast from İstanbul east to Sinop is not all that easy by road. From Sinop east to Hopa, near the Soviet frontier, the road is excellent and very scenic, though with little in the way of historical or artistic interest. The 360-km ride from Samsun to Trabzon can even be done in a day if you wish. You must take a few hours to see the sights in Trabzon, fabled Trebizond, before heading up onto the plateau to Erzurum, or eastward along the coast through the tea plantations to Rize and Hopa.

At Hopa you can climb into the mountains to Artvin, a ride of exceptional beauty. Roads south and east from Artvin are not too good, and may be impassable in winter. Public transport is scarce, as are hotel facilities. Plan to travel from Artvin to Kars or Erzurum only if you have an adventurous spirit and can stand long, bumpy bus rides, or if you have your own car.

Top: The restored Theatre at Aspendos, near Antalya
Left: Detail from the Green Tomb, Bursa
Right: Stained-glass window in Süleymaniye Mosque

Top: The troglodyte dwellings, Göreme
Bottom: Roman busts and modern syntax in the Ephesus museum

Getting There

Air Turkish Airlines has three flights a week from İstanbul to Samsun, twice a week to Trabzon; from Ankara, there are three weekly flights to Samsun, daily flights to Trabzon. In Samsun, THY are at Kazımpaşa Caddesi 11/A (tel (361) 18260 or 13455); a bus (200TL, US$0.28) takes you out to the airport. In Trabzon, the Turkish Airlines office is at Kemerkaya Mahallesi, Meydan Parkı Karşısı (tel (031) 13446 or 11680). The airport bus costs 200TL (US$0.28).

Rail Passenger rail service to Samsun is slow and inconvenient. Everyone takes the bus.

Bus Buses to and along the coast are, as usual, fast, frequent and cheap. Plan to take the bus to Samsun from Ankara (420 km), Kayseri (450 km) or Sivas (340 km). On the eastern reaches of the coast, the route to take is between Trabzon and Erzurum via Gümüşhane.

Boat Turkish Maritime Lines operate car ferries on what amounts to a mini-cruise service between İstanbul and Trabzon, departing İstanbul each Monday evening, arriving in Samsun on Tuesday evening, and departing a few hours later to arrive in Trabzon Wednesday morning. Departure from Trabzon for the return trip is late Wednesday evening, reaching Samsun on Thursday morning, stopping for only about 90 minutes, then embarking again for İstanbul, arriving Friday noon. The price for a reclining Pullman seat from İstanbul to Samsun is 7200TL (US$10.08); to Trabzon, 8500TL (US$11.90). For cabins, prices range from 10,000TL (US$14) to 25,700TL (US$35.98) per person from İstanbul to Samsun; 10,700TL (US$14.98) to 34,300TL (US$48.02) per person to Trabzon. Meals are not included in these prices. The ferry takes cars at a cost of 22,150TL (US$31.01) from İstanbul to Samsun, 29,300TL (US$41.02) to Trabzon.

The cruise is fun, but much of the time you will be steaming at night, with no chance of seeing the passing scenery. Also, food and drink on board tends to be expensive, so pack your own supplies. You can stock up at Samsun, as well. You may find the Pullman seat uncomfortable for sleeping, or noisy, or the room smoky. If you have a sleeping bag you may find it preferable to stake out some deck space and spend the night in the fresh air.

AMASYA

On the way to Samsun, you may pass through Amasya (ah-MAHSS-yah, population 85,000, altitude 412 metres), capital of the province of the same name, and one-time capital of the Pontic kings. Standing on the banks of the river Yeşilırmak, surrounded by high cliffs, Amasya is an old-time town with a number of things to see. Don't just pass right through; stop for a glass of tea or a meal. The town can grow on you, and you may find yourself stopping for the night.

History

Despite its appearance as a small, sleepy provincial capital, Amasya has seen very exciting times. It was a Hittite town, but came into its own as the capital of Pontus. Several of the Pontic kings were buried in great tombs carved into the rock walls which surround the town. In Ottoman times, it was an important power-base when the sultans led military campaigns into Persia, and a tradition developed that the Ottoman crown prince should be taught statecraft in Amasya, and test his knowledge and skill as governor of the province.

Information

Amasya has no proper tourism office, but the museum will sell you a leaflet with a map and information about the town for 200TL (US$0.28).

Things to See

Walk around the town, admiring the old Ottoman houses along the river. There's a tidy little **museum** on the main street, open from 8 am to noon and 1.30 to 5.30 pm; admission costs 200TL (US$0.28). The collection includes artefacts from Pontic, Roman, Byzantine, Seljuk and Ottoman times, and there is an ethnographic exhibit. In the museum garden is a Seljuk *türbe*, now containing some fairly gruesome mummies which date from the Seljuk period and were discovered beneath the Burmalı Cami.

Near the museum is the **Sultan Beyazıt Camii** (1486), Amasya's principal mosque, with its *medrese* and a nice garden. The **Mosque of the Spiral Minaret** (Burmalı Minare Camii, BOOR-mah-luh, 1242), is of Seljuk construction.

Other curious buildings include the **Insane Asylum Seminary**, or Bimarhane Medresesi. The **Mosque of the Blue Seminary** (Gök Medrese Camii, GEURK meh-dreh-seh), built in 1276, has a wonderfully ornate Seljuk doorway once covered in blue tiles. The **Mosque of Beyazıt Paşa** (Beyazıt Paşa Camii), finished in 1419, bears many similarities to the famous early-Ottoman Yeşil Cami in Bursa. The **Seminary of the Chief White Eunuch** (Kapı Ağası Medresesi, kah-PUH ah-ah-suh, 1488) is one of the few religious schools built to an octagonal plan.

Rock Tombs & Citadel You can see the rock-hewn tombs from the town. Climb the path toward them and you'll come to the **Palace of the Maidens** (Kızlar Sarayı, kuhz-LAHR sah-rah-yuh). Though there were indeed harems full of maidens here, the palace which stood here was not theirs but that of the kings of Pontus and later of the Ottoman governors.

Follow the path upward and you will reach the royal tombs of Pontus, cut deep in the rock as early as the 300s BC, and used for cult worship of the deified rulers.

Above the tombs, perched precariously on the cliffs, is the **citadel** *(hisar)*, which can be reached by a path, or by road if you have a car. The remnants of wall date from Pontic times, repaired by the Ottomans. It's from here that an old Russian cannon is fired during the holy month of Ramazan to mark the ending of the fast. The view is magnificent.

Places to Stay - bottom end

Of the cheap places, the *Apaydın Oteli* (AHP-ay-duhn) on the main street charges 2700TL (US$3.78) for a bathless double. The *Aydın Oteli* (ahy-DUHN), right in the centre, charges only 1600TL (US$2.24) for a bathless double. The *Konfor Palas* (kohn-FOHR, Comfort Palace) by the river charges even less: 1550TL (US$2.17), and your room may have a balcony looking onto the river.

Places to Stay - middle

On the outskirts of town is the *Turban Amasya Hotel* (tel (3781) 4054, 5, 6), a small 34-room hotel on the riverbank which has a restaurant and bar, a game room and television lounge, and double rooms with shower for 8500TL (US$11.90), breakfast included. About 25 km north of Amasya on the Samsun road, at Suluova, is the Saraçoğlu Muzaffer Turistik Tesisleri (Muzaffer Saraçoğlu's Touristic Installations) (tel 10), with a hotel charging 6000TL (US$8.40) for a double with bath.

Places to Eat

Look for small restaurants in the narrow market streets off the main square (the one with the statue of Atatürk), such as the *Çiçek Lokantası*, which is very basic but cheap and serviceable. The *Şehir Restaurant*, on the far side of the river from the main square, near the bridge, offers good food and good value. For tea in a nice garden setting, go to the *Belediye Parkı* (Municipal Park), across the river from the main square, by the Belediye Sarayı (City Hall).

Getting There & Away

Amasya is on the busy route between Ankara and Samsun, so buses are frequent. The trip between Amasya and Ankara costs 2200TL (US$3.08), between Amasya and Samsun 800TL (US$1.12).

SAMSUN

Burned to the ground by the Genoese in the 1400s, Samsun (sahm-SOON, population 275,000) has little to show for its long history. It is a major port and commercial centre, and the largest city on the coast. Your reason to stop here would be for a meal or a bed.

Orientation

The bus and railway stations are one km east of the centre, and about ½ km from one another. Come out of the terminal (either one) and cross the coastal road so you can catch a bus heading into town.

The main street, with banks, PTT and restaurants, is Kazım Paşa Caddesi, one block inland from the shore road.

Places to Stay – middle

There is a hotel in the bus terminal, called appropriately the *Terminal Oteli* (TEHR-mee-NAHL) (tel (361) 15519), with 44 double rooms with bath priced at 7000TL (US$9.80).

The city's best is the *Turban Büyük Samsun Oteli* (tel (361) 10750), on the shore in the centre. The 117 air-conditioned rooms rent for 13,700TL (US$19.18) single, 18,150TL (US$25.41) double, breakfast included. There's a swimming pool here.

One block inland from the Büyük Samsun is the small, modern *Hotel Burç* (BOORCH) (tel (361) 15479), Kazım Paşa Caddesi 36 (this street is also called Bankalar Caddesi). The 38 rooms with bath go for 10,000TL (US$14) double. Nearby is the *Vidinli Oteli* (vee-deen-LEE) (tel (361) 16050), Kazım Paşa Caddesi 4, with 65 rooms with shower priced at 9000TL to 10,000TL (US$12.60 to US$14), double.

Getting Away

A bus ticket eastward as far as Ordu costs 1200TL (US$1.68).

SİNOP

West of Samsun 150 km is Sinop (SEE-nohp, population 28,000), which enjoyed a long history as a port, beginning in Hittite times almost 4000 years ago. Successive empires made it a busy trading centre, but the Ottomans preferred to develop Samsun, and under them Sinop became subordinated to its eastern neighbour. Sinop holds memories of its prominence as a Seljuk port in the Alaettin Camii (1214), Alaiye Medrese (now the museum) and Seyyit Bilal Camii.

On the road between Samsun and Sinop you pass through Bafra (BAHF-rah), a tobacco-growing centre.

EAST TO TRABZON

Two of Anatolia's great rivers, the Kızılırmak and the Yeşilırmak, empty into the sea here on either side of Samsun. The rivers have built up fertile deltas which are now filled with corn and tobacco amidst Balkan scenes of bucolic contentment.

Ünye

Ünye (EURN-yeh, population 35,000), 95 km east of Samsun, is a small port town. Five km west of the town are numerous camping places along the beach. The *Turistik Çamlık Motel* (too-rees-TEEK CHAHM-luhk) (tel (3731) 1333), in a pine forest on the shore, is pleasant and inexpensive, with a decent restaurant and obliging staff. A double room with bath and sea view costs 5000TL (US$7), or 7500TL (US$10.50) with a kitchenette.

There are other small hotels in the town such as the *Otel Ürer* (eur-REHR) (tel (3731) 1729), Sahil Caddesi on the shore road, charging 3000TL (US$4.20) single, 6000TL (US$8.40) for a room with bath, breakfast included.

Ordu

Seventy km east of Ünye is Ordu (OHR-doo, population 62,000), another fishing port with some nice old houses and the *Turist Oteli* (too-REEST) (tel (3711) 1466), Sahil Caddesi 4, a bit noisy but not expensive at 4500TL (US$6.30) double. The *Divan Palas* is even cheaper, at 1800TL (US$2.52) double.

Giresun

The town of Giresun (GEE-reh-SOON, population 54,000) was founded 3000 years ago. After the Romans conquered Pontus, they planted cherry trees which made the basis of an important industry which thrives to this day. One theory holds that the ancient name for the town, Cerasus, is the root for many of the names for the fruit – *cherry, cerise* (French), *kiraz* (Turkish) – as well as for the town's modern name. You can see the ruins of a medieval castle here and stay overnight in the *Giresun Oteli* (tel (0511) 2469 or 3017), Atatürk Bulvarı, a modern hotel on the shore one block from the Belediye Sarayı (City Hall). Price for a room with bath is 4800TL (US$6.72) single, 6600TL (US$9.24) double.

From Giresun, it's another 150 km to Trabzon.

TRABZON

Once called Trapezus, and later Trebizond, the modern town of Trabzon (TRAHB-sohn, population 150,000) has a purpose in life. Iran's oil wealth has led to massive purchases of western goods, and many of these goods come to Trabzon by sea, continuing overland by lorry.

Though it is the 20th-century oil boom which has given Trabzon new life, the town actually performed a similar role in the 1800s, when the trade was mostly British. The English-speaking world still thinks of Trebizond as some remote and romantic outpost, though its cosmopolitan days of traders, consulates and international agents are long past.

The main reasons for visiting Trabzon are to see the church of Aya Sofya (1200s), to poke around in the old town, to visit Atatürk's lovely villa on the outskirts, and to make an excursion through the gorgeous alpine scenery to Sumela, a dramatic Byzantine monastery carved out of a sheer rock cliff.

Orientation

Trabzon's airport and bus terminal are east of town. The commercial and governmental centre is at Taksim Meydanı, on a hill above the port. Go here to find hotels, restaurants and other services.

Information

The Tourism Information Office (tel (031) 12722) is at Taksim Caddesi 31, very convenient to most of the town's hotels.

Things to See

Trabzon has lots of old churches, many of which were converted to mosques after the Ottoman conquest of the city. If you stroll along the Uzun Yolu (oo-ZOON yoh-loo, Long Road) west from Taksim, you'll pass the remains of the **Church of St Anne** basilica (Küçük Ayvasıl Kilisesi), built in the 9th century. Then you cross the gorge of the Tabakhane Deresi (stream), turn left into Kale Sokak, and enter the **Citadel** (Kale), the heart of the old part of town. Within the ancient walls is the Ortahisar Camii, which began life in the 900s as the **Church of Panaghia Chrysokephalos**, Trebizond's chief place of worship (the more famous Aya Sofya was built later as a monastery church).

Aya Sofya The Church of the Holy Wisdom (Haghia Sophia or Aya Sofya) is three km west of the centre on a terrace above the coastal highway, reachable by city bus or dolmuş. The church is now a museum.

Built in the 1200s, its design was influenced by eastern Anatolian and Seljuk motifs, though the excellent wall paintings and mosaic floors follow the

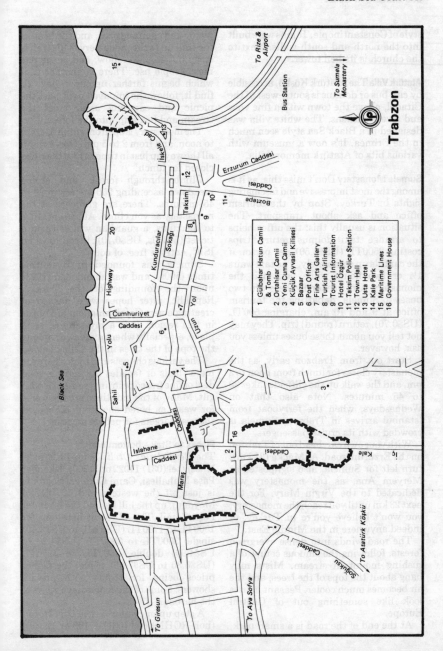

Trabzon

To Rize &
Airport

To Sumela
Monastery

Bus Station

Erzurum Caddesi

Bostepe Caddesi

Taksim

Kunduracılar Sokağı

Cumhuriyet Caddesi

Uzun Yol

Sahil Yolu

Islahane Caddesi

Maraş Caddesi

İç Kale Caddesi

To Giresun

To Aya Sofya

To Atatürk Köşkü

Soğuksu

Black Sea

1 Gülbahar Hatun Camii
   & Tomb
2 Ortahisar Camii
3 Yeni Cuma Camii
4 Küçük Ayvasil Kilisesi
5 Bazaar
6 Post Office
7 Fine Arts Gallery
8 Turkish Airlines
9 Tourist Information
10 Hotel Özgür
11 Taksim Police Station
12 Town Hall
13 Usta Hotel
14 Kale Park
15 Maritime Lines
16 Government House

style of Constantinople. Tombs were built into the north and south walls. Next to the church is its bell tower.

Atatürk Villa The Atatürk Köşkü, accessible by city bus or dolmuş is south-west of the Citadel, above the town with a fine view and lovely gardens. The white villa was designed in a Black Sea style seen much in the Crimea. It's now a museum with various bits of Atatürk memorabilia.

Sumela Monastery Don't miss this, as it is among the most impressive and fascinating sights in Turkey. Stop by the tourism office and ask about transport. The situation is usually this: the office helps to arrange taxi dolmuş return trips costing 2500TL (US$3.50) per person if the car fills up completely. The taxi waits 1½ or two hours while you visit the monastery. On weekends there are two buses to Sumela, departing the tourism office at 9 and 10 am, charging 500TL (US$0.70), return (round) trip. They may not tell you about these buses unless you ask, however.

Start out from Trabzon early, as the monastery closes for lunch from noon to 2 pm, and the walk up the cliffside takes 30 to 45 minutes. Note also that on Wednesdays, when the ferryboat from İstanbul arrives in Trabzon, Sumela is crowded with its cruise passengers.

With your own car, head out of Trabzon on the Erzurum road. At Maçka (31 km), turn left for Sumela, also signposted as Meryem Ana, as the monastery was dedicated to the Virgin Mary. For the next 23 km until you reach the monastery, you won't believe you're in Turkey, or indeed anywhere in the Middle East.

The road winds into dense evergreen forests, following the sinuous course of a rushing mountain stream. Mists may hang about the tops of the trees, and the air becomes much cooler. Peasant houses look like something out of Central Europe.

At the end of the road is a small park,

picnic and camping area, and the head of the trail up to the monastery. This trail is steep but easy to follow, and is the one most people use. There is another trail which begins farther up the valley. To find it, follow the unpaved road past the picnic and camping area, cross the stream and head up into the forest.

The monastery is open only from 8.30 am to noon, and from 2 to 5 pm. Don't climb all the way up just in time to find the ruins closed for lunch!

Climb through forests and alpine meadows, ascending 250 metres in 30 to 45 minutes. There are glimpses of the monastery as you climb. At the entrance to the ruins, a guardian will sell you a ticket (500TL, US$0.70); if you have an ISIC, entry is free, of course.

Sumela was founded in Byzantine times (500s), and was abandoned (1923) upon the founding of the Turkish Republic, after hopes were dashed of creating a new Greek kingdom of Pontus in this region. It is a mysterious, eerie place, especially when mists swirl among the tops of the trees in the valley below.

The various chapels and rooms here are mere shells or façades but have a good deal of fine fresco painting, some of it with gilt. Many of the paintings are the worse for wear, as bored shepherd boys used them as targets for pebble attacks.

Places to Stay – bottom end

The *Benli Palas Oteli* (behn-LEE pah-lahss) (tel (031) 11022 or 11750), İskender Paşa Mahallesi, Cami Çıkmazı Sokak 5, is just off the western end of Taksim Meydanı, up the hill behind the İskender Paşa Camii. The 42 rooms here rent for 1500TL to 1750TL (US$2.10 to US$2.45) single, 3000TL to 3500TL (US$4.20 to US$4.90) double, 4500TL to 5250TL (US$6.30 to US$7.35) triple, the higher prices being for rooms with private showers. Some of the rooms have views of the harbour.

A step up in comfort is the *Otel Horon* (hoh-ROHN) (tel (031) 11199 or 12289),

Sıra Mağazalar 125, a 42-room place on Taksim Meydanı which has a variety of rooms with a variety of plumbing options. Rooms are priced at 4300TL to 5700TL (US$6.02 to US$7.98) single, 6400TL to 8500TL (US$8.96 to US$11.90) double, the lower price being for a room with washbasin, the higher with shower or bath. A room for three, with shower, costs 10,000TL (US$14).

Places to Stay – middle

Best in town is the *Hotel Usta* (OOSS-tah) (tel (031) 12843 or 12195), Telgrafhane Sokak 3, Trabzon 61100, on Taksim Meydanı. There are 72 rooms here, often busy with tour groups, which rent for 7000TL (US$9.80) single, 11,000TL (US$15.40) double, with bath.

Nearby is the *Hotel Özgür* (eurz-GEUR) (tel (031) 11319 or 12778), Taksim Meydanı, with 45 modern-ish rooms, all with bath or shower, renting for 8500TL (US$11.90) single, 11,500TL (US$16.10) double, 14,000TL (US$19.60) triple.

Places to Eat

Look around Taksim and you will find this: the rooftop restaurant in the *Hotel Özgür* is nice, but don't sit down if the restaurant is empty. The *Meydan Kebap ve Yemek Lokantası*, opposite the statue of Atatürk, is a good choice for lunch or dinner. The *Kuyu Restaurant* serves liquor and therefore tends to be a bit noisy (all men) in the evenings. The *Gaziantep Kebabcısı & Baklavacısı* has good, cheap *kebaps* and sweets.

Getting Away

Buses operated by the town of Rize (Rize Belediyesi) shuttle along the coast between Trabzon and Rize frequently, charge 400TL (US$0.56) for a ticket, and give a 50% reduction to holders of the ISIC! The trip from Trabzon all the way to Hopa takes about three hours. If your plan is to go directly from Trabzon to Erzurum, there are direct buses: 10½ hours, 3700TL (US$5.18).

RİZE

Seventy-five km east of Trabzon, Rize (REE-zeh, population 55,000) is at the heart of Turkey's tea plantation area. The steep hillsides which swoop upward from the shore are thickly planted with tea bushes. Local men and women bear large baskets on their backs, taking the leaves to the processing plants. The tea is cured, dried and blended here, then shipped throughout the country. A few years ago there was a shortage of processed tea due, some say, to bad industry planning, and at that time all Turkish eyes were on Rize. In this country, a shortage of tea could spell imminent social collapse.

The bus fare from Rize to Hopa is 600TL (US$0.84).

HOPA

The easternmost Turkish port on the Black Sea coast, Hopa (HOH-pah, population 14,000) is a small town with friendly people who are curious about the few tourists who pass through, and about why they come to Hopa at all. Most of the tourists seem to want to get a look at the Soviet frontier, 30 km to the east, though this is not possible. There is no border crossing point so you can't continue on to Batum, the pretty Soviet seaside resort which was once an Ottoman town.

Places to Stay

Should you find yourself in Hopa, you will probably end up staying at the *Hotel Papila* (PAH-pee-lah) (tel (0571) 1144 or 3641), Orta Hopa Caddesi, right on the shore, a surprisingly modern and comfortable lodging to discover in remote Hopa. The catch is that it's the only such hotel in town, so it gets away with charging big-city prices: 10,000TL (US$14) single, 13,000TL (US$18.20) double. If they're not busy, they're amenable to haggling. The final result may still be high for what you get.

Getting Away

Direct buses from Hopa to Erzurum depart early in the morning, and charge 3500TL (US$4.90) for the long trip. If you miss the direct bus, you can catch a later bus to Artvin (1½ hours, 600TL, US$0.84), then an onward bus from Artvin; but it is altogether better to start out on this trip very early in the day.

ARTVİN

Hopa is in the province of Artvin (ahrt-VEEN), the capital of which is the town of that name (altitude 600 metres, population 18,000), high in the mountains south of Hopa.

The 1½-hour ride to Artvin is wonderfully scenic though something of a dead end: there is not much to see in the town, few tourist facilities, and infrequent and uncomfortable transport to any place except Hopa.

If you're up to it, take the 70-km ride into the mountains. As you approach Artvin you will notice medieval castles guarding the steep mountain passes.

Orientation

The bus station, such as it is, is at Çarşı, the market district at the foot of the high hill which bears the town. You must take a dolmuş or taxi five km up the hill to reach the centre, which is called Hükümet Konağı (heur-keur-MEHT koh-nah-uh, Government House). The Hükümet Konağı is a modern building with a statue of Atatürk in front. The PTT is nearby.

Places to Stay

The *Otel Genye* (GEHN-yeh) is Artvin's best – and an extremely modest – place to stay. The obliging staff will rent you a small, simple but tidy double room with washbasin for 4000TL (US$5.60); shower and flat toilet are down the hall.

Places to Eat

Beneath the Otel Genye is the *Piknik Restaurant*, the local eating and drinking place. It's not great, it's what there is. Dine early. Most of the food is gone by 8 pm, as everyone in Artvin goes to bed early.

Getting Away

You can go by dolmuş to Erzurum from Artvin via Yusufeli and Oltu, bashing over the mountains for 215 km. The journey costs 3000TL (US$4.20). The scenery is extremely beautiful, and even makes up for much of the discomfort.

As for Kars, that's far more difficult to reach as there are several stretches of execrable road (impassable in winter), and very few services. Going by dolmuş or bus, start out early for Şavşat, then continue on to Ardahan, 120 km from Artvin, where there is a hotel and restaurant. If you have your own car, fill your fuel tank in Artvin, pack some food and water, and start early in the day. You can make Ardahan by lunchtime, and Kars (another 110 km) by evening.

Eastern Anatolia

Eastern Turkey is a land of adventure, almost a magical place where each event of the day seems to take on the character of some fabled happening. You might go to bed at night disappointed because Mt Ararat was covered in cloud. But early next morning the mountain will take you by surprise, intruding into your consciousness, shining in the sun outside your hotel window. Or you might be riding along a rough road and suddenly come upon the ruins of a medieval castle, not marked on any map, not described in any guidebook. Every day reveals some new notion of epic events.

The east is not as well-developed as western Turkey. You will see fewer tractors in the fields, more draught animals. Instead of grain-harvesting machinery, you might come across farmers threshing and winnowing in the ancient manner.

The people are no less friendly than in other parts of Turkey but they are not, generally speaking, used to seeing and dealing with foreigners (except in the hotels and tourist offices). It may take a little more time for the friendliness of the adults to emerge. Not so the children. Every single one will simply *have* to find out where you come from, and what language you speak.

Be prepared for the distances. You may ride for hours to get from one town to the next. And when you get to that town, there may not be many hotels to choose from. Travelling in eastern Turkey is certainly not as comfortable as in the west. But if you are adaptable and out for adventure, this is the place to find it.

Touring the Region

The eastern mountains and high plateaux are subject to long and severe winters. I don't recommend travel out east except from May through September, and

preferably in July and August. If you go in May or September, be prepared for some quite chilly nights. A trip to the summit of Nemrut Dağı should not be planned for early morning except in July and August. In other months the mountaintop will be very cold any time, and bitterly cold in early morning. There may also be snow.

Most visitors touring this part of the country make a loop through it, starting from Ankara, Kayseri, Adana or Antakya. Such a trip might follow this itinerary: from Kayseri, head via Sivas and Malatya to Adıyaman, then Kâhta, to see Nemrut Dağı, then to Şanlıurfa, and via Mardin to Diyarbakır for its ancient walls and mosques. Starting from Adana or Antakya, go to Adıyaman and Kâhta via Gaziantep. After seeing Nemrut Dağı, head south to Şanlıurfa, east to Mardin and north to Diyarbakır.

From Diyarbakır, head east through Bitlis and around the southern shore of Van Gölü (Lake Van), stopping to see the Church of the Holy Cross on the island of Akdamar, before reaching the city of Van. Then head north to Ağrı and east to Doğubeyazıt to see Mt Ararat and also the İşak Paşa Sarayı, the dramatic Palace of Ishak Paşa.

From Doğubeyazıt head north to Kars to see the ruins of Ani, then to Erzurum. At Erzurum you can catch a plane westward, or toil through the mountains to Artvin, or head for the Black Sea coast at Trabzon, or start the return journey westward to Sivas and Ankara. This itinerary, from Kayseri or Adana to Van to Kars to Erzurum to Sivas, is about 2500 km, and would take a minimum of. 10 days to complete by bus and/or train; better, two weeks.

Getting There

If you're touring by public transport, you may want to consider flying to or from the eastern region. Buses, as always, go everywhere; there are even direct İstanbul-Erzurum buses. Though there are some trains, they're usually not preferable to the bus.

Air Turkish Airlines flights to the east (per week) are: between İstanbul/Ankara and Diyarbakır (seven), Elazığ (four), Erzurum (seven), Malatya (five), Merzifon (one), Sivas (two), Trabzon (seven), Van (five). In addition, İstanbul Airlines has inaugurated service from İstanbul to Adana, Diyarbakır and Trabzon. Check with the airline for current schedules. Make your flight reservations as early as possible.

Bus Services to and from Ankara are frequent. Routes running east-west are generally not a problem, but service north-south can be infrequent, so allow time and check departures as soon as you can.

Rail From Ankara via Kayseri, there are two major eastern rail destinations: Erzurum and Van. The Erzurum line goes on to Kars and the Soviet frontier, with a connecting train to Moscow. The Van line goes on to Iran, with a connection (sometimes) to Tabriz and Tehran. South of Elazığ, this line branches for Diyarbakır and Kurtalan. The far southern line along the Syrian frontier to Nusaybin is not of much use to tourists.

Except perhaps for the Blue Train, don't expect any of the following trains to be on time; they may be hours late.

To Sivas & Malatya The best train from Ankara via Kayseri to Sivas is the Mavi Tren (Blue Train), which departs Ankara each morning, reaches Sivas after a 6½-hour run, and returns from Sivas to Ankara each evening. Otherwise, the journey from Kayseri to Sivas by normal express train is not bad, taking about 4½ hours. It's another 5½ hours from Sivas to Malatya, and the trains either depart

Sivas before dawn, or arrive in Malatya around midnight, so it's not a convenient service.

To Erzurum From İstanbul and Ankara, trains include the Doğu Expresi (doh-OO), which hauls sleeping cars, a diner and regular coaches and takes about 20 hours overnight between Kayseri and Erzurum. Several trains without sleeping cars, the Mehmetçik Expresi among them, make the trip in the same amount of time. The portion from Erzurum to Kars takes about seven hours by train; it's about four hours by bus.

To Van The best train on this route is the Vangölü Ekspresi (VAHN-gur-lew) which, at the best of times, connects İstanbul and Tehran. From Kayseri it proceeds daily to Sivas, Malatya, Elazığ and Tatvan, hauling couchette cars, coaches and a dining car. At Tatvan, 2nd-class passengers walk aboard a lake steamer; those in 1st-class seats or couchettes can stay in their coach as the whole thing is taken aboard the boat for the trip to Van, at the eastern end of the lake. The journey from Kayseri to Malatya takes 9½ hours, from Malatya to Tatvan another 9½ hours. The steamer-cruise across the lake is yet another four hours.

To Diyarbakır The railway branches south of Elazığ, with the southern line going to Diyarbakır and Kurtalan. The Güney Ekspresi runs from İstanbul, Ankara, Kayseri and Malatya to Diyarbakır, and will carry you from Malatya to Diyarbakır in six hours, from about 6 am to noon.

GAZİANTEP

Known throughout most of its long history as Aintab, this city (altitude 855 metres, population 900,000) was called Antep by the Ottomans. In April 1920, when the Great Powers were carving up the Ottoman lands, Antep was attacked and laid siege to by French forces. The city's Nationalist defenders held out for

10 months before finally surrendering, a feat later recognized by the Grand National Assembly when it granted the city the title of Gazi, meaning Defender of the Faith (or War Hero). Since that time, the city has been called Gaziantep.

Despite its remarkably long history, Gaziantep today is a large, modern city with only two sights to interest visitors: the *kale* (KAH-leh, citadel) and the museum. Other than these, Gaziantep offers a number of comfortable hotels at mid-range prices. As a bonus, you can enjoy a good number of culinary treats: the city and the region are known for excellent grapes and olives, for the soft Arabic 'pizza' called *lahmacun* (LAHH-mah-joon), and for pistachios. This is the pistachio nut (şam fıstığı, SHAHM fuhss-tuh) capital of Turkey. By the way, the phrase *fıstık gibi*, 'like a (pistachio) nut', is the way Turks describe a particularly attractive young woman.

You can bypass this city without great feelings of guilt. If you do stay the night, have some *lahmacun*, buy a supply of delicious pistachios (about 1400TL, US$2 per kilo in the shells; 4500TL, US$6.43 without shells), spend an hour looking at the *kale* and museum the next morning, then get back on the road.

History

Archaeologists have sifted through some of the dirt which forms the artificial hill beneath the *kale*, and have found prehistoric artefacts dating from Neolithic times (7000-5000 BC). But the history begins when small proto-Hittite, or Hatti, city-states grew up (2500-1900 BC). Hittites and Assyrians battled for this region until it was taken by Sargon II, king of Assyria, in 717 BC. The Assyrians ruled for almost a century before being overcome by the Cimmerians, a Crimean people driven from their traditional lands by the Scythians. The Cimmerians swept through Anatolia destroying most everything that lay in their path, and set an example that would be followed by numerous uncreative hordes which showed up in later history.

The Cimmerians cleared out and the Persians took over from 612 to 333 BC. They were followed by Alexander the Great, the Romans and the Byzantines in tiresome succession. The Arabs conquered the town in 638 AD and held it until the Seljuk Turks swept in from the east in the 1070s.

With the Crusades, Antep's history perks up a bit, but most of the action and romance took place in Urfa. The Crusaders didn't stay long before the Seljuks took over again, and Antep remained a city of Seljuk culture, ruled by petty Turkish lords until the coming of the Ottomans under Selim the Grim in 1516.

Orientation

Gaziantep is fairly large, and you will have to take public transport to get from the bus or train station to the centre. For reference purposes, the centre of the city is the intersection of the main roads named Atatürk Bulvarı and Hürriyet Caddesi next to the Hükümet Konağı (hew-kew-MEHT koh-nah-uh), or Provincial Government House. The Devlet Hastanesi or State Hospital, another useful landmark, is a few blocks past the Hükümet Konağı on Hürriyet Caddesi.

Most recommendable hotels are within a block or two of the Hükümet Konağı, as are restaurants. The museum is about half a km from the Hükümet Konağı, a short walk; the *kale* is about half a km from the museum, an easy and pleasant walk. The Otogar (bus terminal) is two km from the Hükümet Konağı; take a 'Devlet Hastanesi' minibus (60TL, US$0.09) or one of the much-less-frequent city buses from the front of the Otogar. Don't listen to the taxi drivers when they say, 'There are no minibuses that take you into town'. The Gar (railway station) is almost as far out. The 'Devlet Hastanesi' minibus passes near the Gar; walk from the Gar to the first

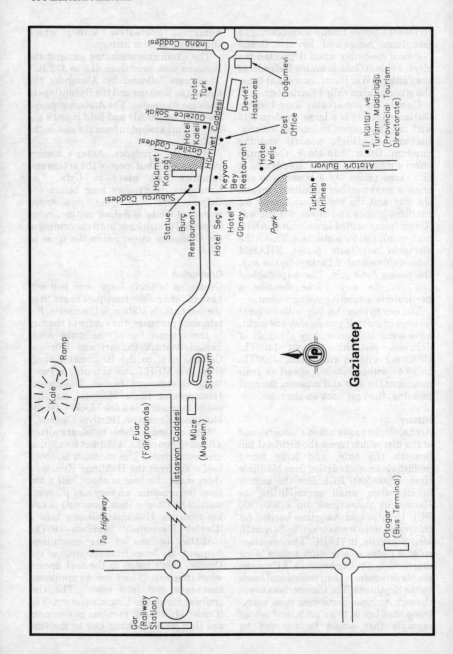

large intersection to find it. You can also take a taxi to the centre for about 400TL (US$0.57).

You can see the hill which bears the *kale* from many places in the city, and thus it serves as a handy landmark. Look for the highest hill, which bears a two-minaret mosque as well as the *kale*.

Information

Gaziantep does not have a Culture & Tourism Ministry office. There is a provincial tourism directorate İl Kültür ve Turizm Müdürlüğü) on Atatürk Bulvarı. Very few of the staff speak anything but Turkish, and few hand-out materials are available.

Things to See

Head for the kale first. The road to it begins just opposite the museum; the museum, for reference purposes, is next to the *stadyum* (stadium).

The citadel was first constructed, as far as we know, by the Emperor Justinian in the 500s, but was rebuilt extensively by the Seljuks in the 1100s and 1200s. The massive doors to the fortified enclosure may well be locked, but at least have a look at them. As you approach the *kale*, bear right around the massive walls. Don't go through what appears to be an enormous stone gateway; this is actually the fosse (dry moat), straddled in ancient times by a drawbridge high above. Around to the right of the fosse you will come to a small mosque, opposite which is a ramp leading up to the citadel doors. If they're open, proceed across the wooden bridge which spans the fosse and into the *kale*.

The surrounding quarter is one of artisans' workshops, old stone houses and little neighbourhood mosques. At one side of the *kale* are gathered the lorries-for-hire, heirs to the ancient carters and teamsters.

Gaziantep's Müze (museum) (tel 11171) is open from 8.30 am to noon and from 1 to 5.30 pm, closed Monday;

admission costs 400TL (US$0.36), half-price on Saturday and Sunday. Surrounded by the requisite sculpture garden, the museum holds something from every period of the province's history, from mastodon bones through Hittite figurines and pottery to Roman mosaics (three fairly good ones) and funeral stones complete with portraits of husband and wife, to an Ottoman ethnography room of *kilims*, carpets and furniture heavily worked in mother-of-pearl.

Places to Stay

Gaziantep accommodation is resolutely middle-range, with nothing much at the bottom and top ends of the price scale. There are no hotels near the Otogar, nor near the Gar. Most of the hotels are within a block or two of the Hükümet Konağı, either on Atatürk Bulvarı, or on Hürriyet Caddesi between the Hükümet Konağı and the Devlet Hastanesi (State Hospital). I'll start with the cheapest places, and end with the best place in town.

Just a few steps from the crossroads at Hükümet Konağı is the *Hotel Seç* (tel (851) 15272) at Atatürk Bulvarı 4/B. Equipped with a lift and central heating, it charges 3500TL (US$5) for a double room without private bath, or 5300TL (US$7.42) with private bath; but watch out for street noise.

Hotel Veliç (tel (851) 22341 or 11726), Atatürk Bulvarı 23, just a few steps farther along, is brighter and more modern, with its own auto park. All rooms have private baths and cost 6000TL (US$8.40) double.

Between the above hotels is the *Hotel Güney* (tel (851) 16886), Atatürk Bulvarı 10, also bright and modern; doubles with private bath cost 6400TL (US$8.96), but the hotel has two bathless rooms which rent for only 3000TL (US$4.20). The hotel has its own car park.

You'll notice an older, unfancy hotel in this area. It cannot be recommended.

Two more hotels are on Hürriyet

Caddesi between the Hükümet Konağı and the Devlet Hastanesi. *Hotel Türk* (tel (851) 19480, 1), Hürriyet Caddesi 27, just across from the Devlet Hastanesi, has only rooms-with-bath, for which it charges 5910TL (US$8.27) single, 7400TL (US$10.36) double.

Best place in town, used to putting up tourists passing through, is the *Hotel Kaleli* (tel (851) 13417 or 12728), Hürriyet Caddesi at Güzelce Sokak 50, between the Hotel Türk and the Hükümet Konağı. For 8500TL (US$11.90) single, 10,500TL (US$14.70) double, or 18,000TL (US$25.20) triple in a suite, you get a hotel with two lifts, large guest rooms with good cross-ventilation, a rooftop restaurant and several private parking slots.

Places to Eat

Gaziantep's recommendable restaurants are likewise clustered at the intersection of Atatürk Bulvarı and Hürriyet Caddesi.

Just across Hürriyet Caddesi from the Hükümet Konağı and its plaza is the *Keyvan Bey Restaurant* (tel 12651), on the upper floor, with an outdoor terrace section festooned with verdure. A full meal here based on *kebap* need cost only 1500TL (US$2.10).

Slightly fancier is the *Burç Restaurant* (tel 13012), at the corner of Suburcu and İstasyon caddesis, on the upper floor. Glassed-in dining rooms have a fine view of the plaza and busy crossroads, and the average meal price rises to 2000TL (US$2.80).

Finally, there's that roof restaurant at the Hotel Kaleli, mentioned above. Green and blue fluorescent lights make everyone look somewhat ghoulish, but it's pleasant and airy for all that, and well above the street noise. A full dinner need cost no more than 2000TL (US$2.80).

Getting There

Unless you have your own car, transportation to and from Gaziantep is by bus or rail. There is an airport here, but as of this writing there are no scheduled flights.

Airports at Adana and Diyarbakır are currently served by Turkish Airlines.

Bus As mentioned, the modern Otogar is two km from the centre. Bus service is, as usual, frequent and far-reaching. Here are some sample cities, times and fares: Adana, 3½ to four hours, 1000TL to 1500TL (US$1.40 to US$2.10); Antakya, 3½ hours, 1500TL (US$2.10); Diyarbakır, five hours, 2000TL (US$2.80); Mardin, 5½ hours, 2000TL to 3000TL (US$2.80 to US$4.20); Şanlıurfa, 2½ hours, 1000TL (US$1.40).

Rail Only one train is a serious contender for your attention, and that is the Mavi Tren (Blue Train) which departs each Wednesday, Friday and Sunday morning at 8.50 am for Ankara and İstanbul (Haydarpaşa). A seat to Ankara costs 2800TL (US$3.92), a *kuşet* (couchette, bunk) 3050TL (US$4.27); to Haydarpaşa, the prices are 4300TL (US$6.02) and 4550TL (US$6.37) respectively.

There is a morning train (6 am) to Akçakale, near Harran, which is not too far from Şanlıurfa, but then you must make your way by taxi (probably) to Şanlıurfa. Take the bus instead of the train. Likewise, an evening *posta* train to Diyarbakır (9 pm) takes an astounding 15 hours, while the bus makes the trip in one-third the time.

NORTHWARD & EASTWARD

You are probably heading north to visit Nemrut Dağı, but just in case your itinerary takes you due east, here's what to expect.

The road from Gaziantep to Şanlıurfa is very hot in summer, yet the land is fertile, with fig orchards, olive trees, cotton and wheat. At Nizip there is a turning south for Karkamış (Carchemish), a Neo-Hittite city which flourished (850 BC) about the time Akhenaton occupied the throne of Egypt. Though Karkamış assumed the role of Hittite capital after the fall of Hattuşaş, there is little left to see, and you must see it with a military escort so you don't get shot as a smuggler, so it's hardly worth the trip.

At Birecik you cross the Euphrates. The town has a ruined fortress, rebuilt and used by the Crusaders.

As you head east, the land becomes rockier and less fertile. The highway is crowded with oil tankers shuttling to and from the Turkish oilfields and refineries in Batman and Siirt. By the time you approach Şanlıurfa, the land is parched, rolling steppe, roasting in the merciless summer sun.

NEMRUT DAĞI

The temples atop 2000-metre-high Nemrut Dağı (NEHM-root dah-uh) are certainly unique. Though the world has many larger and more elaborate temples, none is quite like Nemrut in its megalomania. On a bare mountaintop in south-eastern Anatolia, a petty pre-Roman king cut two ledges in the rock, filled them with colossal statues of himself and the gods (his 'relatives'), then ordered an artificial mountain peak of crushed rock 50 metres high to be piled between them. The king's tomb may well lie beneath those tons of rock. Nobody knows for sure.

Earthquakes have toppled the heads from most of the statues, but many of the colossal bodies sit silently in rows, and the two-metre-high heads watch from the ground. It's something to see.

Plan your visit to Nemrut for a time between late May and mid-October, and preferably for July or August. The dirt road to the summit becomes impassable in spring when the snows melt, turning it to mud. Remember that at any time of year, even in the heat of summer when the sun bakes the valleys below, it will be chilly and windy atop the mountain. This is especially true at sunrise, the coldest hour of the day. Take warm clothing and a windbreaker on your trek to the top, no matter when you go.

History

Nobody knew anything about Nemrut Dağı until 1881, when an Ottoman geologist making a survey was astounded to come across a remote mountaintop full of statues. Archaeological work didn't begin until 1953, when the American School of Oriental Research undertook the project.

From 250 BC, this region was the marchland between the Seleucid empire, successor to the empire of Alexander the Great in Anatolia, and the Parthian empire to the east, also a successor to part of Alexander's lands. A small but strategic land, and a rich and fertile one covered in forests, it had a history of independent thinking ever since the time of King Samos (circa 150 BC). Under the Seleucid Empire, the governor of Commagene declared his kingdom's independence. In 80 BC, with the Seleucids in disarray and Roman power spreading into Anatolia, a Roman ally named Mithridates I Callinicus proclaimed himself king and set up his capital at Arsameia, near the modern village of Eski Kâhta. Mithridates prided himself on his royal ancestry, tracing his forebears back to Seleucus I Nicator, founder of the Seleucid Empire to the west, and to Darius the Great, king of ancient Persia to the east. Thus he saw himself as heir to both glorious traditions. He married a Parthian princess.

Mithridates died in 64 BC and was succeeded by his son Antiochus I Epiphanes (64-32 BC) who, born of a Parthian mother, consolidated the security of his kingdom by immediately signing a non-aggression treaty with Rome, turning his kingdom into a Roman buffer against attack from the Parthians. His good relations with both sides allowed him to grow rich and to revel in delusions of grandeur. As heir to both traditions, he saw himself as equal to the great god-kings of the past. It was Antiochus who ordered built the fabulous temples and funerary mound atop Nemrut.

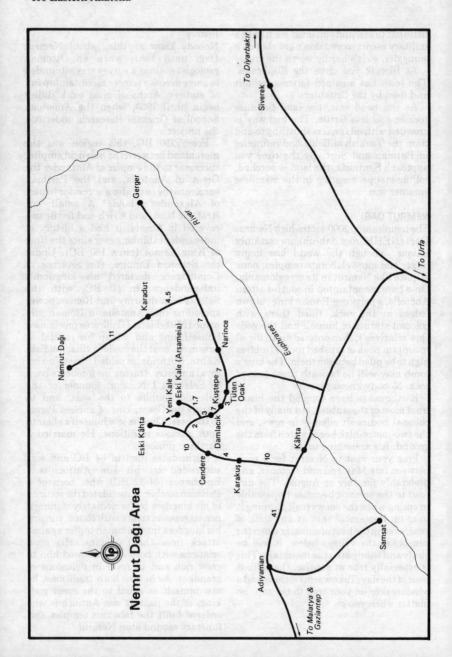

Antiochus must have come to believe in his own divinity, for in the third decade of his reign he sided with the Parthians in a squabble with Rome, and the Romans deposed him in 38 BC. Commagene was alternately ruled directly from Rome or by puppet kings until 72 AD, when Emperor Vespasian incorporated it for good into Roman Asia. So the great days of Commagene were limited to the 26-year reign of Antiochus.

Orientation

The Commagene Nemrut Dağı (not to be confused with a mountain of the same name on the shores of Lake Van) rises between the provincial capital of Malatya to the north and the village of Kâhta, in the province of Adıyaman, to the south, as part of the Anti-Taurus range. Most visitors use the provincial capital of Adıyaman (ah-DUH-yah-mahn, altitude 725 metres, population 70,000) or the nearby village of Kâhta (ky-YAHH-tah, population 32,000) as a base for their ascent, though the route via Malatya is popular as well. These towns are accustomed to tourists and have decent if simple hotels, and minibus drivers who are used to rising at 2 am to haul groups of sightseers up the mountainside in time for sunrise.

The road to the top from Malatya via Tepehan entails an overnight stay in the village of Büyüköz, where there are no hotels for sleeping, only the floors in simple village homes. Also, by taking the Malatya route, visitors miss seeing the several sights along the Kâhta-Nemrut road, such as Arsameia. Cost is about the same by either route. If you decide to go via Malatya, refer to the separate section (below) on that city.

Distances among these points are as follows: Kâhta to the summit of Nemrut 70 km; Kâhta to Adıyaman 35 km; Adıyaman to Gölbaşı 65 km; Gölbaşı to Malatya 121 km; Malatya to the summit of Nemrut 110 km.

Information

The Tourism Information Office in Adıyaman (tel (8781) 1008) is next to the PTT on the main street, which is also the highway. If no one is around, check at the Hükümet Konağı, the Government House.

Things to See

The sights are all along the road between Kâhta and the summit of Nemrut. You can traverse this road by private car or hired minibus. Whichever way you go, pack a bottle of water and some snacks such as dried fruit, biscuits and nuts, for the entire journey can take between six and eight hours, and there are very few services along the way. Plan between two and 2½ hours' driving (or riding) time for the outward trip from Kâhta to the summit. The return trip takes almost as long. Add to these times two or three hours' sightseeing time at the various sites.

Touring by Minibus Some fairly sleazy characters hang around the hotels in Kâhta, trying to browbeat tourists into taking overpriced minibus tours to Nemrut. If someone approaches you aggressively about tours, it's a good policy to ignore them from the start. Instead, strike a bargain with a minibus driver on your own. If you can't fill the minibus, you might do better by joining an organized tour, but choose carefully. For an idea of current prices, or to strike a deal, or to catch a dolmuş to Eski Kâhta, go to Kâhta's minibus garage at the western edge of the town, at the bottom of the hill along the main highway.

There are two standard minibus tours. The short tour takes you from Kâhta to the summit, allows you about an hour there, then comes right down to Kâhta again. The long or complete tour takes you to the summit, and on the trip down stops at Eski Kale (Arsameia), Yeni Kale (next to Eski Kâhta) and Karakuş. A normal price for the short tour is 17,000 to

20,000TL (US$23.80 to US$28), for the long tour 22,000 to 25,000TL (US$30.80 to US$35). A minibus holds about 10 people. If you have enough friends to fill it, you can travel at your own speed, at a very low price.

If you are one of those romantics who plan to stay the night in Eski Kâhta (see below) and ascend at midnight on muleback or on foot, you can get to your base at Eski Kâhta very inexpensively by taking a dolmuş from Kâhta toward Gerger, which passes by Eski Kâhta.

By Private Car Rumour has it that the minibus tour people in Kâhta have tried to make it difficult for people to see the mountain on their own by removing some highway signs. For instance, you won't see any signs marking the way to Eski Kâhta; you must follow the ones which point to Nemrut and Gerger. Rest assured that you can easily do it on your own. Make sure you have plenty of fuel for at least 200 or 250 km of normal driving. Though the return trip is only about 150 km, much of that will be driven in lower gears, which use more fuel. Should you run out of fuel, villagers may be able to sell you a few litres from a barrel or another vehicle's fuel tank.

To Eski Kâhta It's 24 km from Kâhta to Eski Kâhta. After 15 km you come to a fork in the road, with no sign! Take the right fork. The road from Kâhta passes through the villages of Karakuş and Cendere, and the sights begin 10 km after leaving Kâhta. A mound by the roadside at Karakuş, marked with columns, holds the graves of royal ladies from the Kingdom of Commagene. A black eagle (*karakuş*), its head missing, tops one of the columns.

Nineteen km from Kâhta, five km before Eski Kâhta, you'll cross a Roman bridge built in honour of Emperor Septimius Severus (194-211 AD), his wife and sons, long after Commagene had become part of Roman Asia. Of the four

original columns (two at either end), three are still standing, and some historians think that the missing column was removed by one of the sons, Caracalla, when he murdered the other son, Geta, in 212.

As you leave the bridge, a sign points to the right for Nemrut Dağı and Gerger. Even though there's no mention of Eski Kâhta, this road to the right is the one you want.

Eski Kâhta & Yeni Kale You approach Eski Kâhta along the valley of a stream called the Kâhta Çayı. Opposite the town are the ruins of a Mameluke castle (1300s), now called Yeni Kale (yeh-NEE kah-leh, New Fortress), which you can explore. It bears some Arabic inscriptions; the Mamelukes were originally a Turkic people, but they were assimilated into Egyptian society. It's difficult to imagine that this region was once very fertile, cloaked in forests and noisy with the sound of great herds of cattle. Deforestation and consequent erosion have turned it to semi-desert.

Arsameia Just after leaving Eski Kâhta, the road passes through a dramatic, beautiful gorge spanned by an ancient bridge which appears to be Seljuk in design.

Eski Kale About a km up the road from Eski Kâhta, a turnoff to the left takes you (two km) to Eski Kale, the ancient Commagene capital of Arsameia. Walk up the path from the car park, and you'll come to a large stela with a female (?) figure on it; further along are two more stelae, a monumental staircase, and behind them an opening in the rock leading down to a cistern.

Another path leads from the first path to the striking stone relief which portrays the founder of Commagene, Mithridates I Callinicus, shaking hands with the god Heracles. Next to it is a long inscription in Greek, and to the right is a tunnel descending through the rock. The locals will tell you the tunnel goes all the way to the valley floor below, though it has not been cleared of the centuries of rubble yet.

Above the relief on the level top of the hill are the foundations of Mithridates' capital city. The view is magnificent from here. If you stop at Arsameia on your way down from Nemrut, this is the perfect site for a picnic.

Along the Road Driving upward from Eski Kale, you pass through **Damlacık** (three km), with its humble restaurant and camping place, then **Kuştepe** (seven km), then **Tüten Ocak** (three km). Near here a road goes right (south), back to the main highway and Kâhta.

Seven km east of this junction is the hamlet of **Narince**, and another seven km east of Narince is a turning to the left marked for Nemrut, which you want to take; were you to continue straight on, you'd end up in the village of Gerger.

Continue up the mountain through the hamlet of **Karadut**, five km from the last turning. This length of the road is being paved in stone blocks, and it's a welcome change from the bone-jangling rough stretch. On the far (north) side of Karadut is the Motel Nemrut and its camping area, and three km beyond the village is a tea house. From here it is less than eight km to the summit. You're well above treeline when you climb the final ridge and pull into the car park at the summit.

At the Summit Just up from the car park is a ruined stone house where a man sells hot tea, soft drinks and souvenir booklets. Beyond him is the pyramid of stones; it's a hike of less than one km (15 or 20 minutes) over the broken rock to the western temple. Sometimes donkeys are on hand to carry you, but this is not much help since staying on the donkey is almost as difficult as negotiating the rocks on your own.

I, great King Antiochus, have ordered the construction of these temples, the ceremonial road, and the thrones of the gods, on a foundation which will never be demolished . . . . I have done this to prove my faith in the gods. At the end of my life I will enter my eternal rest here, and my spirit will join that of Zeus-Ahura Mazda in heaven.

Antiochus I Epiphanes ordered the construction here of a *hierothesium*, or combination tomb and temple. Approaching from the car park, you see first the western temple, and behind it the conical tumulus, or funerary mound, of fist-sized stones. At the western temple, Antiochus and his fellow gods sit in state, though the bodies have mostly been tumbled down along with the heads. But at the eastern temple the bodies are largely intact, except for the fallen heads, which seem more badly weathered than the heads at the west; on the backs of the eastern statues are inscriptions in Greek.

Both terraces have similar plans, with the syncretistic gods, the 'ancestors' of Antiochus, seated in this order, from left to right: first is Apollo, the sun god, Mithra to the Persians, Helios or Hermes to the Greeks; next is Fortuna, or Tyche; in the centre is Zeus-Ahura Mazda; to the right is King Antiochus; and at the right end is Heracles, also known as Ares or Artagnes. The seated figures are several metres high.

Low walls at the sides of each temple once held carved reliefs showing royal processions of ancient Persia and Greece, Antiochus's 'predecessors'. Statues of eagles represent Zeus.

That flat space next to the eastern temple, with an 'H' at its centre, is a helipad which accepts the arrival of the wealthy, the important and the fortunate.

Places to Stay

You can lodge in Adıyaman, Kâhta, Eski Kâhta, Malatya, or even on the mountain slope – but not everywhere in the same comfort.

Adıyaman Though Adıyaman has some low-end hotels, such as the *Hotel Uyanık* (tel (8781) 1179), the *Hotel Yolaç* (tel (8781) 1301) and the *Konak Oteli* (tel (8781) 2392), there are few advantages to staying here as opposed to staying in Kâhta. In fact, the hotels here often suffer from underuse as most visitors prefer Kâhta, and underuse means musty rooms, inexperienced staff and low maintenance budgets.

As for middle-range places, Adıyaman has two motels. The *Motel Antiochos* (ahn-tee-YOH-kohs) (tel (8781) 1240 or 1184), Atatürk Bulvarı (the main highway), is next to the Mobil petrol station at the western side of the town, on the highway. It's a 43-room place charging 8500TL (US$11.90) per night, double with bath; they have camping facilities and a restaurant, too.

Also on the highway, but 1½ km east of the centre of the town nearer the bus and dolmuş station, is the *Motel Arsemia* (ahr-SEEM-yah) (tel (8781) 2112 or 3131), Atatürk Bulvarı 146, 02100 Adıyaman, where doubles with shower rent for 7500TL (US$10.50). There is a restaurant. Reports have it that the water here goes off during the day. You can camp in the adjoining, tree-less camping area.

Kâhta Low-end places include the *Hotel Mesopotamya* (tel 1296), a block off the highway (follow the signs). It is very simple, with dank and somewhat odorous plumbing but cheap and quiet rooms, and a roof good for very cheap sleeping. (Follow the signs.) Asking price is 4000TL (US$5.60) double with shower, 2000TL (US$2.80) single, but you can haggle if it's not crowded. Beware of the tour touts though.

In the middle range are two hotels on the western outskirts, near the junction with the road to the summit, and one hotel in the town.

Hotel Merhaba (MEHR-hah-bah) (tel 1098, 1139) in the town has a restaurant and 28 rooms-with-bath which rent for 6500TL (US$9.10) double or 4000TL (US$5.60) single, with bath. The Merhaba is nice enough, but is sometimes completely filled by tour groups. It might be good to telephone and reserve a room.

Another group favourite is the tidy *Hotel Nemrut Tur* (tel 1459 or 1863), 02400 Kâhta, on the highway west of town. With a shady terrace restaurant, swimming pool and camping area, it is the compleat lodging-spot, charging 7000TL (US$9.80) double, 4500TL (US$6.30) single, with bath.

Just at the junction with the Nemrut road is the *Hotel Kommagene* (tel 1092), PK 4, 02400 Kâhta, a converted house with fly-screens on the windows, a pleasant atmosphere and prices of 6000TL (US$8.40) double, 3500TL (US$4.90) single, with bath. They have a camping area as well.

At the far western edge of Kâhta, on the Adıyaman highway, is *Nemrut Camping*, with a walled car park and camping area. This is the fanciest camping place in town.

Eski Kâhta This tiny village 25 km north of Kâhta has only one lodging, run by the Demiral (DEH-meer-ahl) family (no phone). For 1500TL (US$2.10) per person you can bed down (it helps to have your own sleeping bag). There's running water from a can. With a camper van, you can camp in their front yard. The Demirals will serve you simple but tasty meals for 700TL (US$1) each, whether you sleep here or not; order well before mealtime. They have beer and soft drinks, but no wine or spirits. Their house was that of Professor Dörfer, a German archaeologist who worked at Nemrut. The Demirals will find a guide whom you can employ to lead you up the mountain, a three or four-hour trek whether you go on foot or on donkey-back.

On Nemrut At the village of Damlacık (DAHM-lah-juhk), five km from Eski

Kâhta along the road to Nemrut, is the *Bahçeli Restaurant ve Kamping*. Expect good tea but rough-and-ready food in the restaurant, and a mere parking place as camping facility. There is running water and a sort of toilet. Also, 35 km from Eski Kâhta, less than 10 km from the mountaintop, is the *Motel Nemrut ve Camping*, a sort of hostel where you can find running water, a simple meal, a roof and a bed for 2500TL (US$3.50) per person. To be sure it's open, contact Mustafa Deniz (tel 1459) in Kâhta.

The newer *Zeus Motel* charges 5000TL (US$7) per person for bed and breakfast. Some of the rooms have three or four beds, and you may find yourself sharing with others unless you're willing to pay for the other beds. Though these prices are high for what you get, they become very reasonable when you realise that the motel has a minibus service from Kâhta to the motel, and also from the motel to the summit. In effect, the trip to the summit is included in the room price. This may not last, I suppose. To check on the current situation, contact the motel's office (*irtibat bürosu*) (tel 1919 or 4775) in Kâhta on the main street, Atatürk Bulvarı 43.

Places to Eat

Besides the dining places in the various hotels (mentioned above), Kâhta has several little restaurants. Typical is the *Kent Restaurant*, on the north side of the main highway in the centre of town. A *hazır yemek* (ready food) restaurant, it fills you up at rock-bottom prices. Two plates of food and a drink will cost about 600TL (US$0.84).

Getting There & Away

Adıyaman and Kâhta are served by frequent buses, but nothing else. There are air and rail services to Malatya (see below).

Bus From Kâhta you can reach Diyarbakır (2½ to three hours, 1600TL, US$2.24) and

Malatya (2½ to three hours, 1700TL, US$2.38). Dolmuşes run between Kâhta and Adıyaman (400TL, US$0.56) throughout the day.

Onward

From Kâhta you have a choice of roads.

North To the north lie Malatya, an agricultural centre without tourist significance, and Divriği and Sivas, two towns important to the history of Seljuk Turkish architecture.

East To the east is Diyarbakır, the most important city in south-eastern Turkey. To the south lies Şanlıurfa, perhaps the most fascinating and pleasant town in the region. If you're heading east rather than north, I'd suggest that you make the detour south to Şanlıurfa, then continue to Mardin and/or Diyarbakır.

On this ride you will enter that fabled cradle of civilisation, the watershed of the Tigris (Dicle, DEEJ-leh) and Euphrates (Fırat, fuh-RAHT) rivers. The shortest route is east from Kâhta to Çaylarbaşı (29 km), and then 11 km more to the highway. Turn right (west) at the highway for Şanlıurfa, 70 km from the junction; or left (east) 23 km to Siverek, and another 90 km to Diyarbakır, a total distance of 153 km.

MALATYA

A modern town grown large and rich on agriculture, Malatya (mah-LAHT-yah, population 252,000, altitude 964 metres) has virtually nothing to offer the tourist except the alternative route up Nemrut Dağı, and apricots. This happens to be the apricot capital of Turkey. An apricot festival is held in late July.

Orientation

Malatya is ranged along its main street for many km. Everything you'll want is in the centre, near the main square with its statue of İnönü and Vilayet (vee-lah-YEHT, Provincial Headquarters) building, and the neighbouring Belediye (beh-leh-DEE-yeh, City Hall).

The bus terminal (Otogar) and train station (İstasyon) are on the outskirts of town, several km from the centre. City buses marked 'Vilayet' operate between the stations and the centre.

Information

The Vilayet holds the local Tourism Information Office (tel (821) 17 733); there is also a small tourist information office in the Otogar. A tourism official will be on hand in the bus terminal, greeting you and urging you to sign up for one of the tours to the top of Nemrut Dağı.

Things to See

Look in the shop windows at all the packages of dried apricots. There is a small museum near the Vilayet (follow the Müze signs).

Going to Nemrut Though this route is less convenient that the route via Kâhta, it makes for a real Turkish adventure. After signing up for a tour with the tourism

official, you start at 10 am by minibus, driving for about six hours to a hut within a few hundred metres of the summit. The road is not the best, but the scenery is marvellous. A guide leads you on a 45-minute hike to the top to see the sunset, then takes you back down to the hut, where you are given a meagre meal and put to sleep on the dirt floor of the hut, in which there are no services of any kind. At 4 am or so, you are awakened to get ready for another hike to the summit to view the sunrise, after which you drive back to Malatya. The entire cost for the minibus is 24,000TL (US$33.60); divided among 10 or 12 people, that comes to 2000TL to 2400TL (US$2.80 to US$3.36) each; you must also pay 2300TL (US$3.22) per person for the night's lodging and two meagre meals in the hut, for a total cost of 4300TL to 4700TL (US$6.02 to US$6.58) for the 30-hour tour. If you do this, take *very* warm clothing, even in summer (you'll be sleeping on a damp dirt floor at the top of a mountain), and some food to supplement the inadequate meals.

You can in fact arrange a trip on your own, but it might turn out to cost more.

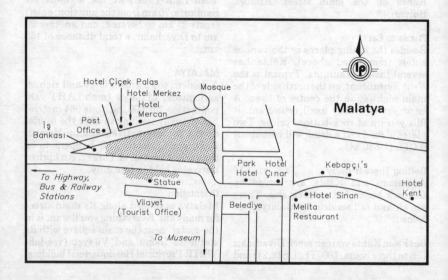

Start by taking the first of the two daily minibuses to the village of Büyüköz (berr-YERRK-erz), via Tepehan. At the end of the run, you must strike a bargain with the driver to take you to the summit, 110 km from Malatya. He must wait, and bring you down to the village again. As the day will be mostly gone by the time you arrive in the village, you will have to spend the night in one of the village homes. The next morning you can catch a minibus back to Malatya.

It may be possible to ascend from Malatya, and find a way to descend via Kâhta. If you have your luggage with you at the summit, try it. Then write me a letter and describe it, so I can tell other readers.

Places to Stay

You must be particularly wary of noise in this town. The last night I stayed here (a week-night), heavy traffic along the main street did not abate until 2 am, and started up again in earnest at 5 am. I got less than four hours' sleep.

Places to Stay - bottom end

A number of small, simple and very inexpensive places are located just east of the PTT, in the centre. The *Mercan Palas Oteli*, (tel (821) 11 570), PTT Caddesi 14, is typical of these, charging 750TL (US$1.05) per person for bathless rooms. Next door to the Mercan Palas are the *Merkez* and the *Çiçek Palas*. Though these places lack the comforts of the more expensive hotels, they are quiet, and quiet is difficult to find in this town.

Places to Stay - middle

The two best hotels in town are just to the east of the Vilayet. *Hotel Sinan* (see-NAHN) (tel (821) 12 907 or 13 007), Atatürk Caddesi 14, has eight floors, a lift, restaurant and bar, and car park, and charges 7500TL (US$10.50) for a double with bath, 5500TL (US$7.70) for a similar single. Being right on the main street, the front rooms suffer from noise.

A bit farther east, up the hill on the opposite side of the main street, is the *Kent Otel* (tel (821) 12 175 or 128 13), Atatürk Caddesi 151. Prices and services are identical to those at the Hotel Sinan.

If these two hotels are full, the clerks may suggest the *Hotel Çınar*, across the road from the Hotel Sinan. While alright in some regards, with friendly staff and well-used rooms renting for 2200TL (US$3.08) double with washbasin, or 2400TL (US$3.36) double with private shower, it suffers badly from the street noise.

Places to Eat

Besides the top two hotels, try the *Restaurant Melita*, next door to the Hotel Sinan, on the upper floor. Clean, bright and cheerful, with attentive and experienced waiter service, it is still surprisingly moderate in price, charging about 2300TL to 2800TL (US$3.22 to US$3.92) for a full dinner.

The main street holds much cheaper *kebapçıs*, such as the *Çınar*, on the main street between the Sinan and Kent hotels, where a meal need cost only 800TL (US$1.12).

Getting There & Away

There are many people interested in buying, selling, trading, growing and eating apricots, so Malatya is served by air, rail and bus.

Air Turkish Airlines (tel (821) 11 922 or 14 053), Dörtyol, Halep Caddesi 1, has flights to and from İstanbul and Ankara on Tuesday, Wednesday, Thursday, Saturday and Sunday. The special bus which runs between the centre and Erhaç airport costs 300TL (US$0.42), and departs 90 minutes before flight departure time.

Rail Malatya's İstasyon can be reached by a dolmuş or city bus of that name. The city is served daily by express train from

İstanbul (Haydarpaşa) and Ankara via Kayseri and Sivas. On Monday, Wednesday and Friday it's the Vangölü Ekspresi, arriving before 6 am and departing at 6 am for Tatvan (and Van). On other days of the week, it's the Güney Ekspresi, on the same schedule, departing for Diyarbakır and Kurtalan.

Malatya and Adana are connected by daily express trains in each direction. From Malatya, departure is at 9.20 am, arriving in Adana at 6.12 pm.

The Vangölü Ekspresi and the Güney Ekspresi, travelling westward, depart Malatya for Sivas, Kayseri, Ankara and İstanbul (Haydarpaşa) at 5 pm – if they're on time.

Bus Several buses a day join Malatya with Sivas (five hours, 2000TL to 2500TL, US$2.80 to US$3.50) and Kayseri (six hours, 2500TL, US$2.80). Adana, Adıyaman, Ankara and Diyarbakır also have frequent service.

SİVAS

The highway comes through Sivas, the railway comes through Sivas, and over the centuries the dozens of invading armies have come through Sivas (SEE-vahss, altitude 1285 metres, population 200,000), often leaving the town in ruins when they left. It started life, so far as we know, in Roman times under the name Megalopolis, later changed to Sebastea, which the Turks shortened to Sivas. Today it is a fairly modern and unexciting place, full of farmers, yet at its centre are a few of the finest Seljuk Turkish buildings ever erected. And outside Sivas, deep in the countryside, is a Seljuk masterpiece hidden among the hills.

History

In recent times Sivas gained fame as the location for the Sivas Congress, which opened on 4 September 1919. Atatürk came here from Samsun and Amasya, seeking to consolidate the Turkish resistance to Allied occupation and partition of the country. He gathered as many delegates from as many parts of the country as possible, and confirmed decisions which had been made at a congress held earlier in Erzurum. These two congresses were the first breath of the revolution, and heralded the War of Independence.

Orientation

The centre of town is Konak Meydanı; near it are most of Sivas's important sights, hotels and the Tourism Information Office (tel (4771) 3535, 2850) in the Vilayet Konağı (vee-lah-YEHT koh-nah-uh), the Provincial Government House.

The railway station (Sivas Gar) is 1½ km south-west of Konak Meydanı along İnönü Bulvarı. After you arrive in Sivas by rail, walk out the front door of the station and out to the bus stop on the station (south) side of İnönü Bulvarı. Any bus running along this major road will trundle you to or from the station. If in doubt, just ask the driver, 'Konak?' (koh-NAHK).

The bus terminal (Sivas Oto Terminalı) is several km south-east of the centre. Transport to and from the terminal is by taxi, with a ride to Konak Meydanı costing 650TL (US$0.91), less to the cheap hotels.

Things to See

All of the sights except one are conveniently grouped in a pleasant park at Konak Meydanı; the other building to see is a short walk away.

Çifte Minare Medrese The Seminary of the Twin Minarets has, as its name explains, a pair (çift) of minarets. Today, that's about all it has, along with its grand Seljuk portal, the medrese building itself being long ruined. It was commissioned by the Mongol vezir who ruled here, and finished in 1271. It is among the greatest monuments of the Seljuk architectural style.

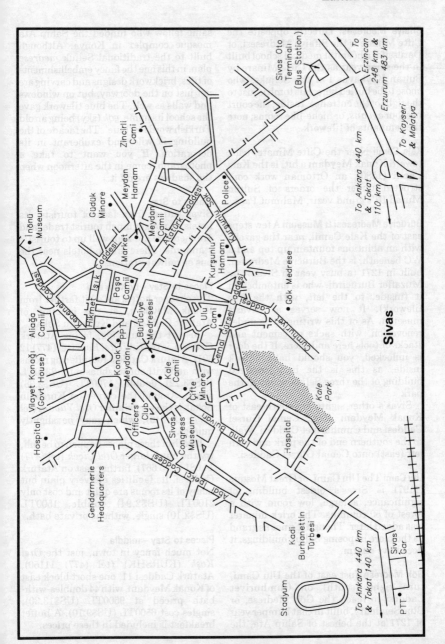

Sivas

To Erzincan 248 km & Erzurum 483 km

To Ankara 440 km & Malatya

To Ankara 440 km & Tokat 110 km

To Kayseri & Malatya

To Ankara 440 km & Tokat 140 km

Sivas Oto Terminali (Bus Station)

Police

Zincirli Camii

Meydan Hamam

Meydan Camii

Güdük Minare

İnönü Museum

Market

Paşa Camii

Bürüciye Medresesi

Aliağa Camii

Hikmet Işık Caddesi

Keçecizar Caddesi

PPT

Konak Meydanı

Vilayet Konağı (Govt House)

Hospital

Officers' Club

Sivas Congress Museum

Gendarmerie Headquarters

Kale Camii

Çifte Minare

Cemal Gürsel Caddesi

Ulu Camii

Kurşunlu Hamam

Gök Medrese

Kale Park

İnönü Bulvarı

Hospital

Kadı Burhanettin Türbesi

Abdi Bekçi Caddesi

Stadyum

Sivas Gar

PTT

Şifaiye Medresesi Directly opposite the Çifte Minare is the Şifaiye Medresesi, or Darüşşifa, a hospital medical school built in the same year as the Çifte Minare by Sultan Keykavus I of the Seljuks, who chose to be buried here. His tomb is just to the right of the entrance. Inside, the court has four *eyvans*, or niche-like rooms; note the remnants of tilework.

Kale Camii Near the Çifte Minare, back toward Konak Meydanı a bit, is the Kale Camii (1580), an Ottoman work constructed under the orders of Sultan Murad III's grand vezir, Mahmut Paşa.

Bürüciye Medresesi & Museum A few steps east of the Kale Camii, near the gazebo with an ablutions fountain up top and a WC beneath, is the Bürüciye Medresesi, built in 1271 (a busy year in Sivas!) by Muzaffer Bürücirdi, who is entombed in it (inside, to the left, with the fine tilework). It now serves as Sivas's museum. As of this writing, it is under renovation, with sacks of cement and stacks of tools here and there. If the door is unlocked, you should have a look inside, as this is the best-preserved building of the three Seljuk works in the park.

Sivas's other sights are south-east of Konak Meydanı along Cemal Gürsel Caddesi and Cumhuriyet Caddesi. Walk to the southern end of the park and turn left (east) onto Cemal Gürsel Caddesi.

Ulu Cami The Ulu Cami, or Great Mosque (1197) is Sivas's oldest building of significance, a large, low room with a forest of 50 columns. The brick minaret was added later. Though it's not as grand as the more imposing Seljuk buildings, it does have charm.

Gök Medrese Just east of the Ulu Cami, turn right (south) on Cumhuriyet Caddesi to reach the Gök Medrese, or Blue Seminary, built in that bumper year of 1271 at the behest of Sahip Ata, the same fellow who funded the Sahip Ata mosque complex in Konya. Although built to the traditional Seljuk *medrese* plan, in this one the fancy embellishments of tiles, brickwork designs and carving are not just on the doorway, but on windows and walls as well. The blue tilework gave the school its name, *gök* (sky) being an old Turkish word for 'blue'. The facade of the building is wild and exuberant in its decoration. If you want to take a photograph, come in the afternoon when the shadows are off it.

Places to Stay

Sivas suffers from lack of tourists. Its hotels do not get much tourist trade, and are therefore not kept well up to touristic standards. There are no hotels near the bus or railway stations.

Places to Stay – bottom end

The cheaper hotels are a bit farther from Konak Meydanı, at the junction of Atatürk Caddesi and Kurşunlu Sokak.

Just at the junction, facing Atatürk Caddesi, is the tidy *Otel Evin* (tel (477) 12 301), Atatürk Caddesi 160, offering rooms with and without washbasin for 2300TL (US$3.22) double, 1700TL (US$2.38) single. Around the corner on Kurşunlu Sokak is the very similar *Otel Yuvam* (tel (477) 13 340), which may be slightly quieter.

If both of these places happen to be full, try the much larger *Otel Çiçek* (tel (477) 14 081 or 15 667), farther east on Atatürk Caddesi. Its facilities are very plain but many of its rooms are quiet and cost only 2100TL (US$2.94) double, 1500TL (US$2.10) single, without private bath.

Places to Stay – middle

Not much fancy in town, just the *Otel Köşk* (KURSHK) (tel (477) 11150), Atatürk Caddesi 11, one short block east of Konak Meydanı, with 44 doubles-with-bath priced at 9500TL (US$13.30); singles cost 6500TL (US$9.10). A buffet breakfast is included in these prices.

Competing with the Köşk for the carriage trade (such as it is) is the *Otel Madımak* (tel (477) 12 489), just around the corner at Belediye Sokak 4. The lobby and restaurant are bright and fancy, though the rooms tend to be plainer and functional. Doubles cost 10,000TL (US$14), singles 6600TL (US$9.24).

The *Otel Sultan* (sool-TAHN) (tel (477) 12 986), Belediye Sokak 18, has 30 double rooms which are sombre and basic, a lift, and hot water heated by the sun. When I stayed there, the sun must not have shone on the heater (though it certainly shined on me), as the water was always cold. Prices are 6850TL (US$9.59) for a double with shower, 6000TL (US$8.40) without; singles cost 4500TL (US$6.30) with bath, 3500TL (US$4.90) without.

Places to Eat

The top two hotels, as usual in these little-touristed towns, have the two fancy restaurants. But for general eating purposes, including breakfast and sweets, try the *Hacı Kasımoğulları Baklava ve Kebap Salonu* at Atatürk Caddesi 17, very near the Otel Köşk. A simple breakfast of yogurt and tea costs a mere 250TL (US$0.35). Lunches and dinners of *kebap*, with some of their own *baklava* for after, cost about 1600TL (US$2.24).

Getting There & Away

As it is on Turkey's main east-west highway, and also a transit point from north to south, Sivas is well served by air, rail and bus.

Air Turkish Airlines (tel (477) 11 147 or 13 687), Belediye Sitesi, H Blok No 7, has flights on Wednesday and Sunday to and from Ankara and İstanbul. There is also a flight from Sivas to Malatya on those same days. An airport bus (350TL, US$0.49) runs you to the airport, departing 105 minutes before flight time.

Rail Sivas is a major rail junction for both east-west and north-south lines. The fastest and most comfortable train is the Mavi Tren (Blue Train), departing Ankara each morning for Malatya via Kayseri and Sivas, returning in the evening.

Otherwise, the two major east-west expresses, the Güney Ekspresi and the Vangölü Ekspresi, pull through Sivas in the middle of the night heading east, and late in the evening heading west, making for inconvenient scheduling.

Prices for rail travel on normal express trains (1st class, 2nd class) are: Ankara (2000TL, US$2.80; 1400TL, US$1.96); Divriği (600TL, US$0.84; 450TL, US$0.63); Diyarbakır or Erzurum (1800TL, US$2.52; 1300TL, US$1.82); Kayseri (800TL, US$1.12; 550TL, US$0.77); Malatya (850TL, US$1.19; 600TL, US$0.84). The Blue Train costs a bit more than the 1st-class rate.

Bus The Sivas Oto Terminalı, like the railway station, has its own PTT branch. This modern bus terminal also has a restaurant and pastry shop, a shoeshine stand and an *emanetçi* (eh-mah-NEHT-chee, baggage checkroom).

Bus traffic is intense in all directions, though many of the buses are passing through, so you can't know what seats are available until a bus arrives. Here's an idea of the schedules and fares: there are buses every hour throughout the day to Kayseri (1300TL, US$1.82, three hours); continuing to Ankara costs a total of 2400TL (US$3.36); to Divriği, a 3½-hour ride, costs 1400TL (US$1.96); to Diyarbakır, the ride takes nine or 10 hours and costs 2200TL (US$3.08). The price for a ticket to Malatya is 1900TL (US$2.66), to Erzurum 2900TL (US$4.06).

DİVRİĞİ

South-east of Sivas, 170 km over roughish roads (but also on the rail line) lies Divriği (DEEV-ree, population 18,000), a town hidden away beyond a mountain pass

1970 metres high, in a fertile valley, and very rarely visited by foreign tourists. Above the town, a ruined castle stands guard over two magnificent Seljuk buildings, the Ulu Cami or Great Mosque, and the Darüşşifa or hospital. Both were built in 1228 by local emir Ahmet Şah and his wife the lady Fatma Turan Melik. They've been beautifully restored and preserved, and there they sit, miles from anywhere, a wonderful work of art hidden away in the boondocks.

Divriği has a few extremely basic lodging places, simple restaurants and banks for changing money.

Things to See
Both of Divriği's architectural treasures are actually part of the same grand structure. Say 'Ulu Cami' (OO-loo jahmee) to anyone in town, and they'll point the way up the hill to the complex.

Ulu Cami The portal of the Ulu Cami is simply incredible, with geometric patterns, medallions, luxuriant stone foliage and intricate Arabic-letter inscriptions in a richness that simply astonishes. It is the sort of doorway which only a provincial emir, with more money than restraint, would ever conceive of building. In a large Seljuk city, this sort of extravagance would have been ridiculed as lacking in taste. Here in Divriği, it's the wonderful, fanciful whim of a petty potentate shaped in stone.

The portal is most of what there is to see. Seljuk buildings were traditionally quite plain outside, other than the portals. There is a side door on the south wall. Past it, to the south-east, is the door to the Darüşşifa.

Darüşşifa Adjoining the Ulu Cami is the hospital, plainer and simpler except for its requisite elaborate portal. The octagonal pool in the court has a spiral run-off, similar to the one in Konya's Karatay Medresesi, which allowed the soothing tinkle of running water to break the silence of the room.

Seljuk Tombs As this was once an important provincial capital, you will notice a number of hexagonal or octagonal drum-like structures throughout the town. These are the traditional Seljuk tombs, or *kümbet*. Ahmet Şah's tomb is near the Ulu Cami, as are several earlier ones from 1196 and another dating from 1240.

A Walk About Town The town is nice, an old-fashioned Turkish mountain town based on agriculture. Its narrow streets are laced with grapevines and paved in stone blocks, its houses still uncrowded by modern construction. It is a pleasant enough place to spend a few hours, which you may have to do if you came by bus or rail.

Places to Stay
Even the lowest of low budgeteers will have to make hard decisions once they look at the hotels in Divriği. But at least there are hotels.

The *Otel Ninni* (tel 1239) charges 1500TL (US$2.10) for a double without water; the common shower and toilet are down one flight from some of the rooms. The *Hotel Değer* next door is even more basic. Both hotels are on the main commercial street in the centre of town.

Getting There
With your own car, you can drive in and out; there is no road through. Over half of the distance from Sivas is on a stabilized road of crushed stone. In spring, late autumn and winter the road may be slippery, washed out, difficult or snowed over.

Rail The rail line from Sivas to Erzurum passes through Divriği, and if you catch the morning Mehmetçik Ekspresi departing Sivas at 6.20 am (though it may be late) you should arrive at a reasonable hour, as the trip is scheduled to take about four hours. The return train of the same name departs Divriği at 8.40 pm, arriving in Sivas a half-hour after midnight. A single ticket costs 600TL (US$0.84) 1st class, 450TL (US$0.63) 2nd class.

You may, of course, continue eastward by train from Divriği to Erzurum, about 6½ hours away, though you will probably have to stay overnight and catch the Mehmetçik the following day.

The Divriği railway station is about two km from the Ulu Cami, south of the centre.

Bus Three or four buses run between Divriği and Sivas daily, continuing to Ankara and İstanbul. The trip between Sivas and Divriği takes about 3½ hours and costs 1500TL (US$2.10). Divriği has no formal bus station, just a large car park next to the market.

Coming from Malatya, you can take a bus as far as Kangal, near the turning for Divriği, and wait for the Divriği bus to stop on its way through.

ŞANLIURFA

Dry, dusty and hot is the way Şanlıurfa (altitude 540 metres, population 207,000) appears at first glance. You may find yourself asking, 'What importance could such a town, in the middle of nowhere, possibly have?' When you get to know Urfa (as it's commonly called), you'll find that it is known for a shady park with several pools, a richness of agricultural produce, a cool and inviting labyrinthine bazaar, and its great historical importance.

Urfa is the Ottoman Empire come alive. In the shadow of a mighty medieval fortress, saintly old men toss chick peas into a pool full of sacred carp, or gather at a cave said to be the birthplace of Abraham. In the cool darkness of the covered bazaar, shopkeepers sit on low platforms in front of their shops, as was the custom in Ottoman times. The chatter of Turkish is joined by a babble of Kurdish and Arabic, with the occasional bit of English, French or German.

You must spend at least one night in Urfa, and allow a full day, or at least a morning, to see the sights and get lost in the bazaar. You may also want to make an excursion south to Harran, the Biblical town of beehive houses near the Syrian frontier, though this can be expensive.

History

The mysterious laws of geography ruled that this dusty spot would be where great empires clashed and clashed again over the centuries. Far from Cairo, Tehran and Constantinople, this was nevertheless where the armies directed from those distant capitals would often meet. Urfa's history, then, is one of being wrecked.

Urfa has been baking in the sun for a long time. It is thought that there was a fortress here, on the hill where the *kale* (citadel) now stands, over 3500 years ago. Called Hurri (cave) by the Babylonians, the people were able to build a powerful state by military conquest because they knew what a chariot was, and how to use it in battle (few of their neighbours had heard of the chariot's invention). But the Hittites finally got the better of the Hurrites, despite the latter's alliance with the pharaohs of Egypt. Around 1370 BC, the Hittites took over. After the fall of Hattuşaş, Urfa came under the domination of Carchemish.

The alliance with Egypt produced an interesting cultural exchange. After Amenhotep IV (Akhenaton) popularised worship of the sun as the unique and only god, a similar worship of Shemesh (the sun) was taken up here. Sun-worship (one would think it might be shade worship instead!) was not just a religious belief, but a political posture: it defied the cultural, political and religious influence of the Hittites, who were too close for comfort, by adopting customs of the Egyptians, who were a safe distance away.

After a period of Assyrian rule, Alexander the Great came through. He and his Macedonian mates named the town Edessa, after a former capital of Macedonia, and it remained capital of a Seleucid province until 132 BC, when the local Aramaean population set up an independent kingdom and renamed the town Orhai. Though Orhai maintained a precarious independence for four centuries, bowing only slightly to the Armenians and Parthians, it finally succumbed to the Romans, as did everyone hereabouts. The Romans did not get it easily, however. Emperor Valerian was badly defeated here in 260 AD, and had a hard time of it over the centuries, keeping the Persians out.

Edessa pursued its contrary history (witness the sun-worship) by adopting Christianity at a very early time (around 200 AD), before it was the official religion of the conquerors. The religion was so new that for Edessan Christians the liturgical language was Aramaic, the language of Jesus, and not the Greek on which the church's greatness was built. Edessa, having pursued Christianity on its own from earliest times, had its own patriarch. It revelled in the Nestorian monophysite heresies as yet another way to thumb its nose at its faraway rulers, whose armies so often tromped through and flattened everything.

Edessa was at the outer edge of the Roman Empire near the frontier with Persia, and as the two great empires clashed, Edessa was shuttled back and forth from one to the other, as in a tug-of-war. In 533 the two empires signed a 'Treaty of Endless Peace', which lasted for seven years. The Romans and Persians kept at it until the Arabs swept in and cleared them all out (637 AD). Edessa enjoyed three centuries of blissful peace under the Arabs, after which everything went to blazes again.

Turks, Arabs, Armenians and Byzantines battled for Edessa from 944 till 1098, when the First Crusade under Count Baldwin of Boulogne arrived to set up the Latin County of Edessa. This odd European feudal state lasted until 1144, when it was conquered by a Seljuk Turkish emir. The 'loss' of Edessa infuriated the Pope, who called for the Second Crusade – which, by the way, never even set foot near Edessa, and in fact accomplished little except to discredit itself. But the Latin county made its mark in history by giving Europeans a look at Eastern architecture. Some of what they saw would turn up later in the Gothic style.

The Seljuk Turkish emir, of the Zengi family, was succeeded by Saladin, then by the Mamelukes. The Ottomans under Selim the Grim conquered most of this region in the early 1500s, but Edessa did not become Urfa until 1637, when the Ottomans finally took over.

As for its modern sobriquet, Urfa became Şanlıurfa ('Glorious Urfa') only about a decade ago. Even since the War of Independence, when 'Heroic Antep' was given its special name, the good citizens of Urfa have been chafing under a relative loss of dignity. Now that their city is 'Glorious,' the inhabitants can look the citizens of 'Heroic' Antep straight in the eye.

Orientation

Except in the bazaar, it is fairly easy to find your way around Urfa. You will see the *kale* to the south as you enter the town along the highway from Gaziantep or Diyarbakır. The Otogar is next to the highway by a streambed (usually dry). City buses (40TL, US$0.06) operate from the Otogar through the centre of town. Ask to go to the Belediye for most hotels and the tourism office, or to Dergâh (dehr-GYAH), also called Gölbaşı (GURL-bah-shuh), for the mosques, pools and bazaar. The latter is 1½ km from the Otogar. A taxi from the Otogar to either place should cost only 400TL (US$0.56).

Once in town from the Otogar, you should be able to walk to everything.

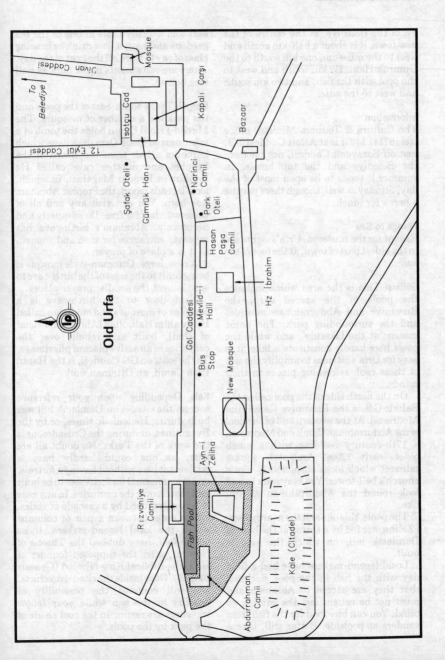

Old Urfa

To Belediye

Divan Caddesi

Mosque

Kapalı Çarşı

İsotçu Cad

12 Eylül Caddesi

Bazaar

Şafak Oteli

Gümrük Hanı

Narinci Camii

Park Oteli

Hasan Paşa Camii

Mevlid-i Halil

Göl Caddesi

Hz İbrahim

Bus Stop

New Mosque

Ayn-i Zeliha

Rızvaniye Camii

Fish Pool

Kale (Citadel)

Abdurrahman Camii

From the Belediye, at the centre of the new town, it is about a half-km north and west to the museum, one km south to the Gümrük Hanı, 1½ km south and west to the pool with the fish, and two km south and west to the *kale*.

Information

The Culture & Tourism Ministry office (tel (8711) 2467) is at Asfalt Caddesi 3/B, just off Sarayönü Caddesi, not far from the Belediye and the top hotels. In summer it tends to be open most of the day, Sunday as well, though there may be a break for lunch.

Things to See

Except for the museum, Urfa's sights are in the oldest part of town, at the foot of the *kale*.

Gölbaşı This is the area which includes the pools of the sacred carp, the Rızvaniye and Abdurrahman mosques and the surrounding park. The name means 'at the lakeside', and while the pools here hardly constitute a lake, it is easy for Urfa's citizens to amplify the size of these cool, refreshing places in their minds.

On the north side of the pool called the Balıklı Göl is the Rızvaniye Camii and Medresesi. At the western end of the pool is the Abdurrahman Camii and Medresesi, a 17th-century building with a much older (early 1200s) Arab-style square minaret which looks suspiciously like a church's bell-tower. You may walk in and look round the Abdurrahman as you like.

The pools, this one and the nearby Ayn-i Zeliha, are fed by a spring at the base of Damlacık hill, on which the *kale* is built.

Local legend-makers have had a field day with the fish in the pool, deciding that they are sacred to Abraham and must not be caught lest the catcher go blind. You can buy food for the fish from vendors at poolside. Better still, take a seat and a shady table in one of the tea gardens and have a cool drink or bracing glass of çay to ward off the heat of the day. There are restaurants in the park as well (see below).

Dergâh To the south-east of the pools and the park are a number of mosques. The Mevlid-i Halil Camii holds the tomb of a saint named Dede Osman, a cave which harbours a hair from the Beard of the Prophet and another cave called Hz İbrahim'in Doğum Mağarası, in which, local legends report, the Prophet Abraham was born. You can visit any and all of these wonders for free. Do so quietly and decorously. Abraham's birth-cave has separate entrances for men and women, as it is a place of prayer.

A new, large, Ottoman-style mosque is being built to the west of the birth-cave to supplement the smaller prayer places.

Next door to the birth-cave is a complex of mosques and *medreses* called Hz İbrahim Halilullah (Abraham, Friend of God), built and rebuilt over the centuries as an active place of pilgrimage. To the east, on Göl Caddesi, is the Hasan Paşa Camii, an Ottoman work.

Kale Depending upon your reference source, the citadel on Damlacık hill was built during Hellenistic times, or by the Byzantines, or during the Crusades, or is the work of the Turks. No doubt all are true, as one could hardly have a settlement here without having a fortress, and it was normal for fortresses to be built and rebuilt over the centuries. In any case it is vast, reached by a cascade of stairs.

You enter between a pair of columns which the local legend-makers, those active folk, have dubbed the Throne of Nemrut, after the supposed founder of Urfa, the Biblical King Nimrod (Genesis 10:8-10). Once inside the citadel precincts, you will confront the possibility of broiling in the sun while your fellow travellers are resting in the cool shade of the park by the pools.

Top: İshan Paşa Palace, Doğubeyazıt
Bottom: Nomad's tent, Doğubeyazıt

Top: Jumbled headstones atop Nemrut Dağı (Mt Nimrod)
Bottom: Mosque inscription, Antalya

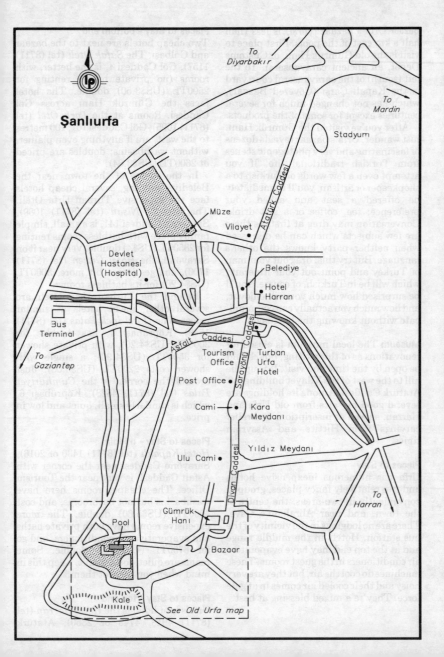

Şanlıurfa

To Diyarbakır

To Mardin

Stadyum

Müze

Vilayet

Atatürk Caddesi

Devlet
Hastanesi
(Hospital)

Belediye

Hotel
Harran

Bus
Terminal

Asfalt   Caddesi

Saraÿönü   Caddesi

To
Gaziantep

Tourism
Office

Turban
Urfa
Hotel

Post Office

Cami

Kara
Meydanı

Yıldız Meydanı

Ulu Cami

Divan Caddesi

To
Harran

Gümrük
Hanı

Pool

Bazaar

Kale

See Old Urfa map

Bazaar Urfa's bazaar *(çarşı)* is less than half a km east of the pools. First place to visit is the old Gümrük Hanı, or Customs Depot, an ancient caravanserai. To the left (south) of the caravanserai courtyard is the Kapalı Çarşı (Covered Bazaar), which has not changed much for several centuries except for some of the products.

After you've visited the Gümrük Hanı, just wander. Urfa's bazaar reveals dozens of fascinating and very photogenic scenes from Turkish traditional life. If you attempt even a few words of Turkish to a shopkeeper or artisan, you'll immediately be offered a seat and asked your preference: tea, coffee or a soft drink. Conversation may drag at first, as there are few subjects which can be discussed when neither party knows the other's language. But try this: drag out your map of Turkey and point out your itinerary, which will be in Turkish, of course. You'll be surprised how much you will enjoy it, and how much you actually can communicate without knowing the language.

Museum The local museum is closed for renovations as of this writing, but should be open by the time you visit. It is up the hill to the west of the Vilayet building, off Atatürk Caddesi. Among its holdings are several good mosaics from old Urfa and Harran, as well as inscriptions and relief carvings from Hittite and Assyrian times.

Places to Stay

Urfa has numerous inexpensive hotels and two relatively fancy places, grouped conveniently in two areas: the centre of the town, and near Abraham's Cave. There are no lodgings in the vicinity of the bus station. Hotels in the middle range and at the top end may have evaporative air conditioners in the guest rooms. These machines do cool the air, but they are very noisy and their cooled air comes in at gale force. They're a mixed blessing at best.

Places to Stay – bottom end

Two cheap hotels are next to the bazaar and Gölbaşı. The *Şafak Oteli* (tel (8711) 1157), Göl Caddesi 4, is the better, with rooms (no private baths) renting for 2500TL (US$3.50) double. The hotel faces the Gümrük Hanı across Göl Caddesi. Rooms at the *Park Otel* (tel (8711) 1095), Göl Caddesi 101, 100 metres to the west, are if anything even plainer, without washbasins; doubles are priced at 2600TL (US$3.64).

In the centre of the town near the Belediye building, several cheap hotels face the expensive Turban Urfa Oteli. The *Otel 11 Nisan* (tel (8711) 1089), Sarayönü Caddesi 141, is a small, simple family place with bathless rooms renting for 2850TL (US$4) double. Very near it on Sarayönü, the *Hotel Güven* (tel (8711) 1700), charges just a bit more, 3000TL (US$4.20) for its bathless rooms.

Behind the Turban Urfa Oteli are several other cheap hotels at similar prices. The *Hotel İpek Palas* (tel (8711) 1546), Köprübaşı 4, has doubles for 3000TL (US$4.20), with private shower for 3500TL (US$4.90); a single with shower costs 2200TL (US$3.08). Just around the corner is the *Cumhuriyet Palas* (tel (8711) 4828), Köprübaşı 6, which is similarly small, quiet and low in price.

Places to Stay – middle

Hotel Kapaklı (tel (8711) 1430 or 2016), Sarayönü Caddesi near the corner with Asfalt Caddesi, is very near the Tourism Office. The cheaper rooms here have washbasins but not bathrooms, and cost 4000TL (US$5.60) double. The more expensive rooms have both private baths and evaporative air conditioners, and go for 6750TL (US$9.45) double. Some rooms are quiet, some aren't. Keep this in mind when you inspect them.

Places to Stay – top end

Urfa's best hotel is the *Hotel Harran* (tel (8711) 4918, 4743 or 2860), Atatürk

Bulvarı, directly across from the Belediye. All 54 rooms have evaporative air conditioners and private bathrooms, and some have television sets and refrigerators. The hotel also has its own terrace restaurant and a Turkish bath. This is a favourite haunt of Arab tourists and businessmen. Rates of 12,000TL (US$16.80) single, 15,000TL (US$21) double.

A few steps to the south is the *Turban Urfa Oteli* (tel (8711) 3520 or 3521), with 53 rooms, all with telephones, twin beds and private shower baths. Some of the guest rooms, as well as the lobby, restaurant and bar, are air conditioned. Prices include breakfast and air conditioning: 7350TL (US$10.29) single, 9750TL (US$13.65) double. A 14% reduction is in order for rooms without air conditioning, and for all rooms October through April. The staff have a reputation for brusqueness.

Places to Eat

Urfa's culinary specialties include *çiğ köfte*, minced uncooked mutton; *içli köfte*, a deep-fried croquette with a mutton filling; *Urfa kebap*, skewered chunks of lamb, or ground lamb rissoles, broiled on charcoal and served with tomatoes, sliced onions and hot peppers. For a snack, try *künefe*, a sweet pastry with a cheese filling.

Places to Eat – bottom end

Inexpensive eateries are plentiful, and the richest concentration of them is near the Hotel İpek Palas and Cumhuriyet Palas on Köprübaşı Çarşısı. The *Güney Lokantası* (tel 2237) at 3/D is an example. Ceiling fans keep the hot air moving, refrigerated cases keep the drinks cold, its location keeps the noise at bay, and the chef fills his steam table with various stews, vegetable dishes, *pilavs* and soups each day. A simple meal of *tas kebap* (mutton and vegetable stew), beans, bread and soft drink costs about 650TL (US$0.91). Other, similar restaurants are only a few steps away.

Perhaps the most pleasant place for an inexpensive meal is in the park at Göbaşı. The *Göl Restaurant & Çay Evi*, next to the Balıklı Göl, has a family dining area, a videocasette player and a prohibition against alcoholic beverages. Tea costs 50TL (US$0.07), Turkish coffee twice as much, soft drinks three times as much as tea. A three-course lunch is 950TL (US$1.33).

If you're in the market for picnic supplies, stop at the *Uğur Pide Fırını* on Göl Caddesi, where delicious flat *pide* bread comes fresh from the wood-fired oven throughout the day. A loaf costs 100TL (US$0.14). The bakery's official address is 'Akarbaşı Çarşısı'.

Places to Eat – mid-range

Urfa is one of those towns in which the best hotels also hold the best restaurants. There is general agreement that the terrace restaurant of the Hotel Harran is the best place to dine. Service is attentive and polite, food is good, alcoholic beverages are served, and the open-air terrace at the back of the hotel several floors up is very pleasant. All this comes at a price, however. A dinner of *tavuk şiş* (chicken brochettes) with a mixed salad, bread and beer will cost about 3500TL (US$4.90).

Getting There

Though Urfa is supposedly served by rail, the station is at Akçakale on the Syrian frontier, 50 km south of the town. The nearest airport is at Diyarbakır. Therefore Urfa is best reached by bus.

Bus As it is on the main highway serving the south-east, Urfa has plenty of bus traffic. The 190-km trip to Diyarbakır takes 2½ or three hours and costs about 1500TL (US$2.10). To Mardin, the 175-km trip along a very busy road presently being widened and improved takes about three hours and costs 1500TL (US$2.10).

HARRAN

And Terah took Abram his son, and Lot the son of Haran his son's son, and Sarai his daughter in law, his son Abram's wife; and they went forth with them from Ur of the Chaldees, to go into the land of Canaan; and they came unto Harran, and dwelt there.

Genesis 11:31

So says the Bible about Harran's most famous resident, who stayed here for a few years back in 1900 BC. It seems certain that Harran is one of the oldest continuously inhabited spots on earth. Today, its ruined walls and Ulu Cami, its crumbling fortress and bee-hive houses give it a feeling of deep antiquity.

Harran's ancient monuments are interesting, though not really impressive. It is more the lifestyle of the residents that you may find fascinating. They live by farming and smuggling, and now await expectantly the completion of the Atatürk Barajı (dam), which will bring water to the irrigation system now under construction. Once the longed-for waters arrive, farming might actually become safer and more profitable than smuggling.

History

Besides Abraham's sojourn, Harran is famous as a centre of worship of Sin, god of the moon. Worship of the sun, moon and planets was popular hereabouts, in Harran and neighbouring Sumatar, from about 800 BC till 830 AD, though Harran's temple to the moon-god was destroyed by the Byzantine Emperor Theodosius in 382 AD. Battles between Arabs and Byzantines amused the townfolk until the coming of the Crusaders. When the Frankish armies approached, the fortress, built (some say) on the ruins of the moon-god's temple, was restored. The Crusaders won, and maintained the fortress for a time before they, too, moved on.

Things to See

Before even reaching the town you'll see the hill surrounded by crumbling walls and topped with ruined buildings. The most impressive of the ruins, in which some good mosaics were found, is the Ulu Cami built in the 700s by Marwan II, last of the Umayyad caliphs.

On the far (east) side of the hill is the fortress, in the midst of the bee-hive houses. As soon as you arrive, children will run up to you and crowd around, demanding coins, candy, cigarettes, empty water bottles and pens. Whether you pass out some treats or not, they'll continue their demands. Expect to have an escort as you tour the ruins.

Several of the residents are happy to welcome foreign visitors, have their photographs taken and show you their homes. A tip is not really expected, but a small gift would be in order, preferably something from your home country. If you take a photograph, send a copy to your hosts.

Getting There

If you have your own car, you must go to Harran for sure. Without a car, you must decide whether the three to four-hour, 100-km return trip by taxi (11,000TL, US$15.40) is worth the money.

Harran is now officially called Altınbaşak, though you will see signs in both names. Leave Urfa by the Akçakale road at the south-east and go 37 km to a turning left (east). From the turning, it's another 10 km to Harran.

MARDİN

East of Urfa 175 km, south of Diyarbakır 100 km, lies Mardin (mahr-DEEN, altitude 1325, population 40,000), an odd antique of a town crowned with a castle and a set of immense radar domes, all overlooking the vast, roasted Syrian plains. There is a certain amount of smuggling trade with Syria (sheep for instance, which are much more expensive in Syria than in Turkey) and Kurdish separatist activity, but other than that, Mardin sizzles and sleeps.

This town had a large Christian community, and there are still a few Syriac Christian families and churches here. On the outskirts is the monastery of Deyrul Zafaran, in which Aramaic – the language of Jesus – is still used as the liturgical tongue.

Mardin is not particularly well equipped with hotels and restaurants, and is perhaps best visited on a day-trip from Diyarbakır if you prize your comforts. Travelling on the cheap, it makes sense to take a bus from Urfa to Mardin, stay the night here if you're in no hurry, then take a minibus north to Diyarbakır.

History

The history of Mardin, like that of Diyarbakır, involves disputes by rival armies over dozens and dozens of centuries, though now nobody cares. A castle stood on this hill from time immemorial. Assyrian Christians settled in this area during the 5th century. In the 6th century, Jacobus Baradeus, bishop of Edessa (Urfa), had a difference of opinion with the patriarch in Constantinople over the divine nature of Christ. The patriarch and official doctrine held that Christ had both a divine and a human nature. The bishop held that he had only one (mono-) nature (physis), that being divine. The bishop was branded a Monophysite heretic, and excommunicated. He promptly founded a church of his own, which came to be called the Jacobite (or Syrian Orthodox) after its founder. At the same time, and for the same reason, the Armenian Orthodox Church and the Coptic Church in Egypt were established as independent. In the case of the Jacobites, control from Constantinople became a non-problem soon afterwards when the Arabs swept in and took control. The Monophysites were able to practice their religion as they chose under the tolerant and unconcerned rule of the Arabs.

The Arabs occupied Mardin between 640 and 1104. After that, it had a succession of Seljuk Turkish, Kurdish, Mongol and Persian overlords until the Ottomans under Sultan Selim the Grim took it in 1517.

Orientation

Perched on the slope of its hill, Mardin has one long main street, Birinci Cadde, running for about two km from the Belediye Garajı at the western end of town through Cumhuriyet Meydanı, the main square, to Konak, a small square with the local government headquarters (Hükümet Konağı) and military buildings, at the eastern end. Everything you'll need is along this street or just off it. City buses (40TL, US$0.06) and Şehiriçi (intra-city) dolmuşes (50TL, US$0.07) run back and forth along the street. If you are driving, leave you car in the car park at Cumhuriyet Meydanı (200TL, US$0.28) and walk to the hotels and things to see.

Information

There is no Tourism Information Office in Mardin because it has few tourists.

Things to See

The prime attraction in the town is the **Sultan İsa Medresesi** (1385). Walk east from the main square to the Hotel Başak Palas, then left (north) up the stairs to a large and imposing doorway. The doorway is what you have come to see, as there is little to see inside; the ancient building is used in part as a private residence. The **Mardin Müzesi** (tel 1664) is set up in one courtyard of the *medrese*. Enter at the door with the flagpole and sign. You may have to shout for the *bekçi* (BEHK-chee, watchman). Hours are 8.30 am to 5.30 pm every day; admission is free. The museum holds bits of statuary, but you've really come to admire the building and the view across the vast, fertile plains to Syria.

The **Kasım Paşa Medresesi** (1400s) is near the western end of the town, below the main street. You'll have to ask for guidance to find it.

The ancient **Ulu Cami** (1000s), an Iraqi Seljuk structure, is below (south of) the main street at Cumhuriyet Meydanı. As Mardin's history has been mostly one of warfare, the mosque has suffered considerably over the centuries, particularly in the Kurdish rebellion of 1832.

Deyrul Zafaran In the rocky hills east of the town, six km along a narrow but good road, is the monastery of Mar Hanania, called Deyrul Zafaran, 'the Saffron Monastery' in Arabic, perhaps from the tawny colour of its stone walls. It was once the seat of the Syrian Orthodox patriarch. Though the patriarchate's seat is now Damascus, the monastery still has the modest trappings due the patriarch, and continues its charitable work of caring for orphans.

You can visit the monastery any day without prior arrangement. As there is no public transport, you must take a taxi from the centre for about 2000TL (US$2.80). Haggle for a set price to include the return journey and about 45 minutes' waiting.

As you drive toward the monastery, you will doubtless notice a hillside on which a motto has been written with white stones: 'Ne Mutlu Türküm Diyene' (What Joy to Him Who Says, 'I am a Turk'). Atatürk originally uttered the phrase as part of his campaign to overcome the Turkish inferiority complex imposed by Europe and America. Here, though, it has a different significance, reiterating the government's commitment to the unity of the country against the efforts of Kurdish separatist groups.

Enter the walled enclosure through a portal bearing a Syriac inscription, and an Orthodox priest will greet you and hand you over to one of the orphans for a guided tour.

First comes the underground chamber, an eerie place with a flat ceiling of huge, closely fitted stones held up by magic, without the aid of mortar. It is thought that this room may have been used ages ago by sun-worshippers, who viewed their 'god' rising through a window at the eastern end. A niche on the southern wall is said to have been for sacrifices.

The guide then leads you to the tombs of the patriarchs and metropolitans who have served here. The doors to the room are 300 years old.

In the chapel, to the left of the altar as you face it, is the patriarch's throne. It bears the names of all the patriarchs who have served here since the monastery was founded in 792. To the right of the altar is the throne of the metropolitan. The present stone altar was carved to replace a wooden one which burnt about a half-century ago. A candle started the fire. The chapel is fairly plain and simple, but the primitive art is wonderful! Note the carved furniture and especially the paintings. Services here use the original Aramaic.

The next rooms on the tour hold several litters used to transport the church dignitaries, and also one of several wells in the monastery. In a small side room is a 300-year-old wooden throne. The mosaic work in the floor is about 1500 years old.

A flight of stairs takes you up to the suite of guest rooms, which is very simple accommodation for travellers and those coming for a period of meditation. The patriarch's suite, a small, simple bedroom and parlour, are here. On the walls of the parlour are pictures of the patriarch (who lives in Damascus) with Pope John Paul II. Another picture shows an earlier patriarch with Atatürk. As you leave the parlour, take a moment to enjoy the fine view of the mountains. Other monasteries, now in ruins, stood farther up the slope. Some of the water for Deyrul Zafaran comes from near these ruins, through underground channels excavated many centuries ago.

At the end of the tour, you may want to tip the guide. He'll refuse at first, but will probably accept when you offer a second or third time.

Places to Stay

All of Mardin's hotels are very basic and very cheap, and few are really pleasant.

East of Cumhuriyet Meydanı are several small, modest hotels, such as the *Yıldız Oteli* (tel 1096), Birinci Cadde 391, where plain rooms without plumbing go for 2200TL (US$3.08) double, 1450TL (US$2.03) single. The public showers are cold water only.

The *Hotel Bayraktar* (tel 1338 or 1645) is on the main street facing Cumhuriyet Meydanı, with its other side overlooking the plains. It is Mardin's best, with 50 rooms on eight floors reached by a lift, and a terrace restaurant where the notables gather. All rooms have showers and rent for 3500TL (US$4.90) double.

In the unlikely event that both of these hotels are full, continue east to the *Hotel Başak Palas* and the even simpler *Hotel Şirin Palas*, on the main street beneath the Sultan İsa Medresesi.

Places to Eat

The only real restaurant is the one in the *Hotel Bayraktar* (tel 1647), which overlooks the square. It is nothing special, but it's what there is. Ask prices here before you order, as my simple meal turned out to be surprisingly expensive at 2000TL (US$2.80).

There are a number of small, very inexpensive eateries east of the Bayraktar along the main street. I would ask prices first here, as well.

Getting There

Several buses a day run from Urfa to Mardin. As for transport to and from Diyarbakır, this is by minibus. They run about every hour between Mardin's Belediye Garajı and Diyarbakır's Mardin Kapısı (Mardin Gate, in the city walls), for 500TL (US$0.70). The 100-km journey takes about 1¾ hours.

DİYARBAKIR

The Tigris (Dicle, DEEJ-leh) flows by the mighty black walls of Diyarbakır (dee-YAHR-bah-kuhr, altitude 660 metres, population 250,000). As with many Turkish cities, this one has grown beyond its ancient walls only in the last few decades. Farming, stock-raising, some oil prospecting and light industry provide Diyarbakır with its income.

The city prides itself especially on its watermelons. 'In olden times', states a brochure printed up for the annual Watermelon Festival (held in late September), 'our watermelons had to be transported by camel as they weighed 90 or 100 kg. They were carved with a sword and sold in the market'. The brochure goes on to say that these days the prize-winning melons at the festival weigh a 'mere' 40 to 60 kg!

Today this city, lying in the midst of a vast, lonely plain, is like a desert oasis full of traders. Many of the men wear the traditional baggy trousers called *şalvar* (SHAHL-vahr), and older women have black head coverings which often serve unofficially as veils. Visiting men from Syria and Iraq have the long robes *(jallabiya)* and headscarves *(keffiye)* of Arab lands, and the women may even be in purdah, wearing the black *chadoor*.

The tawdry chaos of signs at the city's centre, the narrow alleys, the mosques in the Arab style with black-and-white banding in the stone – all these give Diyarbakır a foreign, frontier feeling. The citizens tend to be taciturn and not particularly outgoing in their dealings with foreigners, and the street urchins are pestilential. In summer it's *hot* here; avoid hotel rooms just beneath the building's roof, or rooms that get full late afternoon sun.

History

Considering that Mesopotamia, the land between the Tigris and Euphrates valleys, saw the dawn of the world's first great empires, it's no surprise that Diyarbakır's history begins with the Hurrian Kingdom of Mitanni (circa 1500 BC), and proceeds through domination

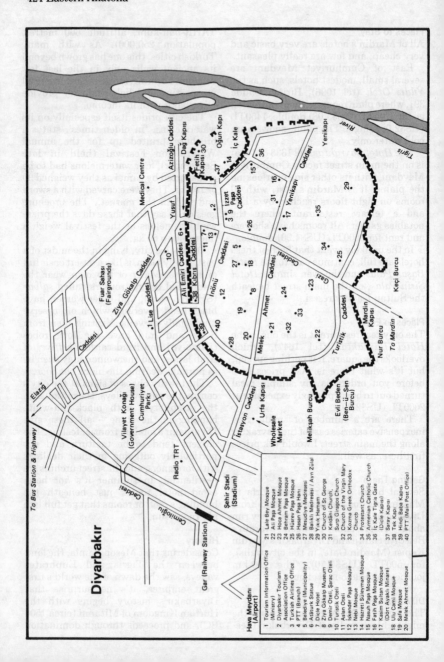

Diyarbakır

To Bus Station & Highway

Elazığ

Cemiloğlu Caddesi

To Mardin

River

Tigris

Azizoğlu Caddesi

Dağ Kapısı

Oğun Kapı

İç Kale

Yenikapı

Medical Centre

Yusuf

Fetih Kapısı

Fuar Sahas (Fairgrounds)

Ziya Gökalp Caddesi

Lise Caddesi

Ali Emiri Caddesi

Kıbrıs Caddesi

İnönü Caddesi

İzzet Paşa Caddesi

Yenikapı Caddesi

Ahmet Caddesi

Gazi Caddesi

Melek Caddesi

Turistik Caddesi

Mardin Kapısı

Keçi Burcu

Nur Burcu

Evli Beden (Ben-ü-Sen Burcu)

Meliksah Burcu

İstasyon Caddesi

Urfa Kapısı

Wholesale Market

Vilayet Konağı (Government House)

Cumhuriyet Parkı

Radio TRT

Şehir Stadı (Stadium)

Gar (Railway Station)

Hava Meydanı (Airport)

1 Tourism Information Office (Ministry)
2 Diyarbakır Tourism Association Office
3 Turkish Airlines Office
4 Dicle (Bank)
5 Belediye (Municipality)
6 Atatürk Statue
7 Dicle Hotel
8 Ziya Gökalp Museum
9 Demir Oteli, Şaraç Oteli
10 Turistik Oteli
11 Aslan Oteli
12 İskender Paşa Mosque
13 Nebi Mosque
14 Hazret Süleyman Mosque
15 Fatih Paşa Mosque
16 Fatih Paşa Mosque
17 Kasım Sultan Mosque (Dört Ayaklı Minare)
18 Ulu Cami Mosque
19 Safa Mosque
20 Melek Ahmet Mosque

21 Lale Bey Mosque
22 Ali Paşa Mosque
23 Hoca Ahmet Mosque
24 Behram Paşa Mosque
25 Hüsrev Paşa Mosque
26 Hasan Paşa Hanı
27 Mesudiye Medresesi
28 Balıklı Medresesi / Ayn Zülal
29 Yıkık Hamam
30 Church of St George
31 Keldâni Church,
    Surp Giragos Church
32 Church of the Virgin Mary
33 Kozma Greek Orthodox
    Church
34 Protestant Church
35 Armenian Catholic Church
36 İç Kale, Tigris Gate
    (Dicle Kapısı)
37 Saray Kapısı
38 Tek Kapı
39 Hindi Baba Kapısı,
40 PTT (Main Post Office)

by the civilisations of Urartu (circa 900 BC), Assyria (1356-612 BC), Persia (600-330 BC), Alexander the Great and his successors the Seleucids. The Romans took over in 115 AD, but because of its strategic position the city changed hands numerous times until it was conquered by the Arabs in 639. Until then it had been known as Amida, but the Arabs settled it with the tribe of Beni Bakr, who named their new home Diyar Bakr, 'The Realm of Bakr'.

I'd like to make this city's history simple for you, and say that when it was conquered by the Seljuks (1085) or the Ottomans (1515) it became a peaceful place, but this isn't so. Because it stands right in the way of invading armies from Anatolia, Persia and Syria, it got clobbered a lot more. It is still a bit unsettled, for south-eastern Turkey has a large Kurdish population. The authorities in Ankara want the Kurds, who are Muslims, to assimilate, and will not permit any talk of secession. Among the Kurds there are nationalists who dream of a Kurdish state encompassing the areas in Turkey, Syria, Iraq and Iran where there are large populations of Kurds.

Orientation

Though the city has grown, your concern is with the old part within the walls, except for the bus and rail stations west of the old city.

Old Diyarbakır has a standard Roman town plan, with the rough circle of walls pierced by four gates at the north, south, east and west. From the gates, avenues travel to the centre, where they all meet. Since Roman times, several sections of wall have been razed and a few new gates opened.

The railway station (Gar) is at the western end of İstasyon Caddesi. From the station, this street travels east to the Urfa Kapısı (OOR-fah kah-puh-suh, Edessa Gate), the city's eastern gate. Inside the walls, the continuation of

İstasyon Caddesi is named Melek Ahmet Caddesi, or sometimes Urfa Caddesi. To go downtown from the station, walk out the front door, go to the first big street, and wait on the left (north-east) corner of the far side for a dolmuş going to Dağ Kapısı.

The bus station (Otogar) is north-east of the city where Elazığ Caddesi (also called Ziya Gökalp Bulvarı) intersects the highway. Travel along Elazığ Caddesi to the centre and you will pass the Turist Oteli just before penetrating the walls at the Dağ Kapısı (DAAH kah-puh-suh, Mountain Gate), the northern gate, sometimes also called the Harput Kapısı. From this gate, Gazi Caddesi leads to the centre. To get downtown from the Otogar, take a dolmuş (60TL, US$0.08) to Dağ Kapısı, 3½ km away. Don't let them tell you that there are no dolmuşes, and that you must take a taxi.

Information

The Tourism Information Office (tel (8311) 12173 or 17840) is in the new city north of the walls at Lise Caddesi 24, Onur Apartımanı. Ask for 'LEE-seh jah-deh-see', which runs west from Elazığ Caddesi about three blocks north of the Dağ Kapısı. The office is about 3½ blocks along.

Things to See

As the old walls are so extensive (almost six km long), perhaps the most delightful way to tour them is in a horse-drawn carriage, called a *fayton* (FAH-yee-tohn, Phaeton). The going rate is about 4000TL (US$5.60), but you may have to haggle for this. Your driver may be able to explain a few things to you in English.

The Walls The historic names for the gates in the walls are the Harput Kapısı (north), Mardin Kapısı (south), Yenikapı (east) and Urfa Kapısı (west). The massive black basalt walls are defended by 72 bastions and towers, many of them gathered around the İç Kale (EECHkaleh, Citadel or Keep) at the north-east corner, overlooking the Tigris. Of the gates, the Harput Kapısı (Dağ Kapısı) is in the best condition. Perhaps the most rewarding area of the walls to explore for inscriptions and decoration is the portion between the İç Kale and the Mardin Kapısı, going westward (away from the river).

Though there were Roman and probably earlier walls here, the present ones date from early Byzantine times (330-500 AD).

Mosques Diyarbakır has many mosques, but the most interesting one is the **Ulu Cami**, built in 1091 and extensively restored in 1155 after having been damaged by fire. The mosque is rectangular in plan – Arab-style, not Ottoman. Its founder was Malik Şah, an early sultan of the Seljuks. Across the courtyard from the Ulu Cami is the **Mesudiye Medresesi**, now used as offices.

Museum Diyarbakır's brand-new museum was under construction as this book went to press. It may be open by the time you arrive.

Places to Stay

Diyarbakır's hotels are fairly simple, with no truly luxurious places.

Places to Stay – bottom end

The area around Dağ Kapısı has numerous little inexpensive hotels. Some are on İnönü Caddesi, along with the more expensive places. The *Hotel Köprücü* (KEURP-reu-jeu) (tel (831) 12963, 4), İnönü Caddesi, Birinci Çıkmaz, is on a tiny dead-end street off İnönü Caddesi near the Büyük Otel. Quiet except for the call of the muezzin, it charges 2300TL (US$3.22) for a double without water, 2900TL (US$4.06) for a room with shower.

Just outside the Dağ Kapısı, on Ali Emiri Caddesi just a few steps from Ziya Gökalp Caddesi, is the clean and convenient *Hotel Mehmetoğlu* (mehh-

MEHT-oh-loo) (tel (831) 12851), Ali Emiri Caddesi 2, where a clean double with shower costs only 3000TL (US$4.20).

On İzzet Paşa Caddesi are two more little hotels, the *Surkent Oteli* (SOOR-kent) (tel (831) 16616), İzzet Paşa Caddesi 19, with surprisingly low prices of 1600TL (US$2.24) single, 2600TL (US$3.64) double, with bath. Nearby, at 20/B, is the *Kenan Oteli* (keh-NAHN) (tel (831) 16614), operated by the same people, charging the same prices.

Moving up in quality a little bit, the first choice is the *Hotel Derya* (DEHR-yah) (tel (831) 14966 or 19735), İnönü Caddesi 13, among the recently renovated places in town, less pretentious than some, offering very good value with rooms priced at 5000TL (US$7) single, 7500TL (US$10.50) double, with shower. Next in line is the *Otel Saraç* (sah-RAHCH) (tel (831) 12365), İzzet Paşa Caddesi 16, almost next door to the Demir. Here the 35 rooms are quite simple, but cost only US$11 or US$12 with shower. *Hotel Ertem* (ehr-TEHM) (tel (831) 12972), just across from the Saraç, is very modest, with beds and nothing else in the rooms, but the price for a double is only 1500TL (US$2.10). It's in the centre of town, but beware the top-floor rooms, which are extremely hot in summer.

Kıbrıs Caddesi is the street along the inside of the walls west of Dağ Kapısı. The *Dicle Otel* (DEEJ-leh) (tel (831) 23066, 7), Kıbrıs Caddesi 3, is on the traffic roundabout at the Dağ Kapısı, a semi-modern place charging 4400TL (US$6.16) single, 6600TL (US$9.24) double, with shower. The older *Hotel Aslan* (ahss-LAHN) (tel (831) 13971), Kıbrıs Caddesi 53, is just a few steps from the Dağ Kapısı, and charges 3300TL (US$4.62) single, 5500TL (US$7.70) double, for older rooms.

Places to Stay – middle

Most of the middle-range hotels are on İnönü Caddesi or on its continuation, İzzet Paşa Caddesi. The *Demir Oteli* (deh-MEER) (tel (831) 12 315), İzzet Paşa Caddesi 8, at the intersection with Gazi Caddesi a short distance south of Dağ Kapısı, is the old standard. The 39-room Demir, popular with tour groups, rents its rooms for 7000TL (US$9.80) single, 9000TL (US$12.60) double.

A hotel nearby charges a bit more for similar rooms, but a fancier lobby. The 75-room *Büyük Otel* (beur-YEURK) (tel (831) 15832, 3), İnönü Caddesi 4, has the trappings, but not the comforts, of a luxury hotel for 9500TL (US$13.30) single, 13,000TL (US$18.20) double, with bath.

Just outside the Dağ Kapısı is the veteran 39-room *Turistik Oteli* (too-rees-TEEK) (tel (831) 12 662), Ziya Gökalp Bulvarı 7, older but well-kept, with more spacious public rooms and guest rooms. Prices reflect this extra comfort: with private bath, singles cost 8900TL (US$12.46), doubles cost 15,200TL (US$21.28), triples cost 19,000TL (US$26.60). Try to get a room at the back, because of the street noise.

Places to Eat

In Diyarbakır, *kebap* places are everywhere, and they solve the dining problem easily and cheaply (700TL to 1400TL, US$0.98 to US$1.96) most of the time. Many are near the junction of İnönü/İzzet Paşa and Gazi caddesis, near the above hotels. The *Hacı Baba Kebapçısı*, a few steps inside the Dağ Kapısı, has a portrait of the Founder at the back, a stuffed sheep in the front window.

A stroll along Kıbrıs Caddesi from Dağ Kapısı and the Hotel Dicle westward will reveal several small, cheap places to eat, including the *Büryan Salonu* for *kebaps*, the 7 *Kardeşler* and the *Kent Restaurant*. The *Babaman Lokantasi* (Bah-bah-mahn) (tel 15887), for example, will serve you a *sebzeli kebap* (vegetable-and-lamb stew), *pilav* and soft drink for 800TL (US$1.12). It even has a *yazlık* or summer dining area on the upper level, overlooking the walls and tea gardens.

For slightly fancier meals, head for the hotel restaurants in the *Demir* (a rooftop place) and the *Turistik*. There are also some *pastanes* in the centre, good for breakfast or a snack.

Getting There & Away

Rail Diyarbakır is connected to Ankara and İstanbul by the Kurtalan Ekspresi which runs eastward on Monday, Wednesday, Friday and Saturday, departing Ankara at 6.40 am. Train service is neither frequent nor dependably on time, and you may prefer to take the bus. For reference, a 1st-class rail ticket from Diyarbakır costs: 3300TL (US$4.62) to Ankara, 2500TL (US$3.50) to Erzurum, 4500TL (US$6.30) to Haydarpaşa (İstanbul), 850TL (US$1.19) to Malatya, 1800TL (US$2.52) to Sivas.

Bus Many bus companies have ticket offices downtown on Kıbrıs Caddesi, or in other spots near the Dağ Kapısı.

From Diyarbakır, a bus ticket costs 7000TL (US$9.80) to Ankara (13 hours), 1600TL (US$2.24) to Kâhta (2½ or three hours), 4000TL (US$5.60) to Mersin (10 hours by night), 2000TL (US$2.80) to Şanlıurfa (2½ hours) and 3500TL (US$4.90) to Van (six hours).

Minibuses to Mardin depart not from the Otogar, but from the Mardin Kapısı (gate in the city walls) about every hour for 500TL (US$0.70).

BİTLİS

Travelling eastward from Diyarbakır along Highway 6, 88 km brings you to the town of Silvan, and another 22 km to Malabadi. Just east of the latter town is the Batman Suyu, a stream spanned by a beautiful hump-backed stone bridge built by the Artukid Turks in 1146. It is thought to have the longest span (37 metres) of any such bridge in existence. With that engaging bend in the middle, it's truly a work of art.

Another 235 km brings you to Bitlis (BEET-lees, altitude 1570 metres, population 32,000), an interesting old town squeezed into the narrow valley of a stream. A castle dominates the town; a nice hump-backed bridge, and another old bridge, span the stream. The Ulu Cami here was built in 1126, the Şerefiye Camii and Saraf Han (a caravanserai) in the 1500s. The town was the capital of a semi-autonomous Kurdish principality in late Ottoman times.

Should you need to stay here, the *Hotel Turist* on the highway in the centre of town is very plain but clean.

Walnut trees surround the town, and in autumn children stand by the highway with bags of nuts for sale. Up the hill at the eastern side of the town, on the left (north) side of the road, is an old caravanserai, the Pabsin Hanı, built by the Seljuks in the 1200s. Feel free to stop and have a look around. It's only 26 km to Tatvan, railhead and western port for lake steamers.

TATVAN

From here you can board a steamer to Van (four hours, 500TL, US$0.70; 400TL with the ISIC) at 8 am, noon or 4 pm. Or you can make the journey more quickly by bus around the southern shore (two hours, 1000TL, US$1.40). Tatvan has no really decent lodgings, though the *Hotel Karaman* will do in a pinch; a small *lokanta* is across the street from it.

Though the church at Akdamar is the most important sight on the lake, there are things to see along the northern shore. Refer to the Van section for details.

AKDAMAR

On the 156-km journey along the southern shore from Tatvan to Van, the scenery is beautiful, but there is no reason to stop except at a point two km west of Gevaş, and there you *must* stop to see the 10th-century Church of the Holy Cross, called the Akdamar Kilisesi in Turkish. One of the marvels of Armenian architecture, it is perched on an island in the lake. Motorboats ferry sightseers over.

You can also make this trip as an excursion from Van.

Things to See

In 921, Gagik Artzruni, king of Vaspurakan, built a palace, church and monastery here on the island of Akdamar (or Akhtamar), three km out in the lake. Little remains of the palace and monastery, but the church walls are in superb condition, and the wonderful relief carvings on them are among the masterworks of Armenian art.

If you are familiar with the Bible stories, you'll immediately recognize Adam and Eve, Jonah and the Whale, David and Goliath, Abraham about to sacrifice Isaac (but he sees the heaven-sent ram, with its horns caught in a bush, just in time!), Daniel in the Lions' Den, Sampson, etc. The paintings inside the church are not in the best of shape, but their vagueness and frailty seem in keeping with the shaded, partly ruined interior. The church and its setting are incomparable – don't miss this place. It's one of the major reasons you've come to Eastern Turkey.

Bring your bathing (swimming) equipment on your outing to Akdamar, as there's lake swimming at Edremit (don't swim if you have sunburn or open cuts or sores, as the alkaloid water will burn you intensely).

Getting There

Dolmuşes run from Van to Gevaş and the ferry dock, departing from near the Hotel Akdamar in Van. The fare is 500TL (US$0.70).

Boats to the island (700TL, US$0.98) run about every 30 minutes if traffic warrants, which it usually does in the warm months. (If it doesn't, you may have to charter a boat for a special trip, at 10,000TL, US$14.) The trip takes about 20 minutes.

VAN

At the south-eastern edge of the vast Van

Gölü (VAHN gew-lew), almost 100 km across the water from Tatvan, lies Van (altitude 1725 metres, population 94,000), eastern railhead on the line to Iran and the largest Turkish city east of Diyarbakır and south of Erzurum. Van has several claims to fame. It was the Urartian capital city, and at the Rock of Van near the lakeshore are long cuneiform inscriptions and the skeletal outlines of an ancient city. Van is also the market centre for the Kurdish tribes who live in the mountain fastnesses of extreme south-eastern Turkey.

Orientation

The very centre of Van is the junction of Cumhuriyet Caddesi and Alpaslan/Çavuştepe Caddesi. This is the centre of the commercial district, near which you will find many cheap hotels, a dolmuş to the Rock of Van, and many bus company ticket offices. The new bus terminal is on the north-western outskirts, at the intersection of Alpaslan Caddesi and Abdurrahman Gazi Caddesi.

There are two railway stations, the İskele İstasyon or lakeside Dock Station, and the Şehir İstasyon or City Station. The city station is due north of the centre; the dock station is several km north-east. The Rock of Van (Van Kalesi), the only significant sight, is about five km west of the centre.

Information

The Tourism Information Office (tel (061) 12018) is at the southern end of Cumhuriyet Caddesi, at No 127; they're not particularly helpful here.

Things to See

There are two major sights to see in Van; they are fascinating and very, very old.

Museum Off Cumhuriyet Caddesi not far from the Bayram Oteli is the museum (müze), with some exhibits dating back before Urartian times. Other exhibits include beautiful Urartian gold jewellery, some with amber and coloured glass; Urartian cylindrical seals; and pots from the Old Bronze Age (circa 5000 BC). The Urartu Süsleme Plakaları (jewellery breastplates) from the 800s to 600s BC are particularly fine, as are the bronze belts. Another exhibit has At Gemleri (horse-bits) from the 800s and 700s BC.

In the ethnographic exhibits upstairs are countless kilims, the flat-woven rugs superbly made by the Kurdish and Turkoman tribes who live in the mountains. At the far end of the room is a sedir or low couch such as is found in village houses, covered with traditional crafts.

The museum is open from 9 am to noon and from 1.30 to 5.30 pm; admission costs 400TL (US$0.56), free with an ISIC. Cameras are not permitted in the museum; you must check yours at the door.

Rock of Van Minibuses to Van Kalesi, the Rock of Van, depart from near the intersection of Cumhuriyet and Alpaslan.

On the north side of the rock is the tomb of a Muslim saint, visited frequently by pilgrims. A stairway from the car park at the north-western corner leads to the top, where you can see the fortifications and several cuneiform inscriptions dating from about 800 BC. On the south side is a narrow walkway (now with an iron railing) leading to several funeral chambers cut from the rock. Before reaching them you pass a long cuneiform inscription.

The view south of the rock reveals a flat space broken by the grass-covered foundations of numerous buildings. This was the site of Tushpa, an Urartian city which flourished almost 3000 years ago. The actual foundations you see, however, are those of the old city of Van, destroyed during the upheavals of WW I and the tragedy of the stillborn Armenian republic. The sight is stunning: a dead city, buried as though in a grave.

Shopping In the shops of Van you will see

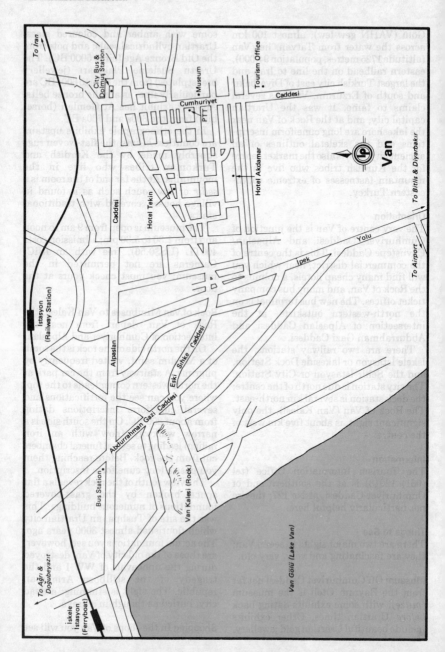

hand-woven craft items – *kilims*, saddle-bags, etc – finer than you've ever seen before. The dealers, however, realize that these finely made things will fetch high prices in Paris, London and New York, so you won't find many bargains. Instead, settle for the finest selection of the finest such items anywhere. Prices for the more normal, common *kilims*, etc will be reasonable. Even if you don't buy (and there is *no obligation* – don't feel pressured!), looking at these crafts is a wonderful experience. Some of the dealers speak English.

Hakkâri The absolute, positive dead end of Turkey is Hakkâri (hah-KYAH-ree, altitude 1700 metres, population 22,000), 210 km south of Van over a zig-zagging mountain road. The scenery is spectacular. There is often trouble in these regions, and the newspapers are full of items about Turkish border guards being killed by smugglers and Kurdish nationalists.

Buses depart daily from Van for Hakkâri. About 58 km from Van, the road passes Güzelsu (Hoşap), with its 17th-century fortress and bridge. At 112 km is Başkale, notable because of its altitude (2450 metres). Yeni Köprü, at 160 km, is the point at which a road goes left for Yüksekova, on the road to Iran, an alternative base for climbs into the mountains. Finally, just over 200 km from Van, you arrive in Hakkâri, which has two small, cheap hotels, the better of which is the *Hotel Çelli*, charging 4000TL (US\$5.60) for a double room; the Çelli also has the best restaurant in town.

Around Lake Van Lake Van is highly alkaline. It was formed when the volcano named Nemrut Dağı (not the one with the statues!) blocked its natural outflow; the water level is now maintained by evaporation, which results in a high mineral concentration in the water. It's not good to drink, but it's fine to swim in, and if you wash your clothes in it, you need no soap!

If you circle the lake, you will pass through **Erciş**, a modern town which covers settlements that date from Urartian times. Continuing west brings you past **Süphan Dağı** (4430 metres high) to **Adilcevaz**, another one-time Urartian town with a ruined castle. At **Ahlat** are numerous *türbes* (tombs), of which the largest is the Ulu Türbe. The castle dates from the reign of Süleyman the Magnificent (mid-1500s).

North of Ahlat some 60 km is **Malazgirt**, the ancient Manzikert, which is hugely important in Turkish history. On 26 August 1071, the Seljuk Turkish Sultan Alp Arslan and his armies decisively defeated the Byzantine emperor, Romanus Diogenes, and took him prisoner. The Byzantine defeat effectively opened Anatolia to Turkish migration and conquest. The Seljuks established themselves in the Sultanate of Rum, and other nomadic Turkish tribes came from Central Asia and Iran to settle here. A band of border warriors following a leader named Osman later spread its influence, and founded a state which would become the vast Ottoman Turkish Empire. It all started here, in 1071, when the heir of the Caesars lost to a Turkish emir.

South-east of Ahlat, near Tatvan, is **Nemrut Dağı** (3050 metres, not to be confused with the Nemrut of the statues, near Adıyaman). This mountain is the volcano which dammed up the outflow of the lake, causing it to take its present vast size of 3750 square km. The crater has a lake in it, and some hot springs.

Places to Stay

Van has a decent, modern, comfortable hotel and a good selection of cheaper places.

Places to Stay – bottom end

The *Bayram Oteli* (BAH-yee-RAHM) (tel (061) 11136, 7), Cumhuriyet Caddesi 1/A, is very near the intersection of Cumhuriyet and Alpaslan. Its 72 rooms with bath go for 3200TL (US\$4.48) single,

4800TL (US$6.72) double. Other services available are a lift, car park, Turkish bath *(hamam)* and TV lounge.

A similar but slightly cheaper place is the *Beşkardeşler Oteli* (BEHSH-kahr-desh-LEHR) (tel (061) 11116), Cumhuriyet Caddesi 34, with 50 bathless rooms for 2750TL (US$3.85) single, 3650TL (US$5.11) double, 5000TL (US$7) triple.

Cheapest of the modernish hotels are the *Kent Oteli* (tel (061) 12404), behind the Türkiye İş Bankası (63 rooms); and the *Çaldıran Oteli* (CHAHL-duh-RAHN) (tel (061) 12718), on Sıhke Caddesi near the Yeni Cami ('New Mosque'), with 48 rooms. Both offer doubles with shower for 4300TL (US$6.02). The Kent has bathless doubles (2800TL, US$3.92) as well.

You can stay at the *Hotel Nuh* for only 750TL (US$1.05) per person, but it is extremely noisy.

Camping There is camping at Edremit, 18 km from Van on the way to Gevaş and Akdamar.

Places to Stay – middle

The best hotel in town is the 75-room *Hotel Akdamar* (AHK-dah-mahr) (tel (061) 3036), Kazım Karabekir Caddesi 56, Van 65200; this street runs west from Cumhuriyet Caddesi near the Tourist Office. The Akdamar's 69 rooms rent for 8000TL (US$11.20) single, 11,200TL (US$15.68) double, with bath. The hotel has lifts, a private car park, a terrace restaurant which is probably the best in town, and a bar.

Next best is the *Tekin Oteli* (teh-KEEN) (tel (061) 13010), Küçük Cami Civarı ('near the Little Mosque') west of Cumhuriyet Caddesi – you can identify the hotel easily by the sign on its roof. There are 52 rooms in this quietish place, renting for 5800TL (US$8.12) double with shower.

A similar choice is the *Büyük Asur Oteli* (beur-YEURK ah-SOOR) (tel (061) 18792, 3), Cumhuriyet Caddesi 126, with 48 rooms with baths, a lift, car park and

restaurant. Room prices are 5000TL (US$7) single, 6300TL (US$8.82) double.

Places to Eat – bottom end

Cumhuriyet Caddesi has numerous *kebapçis*, cheap and good as always. A good, cheap, general-purpose restaurant is the *Birkoç* (BEER-kohch) (tel 11029), off Cumhuriyet Caddesi at Sümerbank Sokak 15 (go to Cumhuriyet Caddesi 79, and then make your way around to the back of this address to find the Birkoç). Most stews are priced at 300TL (US$0.42), meats from 300TL to 465TL (US$0.42 to US$0.65). They pride themselves on their *saç kavurma*, bits of lamb fried and served in a wok-like pan. Or try the *Biryan Restaurant*, which is also very cheap and very good. For breakfast, try the *Seval Kahvaltı Salonu* (seh-VAHL).

Places to Eat – mid-range

The fanciest and probably the best food is at the Hotel Akdamar, where a very good dinner for two can cost 5000TL (US$7), but represents good value for money.

Getting There & Away

As 'capital' of the extreme south-east, Van has ready transport. The bus to Diyarbakır departs four times daily on the seven-hour trip, and costs 2500TL (US$3.50); to Malatya, the trip takes 12 hours. The trip to Erzurum costs 3500TL (US$4.90). To Doğubeyazıt, if you're going by bus, you will take the route via Erciş, Patnos and Ağrı, a distance of 315 km; the bus company may put you in a minibus for the first part of the journey, then switch you to a larger bus at a junction. Hold onto your bus ticket (2000TL, US$2.80).

NORTH FROM VAN

Having come this far, your next goal must be Doğubeyazıt, the town in the shadow of Mt Ararat, at the Iranian frontier on the E23 highway.

Driving a private car, you have an alternative to the Erciş-Patnos-Ağrı route. Where the lake ring road turns westward at the town of Bendimahi, you can, if you like, continue north toward Muradiye, Çaldıran and Ortadirek. The road is unpaved after Çaldıran, badly marked, has no regular public transport, and is extremely rough for the 60 km between Çaldıran and Ortadirek, but it's usually passable and wonderfully scenic. You save a few km as this route is only 184 km long, but you should not drive it after 5 pm. It is officially closed after that hour, and Turkish army patrols are on duty to stop smugglers. They are very friendly if you obey the regulations, but will be uncomfortably strict after 5 pm.

AĞRI

The Turkish name for Mt Ararat is Ağrı Dağı, and the town of Ağrı (ah-RUH, altitude 1640, population 50,000) is 100 km west of the snow-capped peak. There is nothing to hold you here except the few small, very modest hotels (if you arrive at night). Otherwise, head for Doğubeyazıt to the east or Erzurum to the west.

DOĞUBEYAZIT

It's only 35 km between the Iranian frontier and Doğubeyazıt (doh-OO-bah-yah-zuht, population 30,000), a town that is dusty in summer, muddy in winter. The town seems to be made of the dun-coloured earth on which it rests. Behind the town is a range of bare, jagged mountains, before it a table-flat expanse of wheatfield and grazing land. On the far northern side of this flatness rises Mt Ararat (Ağri Dağı, 5165 metres), an enormous volcano capped with ice and often shrouded in dark clouds.

The name Ararat is derived from Urartu. The mountain has figured in legends since time began, most notably as the supposed resting-place of Noah's Ark. But more of that later.

Doğubeyazıt's other attraction is the İşak Paşa Sarayı, a castle-fortress-palace-mosque complex perched on a terrace seven km east of town.

Things to See

Head east for the İşak Paşa Sarayı (ee-SHAHK pah-shah sah-rah-yuh), seven km from town. There are often dolmuşes that pass nearby, especially on weekends. Otherwise, a taxi will demand 2000TL to 3000TL (US$2.80 to US$4.20) for a return-trip tour, waiting time included.

Though ruined, the fortress-like palace has many elements which are in good shape; the mosque is still used for prayers. The building was begun in 1685 by Çolak Abdi Paşa and completed in 1784 by his son, a Kurdish chieftain named İşak (Isaac). The architecture is an amalgam of Seljuk, Ottoman, Georgian, Persian and Armenian styles. A grand main portal leads to a large courtyard. The magnificent gold-plated doors which once hung on the portal were removed by the Russians, who invaded in 1917 and took the doors to a museum in Moscow.

The palace was equipped with a central heating system, running water and a sewerage system. You can visit the mosque and the various palace rooms. Note especially the little *türbe* in a corner of the court, with very fine relief work on it.

Across the valley are a mosque and the ruins of a fortress. The **fortress** foundations may date from Urartian times, though the walls will have been rebuilt by whoever needed to control this mountain pass. The **mosque** is thought to date from the reign of the Ottoman Sultan Selim the Grim (1512-1520), who defeated the Persians decisively near the town of Çaldıran, 70 km south of Doğubeyazıt, in 1514. Selim thus added all of eastern Anatolia to his burgeoning empire, and went on to conquer Syria and Palestine.

The ruined foundations you see rising in low relief from the dusty plain are of **Eski Beyazıt**, the old city, which was probably founded in Urartian times (circa 800 BC).

Mt Ararat The mountain has two peaks when seen from Doğubeyazıt. The right-hand peak, called Great Ararat (Büyük Ağrı), is 5165 metres high; Little Ararat (Küçük Ağrı) rises to about 3925 metres. Best time to view the mountain is at sunrise or early in the morning, before the clouds obscure it.

You can climb Ararat but you need *written* permission from the authorities in Ankara, and then you must have an approved guide. The mountain is dangerous: severe weather, ferocious sheepdogs, rock-and-ice slides, smugglers and outlaws can turn an adventure into a disaster. Getting the necessary permission can take several months.

The only legal way to go up the mountain is with an organized group, which will already have made the necessary official arrangements. Two Turkish agencies operate such trips: Trek Travel, Taksim Meydanı 10/6, İstanbul; and Metro Tourism, Cumhuriyet Caddesi 43/5, Platin Ap, Taksim, İstanbul. In Doğbeyazıt, the Trek & Travel office will arrange a group for about US$100 per person.

Your guide will take you to Eli, a hamlet at 2100 metres, which is the starting point for the trek. You stay at two more camps before the final ascent, for which you should have ice-climbing gear.

Over the years, several people have reported sighting a 'boat shape' high on the mountain, and in 1951 an expedition brought back what was presumed to be a piece of wood from the ark, which had been found in a frozen lake. But so far no one, not even American astronaut James Irwin who climbed the mountain in 1982, has brought back a full report. If it's there, it will be found, for the activity nowadays is intense, with scientists, archaeologists, Fundamentalist Christian sects, the Turkish Mountaineering Federation and various universities all sending expeditions.

Places to Stay – bottom end

The cheap hotels in Doğubeyazıt tend to be very basic indeed. *Hotel Gül* (tel (0278) 1176), Güven Caddesi 28, charges 2000TL (US$2.80) single, 3600TL (US$5.04) double, 4500TL (US$6.30) triple. The *Hotel Kenan* and the *Hotel Beyazıt* charge 3000TL (US$4.20) double, but there are usually free hot showers, and if the sheets aren't clean you can ask that they be changed. Look at several rooms before you decide on one.

The *Hotel İlhan* across the street from the Hotel İsfahan has similar basic accommodation and free hot showers, but charges slightly less.

The several little places along the main street of the town, such as the *Hotel Kahraman*, are used mostly by lorry-drivers travelling to and from Iran, and charge 750TL (US$1.05) for extremely basic accommodation – a bed in a room with four or five sleeping drivers.

Places to Stay – middle

Rising above the mud-brick roofs and television aerials of Doğubeyazıt is the *Hotel İsfahan* (tel (0278) 1159 or 2045), Emniyet Caddesi 26, Doğubeyazıt 04410, with 60 double rooms with showers priced at 5000TL (US$7) single, 8500TL (US$11.90), double 10,600TL (US$14.84) triple. It's modern and comfortable, with its own lift, car park and Turkish baths. The restaurant is the best in town.

The only other place in this class is the *Sim-Er Moteli* (SEEM-ehr) (tel (0278) 1601 or 2254), PK 13, a modern 62-room establishment five km east of town on the E23 highway to Iran. This is the juggernauts' choice, the last lorry-stop before Iran, with fuel pumps, motel, restaurant, 'mini-market' and bar. Besides a place to stay, the Sim-Er gives you a glimpse at the international transport life. With shower, single rooms cost 5500TL (US$7.70), doubles are 9100TL (US$12.74), a set-price meal is 2000TL (US$2.80); children receive a 30% reduction on the room rates.

Places to Eat

The main street holds three or four *kebapçıs*, one of which advertizes (in English) 'All Kinds of Meals Found Here.' The *Gaziantepli Kebap Salonu* is not bad. The restaurants in the two top hotels are good.

Getting Away

From Doğubeyazıt you can go west to Erzurum, a distance of 284 km. If you want to see Kars and the ruins of Ani, you can go north via Iğdır (UH-duhr), Tuzluca and Kağızman, a distance of 236 km. There is minibus service from Doğubeyazıt to Iğdır for 500TL (US$0.70). At Tuzluca there are salt caves you can visit. North of Kağızman, above the village of Çamuşlu Köyü (chah-moosh-LOO kew-yew) are prehistoric rock carvings (*kaya resimleri*, kah-YAH rehseem-leh-ree) which the villagers can show you.

As this route passes very close to the Soviet frontier between Iğdır and Tuzluca, it's important for you to know that the border zone is a no-man's-land 700 metres deep on each side of the frontier line, and that the Soviet border guards will *shoot to kill* anyone who enters that 700-metre strip, on either the Turkish or the Russian side. This is no joke. Don't attempt to approach the border. The Turkish army guards will not appreciate any action which would provoke the Russians, either.

Into Iran Unless you're an international driver who does it frequently and has all the right visas and papers, entry to Iran is difficult. You must have a visa, which can, in theory, be obtained from an Iranian embassy or consulate; but in fact you may wait months and never actually get the visa. For more information see the sections on Visas and Embassies & Consulates in the Facts for the Visitor chapter, or contact your embassy in Ankara for the latest developments. Once in Iran, it's good to have cash US dollars,

which trade easily; but US dollar travellers' cheques cannot be changed.

ERZURUM

Erzurum (EHR-zoo-room, altitude 1950, population 260,000) is the largest city on the high plateau of Eastern Anatolia. It has always been a transportation centre and military headquarters, the command-post for the defense of Anatolia from Russian invasion (and in the days of the empires, from Persian invasion as well). Under the republic, it is assuming a new role as an eastern cultural and commercial city. There is a university here.

Erzurum lacks the colour and complexity of İstanbul or İzmir, but makes up for it with a rough frontier refinement. The severe climate and the spare landscape make one think that this is the beginning of the vast, high steppe of Central Asia. The people, too, reflect the severity of the climate and remoteness of location by their steadfast conservatism. Even though they are not used to seeing a lot of foreigners, they still give travellers a warm welcome. You'll see many more women wearing the veil here, and a few in purdah. The old men go to prayer early and often.

In contrast, the town is also busy with armed forces officers striding purposefully through its streets, and squadrons of troops being trucked here and there. They may well be on their way to a new tree-planting site. When there's no fighting to do, Turkish commanders tend to order that the troops plant trees. The trees are everywhere in Erzurum, and the orderly, modern tree-lined boulevards provide a welcome contrast to the arid, almost lifeless appearance of the surrounding oceans of steppeland.

For tourists, Erzurum is a transfer point with air, rail and bus connections. But when you stay the night (or even two nights) here, you will be able to occupy your free time with visits to some very fine Turkish buildings and a lively market area. You can also take a scenic excursion

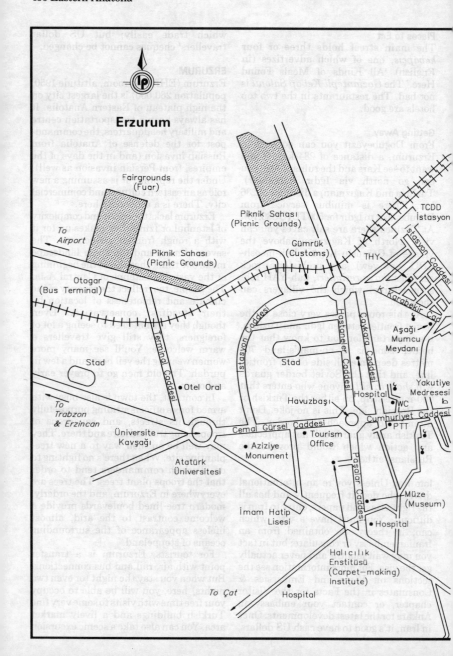

Erzurum

To Airport

To Trabzon & Erzincan

Fairgrounds (Fuar)

Piknik Sahası (Picnic Grounds)

Piknik Sahası (Picnic Grounds)

Gümrük (Customs)

TCDD İstasyon

THY

Otogar (Bus Terminal)

Stad

Otel Oral

Üniversite Kavşağı

Atatürk Üniversitesi

Terminal Caddesi

İstasyon Caddesi

Hastaneler Caddesi

Çaykara Caddesi

Stad

Havuzbaşı

Cemal Gürsel Caddesi

Aziziye Monument

Aşağı Mumcu Meydanı

Yakutiye Medresesi

Hospital

Cumhuriyet Caddesi

WC

PTT

Tourism Office

K Karabekir Cad

İstasyon Caddesi

Pasalar Caddesi

İmam Hatip Lisesi

Müze (Museum)

Hospital

Halıcılık Enstitüsü (Carpet—making) Institute

Hospital

To Çat

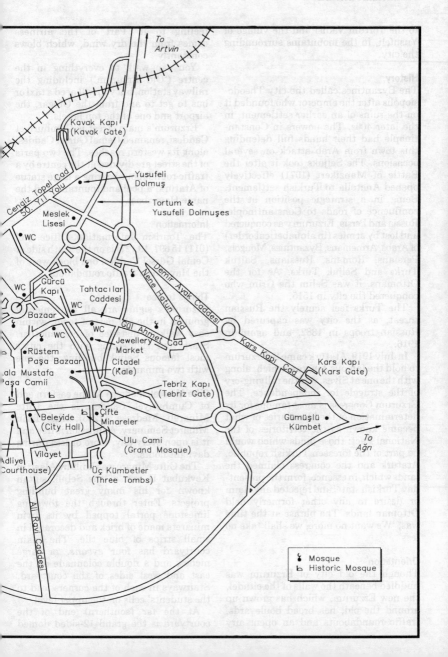

To Artvin

Kavak Kapı
(Kavak Gate)

Yusufeli
Dolmuş

Tortum &
Yusufeli Dolmuşes

Cengiz Topel Cad
50. Yıl Yolu

Meslek
Lisesi

WC

WC

Gürcü
Kapı

Tahtacılar
Caddesi

Demir Ayak Caddesi

Nene Hatun Cad

WC

Bazaar

WC

WC

Gül Ahmet Cad

Kars Kapı Cad

Jewellery
Market

Rüstem
Paşa Bazaar

Citadel
(Kale)

Kars Kapı
(Kars Gate)

Lala Mustafa
Paşa Camii

Tebriz Kapı
(Tebriz Gate)

Beleyide
(City Hall)

Çifte
Minareler

Gümüşlü
Kümbet

To
Ağrı

Ulu Cami
(Grand Mosque)

Vilayet

Adliye
(Courthouse)

Üç Kümbetler
(Three Tombs)

Ali Ravi Caddesi

⌇ Mosque
⌂ Historic Mosque

to the Tortum Vadisi and the village of Yusufeli, in the mountains surrounding the city.

History

The Byzantines called the city Theodosiopolis after the emperor who founded it on the ruins of an earlier settlement, in the later 400s. The powers in Constantinople had their hands full defending this town from Arab attack on several occasions. The Seljuks took it after the Battle of Manzikert (1071) effectively opened Anatolia to Turkish settlement. Being in a strategic position at the confluence of roads to Constantinople, Russia and Persia, Erzurum was conquered and lost by armies (in alphabetical order) of Arabs, Armenians, Byzantines, Mongols, Persians, Romans, Russians, Saltuk Turks and Seljuk Turks. As for the Ottomans, it was Selim the Grim who conquered the city in 1515.

The Turks feel acutely the Russian threat, as the city was captured by Russian troops in 1882, and again in 1916.

In July 1919, Atatürk came to Erzurum to hold the famous congress which, along with the one at Sivas, was the rallying-cry of the struggle for independence. The Erzurum Congress is most famous for its determination of the boundaries of what became known as the territories of the National Pact: those lands which would be part of the foreseen Turkish republic. Atatürk and the congress claimed the lands which, in essence, form the present-day Turkish state, and rejected any claim or desire to any other formerly held Ottoman lands. The phrase at the time was, 'We want no more, we shall take no less'.

Orientation

Though the old city of Erzurum was huddled beneath the walls of the citadel, the new Erzurum, which has grown up around the old, has broad boulevards, traffic roundabouts and an open, airy feeling to it. Part of the airiness comes from the dry wind, which blows constantly.

You can walk to everything in the centre ('Old Erzurum') including the railway station, but you will need a taxi or bus to get to and from the Otogar, the airport and one of the top hotels.

Erzurum's main street is Cumhuriyet Caddesi, renamed Cemal Gürsel Caddesi along its western reaches. The two parts of the street are divided at the centre by a traffic roundabout bearing a large statue of Atatürk, a pool and fountain, and the name Havuzbaşı.

Information

The Tourism Information Office (tel (011) 15 697, 19 127) is on the south side of Cemal Gürsel Caddesi one block west of the Havuzbaşı traffic roundabout.

Things to See

Erzurum's sights are all conveniently grouped in the old part of town, within easy walking distance of one another. Start your sightseeing with the city's most famous Seljuk building, the one with two minarets.

Çifte Minareli Medrese At the eastern end of Cumhuriyet Caddesi is the Çifte Minareli Medrese (1253), the Twin Minaret Seminary. Admission is free and it is open every day, more or less during daylight hours.

The Çifte Minare was built by Alaettin Keykubat II, son of the Seljuk sultan known for his many great building projects. Enter through the towering limestone portal topped by its twin minarets made of brick and decorated in small strips of blue tile. The main courtyard has four *eyvans*, or large niches, and a double colonnade on the east and west sides of the courtyard. Stairways in each of the corners lead to the students' cells on the upper level.

At the far (southern) end of the courtyard is the grand 12-sided domed hall which served as the Tomb of Huant Hatun (Hatuniye Türbesi), the sultan's daughter. Beneath the domed hall is a small room with ingenious vents to allow the entry of light and air. This may have been a *mescit* (chapel), or the tomb proper.

Ulu Cami Next to the Çifte Minareli is the Ulu Cami, or Great Mosque (1179). The contrast between the two buildings is interesting: the Ulu Cami, built by the Saltuklu Turkish emir of Erzurum, is very restrained, though elegant, with seven aisles running north-south and six running east-west, resulting in a forest of columns. You enter from the north along the central (fourth) aisle. As you walk straight in, at the fourth east-west aisle is a stalactite dome with an opening to the heavens. At the far southern end of the central aisle is a very interesting wooden dome and a pair of bull's-eye windows.

Üç Kümbetler To reach the complex of three Seljuk *kümbets*, or tombs, walk south between the Çifte Minareli and the Ulu Cami. Come to a 'T' intersection, turn left, then immediately right, and walk a short block up the hill to the tombs, in a fenced enclosure on the right-hand side. The gate to the enclosure may be locked, but you can see most of what there is to see from the street. They have some good decoration, the best being on the octagonal Emir Sultan Türbesi (1100s).

Erzurum Kalesi Erzurum castle, erected by Theodosius (400s), is on the hilltop to the north of the Çifte Minareli and the Ulu Cami. Walk up the hill toward the curious old clock tower (Saat Kulesi), topped by a Turkish flag, which was actually built as a minaret in the time of the Saltuks but was converted later to its timekeeping function. The clock tower stands by the entrance to the citadel.

Within the citadel you will probably encounter a group of boys playing

football. As soon as they notice you, the game will be broken off and they will run up to ask where you come from, and to try out their one phrase in English, which is usually 'Do you speak English?' or 'What is the time?'

Besides the boys, the citadel harbours a few old cannons with Russian or Ottoman inscriptions, and a disused *mescit*. It is difficult to get to the top of the walls for a view. The boys will recommend that you climb an electricity tower. This is probably not a good idea.

Ottoman Mosques Return to Cumhuriyet Caddesi and head west, and you will pass on the north (right) side the small **Caferiye Camii**, an Ottoman work constructed in 1645 upon the order of Ebubekiroğlu Hacı Cafer.

Cross over the busy intersection, at the south-east corner of which stands the **Vilayet** building, and you come to the **Lala Mustafa Paşa Camii** (1563), at the north-west corner. Lala Mustafa Paşa was a Grand Vezir during the Golden Age of the Ottoman Empire, and his mosque is a classical Ottoman work of the high period. It may have been designed by Sinan or someone in his following.

Yakutiye Medresesi Just to the west of the Lala Mustafa Paşa Camii is the Yakutiye Medresesi, a Mongol theological seminary dating from 1310. This seminary was built by the local Mongol emir. Its portal copies the Seljuk style, as does its minaret. There is a *türbe* behind the school meant to be (but never used as) the emir's tomb. At this writing the school itself is not open to visitors.

Museum The Erzurum Müzesi (tel 11406) is several long blocks south-west of the Yakutiye Medresesi. Walk west along Cumhuriyet Caddesi to the Havuzbaşı roundabout, then turn left (south) and walk up the hill. The museum is just before the next intersection, on the left (east) side of the street. If you're not up to the 15-minute walk, take a taxi for about 350TL (US$0.49), or any bus climbing the hill from Havuzbaşı.

Museum hours are 8 am to noon and 1.30 to 5.30 pm; admission costs 400TL (US$0.56), half-price on Saturday and Sunday, closed Monday. Some of the museum labels are in English.

The museum's collection is interesting primarily for its ethnological displays. There are beautiful carpets and *kilims* galore, a hanging cradle *(beşik)* from the Caucasus *(Kafkas)*, a shepherd's traditional heavy woollen cape, Ottoman costumes and home furnishings, a purloined Russian church bell, a traditional local carpet loom, and an exhibit on the making of prayer-beads *(tespih)* from the lightweight jet-black mineral called *oltutaş*. These can be bought in the market (see below).

Besides the ethnological collection, the museum has some fragments of Seljuk tiles and Urartian pottery, and some pottery and jewellery found in Hellenistic and Roman tombs.

Upstairs (don't bash your head on that low overhang!) are more exhibits, including weaponry, some fine Ottoman suits of chain mail, and a complete coin collection beginning with examples from the Egypt of the Ptolemys through the many Turkish *beyliks* (princedoms) to Ottoman times.

Bazaar Erzurum's market areas are scattered through the old part of the city. Streets are narrow and winding, as usual, and thus it is not easy to direct you on your walk. You can start your wanderings at the Lala Mustafa Paşa Camii, then walk north along the street next to the mosque. You will pass the **Rüstem Paşa Çarşısı**, or Market of Rüstem Pasha, which is the centre for the manufacture and sale of those black *oltutaşı* prayer-beads. For a look at the shops, go to the upper floor.

Just down the street from the Rüstem Paşa Çarşısı is the small **Pervizoğlu Camii**

(1715), with a small, bright blue wooden screen in front. On **Kavaflar Çarşısı Sokak** are many tinsmiths who sell their handmade stoves, heaters and samovars.

Continuing downhill in the market district will bring you, finally, to Istasyon Caddesi, the street to the railway station and the numerous hotels in this district.

Tortum Vadisi & Yusufeli For a look at the countryside around Erzurum, take an excursion into the Kaçkar Mountains through the Valley of Tortum (Tortum Vadisi) to the village of Yusufeli. The valley, about 55 km north of Erzurum, is most beautiful in mid-June, when the orchards of cherries and apricots are in bloom. The lake here was formed by a landslide some three centuries ago. You can visit the 48-metre Tortum Şelalesi (waterfall), which is only worth seeing when the water is not being diverted to the nearby electricity generating plant.

Yusufeli, up in the mountains, has nothing special to see, but is a convenient goal for your excursion. The ride from Erzurum takes 2½ to three hours each way. Start early in order to get back to Erzurum in the same day. If you don't mind primitive accommodation, you can stay the night in the village.

Minibuses through the Tortum Vadisi to Yusufeli do not leave from the Otogar, but from several locations in the old part of town. These locations are not particularly easy to find. The fastest way to find the minibus offices is to have a taxi take you to the Otel Çoruh (choh-ROO), near the Atatürk Endüstri Meslek Lisesi, a technical training high school. Look then for signs with the name Tortum, Yusufeli or Artvin on them. The Artvin-Yusufeli Otobüs İşletmesi, for instance, operates minibuses about every hour as far as Tortum (500TL, US$0.70), with some continuing to Yusufeli (2000TL, US$2.80). Another company here is the Öz Tortum Birlik.

Places to Stay

Erzurum is a low-budget traveller's dream-come-true, with many very cheap places not far from the centre of the town. As for the upper ranges, there are no hotels in the luxury class, but plenty of sufficient, comfortable places.

Places to Stay – bottom end

Erzurum's inexpensive lodging places are scattered throughout the old part of town, and are especially thick along Kâzım Karabekir Caddesi (KYAA-zumm kahrah-beh-KEER), north of the centre, not far from the railway station and the bazaar.

My favourite in the old city is the *Otel Evin* (tel (011) 12349), Ayazpaşa Caddesi, Bedendibi Sokak 12, just down the street from the better-known Hotel Çınar. The Evin has clean beds for 600TL (US\$0.84), and some rooms even have views of the town. Hot water for Turkish splash-baths comes from the simple water heaters in which the *patron* (hotel owner) builds a fire a half-hour before your appointed shower time. The patron, by the way, is a congenial and helpful man.

The *Otel Arı* (tel (011) 13141) is on Ayazpaşa Caddesi, one of the main streets in the bazaar, and charges 1800TL (US\$2.52) double for a room without bath. There are several other, similar hotels on Ayazpaşa as well.

Beginning in Aşağı Mumcu Meydanı, the little square at the eastern end of Kâzım Karabekir Caddesi, you'll see the *Gürcü Kapı Nur Palaz Oteli* (tel (011) 11706), behind the more expensive Hotel Sefer. The hotel has no baths whatsoever, and charges 1200TL (US\$1.68) single, 2000TL (US\$2.80) double for a room.

Walking along Kâzım Karabekir Caddesi, you will come to these hotels:

The 32-room *Hitit Otel* (tel (011) 11204) at No 26, is just off the little square, and charges 2700TL (US\$3.78) for a single with bath, 3000TL (US\$4.20) for a double without bath, 3400TL

(US\$4.76) for a double with bath. It's one of the better places on the street. Right next door is the *Örnek Otel* (tel (011) 11203), a similar place with 35 rooms and very similar prices.

Next along the street is the 55-room *Otel San* (tel (011) 15789) at No 8, charging 3000TL (US\$4.20) for a single with bath, 3400TL (US\$4.76) for a similar double.

The *Otel Polat* (tel (011) 11623), which comes next, has a lift, a family atmosphere, and 60 rooms with bath for 4400TL (US\$6.16) single, 5500TL (US\$7.70) double, 6600TL (US\$9.24) triple.

At the western end of Kâzım Karabekir Caddesi are two more places, very simple, but willing to give reductions in price. The *Otel Serhat* (tel (011) 12139), Gez Mahallesi 49, has only one single room with bath for 1500TL (US\$2.10), but numerous doubles without bath for 2500TL (US\$3.50), before haggling. The nearby *Otel Çam* (tel (011) 13025), Gez Mahallesi BP Karşısı, is quite near the Turkish Airlines office and has very basic rooms without running water for 1000TL (US\$1.40) single, 1900TL (US\$2.66) double, before haggling.

Places to Stay – middle

Otel Oral (tel (011) 19740), Terminal Caddesi 3, is generally regarded as the best hotel in the city. Its 90 rooms and suites all have showers or baths, and telephones, and cost 8535TL (US\$12.55) single, 10,665TL (US\$15.68) double. Though it is indeed comfortable, with a willing staff and good restaurant, it is out of the centre, and you will have to travel everywhere by taxi. Also, being on the main thoroughfare, it suffers from a great deal of noise from heavy vehicles. In the warm months, when you will need to have the windows open for ventilation, request a room at the back *without fail!*

Other hotels are distinctly more modest than the Otel Oral, and are basically at the bottom end. They are mentioned here because their more desirable locations may cause their prices and quality to rise in future.

One middle-range hotel is very near the railway station and the bazaar. It's the 36-room *Hotel Sefer* (tel (011) 13615 or 16714), İstasyon Caddesi near Aşağı Mumcu Meydanı. Modern and convenient, but certainly not fancy, it charges 4400TL (US$6.16) single, 6600TL (US$9.24) double for rooms with bath.

On Cumhuriyet Caddesi in the heart of town are two more choices. The *Kral Hotel* (tel (011) 16973 or 11930), Erzincankapı 18, is across Cumhuriyet Caddesi from the Yakutiye Medresesi. Its 51 rooms with showers currently rent for 4400TL (US$6.16) single, 5500TL (US$7.70) double, 6600TL (US$9.24) triple, but they are open to bargaining. The *Akçay Otel* (tel (011) 17330), Cumhuriyet Caddesi 1, has 32 similar rooms and prices. The entry to the hotel is via Kâmil Ağa Sokak, a small side street opposite the Yakutiye Medresesi and Lala Mustafa Paşa Camii.

Places to Eat

As with hotel prices, meal prices in Erzurum are delightfully low. In fact, all are cheap enough to qualify as bottom-end places, though they are suitable for all tastes and budgets. The only exception might be the dining room of the Otel Oral, and even the Oral is budget-priced compared to a similar place in İstanbul. Restaurants have not sprouted like mushrooms in this town but there are plenty for you to use, mostly along Cumhuriyet Caddesi.

Kebap places are, as usual, the cheapest and best. Just opposite the Akçay Otel on Kâmil Ağa Sokak is the *Mulenruj Kebap Salonu* (that's 'Moulin Rouge'!) (tel (011) 19783) with a large main dining room and a smaller mezzanine at the rear, for couples and families. On the west wall is an ersatz rock grotto with toy electrical power lines on top, connected to a rustic stone waterwheel which, at one time, appears to have

generated the electricity to fire the power lines and light several small bulbs. The whole assemblage does not appear to have worked properly for some time, and its presence in a restaurant is, to me, a total mystery. I guess it's just one of those wonderful Turkish *jeux d'esprit*. The *döner kebap* tends to be a bit salty for my taste, but a meal of it, along with some *kuru fasulye* (beans in tomato sauce), *pilav* and a soft drink came to 1200TL (US$1.68), tip included.

A stroll along Cumhuriyet Caddesi reveals several slightly fancier places, without waterwheels or fake rocks but with similarly low prices. The *Salon Çağın* (tel (011) 19320) is near the traffic roundabout nearest the Yakutiye Medresesi, on the south side of the street. Clean, bright and cheery, it has very tasty food. A light lunch of *sebzeli kebap* (lamb stew with vegetables), bread and soft drink cost a mere 600TL (US$0.84). The *Güzelyurt Restorant* (tel (011) 11514) is much the same, with a menu listing prices of 700TL (US$0.98) for a small filet beefsteak, even less for *şiş kebap* or *pirzola* (lamb chops). A sign in the door says, 'Please do not drive after having used alcohol'.

The *Turistik Tufan Restaurant* (tel 13107), next to the Kral Hotel, has a good situation, with a terrace overlooking the busy street. But it acts as the local men's club, where notables come to drink and dine, and this makes the atmosphere somewhat heavy.

Getting There

Being the major city in eastern Turkey, Erzurum is well served by all modes of transport.

Air Turkish Airlines (tel (011) 18530 or 11904) at 100 Yıl Caddesi, SSK Rant Tesisleri 24, has a daily flight from İstanbul via Ankara to Erzurum, and return. The fare for the one-hour flight from from Ankara to Erzurum is 30,000TL (US$42).

Rail The Erzurum Garı is at the northern end of İstasyon Caddesi, north of the centre about a half km. You can easily walk to or from the station to most hotels except the Oral. Buses depart the station forecourt every half hour and circulate through the city. A taxi should cost less than 700TL (US$1), no matter where you go. Just up the hill along İstasyon Caddesi, at Gürcü Kapı Meydanı, where the bazaar begins, are the offices of numerous bus companies. You can buy your onward tickets here and thus save yourself a trip out to the Otogar.

Bus The Otogar is several km from the centre along the airport road, a 12-minute walk from the Otel Oral. City bus No 2 passes by the Otogar and will take you into town for 50TL (US$0.07). The Otogar has snack shops and a restaurant.

Service to and from Erzurum includes the following destinations, times and fares: Ankara (14 or 15 hours, 5500TL, US$7.70); Diyarbakır (11 hours, 4000TL, US$5.60); Doğubeyazıt (4½ hours, 2000TL, US$2.80); İstanbul (20 or 21 hours, 8000TL, US$11.20); Kars (3½ hours, 1500TL, US$2.10); Sivas (seven or eight hours, 3000TL, US$4.20); Trabzon (eight hours, 3000TL to 3700TL, US$4.20 to US$5.18); Van (seven or eight hours, 3500TL, US$4.90). For Iran, take a bus to Doğubeyazıt, and from there you can catch a minibus to the Iranian frontier.

For dolmuşes to the Tortum Vadisi and Yusufeli, see that section.

Getting Around

Airport Transport From the airport, 10 km out of town, a bus takes you into the centre for 400TL (US$0.56), stopping at the Otogar along the way; if you want to go to the Otel Oral tell the driver, as that is on the way as well. A taxi from the airport to the centre costs about 2000TL (US$2.80).

For the return trip, a bus departs the Turkish Airlines office near the western end of Kâzım Karabekir Caddesi 105 minutes before flight time; if you take a taxi, be at the airport at least 30 minutes before flight time.

KARS

Kars (KAHRSS, altitude 1750 metres, population 80,000) is an odd place. It is chilly and drab most of the time. There are lots of police and soldiers, and every single one of them can tell you without hesitation the precise number of days he has yet to serve in Kars, before he can go west 'to civilisation'. And they will want to talk to you. As a foreigner, you bring them a breath of culture. As for the locals, a harsh climate and a rough history has made them, for the most part, dour and sombre, though not unpolite. The children, as always, are friendly and inquisitive, anxious to try out their 10 words of English on you.

Kars doesn't look at all like a Turkish town. It is dominated by a stark, no-nonsense medieval fortress (rebuilt in 1855) which is still used as part of the city's defenses. Many of the public buildings, and even some of the residences, look Russian, not Turkish. The school gymnasium was obviously built as a Russian Orthodox church.

Kars was indeed held by the Russians for a time (1878-1920), which accounts for the 19th-century Russian aspect of the town. The mood of the inhabitants comes from the fact that Kars, though set in the midst of fertile agricultural land, is a garrison town. What people do here is grow wheat, make carpets and watch out for the Russians.

Orientation

Kars is laid out on a somewhat grandiose grid. The Russians must have had great plans for the town when they laid it out, but as they were unable to keep it, they never realized their goals. Nonetheless, most everything in Kars is within walking distance, except perhaps the railway station.

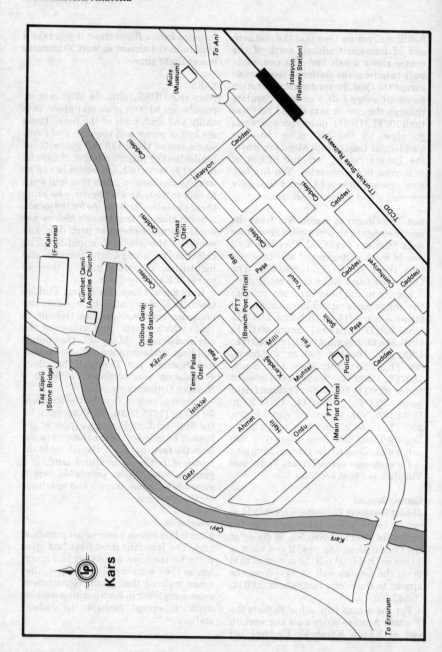

Kars

Information

The Tourism Information Office has been closed for the time being. For information and assistance, go to the museum (see below).

Things to See

You have come to Kars with the intention of visiting Ani. Without that intention, it doesn't make much sense to come here. But while in Kars, there are a few things well worth seeing.

Kars Müzesi First of all is the fine, new little museum, open from 8 am to noon and 1.30 to 5.30 pm, closed Monday. Oldest exhibits date from Old Bronze Age times. The Roman and Greek periods are represented, as are the Seljuks and Ottomans. Several photo exhibits show the excavations at Ani; there are shots of Armenian churches in Kars, as well. The chief exhibit is a pair of carved doors from an orthodox church, and a Russian church bell from the time of Tsar Nicholas II (1894-1917).

You should not miss the ethnographic exhibits upstairs, as this area produces some very fine *kilims*, carpets and *cicims* (embroidered *kilims*). Costumes, saddlebags, jewellery, samovars and a home carpet loom complete the exhibit.

Kümbet Camii Though called the 'Drum-Dome Mosque' in Turkish, this building down by the river was built as the Church of the Apostles by the Bagratid king Abas in 938. The relief carvings on the drum are of the apostles; the porches were added to the ancient structure in the 1800s. As of this writing, the church awaits restoration; you can't see the interior.

Not far from the church is an old bridge, the Taş Köprü, which dates from the 1400s. Ruins of the Ulu Cami and a palace called the Beylerbey Sarayı are beneath the *kale* (fortress). The fortress is not open to visitors.

Places to Stay – bottom end

Hotel Nur Saray, on Fait Bey Caddesi, charges 1900TL (US$2.66) for a double room with washbasin; cold showers are free. Though the Nur Saray is about the best, there are other, similar, cheap places.

Places to Stay – middle

The *Yılmaz Oteli* (yuhl-MAHZ) (tel (0211) 1074 or 2387) has 36 rooms next to the bus terminal. It charges 6300TL (US$8.82) for a double with shower. It is the best place in town.

Places to Eat

Kars is noted for its excellent honey. If you're lucky (or if you ask), you might get it for breakfast.

Places to Eat – bottom end

The town has a number of cheap, suitable restaurants, including the popular *Manolya* on the main street, the *Yeni Nil Kebab Salonu* on Atatürk Caddesi and the *Başkent Lokantası* near the bus station, which has good *döner kebap*.

Places to Eat – mid-range

The best restaurant in town is in the *Yılmaz Hotel*. They serve alcoholic beverages, which is not the case in most places.

Carpet Buying

When I was in Kars, I bought several of the local carpets. The weave of the modern rugs is coarse and the local wool is used undyed, in its natural earthy colours. Any dealer in town can show you some *Kars halıları* (KAHRSS hah-luh-lah-ruh, Kars carpets), and will quote you a price of so-many-liras per square metre. There are several grades of carpets, and thus several different price ranges. Once you've found a carpet you like, and have agreed on a price per square metre (Haggle! You must!), the carpet is measured, yielding the final, exact price.

These are not fine Turkish carpets, but they are very earthy, attractive and sturdy – and not expensive, though heavy and bulky to carry home. I'm not sure I'd trust having them shipped.

Though there are numerous carpet merchants, the best I found was Mr Memduh Yıldız (mehm-DOOH yuhl-DUHZ); just ask, and somebody will point the way to his shop.

Getting There

Rail The Mehmetçik Ekspresi is scheduled to depart Erzurum for Kars each evening at 6 pm, but it is invariably late. The scheduled arrival time in Kars is 10.44 pm, meaning that the trip is supposed to take 5½ hours. A single ticket costs 700TL (US$1) 1st class, 500TL (US$0.70) 2nd class. In the Kars switching yard you might see some marvellous old steam locomotives.

Bus There is direct bus service between Kars and Adana, Ankara, Ardahan, Bursa, Denizli, Diyarbakır, Erzurum, Iğdır, İstanbul, İzmir, Kayseri, Konya, Malatya and Sivas. For Doğubeyazıt, change buses at Iğdır; there is one bus per day to Iğdır, departing at 1 pm (500TL, US$0.70).

Buses take 3½ to four hours to cover the 200 km between Erzurum and Kars. A ticket costs 1000TL to 1500TL (US$1.40 to US$2.10), or about twice the 1st-class train fare.

ANİ

The ruined city at Ani (AH-nee), 44 km east of Kars, is striking. It's a medieval ghost town set in grassy fields overlooking the Arpaçay stream, which forms the boundary between the Turkish Republic and the Soviet Armenian Republic. On the far side, sinister Soviet watchtowers shelter border guards who will shoot to kill if you show an intention of 'violating the sacred borders of the fatherland.' The border no-man's-land extends 700 metres either side of the Aparçay.

The walls of Ani, over a km in length, will impress you as you drive across the wheat-covered plains toward the border.

History

This was the capital of an Urartian state, and later of an Armenian Bagratid kingdom from 953 to 1045, when it was taken by the Byzantines. After the short-lived Armenian kingdom, the city was taken from the Byzantines by the Great Seljuks of Iran, then by the king of Georgia, then by Kurdish emirs. The struggle for the city went on among these groups until the Mongols arrived in 1239 and cleared everybody else out. The Mongols, who were nomads, had no use for city life, and Ani became a ghost city after their victory.

Things to See

Your soldier-guide will take you through the **Alp Arslan Kapısı**, a double gate. Your first view of Ani is stunning, the wrecks of buildings in a ghost city, where once hundreds of thousands lived. Within the walls are the ruins of eight churches, a convent and the **citadel** (İç Kale). The **cathedral** is the most impressive of the churches. Ani became the seat of the Armenian Catholicos in 993; this church was built between 989 and 1010. As the grandest religious edifice in the city, it was transformed into a mosque whenever Muslims held Ani, and back to a church when the Christians took over. Other than the cathedral, the most interesting churches are the **Church of the Holy Saviour** (1036) and the **Church of St Gregory of Tigran Honentz** (1215).

You won't be allowed to visit the citadel. As you walk back toward the Alp Arslan Kapısı, take a good look around and fix it in your memory, for this is the only 'photograph' of Ani you'll take. If you find it constricting to be so limited in your examination of these magnificent remnants, keep in mind that you can look, point, photograph and picnic to your heart's content on the island of

Akdamar near Van, where the Church of the Holy Cross is much better preserved, with much more that is worthy of close examination.

Getting There

To visit Ani, you must have permission from the authorities. The Turks want no trouble with the Russians, so everyone going into the no-man's-land must be accounted for. That's right: Ani lies so close to the border that under normal conditions anyone spotted there would be shot on sight. The Russians make an exception for the ruins, but there are some rules you must follow.

There are only a few buses each day out to Ani Köyü, the hamlet near the ruins. They depart at 6 am and 1 pm; the last bus returning to Kars departs Ani at 4 pm. The road, being a dead-end, has little regular traffic good for hitch-hiking, so you must arrange for transport yourself, and you must have it arranged before you apply to the authorities for permission to visit the site (they'll want to know how you're getting there, and back).

Unless you have a car, or can locate other tourists (Turkish or foreign) in Kars who do have a car, you may want to arrange with a local dolmuş or taxi driver to take you out and back. The going rate is about 7000TL (US$9.80) for the return trip. The museum may help you find a taxi and others to share the trip, but it may end up costing twice the going rate for the taxi. Begin making your arrangements as soon as you arrive in Kars. By the way, there are no services (hotels, restaurants) of any kind at Ani.

Formalities Head for the museum to begin formalities for the visit. Have your passport with you.

After they take down the necessary information, you'll be referred to the Emniyet Müdürlüğü (ehm-nee-YEHT mew-dewr-lew, Security Headquarters), where police officials in green uniforms will approve your application. Usually the approval is routine. Then you set out on the road, and when you reach Ani you report to the soldiers at the Jandarma (zhahn-DAHR-mah, Gendarmerie) post. A soldier will be assigned to guide you around the ruins. If you stay with the soldier and obey the regulations, you will have no trouble.

The regulations include these: no staring or pointing toward the Russian side; no use of binoculars or cameras whatsoever; no taking notes; no picnicking or remaining in one spot for too long; stay together in the group. All this is frightening, but there will be no trouble so long as you scrupulously observe the rules.

Turkish Language Guide

History

From the time when Turks first encountered Islam about the year 670, Turkish had been written in the Arabic alphabet, the letters of the Koran. But the Arabic letters did not suit the sounds of Turkish well, and made the task of literacy very difficult.

Even under the empire, alphabet reform had been proposed in order to promote literacy and progress. But it was Atatürk, of course, who did it in 1928. The story is typical of him: when told that it would take several years of expert consultation to devise a suitable Latin alphabet for Turkish, and then about five years at the least to implement it, he replied, 'The change will be carried out in three months, or not at all'. Needless to say, the new alphabet was ready in six weeks, and three months later the old alphabet was forbidden in public use. And it worked! The president of the republic himself got a slate and chalk, went into the public parks, and held informal classes to teach the citizenry the new letters.

SYNTAX & PRONUNCIATION

Despite daunting oddities such as the soft 'g' (ğ) and undotted 'i' (ı), Turkish is phonetic and simple to pronounce. In a few minutes you can learn to pronounce the sounds reasonably well. The guide below will show you how.

As for grammar, that's another matter entirely. Though supremely logical and unencumbered by genders and mountains of exceptions, Turkish structure is so different from that of the Indo-European languages that it is completely unfamiliar at first. A few hints will help you comprehend road and shop signs, schedules and menus.

Suffixes

A Turkish word consists of a root and one or more suffixes added to it. Though in English we have only a few suffixes (-'s for possessive, -s or -es for plural), Turkish has lots and lots of suffixes. Not only that, these suffixes are subject to an unusual system of 'vowel harmony' whereby most of the vowel sounds in a word are made in a similar manner. What this means is that the suffix might be -lar when attached to one word, but -ler when attached to another; it's the same suffix, though.

Sometimes these suffixes are preceded by a 'buffer letter', a 'y' or an 'n'.

Here are some of the suffixes you'll encounter most frequently.

Noun Suffixes

-a, -e	to
-dan, -den	from
-dır, -dir, -dur, -dür	emphatic (ignore it!)
-(s)ı, -(s)i, -(s)u, -(s)ü	for object-nouns (ignore it!)
-(n)ın, -(n)in	possessive
-lar, -ler	plural
-lı, -li, -lu, -lü	with
-sız, -siz, -suz, -süz	without

Verb Suffixes

-ar, -er, -ır, -ir, -ur, -ür	simple present tense

448

-acak, -ecek, -acağ-, -eceğ-	future tense
-dı, -di, -du, -dü	simple past tense
-ıyor-, -iyor-	continuous (like our '-ing')
-mak, -mek	infinitive ending

Nouns

Suffixes can be added to nouns to modify them. The two you will come across most frequently are -ler and -lar, which form the plural: *otel*, hotel; *oteller*, hotels; *araba*, car; *arabalar*, cars.

Other suffixes modify in other ways: *ev*, house; *Ahmet*, Ahmet; but *Ahmet'in evi*, Ahmet's house. Similarly with *Istanbul* and *banka*: it's *Istanbul Bankası* when the two are used together. You may see -i, -ı, -u, or -ü; -si, -sı, -su, or -sü added to any noun. A *cami* is a mosque; but the *cami* built by Mehmet Pasha is the *Mehmet Paşa Camii*, with two i's. Ask for a *bira* and the waiter will bring you a bottle of whatever type he has; ask for an *Efes Birası* and that's the brand you'll get.

Yet other suffixes on nouns tell you about direction: -a or -e means 'to', as in *otobüs*, 'bus', but *otobüse* (oh-toh-bews-EH), to the bus; *Bodrum'a* (boh-droom-AH), to Bodrum. The suffix -dan or -den means 'from': *Ankara'dan*, from Ankara; *köprüden*, from the bridge. Stress is on these final syllables (-a or -dan) whenever they are used.

Verbs

The infinitive form is with -mak or -mek, as in *gitmek*, to go; *almak*, to take. The stress in the infinitive is always on the last syllable, 'geet-MEHK', 'ahl-MAHK'.

The simple present form is with -r, as in *gider*, 'he/she/it goes', *giderim*, 'I go'. The suffix -iyor means about the same, *gidiyorum*, 'I'm going'. For the future, there's -ecek or -acak, as in *alacak* (ah-lah-JAHK), 'he will take (it)'.

Word Order

The nouns and adjectives usually come first, then the verb; the final suffix on the verb is the subject of the sentence: *İstanbul'a gideceğim*, 'I'll go to İstanbul'; *Halı almak istiyorum*, 'I want to buy (take) a carpet' (literally 'carpet to buy want I').

Pronunciation Key

Most letters are pronounced as they appear. Here are the tricky ones, the vowels and the exceptions.

A, a	short 'a' as in *art* or *bar*
â	very faint 'y' sound in preceding consonant, eg Lâleli is lyaah-leh-LEE
E, e	'eh' as the first vowel in *ever* or *fell*
İ, i	as 'ee' in *see*
I, ı	'uh' or the vowel sound in *were* or *sir*
O, o	same as in English
Ö, ö	same sound as in German, or like English 'ur', as in *fur*
U, u	'oo', like the vowel in *moo* or *blue*
Ü, ü	same as in German, or 'ew' in *few*
C, c	pronounced like English 'j' as in *jet*
Ç, ç	'ch' as in *church*
G, g	always hard like *get*, not soft like *gentle*
ğ	not pronounced; lengthens preceding vowel; ignore it!

H, h   never silent, always unvoiced, as in *half*
J, j   like French 'j', English 'zh', or the 'z' in *azure*
S, s   always 'sss' as in *stress*, not 'zzz' as in *ease*
Ş, ş   'sh' as in *show*
V, v   soft, almost like a 'w'
W, w   exists only in foreign words; not really Turkish
X, x   only in foreign words; Turks use 'ks' instead

An important point for English speakers to remember is that each Turkish letter is pronounced; there are no diphthongs as in English. Thus the name *Mithat* is pronounced 'meet-HOT', not like the English word 'methought', and Turkish *meshut* is 'mess-HOOT', not 'meh-SHOOT'. Watch out for this! Your eye, used to English double-letter sounds, will keep trying to find them in Turkish, where they don't exist.

These examples also demonstrate that the 'h' is pronounced as an unvoiced aspiration (like the first sound in 'have' or 'heart', the sound a Cockney drops), and it is pronounced every time it occurs; it is never combined to make a diphthong. So your Turkish friend is named not 'aa-meht' but 'ahh-MEHT'; the word *rehber*, 'guide', is not 're-ber' but 'rehh-BEHR'. In the old days, English writers used to spell the name *Achmet* just to get people to breathe that 'h', but it didn't work: people said 'otch-met'. Say, 'a HALF'. Now say 'Ah MEHT' the same way.

Common Words & Phrases

Cardinal Numbers

¼	Çeyrek	chehy-REHK
½	Yarım	YAH-ruhm (used alone, as 'I want half')
½	Buçuk	boo-CHOOK (always used with a whole number, as '1½', *bir buçuk*)
1	Bir	BEER
2	İki	ee-KEE
3	Üç	EWCH
4	Dört	DURRT
5	Beş	BEHSH
6	Altı	ahl-TUH
7	Yedi	yeh-DEE
8	Sekiz	seh-KEEZ
9	Dokuz	doh-KOOZ
10	On	OHN
11	On bir	ohn BEER
12	On iki	ohn ee-KEE
13	On üç	ohn EWCH
20	Yirmi	yeer-MEE
30	Otuz	oh-TOOZ
40	Kırk	KUHRK
50	Elli	ehl-LEE
60	Altmış	ahlt-MUSH

70	*Yetmiş*	yeht-MEESH
80	*Seksen*	sehk-SEHN
90	*Doksan*	dohk-SAHN
100	*Yüz*	YEWZ
200	*İki yüz*	ee-KEE yewz
1000	*Bin*	BEEN
2000	*İki bin*	ee-KEE been
10,000	*On bin*	OHN been
1,000,000	*Milyon*	meel-YOHN

Ordinal Numbers

Ordinal numbers consist of the number plus the suffix -inci, -ıncı, -uncu, or -üncü, depending upon 'vowel harmony'

First	*Birinci*	beer-EEN-jee
Second	*İkinci*	ee-KEEN-jee
Sixth	*Altıncı*	ahl-TUHN-juh
Thirteenth	*Onüçüncü*	ohn-ew-CHEWN-jew
Hundredth	*Yüzüncü*	yewz-EWN-jew

Days of the Week

Day	*Gün*	GEWN
Week	*Hafta*	hahf-TAH
Sunday	*Pazar*	pah-ZAHR
Monday	*Pazartesi*	pah-ZAHR-teh-see
Tuesday	*Salı*	sah-LUH
Wednesday	*Çarşamba*	char-shahm-BAH
Thursday	*Perşembe*	pehr-shehm-BEH
Friday	*Cuma*	joo-MAH
Saturday	*Cumartesi*	joo-MAHR-teh-see

Months of the Year

Month	*Ay*	AHY
Year	*Sene*	SEH-neh
Year	*Yıl*	YUHL
January	*Ocak*	oh-JAHK
February	*Şubat*	shoo-BAHT
March	*Mart*	MAHRT
April	*Nisan*	nee-SAHN
May	*Mayıs*	mah-YUSS
June	*Haziran*	HAH-zee-RAHN
July	*Temmuz*	teh-MOOZ
August	*Ağustos*	AH-oo-STOHSS
September	*Eylül*	ehy-LEWL
October	*Ekim*	eh-KEEM
November	*Kasım*	kah-SUHM
December	*Aralık*	AH-rah-LUHK

The Basics

| Yes | *Evet* | eh-VEHT |

No	*Hayır*	HAH-yuhr
Not	*...... degil*	deh-YEEL
None	*Yok*	YOHK
And	*Ve*	VEH
Or	*Veya*	veh-YAH
Good	*İyi*	EE
Bad	*Fenah*	feh-NAH
Beautiful	*Güzel*	gew-ZEHL
Please	*Lütfen*	LEWT-fehn
Pardon me	*Affedersiniz*	AHF-feh-DEHR-see-neez
Pardon	*Pardon*	pahr-DOHN
Help yourself	*Buyurun(uz)*	BOOY-roon-(ooz)
Thank you	*Teşekkür ederim*	teh-sheh-KEWR eh-deh-reem
	Sağ ol	'sowl' (like 'howl')
very much	*Çok teşekkür ederim*	CHOHK ...
Thanks	*Teşekkürler*	teh-sheh-kewr-LEHR
Thanks	*Mersi*	mehr-SEE
You're welcome	*Bir Şey degil*	beer SHEHY deh-YEEL
What?	*Ne?*	NEH
How?	*Nasıl?*	NAH-suhl
Who?	*Kim?*	KEEM
Why?	*Niçin, neden?*	NEE-cheen, NEH-dehn
Which one?	*Hangisi?*	HAHN-gee-see
What's this?	*Bu ne?*	BOO neh
Where is ... ...?	*...... nerede?*	NEH-reh-deh
When?	*Ne zaman?*	NEH zah-mahn
At what time?	*Saat kaçta?*	saht-KAHCH-tah
How much/many?	*Kaç/tane?*	KAHCH/tah-neh
How many liras?	*Kaç lira?*	KAHCH lee-rah
How many hours?	*Kaç saat?*	KAHCH sah-aht
How many minutes?	*Kaç dakika?*	KAHCH dahk-kah
What does it mean?	*Ne demek?*	NEH deh-mehk
This	*Bu(nu)*	boo(NOO)
That	*Şu(nu)*	shoo(NOO)
The other	*o(nu)*	oh(NOO)
Give me	*...... bana verin*	bah-NAH veh-reen
I want	*...... istiyorum*	ees-tee-YOH-room
Hot/cold	*Sıcak/soğuk*	suh-JAHK/soh-OOK
Big/small	*Büyük/küçük*	bew-YEWK/kew-CHEWK
New/old	*Yeni/eski*	yeh-NEE/ehss-KEE
Open/closed	*Açık/kapalı*	ah-CHUHK/kah-pah-LUH

Greetings & Polite Phrases

Hello	*Merhaba*	MEHR-hah-bah
Good morning,	*Günaydın*	gew-nahy-DUHN
Good day	*Günaydın*	gew-nahy-DUHN
Good evening	*İyi akşamlar*	EE ahk-shahm-LAHR
Good night	*İyi geceler*	EE geh-jeh-LEHR

Good-bye	*Allaha ısmarladık*	ah-LAHS-mahr-lah-duhk (said only by the person who is departing to go somewhere – see *Güle Güle*)
Bon voyage	*Güle güle*	gew-LEH gew-LEH
How are you?	*Nasılsınız?*	NAHS-suhl-suh-nuhz (see *İyiyim, teşekkür ederim*)
Very well	*Çok iyiyim*	CHOHK ee-YEE-yeem
Pardon me	*Affedersiniz*	af-feh-DEHR-see-neez
May it contribute to your health	*Afiyet olsun!*	ah-fee-EHT ohl-soon (said to someone sitting down to a meal)
May your life be spared	*Başınız sağ olsun!*	bah-shuh-nuhz SAAH ohl-soon (said to someone who has just experienced a death in the family)
May your soul be safe from harm	*Canınız sağ olsun!*	jah-nuh-nuhz SAAH ohl-soon (said to someone who has just accidentally broken something)
May it be in your past	*Geçmiş olsun!*	gech-MEESH ohl-soon (said to someone who is ill, injured, or otherwise distressed)
Good-bye	*Güle güle*	gew-LEH gew-leh (said only by the person who is staying behind; literally, 'Go smiling' – see *Allah ısmarladık*)
Good morning/ Good day	*Günaydın*	gew-nah-yee-DUHN
I'm fine, thank you	*İyiyim, teşekkür ederim*	ee-YEE-yihm, tesh-ek-KEWR eh-dehr-eem
Please	*Lütfen*	LEWT-fehn (see *Teşekkür ederim*)
May it last for hours	*Saatler olsun!*	saaht-LEHR ohl-soon (said to someone who just emerged from a bath or shower, a shave or a hair cut. It's a corruption of *sınhatler olsun*)
'In your honour' or 'To your health'	*Şerefinize!*	sheh-rehf-ee-neez-EH

Getting Around
Requests

Where is a/the	. . . . . . *nerede?*	NEH-reh-deh
. . . . . . railway station?	*Gar/İstasyon . . . . . .*	GAHR, ees-tah-SYOHN
. . . . . . bus station?	*Otogar . . . . . .*	OH-toh-gahr
. . . . . . cheap hotel?	*Ucuz bir otel . . . . . .*	oo-JOOZ beer oh-TEHL
. . . . . . toilet?	*Tuvalet . . . . . .*	too-vah-LEHT
. . . . . . restaurant?	*Lokanta . . . . . .*	loh-KAHN-tah
. . . . . . post office?	*Postane . . . . . .*	POHSS-tah-neh
. . . . . . policeman?	*Polis memuru . . . . . .*	poh-LEES meh-moo-roo
. . . . . . checkroom?	*Emanetçi . . . . . .*	EH-mah-NEHT-chee

Left	*Sol*	SOHL
Right	*Sağ*	SAH
Straight on	*Doğru*	doh-ROO

Here	*Burada*	BOO-rah-dah
There	*Şurada*	SHOO-rah-dah
Over there	*Orada*	OH-rah-dah
Near	*Yakın*	yah-KUHN
Far	*Uzak*	oo-ZAHK
A ticket to	*. . . . . . bir bilet*	BEER bee-LEHT
A ticket to İstanbul	*İstanbul'a bir bilet*	ih-STAHN-bool-AH
Map	*Harita*	HAH-ree-TAH
Timetable	*Tarife*	tah-ree-FEH
Ticket	*Bilet*	bee-LEHT
Reserved seat	*Numaralı yer*	noo-MAH-rah-LUH yehr
1st class	*Birinci mevki*	beer-EEN-jee mehv-kee
2nd class	*İkinci mevki*	ee-KEEN-jee mehv-kee
For today	*Bugün için*	BOO-gewn ee-cheen
For tomorrow	*Yarın için*	Yah-ruhn ee-cheen
For Friday	*Cuma günü için*	joo-MAH gew-new ee-cheen
Single/one-way	*Gidiş*	gee-DEESH
Return/round-trip	*Gidiş-Dönüş*	gee-DEESH-dew-NURSH

Time

When does it	*Ne zaman . . . . . .*	NEH zah-mahn
. . . . . . depart?	*. . . . . . kalkar?*	kahl-KAHR
. . . . . . arrive?	*. . . . . . gelir?*	geh-LEER
Eight o'clock	*Saat sekiz*	sah-AHT seh-KEEZ
At nine-thirty	*Saat dokuz buçukta*	sah-AHT doh-KOOZ boo-chook-TAH
In 20 minutes	*Yirmi dakikada*	yeer-MEE dahk-kah-dah
How many hours does it take?	*Kaç saat sürer?*	KAHCH sah-aht sew-REHR
. . . . . . hours	*. . . . . . saat*	sah-AHT
. . . . . . minutes	*. . . . . . dakika*	dahk-KAH
Early/late	*Erken/geç*	ehr-KEHN/GECH
Fast/slow	*Çabuk/yavaş*	chah-BOOK/yah-VAHSH
Upper/lower	*Yukarı/aşağı*	yoo-kah-RUH/ah-shah-UH

Rail

Railway	*Demiryolu*	deh-MEER-yoh-loo
Train	*Tren*	tee-REHN
Railway station	*Gar, İstasyon*	GAHR, ees-tahs-YOHN
Sleeping car	*Yataklı vagon*	yah-tahk-LUH vah-gohn
Dining car	*Yemekli vagon*	yeh-mehk-LEE vah-gohn
Couchette	*Kuşet*	koo-SHEHT
No-smoking car	*Sigara içilmeyen vagon*	*see-GAH-rah eech-EEL-mee-yehn*
Computer guichet	*Bilgisayar gişe*	beel-GEE-sah-yahr GEE-sheh
Student (ticket)	*talebe (bileti)*	tah-leh-BEH
Full-fare (ticket)	*tam (bileti)*	TAHM
Daily	*hergün*	HEHR-gurn
Tomorrow	*yarın*	YAHR-uhn

Bus

Bus	*Otobüs, araba*	oh-toh-BEWSS
Bus terminal	*Otogar*	OH-toh-gahr
Direct (bus)	*Direk(t)*	dee-REK
Indirect (route)	*Aktarmalı*	ahk-tahr-mah-LUH

Air

Airplane	*Uçak*	oo-CHAHK
Airport	*Havaalanı*	hah-VAH-ah-lah-nuh
Flight	*Uçuş*	oo-CHOOSH
Gate	*Kapı*	kah-PUH

Boat

Ship	*Gemi*	geh-MEE
Ferryboat	*Feribot*	FEH-ree-boht
Dock	*İskele*	ees-KEH-leh
Cabin	*Kamara*	KAH-mah-rah
Berth	*Yatak*	yah-TAHK
Class	*Mevki, sınıf*	MEHV-kee, suh-nuhf

Highway Terms

God protect me	*Allah Korusun*	ah-LAH koh-roo-soon
Wonder of God	*Maaşallah*	MAASH-ah-lah
Dangerous cargo	*Tehlikeli madde*	teh-LEE-keh-LEE mahd-deh
'Liquid fuel'	*Akaryakıt*	ah-KAHR-yah-kuht
Diesel fuel	*Mazot, motorin*	mah-SOHT, MOH-toh-reen
Petrol, gasoline	*Benzin*	behn-ZEEN
Normal, regular	*Normal*	nohr-MAHL
Super, extra	*Süper*	seur-PEHR
Motor oil	*Motor yağı*	moh-TOHR yah-uh
Air (tyres)	*Hava (lâstik)*	hah-VAH (lyaass-TEEK)
Exhaust (system)	*Egzos(t)*	ehk-ZOHSS
Headlamp	*Far*	FAHR
Brake(s)	*Fren*	FREHN
Steering (-wheel)	*Direksiyon*	dee-REHK-see-YOHN
Electric repairman	*Oto elektrikçi*	oh-TOH ee-lehk-TREEK-chee
Tyre repairman	*Oto lâstikçi*	oh-TOH lyass-TEEK-chee
Car washing	*Yıkama*	yuh-kah-MAH
Lubrication	*Yağlama*	YAH-lah-MAH
Highways	*Karayolları*	KAH-rah-yoh-lah-ruh
Road repairs	*Yol onarımı*	YOHL oh-nah-ruh-muh
Road construction	*Yol yapımı*	YOHL yah-puh-muh
Overtaking lane	*Tırmanma şeridi*	tuhr-MAHN-mah sheh-ree-dee
Low verge (shoulder)	*Düşük banket*	deur-SHEURK bahn-KEHT
Mountain pass	*Geçit, -di*	geh-CHEET, GEH-chee-dee
Switch headlamps	*Farlar kontrol ediniz*	fahr-LAHR kohn-TROHL eh-dee-neez
Careful! Slow!	*Dikkat, yavaş*	dee-KAHT, yah-VAHSH
Vehicles entering	*Araç çıkabilir*	ah-RAHCH chuk-kah-buh-luhr
Military vehicle	*Askerî araç*	ahss-keh-REE ah-rahch
Forbidden zone	*Yasak bölge*	yah-SAHK beurl-geh

Rest area	*Dinlenme parkı*	deen-lehn-MEH pahr-kuh
Spring (potable)	*Çeşme*	CHESH-meh
Motorway, expressway	*Otoyol*	OH-toh-yohl
Long vehicle	*Uzun araç*	oo-ZOON ah-rahch
Wide vehicle	*Geniş araç*	geh-NEESH ah-rahch
Population	*Nufüs*	noo-FEURSS
Altitude	*Rakım*	rah-KUHM

Note: Towns are marked by blue signs with white lettering; villages are marked by white signs with black lettering. Yellow signs with black lettering mark sights of touristic interest. Yellow signs with blue lettering have to do with village development projects.

Accommodation

Where is	... ... *nerede?*	NEH-reh-deh
Where is a hotel?	*Bir otel nerede?*	BEER oh-TEHL NEH-reh-deh?
Where is the toilet?	*Tuvalet nerede?*	too-vah-LEHT NEH-reh-deh?
Where is the manager?	*Patron nerede?*	pah-TROHN NEH-reh-deh?
Where is someone who knows English?	*İngilizce bilen bir kimse nerede?*	EEN-geh-LEEZ-jeh bee-lehn beer KEEM-seh NEH-reh-deh?

To request a room, say one or more of the phrases below, adding ... *istiyorum*, 'I want ....' For example, *İki kişilik oda istiyorum*, 'I want a two-person room', or *Çift yataklı oda istiyorum*, 'I want a twin-bedded room'. If you want to be fully correct, say *istiyoruz* for the plural ('We want ... '). For the courageous, string them together: *Sakin iki kişilik geniş yataklı banyosuz oda istiyoruz*, 'We want a quiet bathless double room with a wide (double) bed'.

Room	*Oda*	OH-dah
Single room	*Bir kişilik oda*	BEER kee-shee-leek OH-dah
Double room	*İki kişilik oda*	ee-KEE kee-shee-leek OH-dah
Triple room	*Üç kişilik oda*	EWCH kee-shee-leek OH-dah
Room with one bed	*Tek yataklı oda*	TEHK yah-tahk-LUH OH-dah
Room with two beds	*İki yataklı oda*	ee-KEE yah-tahk-LUH OH-dahh
Room with twin beds	*Çift yataklı oda*	CHEEFT yah-tahk-LUH OH-dah
Double bed	*Geniş yatak*	geh-NEESH yah-tahk
Room with bath	*Banyolu oda*	BAHN-yoh-LOO OH-dah
Room without bath	*Banyosuz oda*	BAHN-yoh-SOOZ OH-dah
Room with shower	*Duşlu oda*	doosh-LOO OH-dah
Room with washbasin	*Lavabolu oda*	LAH-vah-boh-LOO oh-dah
A quiet room	*Sakin bir oda*	sah-KEEN beer oh-dah
It's very noisy	*Çok gürültülü*	CHOHK gew-rewl-tew-lew
What does it cost?	*Kaç lira?*	KAHCH lee-rah
Cheaper	*Daha ucuz*	dah-HAH oo-jooz
Better	*Daha iyi*	dah-HAH ee
Very expensive	*Çok pahalı*	CHOHK pah-hah-luh
Bath	*Banyo*	BAHN-yoh

Turkish bath	*Hamam*	hah-MAHM
Shower	*Duş*	DOOSH
Soap	*Sabun*	sah-BOON
Shampoo	*Şampuan*	SHAHM-poo-AHN
Towel	*Havlu*	hahv-LOO
Toilet paper	*Tuvalet kağıdı*	too-vah-LEHT kyah-uh-duh
Hot water	*Sıcak su*	suh-JAHK soo
Cold water	*Soğuk su*	soh-OOH soo
Clean	*Temiz*	teh-MEEZ
Not clean	*Temiz değil*	teh-MEEZ deh-YEEL
Laundry	*Çamaşır*	chah-mah-SHUHR
Dry cleaning	*Kuru temizleme*	koo-ROO teh-meez-leh-meh
Central heating	*Kalorifer*	kah-LOH-ree-FEHR
Air conditioning	*Klima*	KLEE-mah
Light(s)	*Işık(lar)*	uh-SHUHK(-LAHR)
Light bulb	*Ampül*	ahm-PEWL

Shopping

Do you have . . . . . . ?	. . . . . . *var mı?*	VAHR muh
We don't have	. . . . . . *yok*	YOHK
Cheap/expensive	*Ucuz/pahalı*	oo-JOOZ/pah-hah-LUH
Price	*Fiyat*	fee-YAHT
Which?	*Hangi?*	HAHN-gee
This one	*Bunu*	boo-NOO
Money	*Para*	PAH-rah
Small change	*Bozuk para*	boh-ZOOK pah-rah
Turkish liras	*Lira*	LEE-rah
Dollars	*Dolar*	doh-LAHR
Very expensive	*Çok pahalı*	CHOHK pah-hah-luh
I'll give you	. . . . . . *vereceğim*	VEH-reh-JEH-yeem
Shop	*Dükkan*	dyook-KAHN
Market	*Çarşı*	chahr-SHUH
This much	*Bu kadar*	BOO kah-dahr
Service charge	*Servis ücreti*	sehr-VEES ewj-reh-tee
Tax	*Vergi*	VEHR-gee

Bank

Identification	*Kimlik*	KEEM-leek
Exchange	*Kambiyo*	KAHM-bee-yoh
Commission	*Komisyon*	koh-mees-YOHN
Charge, fee	*Ücret*	eurj-REHT
Equivalent	*Karşılık*	kahr-shuh-LUHK
Exchange rate	*Kur*	KOOR
Foreign currency	*Döviz*	durr-VEEZ
Purchase	*Alış*	ah-LUSH
Sale	*Veriş*	veh-REESH
Cash	*Efektif*	eh-fehk-TEEF
Cheque	*Çek*	CHEK
Stamp	*Pul*	POOL
Tax	*Vergi*	VEHR-gee

| Working hours | *Çalışma saatleri* | chal-ush-MAH sah-aht-leh-ree |
| Cashier | *Kasa, vezne* | KAH-sah, VEHZ-neh |

Post Office

Where's the post office?	*Postane nerede?*	AH-jah-bah POHS-tah-neh NEH-reh-deh
Post office	*Postane, postahane*	POHSS-tah-NEH
Post office	*PTT*	peh-teh-TEH
Open	*Açık*	ah-CHUHK
Express mail, special delivery	*Ekspres*	ehks-PRESS
Customs	*Gümrük*	gewm-REWK
Money order	*Havale*	hah-vah-LEH
Telephone token (large, small)	*Jeton (Büyük, Küçük)*	kew-CHEWK pah-keht
Closed	*Kapalı*	kah-pah-LUH
Postcard	*Kartpostal*	kahrt-pohs-TAHL
Parcel	*Koli*	KOH-lee
Inspection (prior to mailing)	*Kontrol*	kohn-TROHL
Small packet (mail category)	*Küçük Paket*	kew-CHEWK pah-keht
Printed matter (mail category)	*Matbua*	MAHT-boo-ah
Letter	*Mektup*	meht-TOOP
Parcel	*Paket*	pah-KEHT
Poste Restante, General Delivery	*Postrestant*	pohst-rehs-TAHNT
Postage stamp	*Pul*	POOL
Registered mail	*Kayıtlı*	KA-yuht-luh
By plane (air mail)	*Uçakla* or *Uçak İle*	oo-CHAHK-lah, oo-CHAHK-ee-leh

Menu Translator

Except in the fanciest restaurants, Turks don't have much use for menus. This is a society in which the waiter (*garson*, gahr-SOHN) is supposed to know his business and to help you order. Nonetheless, the waiter will bring a menu (*menü* (meh-NEW) or *yemek listesi* (yeh-MEHK lees-teh-see) if you ask for one. The menu will at least give you some prices so you'll know what you will be asked to pay.

Otherwise, you may choose from the menu several times only to get the response *Yok!* (YOHK, None!). The menu, as I said, is not much use. Instead, the waiter will probably say *Gel! Gel!* (Come, come!) and lead you into the kitchen for a look. In the glass-fronted refrigerator cabinets you'll see the *şiş kebap, köfte, bonfile* steaks, lamb chops, liver, kidneys and fish which are in supply. Also in the cabinet may be the cheeses, salads and vegetable dishes, if meant to be served cold. Then he'll lead you right to the fire for a look at the stews, soups, pastas and *pilavs*. With sign language, you'll have everything you want in no time. It's a good idea to ask prices.

Some general words to know are:

Lokanta	loh-KAHN-tah	Restaurant
Pastane	PAHSS-tah-neh	Pastry-shop
Fırın	FUH-ruhn	'Oven' (bakery)
Pideci	PEE-deh-jee	'Pizza' place
Köfteci	KURF-teh-jee	Köfte restaurant
Kebapçı	keh-BAHP-chuh	Kebap restaurant
Büfe	bew-FEH	Snack shop
İçkili	eech-kee-LEE	Alcoholic drinks served
İçkisiz	eech-kee-SEEZ	No alcohol served
Aile salonu	ah-yee-LEH sah-loh-noo	Family (ladies) dining room
Aileye mahsustur	ah-yee-LEH mah-SOOS-tuhr	No single men allowed
Kahvahltı	KAHH-vahl-TUH	Breakfast
Öğle yemeği	ury-LEH yeh-meh-yee	Lunch
Akşam yemeği	ahk-SHAHM yeh-meh-yee	Supper
Yemek	yeh-MEHK	To eat; meal, dish
Porsyon	pohr-SYOHN	Portion, serving
Çatal	chah-TAHL	Fork
Bıçak	buh-CHAHK	Knife
Kaşık	kah-SHUHK	Spoon
Tabak	tah-BAHK	Plate
Bardak	bahr-DAHK	Glass
Hesap	heh-SAHP	Bill, check
Servis ücreti	sehr-VEES ewj-reh-tee	Service charge
Vergi	VEHR-gee	Tax
Bahşiş	bah-SHEESH	Tip
Yanlış	yahn-LUSH	Error
Bozuk para	boh-ZOOK pah-rah	Small change

Here is a guide to restaurant words, arranged (more or less) in the order of a Turkish menu and a Turkish meal. I've given the names of the courses (*çorba, et,* etc) in the singular form; you may see them in the plural (*çorbalar, etler,* etc).

Çorba (CHOHR-bah, Soup)

Balık çorbası	bah-LUHK	Fish soup
Domates çorbası	doh-MAH-tess	Tomato soup
Düğün çorbası	dew-EWN	Egg-and-lemon soup
Et suyu (yumurtalı)	EHT soo-yoo, yoo-moor-tah-LUH	Mutton broth with egg
Ezo gelin çorbası	EH-zoh GEH-leen	Lentil & rice soup
Haşlama	hahsh-lah-MAH	Broth with mutton
İşkembe çorbası	eesh-KEHM-beh	Tripe soup
Mercimek çorbası	mehr-jee-MEHK	Lentil soup
Paça	PAH-chah	Trotter soup
Sebze çorbası	SEHB-zeh	Vegetable soup

Şehriye çorbası	shehh-ree-YEH	Vermicelli soup
Tavuk çorbası	tah-VOOK	Chicken soup
Yayla çorbası	YAHY-lah	Yogurt & barley soup

Meze (MEH-zeh, Hors d'Oeuvres)

Meze can include almost anything, and you can easily – and delightfully – make an entire meal of *meze*. Often you will be brought a tray from which you can choose those you want.

Beyaz peynir	bey-AHZ pehy-neer	White cheese
Börek	bur-REHK	Flaky pastry
Kabak dolması	kah-BAHK	Stuffed squash/marrow
Patlıcan salatası	paht-luh-JAHN	Aubergine/eggplant puree
Pilaki, Piyaz	pee-LAH-kee	Cold white beans vinaigrette
Tarama salatası	tah-rah-MAH	Red caviar in mayonnaise
Yalancı dolması	yah-LAHN-juh	See *Yaprak dolması*
Yaprak dolması	yah-PRAHK dohl-mah-suh	Stuffed vine leaves
(etli)	eht-LEE	with lamb (hot)
(zeytinyağlı)	zehy-teen-yah-LUH	with rice (cold)

Balık (bah-LUHK, Fish)

A menu is no use in ordering fish. You must ask the waiter what's fresh, and then ask the approximate price. The fish will be weighed, and the price computed at the day's per-kilo rate. Sometimes you can haggle. Buy fish in season (*mevsimli*, mehv-seem-LEE), as fish out of season are very expensive.

Alabalık	ah-LAH-bah-luhk	Trout
Barbunya	bahr-BOON-yah	Red mullet
Dil balığı	DEEL bah-luh	Sole
Hamsi	HAHM-see	Anchovy (fresh)
Havyar	hahv-YAHR	Caviar
Istakoz	uhss-tah-KOHZ	Lobster
Kalkan	kahl-KAHN	Turbot
Karagöz	kah-rah-GURZ	Black bream
Karides	kah-REE-dess	Shrimp
Kefal	keh-FAHL	Grey mullet
Kılıç	kuh-LUHCH	Swordfish
Levrek	lehv-REHK	Sea bass
Lüfer	lew-FEHR	Bluefish
Mercan	mehr-JAHN	Red coralfish
Midye	MEED-yeh	Mussels
Palamut	PAH-lah-moot	Tunny, bonito
Pisi	PEE-see	Plaice
Sardalya	sahr-DAHL-yah	Sardine (fresh)
Tarama	tah-rah-MAH	Roe, red caviar
Trança	TRAHN-chah	Aegean tuna
Uskumru	oos-KOOM-roo	Mackerel
Yengeç	yehn-GECH	Crab

Et ve Kebap (EHT veh keh-BAHP, Meat & Kebab)
In *kebap* (keh-BAHP) the meat is always lamb, ground or in chunks; preparation, spices and extras (onions, peppers, *pide*) make the difference among the *kebaps*. Some may be ordered *yoğurtlu* (yoh-oort-LOO), with a side-serving of yogurt.

Adana kebap	ah-DAH-nah	Spicy-hot roast köfte
Böbrek	bur-BREHK	Kidney
Bonfile	bohn-fee-LEH	Small filet beefsteak
Bursa kebap	BOOR-sah	Döner with tomato sauce
Çerkez tavuğu	cher-KEHZ tah-voo	Chicken in walnut sauce
Çöp kebap	CHURP	Tiny bits of skewered lamb
Ciğer	jee-EHR	Liver
Dana	DAH-nah	Veal
Döner kebap	dur-NEHR	Spit-roasted lamb slices
Domuz	doh-MOOZ	Pork (forbidden to Muslims)
Etli pide, ekmek	eht-LEE PEE-deh, ehk-MEHK	Flat bread with ground lamb
Güveç	gew-VECH	Meat & vegetable stew
Kağıt kebap	kyah-UHT	Lamb & vegetables in paper
Karışık ızgara	kah-ruh-shuk uhz-gah-rah	Mixed grill (lamb)
Koç yumurtası	KOHCH yoo-moor-tah-suh	Ram's 'eggs' (testicles)
Köfte	KURF-teh	Grilled ground lamb patties
Kuzu (süt)	koo-ZOO (SEWT)	Milk-fed lamb
Orman kebap	ohr-MAHN	Roast lamb with onions
Pastırma	pahss-TUHR-mah	Sun-dried, spiced beef
Patlıcan kebap	paht-luh-JAHN	Aubergine/eggplant & meat
Piliç	pee-LEECH	Roasting chicken
Pirzola	peer-ZOH-lah	Cutlet (usually lamb)
Saç kavurma	SAHTCH kah-voor-mah	Wok-fried lamb
Şatobriyan	sha-TOH-bree-YAHN	Chateaubriand
Sığır	suh-UHR	Beef
Şinitzel	shee-NEET-zehl	Wienerschnitzel
Şiş kebap	SHEESH	Roast skewered lamb
Tandır kebap	tahn-DUHR	Pit-roasted lamb
Tas kebap	TAHSS	Lamb stew
Tavuk	tah-VOOK	Boiling chicken

Salata (sah-LAH-tah, Salad)
Each one of the names below would be followed by the word *salata* or *salatası*. You may be asked if you prefer it *sirkeli* (SEER-keh-LEE), with vinegar or *limonlu* (LEE-mohn-LOO), with lemon juice; most salads (except *söğüş*) come with olive oil. If you don't like hot peppers, say *Bibersiz* (BEE-behr-SEEZ), though this often doesn't work.

Amerikan	ah-meh-ree-KAHN	Mayonnaise, peas, carrots
Beyin	behy-EEN	Sheep's brain

Çoban	choh-BAHN	Chopped mixed salad
Domates salatalık	doh-MAH-tess sah-LAH-tah-luhk	Tomato & cucumber salad
Karışık	kah-ruh-SHUHK	Chopped mixed salad
Marul	mah-ROOL	Romaine lettuce
Patlıcan	paht-luh-JAHN	Roast aubergine/eggplant puree
Rus	ROOSS	Mayonnaise, peas, carrots
Söğüş	sur-EWSH	Sliced vegetables, no sauce
Turşu	toor-SHOO	Pickled vegetables
Yeşil	yeh-SHEEL	Green salad

Sebze (sehb-ZEH, Vegetable)

Bamya	BAHM-yah	Okra
Barbunye	bahr-BOON-yeh	Red beans
Bezelye	beh-ZEHL-yeh	Peas
Biber	bee-BEHR	Peppers
Domates	doh-MAH-tess	Tomato
Havuç	hah-VOOCH	Carrot
Hıyar	huh-YAHR	Cucumber
Ispınak	uhs-spuh-NAHK	Spinach
Kabak	kah-BAHK	Marrow/squash
Karnabahar	kahr-NAH-bah-hahr	Cauliflower
Kuru fasulye	koo-ROO fah-sool-yah	White beans
Lahana	lah-HAH-nah	Cabbage
Patates	pah-TAH-tess	Potato
Salatalık	sah-LAH-tah-luhk	Cucumber
Soğan	soh-AHN	Onion
Taze fasulye	tah-ZEH fah-sool-yah	Green beans
Turp	TOORP	Radish

Meyva (mehy-VAH, Fruit)

Armut	ahr-MOOT	Pear
Ayva	ahy-VAH	Quince
Çilek	chee-LEHK	Strawberries
Elma	ehl-MAH	Apple
Greyfurut	GREY-foo-root	Grapefruit
İncir	een-JEER	Fig
Karpuz	kahr-POOZ	Watermelon
Kavun	kah-VOON	Yellow melon
Kayısı	kahy-SUH	Apricot
Kiraz	kee-RAHZ	Cherry
Mandalin	mahn-dah-LEEN	Tangerine, Mandarin
Muz	MOOZ	Banana
Nar	NAHR	Pomegranate
Portakal	pohr-tah-KAHL	Orange
Şeftali	shef-tah-LEE	Peach
Üzüm	ew-ZEWM	Grapes
Vişne	VEESH-neh	Morello (sour cherry)

Tatlı (taht-LUH, Sweets/Desserts)

Aşure	ah-shoo-REH	Walnut, raisin, pea pudding
Baklava	bahk-lah-VAH	Many-layer pie, honey, nuts
Burma kadayıf	boor-MAH kah-dah-yuhf	Shredded wheat with pistachios & honey
Dondurma	dohn-DOOR-mah	Ice cream
Ekmek kadayıf	ehk-MEHK kah-dah-yuhf	Crumpet in syrup
Fırın sütlaç	foo-roon SEWT-lach	Baked rice pudding (cold)
Güllaç	gewl-LACH	Flaky pastry, nuts, milk
Helva	hehl-VAH	Semolina sweet
Hurma tatlısı	hoor-MAH	Semolina cake in syrup
Kabak tatlısı	kah-BAHK	Candied marrow/squash
Kadın göbegi	kah-DEEN gur-beh-yee	'Lady's navel', doughnut in syrup
Kazandibi	kah-ZAHN-dee-bee	'Bottom of the pot', baked pudding (cold)
Kek	KEHK	Cake
Keşkül	kehsh-KEWL	Milk & nut pudding
Komposto	kohm-POHSS-toh	Stewed fruit
Krem karamel	KREHM kah-rah-MEHL	Baked caramel custard
Krem şokolada	KREHM shoh-koh-LAH-dah	Chocolate pudding
Lokum	loh-KOOM	Turkish Delight
Meyve	mehy-VEH	Fruit
Muhallebi	moo-HAH-leh-bee	Rice flour & rosewater pudding
Pasta	PAHSS-tah	Pastry
Peynir tatlısı	pehy-NEER TAHT-luh-suh	Cheese cake
Sütlaç	sewt-LAHCH	Rice pudding
Tavuk gögsü	tah-VOOK gur-sew	Sweet of milk, rice, chicken
Tel kadayıf	TEHL kah-dah-yuhf	Shredded wheat in syrup
Yogurt tatlısı	yoh-OORT taht-luh-suh	Yogurt & egg pudding
Zerde	zehr-DEH	Saffron & rice sweet

Other Dishes & Condiments

Bal	BAHL	Honey
Beyaz peynir	bey-AHZ pey-neer	White (sheep's cheese)
Bisküvi	BEES-koo-VEE	Biscuits
Börek (-gi)	bur-REHK	Flaky or fried pastry
Kıymalı	kuhy-mah-LUH	With ground lamb
Peynirli	pehy-neer-LEE	With white cheese
Sigara	see-GAH-rah	'Cigarette' fritters
Su	SOO	Water
Buz	BOOZ	Ice
Cacık	jah-JUHK	Yogurt & grated cucumber
... Dolma(sı)	DOHL-mah(-suh)	Stuffed (vegetable)

Biber . . .	bee-BEHR	Green pepper
Kabak . . .	kah-BAHK	Marrow/squash
Lahana . . .	lah-HAH-nah	Cabbage leaves
Yalancı . . .	yah-LAHN-juh	Vine leaves
Yaprak . . .	yah-PRAHK	Vine leaves
Ekmek	ehk-MEHK	Bread
Hardal	hahr-DAHL	Mustard
İmam bayıldı	ee-MAHM bah-yuhl-duh	Aubergine/eggplant baked with onions & tomatoes
Kara biber	kah-RAH bee-behr	Black pepper
Karnıyarık	KAHR-nuh-yah-RUHK	Aubergine & lamb (hot)
Kaşar peynir	kah-SHAHR pey-neer	Mild yellow cheese
Limon	lee-MOHN	Lemon
Makarna	mah-KAHR-nah	Macaroni, noodles
Musakka	moo-sah-KAH	Aubergine & lamb pie
Pasta	PAHSS-tah	Pastry (not noodles)
Peynir	pehy-NEER	Cheese
Pide	PEE-deh	Pizza; flat bread
Reçel	reh-CHEHL	Fruit jam
Sarmısak	SAHR-muh-SAHK	Garlic
Şeker	sheh-KEHR	Sugar; candy; sweets
Sirke	SEER-keh	Vinegar
Siyah biber	see-YAH bee-behr	Black pepper
Spaket	spah-KEHT	Spaghetti
Tereyağı	TEH-reh-yah	Butter
Tuz	TOOZ	Salt
Yağ	YAH	Oil, fat
Yogurt	yoh-OORT	Yogurt
Zeytin	zehy-TEEN	Olives
Zeytinyağı	zehy-TEEN-yah-uh	Olive oil

İcki, Meşrubat (eech-KEE, mehsh-roo-BAHT, Drinks)

İcki usually refers to alcoholic beverages, *meşrubat* to soft drinks. If your waiter says *İçecek?* or *Ne içeceksiniz?*, he's asking what you'd like to drink.

As for Turkish coffee, you must order it by sweetness; the sugar is mixed in during the brewing, not afterwards. When the waiter asks *Kahve?* (kahh-VEH), say *sade* (sah-DEH) if you want no sugar; *az* (AHZ) if you want just a bit; *orta* (ohr-TAH) for a middling amount; *çok* or *şekerli* or even *çok şekerli* (CHOHK sheh-kehr-LEE) if you want lots of sugar. When the coffee arrives, the waiter may well have confused the cups, and you may find yourself exchanging with your dinner-mates.

Nescafé is readily found throughout Turkey but tends to be expensive, often 500TL (US$0.70) per cup.

Aslan sütü	ahs-LAHN sew-tew	'Lion's milk' (*rakı*)
Ayran	AH-yee-RAHN	Yogurt drink
Bira	BEE-rah	Beer
Beyaz	bey-AHZ	Light
Siyah	see-YAH	Dark
Boza	BOH-zah	Thick millet drink

Buz	BOOZ	Ice
Çay	CHAH-yee	Tea
Cin	JEEN	Gin
Kahve(si)	kah-VEH(-see)	Coffee
Türk	TEWRK	Turkish
Fransız	frahn-SUHZ	Coffee & milk
Amerikan	ah-meh-ree-KAHN	American coffee
Limonata	lee-moh-NAH-tah	Lemonade
Maden sodası	mah-DEHN soh-dah-suh	Fizzy mineral water
Maden suyu	mah-DEHN soo-yoo	Mineral water
Neskafe	NEHSS-kah-feh	Instant coffee
Rakı	rah-KUH	Anise-flavoured brandy
Sahlep	sah-LEHP	Hot milk & tapioca root
Şarap	shah-RAHP	Wine
Beyaz	bey-AHZ	White
Kırmızı	kuhr-muh-ZUH	Red
Köpüklü	kur-pewk-LEW	Sparkling
Roze	roh-ZEH	Rose
Su	SOO	Water
Süt	SEWT	Milk
Vermut	vehr-MOOT	Vermouth
Viski	VEE-skee	Whisky
Votka	VOHT-kah	Vodka

Cooking Terms

Buğlama	BOO-lah-MAH	Steamed, poached
Etli	eht-LEE	With meat
Ezme(si)	ehz-MEH(-see)	Puree
Fırın	fuh-RUHN	Baked, oven-roasted
Haşlama	hahsh-lah-MAH	Boiled, stewed
İyi pişmiş	ee-YEE peesh-meesh	Well-done, -cooked
Izgara	uhz-GAH-rah	Charcoal grilled
Kıymalı	kuhy-mah-LUH	With ground lamb
Kızartma	kuh-ZAHRT-mah	Broiled
Peynirli	pehy-neer-LEE	With cheese
Pişkin	peesh-KEEN	Well-done, -cooked
Rosto	ROHSS-toh	Roasted
Salçalı	sahl-chah-LUH	With savoury tomato sauce
Sıcak	suh-JAHK	Hot, warm
Soğuk	soh-OOK	Cold
Soslu	sohss-LOO	With sauce
Terbiyeli	TEHR-bee-yeh-LEE	With sauce
Yogurtlu	YOH-oort-LOO	With yogurt
Yumurtalı	yoo-moor-tah-LUH	With egg

Index

Temperature

To convert °C to °F multipy by 1.8 and add 32

To convert °F to °C subtract 32 and multipy by 5/9

Length, Distance & Area

	multipy by
inches to centimetres	2.54
centimetres to inches	0.39
feet to metres	0.30
metres to feet	3.28
yards to metres	0.91
metres to yards	1.09
miles to kilometres	1.61
kilometres to miles	0.62
acres to hectares	0.40
hectares to acres	2.47

Weight

	multipy by
ounces to grams	28.35
grams to ounces	0.035
pounds to kilograms	0.45
kilograms to pounds	2.21
British tons to kilograms	1016
US tons to kilograms	907

A British ton is 2240 lbs, a US ton is 2000 lbs

Volume

	multipy by
liperial gallons to litres	4.55
litres to imperial gallons	0.22
US gallons to litres	3.79
litres to US gallons	0.26

5 imperial gallons equals 6 US gallons
a litre is slightly more than a US quart, slightly less
than a British one

Lonely Planet

Lonely Planet published its first book in 1973. Tony and Maureen Wheeler had made a lengthy overland trip from England to Australia and, in response to numerous 'how do you do it?' questions, Tony wrote and they published *Across Asia on the Cheap*. It became an instant local best-seller and inspired thoughts of a second travel guide. A year and a half in South-East Asia resulted in their second book, *South-East Asia on a Shoestring*, which they put together in a backstreet Chinese hotel in Singapore in 1975. The 'yellow book', as it quickly became known, soon became *the* guide to the region and has now gone through five editions, always with its familiar yellow cover.

Soon other writers started to come to them with ideas for similar books – books that went off the beaten track and took an adventurous approach to travel, books that 'assumed you knew how to get your luggage off the carousel,' as one reviewer described them. Lonely Planet soon grew from a kitchen table operation to a spare room and then to its own office. It also started to develop an international reputation as the Lonely Planet logo began to appear in more and more countries. Always the emphasis has been on travel for travellers and Tony and Maureen still manage to fit in a number of trips each year and play a very active part in the writing and updating of Lonely Planet's guides.

Today over 20 people work at the Lonely Planet office in Melbourne, Australia and there are another half dozen at the company's US office in Oakland, California. Keeping guidebooks up to date is a constant battle and although the basic element in that struggle is still an ear to the ground and lots of walking, modern technology also plays its part. All Lonely Planet guidebooks are now stored and updated on computer. In some cases authors take lap-top computers into the field with them. Lonely Planet is also using computers to draw maps and eventually many of the maps will also be stored on disk.

At first Lonely Planet specialised extensively in the Asia region but these days it is also developing major ranges of guidebooks to the Pacific region, to South America and to Africa. The list of walking guides is also growing and Lonely Planet is producing a unique series of phrasebooks to 'unusual' languages. In 1982 the company's *India – a travel survival kit* won the Thomas Cook Guidebook of the Year award, the major international award for travel guidebooks and the company's business achievements have been recognised by twice winning Australian Export Achievement Awards, in 1982 and 1986.

The people at Lonely Planet strongly feel that travellers can make a positive contribution to the countries they visit both by better appreciation of cultures and by the money they spend. In addition the company tries to make a direct contribution to the countries and regions it covers. Since 1986 a percentage of the income from each book has gone to aid groups and associations. This has included donations to famine relief in Africa, to aid projects in India, to agricultural projects in Nicaragua and other Central American countries and to Greenpeace's efforts to halt French nuclear testing in the Pacific. In 1987 $30,000 was donated by Lonely Planet to these projects.

Lonely Planet Newsletter

We collect an enormous amount of information here at Lonely Planet. Apart from our research there's a steady stream of letters from people out on the road. To make the most of all this info we produce a quarterly Newsletter (approx Feb, May, Aug, and Nov).

The Newsletter is packed with down-to-earth information from the pens of hundreds of travellers who write from first-hand experience. Whether you want the latest facts, travel stories, or simply to reminisce, the Newsletter will keep you in touch with what is going on.

Where else could you find out:
- about boat trips on the Yalu River?
- where to stay if you want to live in a typical Thai village?
- how long it takes to get a Nepalese trekking permit?
- that Israeli youth hostel stamps will get you deported from Syria?

One year's subscription is $10.00 (that's US$ in the USA or A$ in Australia), payable by cheque, money order, Amex, Visa, Bankcard or MasterCard.

Order Form

Please send me four issues of the Lonely Planet Newsletter. (Subscription starts with next issue. 1987 price – subject to change.)

Name and address (print) ....

....

....

Tick one

☐ Cheque enclosed (payable to Lonely Planet Publications)
☐ Money Order enclosed (payable to Lonely Planet Publications)
Charge my ☐ Amex, ☐ Visa, ☐ Bankcard, ☐ MasterCard for the amount of $.....................

Card No ....   Expiry Date ....

Cardholder's Name (print) ....

Signature ....   Date ....

Return this form to:

Lonely Planet Publications   *or*   Lonely Planet Publications
PO Box 2001A   PO Box 88
Berkeley   South Yarra
CA 94702   Victoria 3141
USA   Australia

Lonely Planet Guides to the Middle East

Egypt & the Sudan – a travel survival kit
The sights of Egypt and the Sudan have impressed visitors for more than 50 centuries. This guide takes you beyond the spectacular pyramids to discover the villages of the Nile, diving in the Red Sea and many other other attractions.

Israel – a travel survival kit
This is a comprehensive guidebook to a small, fascinating country that is packed with things to see and do. This guide will help you unravel its political and religious significance – and enjoy your stay.

Jordan & Syria – a travel survival kit
Roman cities, ancient Petra, Crusader castles – these sights, amongst many others, combine with Arab hospitality to make this undiscovered region a fascinating and enjoyable destination.

Yemen – a travel survival kit
The fertile mountains and plateaus of the Arabian Peninsula have preserved a treasure trove for adventurous travellers – superb architecture, dramatic countryside and friendly people.

West Asia on a shoestring
A complete guide to the overland trip from Bangladesh to Turkey. Information for budget travellers to Afghanistan, Bangladesh, Bhutan, India, Iran, Maldives, Nepal, Pakistan, Sri Lanka, Turkey and the Middle East.

Lonely Planet Guides to the Indian sub-continent

Kathmandu & the Kingdom of Nepal – a travel survival kit
Few travellers can resist the lure of magical Kathmandu and its surrounding mountains. This guidebook takes you round the temples, to the foothills of the Himalaya, and to the Terai.

Trekking in the Nepal Himalaya
Complete trekking information for Nepal, including day-by-day route descriptions and detailed maps – this book has a wealth of advice for both independent and group trekkers.

India – a travel survival kit
An award-winning guidebook that is recognised as the outstanding contemporary guide to the subcontinent. Looking for a houseboat in Kashmir? Trying to post a parcel? This definitive guidebook has all the facts.

Kashmir, Ladakh & Zanskar – a travel survival kit
This book contains detailed information on three contrasting Himalayan regions in the Indian state of Jammu and Kashmir – the narrow valley of Zanskar, reclusive Ladakh, and the beautiful Vale of Kashmir.

Pakistan – a travel survival kit
Pakistan has been called 'the unknown land of the Indus' and many people don't realise the great variety of experiences it offers – from bustling Karachi, to ancient cities and tranquil mountain valleys.

Bangladesh – a travel survival kit
The adventurous traveller in Bangladesh can explore tropical forests and beaches, superb hill country, and ancient Buddhist ruins. This guide covers all these alternatives – and many more.

Sri Lanka – a travel survival kit
This guide takes a complete look at the island Marco Polo described as 'the finest in the world'. In one handy package you'll find ancient cities, superb countryside, and beautiful beaches.

Also available:
Nepal Phrasebook and *Sri Lanka Phrasebook*

Lonely Planet guides to South-East Asia

South-East Asia on a shoestring
For over 10 years this has been known as the 'yellow bible' to travellers in South-East Asia. The fifth edition has updated information on Brunei, Burma, Hong Kong, Indonesia, Macau, Malaysia, Papua New Guinea, the Philippines, Singapore, and Thailand.

Indonesia – a travel survival kit
This comprehensive guidebook covers the entire Indonesian archipelago, from Irian Jaya to Sumatra, including Bali and Lombok. Some of the most remarkable sights and sounds in South-East Asia can be found amongst these countless islands.

Bali & Lombok – a travel survival kit
Bali is a picturesque tropical island with a fascinating culture and an almost fairytale unreality – dense tropical jungle, superb temples, great beaches and surf, and traditional villages.

Malaysia, Singapore and Brunei – a travel survival kit
These three nations offer amazing geographic and cultural variety – from hill stations to beaches, from Dyak longhouses to futuristic cities – this is Asia at its most accessible.

Burma – a travel survival kit
Burma is one of Asia's friendliest and most interesting countries, but for traveller's there's one catch – you can only stay for seven days. This book shows you how to make the most of your visit.

Thailand – a travel survival kit
Beyond the Buddhist temples and Bangkok bars there is much to see in fascinating Thailand. This extensively researched guide presents an inside look at Thailand's culture, people and language.

Also available:

Thailand Phrasebook and *Indonesia Phrasebook*
Both these small but indispensable guidebooks provide practical phrases for travellers. The *Thailand Phrasebook* includes Thai script to enable you to 'point and show'. Indonesian is almost identical to Malay so the *Indonesian Phrasebook* is doubly useful.

Lonely Planet guides to North-East Asia

China – a travel survival kit
Travelling on your own in China can be exciting and rewarding; it can also be exhausting and frustrating – getting a seat on a train or finding a cheap bed in a hotel isn't always easy. But it can be done and this detailed and comprehensive book tells you how.

Tibet – a travel survival kit
After centuries of isolation, this extraordinary region is now open to individual travellers. This comprehensive guidebook has concise background information, and all the facts on how to get around, where to stay, where to eat, what to see . . . and more.

Japan – a travel survival kit
Japan offers many contrasts but few visitors get past the modern facade to see the traditional side of the country. This book covers the cities, but also tells you how to find the 'real' Japan and get the most from your visit.

Taiwan – a travel survival kit
Taiwan offers not only spectacular scenery but also an exciting blend or trditional Chinese culture in an export-oriented society. This guide is packed with valuable information and the extensive use of both Chinese script and Pinyin help to overcome the language barrier.

North-East Asia on a shoestring
Shoestring guides give essential information for low-budget travel in an extended region. This book includes up-to-date information on six unique states: China, Hong Kong, Japan, Korea, Macau, and Taiwan.

Also available

China Phrasebook
A small, indispensable book with common words, useful phrases and word lists to help you through almost any situation. This book gives the Pinyin spellings for Mandarin as well as the Chinese characters.

Tibet Phrasebook
This handy pocket-sized book gives you all the words and phrases you'll need when you're out in the back blocks, and also incorporates Tibetan script.

Lonely Planet Publications are available around the world - a list of distributors follows.

Lonely Planet travel guides

Africa on a Shoestring
Alaska – a travel survival kit
Australia – a travel survival kit
Bali & Lombok – a travel survival kit
Bangladesh – a travel survival kit
Burma – a travel survival kit
Bushwalking in Papua New Guinea
Canada – a travel survival kit
China – a travel survival kit
Chile & Easter Island – a travel survival kit
East Africa – a travel survival kit
Ecuador & the Galapagos Islands
Egypt & the Sudan – a travel survival kit
Fiji – a travel survival kit
Hong Kong, Macau & Canton – a travel survival kit
India – a travel survival kit
Indonesia – a travel survival kit
Japan – a travel survival kit
Jordan & Syria – a travel survival kit
Kashmir, Ladakh & Zanskar – a travel survival kit
Kathmandu & the Kingdom of Nepal
Malaysia, Singapore & Brunei
Mexico – a travel survival kit
New Zealand – a travel survival kit
North-East Asia on a Shoestring
Pakistan – a travel survival kit
Papua New Guinea – a travel survival kit
Peru – a travel survival kit
Philippines – a travel survival kit
Raratonga & the Cook Islands – a travel survival kit
South America on a Shoestring
Sri Lanka – a travel survival kit
Tahiti – a travel survival kit
Thailand – a travel survival kit
Tibet – a travel survival kit
Tramping in New Zealand
Travel with Children
Travellers Tales
Trekking in the Indian Himalaya
Trekking in the Nepal Himalaya
Turkey – a travel survival kit
West Asia on a Shoestring

Lonely Planet phrasebooks

Indonesia Phrasebook
China Phrasebook
Nepal Phrasebook
Papua New Guinea Phrasebook
Sri Lanka Phrasebook
Thailand Phrasebook
Tibet Phrasebook

Lonely Planet Distribution

Lonely Planet travel guides are available round the world. If you can't find them, ask your bookshop to order them from one of the distributors listed below. For countries not listed, or if you would like a free copy of our latest booklist, write to Lonely Planet in Australia.

Lonely Planet Distributors

Australia
Lonely Planet Publications, PO Box 88, South Yarra, Victoria 3141.

Canada
Raincoast Books, 112 East 3rd Avenue, Vancouver, British Columbia V5T 1C8.

Denmark, France & Norway
Scanvil Books aps, Store Kongensgade 59 A, DK-1264 Copenhagen K.

Hong Kong
The Book Society, GPO Box 7804.

India & Nepal
UBS Distributors, 5 Ansari Rd, New Delhi – 110002

Israel
Geographical Tours Ltd, 8 Tverya St, Tel Aviv 63144.

Japan
Intercontinental Marketing Corp, IPO Box 5056, Tokyo 100-31.

Netherlands
Nilsson & Lamm bv, Postbus 195, Pampuslaan 212, 1380 AD Weesp.

New Zealand
Roulston Greene Publishing Associates Ltd, Private Bag, Takapuna, Auckland 9.

Papua New Guinea see Australia

Singapore & Malaysia
MPH Distributors, 601 Sims Drive, £03-21, Singapore 1438.

Spain
Altair, Balmes 69, 08007 Barcelona.

Sweden
Esselte Kartcentrum AB, Vasagatan 16, S-111 20 Stockholm.

Thailand
Chalermnit, 108 Sukhumvit 53, Bangkok 10110.

UK
Roger Lascelles, 47 York Rd, Brentford, Middlesex, TW8 0QP

USA
Lonely Planet Publications, PO Box 2001A, Berkeley, CA 94702.

West Germany
Buchvertrieb Gerda Schettler, Postfach 64, D3415 Hattorf a H.